Get Published

Get Published

Top Magazine Editors Tell You How

Completely Revised and Updated

Diane Gage and Marcia Coppess

An Owl Book

Henry Holt and Company
New York

Henry Holt and Company, Inc.
Publishers since 1866
115 West 18th Street
New York, New York 10011

Henry Holt ® is a registered trademark of
Henry Holt and Company, Inc.

Published in Canada by Fitzhenry & Whiteside Ltd.,
195 Allstate Parkway, Markham, Ontario L3R 4T8.

Library of Congress Cataloging-in-Publication Data
Gage, Diane.
Get Published : top magazine editors tell you how / Diane Gage and Marcia Coppess. — Completely rev. and updated.
p. cm.
"An Owl Book."
Includes index.
1. Authorship—Marketing—Handbooks, manuals, etc. 2. Authorship—Marketing—Directories. 3. American periodicals—Directories. I. Coppess, Marcia. II. Title.
PN161.G33 1993
808'.02—dc20 93-17650
CIP

ISBN 0-8050-2689-4

First published in hardcover in 1986
by Henry Holt and Company, Inc.

First Revised Owl Book Edition—1994

Designed by Terry Fetterly Smrt

Printed in the United States of America
All first editions are printed on acid-free paper. ∞
5 7 9 10 8 6 4

To the writers who
wish they would
but haven't,
want to
but think they can't,
or did once
and wish they could again,
this book is dedicated.

Contents

Acknowledgments . . . xii
Introduction . . . xv

Part I Getting It on Paper

1 Increasing Sales by Knowing Your Market . . . 3
2 Spotting and Shaping Ideas . . . 17
3 Crafting Eye-catching Queries . . . 29
4 Tracking Down and Interviewing Expert Sources 63
5 Writing Articles That Command Attention . . . 81
6 Using the Library to Your Advantage . . . 109
7 Taking Care of Business . . . 119

Part II Getting It in Print

Alaska Airlines Magazine . . . 147
Americana . . . 152
American Health . . . 155
The American Legion Magazine . . . 160
American Visions . . . 165
American Way . . . 169
America West . . . 172
American Woman . . . 176
The Atlantic . . . 181
Audubon . . . 186
Better Homes and Gardens . . . 190
Black Elegance . . . 194
Black Enterprise . . . 198
Boys' Life . . . 204
Bridal Guide . . . 208
Bride's & Your New Home . . . 211
Brides Today . . . 217
child . . . 222
Christianity Today . . . 225
Condé Nast Traveler . . . 230
Cooking Light . . . 233

Cosmopolitan 237
The Costco Connection 241
Country Victorian Decorating & Lifestyle 245
D&B Reports 249
Eating Well 253
Emerge 258
Endless Vacation 263
Entrepreneur 268
Essence 271
Exploring 275
Family Circle 279
Family Fun 284
Field & Stream 288
First for Women 292
Fitness 295
Friendly Exchange 300
Glamour 304
Good Housekeeping 309
Guideposts 315
Harper's 321
Harrowsmith Country Life 324
Health 329
Hemispheres 333
Highlights for Children 338
Home 343
International Wildlife/National Wildlife 347
Islands 353
Ladies' Home Journal 358
Lear's 361
Longevity 365
McCall's 369
Men's Health 373
Military Lifestyle 377
Mirabella 382
Modern Bride 384
Modern Maturity 387
Mother Jones 391
Ms. 394
National Geographic 398
Nation's Business 402
New Body 406

New Woman 409
Off Duty 413
Omni 417
Outside 422
Parade 426
Parenting 430
Parents 436
Popular Mechanics 440
Popular Science 445
Profiles 448
Psychology Today 453
Reader's Digest 457
Redbook 463
Robb Report 468
Scouting 473
Sesame Street Parents' Guide 477
Seventeen 482
Shape 485
Sierra 489
Ski 494
Sky 499
Smithsonian 503
Snow Country 507
Spirit 511
Sport 516
Sports Afield 520
Tennis 523
Upscale 527
USAir Magazine 532
USA Weekend 536
Weight Watchers Magazine 540
Woman's Day 544
Woman's World 548
Women's Sports & Fitness 551
Working Mother 555
YM 559
Young Sisters and Brothers 562
Your Health & Fitness 567

Index 573

Acknowledgments

A lot of acknowledgments say that a book would not have been possible without a particular individual. In our case, those are more than just words. Beth Labko, our editorial coordinator, was a human *Get Published* headquarters. The thousands of facts and details required for a book like this somehow made their way into logical order in Beth's mind. She charmed the editors as our firstline contact, edited with flair and authority, knew where to reach for a lost file, made and returned phone calls, kept up with nonstop FAXes, and still managed to cheer us on and see the manuscript to completion. We are forever grateful for the hours of tireless overtime she invested in this project.

We also extend our thanks to Ann and Roger Omae for their hospitality while we trekked through New York; Deborah Purdy for her writing assistance; Katherine Huggler for her detailed copyediting; Terry Smrt for her layout and design expertise—not to mention her patience and perseverance; our agent, Deborah Schneider, of Gelfman, Schneider and Associates, for continuing to believe in the book; and to Alison Juram, our editor, for her enthusiasm throughout the entire project.

Of course there would not be a book like this if more than 100 busy magazine editors had not been willing to sit with us and explain the individual needs and preferences of their magazines.

And we are indebted to the more than one dozen professional writers who gave freely of the kind of knowledge and advice that only comes with years of commitment to the business of writing.

We thank them.

Remarkably, the men in our lives supported us again through this book that consumed our lives.

All my love to my wonderfully caring husband, Gene, and my adorable son, Kevin, who patiently supported me while home life was eclipsed by a looming deadline. Thank you for always standing by me and cheering me on to pursue my dreams.

—Diane

Michael, you are an angel disguised as a mild-mannered husband. Thank you for tolerating the inevitable chaos of this book. Thanks to Joe, who steadfastly maintained his belief in me. And to my heroines of the BSP, who have achieved far greater things in their work than any acknowledgment could ever express: I am proud to know you.

—Marcia

Introduction

If you are a writer, you know it. You know it because you seldom do anything without the experience triggering a story idea. While everyone else sleeps in on Saturday morning, you rise early to write three pages without being interrupted. Even though you sometimes threaten to quit, you know you can't. There's no match to the triumph you feel when the words you've inserted, deleted, rearranged, transposed, expanded, and pared down finally embrace the rhythm, emotion, and meaning you've struggled to achieve.

Whether you've always believed that you can write or just suspect that you have talent, you won't be a writer until you actually write. Some noble souls can write just for their own benefit, but if you're like most, you write to be published.

Magazines are a large and diverse part of the publishing world. Although you can gain entry to a magazine by writing one good article, to develop a long-term relationship with an editor you must learn all you can about the personality of the magazine. And to strengthen your foothold in the field, you should know how the entire magazine industry works.

We wanted to learn more, too, and the result is this freshly updated version of *Get Published.* While other books that draw upon a writer's own experience in magazine-article writing offer useful information, we think that the best way to learn about writing well-targeted articles for a particular magazine is to hear about the magazine directly from its editor. Few writers get that opportunity, however, until they've written an article or two for a magazine. Although virtually all editors advise writers to read their publication to learn what they need, it's not the same as getting advice straight from the editor.

For *Get Published*, we interviewed editors of the nation's best freelance magazine markets to gather their opinions, demands, and preferences. How did we decide which of the thousands of magazines were best for writers? We started with a lengthy list of possible candidates. Then we learned all we could about each magazine. We aimed high, beginning with eight criteria:

- Pays on acceptance
- Purchases only First North American Serial Rights
- Pays at least 50 cents a word
- Has a good reputation among the general public and writers
- Has a substantial circulation base

- Is a showcase for a writer's work
- Buys a lot from freelancers
- Has a positive attitude toward freelance writers

From there it became a bit more subjective. If a magazine did not pay as much as another, but was a showcase for a writer's work or bought a lot of articles, we chose it over one that paid well but used few writers. If a magazine couldn't or wouldn't answer all our questions, we decided against it. Specialty magazines that are well known in their category but don't pay well were included. New magazines and those in transition were left out because their information was certain to change. And, finally, we relied on experience and the gut feelings we've developed as freelancers.

Some magazines that pay well and showcase a writer's work are missing from the book. For instance, although many city and regional publications are terrific markets for writers, we chose not to address that group because this is a book about national markets. We also excluded pornographic magazines, regardless of the types of articles they buy. And—a new trend since the last edition of the book—several major magazines that buy freelance material declined to be interviewed, stating that they already received too many unsolicited submissions.

Why would editors, who have one of the world's most hectic professions, take time to be interviewed for this book and share candid information about their publications? Because most are as interested in finding writers with good ideas for their magazines as writers are eager to sell their words.

We designed *Get Published* to bridge the gap for writers who are just starting out, for those who have studied their target magazines but do not yet have a relationship with an editor, and for authors who have sold to several magazines but want to broaden their market base. You'll find quotes from editors and successful freelance writers in chapters on marketing yourself and your work, idea development and slanting, query letters, interviewing, researching, writing, and running your freelance business.

The heart of this book lies in the chapters on each of the top national magazines. We've included demographics, pay rates, and other important details about each market. But the best information is found in the comments from the editors themselves. Their remarks are frank and to the point; they're also insightful, revealing, and sometimes hopeful. We think that what they say will provide you with the in-depth information you need to increase your sales to major national magazines.

Once you know what magazine editors say about marketing articles to their specific publications, and you begin to apply that knowledge to your work, it will become easier to sell what you write. Seeing your byline in print is possible, especially when you take advantage of tips from the nation's top editors and you persevere to meet their needs.

Part I

Getting It on Paper

CHAPTER 1

Increasing Sales by Knowing Your Market

How often have you picked up your favorite magazine only to discover that the idea you thought of six months ago has earned someone else a cover story? As you turn the pages and read what could have been your words, you grumble to yourself, "Gee, I could have written that." Perhaps you could have. But instead you should ask, "Could I have sold that?"

The key to a byline is identifying your markets and then selling your ideas and abilities to the right buyer. You'll only be successful at selling magazine articles when you regard ideas as marketable products and target magazines as prospective clients that have needs you can fill.

Freelanced articles account for a large portion of the editorial content (also simply called "editorial") found in magazines. Many editors attest that magazines need writers. So, even if you are just starting out, there is the chance for you to sell your work if you have just the right idea for the perfect market. If you continue to feed editors good ideas backed up with a fresh approach and dependability, you can score more and more bylines in increasingly prestigious—and better paying—publications.

However, it's also true that many editors don't depend on finding ideas in the unsolicited mail. They rely instead on a handful of favorite writers. Increasingly, editors develop article ideas for their magazines in meetings with their staffs, then assign articles to writers with whom they have already worked or whose work they know. You can be invited to join that exclusive "stable" of writers if you are willing to spend the time now to learn how to market your article ideas and yourself appropriately.

Marketing Your Writing

Just as freelancing is a business of writing, it is also a business of marketing. Writers market a product (an article) to the appropriate buyer (the magazine) by submitting a proposal (a query). As in any business, you must invest in the business in order to make it profitable. In this case, time, energy, and research constitute much of the investment.

Since freelancing is such an individual pursuit, no two writers work in exactly the same way. But successful writers do have certain standards and habits in common. Most frequently, they share the attitude that writing is a business and that writers are professionals in that business.

Professional writers Dan Baum and his wife, Margaret Knox, of Missoula, Montana, started freelancing the day they married. Now, they both concentrate on wilderness, wildlife, and environmental journalism, selling to such markets as *Sierra, Mother Jones, Smithsonian,* and *The Nation.* Baum says, "At least half of our time is spent running the business—marketing, billing, following up on stories, and generating new business. We keep an office downtown and run this operation as a business, file taxes as a business, and have business cards."

The Competition Is Stiff, but You Can Rise Above It

Each day, national magazines receive piles of unsolicited queries and manuscripts from freelancers throughout the country. *Family Circle* receives about 10,000 submissions a year, yet only buys 200; *Parade* estimates that its submissions number 12,000, from which only 150 see print; and *USAir* gets 2,500 queries but assigns only about 130 articles. Yet despite the overwhelming numbers of queries and manuscripts that cross their desks, editors bemoan the lack of good proposals that hide among those submissions. You can overcome their objections by learning as much as possible about the markets you want to tackle and by writing proposals that truly meet their needs. The more experience you get selling, the more you'll be recognized as a known commodity.

In recent years, as budgets have diminished and staffs have been cut, magazine editors have become less likely to use valuable staff time reading queries from people they don't know. Unsolicited manuscripts, fully written without any input from the editors, are almost universally unwelcome. There simply isn't the time, and the payoff isn't great enough for an editor to wade through the "slush pile," as it is called.

"Our slush pile is read by editorial assistants," says Nelson Aldrich, Jr., articles editor of *Lear's.* "They haven't found anything in the last 18 months that has led to an article assignment. They may find a proposal from an established writer who is introducing himself to us. But *Lear's* is, in reality, closed to beginning writers.

The way someone gets an assignment here is by finding someone I already know and getting a personal reference."

If you are plotting the expansion of your writing career, keep in mind that you won't be the only one reviewing your article when it hits the newsstands. The successful completion of one assignment may bring phone calls and assignments from that magazine and others. Since good writers don't always venture into another magazine's territory, editors go hunting for them. They scour countless magazines and newspapers to keep abreast of trends, monitor the competition, and identify local stories with national potential.

Along the way, they take note of writers whose work they admire. Because the brief biographical statement at the end of an article often mentions where the author lives, it's a simple matter for the editor to give the writer a call and invite him or her to submit some ideas and writing samples.

Editors make other kinds of phone calls, too. Some editors ask writers to submit clips (writing samples) with the name and telephone number of the assigning editor marked on them. They then call the editors to see how much work a manuscript needed when it was turned in, and whether the writer was a professional and pleasant person to work with.

Cornering Your Markets

There it is. It teases you. You resist its call, but in the end it wins. Like dieters who can't keep away from the refrigerator, writers are drawn to newsstands filled with racks and racks of glossy magazines that tantalize them with colorful covers and enticing cover lines. It's tempting to sample them all and walk away with an armload of reading, but there's a point at which you must stop gorging yourself on others' articles and begin writing your own.

There are approximately 11,000 consumer and trade periodicals published in the United States. There may be dozens in which you'd love to see your byline. But your chances of getting published will be increased if you concentrate your energies on three or four magazines, get to know their needs, and then work until you can meet those needs. Although you shouldn't disregard the potential of occasionally writing for other magazines—sometimes a good idea simply isn't right for the markets in which you usually like to concentrate—it's important to become expert on a few select markets.

Who Reads This Stuff?

Advertisers spend a lot of money deciding in which publications to place their ads. Magazines depend on the advertising revenue to keep afloat. So how does that relate to you and the articles you want to write? It's simple: if you can understand to whom the magazine is targeted—and therefore to whom the advertisers hope to sell their products—you're a long way on the march to understanding the types of articles the editors seek.

By now you've probably heard of "Baby Boomers," the "Thirtysomethings," and maybe even the "Twentysomethings," "Generation X," or the "Grunge Generation." These names represent certain demographic groups that advertisers identify in their never-ending attempt to put their hands on the nation's pulse and pursestrings.

Some other groups to which advertisers and editors pay attention are the "Retired Wealthy," the "Family Leisure" group, the "Outdoor/Adventure" market, the "Sandwich Generation" (those who are responsible for both children and aging parents), and the "Green" market (those concerned with the environment and conservation).

In addition to the "nicknamed" groups, advertisers sometimes think simply in terms of age, gender, or income, such as women between 25 and 44 years old, or those with sufficient disposable income to allow luxury travel. As you read through the chapters on individual magazines in this book, you'll note that some of the first information listed is demographic: that's so you can tell quickly whether you are aiming for the right market. In narrowing your focus to three or four target magazines, choose publications that cover your special interests and that you enjoy reading. You'll find your study of them more pleasurable, and article ideas for those magazines will come more easily. Yet breaking into those magazines may still take time.

With all the subjects that a magazine covers, and the high number of proposals it receives, don't feel dejected if you learn that the idea you thought was unique is already in the works. That only shows that you know your market and that an editor can depend on you to deliver a well-slanted article.

If you consistently send good article ideas and follow up assignments with manuscripts that deliver what you promise, editors will learn that you are a reliable source. Occasionally, an editor will assign a short piece to you if he or she thinks you have potential. Then the editor will watch to see how well you follow directions, use your own creativity, meet the deadline, and deliver a professional-looking package. Or, if your ideas aren't quite right but your queries are sharp, your name may be given to an associate or assistant editor who will encourage you to query him directly in the future. If that happens, take advantage of the invitation and send your new contact another story idea.

What's Your Specialty?

If you were looking for a lawyer to represent you, chances are you'd retain someone who specialized in your particular legal problem. In many fields, the most successful people are those who gather enough knowledge in one aspect of their profession to make them indispensable to their clients.

One way to make yourself indispensable to an editor is by becoming an expert. You may think that you're not an expert on anything. But expertise doesn't have to mean earning an advanced degree in a difficult subject, or becoming famous for your knowledge about something.

Expertise is experience combined with skill—and experience is living, watching, talking, and seeing the world from a unique perspective. Your expertise may be in raising kids, managing a company, or being a good employee. It may be in growing citrus trees, inventing something, or trying out a new "widget" to find out how it works. You are probably an expert on countless things that can become article ideas if you learn to recognize them.

Many writers establish themselves as specialists in one or two disciplines such as science, finance, or travel, and develop insights and professional contacts that magazine editors value. Once these writers demonstrate their expertise, editors often call them to request articles on subjects in their particular fields.

Successful writer Sherry Suib Cohen of New York was a teacher, mother, and wife for 15 years before she began freelancing. Now, more than 15 years into her second career, she has written 14 books, and has been published in nearly every major women's magazine. She is a contributing editor at *New Woman* and writes for *Glamour, Ladies' Home Journal, Family Circle, Seventeen,* and *Woman's Day.* And she still specializes in articles examining issues of interest to women—similar to the articles she began with, but on a much larger scale, for an enormous audience, and with enviable compensation.

Elaine Whiteley, a professional writer from Oceanside, California, has cornered her market at *Ladies' Home Journal* and other women's and religious magazines by specializing in elaborately researched articles on sensational local stories that have national significance. Her first article told of a little girl whose father awoke in time to foil someone trying to kidnap her from her bed. Her second piece, for *Ladies' Home Journal*, concerned baby sitters who maim and kill. Not simply a dramatic story, it included case histories, interviews with authorities, and statistics to back up the drama of the topic.

Although it's advantageous to set yourself up as an expert in one or two areas, don't think that specializing excludes you from writing about other fields.

Jon Krakauer is a writer from Seattle who works for *Smithsonian, Outside, Rolling Stone,* and *Men's Journal*, among others. He began his freelance career by writing for small mountain climbing magazines. "I heard people talking about specialists versus generalists, and knew that I could never make a living writing on only outdoor topics. So, while some editors consider me an outdoor adventure writer, other editors think I'm an arts writer. I fear that once a magazine typecasts me, I'll have to plead to write in another area," he says.

Don't Be Afraid to Aim High

If you have never written for magazines before, but have talent, professionalism, dedication, and good ideas, there's no rule that says you must write for a small-circulation magazine or regional publication before you attempt to write for national markets. Your competition will be lighter at smaller markets and you may be able to earn valuable clippings more quickly. But the basic requirements for selling an article are the same for any magazine. The fact that a magazine is small does not mean it has lower standards, nor does a magazine's success or large circulation always mean that it won't recognize and buy good writing from a writer unknown to its staff.

On the other hand, Dan Hurley, a professional from Upper Montclair, New Jersey, who writes for *Good Housekeeping, Parents, TV Guide,* and *The New York Times*, thinks aiming high has its merits. "Don't be afraid to start at the top," he advises writers who are just starting out. "But be cautious; success is not instantaneous."

Hurley worked for tabloids when he began, then started writing for the American Bar Association. When he wrote an article on crime prevention, he decided it had enough strength to go beyond the ABA, and pitched it to *The New York Times.* The idea was rejected, but Hurley tried other national magazines until his proposal became an assignment at *Psychology Today.* His career took off, and three years later he became a contributing editor at *Psychology Today.*

Persistence counts. So does studying your craft to gain insights and taking assignments at smaller markets to gain experience that can help pave your way to larger, better-paying jobs. "Taking a writing course was a marvelous way for me to start," says writer Sherry Cohen. "It may sound pedestrian, but I never could have broken into the big time if I hadn't taken that class and then had the opportunity to compile clips from local publications in Mamaroneck and Westchester, New York. They sent me to cover local stories on topics such as teen runaways and sex in the suburbs—and that earned me an enormous amount of experience in interviewing and asking hard questions."

Write for the Magazine, Not for Yourself

If you want to sell your writing, one of the first things you must know is the difference between writing for an editor and writing for your ego. Successful writers understand that they are writing to be published, not to unload opinions and biases.

Writer Jon Krakauer says, "I wanted to hit myself in the head when it finally dawned on me that to be successful I had to give magazines what *they* wanted, not what I wanted. When I first started writing, I thought magazines just needed to open their minds to my ideas. You can try that later, but not while you're still an unknown commodity."

As mentioned earlier, magazines go to great lengths to perform market research to identify their target markets. Among other things, demographics tell them where readers live, their education and income levels, how many children they have, and what they do with their discretionary income and leisure time.

Those details, coupled with reader satisfaction surveys, give magazine editors the information they need to design editorial that will capture the interests of their readers and the pocketbooks of their advertisers. It's a science and an art that they spend many hours and thousands of dollars perfecting. The last thing editors need are writers trying to persuade them to test new editorial directions.

If you want to sell to magazines, give them more of what they do, only better.

Read the Magazine!

"Success is being able to figure out what each magazine wants and who their audience is, and then writing for that audience," says Krakauer. "Most writers don't appreciate how specifically focused every magazine is on a particular segment of the market."

To analyze what the magazine is doing with its editorial, see what it does to differentiate itself from its closest competitors. Write the editorial office for a copy of the magazine's writer's guidelines and call or write the advertising office for a media kit to see the demographic statistics for yourself.

Then, invest some time and money in the next few issues. With each new issue, monitor the magazine to determine any changes in staff, editorial slant, and design. Also study the advertising to gain a sense of the products the magazine thinks its readers will buy. In other words—study your market. Just as you wouldn't apply for a job without having the proper credentials and background, don't attempt to sell an article to a magazine unless your idea and your writing style is a perfect fit for that publication.

If there was one request the more than 100 editors interviewed in this book made almost unanimously, it was "Read the magazine!" Editors quickly tire of getting story suggestions from writers whose only acquaintance with their publication is the masthead that lists the names of the editors. They don't even want proposals from writers who read the magazine but only flip through its pages and read one or two articles. What they want instead is a writer who knows their publication intimately.

Editors expect writers to understand how their magazine divides its editorial into features and departments or columns; to have a good idea of the purpose of each department; and to be able to identify what topics are broad enough or interesting enough to warrant feature coverage. It is only by studying at least six of the most current issues of the magazine that you can begin to grasp the unique niche each magazine is trying to carve, learn how it approaches topics, and understand the style and voice of the writing.

To be able to do all that, you need to start reading the magazines you'd like to sell to—not as a casual reader—but as a potential writer for that magazine. While you review the magazine, take note of the following:

- **Date.** How often is the magazine published? Is it weekly, monthly, bimonthly, or quarterly? This will give you an idea of the amount of freelance material the magazine uses, how much of the material it covers is time-sensitive, and how far in advance you need to query for seasonal material.
- **Cover Lines.** Editors agonize over the words and phrases they put on covers because those cover lines, or "blurbs," as they are called, attract newsstand sales and draw readers into their magazines. Analyze those lines. They will give you a wealth of insight into the top editors' feelings of what's hot. Then ask yourself, "How can my idea be worded as a cover line? Does it have that special twist that will make readers pick up the magazine at the grocery store check-out line? Is it new,

bold, sexy, startling, political, debatable? Before you look inside the magazine, note the cover illustration. Is it a photo of a person, an airplane, an exotic island, food, or a celebrity? That will give you a quick indication of what the editors—and their readers—are interested in.

- **Table of Contents.** The listing of articles and departments at the beginning of the magazine can give you terrific clues about the "editorial mix" of a magazine. Determine if there is a pattern. For example, does an in-flight magazine include two travel pieces, one art piece, and one business piece each month? Does a teen publication always run two boy/girl relationship articles, one school piece, and one friend piece in each issue? You'll learn what types of articles a magazine wants most by noting the major categories of subjects covered.

  Take special note of how the table of contents is divided. Does your idea fit into any of the categories listed? Does it have a large enough scope to become a major feature? Can you create a title and blurb about your article that matches the intensity and tone of the articles listed?

  Next, review the departments and columns. The terms "department" and "columns" are used interchangeably. While a magazine might prefer one or the other, there is no true distinction for how the two terms differ in the magazine world as a whole. How many are there? What are the topic categories? Which are always written by the same writer or expert? (Don't even attempt to sell to those—they are sewn up!) Do any seem to be open to freelancers? If a department includes several small articles or news briefs, look at the articles in those departments to see if they include bylines and then cross-reference those bylines with the names included in the magazine's staff box to find in-house departments. Then check to see if the name on the piece is listed as a contributing editor—this is a writer who writes regularly for the magazine and is often paid a monthly retainer for his or her contributions. If the names change with every issue, or if a bio states that the author is a freelancer, you've found an open spot in the magazine.

- **Staff Box.** The staff box, or masthead, is the "who's who" of the magazine. Each magazine's hierarchy is different, just as different companies have different titles and echelons. In general, you'll find the following editorial titles:

  Editor-in-Chief
  Managing Editor
  Articles Editor

Associate Editor/Senior Editor/Deputy Editor
Special Department Editor (Food, Beauty, etc.)
Editorial Assistant

Typically, you should query the articles editor for a feature. If the magazine does not list that position, you may select a name from among the senior or associate editors. It makes sense to invest a few cents and call the magazine's switchboard or an assistant in the article department to determine who among those editors would be best to query. Often, different associate or senior editors have specific responsibilities or areas of interest. If one editor at a woman's magazine handles health topics, it's much more expedient to get her name right than to send it to the wrong editor and depend on that person to pass it along.

- **Front Matter.** The front matter of a magazine often includes the editorial, news briefs, and some regular columns—plus a lot of advertising. This is the best break-in section, so take note of the opportunities.

  Identify the goal of each department and how it differs from the major features. Also look at length and format. Some departments are short news briefs; others can be quite lengthy pieces on a single topic. You'll have more success selling news briefs and tidbits than longer pieces at first because editors are more willing to take a chance on a new writer if the assignment is a short one. That way, if you need more direction than anticipated or if the piece doesn't turn out as they envision, they've lost less time and money. But if you prove yourself on a small piece, the chances of earning a bigger assignment increase.

- **Well.** The center portion of the magazine is referred to as the well. It includes feature articles—often two-page spreads or longer—and little or no advertising. Editors place their most important editorial here where it receives more design attention, length, and color photography or illustration. So, take note of what they consider the most essential stories, and mirror what they are doing in terms of research, style, and format if you are trying to sell a major piece.

  Ask yourself, do the pieces include subheads, sidebars, graphs, or boxed information? How are the articles reported—do they include anecdotes, lots of quotes, or do they demonstrate the author's point of view? If the magazine covers travel, ascertain whether the features are destination-oriented (meaning they give a lot of information on where to stay and what to do) or more experiential. If you're looking at a food piece, is the style more about the experience of eating the food, or is it about how to prepare the food coupled with a number of recipes? That's the kind of analysis that will allow you to hit a bull's eye, instead of continuing to miss the mark with approaches to articles that won't work for the market you are trying to capture.

Some large magazines include two or three features separated by shorter articles called "well-breakers." If your idea is feature material but doesn't warrant great length, it may be a good candidate for a well-breaker.

This information about the well is meant to help you understand the physical structure of a magazine—not so you will tell an editor where your article belongs! Most editors will not appreciate being told that the piece you are proposing would be a perfect two-page spread for the well of the magazine. That's their decision. But they *do* want you to know enough about their magazine to be able to propose a feature or note that your idea might work for a particular column or department. When it comes to departments, the more specific you can be about where your piece fits, the better chance you'll have of getting an editor's attention.

- **Back Matter.** As with the front matter, this section includes a lot of advertising. It may also incorporate a directory of product outlets or classified ad section. However, you'll also find it to be the home of additional departments and columns, short special-interest articles, and regional sections. Many magazines also include a final-page essay. Are there columns to which you can contribute or short pieces you can write? Is the essay page something you can see yourself penning?

Keep Up with What's Up in the Magazine World

It's important to nurture the relationships you have with editors at different magazines and to strengthen new ones when an editor comes on staff at a magazine to which you've been contributing. But often, just when it seems that you've solidified a relationship, the editor moves on!

Job-shuffling goes on continually among magazine editors. Writers who want to build good will with editors should stay up-to-date on editorial changes. But since the magazine you see on the newsstand in June was "put to bed" at least three months earlier, its masthead may be out of date by the time you read it.

One way to keep up with the latest staff changes is to read *Folio,* the trade publication of the magazine world, and *Publishers Weekly,* the trade publication of book publishing. Both magazines report on promotions, changes in management, and hot new talent and trends in their respective industries. Other good sources of market information are *Writer's Digest* and *The Writer.*

Keeping track of changes in the staff will serve you well, not only when sending query letters, but also as you continue to build your freelance business. If you notice one month that there is a new editor-in-chief, be on the lookout for major changes at that magazine. It's not uncommon for editorial slant and graphic design to take on a completely new feeling under the tutelage of new top brass.

When editors in other positions move on, it's also important to note who takes their place and to attempt to get to know the new editor. Then, watch for where the former editor's name pops up. Having had a previous contact with that editor, you may inherit a new market if you take the time to learn about it.

Staying abreast of what's happening will enable you to send a quick note of congratulations when an editor you've worked with earns a promotion or the magazine debuts a new design. It's also sound strategy to occasionally let an editor know when a piece in a magazine really captured your interest or touched a subject in a particularly skilled way. Just like the rest of us, editors remember those who show sincere interest in their work. It's not brown-nosing; it's plain old-fashioned good business.

"It's important to cultivate relationships with editors," says writer Paula Jhung, of Rancho Santa Fe, California, whose byline has appeared in *Home, Country Accents, 1001 Home Ideas, Select Home, Family Circle,* and *Weight Watchers.* "At first I thought I'd be bugging them if I communicated other than sending query letters. But now I occasionally send editors I work with bits of information they might be able to use in an upcoming piece, Christmas cards, and comments on articles they've run."

Jhung's gestures are backed up with good solid work that goes above and beyond what her editors expect. "I always try to give the editor a little bit more," she says. "I send in my piece a few days before deadline, include a sidebar of information the editor hasn't asked for, or quote a few celebrity sources in the piece to give it that extra flair. When you do those kinds of things, editors remember you and you're apt to get more assignments."

But don't despair if, instead of being in the stable, you find yourself locked out of the barn. Today, your only contact may be an editorial assistant at a small magazine. But in a few years that assistant may become the articles editor of a major magazine. If you solidify your relationship with him or her now, your career may expand along with theirs.

Getting to the Core of the Big Apple

Some established writers find that spending a few days or a week in New York City each year is well worth the expense, since it provides them with enough work to keep them busy until their next trip. Once you have several years of experience and a credible portfolio, you may decide to write to your stable of editors and a few new editors you want to get to know, telling them that you're coming to town and that you'll have a suitcase full of ideas to discuss. Before you go, however, you'll need to spend several weeks preparing numerous queries for each market, ensuring that you don't repeat recently published ideas.

It takes a fair amount of work to prepare for an editor visit (unless you live within driving distance of New York City). But the time and cost can really pay off when an editor is able to get to know you as a person.

"I believe in personal contact," says freelancer David Roberts of Cambridge, Massachusetts, who writes for *National Geographic, Smithsonian,* and *The Atlantic,* among others. "During the crucial period when I was going from marginal to successful, I went to New York once a month and Washington, D.C. four times a year. I'd call my editors and say that I was going to be in town and ask them if they had time for coffee or tea. There was never a case in which a personal visit to an editor to whom I'd only talked on the phone failed to improve the whole relationship."

Be forewarned that you may not go home with solid assignments. In fact, more often than not, an editor will want either to take your written idea and pass it among the other editors or will ask you to submit an expanded outline. The outlines will be necessary because an idea you present may metamorphose into a completely different article when it blends with what the editor has in mind for the future. Your idea on controlling clutter may expand until you find yourself writing "100 Ways to Clean Up Now!"

When you return to your office, note which ideas are under consideration with which editors, and follow up with a letter stating your understanding. If you've promised an outline or two to an editor, set a deadline for yourself (while the idea is hot) and tell the editor in your letter when he or she can expect your outline. Then get it there, and watch your sales successes soar!

CHAPTER 2

Spotting and Shaping Ideas

Writers are frequently asked, "Where do you get all those ideas?" People are fascinated by a writer who simultaneously sells three distinctly different story ideas—one about child care, another about mountain climbing, and a third about how to grow pesticide-free vegetables—to three different magazines.

For a seasoned writer, finding good ideas isn't the problem—it's carving out the time to turn them into article proposals. More than anything else, writing is an ache that never dulls when you're away from your work. It's an obsession with the pursuit of an idea.

When you write for a living, or aspire to, you view life in terms of the next article or book you want to write. As soon as you hear anything a little offbeat, you think, "How can I turn this into an article?" For writers, there are no vacations or time off—only opportunities to uncover new projects.

As your senses sharpen and your curiosity heightens, you see story ideas everywhere. Although you appear to read the newspaper like everyone else, you clip and save articles instead of coupons. And, while others enjoy the conversation during a dinner party, a simple comment whets your appetite, and you sneak out your pen to take notes on your napkin.

Put Your Experiences up in Lights

Just as a newspaper reporter spends years sharpening his "nose for news," a magazine writer works to develop an acute ability to sniff out a feature. Often, there's no more to recognizing potential ideas than paying attention to the happenings in your life and in the lives of those around you. If you or someone you know experiences something, has a problem with someone, or needs advice to overcome an obstacle, chances are you can turn those needs and desires into an article to entertain or inform others.

For instance, one writer who was planning her wedding became frustrated by dictatorial vendors. When she told a freelancer friend about the restrictions the wedding photographer was placing on her, an idea presented itself. "Write an article about how to prevent wedding vendors from pushing you around," said the second writer, who was a little more distant from the subject. The two writers collaborated on the piece, "Look, It's *My* Wedding" for *Bride's.*

As another example, when this book's co-author Diane Gage adopted her son in an open adoption in which she and her husband developed a relationship with the birth mother, she turned the experience into a story for *Good Housekeeping.* "Thank You, Melissa," told of the very special friendship that grew between the two women and the support and gifts they gave to one another during this very emotional time.

Similarly, when this book's other co-author Marcia Coppess was dating her future husband, who was then in law school, she parlayed her frustration of putting up with a boyfriend whose nose was constantly in books into a piece called "Life With Student." It shared the griefs and gripes of a nonstudent partner with others in the same situation.

Yet another freelance writer who was the victim of continuous obscene phone calls decided not to get mad but to turn the experience into a how-to piece for other women on how to handle such calls. A woman writer who owned a jewelry store with her husband knew that other married people in business together had to experience the same feelings of couple claustrophobia. She revealed how she and her husband solved the problem of too much togetherness in the *Good Housekeeping* column, "My Problem," with an article called "My Husband and I Shared Too Much."

Elaine Whiteley, a regular writer for *Ladies' Home Journal* and other women's and inspirational magazines, turned tragedy into triumph when she wrote a piece about her son's head injury. The article, "Child of Promise," which appeared in *The Ensign,* a Mormon magazine, gave other parents hope and courage. She tempered the article with the reality and comfort that, although her son would be different, he brought special love and understanding into their hearts.

Legend has it that when the granddaughter of the composer Bach asked him where he found ideas for his compositions, the master artist replied that it was all he could do not to trip over them when he got out of bed in the morning. The point is, if you are single, married, have kids, own a business, go on vacation, go to school, have a hobby, work to get along with other people—shoot, if you're alive—chances are you are going through experiences that, with some careful thought and a little research, could metamorphose into intriguing article ideas.

Fran Carpentier, the enthusiastic senior articles editor of *Parade*, concurs that writers should consider their interests, background, and knowledge when looking for article ideas. "A lot of writers hold aces, but they just don't play them the way they should," she says. "Do you have any particular training or background or a long-time, well-nurtured interest that makes you the best person to write a particular story or to cover a specific beat? If so, use that to develop story ideas that will inspire confidence in you as a writer from the editors with whom you work."

Getting Inspiration from Newspapers

As a writer, you can expect to spend a great deal of time poring over newspapers, magazines, books, newsletters, and press releases, not only to keep up with trends and the news of the day, but to extract nuggets of information and ideas from articles written on other topics.

To preserve the inspiration of the moment for a time when they can write, many writers save newspaper and magazine articles that they consider to be potential article ideas. They refer to the clips for research leads and for help in generating ideas.

Paula Jhung, a writer who specializes in home decorating and health, keeps a file on anything that appeals to her. "I build files from newspaper articles, notes on something I've heard, and other articles I see," she says. "Then, if I have a question about a home decorating problem, I figure that others might also. I use the newspapers as a starting point to try to find an expert to talk over the problem with and get some good ideas. A query usually begins to gel after that."

Co-authors Gage and Coppess turned a mention in the local news section of their daily newspaper into a story for *Family Circle*. The newspaper article was about a widow's involvement in a grassroots movement to restore education benefits to children whose fathers were killed during the Vietnam War. It seemed to have national potential. *Family Circle* agreed and combined the article with three other stories for the piece, "Women Who Made the Difference." That title later became a regular column open to freelancers. (See the *Family Circle* chapter in Part II for details.)

Studying your local newspaper to keep abreast of hometown articles that can grow into national magazine stories is also a proven technique for idea generation. Rebecca Greer, articles editor of *Woman's Day*, says she is always in need of perceptive writers who keep aware of the world around them. "A dramatic narrative about someone who has been rescued from an accident or saved by a medical miracle is one of the best opportunities for an unknown writer," she says. "I'm looking for the writer from, say, North Carolina, who will send in a newspaper clipping from her local paper about a successful day care program or a dramatic rescue. The writer will pair the clipping with a well-written article proposal in which she suggests an angle and assures us that she has already contacted the people involved and has permission to interview them.

"I can hire my choice of writers to do an article on cancer," Greer continues. "But for dramatic, true stories with heartwarming angles, I look to writers outside of New York City. I am astounded at how few writers take advantage of what they know—viewpoints that we cannot get from our regular stable of contributors."

Reading a brief article in the *San Diego Union/Tribune* became fodder for a *Good Housekeeping* article for co-author Diane Gage. The piece told how a birth father in a small town 100 miles from San Diego had found his son, who had been given up for adoption 18 years earlier, and that a reunion was planned. A call to the school where the father worked put Gage in touch with the man, who was delighted to share his story. The adoptive family and their teenage son in North Carolina also agreed to be interviewed.

And freelancer Elaine Whiteley created a *Ladies' Home Journal* magazine story out of a television news report she saw about a woman whose young daughter had been shot by a playmate who had found a gun in her parents' bedroom. Her daughter's recovery became a Christmas miracle that made a perfect holiday inspirational piece.

Gleaning Ideas from Magazines

A reliable source of ideas that is often overlooked by freelancers is the target magazine itself. Since most magazines have a few subjects of such great interest to their readers that they cover them regularly, identifying those subjects and keeping alert for unusual stories can yield assignments.

"Old issues of magazines are some of the best possible places to find ideas," says freelancer/editor Sherry Suib Cohen, whose byline has been countlessly repeated in *New Woman, Glamour, Ladies' Home Journal, Family Circle,* and *Seventeen.* "There is nothing new under the sun; you can go back through 15 years of *Cosmo,* or any magazine for that matter, and give new twists to old ideas."

Freelancer Ben Wynne of Jackson, Mississippi wanted to write for an in-flight magazine, so he studied Delta Airline's *Sky* magazine. "I read a number of issues to see what types of articles it bought in the past," says Wynne. "I saw that the magazine had done several articles on the 100th anniversary of something—one being the L.A. Dodgers. So, I began looking through an almanac for a hook on an anniversary story. I discovered that the centennial anniversary of the Ferris wheel was approaching. From the back of a matchbook cover I learned that also coming up was the 100th anniversary of the first car. I sold both ideas to *Sky*." (See Wynne's Ferris Wheel query letter reproduced in Chapter 3.)

That's not to say that magazines only want you to feed them ideas they have covered. If *Outside* publishes an article on new spots for mountain biking one month, you should not dash off a query on the same topic. Although magazines repeat general topics, they don't want to approach the stories in the same way twice.

A magazine may feature health topics in each issue. But, unless there is some significant new information or research released, an editor won't cover the same topic for another 12 to 18 months. Still, within a week of publishing an article on a certain subject, editors can expect a handful of queries on that same subject—from writers who apparently believe they could have done a better job than the original writer.

The same "no repeat performance" rule applies to articles that appear in rival magazines. Editors say they frequently receive queries that suggest topics covered in a current issue of a competing magazine. Sometimes, writers even quote the authority cited in the original article. Naturally, no editor will consider running an article so similar to the competition's. If the topic intrigues you, do your homework and find a fresh angle.

Additional Sources of Revelation

Newspapers, magazines, and radio and television news broadcasts are terrific sources of ideas just waiting to be developed. Many news or feature stories you hear on the radio or see on television can be retooled as magazine pieces. Keep a notepad near the TV(s) and radio(s) in your home and car so you can jot down ideas and the names of the experts or people interviewed.

And don't forget the sources from which many radio and TV news departments get their ideas—the many public relations departments and agencies working for businesses and organizations throughout the country. Public relations professionals spend a good portion of their hours turning the expertise of their clients into news releases that will capture the interest of the media. Getting such news releases is often as simple as calling the public relations departments of these organizations and asking to be included on their mailing lists.

The public relations or public information offices of universities, hospitals, agencies, and corporations are often delighted to include freelancers in their media lineup. In fact, many buy mailing lists of writers' organizations and send to writers with a background in their topic the same press information that they send to reporters and producers. You can turn the tables by contacting them first.

You might also want to get in touch with some of the larger or more specialized public relations agencies who represent clients with specialties that interest you. If you are a food writer, for example, it would behoove you to be on the mailing list of the Culinary Institute of America, the U.S. Food and Drug Administration, the American Dairy Council, the American Dietetic Association, various food producers and distributors, and wineries, to name a few. You could also learn which public relations agencies handle food clients by purchasing a directory from the Public Relations Society of America or the International Association of Business Communicators.

Professional and fraternal organizations are equally inspiring sources when it comes to germinating ideas that can grow into articles. Find a few organizations that represent subject categories of interest to you and ask to be included on their mailing lists for news releases and announcements of seminars and trade shows. (See Chapters 4 and 5 to learn how to find these groups.)

Attending seminars and trade shows can fill your head with scores of ideas. Even if you can't attend in person, obtaining the conference or trade booth program or bulletin (which you can receive by mail) is almost as good as being there. The titles and summaries of speeches and the bios on the speakers may trigger questions and curiosity that can be the beginning of a wonderful article. From there, all it takes is a few phone calls to follow up on your idea.

Timing Is Everything

With the plethora of magazines published and the number of ideas gobbled up in each issue, it's imperative that freelancers know what is and is not being covered, so their ideas can be as fresh as possible.

Along with reading magazines and newspapers, you can search for new ideas in professional journals and specialized newsletters. Many writers schedule regular trips to the library to study the specialty published in their area of interest. Some of the ripest ideas waiting to be plucked are found in abstracts. In a few hundred words, an abstract summarizes the latest reports in a particular field. Thousands of potential feature articles are hiding in such publications as *Chemical Abstracts*, *Dissertation Abstracts*

International, Biological Abstracts, and *Social Science Abstracts.* (For more information on abstracts and their use in research, see Chapter 5.)

Before you go too far with any idea, however, check the *Reader's Guide to Periodical Literature* or InfoTrac® in your local library to see if the angle you're taking has been done recently. If you find that your topic was covered within the last year by magazines that rival your market, reconsider either the slant on your topic or the market you've chosen.

Angle, Not Idea!

Once you've become attuned to seeing life's incidents through the eyes of a writer and extracting original ideas from articles and news reports, it's time to find an angle that is different enough from all other articles written on the topic to be unique. Put your idea on a pedestal and, like a sculptor inspecting an uncut stone from every side to find its various shapes waiting to be revealed, critically regard your raw idea from various vantage points. Then, focus on the clearest approach to creating your article "masterpiece."

While this book's co-authors Gage and Coppess were riding the train into New York City to interview an editor for the first edition of this book, one of them worried aloud and then remarked, "I can't believe how much I worry like my mom!" Seconds later, their eyes met with that writer "ah-ha"—the moment when you realize you've taken an everyday occurrence that begs for attention and turned it into a publishable idea. The two spun that offhand comment about worrying into an article idea about how often children emulate their parents' most bothersome characteristics. The resulting article "Are You Picking Up Your Parents' Bad Habits?" was published in *Seventeen.*

The idea for that *Seventeen* article wouldn't even have begun to spark an editor's interest if it had been left in its raw form—stated just as an idea about how kids emulate their parents. Big deal, right? But the idea immediately caught the attention of the magazine's editors by being tweaked to an angle about "picking up parents' bad habits."

Here's another example of how to hone in on what can seem like an elusive angle. You may know more about nutrition than anyone else on earth. But knowledge alone won't garner assignments. Nor will general musings about the number and quantity of daily vitamins an adult needs. That's just an idea. To sell an article, a writer must develop a new twist on a topic—especially one that's been written about a lot. For example, how many people will be interested in an overview on the dangers of lead paint? By contrast, consider how many will read every word of a piece called, "How You Can Protect Your Family From Lead Poisoning."

Parade Senior Editor Fran Carpentier says that it's crucial for writers to recognize the difference between a subject (or topic or idea) and an angle. The editor tells a story of a proposal she initially rejected from a New Jersey writer about the growing movement to teach cardiopulmonary resuscitation (CPR) skills in junior high and grammar schools.

"After the freelancer received a rejection notice, she somehow managed to get on the phone and asked to come in to see me. I don't know how she succeeded—it takes even my dentist five weeks to get through," Carpentier laughs. "But she was insistent that the topic was important. When she came in, she began telling me stories about a nine-year-old trained in CPR who saved her choking two-year-old brother, and a five-year-old who saved his grandmother. I almost got whiplash from raising my head to say, 'Why didn't you tell me you wanted to write an article about *kids who save lives*!?' The writer was able to find similar success stories from across the country. Hence, she got the assignment. Her article was as good as those turned in by the regular pros I work with."

How can you tell the difference between an angle and an idea, or subject? Some hints: you can give a title to an angle; an idea or subject takes at least 30 words to explain. You may envision the style and format the angle will take; the idea seems interesting, but you're not sure how you'd write it. You have a good hunch about what type of magazine may be interested in the angle; the idea or subject just seems like something that would appeal to any reader.

Listed next are five idea/subject examples. Challenge yourself to narrow each into angles for two or more magazines:

- Communication
- Race relations
- Toilet training
- Graduate school
- Boats

One way to develop an angle is to take a three-step approach: begin with a local issue that is familiar to you. What's happening in your own backyard? Assume that in your town the city council election campaigns seem to be based on race rather than on the merits of the candidates. A possible subject or topic, among others, is race relations. Why has this council contest taken such a turn? What has led up to this situation?

Second, look for the universal message in your topic idea. Is it that people of color apparently need to be elected to local office if they are to receive equal attention from City Hall? Is it that some cities are going through a generational transition from white-male-dominated politics to multicultural representation? Or is it that sometimes a white male *is* the best candidate for the job, but people fail to realize it?

Now you're close to an angle—all from the original idea of race relations. Your third step is to find people to populate your article. People want to read about people; magazine editors want articles told through true experiences of real people. It won't do, in most cases, to write a scholarly article on the challenges of establishing qualified multicultural city governments. Most editors would yawn at the thought.

But what about a piece that compares and contrasts city council elections in two different cities, where the facts were the same but the outcomes were different? Could you build an article around that? What form might it take? What's a possible working title or cover line for the magazine? Do you imagine it as an essay, as reportage, or as a long piece about the larger subject and two sidebars about the contrasting council elections?

Now you have an angle, and also a possible format for the article. With the knowledge gained from the previous chapter about identifying markets, your remaining task is to seek out the publication that would most likely want to give its readers this thought-provoking article.

Take the Angle Test

If you can remember the phrase, "Angle, not idea," you'll increase your chances of receiving magazine acceptance letters and phone calls. There aren't many fresh ideas or subjects, but there are endless fresh angles on familiar ideas. Editors want a specific slant that makes a story different from the scores of others already suggested by other magazine writers.

The following list contains a few examples of broad article ideas, each with its unique angle of focus that actually caught an editor's attention and got these articles published:

IDEA: Helping kids cope with surgery.
ANGLE: Hospital teaches kids to play mind games to take their thoughts away from their medical problems.
IDEA: Careful listening improves communications.
ANGLE: Overcoming 12 roadblocks that impede active listening.
IDEA: How to win awards for your work.
ANGLE: How to market your award-winning status to earn new business.

IDEA: The more you know your spouse, the better you'll get along.
ANGLE: A quiz, "How Well Do You Know Your Mate?" that asks questions like—what the name of his dog was when he was growing up; what her favorite color is; and what his worst childhood memory was.

Now, try your hand at crafting angles. Here are a few more ideas that need to be shaped into angles. How would you make these subjects marketable to a magazine?

1. **IDEA:** Why men and women fight
   ANGLE: ________________________________

2. **IDEA:** New childhood cancer treatments
   ANGLE: ________________________________

3. **IDEA:** How to handle emotions in the workplace
   ANGLE: ________________________________

Here are the angles on these same broad ideas that sold to national magazines:

1. "Relationship Waves: Riding Out the Low Times to Reach the Crest Again"
2. "The Good News About Childhood Cancer"
3. "Bare Your Emotions: Why Not? Allowing Employees to Express Emotions Might Motivate Them"

Know Thy Reader

When shaping an idea, it also pays to know your audience. Many new writers who hear the adage, "Write about what you know," take that advice literally without considering the audience that one day might read what they write. The advice might be better phrased, "Write about what your readers want to know." Remember, a writer is a salesperson selling a product to a client with specific needs. You must analyze those needs before trying (fruitlessly) to sell an article on tax reform to *New Body*.

Without doing your homework, you might believe that a story idea you cooked up for *Ski* would work just as well for *Snow Country*. But, although their editorial emphases are similar, the two magazines are far from identical. While *Ski* fascinates readers with the flavor and ambiance of a chic or unique ski resort, *Snow*

Country also delves into the environmental, political, and community aspects of life in snow country.

Some ideas, however, can sell to several markets if you simply change the angle. For instance, *Better Homes and Gardens* and *Country Victorian Decorating & Lifestyle* both publish articles on home decorating and gardening, among other topics. So, if your subject was wicker garden furniture, both magazines would be potential markets. But to *Better Homes and Gardens* you'd need to pitch an article called "How to Care for Wicker" or "Restoring Flea Market Wicker." *Country Victorian Decorating & Lifestyle* wouldn't be interested in those ideas, but might respond to a piece on upholstered Victorian wicker and how to use it in a 1990s home.

Milking Your Idea for All It's Worth

With all the work you'll invest in gathering story ideas, finding experts, and learning about a topic, it makes financial sense to get as much mileage out of one subject as possible. That doesn't mean that you should submit the same query to a number of magazines. Simultaneous submissions are suicide at most magazines. They simply don't work, because all magazines, like all people, have different approaches and responses to the same topic.

But you *can* develop five different angles from the same subject. Let's say that you learn about a restaurant that employs multihandicapped people. The first idea that comes to mind is a warm, fuzzy piece about the restaurant and its work in general. It might work for a women's magazine or even for *Parade*, but what else could you do with it?

In the course of your research on the piece, you learn that the restaurant owner had a brother with Down's Syndrome who died. You could do a piece on this owner and the legacy she has built for her brother. You may also learn that this owner was a very successful entrepreneur before selling out to begin this restaurant. What an interesting profile on someone's choice of lifestyle! Would that idea work for an in-flight magazine? And what about the employment crisis that restaurants are experiencing as the number of available teen workers shrinks? Your information could be incorporated into an article on solving employment woes for a business magazine or a restaurant trade magazine.

Home decorating writer Paula Jhung took an article she did on how to reduce noise in the home and dissected it into at least two additional articles: how to soundproof a house, and how to keep down the clattering in the kitchen. The subject of housework has been a constant feeder for her bank account. She also once wrote about the psychology of housework for the *Los Angeles Times* and parlayed the same subject into a series for the *San Diego Union*, including pieces on clutter, living with less, and preventive measures to reduce housework. She is also working on a book on the topic.

"There are never enough good ideas," says Mark Bryant, editor of *Outside*. "We're very selective, so we overlook a lot of good stories in search of great ones. Despite the fact that we receive dozens of queries a day, I often have to scramble and scratch before an editorial meeting to scare up proposals and ideas that are of the high quality we seek. Any writer who can match intriguing ideas with superior writing will always be in demand."

CHAPTER 3

Crafting Eye-catching Queries

A famous American theatrical producer once said, "If you can't write your idea on the back of my calling card, you don't have a clear idea." While magazine editors allow article proposals—called query letters—to take up more space than the back of a calling card, they demand concise writing and draw the line at the bottom of one page. It's your job to compress onto that one page the most pertinent information about your idea, the reason the editor should buy the article, and the credentials that prove you're the best person to write it.

Virtually all editors welcome a concise query with an intriguing idea that states its case quickly. If the idea is buried in a long query, an editor often will not take the time to decipher it.

"Give me all the pertinent details I need to know up front," says David Neff, executive editor of *Christianity Today.* "The inverted pyramid news style works well for queries." (The inverted pyramid style presents facts in order of their importance, with the most important fact leading the article. That way, if the article must be shortened later to fit onto a page, the less important information gets cut from the bottom, or end, first.)

Although most busy editors resent wading through rambling text in search of a writer's idea, they are more concerned about the content of a query than its length. In addition to selling your product, a query reflects your writing style and ability. A good product may sell in spite of the salesman, but a writer's ability is equally as important as his idea.

A query letter is often the sole criterion by which an editor judges a writer's ability and professionalism. Carolyn Kitch, senior editor at *Good Housekeeping,* says, "People forget that an article proposal is a writing sample. If a writer promises a piece on some powerful, suspenseful rescue and the query is dull and hard to understand, I know the writer will have trouble writing in the dramatic narrative format."

Pre-query Research

"Under-reported queries don't sell," says freelancer Dan Baum, who writes from an office in Missoula, Montana. "It took a while to learn that it takes almost as much research and reporting to write a winning query as it does to complete the article."

Baum often tries to sell his articles first to a newspaper, to pay for the time he'll need to research sufficiently to create a good query.

As stated in Chapter 1, before you begin writing that query, you must determine that your idea is appropriate for your target magazine, and that an article on the same topic with the same approach hasn't been published in your market or a close competitor for at least two years. Unless you have breaking news or research that warrants a new look at the topic, a recent article in a competing magazine is the death knell to your idea. How do you find that out? One way is by reading the magazine and its close competitors and knowing what they have published.

Dan Hurley, a New Jersey writer who has been published in *Good Housekeeping, TV Guide, Parents,* and *Family Circle,* among others, says, "I read three or four back issues and sometimes make a general list of the categories of articles a magazine publishes. Once I know what the magazine wants, I work hard on the first paragraph of my query. It often is very similar to the first paragraph of the eventual article. It has to pique the editor's interest right off the bat because they get hundreds of these letters."

The other way to determine whether your article idea has been published somewhere recently is to look up your subject in the automated InfoTrac® or the *Reader's Guide to Periodical Literature,* which can be found in the reference section of your local library. (For more on libraries, see Chapter 6.)

If you discover recently published articles on your idea, particularly in competing magazines, your timing may be wrong. But it's better to discover this now, rather than after you've invested your time in drafting a query letter.

Once you've determined that your idea and your timing is right for your selected magazine, conduct some preliminary research so that you will be able to write an effective query letter. Some writers do a few brief interviews with experts or people who will be featured in the article to highlight major points; others do a major portion of their article research before querying.

Your query letter will be more convincing and timely if you offer names and titles of any people you plan to interview and tell why they are experts on the subject. But before you promise an editor an interview, get permission to conduct the interview from those people. Once you receive an assignment, it's embarrassing to have to explain later that the person on which your story hinges refuses to grant an interview. If your story concerns a true-life drama or a story available only through one person, be sure to get their go-ahead—preferably on paper—before you query. Otherwise, you may learn later that they are in litigation or working with another writer on a book or movie deal.

Almost as bad as promising an interview you can't get is suggesting a story about a subject in which you really are not interested. When you propose an idea you really aren't sold on, your lack of enthusiasm will show. You may even have trouble completing the piece—and that can ruin your relationship with the magazine.

Create a Title to Hone Your Angle

So, now you know a few things to avoid. What *should* you do to develop that sparkling query that will shout out at an editor and win you an assignment?

"Think headline. Think enticing, sexy, provocative," says Fran Carpentier, senior articles editor of *Parade*. "Be honest," she says. "Would *you* want to read this story?"

A working title will force you to think of an angle instead of just a subject. For instance, jealousy is a topic frequently covered by teen magazines. Yet, proposing a flat article on jealousy probably won't get you very far. What about proposing an article entitled, "When You're Jealous of Your Best Friend"? That one sold to *Seventeen* because it had the right balance: a topic of frequent interest to the reader, and a unique twist that made it different from previous stories.

Don't get too attached to your working title; editors know what titles work for their magazines, and it's rare when they use an initial working title. But taking the time to develop it is a worthwhile sales tool.

Two Who's and Two What's Are All It Takes

There are many ways to write a query letter, but regardless of the style, a query is more than a letter; it's a business proposal. Writing a query letter is like making a sales call. An effective query offers a brief synopsis of the subject, explains what the article will cover and who will be interviewed for it, and concludes with a summary of the special knowledge or background that makes the writer the best person to write the article.

You can streamline your query writing by remembering the two who's and two what's of query letters:

- **Start with a what.** What do you want to write about? Tell the editor immediately in some interesting, amusing, or poignant way why he or she should read further. Try using an intriguing quote, a very brief anecdote, or perhaps a statistic that is certain to raise an eyebrow. But only use those tools if they are real grabbers. Sometimes, the most compelling way to sell a story is to write a straight, brief paragraph that states the fact you want to explore.
- **Follow with a who.** Whom will you interview? Who says so? Who disagrees? From whom have you already secured a revealing interview?
- **Then another what.** What will you prove? What do your experts say about it? On what parts do they disagree? What are the details behind your idea? Try telling the editor what you'll do by writing a four- or five-point list in bulleted form. (Bullets are dots, squares, asterisks, or some other symbol to highlight and delineate points.)

  Note, though, that you may find that it makes sense to switch the order of the second and third parts of your query, depending on the subject and the approach you want to take.
- **Finally, *who* are you?** Why are you the person to write this article? This is a paragraph that usually begins with, "I have written for...," or something similar.

  If you haven't yet sold an article to a magazine, why are you qualified to write on this topic? Do you have access to an exclusive interview? Is this an area you've studied or followed for several years? Do you have a personal perspective to bring to a universal issue?

Unsolicited Manuscripts and Simultaneous Submissions

Some writers bypass the query stage and send in an entire article, thinking that it will sell easier and faster. But submitting an unsolicited manuscript is considered amateurish by nearly all editors. (A few editors are open to unsolicited manuscripts. Their particular interests are noted in the chapters about their magazines.) Today, slimmer staffs mean that fewer editors have more responsibilities, so some magazines refuse even to review unsolicited material. It's considered a big a waste of time, not to mention unprofessional.

There are four exceptions to the "no unsolicited manuscripts" rule. They are: humor, essays, opinion, and fiction. Those styles of writing can be judged only by reading the finished product. A query that says, "I'm going to write a story that will make you fall out of your chair laughing" proves nothing. The editor must read the manuscript and risk the fall.

In most nonfiction departments, your prized manuscript may be tossed into the "slush pile" until someone has a free moment to scan it before sending it back to you. There's a sound reason behind that policy. Ideally, an article is a collaboration between an editor and a writer. While the writer may come up with the angle, an editor will suggest a little more in one area and steer clear of other areas. When unexpected information or research comes up midway through the piece, the two parties talk over how to handle it: the writer has more information about the subject, while the editor knows what his readers want to know and what has been covered in the past.

Later, when the manuscript is edited, the editor turns to the writer for clarification, but relies on his own skill to polish the author's prose. So in the end, whose article is it? The professional freelancer is grateful to a good editor, who almost always makes the writer sound better. And the editor appreciates the opportunity to work with a writer who has good solid writing skills but also is open to changes and improvements to his story.

Fran Carpentier of *Parade*, explains, "Together, you the writer and we the editors are smarter than any one of us alone. We are not adversaries, and it's best when we work together."

When you go ahead and submit a completed manuscript, you circumvent the guidance you would have had from an editor. Now you have only one chance, and the editor sees only one version of an idea that could have taken any number of turns. The odds of your approach being just right without some editorial input are too slim, considering the time you must invest in writing the article.

After you've worked so hard to prepare a sparkling query, it may be tempting to submit it to as many magazines as you can think of. But most editors frown upon simultaneous submissions. They want ideas that no other magazine has touched upon, so they are seldom willing to consider queries they know other editors are reading at the same time. Though the custom seems unfair to writers, it can hurt your reputation if you ignore it.

Here's a thought about simultaneous submissions from the *Better Homes and Gardens* Freelance Fact Sheet: "If you expect to sell the same article to several publications, do not send it to us. It is not journalistically ethical to send copies of the same article simultaneously to more than one publication, with the purpose of making a sale to the first that accepts it. This practice is likely to result in serious embarrassment."

"Simultaneous submissions are usually a turn-off," says Sharyn Skeeter, editor-in-chief of *Black Elegance.* "It depends, however; if the magazine is not a competitor or my readers won't ever see the piece it doesn't matter to me. But I *do* want to know if it is happening."

Terri Barnes, editor of *USAir*, becomes frustrated with writers who categorize in-flight and travel magazines as one amorphous group. "They often send the same idea to 20 magazines without discerning the differences between the magazines," she says. "If they would spend more time on fewer magazines, they'd probably be more effective."

Getting in Form

Many editors have idiosyncratic preferences about queries. You'll learn those as you read the Part II chapters in this book and when you develop relationships with the editors in your target markets. But from the information received by the co-authors of this book while interviewing the many editors quoted in Part II, four basic proposal styles that work were identified, as well as a fifth style reserved for very seasoned, established writers.

A cover letter, which can accompany any of these query styles, is one of the most graceful ways to include a personal note to an editor you know without interrupting the flow of the query. And since the editor will most likely keep the letter in an "in" basket while the proposal circulates among other editors for their comments, it will serve as a reminder that you await a reply.

The five query styles exampled in this chapter differ slightly from those featured in earlier versions of *Get Published.* The Business Proposal, in particular, has changed significantly. It is a style now greatly preferred by many editors, while the more detailed Summary Query now comes in second.

Sample Query Letters That Sold

What follows are a number of letters written by freelancers across the nation that resulted in assignments from major magazines. Take the time to study their style, form, and the content. Notice the differences between the Summary Query and the Business Proposal. Think about when you might send a Short Take to one of your target magazines—and for what column it might work. While both Outline Queries are the results of editors' requests for information, think about how an outline query might take shape as a first query to an editor.

1. The Business Proposal. With the busy pace at today's understaffed magazine offices, many editors now prefer the Business Proposal. It is a straightforward letter stating up front what you want to write. The topic is followed by your approach and the names of experts or other appropriate sources. The letter ends with your credentials and a cordial invitation to call. It is kept to one page in length.

There is no sample lead, no quotes, no anecdotes. Just the facts—fast and straight. Yet, while many editors say they want a fast-read query, they still require all of the elements of the story. Without those, they can't make a decision—and a tough decision frequently becomes a "no" when an editor doesn't have enough to go on.

Clips are important with a Business Proposal. Since your query will not demonstrate your ability to create beautiful prose, the article samples you attach must do the trick for you. Be sure to choose a sample or two that are close in tone to the article you want to write. If you do not have clips, write the first page of your proposed article in the style you anticipate using, and attach it to your letter.

Business Proposal Sample (typed on letterhead)

(Date)

Harry Bacas
Senior Editor
Nation's Business
1615 "H" Street, N.W.
Washington, DC 20062

Dear Mr. Bacas:

Managers of small businesses seem to carry all the company's problems on their shoulders. But being a leader doesn't mean running a one-man show and taking ownership of every problem.

In an article for *Nation's Business* titled, "The High Cost of Running a One-Man Show," business managers will learn to recognize who really owns a problem and how they can delegate responsibility accordingly.

The article will show readers the wisdom in learning to abdicate the one-man show role. It will address the problems of over-supervising and the benefits of working within a team framework. Leaders can learn to move from being problem solvers to being facilitators who see that issues get resolved.

There is a big difference between the two approaches; the latter leads to a more participative process between the leader and his or her staff. Learning these methods frees managers to do the more specialized work for which they were trained.

I have interviewed Sidney Wool, director of the L.E.T. Program for Effectiveness training in Solana Beach, California, and Fred Pryor, CEO of Pryor Resources, Inc., a management consulting firm in Shawnee Mission, Kansas. In addition to experts, I'll talk to owners and managers of small- to medium-size businesses to discover how they deal with the issue.

I have written for *Entrepreneur, Income Opportunities, Reader's Digest, McCall's, Family Circle, Good Housekeeping* and *Health.*

Sincerely,

Diane Gage

* * *

2. The Summary Query. Some editors still prefer the Summary Query, a proposal that mirrors the article you want to write. It usually opens with a sample lead paragraph that might include a colorful anecdote, quote, or statistic. The body of the query provides examples of the information the article would offer, such as new trends and the names of people you plan to interview. The last paragraph summarizes your writing experience and any credentials that qualify you to write the piece.

Like the Business Proposal, a Summary Query should be as specific as you can make it within the confines of one to two pages. Let the editor know the style of article you have in mind. Will it be news-packed reportage, a question-and-answer interview, or a first-person experience?

Hit your editor with a lead that intrigues him. Then tell a story that he can't stop reading and convince him that you have enough information on your topic to warrant an assignment.

The Summary Query can take on two forms, depending on your needs: the first has a cover letter attached that is used to mention a previous assignment, make a personal comment to the editor, or to emphasize the access you have to a person you think the editor would like to feature in his magazine; the second page then begins with the article title, centered a couple of inches down the page, and the query.

The second form of a Summary Query is set up like a traditional business letter: date, name of editor, title, magazine name, address, and a salutation. It then launches directly into your sparkling lead. It may seem odd at first to dispense with a greeting and, instead, start with "Johnny was six days old when...." but that's standard in this business, and an editor will not think it odd at all. In fact, a letter beginning with, "I admire your magazine so much that I'd like to write for it. Here is my idea," will tip off the editor that you're new to the game.

There are several formats the Summary Query can take. It can be typed as a standard letter or it can be typed in article style with a headline and byline and accompanied by a brief cover letter that simply tells the editor a query is enclosed. If you choose the latter, make sure that the page with the actual query on it is printed on letterhead so your telephone number is easily accessible should your cover letter get separated from the query. Following are three Summary Query samples:

Summary Query Sample #1 (typed on letterhead)

(Date)

Lidia de Leon, Editor
SKY
Halsey Publishing Company
12955 Biscayne Boulevard
North Miami, FL 33181

Dear Ms. de Leon,

George Washington Gale Ferris was disparaged by more than a few people as "The man with wheels in his head" when he conceived a wild notion in the spring of 1892. An architect and bridge builder, Ferris attended a meeting in Chicago where the upcoming Columbian Exposition of 1893 was discussed. A general consensus held that the Chicago Midway needed a centerpiece, a focal point to rival the Eiffel Tower that had been unveiled at the Paris Exposition three years earlier. "Towers of various kinds have been proposed," stated the mandate, "but towers are not original. Mere bigness is not what is wanted—something novel, daring, and unique must be designed and built if American engineers are to retain their prestige and standing." Acting on this sentiment, Ferris came up with a unique design, a design that would entertain generations of Americans at county fairs and amusement parks and one that continues to bear his name today.

George Washington Gale Ferris was the father of the Ferris Wheel. The first "Great Wheel" was designed by Ferris in 1892 and put on line at the Columbian World Exposition of 1893. It created an immediate sensation and was lauded as a "glorious triumph of American industry and skill." It was 250 feet in diameter with each car being 27 feet long and 13 feet wide. At full capacity the wheel held about 2100 passengers and by the end of the Exposition over one and a half million fairgoers had ridden it. It was a smashing success and was reported as such throughout the country. A member of one of the foreign delegations that were headquartered near the wheel summed up the experience when he observed, "When it was seen that the wheel was moving, the foreigners from many nations came running from all sides, shouting vociferously and gesticulating wildly. The wheel had been an enigma to them." Others stated that the wheel attained it greatest majesty at night when it was outlined by 3,000 incandescent lights donated by the Western Electric Company of Chicago.

I am a freelance writer who would dearly love to prepare an article for SKY Magazine on Mr. Ferris and the original Ferris Wheel for publication next year. I believe this would be appropriate because 1992 marks the hundredth anniversary of the Ferris Wheel. I have access to all relative information through a variety of sources, including the Chicago Historical Society and the Nevada State Historical Society (where many of Ferris' papers are held).

If SKY Magazine is interested in an article of this nature I would appreciate the opportunity to write it. Thank you very much for your time and consideration.

Best Wishes,

Ben Wynne

(Reprinted with permission from Ben Wynne)

* * *

Summary Query Sample #2 (typed on letterhead and sent with cover note)

(Date)

WOMAN'S DAY Article Proposal

"A Parent's Worst Nightmare"
by Elaine F. Whiteley

Rebecca and Kenneth Routon awoke one night to every parent's worst nightmare. An intruder had entered their

Tustin, California home through an unlocked patio door and carried their nine-year-old daughter Jennifer from her bedroom. Groggy with sleep, Rebecca heard their 15-year-old son, Joshua, shouting for help. But before she could move, Kenneth leaped out of bed and ran into the hallway. Joshua pointed to the stairs and yelled, "Dad! Someone is taking Jennifer downstairs!"

The unarmed father raced down the stairs and out the patio door. In the moonlight he could see Jennifer kicking and screaming hysterically as the man dragged her across the lawn. "Let her go!" Kenneth hollered.

The kidnapper whirled around, his left arm hooked around the girl's neck. He pressed a knife against the soft flesh of her throat and rasped, "Come any closer and I'll kill her!"

Kenneth didn't hesitate. "I knew if I didn't get to her soon, she'd be dead anyway," he explains. Screaming, "You'll have to kill me first!" he hurled himself at the assailant. The man slashed out at Kenneth. The sharp blade cut his arm, but he felt no pain. "It didn't matter what it took," Kenneth relates. "As long as I was alive I wouldn't let him take my little girl."

The article I propose will share with readers of WOMAN'S DAY the details of this exciting story. I will include:

- Rebecca's part in the drama, including her feelings of horror and helplessness when she realized her daughter had nearly been kidnapped;
- Further details of Jennifer's rescue and the intruder's arrest after Kenneth knocked him unconscious;
- The trial at which Jennifer's testimony of how she desperately pled with her abductor not to kill her moved the jurors to tears;
- Mention of the many cards and letters the Routons have received from across the nation praising the rescue.

As a freelance writer, I've sold my work to a children's magazine, THE FRIEND, a clip of which I'm enclosing. If you wish, I can provide photos of the Routon family. Interested? I'll look forward to hearing from you.

(Reprinted with permission of Elaine Whiteley)

* * *

Summary Query Sample #3 (typed on letterhead and sent with cover note)

(Date)

LADIES' HOME JOURNAL ARTICLE PROPOSAL

"Baby Sitters Who Maim and Kill"
by Elaine F. Whiteley

Jane Snead, a Virginia mother, thought she had found the perfect baby sitter for her six-week-old daughter Ashley. Martha Guba, a pleasant, older woman told Jane, "I charge a little more, but I give that extra loving care."

By the time Ashley turned 10 months old, she screamed every time her mother dropped her off at the sitter's house. But because Martha seemed devoted to the baby, Jane thought her child was just being manipulative. Then Jane received a frantic phone call at work. Something was terribly wrong with her baby and the paramedics were rushing the child to the hospital. Ashley died before Jane could reach her. To the mother's horror, she learned the baby sitter had given the child a massive overdose of an antidepressant to keep her from fussing.

Jane's shocking story is hardly an isolated incident. In "Baby Sitters Who Maim and Kill," I will share the stories of nine women from six states whose children were seriously injured or killed by their baby sitters. These mothers, all from middle to upper-income families, felt they had placed their children in loving homes.

I believe a similar format to the one used in the article "In Families Like Ours," printed in your April issue, would work well for the proposed piece. I will offer:

- Statistics and facts illustrating the extent of abuse in family day care.
- Reasons why some home day-care providers abuse children in their care. (Generally for the same reasons parents do. In some cases, the sitters shook the children, not realizing it could cause serious injury or death.)
- Warning signs to look for that may indicate abuse.
- Problems within the system.
- Suggestions on how parents can protect their children.
- Tips for finding safe home day care.
- Solutions that will prevent abuse.

Attached is a list of experts I will quote.

I will also provide three service sidebars. The first will summarize steps parents should look for in choosing home day care. The second, the address of where to write for more information concerning a newly formed support group for parents of children abused in day care. And last, a coupon readers can clip and mail to their representatives in Congress encouraging their support for a child care bill that will mandate tougher home day care regulations.

Although the majority of women who provide home day care give excellent, loving service, there are some who do not. Deborah Daro, director of research for the National Committee for the Prevention of Child Abuse, estimates that in the United States, eight to nine thousand children are maimed or killed each year by home day-care providers. The situation will only get worse as the number of working mothers increases.

Part of the problem is the lack of state and federal regulations governing day care. Legislation proposing to set up minimum standards for the health and safety of children in home day care is scheduled to go before Congress when it convenes in January. If passed, the bill will ensure that every day-care provider receives training in child abuse development and understand how to discipline children without abuse.

In addition, the bill provides safeguards to alert parents if their baby sitter has ever been convicted of criminal activities or child abuse. In Jane Snead's case, her baby sitter had been convicted 10 years before for abusing her own two children. Yet, the sitter's name appeared on a list of day-care providers kept by the Fairfax County Office of Children.

As a freelance writer, I've had a story appear in a children's magazine, THE FRIEND, a clip of which I'm enclosing. I've also recently sold an article to WOMAN'S DAY.

The proposed article, "Baby Sitters Who Maim and Kill," concerns a vital issue of our times. Are you interested?

(Reprinted with permission of Elaine F. Whiteley)

* * *

3. The Outline Query. If your article proposal includes 10 main points, or gives the five major aspects of a subject, the Outline Query may work for you. This outline is different from the academic A-B-C outline you learned in high school composition class. It starts with a two- or three-sentence synopsis of your idea. Then it highlights major points of your article in simple phrases.

To emphasize the points, indent each phrase and use dashes, numbers, or bullets (heavy, solid dots) at the beginning of each phrase.

Next are two examples of Outline Queries. First is a proposal sent by book co-author Marcia Coppess following a New York visit during which she met with Jane Chestnutt, editor-in-chief of *Woman's Day.* (Chestnutt was then health and beauty editor.) The two discussed several ideas on dental topics, and the editor requested a couple of approaches. This is the approach that sold:

Outline Query Sample #1 (typed on letterhead)

(Date)

Jane Chestnutt
Health and Beauty Editor
Woman's Day
1515 Broadway
New York, NY 10036

Dear Jane:

I haven't forgotten you, or the ideas we discussed. I've been collecting material since we met, and have talked with a number of the nation's top dental researchers about what is hot in their field.

You asked what five things a dentist could do that a patient might not know to ask. I directed that question to a handful of dentists and educators. I have plenty of tips, and can provide a list of five, 10 or 20 things, depending on what you need. Some examples:
A dentist can:

- Take your blood pressure
- Recommend or fit you for an anti-snoring device
- Perform a complete head-and-neck cancer check
- Diagnose diabetes (Dentists are often the first to notice the likelihood of the diagnosis)
- Fit a youngster for an athletic mouthguard
- Fit and insert idental-fication tags on a back tooth
- Take and maintain a complete medical history
- Provide a second opinion before a patient undergoes extensive treatment

I have plenty of material to cover dentistry as a "Breakthroughs in Dentistry" piece or as "Ten Things Your Dentist Can Do For

You That You Might Not Think To Ask." Give a call when you'd like to discuss these ideas. Thanks for your interest, Jane.

Sincerely,

Marcia Coppess

* * *

Next is an example of an Outline Query and cover letter that book co-author Diane Gage sent to *Good Housekeeping* after she had completed the research on a story on day care in the '90s assigned to her by the magazine.

Outline Query Sample #2 (printed on letterhead)

(Date)

Mary Ann Littell
Director/Editor
Infants and Children Laboratory
GOOD HOUSEKEEPING
959 Eighth Ave.
New York, NY 10019

Dear Mary Ann:

I have finished my series of interviews with Anne Mitchell of Bank Street College of Education for the "Day Care in the '90s" article and have enclosed an outline for your review.

Please give me a call as soon as you can to discuss the outline and let me know any changes you'd like to make.

In addition to interviewing Anne, I sent away for a number of articles and reports which provided me with direction for my questions and topics I felt we needed to cover. I'll be including some information from that research, but most of the editorial material will come from Anne, who has been terrific to work with.

I look forward to talking with you.

Sincerely,

Diane Gage

GOOD HOUSEKEEPING

Article Outline

"Day Care in the '90s"

I. Overview

a. Economy changing in a way that most families require more than one job to support themselves.

b. Two out of three mothers are working outside the home.

c. Organized child care system has responded to meet rising demand. There are a number of problems that remain as challenges for this decade. There is a shortage of quality day care, especially in infant and toddler care. Most day care workers are underpaid, and many families have a difficult time affording day care. There are no national standards and quality varies greatly by state.

II. Day Care Options/Hours in Day Care

a. 1990 stats on where children are cared for e.g. family day care, center-based care, relatives, in-home (nannies).

b. The number of children in child care centers is dramatically up for children ages 3-5, due to parents' desire for education for their children.

c. Public schools provide programs for kids with special needs under age 5, economically disadvantaged children and after-school programs for children over age 5.

d. More than half of the children in centers or family day care spend more than 35 hours a week in day care.

III. Costs

a. Parents who buy full-time day care typically spend just slightly less on child care than they do on their mortgage.

b. Families can afford about 10% of their income spent on day care; but they actually pay about 20%.

c. The cost of day care varies by locale. On average, centers cost about $357 a month and family day care costs about $369 a month.

d. Coverage of the following:
- Child Care Development Block Grant
- Dependent Care Tax Credit
- Flexible Spending Accounts
- Earned Income Tax Credit

IV. Child Care Provision in the Workplace

a. Employers are increasingly recognizing that child care is a major family issue that affects workers' productivity and job satisfaction.

b. Percentage of day care provided in the workplace.

c. Coverage of Dependent Care Assistance Plan and flex-time.

V. Quality of Care

a. Many state child care regulations don't ensure quality.

b. Quality day care means a clean and safe environment with appropriate equipment and enough adults who know what they are doing working with the kids.

c. Day care centers must be vigilant about handwashing. Colds, upper respiratory infections and communicable diseases are vastly reduced when good handwashing practices are in place.

d. Research shows that the quality of day care is based on the training and education of teachers and a small staff/child ratio to provide more individualized attention.

e. The National Association for the Education of Young Children has an accreditation program for centers. Only 3,000-5,000 out of the 80,000 nationwide are accredited.

VI. The Threat of Child Abuse

a. Children are more at risk for child abuse by members of their families than by child care providers.

b. Only 1.5 percent of the 2.5 million children in day care are abused. Child care programs are not high-risk places for physical or sexual abuse.

VII. Parents & Guilt

a. Having moms work is not bad for kids. If parents feel good about themselves, that is good for their kids.

b. Part of being a good parent is knowing how to find good child care.

c. The relationship parents have with their children's care givers is more important than the number of hours spent in day care.

d. Parents have the first and most enduring, meaningful relationship. It is essential that families make sure they have a family life as well as a work life.

* * *

4. The Short Take. This format is especially effective for querying the editor of a news-brief section when you're trying to break in, such as those found in *American Visions*' "Arts Scene," *Harrowsmith Country Life*'s "Gazette," or *Snow Country*'s "Snow Country Store." This approach also works with an editor whom you want to impress with your breadth of knowledge in an area or for a particular column.

Instead of submitting one fully-developed query, offer three to five ideas and devote a couple of short, titled paragraphs to each. After your last idea, state your qualifications and tell the editor that you will send a more fully developed proposal for any or all of the "Short Takes" at his request. In the case of using Short Takes to propose longer pieces, expect the editor to ask for expanded proposals on anything in which he is interested. Though some editors don't mind receiving up to 10 Short Takes at once, it is best to submit only a few the first time to see whether your editor is open to the approach. A disadvantage of this type of query is the possibility that the editor may pick only what he considers the best idea in the group. You may have to forfeit the other ideas at that magazine—one or two of which may have worked if presented alone—in exchange for impressing the editor with your boundless imagination.

Writer Paula Jhung always combines a basic Summary Query on one topic with a few Short Takes. (See one of her queries later in this chapter.) Jhung ends her article proposals with two or three other ideas. She writes them in quick sentences, outlining a point or two about each. This sends a message to the editor that Jhung is serious about writing for the magazine.

Short Take Query Sample (typed on letterhead)

(Date)

Susan Sulich
Articles Editor
BRIDAL GUIDE
441 Lexington Ave.
New York, NY 10017

Dear Susan:

Thanks for asking me to send you some article ideas. Here are three wedding how-to ideas for you to consider.

1. THE SENSUOUS WEDDING

In "The Sensuous Wedding," I will describe how to take into account little details that make a wedding memorable by learning to appeal to the senses. It might be the luxurious texture of plush velvet dresses, the visual delight of a brilliant bouquet, the warm, cozy smell of hot apple cider, or the emotional tug of a long-forgotten love song.

One San Diego couple worked to make their wedding as warm and cozy as a Victorian Christmas card. When guests walked through the door to their reception, they were met by the smell of hot apple cider and the sounds of Bing Crosby singing "White Christmas." The yuletide spirit was complete when guests found tiny, beautifully wrapped Christmas presents at their table settings.

Another bride used ultra-romantic prelude music that brought tears to many guests' eyes. Then, when the last bridesmaid had made her way to the altar, the church doors closed tightly. After a dramatic pause and the flair of trumpets, the doors opened to reveal the bride and her father.

Sensual weddings make lasting impressions, creating memories in the hearts and minds of family and friends for a long time to come.

2. GETTING TO KNOW YOU: WEDDING PARTY PLEASERS

Your wedding party is large. But the members' acquaintance of one another is small. Why not build a rapport between them before the big day?

Here are some ideas. Consultant Lisa DeMarco suggests throwing a "bridal party party" at least a month before the wedding to help transform acquaintances into friends. One couple asked their attendants to be in the wedding by mailing them fortune cookies that included the personal request.

Another bride created a music video for her bridesmaids—a group of longtime friends. Yet another bride wrote a poem about friendship for her bridesmaids who did not know one another before the wedding.

"Wedding Party Pleasers" will show couples fun ways to break the ice and build a stronger bond in their own friendships with these loved ones as well.

3. THE ENCHANTING ELEMENT OF SURPRISE

She surprised him before the wedding by sending an embroidered handkerchief to his room. It read "Forever My Prince." He surprised her by singing their special song at the reception. They surprised their families by writing vows dedicated to them alone.

In "The Enchanting Element of Surprise," I will share how many couples are delighting friends, family, guests, and one another, by including some loving mischief in their wedding day.

The examples included in the article can be both naughty and nice. For example, one wedding party attendant decorated the bride and groom's hotel suite and included a basket of champagne, chocolates, and lingerie items. But before she left the hotel room, she also left a flannel nightgown on the king-size bed.

A couple might choose to have their parents' wedding song played as one of the first dance numbers. Or if a good friend or relative has just celebrated a birthday, they might invite everyone to join in a chorus of "Happy Birthday."

Special touches like these, and many more to be discovered from interviews of bridal consultants and brides, make the wedding party and guests feel special and included in the fun and festivities.

I look forward to hearing from you about these ideas.

Sincerely,

Deborah Brada

(Reprinted with permission from Deborah Brada.)

* * *

5. The Fishing Expedition. A seasoned writer with impressive credits who wants to develop a relationship with a new editor may send a letter of introduction rather than a query. The letter summarizes the writer's publishing credentials, outlines his areas of expertise, includes solid clips, and indicates that he is already knowledgeable about the magazine and eager to work for the editor. This query style is used in the travel-writing field by writers who can, for instance, offer 13 years as a resident of and writer about Indonesia. However, while the Fishing Expedition query may result in an assignment for a well-published writer, it will not work for the writer who has not yet established a track record. Don't reveal your naïveté by trying this type of letter before you've earned a stack of good clips to back it up.

Fishing Expedition Sample (typed on letterhead)

(Date)

Deborah Harding, Editor-in-Chief
Shelter Magazine Division
GCR Publishing Group
1700 Broadway
New York, NY 10019

Dear Ms. Harding,

Congratulations on your new position at GCR. Diane Gage forwarded your letter to me since I specialize in homes. You may remember Diane and I collaborated on a series of decorating articles for BRIDAL GUIDE in 1990.

A little about myself: I have a background in interior design and have been writing about homes since 1981. I wrote a remodeling column for THE SAN DIEGO UNION for a number of years, and am now a frequent contributor to the LOS ANGELES TIMES. I was also a regular at 1,001 HOME IDEAS, most often in their "1,001 Ways To Save" department. My work has appeared in HOME MAGAZINE, among others, including shorts in the "Reader's Idea Exchange" of FAMILY CIRCLE. I have a book and a syndicated column under consideration as well. I was also a scout for HOMESTYLES, where I tracked and photographed homes built from the publication's blueprints. My photography skills are limited, but I have access to a nationally published interior design photographer.

I love the look of COUNTRY ACCENTS and COUNTRY VICTORIAN ACCENTS and would like to be a part of your team. I live in an area of truly beautiful homes and know of a number of good candidates for COUNTRY ACCENTS. One is a house built by Douglas Fairbanks and Mary Pickford for the manager of their cattle ranch. It and the main house were designed by architect Wallace Neff, who designed homes for Cary Grant, Charlie Chaplin, Joan Bennett, Groucho Marx, Darryl Zanuck, and Jack Lemmon, among others.

While the Fairbanks house had never been structurally changed, it had fallen into disrepair over the years. The current owners, Mary and Bill Culver, have restored it to its former charm. They have also added a large organic garden where they grow vegetables and herbs for themselves and for a local cooking school. Mary makes dried wreaths and arrangements from the garden as well.

On the following pages I've proposed a lead, working title, and some highlights of the piece. I start with the history of the place, then go on to tell what the new owners have done and how they did it.

I've included a copy of a photo from the early days as well as some snapshots taken recently. The interior design may look a little spare for COUNTRY ACCENTS but there's a wealth of good things that can be massed for effect.

Sincerely,

Paula Jhung

(reprinted with permission of Paula Jhung)

* * *

After All That, Who Needs to Query?

With a lot of work and a little luck, you'll discover that your phone begins to ring, bringing with it assignments from editors you've begun to work for, as well as calls from other editors who want to see something from you, or who suggest that you write a particular story for their publication. Since the writers featured in this book are well established in their careers, few of them have to write queries any more. Instead editors call them with assignments.

"I rarely do queries," says Gurney Williams, III, former editor of *Popular Mechanics* and *Omni*, and now a freelancer for many major magazines. "Most of my articles are assignments. But, once in a while, an editor will call and say he wants me to do a piece. He will want a brief summary of what I would do with the topic—sort of a pseudoquery. It has never led to an editor saying no to my approach.

"Queries are dead time," the writer-turned-editor-turned-writer Williams says. "Just remember that they make no money and take a fair amount of work to do. So, while you need to be thorough—especially when you're just starting out in this business and are unknown—but watch how much time you put into it and use self-restraint."

Good advice from someone who has sat on both sides of the desk. And, if you make your queries as thorough as possible and as quickly as possible, you'll have more time for more queries. Then one day you'll realize that you can't remember the last time you wrote one of those old things!

How to Shorten a Lengthy Query

The overwhelming majority of editors prefer queries no longer than one page, though many agree that some queries have to spill onto the second page. However, three-page proposals will seldom get the results you seek. When your query runs too long, consider these points:

- **Title.** Does your proposed article offer a working title? A title forces you to narrow your topic and helps an editor understand what you want to say—without a lot of words.
- **Anecdotes.** How many anecdotes have you included? How long are they? An anecdote can be a good beginning, but it should be no more than two or three sentences long. Leave the best and cut the rest.
- **Quotes.** How long are the quotes you feature? One quote from a primary source is plenty. Lengthy quotes serve no purpose.

- **Bullets.** Did you summarize the points you'll cover rather than explaining them at length? Of course, you should tell your editor what you plan to cover and how you plan to do that. But save space by "bulleting" your points, as in this list:

  In "How to Shorten a Lengthy Query," readers learn to:

  - Write a working title to narrow their topic
  - Eliminate unnecessary anecdotes
  - Slim down the quotes they use
  - Use bullets instead of long-winded paragraphs
  - Attach copies of published articles instead of writing a long biographical paragraph

- **Clips.** Did you attach three clips of published work? This will shorten your biographical paragraph to, "Some copies of my recent work are attached."

The Basics Count

"The query is your opening gambit. It's worth spending time to make it the most professional presentation possible," says Duncan Barnes, editor of *Field & Stream.*

Your idea may be extremely timely or important, but many editors will refuse even to consider it unless it is submitted as a polished query package. Editors complain about three aspects of a query package most often: (1) the physical appearance of the query; (2) the grammar, spelling, and punctuation; (3) the quality of the writer's clippings of published work.

- **Appearance.** Although query formats vary, proposals are usually set up like business letters, with the writer's return address and phone number, the date, the editor's name and title, magazine name and address, and a salutation. (Check the masthead of the current issue of the magazine you are querying, or give a quick call to the magazine's editorial department to verify that the editor to whom you are writing is still on staff and still holds the same position as listed in this book's Part II chapters or in whatever other reference you're using to glean this type of information.)

  Your letter must be typed or word-processed; not even the very neatest handwriting is acceptable. If you don't have access to a computer and can't afford to buy one, it's worth the couple of dollars it may cost to pay a professional to prepare your letter. Many typists work out of their homes and charge a fair price. Or you may want to rent computer time from a friend, business, or library. Some business printing chains offer computers for hire by the hour, too.

Maria Anton, senior managing editor of *Entrepreneur*, comments, "I often receive unprofessional looking queries —they are typed on old typewriters and are hard to read. I won't pass up a query just because of its looks, but if a person can't even produce a professional-looking letter, I wonder how good their story will be.

"Serious writers look good," she continues. "Their letters are crisp and clean. I think the appearance of the page reflects how professional they are. Serious writers invest in good equipment."

If you work on a computer or plan to buy one, be aware that editors, who read scores of queries every day, do not look kindly upon writers who use poor-quality dot-matrix printers. If you wonder why your queries are receiving replies so slowly, it may be that a tired-eyed editor keeps allowing that dot-matrix letter to sift back to the bottom of the in basket. Since the price of computers and software has dropped so dramatically, try to buy an adequate computer and good-quality printer. Graphics and other extras aren't necessary; you just need to be able to produce a professional-looking page.

Editors also frown upon any photocopied query letters, complaining that copies are often difficult to read because of the poor quality of reproduction. Copies also make an editor feel as though he is just one of many editors evaluating your idea—and remember that few editors are willing to tolerate multiple submissions.

Personal letterhead, if it is done correctly, projects a professional image to an editor unfamiliar with your work. If you use black ink and a standard 20-pound paper, white or colored, the cost can be minimized. (Colored ink and special printing processes cost more.) If your budget allows it, consider investing in personalized 9" x 12" catalog envelopes (number 10½), since you will use those most often to submit queries, manuscripts, and clips in a flat package.

Alternatively, have labels printed with your name and address, with room to address the rest of the label to a magazine. If you work on a computer or word processor, you can select labels that your printer can accommodate.

You may also want to have business-size envelopes (number 10) printed with your return address for other correspondence with editors and story contacts. And, as you become a more active freelancer, you'll discover that having business cards, with your name, address, and phone and FAX numbers, saves a lot of time and confusion when giving your name to prospective sources and interviewees.

But beware. Editors have specific biases that might work against you about letterhead and business cards. A number of editors even mistrust writers who take the straightforward approach of putting "Writer" or "Freelance Writer" under their name. It seems that the sheer numbers of writer "wannabes" has prejudiced editors against even a simple statement of profession. Some writers, however, put a description of the type of work they do, such as "writing/editing" because they want to use their cards broadly to solicit new business.

It is essential that your magazine proposal include a self-addressed, stamped envelope (SASE). Because of the huge expense a magazine would incur if it paid the postage needed to respond to the thousands of queries it receives each year, nearly all editors refuse to reply unless a writer sends an SASE. Some editors will use the SASE to return your query with a rejection note naming the article and the reason why they can't use it; others simply insert a preprinted, all-purpose rejection slip in it. Don't take that personally—it's just another indication of an editor's lack of time.

- **Grammar, Spelling, and Punctuation.** Most writers know that good grammar, spelling, and punctuation are the basic requirements of writing a query letter. But in the fervor of trying to sell an editor on an idea, some writers are not as careful as they should be.

  If you know that you're weak in the basics, take a grammar class at your local college or adult education center. Get in the habit of referring to the dictionary when you have even the slightest doubt about a word. Read grammar books to learn the rules, and great nonfiction and fiction works to see a variety of vocabularies and styles. Consider having a friend proofread your query, and learn to proofread your own work by reading it aloud before submitting it. (Your ear may hear what your eye did not see.)

  If you want the support of another "eye" watching your grammar and spelling, there are several tutoring programs and checkers available on software. Depending on the grammar checker, you may customize the software to allow for colloquialisms or to watch out for sentence fragments. A few grammar checkers (and their toll-free telephone contact numbers) include:

- CORRECT GRAMMAR® (800) 523-3520
- Grammatik 5® (800) 872-9933
- PowerEdit™ (800) 800-4254
- RightWriter® (800) 992-0244

Even if you've used your spelling checker, grammar checker, and any other toys you have on your computer, it's best to proofread your final draft at least twice. Printing out the manuscript and seeing the words on a page may help.

The first time you proofread, read the query through for overall content. Be sure that your thoughts flow easily and have a sense of order, and that transitions between sentences and paragraphs are smooth. This is also the time when you can catch mismatched verbs and pronouns and overused adjectives. Then go back and proofread word by word to check for spelling, grammar, and punctuation.

Do everything you can to improve your own use of the language. Remember, your best idea will go nowhere if all the editor sees is a query full of mistakes.

- **Clips.** With your query, send a synopsis of your publishing background and photocopies of a few (no more than three) articles you have had published. Be sure that your copies are neat and that they include the name and date of the magazine. If you haven't been published, don't grasp at straws by listing college writing classes or including articles you wrote for your high school newspaper. It's far better to present yourself as a new writer with talent than to emphasize your lack of published work.

  Writer Dan Hurley advises, "Write for any Podunk paper you can so you get clips when you're starting out. They are all stepping stones to bigger assignments."

  When given a choice, editors prefer to review clips of articles that are similar in tone or content to the piece you propose to them. That gives them an idea of how well you communicate the type of information their magazines cover.

  But, being editors, they know that the clips you send to them can be vastly different from the manuscripts you originally submitted to those magazines. Therefore, some editors use clips only as a general guideline of the type of writing you've done, not as a true writing sample.

  "Many writers, especially new writers, are edited very heavily, so their clips are misleading," observes Kate White, editor-in-chief of *McCall's.* She adds, only half-jokingly, "In fact, a couple of editor friends and I have thought of starting a computerized Universal Product Code that would appear at the end of every article to indicate to other editors how much the writer had been edited. The lines of the code would tell us whether the piece needed a total rewrite or just minor editing.

"Sloppy writers can sell to a magazine once, but not again," White continues. "Editors sometimes buy an article—based on a good query and impressive clips—and discover that the piece has to be completely rewritten. Although the writer never works for that editor again, there is nothing to prevent him from using his clip from that magazine to get assignments from editors at other publications. Naturally, those editors later discover that the person has to be heavily edited."

If you haven't collected a sampling of good clips yet, one way to gain an editor's trust is by writing a strong sample lead in your query. Some freelancers find that writing the first page of their proposed article and attaching it to their query demonstrates their ability to write clear, concise copy and wins an editor's respect and confidence.

Others break in with an idea that is just odd enough to grab the editor's busy eye. "When you're starting out, no major magazine is going to fly you to Paris on assignment," says Robert Goldberg, a New Jersey TV critic for *The Wall Street Journal*, and a writer who has had bylines in *Vogue, Premiere, Cosmopolitan, Sports Illustrated, Rolling Stone,* and other magazines. He suggests proposing articles on the offbeat, while still remembering what the magazines are looking for.

"Early in my career, I was able to break into *Rolling Stone* with an article on a guy who does rock and roll insurance for big musical tours," Goldberg recalls. "I wrote about 2,000 words on it, and have continued to write for the magazine."

How Time Flies

Editors would like to respond to article proposals more quickly than they do, but production schedules, editing demands, and the tremendous numbers of unsolicited submissions they receive make the average response time to query letters about six weeks.

Andrea Feld, managing editor of *Bride's & Your New Home*, explains, "In each production cycle, we have a little bit of time during which we are able to focus on the piles of queries that accumulate. The rest of the time we're writing and editing the issue, and we have our own deadlines. So it's very hard for us to respond quickly."

A balance of patience and perseverance is the most valuable attribute a writer can have. You won't win any friends in publishing circles if you pester editors for a reply. Writers who sell their work on a regular basis respect editors but do not let them intimidate them. They know that bothering editors by phone or FAX only works against them, yet they do not hesitate to pick up the phone to discuss a piece on which they are working. And, if an editor invites a writer to call with ideas, the smart writer takes him up on it—and fast!

If your story is urgent, or if it is about one of those dramatic rescues, miracle recoveries, or first-in-history breakthroughs, every other writer who is as ambitious as you are will want the piece. In that situation (one that only comes along every few years at most), you may want to call an editor. But first prepare a brief sentence explanation of why you're calling that emphasizes the uniqueness of the story and the details you can offer. If you rehearse the explanation a few times, you'll be able to discuss it more clearly when you call, without feeling jittery or tongue-tied.

If the editor is interested, offer to FAX the proposal that day, and ask if there's one particular angle that he or she sees as the best possibility. But if the editor turns your idea down, thank him or her for their time and get off the phone. There are few things editors like less than writers who interrupt them with a phone call and then stay on the line after their business is completed.

Writers are expected to be able to put their thoughts in writing, so most editors are amazed and annoyed when writers they have never met or barely know call to pitch an idea. Although an editor may be cordial on the phone, his opinion of you will diminish if you interrupt his day by calling with a query he is not prepared to consider. Besides, what will a phone query gain you? If the idea holds the slightest bit of promise, he will undoubtedly ask you to send him a query anyway.

The Numbers Game

Are you one of those writers who hovers around the mailbox, nervously awaiting replies to your queries? If so, you know how depressed you feel when the proposal on which you based all your hope returns home empty-handed. Rejections are never a cause for celebration, but they'll bother you a lot less if you have a number of queries circulating at all times.

One editor who decided to freelance full-time asked a successful freelancer friend how she maintained her steady stream of assignments. The writer replied that her method was to have 20 pieces of paper in the mail at all times. That included not only queries, but assigned articles, expense reports, invoices, research she had requested for future articles, and other correspondence with editors.

That's an ambitious goal, and one that not everyone can attain. But a goal of any sort is important. You might decide that your goal will be to devote three days a month to writing queries, or to submit two queries a month to magazines. Whatever goal you choose, commit yourself to it, and stick with it.

Since not every query you send will be accepted the first time, you'll need to retarget the rejected ones as they come back, and submit them to new markets. If you set a goal of writing two queries a month, you will produce 12 new queries in six months, and will probably submit several of those to different markets two, three, or more times each. Chances are, if you study your markets, write tight queries, and target them correctly each time you submit them, some of those ideas will become assignments.

But what happens when an editor who requested a manuscript rejects it after you submit it? It could be that the magazine turned down the article for reasons other than the manuscript's quality. If so, why not submit the idea elsewhere? Resist the temptation to send in the completed manuscript, and instead submit another query.

If an editor rejects your article or proposal because the angle is wrong for his or her magazine, you have a choice: either give your idea a new direction and query another magazine, or, if you're convinced that your approach is the right one, research further and find a more appropriate audience for your article.

For example, let's say that you met a woman who survived a rare disease thanks to a new medical procedure. Your first inclination is to write a moving account of her courage during the ordeal. You submit a query to *Woman's Day*, whose editor replies that although the idea has merit, the disease is so uncommon that she fears her readers will not relate to the story. You really want to break into women's magazines, so you reslant the story as a medical breakthrough and propose it as a health column to *Redbook. Redbook* passes on the idea, too, this time because the approach is too scientific. You take your cue and submit a more medical slant to *Health.*

This is a good example of how, although you should continue to concentrate on your three or four target markets, some stories simply belong in other magazines. The astute writer will not just sulk over a rejection; he or she will consider the possible reasons why the article idea did not land at the first magazine queried, then analyze the query and either strengthen or change the story.

If there are no time constraints on your idea, wait six weeks for a reply from the time the editor should have received your query.

Then, if you haven't heard, send a photocopy of the original query along with a short note that indicates the original date when you submitted the query.

If your follow-up letter gets no response, it's appropriate to call the magazine. If one or two calls don't get you an answer, send a polite letter telling the editor that you are removing your proposal from consideration. Then submit the query elsewhere.

Because it may take weeks to get a go-ahead on a project, don't send off just one query and sit idle until you receive a reply. Work until you have several queries out at once. Then, as those queries win assignments, replenish the supply of ideas circulating.

A Bit on Contracts, Assignment Letters, and Kill Fees

Although these topics are covered more fully in Chapter 7, they warrant a mention here as well. The contracts you sign and agreements you make as a professional writer can make a difference of hundreds and even thousands of dollars, so it pays to learn the basics before you sign on that dotted line.

An editor who wants your article will send you an assignment letter or will call to request the piece. But even editors who call with the good news usually follow up with a confirmation letter to indicate the length of the piece and the due date, and to suggest a specific focus for the piece. The confirmation letter will state whether the article is being requested on speculation—meaning that the magazine is interested but is under no obligation to buy the piece. Or it will say that it is on assignment with a guaranteed "kill fee." A kill fee is a specified amount—usually 15 to 30 percent of the article fee—that is paid if the article doesn't meet the magazine's expectations or is "killed" (not published) for any other reason.

Some editors send a contract in lieu of a confirmation letter. Others send the letter and follow up with the formal contract once the piece is written. Regardless of the magazine's method, be sure that you have some written form of agreement before you invest more time in the piece. As noted in Chapter 7, where you'll find samples of contracts, you can often prevent delayed payments by asking for a contract before you begin to work.

Many established writers will not consider writing on spec, but a good number of new writers regard it as an unavoidable steppingstone in building a portfolio. It's a risk, but one that is worth taking at the beginning of a writer's career.

But be careful not to exploit yourself. Once you have a healthy track record, you will probably write only on assignment—especially for those editors who have bought your work before. Don't let your eagerness to publish tarnish your image as a professional with a valuable product to sell. How many other professionals work on spec? Teachers are not paid only if their pupils learn, nor are physicians paid only when the patient gets well.

To editors, spec work is a form of protection for times when a writer cannot deliver what the editor expected. But to a few editors who have less respect for writers, it's a way to review a lot of work and to pick and choose. Be wary and be wise. Your skill with words is a great part of your business "inventory."

Thanks, No

When you labor over a query and then send it to your favorite magazine only to have it boomerang to your mailbox within days, it's hard to believe that anyone on the staff bothered to look at it. It's a writer's reality that the first few queries will probably not make it past the editorial assistant's desk.

This book's co-author Coppess sent 72 queries in her first year of freelancing; she received only seven assignments to show for her work.

Often, the first person to read your query will be an editorial assistant whose job is to eliminate proposals that are glaringly wrong for the publication. This person then passes the remaining queries to associate or senior editors, according to who handles what topics or columns at the magazine. Finally, the articles editor or executive editor is given a pared-down stack of query ideas and—frequently at an editorial meeting—discusses the ideas with other editors.

Although it's true that many queries never get beyond an editorial assistant fresh out of college, some top editors still exercise their prerogative to review every piece of paper that floats over the transom. (Over-the-transom submissions are any articles or proposals that are sent unsolicited to a magazine.)

If you receive a rejection slip from a magazine, don't say what some writers have been heard to sigh: "They rejected me." Remember, the editor rejected your idea, not you.

Writer Dan Hurley says, "The single most important concept that a beginning writer can grasp is to understand about rejection slips. As a beginner, you will get more rejections than assignments. That doesn't mean you're not good; you just don't have skill in the craft of query-writing yet. Any salesperson will tell you that you have to accept a quota of rejections. So just know that with each rejection you're getting closer to achieving your success!"

By the way, many beginning writers fear that the ideas they send to a magazine will be "stolen" by the editorial staff and written in house or given to a favored writer. In the authors' experience, that rarely happens. Instead, several queries on the same topic submitted by different writers arrive at the same time. The best may be accepted and the others rejected, leaving the remaining writers wondering whether their idea was scooped.

Other writers come up with ideas that simply miss the mark.

David Roberts, a freelancer in Cambridge, Massachusetts, recalls that, before he was published in *The Atlantic*, he submitted an article there on speculation. The topic: "The Myth of the Fat Eskimo." Roberts had recently completed a summer study program at Stanford that concerned British Victorian ideas on the Arctic and was enamored with his topic, which dealt with the subtle racism implied in the Victorian view of Eskimos.

"Mike Curtis sent me the very best rejection letter I've ever received," Roberts laughs. "It simply said, 'This is a marvelous answer to a question no one has asked.'" It made Roberts laugh at himself and realize that his esoteric interests would not always find their way into print.

"Rejections are less personal than you think," says Roberts. "If I make six calls to an editor and he doesn't return any of them, I start to think, 'What did I do to get him angry? I must have been testy last time.' Then I find out the real reason he hasn't called is because he had 86 other calls and a publication to put out!"

If you receive a note of rejection—polite and personal or photocopied and unsigned—take a few minutes to consider why your idea was not suited to the magazine. Then select a new market, perhaps do a little more research or another interview, refocus the angle, and put the query back in the mail. When that idea or another one of your ideas sells, you'll realize that the thrill of one victory can help you forget scores of defeats!

For example, Gage and Coppess, co-authors of this book, proposed an article in 1984 about a growing body of research showing that those who grow up with alcoholic parents remain deeply affected by their past in their adult lives. During a nine-month period, this article idea was submitted to five major women's magazines, and five polite rejections were returned. Each one echoed the one before it—alcoholism had been written about many times.

The problem: the startling information about the generational waterfall effect of the disorder was buried deep in a three-page query. After five rejections it would have been easy to file that idea in a drawer somewhere. But the information was unique. No one suspected—neither the editors nor us—that a major societal trend was just then beginning, the Adult Children of Alcoholics movement. The query was reworked one more time—and the piece sold to *McCall's.* The response was immediate and enthusiastic: the experts interviewed for the piece appeared on major television and radio shows, a synopsis of the story went out on the major wire services, and—most rewarding of all to Gage and Coppess—the fledgling organization of Adult Children of Alcoholics was flooded with requests for help and information.

Madeleine L'Engle, author of many books, including the novel *A Wrinkle in Time,* has a personal Cinderella story that proves determination and talent can combine to overcome scores of rejections.

"That book almost never got published," L'Engle recounts. "You name any major publisher, and without exception they rejected it. When Farrar, Straus, and Giroux finally accepted it, they told me that they were buying it because they liked the book—not because they thought it was going to sell."

A Wrinkle in Time went on to win an American Library Association Newbery Medal in children's literature, and became the first of a trilogy of books which, along with her other works, have caused L'Engle to be a much-loved writer and sought-after conference leader.

CHAPTER 4

Tracking Down and Interviewing Expert Sources

One thing is certain about magazine writing: you can't begin until you have the raw material from which to pen your prose. As a writer, it's your charge to find enough information to create the number of words your target magazine desires, gain a thorough understanding of the subject, discern what's important and what's not, and then impart intriguing new insights to keep the promise of the fresh angle that won you an assignment.

Writing for magazines means getting current information directly from the experts themselves. You can't depend on other magazine articles or books in which the information is months or years old by the time it hits the newsstand or bookshelf. While those resources can help you find out who knows what or get your bearings on a topic, most magazine editors want you to talk to people immediately involved with the subject. Quoting experts from other printed sources is almost always unacceptable. You must interview them yourself to get truly up-to-the-minute research—editors want the freshest quotes and statistics straight from the source. Whether you're working on a how-to piece, a report on a current event, a profile, a Q&A, or a travel destination piece, you'll need to know how to find and interview sources who can provide timely information.

Sources need to be national in scope and recognition. Editors don't want just any expert's say-so on a topic. They want *the* expert, or at least someone who has vast experience in the area. "Just because someone is a psychologist, a scientist, or happens to have the right initials after his name doesn't make him an authority on the topic," asserts Rebecca Greer, articles editor of *Woman's Day*. "Probably three out of four queries we receive are from people who quote local doctors, psychologists, or other experts down the street, while we look for national authorities."

Even an essay or experiential article means gathering your own thoughts or taking part in an activity or event before you actually sit down and write. Some authors of personal pieces sit down and "interview" themselves—before they start writing, they pour out all their ideas onto the computer screen (or paper) to make sure they have included all they want to say.

Where to Start the Hunt for Experts

One smart way to begin research is to see what's been written on your topic to date. That exercise will give you the latest information on the subject so that you can start researching your piece from a knowledgeable base. It will also tell you "who's who" in the field you're researching so that you can spot the hottest experts you want to interview.

"Doing homework is crucial to get below the superficial level of what has already been published," says David Roberts of Cambridge, Massachusetts, who has written for *National Geographic* and *Smithsonian*, and is contributing editor to *Outside* and *Men's Journal*. "It also helps a writer ask good questions. For example, if I asked a professional archaeologist to tell me about Anasazi, that would be considered a dumb question. But if I asked, 'Why do you have rectangular kivas at Betatakin and circular ones at Keet Seel?' I demonstrate that I know something about the two jewels of the Navajo National Monument in northeastern Arizona."

Writer Gurney Williams, III, worked as an editor for *Omni* and *Popular Science* before beginning to freelance for such magazines as *Family Circle, Omni, Good Housekeeping, Reader's Digest,* and *Smithsonian.* He starts most of his research by consulting the database Dialog® for consumer articles written on his topic. He requests full text when available and, if only a summary is included on the computer, he calls the database's toll-free number to request that the full article be sent to him. While there is a charge per article, Williams finds the service to be timesaving and he bills the magazine for his on-line research time as well as for copies of articles mailed to him. (See Chapter 6 for more details on database searches.)

Freelancer Gail A. Levey, a regular contributor of nutrition articles to *Parade,* also initiates much of her research by scoping out the latest work. "For medical and science stories, such as one I once wrote on the latest in weight control, I usually begin with a computerized literature search at a medical school, college library, or through the National Center for Nutrition and Dietetics in Chicago. I look back through five years of abstracts on the topic because the most active researchers keep publishing and I'll get the majority of timely research that way. Reviewing abstracts allows me to identify names of experts I want to interview and gives me an update on the topic. Then I choose several titles and pull hard copies of the articles to read.

"Once I've identified the key researchers, I call them to ask if there are any new studies they've conducted or know about that they can mail or FAX to me," Levey adds.

Expediting Access to the Experts

To find those national authorities, you don't have to live in a big city or, for that matter, even leave your home. Start by visiting or calling a library to find the name of the appropriate special interest group with the help of the *Encyclopedia of Associations.* You might also want to locate a clearinghouse on your topic by contacting the state offices of consumer affairs, social service, or health. (See Chapter 6 for more details on these and other ways to locate experts.)

Thomas Mann is a reference librarian in the magnificent Main Reading Room of the Library of Congress in Washington, D.C., and author of *A Guide to Library Research Methods.* "There is an amazing number of special interest groups," he says. "There's one for people who grow Siberian irises, another for those who play chess by mail, and yet another for those who make frozen onion rings. Whatever your subject, there is probably an association that relates to it. And once you start asking questions of people in the network, they'll refer you to more experts.

"The other way to find experts is to look up your topic in journal articles and books," Mann continues. "You can find the authors or experts by looking in directories of university faculty or scholars, or by looking at PhoneDisc®, a CD ROM computer disk that lists the name of almost every person in any phone book in the country."

Sometimes finding your expert is as simple as calling information in the city where the person lives and asking for the name of the university or organization where the individual works. If information doesn't have a listing, a call to the city's Chamber of Commerce might put you in touch.

"Since I work in the nutrition field and get notices of upcoming conferences, I look through those to see if anyone is presenting a piece of research on my topic," says Levey.

When she is conducting research on a nonmedical topic and scientific papers aren't needed, such as the piece she wrote on picking and storing fruits and vegetables, Levey does not feel it's necessary to conduct an in-depth computer search on the topic. "For that kind of article, I go to the library and look through the *Encyclopedia of Associations*, which lists the associations for virtually every industry," she says. "For the produce article, I called the United Fresh Vegetable Association and the Produce Marketing Association. If I were writing on food labeling, I'd call the National Food Processors Association. I ask for the press office, tell them who I am writing for and my deadline, and they give me information as well as the names and telephone numbers of experts in the field."

Levey says it's essential, even when going through a professional association, to make sure the names of the authorities they offer are people who actually are doing the latest research in the field. "I like to know the main people in the field who are working at a university or who have a medical center affiliation," she says. "That tells me that they are teaching and that therefore their information is up-to-date. I can also find such people by using a reference book called *Science Sources,* which is produced by the American Association for the Advancement of Science. It lists public information officers at universities, professional associations, and all the units of government that have to do with science, as well as congressional committees working on scientific topics. For several articles, I found the contact at the Agricultural Research Council, which funds nutrition research all over the country."

Don't be afraid to use the telephone for research. It can help you find the statistics you need, allow you to interview a scientist 3,000 miles away, and put you in touch with a government agency representative who can send you a computer-generated abstract of research completed on your topic.

Each phone call you make can direct you to additional contacts. And though the first person you call may not be able to help you, he may recommend a second authority, who could give you helpful information. That second interview may then lead you to a third contact who ends up delivering the most valuable interview of all. If you have interviewed a good source on a controversial topic, ask for names of one or two people your expert can suggest who will *not* agree with him.

"A real problem for many people doing research is that they are too shy to make that first phone call to an expert," says Thomas Mann of the Library of Congress. "They assume that if the information can't be found in the library, it won't be available to them, period. That's just not true. The goal of research is not to play library games, but to find what you need. Often, that can be done by a few phone calls rather than going to the library. 'People' resources are just as important as printed ones."

Interviewees can also be tracked down when you visit places for firsthand experiences and insights and talk to folks who witnessed an event or authorities who can give you their perspective.

How to Ask for an Interview

Asking for an interview can be tricky for new writers, especially if you're gathering information for a query and have yet to get an assignment from a magazine, or if you're doing a piece on speculation. Many experts are savvy about how magazines work because they have written articles themselves or have been interviewed repeatedly. They may only want to give you their time if you are on assignment. As a new writer it is essential to come across as professional and self-assured as possible, without sounding cocky, to get the interviewee to grant you the time and information you need.

Before you call a specialist to ask for his or her time, think about how you will present yourself and your topic. Remember, first impressions are lasting and could color your entire interaction with your source. Here are a few tips to follow as you start the interviewing process:

1. Introduce yourself as a writer—even if you work in another field and only write part-time. Of course, mention if you also are an expert in the field about which you are writing as with dietitian/writer Levey.
2. Be specific about the angle of the story you are pursuing so the specialist can keep information on target.
3. Tell the expert the name of the magazine for which you are planning to query or write. Understand its format and style so you can let the expert know the audience to whom he or she will be directing comments.
4. Let the expert know exactly how much time you expect the interview to take, so he or she can set aside enough time and so you can assure a busy person you won't monopolize too much of their time.
5. Decide if you will give the expert a chance to see or hear their quotes in context once you have written the piece. Often experts have been misquoted, or believe they have, and either are hesitant to grant an interview or hold back during the interview. Agreeing to call and read their quotes to them or FAX them their quotes reassures experts that they will be quoted correctly. (More about the pros and cons of this action later.)

The following conversation is a sample introduction you can adapt to fit your needs when you call an expert to arrange for an interview. If you're calling before you write the query, ask for a few minutes of the person's time to get enough information for the proposal. Let the expert know that you will call back for a more in-depth interview after you have interested the magazine in the idea. This saves you and the specialist time and will save you long-distance telephone expense of conducting an interview for an article that may never sell.

Sample Introduction:

"Hello, Dr. Gordon (or Dr. Gordon's secretary or assistant), my name is Sandra Jacobs. I'm a freelance writer from Denver. I'm preparing an article proposal for *Parenting* magazine on when to get involved in your child's school problems. The American Psychological Association suggested that you would be an ideal psychologist for me to interview because of your background in working with families and the book you published on parent/teacher relationships."

(Dr. Gordon or associate responds.)

"I'd like to schedule a 10- to 15-minute interview with you now so I can incorporate some of your latest findings and quotes into a proposal. Then, if *Parenting* accepts my idea, I'll make another appointment with you for a more in-depth interview. It will take six to eight weeks before I hear if the magazine is interested."

(Dr. Gordon or associate responds positively and suggests a time for the interview.)

"That works well with my schedule. Thanks for your time. I'll call next Wednesday at 3 p.m."

When you set an appointment for an interview, ask a secretary, associate, or the public information or public relations office to mail or FAX to you any background information on the interviewee or his expertise. Request the individual's résumé (if needed for a profile piece) and any press releases and articles that have been written about or by him or the topic in the recent past. You should confirm the name of the person's book on the topic so you can get a copy from the library. It is very flattering to an author for an interviewer to review his book and to intelligently comment on it. When you show interest in an expert's work, chances are you'll get a better interview.

If the person you need to interview is not the expert on the topic but someone you want to talk to for his personal story or for a brief anecdote to illustrate the topic, you would go about asking for an interview in much the same way. Let the individual know who you are, what topic you are writing about, or that you are interested in telling his personal story, and what magazine you are targeting.

It's important to note that it is rare for an expert to ask for monetary compensation for an interview. Most are happy to impart information in exchange for the publicity they'll garner for their work, the notoriety the piece will bring to them, increased sales of their book, or simply because it is both a part of their job to grant interviews and they like to share their insights to help others. If the expert wants to be paid you may do so, though most writers would move on to another highly regarded individual in the field.

For a brief anecdote or quote from a layperson, monetary compensation should not be an issue. However, if you want to tell a person's story, whether it is an adventure, rescue, weight-loss story, or comeback, the individual may expect remuneration. There is no set rule here. Some magazines offer subjects a stipend in return for being the first magazine to tell their story. That amount of money varies and may be negotiated through you as the writer, or the magazine may want to work it out with the individual(s) involved. If the magazine doesn't offer an extra sum to the person whose story you're telling, and you decide that you'd like to share part of your fee, you have every right to do so.

Before You Ask Your First Question

Being prepared for an interview allows you to get better information more quickly. You'll also come across more professionally to the interview subject. Here are a few suggestions on how to prepare before you ask your first question.

1. Ask for a reasonable amount of time—not so short that you don't get what you want and not so long that the source is reluctant to grant you the interview.
2. Make sure your subject understands whether you plan to conduct the interview over the phone or in person. As mentioned earlier, if the subject lives far from you, the phone is often the only alternative. Sometimes, however, if you are writing on assignment for a magazine, the publication will pay for transportation and other expenses. In-person interviews can give you insights into an individual's persona, office, or home environment that are necessary for some stories.
3. If you are conducting an in-person interview, get full directions to the person's office and inquire about parking

availability. (Avoid interviewing subjects in restaurants. The clank of dishes and other conversations make note-taking and deciphering taped transcripts a real bear.)

4. Verify your interview appointment the day before or the morning of the interview as a friendly reminder and to make sure the person's schedule hasn't changed.
5. Before your interview, review any background information you may have requested when arranging the interview. Highlight the important details and take a few notes to formulate subject areas you want to cover. Some writers also draft their questions and send them to the interview source ahead of time. It just depends on your style. Regardless, it is always important that the interviewee knows the major points you want to cover in advance, so he can be of the right mindset when you do the interview and have necessary information at his fingertips.
6. Think of ways you can personalize the first few minutes of the interview to put you and the interviewee at ease. How will you describe the purpose of your interview? Can you comment in general about the person's work or accomplishments? Do you want to tell the interviewee why the topic is so important to the magazine's readers, or what sharing their story will mean to others reading it? If you are doing a profile piece, making a few comments about the person's work or background will immediately assure him that you are prepared and not coming into the interview cold.

   "Try not to be terrified of the person you are interviewing, even if he or she is a well-known doctor or celebrity," says Sherry Suib Cohen, a contributing editor to *New Woman* who also writes for *Glamour, Ladies' Home Journal, Family Circle, Woman's Day,* and *Seventeen.* "People love to tell you about themselves or a subject that fascinates them."

   Home decorating writer Paula Jhung says she never uses the word "interview" when requesting information from experts. "Asking for an interview puts people on guard," she believes. "They think they have to say something terribly intelligent or they have to rehearse. To try to get off-the-cuff, spontaneous comments, I say, 'May I ask you a few questions for a possible article about . . . ' Before I begin asking questions, I flatter them by referring to something I've read about them or their work."
7. Make sure you have plenty of paper and pens at your disposal, that your tape recorder, if you use one, is working, and that you have enough tapes and batteries or the AC adapter. If you take

notes on a computer, make sure you back up your work regularly. If you are taking a laptop or notebook computer to the interview, check to see that your battery is charged and that the AC adapter is packed.

8. Before you tape a conversation on the phone or in person, ask permission to do so. If the interviewee is hesitant, explain that you use the tape recorder to help you verify the accuracy of your notes. As you begin taping, however, ask permission of the interviewee, so that you'll have his or her consent documented. If the person does not want to be taped, respect his or her wishes.
9. If you agree with the practice and it works for the type of article you're writing, let your source know that you will read him his quotes in context to make sure the piece is accurate once the story is written. This is a controversial point discussed further under the "Checking Quotes and Facts" subhead later in this chapter.

Treat Your Sources Well

Securing an interview that will give you enough information to write an enticing query or add facts to your article can be difficult. Experts are often bombarded with requests for interviews and are not eager to spend time talking with writers who don't have firm assignments. Even when you have an assignment, many people refuse to be interviewed because they believe they've been misquoted by journalists in the past.

It does pay to treat your sources well—both experts and otherwise—because, except for essays or experiential stories, they are the backbone of most articles. "The key is to find an expert who has perspective, talks a lot and well, and, if possible, is funny," says Seattle freelancer Jon Krakauer whose credits include *Smithsonian, Rolling Stone, Outside, Architectural Digest,* and *Men's Journal.* "One good quotable person can save a story."

When you interview a national authority, you'll talk with a busy person who is volunteering his time to assist you, so demonstrate your professionalism and your respect for his time by calling or arriving on time, doing your homework to understand the information, and preparing a list of questions before you begin the interview.

If the person you're interviewing has warned you in advance that he or she will have only 10 minutes to talk with you, consider mailing a list of no more than 10 questions to him or her a week before the interview. This will help your expert prepare his answers, save time in explaining your purpose, and impress him with your preparedness and the fact that you value his time.

"Be well-prepared for your interview," says writer Levey. "There is nothing an interviewee likes less than feeling he has to spoon feed the writer. The role of an expert is to give the article credibility and to tell the audience the most important points—not to teach the writer the subject. As a spokesperson for the American Dietetic Association, and thus an interviewee myself, I want the writer to have a good working knowledge of the subject and to know the level of understanding of the magazine's audience. You need to be able to articulate your angle and be aware of how deeply you want to dive into the subject. You can't just ask someone to talk about kids and cholesterol—what exactly do you want to cover?"

Levey also encourages writers to verify the interviewee's name, title, address, phone and FAX numbers, and to confirm spellings before you start to ask questions. If you wait until the end of the conversation, you may forget.

"I always ask for work and home phone numbers, promising only to call at home if I have to check something urgently," says writer Levey. "But, some experts prefer to be called at home."

Levey also suggests that if an expert gives you a number of titles and professional associations, you ask which one he or she prefers, since most magazines are tight on space and can't always list every credit.

Although you want to show the interviewee that you've done your research on his or her subject, don't hesitate to ask questions that you fear are elementary. You must thoroughly understand the subject before you can translate what you learn into an interesting and understandable article. Scientists, doctors, lawyers, engineers, and other specialists often talk in jargon and complicated terms. It's better to ask them to define and spell unfamiliar words when they use them, than to have to call back later because your notes are meaningless or your editor has asked you to decode your indecipherable prose.

Go into your interview knowing what you want your subject to tell you, or the direction in which you want the questions to lead. Don't let yourself get trapped by a long-winded interviewee who gets sidetracked on interesting but irrelevant yarns. Remember, he or she may be the expert on the topic, but you're the writer and the one who decides what to include in the article.

Always keep track of the time during an interview and plan to stop several minutes early to ask the individual if there are any questions you didn't ask that you should have or if he has anything to add. Often, if you stop on time but the interviewee has more to say, he or she will encourage you to continue, even though he only promised you a certain amount of time.

Taking Notes

As the number of interviews you conduct increases, you'll discover that it makes sense to invest in a tape recorder and a phone adapter to tape phone interviews. Taping a phone interview saves you from simultaneously trying to hold a phone, take notes, and plan your next question. Without a recorder you may miss valuable information or star-spangled quotes, or will lose your train of thought as you scribble illegible notes. But always remember: a few minutes into the interview, stop the conversation to make sure that your tape recorder is working!

Some freelancers don't find taping to be a useful method. "The hardest thing about interviewing is to listen and write at the same time—to keep the conversation on track, and yet be open to something unexpected," says writer David Roberts. "Tape recorders make you lazy and are inhibiting for the subject," he contends.

Roberts' friend and colleague writer, Jon Krakauer, differs on this point. "I believe in taping interviews because, unless you do, it's tough to get turns of phrases and regional ways of speech that make good dialogue," he says. "I find that if I don't tape and instead rely on notetaking, I don't really hear the conversation because I'm so busy making sure I get down every word. And though transcribing tapes is time-consuming, when I listen to the interview again, I hear ideas I completely missed before, and new ideas for the article pop into my head."

If your phone has a speaker-phone option, it may pay to use it to free up your hands and alleviate shoulder pain, as long as the person you are interviewing doesn't mind this less personal approach. You may want to explain that using the speaker phone allows you to get the information down more accurately. Or you may want to follow the lead of Dan Baum and Margaret Knox, environmental journalists in Missoula, Montana, and use headsets when interviewing to keep your hands free and to avoid the squawk-box effect of speaker phones.

More and more writers have learned to take notes on the computer while they interview over the phone, and some even take portable computers with them to interviews. While at first you may think that this approach seems impersonal, writers become quick at the keyboard and can often type while looking at the interviewer (much like a court reporter). And with silent keyboards, the computer is less of a distraction than most people think. In fact, many subjects are impressed that the writer brought a computer along and feel reassured that their words will be taken down more carefully than if the interviewer were trying to write by hand.

Some freelancers continue to tape conversations even when they take notes on the computer to have a back-up and to verify the exact wording of quotes. When you take notes on the computer as you interview, you save yourself from the laborious, time-consuming task of transcribing all the notes.

"Margaret and I take notes on computer because it's faster, allows us to get more of the conversation word-for-word, and eliminates all those scraps of paper," says husband and fellow writer Baum. "We are careful to save every 10 minutes during the conversation so there is less of a chance of losing notes. And we always back up the notes on the hard drive and the floppy disk after the interview."

What if the authority you interview speaks as fast as an auctioneer? Your high school shorthand class or the secret code you invented with a friend 20 years ago may come in very handy—whether taking notes by hand or on computer. Simple abbreviations like "cld" for could or "nt" for night will save your hand for statements you'll want to get down word-for-word.

If, as you take notes, you hear something that you think would make a great lead to the article, such as a terrific anecdote or intriguing statistic, put an asterisk by the information. Later, when you are ready to write, it will be much easier to start if you already have a leg up on material to be shaped into a lead.

After your interview, try to review your notes as soon as possible. While the information is fresh in your mind, you can fill in any blanks, decipher scrawled notes, and clarify quotes. If you can't understand something, call back the person immediately to verify information. Then, even if you have to wait days or weeks to write the article, your notes will be as clear as possible and make sense. And, the better the notes, the better the writing.

Getting Good Quotes

Writers are after pearls of wisdom, turns of phrases, colorful quotes, and wonderful insights to make their writing come alive. Some people are eager to share information and talk openly and freely. Others are reserved or hesitant to impart what they know, and they need a good interviewer to pull the best out of them.

As mentioned earlier, the easiest way to get someone to talk is to show them that you are interested in them or their topic, and by knowing something about them before you begin. That way, the interviewee realizes that he doesn't have to start at the beginning with information or stories he has repeated countless times or by wasting time giving mundane information that could easily be found elsewhere.

As you are conducting the interview, you can continue to show your interest by what you say and how you act. If during an interview (either on phone or in person), you simply ask questions and wait for answers without giving your source any input, chances are he will tire early. But if you sound involved by making comments, laughing when appropriate, and showing genuine interest, you'll spur on the person. Like an audience of any storyteller or entertainer, you've got to encourage your interviewee by showing appreciation. Why not say, "Good quote" or "That's just the type of detail I need" on occasion when your source gives you a quote you know you'll treasure?

It's said that an interview is a conversation the writer controls. While striking up a conversation is one way to get good quotes, be careful not to get too much into the dialogue that you take over. Dominating the interview will not get you the goods you want. And becoming so engrossed that you actually answer the questions you ask and put words in your source's mouth is obviously counterproductive. If the person you are interviewing doesn't answer a question immediately, bite your tongue, and let the question hang in the air for a few minutes. Chances are the person will give you an answer if you are patient and give him time to ponder. If too much time passes, move on and try posing the question differently later.

Different types of writing require a variety of interview approaches. Freelancer Roberts says that for the type of writing he does it helps to be confrontational. "In a story I did on the Anasazi, I knew the Hopi were direct descendants of them. I told the Hopi's cultural spokesperson that the archaeologist didn't think much of their oral traditions. He blew up and let me know what the archaeologist didn't know. Because of that prickly technique, I prompted a wonderful dialogue. Most writers would have just gone for the romantic side of the story. But I like paradox, contradictions, and complexity."

Writer Elaine Whiteley is on the opposite end of the writing and interviewing spectrum. Her stories of people overcoming personal ordeals—like parents whose children have been maimed or killed by baby sitters, or children molested by school teachers (both published by *Ladies' Home Journal*)—demand that her sources trust her implicitly with sensitive personal information.

"When I interview people, I listen to them not only with my ears, but with my heart," says Whiteley. "I try to feel what they are feeling. I truly care that they have had terrible sorrow and anguish in their lives."

Whiteley also keeps the trust of her sources by making sure she never betrays the people she interviews. "If someone says something to me in the heat of the moment that would be embarrassing or harmful to them once it was in print, I won't use it—even if it was a juicy quote," she says. "And, when I show them the final draft before it goes to the magazine, I always let my sources know up front that I won't use anything they don't want me to."

Regardless of what type of interview you conduct, cherish the words you are given and your sources' ideas and opinions. The greatest respect a writer can give an interviewee is to maintain the integrity of what he or she said through careful writing and accurate quotes.

When Is Enough Research Enough?

How do you know when you've learned enough to write either the query or article you've been researching? Naturally, the answer varies with each project.

For a query, you need to do a bit of research in order to write a marketable proposal. In query research, the general guideline is: learn enough to impress the editor with your knowledge, but don't waste your time with numerous lengthy interviews when you don't know if the editor will request a different angle, or whether you'll write the piece at all.

"Before I write my query letter, I briefly interview three to four experts to get a feel for the subject," says Elaine Whiteley. "They bring out points that help me understand the information better. Then I go to the library and read information already written on the topic before I do in-depth interviews for the final piece."

When actually writing the article, you'll know you've researched your topic sufficiently when, as you exhaust your list of sources and complete your interviews, you hear information you've already gained from previous research. Another clue is when you read other articles or papers on your topic and discover that you've collected more information than they cover. If you still have unanswered questions or are relying on only one source, however, you have more work ahead of you.

There are two hazards of research: wasting time getting too much information on all facets of your topic so that you lose focus and can't zero-in on your particular angle; and not spending enough time in the research phase so that your ultimate article lacks the depth and breadth the editor and reader expect.

Most veteran writers will tell you that they always get more details and facts than they could ever use in the short space of a magazine article. That's because it is only when you have all the data in front of you that you can decide the most vital pieces of information to include within your space constraints. But even so, you always have to keep the narrow angle of your topic in mind.

"To really understand your topic, you need to amass a zillion times more research than what you actually need and then whittle it down to a 1,000- or 2,000-word article," writer Levey says.

"Study the market you're writing for to understand how many sources appear in a typical article," says writer and former editor Williams. "Some magazines require only a few sources, while others want 10 experts quoted in the course of a full feature."

Writers Margaret Knox and Dan Baum, though married, write independently on wilderness and political topics. They admit that they end up with desks piled high with research. "If we're mentioning a court case, we try to get the indictment or complaint to back up our story, and we always want any studies anyone can offer," says Knox. "By the end of the story, we always have a large box of paper."

"I was trained at *The Wall Street Journal* to not trust anything anyone says," says Baum. "If someone gives me an interview and they have information on paper, I get the paper as well, whether it is a newspaper article, a memo, or a court ruling. We have a Federal Express account and ask interviewees to send the material to us. We may run up several hundred dollars in charges, but the magazines we work for reimburse us for overnight mail, FAX, and postage charges."

Checking Quotes and Facts

If you want to be considered credible and professional by your sources as well as by the magazine editor, fact check your article before you submit it. At the very least, that means calling sources or looking at written reports to verify dates, statistics, spellings of names, titles, ages, and locations included in your final draft.

Some writers go a step further and call the interview sources to review their quotes, or FAX their quotes to them. Most, however, do not send the sources the entire article because experts tend to want to add information or rewrite paragraphs that do not include their quotes. How you choose to fact check is up to you—just make sure the information is right.

Letting experts hear or see their quotes is a controversial subject among writers. Many are afraid they'll lose the freedom a writer cherishes if they are tied to the whim of their sources.

Others who write investigative pieces would never think of checking a quote that a source might later want to change.

But freelancers who are writing reportage, how-to pieces, true-life dramas, personal profiles, or other articles dependent on quotes from experts or on the accuracy of someone's dramatic story wouldn't think of submitting an article without letting the person they interviewed verify their quotes. Not only does checking quotes ensure that the information is correct and didn't get misconstrued, it protects a writer's reputation with the magazine. Few things are more embarrassing for a writer than to have a magazine's fact-checking department find an error or, worse yet, to have an expert call the magazine to complain that information was inaccurately reported.

"When I finish an article, I always call the people I've interviewed to read them their quotes," says Levey. "I want to protect my sources for their reputation and because, no doubt, I'll want to interview them again."

Most magazines want writers to turn in a source list of experts and any person quoted. The list should be alphabetized and include names, titles, businesses, addresses, and phone and FAX numbers. If you've used a pseudonym for an individual mentioned in an anecdote, include the real name in the source list with the pseudonym in parentheses.

Some magazines also request that writers turn in a second, annotated version of their manuscript along with a clean draft. This is much like a footnoting system.

First, you number your interviews and all other pieces of research submitted for fact-checking purposes. Next, you put a subnumber (1a, 1b) next to each relevant quote or fact you incorporated in the article. You can do this by hand-writing the numbers in the margins next to the fact, or by using a footnote option your word-processing software may offer. Then, you go through the manuscript and put the corresponding number from the actual research next to the fact and quote as it appears in the manuscript.

Here's an example:

> There are 11,000 consumer and trade journals published in the United States.[1c] While as a writer, you'd love your byline to appear in each and every one of them, it's best to pick two or three target markets and intimately learn the needs of those few, say co-authors Diane Gage and Marcia Coppess.[2f]

If you had written that paragraph, the number 1c would correspond to the notes from the research you did with the Gale Directory of Publications and Broadcast Media. It would be the first set of notes and the third point on those notes. The number 2f would be from your second set of notes (from an interview with Gage and Coppess) and would refer to the sixth point in those notes.

Freelancer Whiteley's fact-checking system earned her praise from *Ladies' Home Journal* as the most thorough they had seen. "I put all my notes in a huge binder, alphabetized by the name of the source, and with all the pages numbered," says Whiteley. "On my annotated final draft, I write the name of the source and the page number, to facilitate the magazine's fact-checking process. Because I transcribe all my tapes verbatim, I might turn in one or two three-ring binders of notes. I prefer to be thorough than to turn in misinformation. When I write for a magazine, I represent that magazine. I feel a great obligation to do the best I can because my work reflects the reputation of the publication."

Once your article is published, you can keep your sources satisfied by sending them a photocopy of the magazine in which the piece appeared, or a tear sheet, which is an unbound copy of your article. (You can request a few from the magazine). There's no need to go out and buy a dozen copies of the magazine to send each source the entire publication, unless of course, you are feeling particularly generous.

"I often write labels for the people I interviewed and arrange for the magazine to send them copies," says Gail Levey.

It's a simple gesture, but few writers do it. You'll be surprised at how appreciative your sources will be and how they'll remember you as a competent and considerate writer the next time you ask for their insights and time.

CHAPTER 5

Writing Articles That Command Attention

The hardest thing about writing is writing. Converting thoughts and notes into words that create clear images in readers' minds rarely comes without a struggle.

Writing can be a lonely, frustrating process. There are no easy formulas for transforming blank sheets of paper into a readable, entertaining, and informative manuscript. Many would-be writers, who breeze through idea development, querying, and research, fail at writing because they can't endure the arduous process of putting words on paper and then reworking those words until they express exactly what they were supposed to, in the way the writer wanted them to, and in a way that will please the editor.

As Red Smith, the late author and *New York Times* sports columnist put it, "Writing is easy. All you do is sit in front of a typewriter and open a vein."

Like most writers, Smith knew that writing can feel like sweating blood. And the computer age hasn't made it any easier. While the writers of yesterday had wads of paper overflowing from the trash can and pooled around their feet, today's journalists hold down the delete button, watching work disappear that just didn't live up to their ideals.

Unblocking Writer's Block

Professional writers, who can't afford to miss a deadline by letting the ultra-perfectionist or super-procrastinator inside them take over, know that putting something—anything—down on paper is better than writing nothing at all. Some people spend hours staring at a blank computer screen or give up for the day, after numerous false starts, and blame their inertia on "writer's block." Other writers have just as frustrating a day yet still manage to get work done. They realize that what they write on an off day can be cleaned up on another day, when their thoughts are flowing more clearly. For them, writer's block isn't an excuse to avoid the computer. It's an occupational hazard.

Avoiding the computer keyboard or the blank piece of paper doesn't make things better; it just prolongs the agony. If you give the actual writing process the attention it deserves and press on beyond those difficult moments, the reward of seeing your byline in print and receiving a paycheck will be satisfying and fulfilling.

Writers have devised a variety of ways to get themselves to their desks and working. We joke that, although there are many items you need or want to be a good writer, the most valuable item in which you need to invest—more than a fancy computer, great thesaurus, or inspirational writing class—is a timed-release seat belt for your office chair. You'd sit down in the morning, and the belt wouldn't release you until a pre-programmed time. The point is, if you don't stay in your seat in front of the computer screen or paper, you'll never get anything written. Most writers are great procrastinators. Maybe it's fear, maybe it's anxiety. Whatever it is, most will tell you they make every excuse not to write.

"I do everything to avoid it," says full-time freelancer Jon Krakauer of Seattle. "The dishes, laundry, housecleaning—everything else gets done first. Then, when there is no other way to avoid it, I immerse myself in writing. It's not the smartest way to work, but as the a deadline looms and I finally make myself sit down to write, I'll spend a week tinkering around to make the first paragraph right. Then I'll write 5,000 words over three days and barely sleep."

Writer David Roberts of Cambridge, Massachusetts, takes a more methodical approach to his writing, doing a little at a time until the piece is done prior to his deadline. "I have never had writer's block," he says. "Maybe it's narcissism and I love my own prose too much, or maybe it's because I'm disciplined. There are days when I don't want to write, but I say, 'Damn it, do it. Get going.' And I do. I've always told people that having an overwhelming belief in your talent—or maybe a pigheaded belief in yourself—is more important than being a good writer."

Writers Margaret Knox and Dan Baum, who are married but earn separate bylines, say that every time one of them has a major article to write, the same behavior pattern emerges. "We start pacing around the office, the desk becomes messier, and we endure a few frantic evenings at home when one of us thinks that he or she is not going to get the article done," says Baum. "We both do the same thing, so when one of us starts feeling panicked, we get home and say, 'I'm in my pre-breakthrough freak-out mode now. Please be extra nice to me.' We fear that we'll never find enough material, we'll never get organized, and are coming to the end of our careers. Now, when that happens, we recognize it as part of the creative process. Writing can feel like a grind while you gather information, fact check, deal with editors, and take care of business. But it can also be exhilarating, and getting through the writing process itself is the most rewarding part."

Some writers say they have to have complete silence to write—even a soft radio in the background gets their minds off their work. Others play white-noise-type of music—the sounds of waves lapping on a shore or wind rustling through trees—to give their writing a backdrop. Still others—maybe those who come from a newspaper bullpen background—could write in the midst of Armageddon.

If you want to write, you must know how you work best and be tough on yourself to persevere. If you are best at 5 a.m., don't try to write at midnight. Instead, go to bed at a decent time and set the alarm clock for an early hour. But if the wee hours of the morning are when you really get cooking, arrange your day so that you can have the time between 1 a.m. and 3 a.m. to get your work done.

If your family and friends applaud your writing but can't seem to leave you alone long enough to let you do it, set some boundaries. You might make a policy that you don't answer your phone during certain hours of the day, but that your family will have a secret code to get your attention, such as ringing twice, hanging up, and calling back. You might have to do as one doctor did, and set aside two hours a night when the kids are in bed—say from 9 p.m. to 11 p.m.—to write.

You'll never *find* the time to write. You'll have to *make* it. Likewise, you've got to make space to write. If you're trying to make writing your full-time or part-time job, it's worth it to set up shop in a den, corner of the garage, or portion of the bedroom. You need a place to go to do your job, where you can have easy access to your computer, research books, and notes. The location doesn't have to be big or fancy, but make it easy to begin work. Don't try to write on the kitchen table, which has to be cleaned of writing materials to feed the family. Find a place where the computer or materials can be placed, begging you to come to it any time you find a few spare moments.

Use the Magazine as Your Stylebook

To perfect the craft of magazine writing, think back to the advice all editors urge when trying to market your work to their publication—read the magazine! This time, however, rather than looking at it through the eyes of a salesperson identifying the types of topics the magazine buys for its different sections, look at it as a wordsmith who is actually fulfilling the order. Study the magazine in this vein by dissecting how your type of article is assembled.

"When I wanted to write for *Smithsonian*, I got a half-dozen back issues and read them from front to back," says writer Krakauer. "I tried to figure out what the writers did, the type of vocabulary they used, the colloquialisms woven in—all the stuff that makes writing tight."

While the principles of article anatomy hold true for virtually every magazine you'll read, each publication has its own nuances and preferences when it comes to how it likes its articles crafted. It's not that the writing is formulaic, but there are certain styles and techniques that each publication develops. And when they find what works, they usually want more of the same.

Use your target or assignment magazine as your stylebook. Analyze exactly how its articles work. When writer Elaine Whiteley earned her first assignment from *Ladies' Home Journal*, she started by reading two-years' worth of back issues to analyze the articles' form and substance. To imprint that on her brain, she chose three articles that resembled the true-life drama she was going to write, and typed them word-for-word.

"Typing the articles verbatim allowed me to get a sense of what the writers did to make their pieces work for *Ladies' Home Journal*," says Whiteley. "I studied the way the leads were formulated and how transitions and endings were written. I learned that the magazine likes to use statistics and how they incorporated them into the piece. I also saw how many case histories were used and how quotes from authorities were included to illustrate a point."

She also paid attention to how experts' credentials were cited, and the types of sidebars or reader service information that accompanied the pieces. Because she painstakingly put the magazine's work under the magnifying glass, her initial sale as a beginning writer hit the magazine's quality mark the first time—much to the editors' amazement.

Here is a checklist of questions you can ask yourself about articles in your target magazine:

1. What types of titles do the articles have? Play on words? Alliterations? Two-part titles? Titles with subheads or decks? (A deck is a publishing term for a part of a headline that may carry two or three stacked lines.)
2. Do most pieces begin with a lead that includes an anecdote, a quote, a statistic, a controversial statement, or a startling

juxtaposition? Does the lead create a scene or in some way summarize what lies ahead?

3. Is the voice of the articles lively and chatty or serious and staid?
4. Is the magazine familiar with its readers or more formal and distant? Academic or colloquial?
5. Are specialists cited throughout the articles? If so, how are they listed—first name, credential, title, affiliation?
6. How are sources in anecdotes listed? Does the magazine give first and last names, ages, occupations, locales?
7. Are most pieces divided by subheads?
8. Does the magazine give a lot of facts and statistics?
9. Does the type of piece you are writing use the first person? Third person? Or both, depending on the piece?
10. Are any boxed items and sidebars used for additional information?

A Look at Article Genre

There are several different genre of articles, one of which you will either suggest in your query or the editor will stipulate when you are given the green light to write the piece. Here is a simple breakdown:

- **Essay** pieces use the writer's voice and viewpoint to analyze or interpret a subject. An essay is limited to the author's perspective or insights. As Lewis Lapham, editor of *Harper's* says, "Essay writing is thinking out loud. You can never be sure where it will end up. It's an adventure. It is always personal and, if done well, both the reader and the writer learn something from the enterprise."

  Essays are usually written in the first person, but they can be done in the third person as well. For instance, a political essay, while espousing a clear position on an issue, may not involve the author in the text. Conversely, an essay for *child*'s "Child of Mine" feature would be an intensely personal look at one's offspring. Many magazines prefer to run a light back-of-the-book essay to close their publication.
- **First Person** is a style that uses verbs and pronouns in the "I" form. This is one instance where the writer is definitely the center of attention. First person is often used to tell a story.

If you are telling someone else's story and the editor asks you to write a first-person as-told-to article, you will write the article as if you are the main character of the story. The byline will feature the subject's name first, followed by "As told to (your name)."

- **Opinion/Editorial** pieces give the writer a chance to share strong beliefs and convictions about a specific topic. They can be written in the first or third person, and often include such journalistic tools as statistics and quotes from others, as well as an opinion.
- **Reportage** gives an account of events in a news format. It is straight journalism, incorporating facts, expert quotes, statistics, and anecdotes. The author does not appear in the article.
- **Third Person** is the most common style of writing requested by magazines. It includes third-person pronouns and verbs. The writer's voice typically is not heard. However, it can take on many forms: drama, reportage, or narrative.

Going to School on Article Anatomy

To write magazine articles well, it's essential to understand how they are constructed. Every magazine article has a beginning, a middle, and an end. Following next are the general elements of a magazine article:

Note: Some of the components will apply to some article styles and not to others; this should be evident by the descriptions.

- **Title.** It's just a few short words, but a title (or headline) can take longer to write than full pages of prose. It's an art to be able to write a good one, which is why most magazine editors end up changing the headlines writers create for their pieces. Still, take your time to fuss and fret over what you are going to title your piece. Look at the magazine for which you are writing and identify the types of titles it uses. Does the publication like short, staccato titles, or longer ones with tempo? Does it play on words and revive old puns? Do most titles include a verb to impart action, or are they more like quick labels?
- **Subhead or Deck.** Some magazines use either a deck or a subhead after the title to further explain the intent of an article. A subhead is a second, more elaborative part of the title. An example of title and subhead is "Fields of Greens: Making the Best of Summer's Salads."

A deck can be a sentence or two that summarizes the theme of the piece. An example of a title with a deck is "Growing Greens" and "Today's gardeners vie for unusual lettuce varieties to add zest to summer salads."

If your magazine uses a deck as a matter of style on most articles, it pays to submit your piece with one. Though it may get changed, it demonstrates to the editor that you are aware of the magazine's style and are doing your best to mimic it.

- **Lead.** The beginning sentence or paragraph of an article is called the lead. Its sole purpose is to lure the reader into the article with an interesting fact, an enticing anecdote, a unique turn of phrase, or tantalizing information.

Writing the lead to your article is unquestionably the hardest part of writing. When you've spent days, weeks, or months gathering information for your assignment, it can seem impossible to know where to start your tale. It's equally frustrating to figure out how to relay the information in an exciting, intriguing way that will draw in the reader.

If you've done what was suggested in the previous chapter on interviewing and listened for an especially funny, interesting, or startling anecdote, quote or statistic, and then noted it with an asterisk that stands for "potential lead," your problem may be nearly solved. Go back through your notes and look at all the places you've highlighted, and determine if any one of those points might be a launching pad for your story. Chances are, you'll find one that works, at least to get you started.

Writer Paula Jhung warms up to creating her leads by free-writing on a big yellow pad everything she has learned or can think of about her topic. "Often what I write is garbage, but on occasion some fresh and original gems come out that can be the lead or the root of a story," she says.

Writer Krakauer concurs that figuring out how to hook the reader into his story is the hardest part of writing. "I look at my yellow pad of outlined points and identify a starting point that allows the story to flow most naturally," he says.

Whatever way you work, remember your goal is to get going. Many writers say that it isn't until their story is written that they go back and write the perfect lead. That's the flexibility of writing. Any portion of your work can be polished at any time. You don't have to perfect each part of your article before you move on. Until the day your manuscript leaves your hands at the mailbox, you've got every chance you need to hone it to perfection.

- **Billboard Paragraph.** Soon after you write your lead, it's time to write what is referred to as the "billboard" or "orientation" paragraph. Like the topic sentence of a paragraph, this block of copy serves as the topic paragraph for the entire article. It tells the reader what the story is about and where it is going to take him. This is where the journalist sets up the five Ws and one H—the who, what, when, where, why, and how of the story. While in a newspaper article these elements are supposed to be near the beginning of the story, magazine article writing is a little more lax. You can begin unveiling them here, and finish in the body of the piece. However, you must cover the full information in a comprehensive way.

  The billboard paragraph is the most important section of an article because it outlines the purpose and lets the reader know what to expect. It is the motivation for the reader to invest his time in your words.

- **Body.** The middle, or body, of an article fulfills the promise of the billboard paragraph. It gives general background information, develops major points, and keeps the reader engrossed by using quotations, anecdotes, observations, statistics, tips, or how-to information. This is also the place to present pros and cons of an issue.

  As you write the body of the article, be sure to include the sources of facts and figures as you cite them. Don't bore readers with a long list of statistics; instead, just sprinkle them throughout the article. When you include quotations from more than one person, attribute the comments in each paragraph so that the reader knows who is saying what.

  Note that if you have interesting information that enhances your piece and is related to its subject but not essential, consider writing a sidebar. (See description later in this section.) You don't have to cram everything into the body of the article. Sometimes, information gets more attention if it is called out with a separate treatment.

- **Summary.** The closing paragraphs of an article resolve the problem, offer solutions, restate the theme, recommend action, or summarize the information. They offer details about the impact of the subject on future issues, and summarize the significance of all you have written. This is where you present the final conclusion or opinion.

- **Ending.** Readers want to feel fulfilled when they finish an article. Therefore, the last few sentences should make people feel satisfied about the time they've invested in reading. Many articles end with a thought-provoking message, a fitting quote or anecdote, or a memorable punch line. Remember, everything that is written must have a payoff—some kind of message. It's what some magazines call a "take-away." You, of course, should know the take-away you'll offer before you complete the piece.

"The ending statement should touch the heart or at least leave an imprint on the reader's mind," says writer Elaine Whiteley.

- **Sidebar.** A sidebar is usually a shorter article (often about 500 words) that highlights or expands one point. Sidebars run adjacent to or at the end of the articles to which they refer, and are set apart by a box or different-colored or shaded background, and a separate headline.

  Sidebars are also used to list product or consumer information that would become unwieldy if included in the text. For instance, the names and addresses of hotels in a city featured in a travel article would be more useful and readable in a sidebar.

Start by Organizing Your Notes

It's the moment of truth. There you are, all alone, surrounded by stacks of yellow paper, reams of computer notes covered with details from interviews, library research printouts, books, pamphlets, and public relations press kits. You may even have photos, musical cassettes, or product samples.

It's time to tame the raw data into obeying the magazine's rules and format. How do you wade through perhaps millions of words to find just the few thousand you need to tell the story?

One of the first things to do is refer back to your query. It should serve as an abstract of your article. It will remind you of your angle and the points you said you'd cover when you sold the editor on your idea.

As you review your notes and compare the fresh information you've gathered to what you promised in your query, you'll undoubtedly see that your research revealed many new points of which you were unaware when you wrote the proposal. If you discovered a major issue along the research trail and think it may change the scope of your article, don't write the piece with a new point of view before talking it over with the editor. He may like the new focus better, or suggest that you save the information for a follow-up piece or sidebar.

Occasionally, your new facts may sour the editor on the idea. Although that would result in a kill fee (usually between 15 and 30 percent of the full payment) instead of a published article, it's better to discuss it now than to be surprised after you've invested a lot of time and work.

If the editor didn't offer specific opinions when he assigned the piece and your article could be approached from three or four directions, decide which angle you want to take, then call the editor. You don't need to give him a play-by-play description of your plans. Simply say, "I've finished researching and was going to start writing the piece, but thought I'd run the angle by you first." Most editors will appreciate the chance to participate in the article's formation.

Some editors request a brief outline of your piece once the research is completed and before you start writing, to update them on where your research has taken you. Even if the editor doesn't request it, taking the time to organize your research and identify what you want to accomplish in your article can make the writing process easier. The outline can be as detailed or as sketchy as you like, but should at least include a listing of major points the article will cover, in the order in which you plan to cover them. (Once you start writing, the order will probably change. But, again, an outline will get you going.)

To write the outline and the piece itself, most writers begin by reading their notes just prior to actually writing. A good rule of thumb is to try to have several hours of uninterrupted time when you begin the reviewing notes/writing process. Use a highlighter to mark the salient points in your notes.

"I highlight interesting quotes and observations and then list on a single page the points I want to make in my article," says writer Krakauer.

Freelancer Whiteley takes the review/outline process another step further. She rereads all the interviews and makes an outline of major points she needs to cover. (Her articles often run to 3,000 words or longer.) She highlights each major section of her outline in a different color marker. Then she goes back through and highlights important information and quotes, color coding them according to her outline.

If she is writing a major piece, she jots down each topic of her outline in big print on a white piece of paper. She spreads the topics out on a large table and then puts the notes that correspond with each section in the correct pile according to the topic. That way when she is writing, she knows right where to go to find the information that pertains to the specific sections of her article.

In some cases, when you have notes for different sections interspersed on one page, you may want to make as many photocopies of that page as there are topics. For example, if three items from your outline are from one page of notes, you'd make three copies. Then you would put each copy in the corresponding pile and keep the original intact in your master file. Be sure to write the source's name on the top of each copied page so you know where the information comes from.

Another way to code notes is to number the paragraphs according to the number of the section in your outline to which your notes pertain. Some writers cut apart their notes and tape them back together following the order of the outline. Yet others use their computers to organize notes, by moving similar sections of information together with the "Move," highlighting, or "Block" function of their software. Whatever your method, you'll save time in the long run by planning and organizing your article before you start writing it.

Getting Through the First Draft

It has often been said that every writer has two literary personalities—the creator and the critic. While some writers have to perfect each sentence before proceeding to the next, many contend that they are most creative when they let all their thoughts spill out to create a first rough draft before they let the critic within take over and edit.

"The first thing I have to do when I'm writing is come up with a good lead; I can't go on until that is accomplished," says writer Whiteley. "Unlike all the books I've read on writing, I'm not the type of writer who can just get the first draft down as fast as possible. I work on a small section at a time—about one-half page—and get it to the part where I feel good about it, then proceed to the next section. I have to do that to feel encouraged along the way. Otherwise, I get too frustrated and want to give up."

Freelancer Krakauer, however, prefers to rework the lead and first page until they are perfect and then whip out the rest of the rough draft quickly as possible. "I might rewrite the first paragraph or first page a hundred times before moving on," he says. "I know it makes no sense, because by the time I am done with the piece, I'll probably go back and change it. But that's how I work. After the lead is written I buzz through everything else. Once I have a draft down on paper, I enjoy tinkering around with it until it's just how I want it. But the first draft can be painful."

Getting in Style

Perhaps a few truly great writers are born with a distinct, fluid writing style pulsing through their veins. But most of us can't sculpt sentences into unique shapes, or create a perfect writing rhythm without a lot of painful practice. Even as you successfully sell your work, you'll continue to refine your ability. You'll learn from editors who make your work better, from writers you admire, and from books that detail ways to improve your talent.

"I don't think it's possible to write well without reading compulsively," says Krakauer. "When I read a passage in a book or article that is really great, I reread it over and over, asking myself why it was so moving or impressive. When I have those answers, I know I have learned a new trick.

"Good writing is like music," he continues. "It has rhythm, pace and poetry. You can learn to write by ear by reading a lot. It also pays to listen to people read aloud; I go to readings all the time. The more you listen to writing and the more you write, the more you learn what works and what doesn't. Writing is hard. To do it well is incredibly difficult."

Whiteley also believes that being a voracious reader helped her learn to write. "You sort of pick up through osmosis how other writers home in on their stories," she says. This mother of 10 also believes that life is one of the best writing teachers. "I couldn't write 20 years ago as I do now because I didn't have an experienced scope of emotions. If you've felt pain in your life, it's easier to understand the pain of others. The same holds true for joy and humor."

But you can't just admire the work of others. There is no substitute for practice. *Harper's* Editor Lewis Lapham suggests that one of the best things a beginning writer can do is to write a lot. "Joyce Carol Oates should be a great inspiration to the aspiring writer because she writes a great deal," he says. "Some of her stories succeed to a greater extent than others, but she just keeps writing."

New York writer Gail Levey says when she started writing just after earning her master's degree in nutrition, she knew she could write well. But, after writing all those academic papers, she had to change the way she wrote to fit the audiences to which she was now targeting.

"My first articles were more academic," she recalls. "Then when I became the nutrition researcher for Earl Ubell, the health editor for *Parade*, I read and reread all his work. I realized my style needed modification, and I worked hard to write more for the lay public. Today, I write like I speak—descriptive yet simple—and since I do a lot of public speaking, the two are complementary."

Bob Strohm, editor-in-chief of *National Wildlife* and *International Wildlife*, recalls a saying of one editor at his publication, "Never underestimate a reader's intelligence, but never overestimate his comprehension."

In other words, write well, but write simply. Don't use jargon or special phrases known only to certain professions unless you define them for the reader. If a medical specialist, for example, talks in "medical-ese," reinterpret that into everyday language for the reader. After all, a writer is a conduit whose job it is to impart information from one or more sources into clear yet interesting language for the reader.

No matter how you develop your style, work hard. Editors want writers who exude passion in their work—either by working hard to get the best reported article, poring yourself into an essay or opinion piece, or going the extra length to push for pithy quotes.

"We seek writers who can bring vision to a story. That's key," says *Parade* Senior Articles Editor Fran Carpentier. "In the end, we are buying a combination of the writer's reporting skill and his innate talent to weave a story."

Creativity Can Be Learned

A difficult lesson that many new nonfiction writers have to learn—particularly if their training is in journalism or the sciences—is that creativity is as integral a part of nonfiction as it is of fiction. No, you don't have to fabricate entire lives, histories, or futures. But you must be descriptive, provocative, and sensual. You must use your imagination so that readers can not only see your words, but feel, hear, and smell them as well.

The best piece of writing touches the reader's life. It speaks directly to his own personal experience, concerns, and emotions. This makes a piece memorable and of lasting impact.

Let your imagination run free, but don't exaggerate a point by using contrived metaphors and similes, and don't try to impress your editor by using long, complicated words. More often than not, direct, uncluttered writing works best.

Simple writing does not mean boring writing. Make sure that you vary the length and structure of your sentences to create an interesting rhythm with a pleasant tempo. Your writing should be descriptive, but you mustn't overwrite. As you continue to comb back through your writing, peel away excess words to strengthen your sentences and clarify your thoughts.

Try also to choose active verbs over passive ones or verbs of being (is, was, or will be). Instead of saying, "He was selected for the experiment by the professor," say, "The professor selected him for the experiment." Rather than "The cat was on the chair," try, "The cat lounged on the chair." But don't reach too far for an unusual verb. Sometimes items simply sit, flowers simply bloom, and people simply say. Be critical of the pretty words you use; a plain one may be more effective.

Some editors complain that otherwise creative people become stilted when they write for publication. Others who write marvelously vivid and thoughtful query letters revert to a drab business style in their manuscripts.

When writing dialogue, try to impart any inflections, colloquialisms, and other idiosyncrasies of the people you quote to give a sense of their personality, background, or culture. Listen as closely as you can to the way people talk, so that you don't have flat, homogenized quotes. Use distinctive expressions if you think they'll help the flavor of your article.

Try to get a feeling for your topic and those involved with it. Rather than relying on journal and newspaper articles, interview a scientist who can speak passionately about the effects of a new drug. Whenever possible, look into the eyes of a person involved in a heart-wrenching drama rather than interviewing him or her by phone.

Revving Up Your Creative Engine

If you're stuck in neutral, relying on the same old nouns, verbs, and adjectives to tell a story, take a gander at the many writing how-to books you'll find in the library or bookstore—and try performing the exercises they include. Or give your muse a jump start with an exercise refined by Susan Victoria "Noonie" Benford, a writer in Cardiff, California. She lived for years with her grandparents who teased her with puns and wordplay. When she started writing, first for passion, and later to make a living, Benford developed a writing workout based on programmed word association to "rev" her creative juices.

To generate a list of verbs, adjectives, and adverbs from which you can draw to make a piece of writing come alive, start by identifying the topic of the paragraph or section of your article. Brainstorm a list of related words to that topic.

For example, in a travel destination article about San Diego, California for *USAir*, writers Benford and this book's co-author Diane Gage were at a loss for descriptive copy under a section that talked about the city's growth rate. To make their words come alive, they used programmed word association. First, they identified that San Diego had become so popular because of its year-round temperate climate. They used "climate" as the springboard for creativity and came up with the following list of climate-related words:

cloud	rain	humidity
downpour	torrential	sunny
hazy	forecast	weather
stormy	horizon	drizzle
fog	seasonal	mild
temperature	tropical	highs
lows	coastal	wind

Next, they started writing, but instead of putting down the first verb, adjective, or adverb that came to mind, they looked at their word list to see if another word would paint a more vivid, exciting picture.

The following paragraph is an example of the finished product. The words that resulted from the programmed word association exercise are underlined so you can see how they were woven in. The original wording that came to mind is in parentheses so you can compare what the writing would have sounded like without the extra effort. The original copy wasn't bad, but the new copy gained punch and flavor:

> "One of the hottest (most debated) topics among San Diegans is growth management. How can a community, which has named itself 'America's Finest City,' and which claims one of the most sought-after climates in the world, maintain a high quality of life while accommodating a growth rate that is expected to outpace New York and Los Angeles? The issue, which San Diego has addressed but not resolved, is clouding the horizon (causing much anxiety). But for now, San Diego's forecast is sunny (future looks bright)."

You won't have to use programmed word association at every turn in your writing, but it is a fun way to infuse your work with creativity when it's beginning to sound bland. Be careful, however, not to overdo it. A little goes a long way.

Editing Your Work

The writing you find in a magazine has been carefully plotted and polished to perfection, both by the writer and the editor. There are few pieces of writing that just pour forth from a writer's brain onto the page in perfect form. It's a rare writer who doesn't spend as much time massaging copy into form as he does getting the raw words down on paper. As many editors have said, "Writing is actually rewriting."

Once you've exhausted your creative energies, unharness the critic within you and edit your work. Look for redundant phrases, overused words, incorrect verb tenses, misplaced modifiers, and incorrect use of pronouns. Don't settle for mediocre writing. Think quality. When you write for top national magazines, you are competing with some of the best writers out there. Never let yourself do less than your best.

"We never send an article off without letting the other review it first," says Margaret Knox, who is lucky enough to have a husband who is also a writer/editor. "Though we write separately, we are there for each other, talking about the story, shaping it, and editing it. Our work is highly collaborative."

And there is nothing wrong with that. Don't think that just because you're a writer, you have to work in solitude. There's no shame in letting others evaluate and critique your work before you submit it to a higher authority.

One of the hardest things for a writer to do is to cut his own work. Even editors who want descriptive writing want it tight. You must force yourself to cut the fat—especially if your first draft always seems to be twice as long as the requested word length.

One way to pare your words is by starting with the big picture. Are there entire sections that could be cut without destroying the purpose and meaning of your article? It could be that, with just a little surgery to smooth transitions, you could delete a huge block of words and the reader would never miss it. Next, evaluate paragraphs and decide which ones could be eliminated. Then proceed to do away with unnecessary sentences and finally meaningless words.

Another editing approach is to comb the entire manuscript for unnecessary words. The search then expands to unnecessary sentences and phrases until finally entire paragraphs or sections are eliminated.

Word count matters to editors. If you have been assigned a 1,500-word piece, don't send in 3,000. And don't even turn in 2,000 without calling the editor and asking if the extra 500 words is okay. At most, your final draft should be within a mere 100 or 200 words of the assigned length.

"When I make an assignment, I am very specific," says Debi Lewis-Kearns, editor of *Brides Today*. "I really mean it when I tell you to write 750 words. Don't send me a note that says, 'Sorry, I couldn't stop myself,' with a manuscript that is three times the length I need."

Parting with your prose can be a difficult task and it sometimes seems like you can't cut a word without destroying the meaning and integrity of your piece. But many editors say that every piece of writing can be cut by 20 percent. If you can't bring yourself to edit your work, ask a friend or hired gun to do the job for you. You'll be amazed to see how someone unattached to the work can easily spot excess verbiage and thoughts. And, though you may hate to do the surgery necessary, if you want your piece to survive, it has to be done.

"To avoid over-reporting, we sit down halfway through the writing process and talk the piece through," says Dan Baum of the writing style he and his wife Margaret Knox have developed. "If you evaluate where you have been and where you are going in the process, you can drop certain angles or sections that would waste time and money because they'd make the piece too long and would have to be cut anyway. Sometimes, just writing the lead plus a rough outline underneath it will tell you what you need and what you don't."

One word of caution: don't throw out or delete your edited work. Save the old lengthy manuscript in a file folder, or a block of text you've deleted in a separate computer file. You may even want to save your first long draft under another name on the computer so that you have that raw writing to refer to if you change your mind and want to reinstate a piece of information.

Saving that text will pay off, even after you submit your piece to the magazine. It never fails. If you bite your lip and cut a section or sentence, the editor will call and wonder why you didn't include that fact or thought. If you've carefully saved it, you won't have to reinvent the work.

Although it's painful and time-consuming, editing and cutting is part of the writing process. The more you do of it, the less your editor will have to do, and the more repeat assignments you'll receive. Many an editor has bemoaned the fact that writers want them to be journalism teachers. In fact, one editor said she has received manuscripts with question marks in the margins as if the writer expected her and her staff to critique the writing. She, like most editors, does not have the time to coach freelancers through the writing process.

Editors do not consider it their job to teach you how to write, hold your hand, or tell you that deadlines are real. This is a business and they want to work with professionals.

Through the Mill

At almost all costs—sleepless nights, long days at the office, wake-up calls before dawn, and express mail charges—do what it takes to turn in your manuscript on time. The deadlines editors set are not arbitrary. Typically, they have in mind a certain issue in which they want to slot your piece. If you're even a day late, you can throw off their entire schedule.

"Every editor lives under the Damoclean sword, which is the shipping date to the printer," says *Omni* Editor Keith Ferrell. "We make our money by being timely. Every day that a writer misses the deadline, he runs the risk of his piece not making it into the magazine."

Most writers use every second they have to write and edit their work, and with the advent of express mail, they push the deadline to its limits. It's a common occurrence for a writer to rush to meet the 5 p.m. express mail deadline the day before the article is due, when the editor has given him two months to write the story. This book's co-author Diane Gage once had two articles due on the same date, and in typical writer fashion she was completing both the day before. When she missed the overnight mail drop-off deadline, she took the only other alternative—airplane freight. It cost her more than $80 to send her two articles from San Diego to New York. But the cost was worth it to maintain her reputation as a writer who delivers on time.

With FAX machines, writers can get off the hook for a day, if needed. If you just can't get to the overnight mailbox in time, you can FAX your article on the due date so the editor can begin the editing process, and then express mail the original so it arrives just one day tardy. But why not do what writer Paula Jhung does and plan your life so that the piece can arrive a day early? A writer who is ahead of schedule? Now that would make an editor remember you!

Rewriting Until It's Right

So, once your manuscript scurries into the editor's office with not a moment to spare, what happens next? What process does the article go through from the time it leaves your hands until you see your words shining out from the slick pages of a magazine?

While magazines differ in dividing their editorial responsibilities, there are basic steps each magazine takes before a writer's work sees print. Generally, the editor who assigned the piece, or his assistant, will receive your manuscript package and be the first one to read your article. If he has immediate questions or sees glaring holes in your manuscript, chances are that the editor will call you to discuss the problems before editing it. But, if your piece lives up to your promises, the editing process begins.

At a large magazine, several editors may read and comment on your manuscript, but it is typically the editor who assigned the piece who actually line-edits your work. (Line-editing means combing a manuscript to improve content, format, style, and voice. Copyediting, later, means fine-toothing the manuscript for grammar, spelling, punctuation, and other structural problems). At a smaller magazine, one editor may be responsible for the entire editing process, from initial review to shaping the piece into final form.

The amount of editing varies, depending on the writer's ability, but all manuscripts are edited for content, style, clarity, grammar, punctuation, and length. Some articles need paragraphs rearranged and entire sections deleted, while others require only minor editing and a few simple insertions to strengthen a point here or there. Don't be surprised, however, when you receive galleys to approve and discover that, while you recognize the words, the story isn't the one you wrote. Every magazine has its own personality and voice, and many editors perform major surgery on freelanced articles in order to make them speak with the appropriate voice.

Helen Gurley Brown, editor of *Cosmopolitan*, says, "Our major strength is not just the subject matter of the stories we assign; it's what we do with an article that makes it sing and be terrific. If necessary, we take our articles apart and put them back together again."

Even if you submit a well-written piece, it's common for an editor or the magazine's fact-checking department to ask you to provide more information on a particular point, to rewrite a section, or even to rework the entire manuscript. It's a given that a second set of eyes is going to see that your paragraph on page six would make a better lead, that you missed a transition, or that you've included too many anecdotes.

Part of being a professional means not whining and moaning when an editor does his job and edits your work. If an important point has been deleted or misconstrued, it's your duty to tell the editor. But don't be so in love with your words that you want it your way, no matter what.

"Once you learn that the editorial staff has to cut your work, loosen up about it so we can make it fit and make the page look nice," says *Brides Today* Editor Debi Lewis-Kearns. "Don't hold on so tightly to the words you've written."

Gurney Williams, III, a writer in Rye, New York, says that one of the hardest things to deal with as a writer is the layers of editors who look at your work and want changes. "It strikes terror in any writer's heart when one editor requests changes and you make them, and then the manuscript goes back and is read by a higher-level person, who also wants changes, and then finally the editor-in-chief looks at it and wants you to change the lead. It can be very frustrating, but if you want to keep the market, you clench your teeth and keep going. However, if that happens a few times with one particular magazine it may not be worth your time no matter how good of a market it is. I have had to cut bait at a few magazines."

If a writer's worst fear happens—your manuscript gets rejected or killed—don't turn around and kill the messenger. "The hardest thing for a writer to deal with is rejection," says freelancer Roberts. "If you go into a tailspin, become depressed, or let the editor see your anger, you won't make it as a writer. I am feisty and competitive, so I get pig-headed and set out to prove the editor wrong by bouncing back with an even better piece of work."

When a relationship with a magazine gets tested, writer Baum suggests trying to walk in the editor's shoes. "Keep in mind the grueling and impossible job most editors have," he says. "They are under incredible pressure to meet deadlines and keep their jobs. Even if an editor completely transforms your copy or demands enormous changes, it pays in the end to try your best to serve your client."

That doesn't mean writers have to accept unprofessional practices from editors. "If an editor has promised to show me changes and doesn't, or if a magazine continually pays late, I drop the magazine," says writer Margaret Knox. "I expect editors to live by the same standards they want me to uphold."

While the writer/editor relationship may become strained at times, editors do not want adversarial relationships with writers and vice versa. Writers depend on editors for assignments, but editors need good writers just as much. "I would be out of a job without you," says Carpentier of *Parade.* "There is a real excitement in the creative process between the writer and editor as they work to make a piece just right. It's nice to see that collaborative intellect at work."

When you are asked to rewrite, analyze the reasons. Was your material poorly organized? Did it fail to deliver what you had promised? Once you've rewritten the piece and the magazine publishes it, compare your final draft with the printed version. You can learn a ton by identifying exactly how an editor changed your manuscript.

Many editors stress that rewriting should be considered a routine part of the article-writing process—not a personal threat or condemnation. The way a writer responds to an editor's rewrite request often immediately sets an experienced freelancer apart from a naïve one. The savvy writer does not complain, while the inexperienced one grumbles as if to say, "Rewrite? For what you paid me?"

Even after you've cleared up questions and rewritten the entire manuscript, your article will be reviewed again and again by the editor before it receives his final approval. But then it's his turn to get edited. Your piece, into which the editor has put hours of his own talent, goes to a copy editor. That person will review the manuscript, not page-by-page or even word-by-word, but character-by-character. He or she will hunt for misspellings, misused phrases, unnecessary or incorrect punctuation, and a host of other technical problems that have eluded you, your editor, and the many other editors or assistants who have pored over your article numerous times. Finally, when the copy editor is content that your manuscript commits no sins of style, your bruised and battered—but much improved—article will make its way into design and production. Even there, you may be asked to cut five lines in the third section or add three lines to the end to make the article fit on the designed page. Then—it's off to press and finally into the hands of the readers!

Package Perfection

Looks aren't everything, but a neat, well-presented manuscript package plays a part in convincing an editor that you are serious about your work. From an editor's standpoint, a sloppy manuscript with typos, misspellings, and other flaws hints that the author may be careless in research and writing, too.

Following next are a few points to pay attention to for preparing a neat, professional manuscript:

- **Paper Size.** Your manuscript should be typed on 8-½" x 11", 20-pound white paper. Do not use erasable paper because the type smudges and an entire sentence can be wiped out when an editor attempts to erase an editing mark.
- **Type Size.** Editors say that pica type, not elite, makes reading manuscripts easier. On the computer, this would be at least 10-point type.
- **Type Clarity.** If you're using a typewriter, make sure the ribbon is fresh; in the case of a laser printer, make sure your cartridge has been replaced and the type is pristine.
- **Title Page Data.** In the upper left corner of your first page, type your name, address, telephone and FAX numbers, and social security number (for accounting purposes). Some writers also include the rights they are selling, but that's not essential, since rights are outlined in the magazine's contract or assignment letter. In the upper right corner, type the approximate number of words in your manuscript.

- **Title Location.** Type your manuscript title at least one-third of the way down on the first page, leaving plenty of white space for your editor to make notes and comments. Include your byline directly under the title.
- **Top-of-the-Page Slug.** On each subsequent page, include a heading in the upper left corner that includes your last name, the title of your manuscript, and the page number. (A slug is a code for the title. For instance, the title "Stress and the Nine-to-Five Job" with the byline Joyce Taylor would carry a slug that read Stress/Taylor/2.)
- **Double-spaced Copy.** Your article manuscript lines should be double-spaced, with at least one-inch margins on the top, bottom, and sides. It is better to allow a wider margin at the bottom of a page than to let your text almost run off the page—and the added space gives the editor more room to do his work.
- **Final Edits.** If you work on a computer, any last minute changes can be easily made and a fresh copy of your manuscript printed. However, if you notice a simple typing, spelling, or grammatical error, make the change in pencil, not ink, directly above the word. (If you are unfamiliar with copyediting symbols, there are a variety of books available to introduce you to them. *The Chicago Manual of Style* is a good source.) Most editors don't mind seeing a minimal amount of pencilled corrections, but don't get carried away.
- **Submission of Original Copy.** Keep a copy of the manuscript for your files, but send the original to the editor. An original manuscript looks more crisp than a photocopied one, and your editor deserves your best. Your copy, plus a saved diskette file if your writing was done on computer, can serve as a backup in case the original is lost in the mail or misplaced in the magazine's office. You'll need to refer to your copy, too, when the editor calls you with questions or wants to go over specific statements or paragraphs.
- **Manuscript Condition.** Editors prefer paper-clipped, not stapled, manuscripts. It's best to mail your manuscript flat in a 9" x 12" envelope so the editor doesn't have to struggle with a manuscript that has been folded in thirds and mailed in a letter-sized envelope.
- **Photos.** If you're sending photos, keep them from bending during transport by placing them between two pieces of cardboard secured by a rubber band. Slip each photo into a plastic page protector (available at any stationery store) to

avoid scratches. Transparencies should be protected by cardboard as well, and can be sent in flat plastic slide holders that you can buy at a photography store.

- **Source List and Research Material.** If requested, send copies of your research material (also in concise and easily legible condition) with the manuscript so the editor can fact check. Include a list of the names and addresses of contacts and interviewees, copies of reports or journal articles, and other pertinent information.
- **Invoice.** When an editor agrees to pay expenses, you are expected to account for them. Insert an invoice for your work with your final product. As with any bill, include your name, address, phone number, social security number, a description of services rendered (in this case, the title of your article), and the amount due. If you already have receipts for expenses, include those amounts on your invoice and attach the receipts to the bill (keep copies of receipts and invoices). Or, wait until your phone bill arrives and send a second invoice exclusively for expenses. Most magazines request original receipts but will accept photocopies of phone bills, since you may be billing several magazines for calls incurred during one billing cycle.

Finally, double-check with the editor that your manuscript arrived safely. One week after your manuscript should have landed at the magazine, call the editor's office to make sure that it did. The editor's secretary or assistant should know or can check for you. It's better to follow up and be certain that your manuscript arrived at its destination than to learn later that it was lost in the mail and have to deal with an angry editor.

Writing/Critique Groups

If you haven't already done so, join a writers' critique group. Such groups, which may meet weekly or monthly, offer you the opportunity to share your work with other writers. Though group formats vary, most involve either exchanging manuscripts or works-in-progress and giving comments individually, or listening to one writer read his work and then offering suggestions and impressions as a group.

"It's not enough to just want to be a writer, you need to take time to hone your skill," says Annie Stine, deputy editor of *Sierra*. "Take classes or join writing support groups to practice the craft and let others critique what you have written. It really helps to get other perspectives on your own work and to see what others are doing."

You'll only get from a writing support group the energy you put into it. Don't be afraid of criticism, suggestions to rewrite or heavily edit, or others' remarks about your work. They are only opinions, not indictments, and you are free to take the thoughts that help you, improve your work, and leave the rest behind. If, however, you discover that your group either always loves your work or takes great joy in destroying it, find a new group or start one of your own. A critique session should alternately bolster your confidence and remind you of the difficulty of writing. If either aspect is missing, you're losing out.

Another way to improve your writing ability is by joining a national writers' organization. Many publish newsletters that offer articles on writing techniques and address problems that writers share. Several organizations extend critiquing services, seminars, and correspondence classes. But critique groups and writers' organizations will carry you only so far; you have to bear your own weight the rest of the way.

Information on Writers' Organizations

The remainder of this chapter is a listing of national writers' organizations that you may consider joining. Some have regional and/or local chapters in various communities, and most charge a membership fee. To learn of writing groups in your area, try contacting local colleges and universities, local newspapers, and any agents or publishers who work nearby.

When you decide to join a writers' group, identify what you want from the organization. You may discover that membership in one national group as well as in a local one will give you the right balance between financial/professional services and regular contact with other writers.

Many writers' organizations have specific criteria for membership, such as a certain number of articles published in national magazines, authorship of a book, or editorship of a publication. The following listing introduces some of the larger national groups, to which you can write for additional information:

American Society of Journalists and Authors, Inc.
1501 Broadway, Suite 1907
New York, NY 10036
(212) 997-0947

The American Society of Journalists and Authors, Inc. (ASJA), is a nationwide organization of more than 800 independent nonfiction writers who have been freelancing on a regular basis, full- or part-time for at least two years. To join ASJA, you must meet those criteria and must have sold a specific number of bylined magazine articles or books.

Benefits and services offered to members include market information, exclusive referral services, regular meetings with editors and others in the field, group health insurance, and a wide variety of discount services. There are regional chapters of ASJA in some areas of the U.S.

The Authors Guild
330 West 42nd Street, 29th Floor
New York, NY 10036
(212) 563-5904

The Authors Guild is an organization of professional writers whose purpose and function is to protect and promote the professional and economic interests of its members. Areas of concern include book contracts, copyrights, subsidiary rights, free expression, and taxes.

Membership is open to any author who has had a book published by an established American publisher within seven years prior to application, or to any author who has had three fiction or nonfiction works published by magazines of general circulation within 18 months.

The Guild publishes a quarterly bulletin for members and conducts panel meetings with experts in publishing. Members are eligible for a group health insurance plan through a separate organization.

Council of Writers Organizations
972 Valley Road
Marquette, MI 49855
(906) 249-3156

The Council of Writers Organizations is a consortium of approximately twenty writers' groups which acts as a national watchdog on writers' issues, and offers a communications network on issues of interest to writers and writing services. Membership is available to all national and regional writers' groups. Those comprising the Council include: Washington Independent Writers, Independent Writers of Southern California, Outdoor Writers Association of America, Society of American Travel Writers, and the American Society of Indexers. Annual dues are $300.

Major medical, term life, and accident group insurance is available through member groups. Home equipment group insurance coverage includes camera equipment and computers. CWO member groups can also take advantage of Avis Rent-a-Car discounts.

The Council publishes a monthly newsletter, *WordWrap*.

National League of American Pen Women
1300 17th Street, N.W.
Washington, D.C. 20036
(202) 785-1997

The objective of the National League of American Pen Women, founded in 1897, is to conduct and promote literary and educational work of professional recognition and charitable activities in the fields of arts, letters, and music.

The work of members is often published in *The Penwomen*, the League's official magazine.

The National Writers Club
1450 South Havana, Suite 424
Aurora, CO 80012
(303) 751-7844

The National Writers Club, founded in 1937, represents approximately 3,000 freelance writers. Two classes of membership are available: 1) an associate membership open to anyone with a serious interest in writing, and 2) a professional membership, which requires a record of publication.

The National Writers Club provides manuscript criticism and marketing assistance for its members. The Club sponsors workshops, an annual conference, and many regional conferences, as well as contests for poetry, book-length manuscripts, short stories, and articles.

The Club's official publication, *Authorship*, is published six times a year. Other publications include *Freelancers Market*, *Flashmarket News*, and a number of writer's research reports covering in-depth information on topics related to writing and publishing.

The National Writers Union
873 Broadway, Suite 203
New York, NY 10003
(212) 927-1208

In 1980, a group of writers met in New York City to form the National Writers Union. In its statement of purpose, the Union says that it is committed to "the protection and advancement of American writers, to the nurturing of American literature, and to the cause of free expression in American life."

The Union wants to eliminate the work-for-hire clause from copyright law, to improve wages for magazine and newspaper writers, and eliminate the kill fee in magazine contracts with writers.

The National Writers Union has local chapters in several major cities. Like some other large national writers' organizations, it offers group health insurance, discounts in office supplies, computers, and car rentals, and publishes a newsletter. Membership is open to any writer who has published a book, play, three articles, five poems, one short story, or an equivalent amount of newsletter publicity or advertising copy. Also eligible are writers whose work is unpublished, but who are actively writing and attempting to publish.

PEN American Center
568 Broadway
New York, NY 10012
(212) 255-1977

An international association of writers, whose members include poets, playwrights, novelists, essayists, and literary editors, PEN is dedicated to defending freedom of expression.

PEN sponsors a number of symposia and conferences on writing, publishing, and censorship. Prizes and awards are given annually to honor excellence in the world of letters. PEN sends out a quarterly newsletter and other publications dealing with censorship and translation.

CHAPTER 6

Using the Library to Your Advantage

It's true that editors want current information from living, breathing sources, but that doesn't mean you should stay out of the library completely. Writers use the library to identify sources and to get facts and statistics they need for background research or to embellish a piece.

Increasingly, libraries are modern, computerized information centers with the latest resources, research, and references. Even if they are housed in ancient halls of wood and marble, most have resources that can lead you to current information on your subject.

Tapping the Talents of Librarians

The most precious resource the library offers isn't a book, a guide, or a card catalog. It is a highly trained research specialist called the reference librarian, a person who has earned a bachelor's degree, plus a master's degree in library science, and has thus spent six or more years in college learning how to use catalogs and reference books to uncover the rich information to be found in libraries.

"A reference librarian can answer a huge number of questions," according to Lois Horowitz, a San Diego librarian and author of *Knowing Where to Look: The Ultimate Guide to Research.* "But keep in mind that the whole library is a reference section, not just that little area with directories and a reference librarian."

People are reluctant to ask librarians for help, but a librarian's job is to answer questions, either in person or over the phone," adds Tom Gaughan, editor of *American Libraries,* a membership magazine of the American Library Association, located in Chicago, Illinois. "They look forward to those questions because every time they answer one, they learn something new."

Gaughan notes that the reference librarian can be a writer's best friend. "There is so much information out there, and the librarian knows how to look for it systematically," he says. "Any research question a writer has isn't so complex or obscure that it hasn't been asked before. Chances are it's a walk on the beach for a librarian."

A librarian can help you locate a book that is categorized in a confusing way, refer you to a government publication about your topic, or request an interlibrary search for a book his library doesn't have. He can aid you in your hunt for an expert to interview, direct you to archives if you need historical background, and join you in seeking out an elusive fact.

But you don't always have to leave your office to get assistance from a librarian. Large libraries receive hundreds of telephone calls a day asking for the address and phone number of an out-of-state professional association, biographical information about a famous person, the date of an historic event, the capital of a country, a statistic, or verification of a famous quote.

Librarians say that of the two to four hours a day they spend behind the reference desk, much of that time is spent on the phone. They expect a question when the phone rings, so don't apologize or give a lengthy explanation of why you need the fact. Simply ask your question directly and courteously, and they'll do all they can to find you an answer. If the question is an easy one, they'll answer it while you wait; if it will take more research, they'll usually offer to call you back.

"A rule of thumb librarians operate by is that they will answer three questions at a time over the phone, provided extensive research is not involved," says Lois Horowitz.

A phone call is appropriate for a quick question or for verification of a fact or two. For more detailed answers, you'll need to visit the library in person.

Checking Reference Guides

There are certain types of reference works with which every writer or researcher should be familiar. This book can offer just a quick overview of some of the research materials available. There are entire books, however, that provide exhaustive lists of major reference works, libraries, and sundry informational sources to which you may refer when researching your magazine articles. Some of these are: *A Guide to Library Research Methods*; *Guide to the Use of Books in Libraries*; *Knowing Where to Look: The Ultimate Guide to Research*; *Guide to Reference Books*; and *Writer's Resource Guide.*

If your subject is particularly difficult to research, consult *Subject Collections,* a directory that tells which libraries specialize in collecting certain subject areas. "If you wanted to know if any library has a special collection on the history of printing, it will tell you," says Thomas Mann, a reference librarian in the Main Reading Room of the Library of Congress in Washington, D.C. "There are more than 10,000 special collections."

The *Directory of Special Libraries and Information Centers* can also lead you to special libraries, research libraries, information centers, archives, and data centers maintained by government agencies, businesses, industries, newspapers, educational institutions, nonprofit organizations, and societies in the field of technology, science, medicine, law, art, religion, history, social sciences, and humanistic studies. The book indicates whether the library or center in question is open to the public, whether you must make an appointment, and whether the library participates in interlibrary loan arrangements.

Examples of just two special collection libraries included in the directory are the Lila Acheson Wallace Library at the Juilliard School in New York City, which has collections on music, drama, theater, and dance, as well as first and rare editions of musical scores, and the Sutro Library in San Francisco, best known for its collections of genealogical research materials.

Other good sources are the *Medical Library Association Directory* and the *North American Film and Video Directory.*

When you're looking for information about people, check the *Biography Index,* a cumulative index of biographical material in magazines, selected professional trade journals and books. "You could find an article on Sting in *Playboy* or a piece on Nathan Hale in *American History,*" says Editor Tom Gaughan of *American Libraries.*

If you are looking for a book and can't find it in your library, ask your librarian to locate it for you through interlibrary loan. If you need to find the exact author, title, and publisher or if you are wondering if a book on your subject has been written, check *Books in Print,* a resource that lists books in three ways—by author, subject, and title. According to librarian Mann, about one million book titles currently in print produced by over 40,000 publishing houses are included in that reference guide. There's also a *Forthcoming Books in Print* for books that are scheduled for publication soon.

The average library can not hold even a fraction of the books written. The largest collections of books available in one place can be found at the Library of Congress in Washington, D.C., which Mann says is supposed to receive two copies of everything published. "However, we keep only about half of what we receive on copyright deposit," he notes. "We have more than 100 million items to date."

The Library of Congress acquires items at the rate of about 10 per minute. Originally meant to collect and preserve state and government publications for the use of Congress, it now is an international information center and one of the world's greatest libraries.

The Library of Congress *Book Catalog* is available on a computer network called the Internet® System. If a book you are interested in isn't available at your local library, the librarian can request it from the closest library through a computer network called OCLC®, which includes about 14,000 libraries in the U.S. and abroad.

How to Search for Your Subject

The best way to start researching your topic in the library is to conduct a search, either manually if your library still retains a card catalog, or via computer or compact disk databases. There is a systematic way to conduct a subject search in a library.

"There are several methods of doing subject searches, all of which are capable of turning up things the others can't," says Mann. "The *Library of Congress Subject Headings* list is contained in a four-volume set that is updated annually and is always located near the library catalog. It gives the standardized subject category terms under which most libraries file information. These headings round up all sorts of books on the same subject, regardless of the words in the title. For example, if a writer wanted information on the subject 'death penalty' he might decide to look under those words or try 'capital punishment' or 'legal execution.' By looking in the *Library of Congress Subject Headings*, the writer would know that the library files information on that topic under the category 'capital punishment' and not under 'death penalty.'"

Smaller libraries use what is called the *Sears List of Subject Headings*, a condensed version of the larger *Library of Congress Subject Headings.*

Another way to look up topics using a computer database is through a key word search. "When you do a key word search, it's important to always check the category list that corresponds with the database you are searching. Many databases have different lists; for example, there is one for education and another for psychology, and so on," says Mann.

Citation searches are another way to find what you need. Citation indexes list books, journals, or dissertations on various subjects and tell you who has cited those sources in footnotes.

Computer Databases, Microfilm, and Compact Disc Searches

Electronic media are extremely useful research tools available at the library that shouldn't be ignored. "Ask your reference librarian how to use microfilm, computers, and compact disks available in the library to conduct searches; otherwise they can become invisible to a researcher," says Lois Horowitz who, in addition to being an author, is head of the Order Section at the San Diego Public Library. "It's hard to imagine that so much information can be on such a small piece of film or disk. One small box of microfilm replaces an entire wall of books. In fact, the nationwide telephone directories on microfilm are housed in a shoebox-sized container."

Horowitz goes on to say that more and more newspapers are now available in full text on computer disk. "Several newspapers are also indexed on compact disk in full text. For example, the *National Newspaper Index* cites articles from five newspapers: *The Wall Street Journal, New York Times, Los Angeles Times, Christian Science Monitor,* and *San Francisco Chronicle.* If you wanted to identify an article through a newspaper index, you would perform a key word search," she says.

When searching for magazine articles, the standard resource has been the *Reader's Guide to Periodical Literature,* an index that categorizes the content of more than 250 magazines. This resource is available in book form and in an expanded version on disk, called the Wilsondisc® (for the name of the publisher of that reference guide). "This disk combines a cross-section of 1,000 popular periodicals covered by four to five science and technical indexes," says Horowitz.

InfoTrac® is another computerized periodical index available on compact disk. It provides five times the number of magazines as the *Reader's Guide* and also includes abstracts of some articles to give researchers the flavor of the piece before they set out to find the entire article. Compact disk databases such as InfoTrac® are offered at a fixed fee and are updated monthly, whereas computerized databases are on line, meaning you get fresh information about what's available on a daily basis. Be aware that you also pay by the minute to conduct a search on a computerized database. By comparison, the most recent print index is two to three months old.

"InfoTrac® has become a cheaper way for libraries to conduct searches, so most public libraries have gotten away from on-line computer database searches," explains Horowitz. "But if you are doing extensive research and want to cover all your bases, and you can't get all the coverage you need through some other format, you might consider using one. Some public libraries offer the service, but with the availability of compact disks, they are getting away from it."

University and law libraries are more likely to offer computer database searches, as are regional research centers for libraries in a specific geographical area. There are also specialized research firms and individual professional researchers that conduct searches, to which the library may be able to refer you.

To identify which database to use, consult your library. There are directories of the approximately 7,000 on-line databases listed by subject category. Dialog®, the largest of the accessible database companies, has over 400 different databases a writer can tap into. Many university libraries and public libraries are hooked up to this source. Several other general databases include CompuServe® and The Source®. NEXIS® is a general database that gives full text, not just bibliographic citations, of more than 1,000 journals, reports, and newsletters, and LEXIS® is a legal database that offers the same type of full-text service.

Librarian Mann warns writers that published bibliographies and indexes are as important as computer-generated ones. "Don't assume everything in print is on a computer or compact disk," he says. "Computers usually cover only recent literature; compact disks usually cover only from the 1980s. Some indexes and bibliographies will never be put into electronic form because of the costs and copyright restrictions. Often, published materials provide windows into earlier literature that are much better than computer databases. You can do a very good computer search and still wind up with shallow research on some subjects."

Other Important Library Tools

It's impossible to provide an exhaustive list of the wealth of available library references in such a short chapter as this. The following is a partial list of some of the references found in most libraries. They can give you a head start in the research process; your librarian can help you discover many more.

- **Abstracts** are an extension of periodical indexes. These monthly or quarterly indexes, in published form or on computer, offer a short summary of the content of articles that appear in magazines and professional journals. They allow you to determine what the article is about without having to read the entire article. They can be used as reference tools or as grist for the writer's idea mill. You'll find abstracts either in the library's reference section or in the department that contains your subject.

There are the popular computerized magazine abstracts mentioned earlier (InfoTrac® etc.) as well as specialized abstracts summarizing what has been published in one discipline, such as geology, medicine, or chemistry. These are good first sources when you want to read briefly what has been written by professionals in a given field, though they are typically very academic. Some well-known abstracts are: *Psychological Abstracts*; *Sociological Abstracts*; and *Communications Abstracts*.

- **Biographical Dictionaries/Indexes** let you find out who did what, and when. Some of these dictionaries and indexes list the movers and shakers in science, business, politics, and other areas. Others are categorized by religion, time period, nation, ethnic group, or vocation. The most famous of these books is *Who's Who,* a British publication that lists short biographical statements about those whom it deems to be the world's most illustrious people. *The New York Times Biographical Edition* compiles articles about people in the news, including notices of successes and deaths. Other biographical dictionaries are: *American Men and Women of Science; Current Biography*; *Who's Who in America*; and *Directory of American Scholars.* As mentioned earlier, the *Biography Index,* which is set up like the *Reader's Guide to Periodical Literature,* lists references to persons of note mentioned in books and magazines.
- **Clearinghouses**, which amass information on social services and self-help, are available from many offices of social services, health and welfare, or consumer affairs. They can provide contact names and phone numbers to many organizations.
- **Dictionaries** go beyond familiar word dictionaries such as *Webster's Collegiate Dictionary.* There are many dictionaries on specific subject areas—and you can use those to learn more than spelling and meaning. They can be great sources of general information about special interests such as antiques, ballet, biochemistry, geography, and philosophy.
- **Directories** let you find the person or organization you need to fill your article with information—whether it is a chemist in Kentucky, an architect in Arkansas, or a minister in Missouri. As a writer, you may need to find such a specialist to verify facts or to balance an East Coast source with one

from the Midwest. To locate that source, there are many directories that are more specific than the telephone book. Most include addresses and telephone numbers as well as other information, such as the person's profession or specialty.

The following are six useful directories for writers: *Directories in Print* (a reference guide to other directories); *The National Directory of Addresses and Telephone Numbers* (which includes major corporations, state and federal government agencies, and other information sources); *The National Directory of Toll-Free Phone Numbers*; *The Research Centers Directory* (which describes more than 5,000 research institutions); *The Encyclopedia of Associations* (which offers the names and locations of 20,000 professional and fraternal associations); and *Washington Information Directory* (which lists information and contact names about federal government agencies and other organizations in the nation's capital).

There are a variety of other directories, such as: *The Directory of Medical Specialists*; *The Congressional Staff Directory*; *The Encyclopedia of Business Information*; and *The Lively Arts Information Directory*. Another directory, *Science Sources,* lists all colleges and universities that have anything to do with science.

In addition, your local library probably has a wide selection of telephone directories to major cities in the United States and of the capital cities of the world.

- **Fact Sources** provide general information on an endless number of subjects. Almanacs and fact books can be great resources for little-known facts and offbeat statistics. *Information Please Almanac, The World Almanac and Book of Facts, New York Times Reference Guide,* and *The Book of Lists* are four well-known general information books. Other useful references are *Famous First Facts, Facts on File, Editorials on File, The Congressional Record,* and *Congressional Quarterly Almanac.*
- **Government Publications** are plentiful since the United States is the most prolific publisher in the world. Its U.S. Government Printing Office produces countless pamphlets, books, reports, and papers on virtually every subject. But, although most large cities designate a certain library as their official publications depository, less than half of the government's output ever reaches those depositories. Large cities have government bookstores that house only a few thousand publications, but will order any public document the government has published and still has in print.

To keep abreast of some of the latest government releases, review the *Monthly Catalog of United States Government Publications*, which is updated monthly and available both on compact disk and in paper form at most large libraries. Also available is the *United States Government Organization Manual*, which gives information on the organization, activities, and officials of various departments, bureaus, offices, and commissions.

- **Indexes** are often a writer's first stop at the library when working on a query or magazine article. Indexes offer the names and publication dates of newspaper, periodical, or journal articles, usually categorized by subject and author. Unlike abstracts, they do not give any information to summarize the article content.

  Earlier in this chapter, the *Reader's Guide to Periodical Literature*, the Wilsondisc®, and InfoTrac® were mentioned. Other helpful indexes are: *Index Medicus*; *Index to Legal Periodicals*; *Business Periodicals Index*; and *New York Times Index*. Also, *Public Affairs Information Service Bulletin* is an exhaustive index of articles, books, and government reports about social topics, economics, and international relations.

- **Public Opinion Polls** providing information on how people feel about current events, newsmakers, and social trends can be found through polling organizations. These companies call or approach people on the street to learn such information as how the public thinks the president is faring, how many teenagers have smoked marijuana, and how much meat the average American consumes per month. Two of the best known pollsters are the Harris Poll and the Gallup Poll. Many polls are published; others are commissioned by industry and never see daylight. The monthly Gallup Report can be found in most large libraries.

- **Quotation Sources** let you verify a quote from a famous person or find the old adage that would make a perfect lead to your article. Libraries usually have an entire shelf of quotation books. The most famous is probably *Bartlett's Familiar Quotations*. But Burton Stevenson compiled several others, including *The Home Book of Quotations, Classical and Modern*; *The Home Book of Proverbs, Maxims and Familiar Phrases*; and *The Home Book of Biblical Quotations*.

- **Statistics** add credibility and a sense of timeliness to an article. Government statistical indexes are often most efficient and useful. Good sources are: *Statistical Abstract of* *the United States*; *American Statistics Index*; *Index to International Statistics*; *Historical Statistics of the United States*; and *A Comprehensive Guide and Index to the Statistical Publications of the United States Government*; as well as the publications of the United States Bureau of the Census, presenting quantitative summary statistics on the political, social, and economic organization of the United States.

- **United Nations Publications** include a vast number of fine research papers on such subjects as world hunger, single mothers, and trends in agriculture. United Nations publications are often available in local libraries and are listed in the central card catalog under their subject headings. For a free catalog of publications and price lists, write to: Unipub, Inc., Box 433, Murray Hill Station, New York, NY 10016.

CHAPTER 7

Taking Care of Business

Writing is a career, a profession, and an art—not just one, but all three. It is a career because you have to prepare for it, hope to make a living at it, and often you must start at the bottom and work your way up. It is a profession because of its intellectual requirements and the respect you gain when you become successful at it. It is also an art—and this is what sets it apart from other careers or professions—because it requires something on a spiritual or creative level that isn't always necessary to succeed in other fields.

There are countless people who think they want to be writers, but who are actually attracted to the glamorous myth that surrounds the art. Those who really want to write will write, and they'll learn quickly that if those luxurious trappings do appear, it typically won't be until after years of hard work and little recognition. Those who come seeking glamour, on the other hand, will give up long before they have a chance to earn it.

Being an artist isn't all the pain and drudgery that some would have you believe. Those who dream of living in dusty, airless garrets and subsisting on cans of cold beans are fantasizing their own version of the "writer myth." They relish impersonating the eccentric writer with disheveled clothing and unbrushed hair, who creates his art in a 48-hour flurry of uninterrupted hysteria, then drops from exhaustion and doesn't write again for a year. That lifestyle, though it may make good copy, doesn't encourage a writer to regularly and dependably produce salable work.

Eccentric writers forget that writing is one more thing: it's a small business, whether you conduct it full time in a rented office across town or during evenings and Saturday mornings in a corner of the garage. If you plan to make your living or to augment your income with proceeds from your writing, you must enter this small business as you would any other.

Magazine payment has not kept in step with the cost of living in recent years. In fact, most magazines pay roughly the same as they did a decade ago. Many demand more from the writer for that same amount. Today, a writer is less likely to be protected from lawsuits under the legal wings of the magazine, is expected to provide detailed fact-checking information, and sometimes must endure unreasonable lags between submission of the article and payment for it.

A 1990 survey of more than 800 professional writers who are members of the American Society of Journalists and Authors found that the average full-time freelancing ASJA member made about $20,000. That's not a great living, especially if you're a sole or primary breadwinner. In reality, most full-time writers make it with a combination of magazine articles, reprints, public relations or corporate writing, and books. To survive solely on magazine article sales, one would have to reach the pinnacle of editors' preferences at a handful of magazines that pay top dollar.

Dan Hurley, a writer for *Good Housekeeping, TV Guide, Family Circle,* and other national magazines comments, "When you're first starting out, it may take you one or two weeks to get a good idea together and write the query. Then there will be a three- or four-week lull while you wait to hear. If you get the assignment, it will be six weeks before you can complete it, then you'll be asked to revise it. That's another two weeks—and you're up to 13 or 14 weeks to finish an article. And what do you get for your trouble?" he asks. "If you've been really lucky and have broken into a good market, you'll be paid a dollar a word, so you might get $2,000. That's for more than three month's work, if you've done nothing else. If you're more typical, you'll make $500 or so for that length of time.

"You have to learn to juggle," he says. "Have a proposal in at one place, be doing research for another article, be writing another, and doing last revisions on yet another. That is the only way you will survive as a freelancer."

Unfortunately, too many new writers care more about seeing their names in print than they do about demanding fair value for work done. Although there may be something honorable to be said for such an attitude, landlords and creditors are not very understanding when you try to pay the bills with bylines. If you have an adequate income and care about nothing more than getting an article published on the side, you need not bother learning the business. However, if you're serious about a full- or part-time career in freelancing, prepare for some investments. Writing, like most small businesses, requires a certain cash outlay. The amount can vary tremendously, depending on whether you're comfortable working on Grandpa's Underwood or whether you decide to invest in a computer system; whether you can work on a door laid over a pair of sawhorses in the garage or must have an elegantly decorated office with a view. It also depends on how much you work and the type of writing you do. (Travel writing, for instance, is expensive when you start out, since few magazines pay expenses to fledgling writers.)

Editors say that if writers want to be treated as professionals, they need to take themselves more seriously. And that includes being trained to run a writing business.

"It's hard, but you can make a living at this," says writer Dan Baum. "You have to be willing to be a business person."

One challenge of this profession is that there are so few continuing education courses or journalism schools that offer the sort of training that covers all the facets of the business of freelance writing. Although a degree in business administration or accounting will help you with your balance sheet, it won't teach you how to market your work. You'd need a degree in marketing or public relations to do that. But you also need to know how to write, for which you might want a journalism, literature, or English degree.

A formal education in any of those areas can help you understand certain aspects of the business and will broaden the number of subjects about which you can write. But writing is a trade you learn by seeking out information, learning it, and practicing what you learn.

Writer Dan Hurley notes, "Your skill as a writer is very important, but tenacity is more important."

Writing is a career in which the time-honored tradition of learning from those with more experience is employed. Many established writers are willing to meet with a novice writer—at the experienced writer's convenience and the new writer's expense—to discuss getting started, developing a business, and other topics a journalism school isn't likely to teach. If you're starting out, you may also want to work as an editor or researcher for an established writer to absorb as many insights as you can before striking out on your own.

The Pros and Cons of Freelancing

It is a rare and lucky writer who is discovered when an editor stumbles upon the writer's work in a college newspaper or tiny anthology. Most writers have to bring themselves to the attention of editors by consistently improving their submissions and presenting themselves and their work in a professional way.

Without that responsible work sense and perseverance, others of less talent will sell more, simply because they have business savvy.

There are many advantages to being a self-employed writer. You don't have to dress in any special way when working alone (although you should dress professionally when meeting with an editor or interviewing someone). You aren't required to stick to a predetermined, rigid schedule, but can work any hours you like. And you don't have co-workers to distract you, no office politics to irritate you, or the boss to hound you.

But for every advantage, there is a disadvantage. The lack of a rigid schedule is the most common complaint for most writers. It's tough on warm summer mornings to force yourself to walk into the den and sit down to write, or head out to the library. Or when a friend calls on Saturday morning and asks you to play golf, it's hard to explain that you've got an article to write instead. Even if you write full time, it can be difficult to keep yourself at your seat when your mood is bad, you've got errands to run, or you simply don't have the concentration for work. On an off day in any other job, you could attend a meeting or pause in the halls or by another's desk to share the latest gossip—and you would still get paid!

But at your home office, while you can take all the breaks you want, you won't see any profits unless you produce. There's no one to tell you to get back to work if you stall too long, and no one to nag you if you spend 45 minutes reading the newspaper when you've promised yourself that you'll only scan it for story leads. Your editor won't know if you take the morning to chat on the phone with a friend. And the office won't call to see where you are if you turn off the alarm and roll over to catch a few more winks or just don't show up for work. But what *will* happen is worse: your checkbook will suffer and editors will learn that they can't count on you to meet their deadlines. When you begin writing at home, you may be tempted to fulfill that Bohemian fantasy of a writer who works half a day, then saunters off to the beach. But when you discover that the assignments are slow in coming, or aren't coming at all, you'll get back to work in a hurry.

A Writer's Workday

Writer Gurney Williams, III, worked as an editor for a number of years at *Popular Mechanics* and *Omni* and now freelances for *Family Circle, Omni, Longevity, Reader's Digest,* and *Smithsonian,* among others. He shares his metamorphosis from neophyte businessperson to a careful accountant of his time and money:

"When I first started freelancing again in 1986, I was overly concerned about whether I had enough work. I was keeping track of my assignments on the back of envelopes and adding up how much I would make from each assignment compared to what I needed to live. That finally triggered my purchase of a computer spreadsheet program that helps me track all of that.

"I am careful about time management. I track workdays with my spreadsheet and I let my computer act as a time clock. I carefully watch income versus time for every project I do, so at any time I can look at what I am making per day as well as what I am making on any individual assignment per day.

"The computer program really helps a lot," he continues. "I also use a datebook that has every hour of the day open. I fill in what I am doing for every 15-minute period. I generally work on three or four things a day. So I'll work on one project for two hours, then mark off that time slot. I update the program nightly.

"Using this time management system is a little like having someone watching me," Williams says. "I don't know why I need it. With a family of three kids to support, it's hard to make myself not work!"

This book's co-author Marcia Coppess adjusts her schedule according to her day's tasks. When she is doing a lot of interviews plus phone research, her day may start at 6:30 a.m. in California so she can interview someone in New England at 9:30 a.m., Eastern Standard Time. Since she prefers to interview a number of experts during a short period, she may conduct five hour-long interviews in one workday. She uses the time between interviews to review her notes, fill in blanks, and think of additional questions before calling her next contact. She uses a phone adapter to record all interviews and either transcribes them herself or hires someone to do it for her.

Paula Jhung, a home decorating and health writer, works five days a week from 9 a.m. to 4 p.m., with time off during midday for lunch. Most successful writers keep regular hours—and only a few count the early morning hours as "regular." The typical pro, it seems, ends up working a nine-to-five job with overtime, whether he works at home or in a high rise.

Payment, Please

Although they won't mention it, many editors have some leeway in the amount they can pay you. On your first assignment, you may choose to accept the fee offered. But as you progress through that magazine and others and acquire a solid standing as a writer, keep your eye on the fees you accept. No matter where you begin—$50 or $500 for 500 words—your goal should be to be paid the most you are worth. Most writers aim to be paid one dollar per word or more; however, you're likely to be offered less by smaller publications. After you've completed two to three assignments with a magazine, it's fair to ask for more money on the next assignment.

"I've been surprised at how easy it is to get a little more money," says Jhung. "If an editor offers an amount I think is low, I have a long pause and say, 'Oh, I was thinking more in the line of such-and-such.' Nine times out of 10 the editor says that it's no problem."

An unpleasant task of the small business person is bill collecting. Publishers, who often work within slim budgets, may pass over you in the payment line to satisfy clients who can cause them more damage, such as printers, distributors, and suppliers. Writers tend to be last on the list. So, even if your contract states that payment is on acceptance, there's a good chance that it may stretch to four weeks or even four months after acceptance—and acceptance comes after all revising, editing, and fact checking is completed.

What's the solution? Some established writers now request a percentage of their fee as they begin work. Others get an advance against expenses if their research will be costly. Many writers enclose an invoice when they send their manuscript, on the theory that anything that makes an editor's job easier is bound to be dealt with first.

You can prevent delays by requesting your contract before you begin work. Some magazines try to handle contracts after you turn in the work—leaving you legally unprotected and financially at their mercy if they stall on processing the contract and payment. When you receive an assignment, ask the editor when you should expect payment. (At some publications, it's as simple as sending in an invoice before the accounting department cuts the checks for the month.) Take note of your expected payment date. If you're not paid within a week of that time, it's fair to call the editor and ask him to follow up for you—or to offer to call the accounts payable department on your own. This is typical business practice and nothing that another professional wouldn't do. So get out of your garret and get paid!

Many magazines pay reasonable expenses you incur while researching and writing an article on assignment for them. "Reasonable" usually means long-distance phone bills, FAX or express mail expenses, mileage or transportation to an out-of-town interview, and photocopying expenses. It doesn't, however, include charges for the paper you use in preparing the article, or an extravagant lunch interview. A writer who bills a magazine for unreasonable expenses works for that magazine only once. When you receive an assignment, confirm that your editor will pay expenses. Many articles require a number of phone calls, but if the cost is $100 or less, an editor will readily agree. However, if your needs will be greater than that, talk about it up front. It will help if you warn your editor of your expenditures by saying, "I think there will be a lot of phone work on this piece. Shall I let you know if my long-distance costs go beyond $150?" or "In order to do the best job for you, I'll have to travel to where the article takes place. Can you authorize two days' expenses, plus mileage?" Then, make sure that expenses are discussed in your contract or confirmation letter. That will give you and your editor a guideline and will prevent haggling and heated debates when your editor receives a bill he or she is not prepared to pay.

Most magazines won't pay for expenses that aren't supported by original receipts, so keep scrupulous records of all you do for each article and make copies of all receipts for your own files. Since the majority of your expenses will be phone or travel costs, you may have to wait until a phone or credit card bill arrives in the mail before billing the magazine. Then photocopy the bill and underline or highlight the expenses for which the magazine is responsible.

Easier still are accounting services offered by some long distance carriers. You can pay a nominal amount for the service, which enables you to assign a numerical code to every client. At the end of the billing cycle, your bill arrives with every client's charges on a separate page. Attach your receipts and phone bill to an invoice that sums up each of your expenses by category (i.e., phone—$23.47; gas mileage—$45; lunch interview with Smith—$17). Keep a copy of the invoice you prepare, along with the original phone bill (since it may include phone calls made for several other purposes). Then mail your invoice, your original receipts, and an annotated copy of the phone bill with a brief note to your editor.

Setting Up Shop

Some people aren't concerned about the location or condition of their offices; others have to have every idle file out of sight before they can get to work. Some visit their local office supply store and buy a standard desk and chair. Others fill a room with antiques or memorabilia.

Since writer Jhung began her career as an interior designer, having her own office was important to her. "We built it about 10 years ago," she says. "It is about 100 feet from the house, down in a gully. I find that the physical distance from our living quarters works well for me."

There are lots of bookcases in Jhung's office—some free-standing, some built-in. She has one desk for writing and another side desk to hold her computer. A separate phone line saves her from personal calls during her workday.

Your office should be a pleasant spot in which you enjoy working. It should have plenty of natural light and air circulation. A desk lamp or other form of lighting will help if you plan to work during the evening. The office should have enough room for a desk and chair, one or more filing cabinets, and shelves or a bookcase. (A closet can be converted to accommodate much of your filing and books by adding shelves and filing cabinets.)

Optimally, the room should be large enough for a couple of chairs and another table, in addition to your desk and chair. You'll appreciate the chairs and table when you have someone over to interview, or when you've been working hard on a manuscript and need to edit it, but can't bear to sit at your desk any longer.

When you begin your writing career, you may be content with balancing a manual typewriter on your lap while you spread notes across the living room floor. But as you begin to juggle two, three, or more concurrent assignments, develop contacts and get on mailing lists, and establish idea files and regular correspondence with a handful of editors, you'll want to hang out a shingle and create yourself an official workplace. The following points provide some insight to freelance business basics:

- **Equipment.** While it's true that you can write anywhere and under nearly any circumstances, this book's authors believe that you'll be most comfortable and probably most productive if you meet office equipment and organization needs. Your first priority should be a suitable computer and printer or typewriter.

  Editors understand that not everyone can afford the latest computer and laser printer. But no matter the brand or level of sophistication, the criterion for a word processor of any sort is an ability to produce legible copy. A typewriter that prints light pages covered with broken letters or uneven lines is simply not acceptable. Consider renting time at a business that offers that service, or having your queries and final manuscripts professionally word-processed.

  If you've thought about investing in a computer, but haven't been convinced of its usefulness, go to a computer showroom and ask the salesperson to demonstrate word-processing capabilities, or take an introductory computer course at a local college. Then consider the advantages of those features next time you write queries or articles.

You'll see that the easy accessibility of work saved in a computer file can give you unlimited flexibility in using all of the article ideas you are currently circulating. It can also keep your queries in storage—ready for reslanting and resubmission if they are rejected from your first market. Make sure that each time you resend a query you personalize the inside address and salutation. Computer file storage also can save you countless hours of rekeying a manuscript when you need to move entire blocks of copy from one section to the next, or when you decide that the material you have written is good but belongs in a separate article or sidebar.

Other than an adequate computer, a sturdy desk and a good chair become essential as you increase the number of hours you spend at them. It doesn't really matter where you sit or what you work on, as long as your working space is large and strong enough to allow you to spread out your notes or to have reference books nearby.

Another requirement is a telephone within easy reach. It's inconvenient to conduct all your interviews from a phone hung on the kitchen wall, so install an extension (or your own line) at your desk. While you're buying a new phone, consider an answering machine. You can't be at your desk all the time; there will be entire days when you'll be out on interviews or doing research, and it hurts to miss a call from an editor or an important contact. An answering machine is especially important if you work full-time elsewhere and write on nights and weekends.

You'll discover that a small, reliable tape recorder with a telephone recording device will be invaluable. Also, a transcribing unit or foot pedal for your tape recorder will save a lot of time and bother when you transcribe lengthy interviews. Typing your interview notes directly into your computer also saves countless hours of transcribing or listening to tapes.

Magazine editors know that few people who write well are accomplished photographers, so they seldom purchase both photos and article from the same person. The exceptions are outdoor and travel writers, who often learn both crafts, since those articles are commonly purchased only if photos are available with the manuscript.

Nevertheless, it may be smart for you to take a photography class and to consider investing in a 35-mm camera and one or two good lenses. You may occasionally photograph a place, subject, or person and enclose the visuals with your query to emphasize the unique angle of your article. Although the editor will eventually send out a professional photographer to take the final, published photo, your photograph can clinch an assignment in situations in which one snapshot is worth more words than you can pack into a query.

- **Library.** To save yourself the embarrassment of having your manuscripts heavily copyedited, you should begin a small library of reference books, and refer to them regularly. These books should include: a good dictionary such as *Webster's Collegiate Dictionary*; a thesaurus or word finder, like the standard *Roget's Thesaurus* or equally useful *The Synonym Finder* (most word-processing programs include a very simple on-screen thesaurus for easy computer reference); and a stylebook—*The Associated Press Stylebook* is preferred by newspaper journalists, while *The Chicago Manual of Style* is the choice of the book publishing industry. Strunk and White's *The Elements of Style* is a classic that is helpful for all types of writing.

  In addition to the basic word and style reference books, you should have telephone directories to your city and to the nearest major metropolitan area. Extremely useful to have is a New York City telephone book. No matter where you live, it will save repeated calls to directory assistance. Ask your telephone company to help you get directories. Other directories, such as *The Official Guide to Toll-Free Phone Numbers*, can be helpful.

  Additional resource books include the *Bible*, *Bartlett's Familiar Quotations* (and similar books), and an almanac or book of facts. Refer to Chapter 6 for other useful library and reference books.

For names of more reference materials than are named in this book, you may want to collect writer's guidelines and other notices and information about the magazines in which you are interested. (For example, early in her career, this book's co-author Marcia Coppess kept a three-ring binder which was separated into three categories: guidelines; newsletters and articles containing useful information about her target magazines; and mailing lists and various market lists she had assembled. She referred to the binder as her own personal reference source while preparing queries.

But even more helpful than a binder full of guidelines is a collection of current magazines. It's wise to subscribe to your target magazines, and to save at least the current year's issues. But those three or four magazines probably aren't the only ones you'll want to read. Without a planned storage method, you will soon find yourself surrounded by stacks of yellowing periodicals.

The solution may be to store your personal library of periodicals alphabetically in vertical magazine files, which can be purchased in plastic, acrylic, or cardboard types at an office supply store. Since they fit upright on a bookshelf or closet shelf, you'll be able to keep the floor of your office much neater. You also have an immediate reference when you want to know whether a particular magazine publishes certain types of articles or whether it has covered your topic in recent months.

On your bookshelf, next to your binder of current magazine information, reference books, and collection of current magazines, should go your portfolio of published pieces. When you visit an editor in person or are considered for other nonmagazine writing assignments, bring along your portfolio to showcase your work.

Your portfolio book can be a three-ring binder, scrapbook, or similar book. A binder is usually preferable because you can place your clips inside vinyl or plastic jackets to protect the article clips and make the pages easy to turn and because you can expand binder contents so easily. Clips must be pasted or taped into a traditional scrapbook and they just don't hold up very well.

If you are a specialist (a person who writes on only one topic), your portfolio should demonstrate your breadth of knowledge in the field. If you are a generalist (a person who writes on a number of topics), it should highlight the variety of work you have done. The cover of the magazine in which your piece appeared can serve as a colorful break from a book full of black-and-white pages. So cut them out when you clip your articles and place them in front of each article.

File, Don't Pile

The way you handle two housekeeping tasks in your writing business—filing and tracking your queries and manuscripts—will make the difference between a chaotic or an orderly office operation for you. Once you've been at your writing for a year or more you will have files stacked in corners and manuscripts lost in the shuffle unless you devise a good system early.

For instance, if your filing cabinet is across the room, you will gather little piles on the floor around your desk instead of walking across the room to do your filing. A messy office costs money, time, and brain power. When you must spend 10 minutes looking for a file, or five minutes hunting down an expert's phone number, you're wasting time that could be spent more productively.

Other than a lack of proper equipment and furniture, many writers suffer from an inability to throw away paper. They often think that one day they will use that newspaper item or an article torn from a newsletter, so they keep them forever. But no one needs a stack of newspapers dating back three years—that's what a library is for! Although you may not need a four-drawer filing cabinet yet, a two-drawer cabinet is a must for a serious writer. The filing system you devise should allow you to place your hand on a given file at any moment. It doesn't look good when an editor calls to discuss an article or to assign a piece on which you queried him, and you take four minutes just to find the right file. No matter what system you devise, it needs to make sense to you.

Your papers will typically fall into seven categories:

1. receipts and financial records
2. ideas to pursue
3. ongoing research
4. queries pending assignment
5. articles in progress
6. completed manuscripts
7. tear sheets of published articles.

Some people prefer to have one file for every project. Into that folder go the original query, interview notes, rough drafts, a copy of the final manuscript, the published piece, and receipts and invoices from that article work. Others break up their files by category. All bookkeeping and receipts may go into a single "Finances" file or into 12 separate "Finance" files, one for each month of the year. All unanswered queries may go into a "Queries Awaiting Reply" file on top of the desk; interview notes, research material, and rough drafts may be filed in a drawer.

Co-author of this book, Diane Gage, has six file drawers in her office, as well as a four-drawer filing cabinet and a metal bookcase to hold labeled archive boxes in her basement. Her office file drawers have space left in them to accommodate future files. Each of the drawers is labeled according to the purpose of its contents. Files within each drawer are alphabetized, and a different colored label is used for each drawer, so she knows where each file belongs at a glance. (Green labels are used for accounting files, red for magazine articles, etc.)

Two drawers are labeled "Magazine Projects." Into those go files containing queries, articles in progress, research and interview notes, and completed manuscripts. Some files only contain notes about a topic Gage may want to cover one day—this prevents her from losing those ideas and reminds her of them each time she opens the drawers to retrieve something else. When those drawers fill up, Gage removes any files pertaining to completed work that she is reasonably certain she will not need, and files them in the archive file boxes in her basement.

Two more drawers are labeled "Book Projects." The files from each of her on-going books are assigned a colored label and are separated by chapter and sometimes by topics within chapters. A fifth drawer is called "Writing How-To and Background." All information Gage collects on writing, such as articles or newsletters, as well as samples of writing she admires, goes into that drawer. This drawer also contains clippings of her published articles, her résumé, and other promotional materials. The last drawer, labeled "Business," contains contracts, receipts, warranties, and instructions on equipment.

Basement archive file boxes are labeled according to their contents, so she can easily find research notes and names of sources that could be resurrected for future work. The basement file cabinet holds lesson outlines and writing handouts ready to go for classes and seminars she teaches.

If you have one or two projects to which you must refer constantly, or if you know that an editor will be calling with questions about a particular project, keep those files in a vertical file on your desk. But be aware that desktop files usually just serve as junk collectors.

Of course, you should play it safe and file at least one original printed copy of everything you write. In addition, make a file for photocopies of your clips. If you have 20 or more copies made at once of your best three or four clips, you will have a steady supply to accompany queries, and won't have to run to the copying service or be tempted to send an original clip when you run out of copies.

It's also a good idea to photocopy the source lists you submit to editors for fact-checking purposes. Maintain a file of the names, addresses, and telephone numbers of the experts you interview, and you'll create your own personal directory of experts on various topics. And there's no rule that says you can't interview the same person for a number of stories on different topics for separate magazines when the person proves to be helpful and articulate.

Keeping Records

Face it. No matter how long you put it off, you're going to have to do your taxes sooner or later. And when you do, you'll be glad that you've kept good records during the year.

A freelance writing business is a financial drain during its first years, since those will be the years during which you'll purchase a computer, office furniture, and all the other gadgets that writers eventually collect, such as FAX machines, tape recorders, telephone answering machines, transcribing units, and cameras.

But even during an average year, bookkeeping is bothersome, since the majority of your purchases will be less than $20, and they will happen regularly. By the end of the year, you'll collect a pile of receipts for many small-ticket items—a few pages of photocopying, a box of large padded envelopes, or a magazine bought at the supermarket. If you don't keep track of them as you go along, you'll have a nightmare on your hands at tax time.

As with filing and storing your work, you must find the bookkeeping system that works best for you. Some people actually prefer the shoebox method—they toss everything in a box and rummage through it every April. They'd rather suffer once a year than deal with the paperwork on a regular basis. Others adapt computer accounting or checkwriting programs for their home writing business. Most people realize that if they keep their records in some sort of order during the year, their tax preparation will go much more smoothly.

Marcia Coppess, co-author of this book, has used the same simple method for years. It has three components: an accordion file, a ledger, and an invoice file.

Each division of the accordion file is marked according to the various expense categories allowed on the Federal IRS form Schedule C, for business income and deductions. Into those accordion divisions go all receipts she collects during the month, from photocopying receipts for 30¢ to receipts for the purchase of a computer or desk. She periodically pulls out the receipts and enters their amounts into the ledger.

The ledger has a column marked for each major category of expense she incurs during the year—matching Schedule C again—such as telephone expenses, travel, office supplies, dues and publications, and utilities.

The invoice file holds a page or two from the ledger. On those pages, Coppess can enter the date, publication, article or service, and payment. Copies of invoices, signed contracts, and payment stubs stay in the file and ledger pages recording income can be updated every time a check arrives.

At any time of the year, her receipts are in order by month, so Coppess can estimate her expenses. They are also entered in the ledger by category, which she can transfer onto the IRS Schedule C. And her income is listed in one place, so she can easily total it. The entire bookkeeping system takes up very little space and time.

Some Tax Tips from a Pro

Michael Dreyer, C.P.A., of the accounting firm of Dreyer, Edmonds, and Associates in Los Angeles, has been helping small businesses organize and attend to tax details for more than 20 years. In 1987, he made the *Money* magazine list of the nation's best tax practitioners, an award based on selection among peers.

Dreyer recommends having a nest egg of six month's net income before anyone steps out into a writing business that is likely to have, shall we say, *wide* fluctuations of income at the start. He also suggests that a writer invest in a good computer and the necessary software to begin work.

"The professional writer should be able to comfortably purchase the minimum hardware necessary because word processing equipment is dropping in price so rapidly," he says. "And that seems to be the minimum investment required to start the business."

But there's plenty more to think about when it comes to tracking your business' growth, your income, and the expense of running a small business. In the following question/answer paragraphs, Dreyer answers 10 often-asked questions about starting a writing business and maintaining the proper tax status:

1. **How does a writer prove that his work is a business and not a hobby?**

   The main rule here is intent to make money. You should be able to show published articles, queries that went out, and other correspondence with editors that demonstrate that you made an effort to market your product and make money, whether you succeeded or not.

2. **What is the most common mistake small business owners make in keeping track of their business income and expenses?**

   That's an easy one to name. The problem is that too many people mingle their business finances with their personal ones. Then they destroy everything in the house just prior to April 15 trying to justify their business. The solution is equally easy: simply keep a separate set of books and a separate checking account for your business.

3. **How can a writer spend the least amount of time on bookkeeping while doing all that's necessary?**

First, try to pay with a credit card as often as is practical. Every time you empty your wallet of receipts, make a notation on every receipt—a "B" for business use or a "P" for personal expenditure. When you pay your monthly bill, pay the "B" portion with a business check and the "P" portion with a personal check.

If you don't have a business checking account, calculate the two amounts and record the business expenditures in your business ledger. Keep an envelope for cash receipts. Periodically record them in the ledger and reimburse yourself if you paid for them with personal funds. If you plan to do your books manually, meet with a bookkeeper and have him set up a spreadsheet system.

If you choose to use a software accounting program, look for a simple spreadsheet and check-recording program that will prepare an income statement for you at the end of the year. Quicken® is a program that is easy and does what you'll require.

4. **When or why should a writer consider incorporating?**

It is rare that a writer needs to incorporate himself. Unless you have become very profitable—such as netting $150,000 a year after expenses—it isn't necessary.

5. **How much can a writer deduct in education expenses compared to his income?**

Since writers frequently must learn a lot about their trade by reading books and attending conferences and seminars, I'd consider any expense of that type to be a legitimate business expense, says the accountant. A distinction is drawn, however, between attending seminars to *prepare* to be a writer and attending them to *improve* your income potential by becoming a better writer. The first is not deductible; the second is. The rule, again, is that you must be able to show an intent to make a profit at writing.

6. **When is a subcontractor considered an employee for tax purposes, and when is he an independent contractor?**

When you hire researchers, typists, or other assistants, the question is whether they work independently from you or directly under your supervision. For instance, any kind of researcher would be considered an independent contractor if you give him some topics and he conducts research on his own schedule, in his place of business, and with his own methods. Likewise, a typist who transcribes interview notes in his home on his computer is independent. Remember that independent contractors must be sent an annual IRS form 1099 if they are paid more than $600 in any year.

But an assistant who comes to your office for 10 hours a week and files, makes phone calls, and does billing is likely an employee because you set his work schedule, provide him work space, and supervise his work activity. You are then responsible for withholding the following: Social Security, Medicare, state disability insurance, and federal, state, and local taxes (if applicable). As an employer, you must also match the amount paid by the employee for Social Security and Medicare taxes. And, you must pay the worker's compensation insurance, unemployment insurance, and other state taxes (if applicable). It is up to you whether you want to pay for vacation time, overtime, health insurance, or other benefits.

7. **How can a writer get insurance for himself and his family? And should he buy disability, libel, and other special coverages in addition to health insurance?**

It is difficult to get insurance at all if you are self-employed. Often, sole practitioners find their best insurance deals through professional organizations to which they have the opportunity to belong.

Disability, libel, and other special coverages are a matter of peace of mind, he adds. Since self-employed people are not eligible for state unemployment benefits, some people choose to purchase a separate disability policy. Others keep enough in savings to give them a sense of security.

8. **How does a home office qualify for a deduction, and what can and can't be deducted?**

The home office you create must be the 'focal point' of your business. It can not be used also as a den or guest room. It should be set aside solely and completely for your use as a professional writer. Once that is established, everything it takes to run that office is deductible, including electricity, a *separate* telephone line, computer costs, and capital expenses such as furniture or improvements. You may deduct that portion of your home devoted to office space, but may not deduct an additional part of the house just because you occasionally interview someone in the living room or have a client to dinner in your home.

Also, choosing to deduct part of your mortgage payment as an operating expense may not be worth the trouble. When you sell your home, your business has to take a portion of the capital gain you realize from the sale. Since most writers don't keep a large cash reserve, that could be a big burden. So many people choose to deduct other office items, but not the office itself.

9. **What are the rules concerning travel and entertainment?**

   For travel expenses, you must demonstrate that your destination and activities were germane to an article or project, directly. There must be more than just a casual connection between the expenditures and your writing. And you should spend more than half your time while traveling on business, not vacation.

   Regarding entertainment, a specific business purpose must be discussed during a meal. You can't simply go out with writer friends and visit. But a group that meets at a restaurant to swap market ideas would be able to deduct the meal cost. As a general rule, the more successful you are at what you do, the more you can deduct entertainment and meal expenses. But no matter how often or seldom you entertain, you must have the names of those with whom you ate and the business purpose written on the receipt. Make your records when you pay so you won't have to recall later.

10. **Who has to pay quarterly income taxes?**

    Anyone who anticipates having a total tax liability of $500 or more in a year must file their taxes quarterly rather than on April 15.

    Find out how much you'll owe by requesting withholding information pamphlets from your state tax board and the IRS. The IRS will give you the forms you need to file quarterly and answer specific questions.

    As an independent writer, you no longer have a job at which your employer withholds tax from your pay. So set aside a portion of your income on a regular basis to pay taxes to the IRS. You must set up your own system because no one else will do it for you.

Dreyer's final advice to the small businesses owner is said with a smile: Be imaginative with your deductions. Stay aware of all that might be reasonable to deduct as a business expense. You'll be surprised at how much there is.

What to Deduct

To learn more about what you may deduct as a business expense, consult with an accountant or read IRS publications on tax regulations for small businesses. We suggest that, as you shop for an accountant, you look for one who has experience in working with home-based, sole-proprietor businesses. There are a variety of deductions you may claim. The following is only a partial listing:

- **Office Supplies**
  Audio recording tapes
  Business card file
  Calendars, electronic reminders, and other organizing materials
  Computer diskettes and their containers
  Files and desk organizers
  Film, photo supplies, and processing fees
  Ink cartridges for computer printer or typewriter
  Miscellaneous printing, FAXing and photocopying fees
  Paper clips, pencils, pens, staples, tape
  Pencil sharpener
  Postage
  Postage scale
  Stationery and paper goods
- **Equipment**
  Camera, lenses, and miscellaneous equipment
  Computer and software
  Facsimile machine (FAX)
  Office furniture
  Photocopier
  Tape recorder
  Telephone
  Telephone answering machine
  Transcribing unit
  Typewriter
- **Professional Dues and Educational Materials**
  Books, magazines, and subscriptions
  Classes and seminars
  Library card
  Newsletters
  Organization membership dues
  Research fees for database subscriptions and searches

- **Travel and Entertainment** (if not reimbursed by magazine)
  Airplane or other transportation to interviews or meetings with editors or sources
  Hotel accommodations
  Meals
  Mileage
  Miscellaneous transportation (taxi, bus, subway)
- **Miscellaneous**
  Bank charges for business checking and savings accounts
  Car maintenance (a percentage of routine repairs)
  Dues and subscriptions to professional organizations and journals
  Equipment repairs
  Fees for traveler's checks on business trips
  Interest and depreciation on equipment and other capital expenses
  Legal and professional assistance
  Long-distance telephone costs, including fees for long-distance telephone services used for business
  Maintenance service contracts
  Office maintenance costs
  Office-only telephone line service
  Safe deposit box for contracts
  Wages to researchers, transcribers, and assistants

Rights and Contracts

It's natural, especially if you're a new writer, to be so thrilled to receive an editor's call requesting an article that you forget to ask about the rights the magazine is purchasing, the payment, and when the editor will send the contract. Excited or not, you should always request a written agreement between you and the publication *before* you begin writing.

After calling you to assign an article, an editor may follow up a few days later with an assignment letter that serves as the only contract you'll receive. The letter is often informal, but should include the following points of agreement: working title of article; word length; due date; rights purchased; payment; kill fee; and expenses approved.

Some magazines augment the assignment letter with a contract. Usually you will receive two copies of the contract—one to keep and one to return to the editor with the date, your signature, and your Social Security number.

But if an editor tells you that his magazine does not work on contract, or that he will send the contract after he sees your finished manuscript, be prepared to offer your customized contract cheerfully. Beware of any magazine that works without a contract because that leaves you unprotected. There are two samples of good contracts included in the coming pages; you can find others by talking with writers at meetings, or by customizing a contract you receive from another magazine.

The types of contracts that magazines use are as varied as their editorial focuses. Some are straightforward one-page agreements, while others are detailed multipage documents. Be certain to read each clause carefully. If you don't understand a point, call your editor for an explanation.

Different magazines will request different rights from you. Don't assume that just because certain rights are claimed in the contract, you are obligated to those terms. A contract is not a contract until there is both an offer *and* acceptance.

Editors are accustomed to writers asking for changes in the standard contract they offer. Some magazines have two or three versions of their contract, and send out the A, B, or C version according to the experience of the writer. If you see something in your contract that is unacceptable, there is no harm in telling the editor that you want to line out that clause or replace it with one of your own wording.

The following types of rights most frequently appear in magazine article contracts:

- **First North American Serial Rights** gives the magazine (known as the serial) the right to be the first publication in North America to print your article. All other rights belong to you, including the right to resell the piece to a second publication or a syndicate after a specified period of time has elapsed.
- **All Rights** gives the magazine exclusive and total rights to use your article. A magazine might request these rights if it believes your article has book or movie potential, or if the piece will break new ground and the magazine wants to ensure exclusivity. The agreement is not always in your best interest, since the magazine holds the right to conduct any negotiations and agree to any fees for subsequent sales, although it usually splits the proceeds with you. However, the advantage to selling all rights can be that the magazine pays you more for the article, and exercises its greater powers to resell than you would be able to.
- **One-time Rights** gives the magazine the right to publish your work, with no guarantee that it will be the first or only periodical to publish it. This type of agreement is most often

used by a writer who sells the same article to many newspapers in nonoverlapping circulation areas. It is also commonly used in the sale of photographs.

- **Reprint Rights or Second Serial Rights** gives the magazine the right to publish your work after it has been printed elsewhere.
- **Work-for-Hire** gives the magazine all rights, *plus the copyright*, to your work. Since you are, in effect, working as hired help, the magazine is under no obligation to give you a byline, consult you about editing changes, or notify you if the article is sold for a fee elsewhere. Carefully weigh your decision to write on a work-for-hire basis. When you sign a work-for-hire agreement, you are signing away every right to any recognition or payment for your creation.

Looking to the Future

There are three particularly interesting issues about contracts that cause writers and editors to join different camps. You may want to consider what your policy will be about them now, so that you will be prepared with an explanation if the time comes to change a contract to your terms. The three issues are:

1. **Electronic and international rights.** The advent of databases and electronic subscriptions has changed the magazine and book world. Increasingly, magazine contracts claim the right to sell your article electronically, through film, video, or cassette, and to other countries. Often this promises that the writer gets half of any fees earned from the additional sales—although you have no way of knowing what has been sold or when.

   Contracts may ask for rights to reprint in anthologies, other magazines and newspapers, and a subscription database called the National Writers Union Agents and Publishers Data Base—often without further payment.
2. **Indemnification clauses.** What would our lives be like without lawyers to worry themselves over every little thing? Many, if not most, publishing contracts contain some form of indemnification clause. To indemnify means to hold harmless. In the case of magazine contracts, these clauses ask the writer to promise to hold the magazine harmless from any lawsuit that might arise from the article the freelancer has been assigned to write. Further, most claim the right to choose whatever legal action they deem

appropriate to dispense with the claim, and to pass the cost of that legal action on to—guess who?—you.

In the more fair and balanced contracts, the writer agrees to indemnify the magazine for damages knowingly caused by the writer, such as libel or plagiarism. That is a fair request, and something to which a conscientious and competent writer will agree.

In a worst-case scenario with a bad contract, however, the author would pay legal fees or, more likely, whatever lump sum the magazine's lawyers promised to the claimant to end the suit—even if the piece were heavily rewritten in-house and the writer was not allowed a peek at the galleys. You could be liable for $10,000 in legal fees or fines for an article for which you were paid $500.

Worried? You should be. Be aware of these clauses. In some cases, the chances of a lawsuit are dim; in others, they are greater. Consider carefully whether the fee for the piece you are assigned is worth that risk.

3. **Kill fees.** Throughout this book we discuss kill fees as if they are an assumption of a good magazine deal. But think again: should they be? Kill fees are designed to protect editors from assignments made to writers unable to handle their jobs, and to protect writers from editors who change their minds midstream about an article's content or the writer's approach and style.

   However, the National Writers Union, a 3,200-member union associated with the AFL-CIO, is circulating a contract that does not allow for a kill fee. If the assignment is made, the author is paid, period. The NWU is working with individual magazines in an attempt to get them to adopt this contract as their standard, and is also asking writers to step forward and request that their editors accept it.

   As the contract is now written, a magazine is not protected from incompetent writers—most editors object to that. But some writers argue that the editor's job is to hire only the best writer for the job, which *would* protect them from incompetent writers. Time will tell how well this idea flies. (Copies of the NWU Standard Journalism Contract and the American Society of Journalists and Authors' Contract follow.) As a business owner, it is up to you to decide on the legal agreements you make.

Suggested Letter of Agreement

originating with the writer (to be used when publication does not issue written confirmation of assignment)

DATE

EDITOR'S NAME & TITLE
PUBLICATION
ADDRESS

Dear EDITOR'S NAME:

This will confirm our agreement that I will research and write an article of approximately NUMBER words on the subject of BRIEF DESCRIPTION, accord with our discussion of DATE.

The deadline for delivery of this article to you is DATE.

It is understood that my fee for this article shall be $ AMOUNT, with one-third payable in advance and the remainder upon acceptance.[1] I will be responsible for up to two revisions.

PUBLICATION shall be entitled to first North American publication rights in the article.[2]

It is further understood that you shall reimburse me for routine expenses incurred in the researching and writing of the article, including long-distance telephone calls, and that extraordinary expenses, should any such be anticipated, will be discussed with you before they are incurred.[3]

It is also agreed that you will submit proofs of the article for my examination, sufficiently in advance of publication to permit correction of errors.

This letter is intended to cover the main points of our agreement. Should any disagreement arise on these or other matters, we agree to rely upon the guidelines set forth in the Code of Ethics and Fair Practices of the American Society of Journalists and Authors. Should any controversy persist, such controversy shall be submitted to arbitration before the American Arbitration Association in accordance with its rules, and judgment confirming the arbitrator's award may be entered in any court of competent jurisdiction.

Please confirm our mutual understanding by signing the copy of this agreement and returning it to me.

Sincerely,

(signed)

WRITER'S NAME

PUBLICATION
by ____
NAME AND TITLE

Date ____

NOTES

[1]If the publication absolutely refuses to pay the advance, you may want to substitute the following wording: "If this assignment does not work out, a sum of one-third the agreed-upon fee shall be paid to me."

[2]If discussion included sale of other rights, this clause should specify basic fee for first North American rights, additional fees and express rights each covers, and total amount.

[3]Any other condition agreed upon, such as inclusion of travel expenses or a maximum dollar amount for which the writer will be compensated, should also be specified.

(Reprinted with permission of the American Society of Journalists and Authors, Inc. from the ASJA Handbook: A Writer's Guide to Ethical and Economic Issues *[$12.95 direct from ASJA, 1501 Broadway, #302, NY NY 10036].)*

* * *

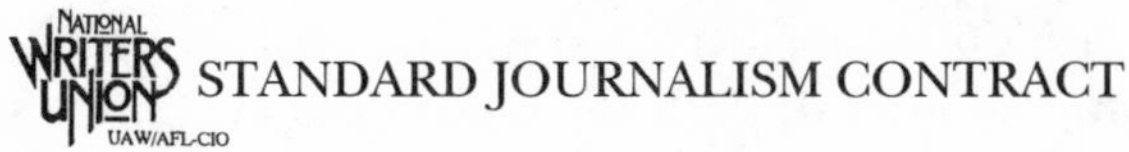

NATIONAL WRITERS UNION STANDARD JOURNALISM CONTRACT
UAW/AFL-CIO

Contract between (Writer)__________________________________
and (Publisher): __________________________________

1. The Writer agrees to prepare an Article of _____ words on the subject of:

____
____
____

for delivery on or before ______________ (date). The Writer also agrees to provide one revision of the Article.

2. The Publisher agrees to pay the Writer a fee of $__________ within 30 days of initial receipt of the Article as assigned above. (In other words, an original and coherent manuscript of approximately the above word count on the subject assigned, and for which appropriate research was completed.)

3. The Publisher agrees that the above fee purchases one-time North American print publication rights. All other publication rights will be negotiated separately by the Writer and the Publisher.

4. The Publisher agrees to reimburse the Writer for all previously agreed-upon and documented expenses within 15 days of submission of receipts.

5. The Publisher agrees to make every reasonable effort to make available to the Writer the final, edited version of the Article while there is still time to make changes. In the event of a disagreement over the final form of the Article, the Writer reserves the right to withdraw his/her name from the Article prejudicing the agreed-upon fee.

6. The Writer guarantees that the Article will not contain material that is consciously libelous or defamatory. In return, the Publisher agrees to provide and pay for counsel to defend the Writer in any litigation arising as a result of the Article.

7. In the event of a dispute between the Writer and the Publisher that cannot be resolved through the National Writers Union grievance process, the Writer will have the option of seeking to resolve the matter by arbitration or in court. If arbitration is chosen, the Writer may be represented by the National Writers Union in any procedures before the arbitrator. The arbitrator's fee shall be shared 50% by the Publisher and 50% by the Writer. Any decision reached by the arbitrator may be appealed pursuant to applicable law.

____________________	____________________
Writer or Writer's Representative	Publisher's Representative
Date: ____________	Date: ____________

(Reprinted with permission of the National Writers Union, 873 Broadway, Suite 203, New York, NY 10003.)

* * *

Ready, Set, Get Published

By now you've realized that freelance writing is more than picking up a pencil or tapping on a keyboard to put words on a page. It's more than wanting to write, or blanketing the market with unfocused queries. It's work—and lots of it!

You now know that writing for national magazines requires learning the most you can about your target magazines and having the professional commitment to meet editors' needs and deadlines. Of course, the best way to learn about a publication is by talking about it directly with its editor. But since such personal contact is rarely possible for a beginning writer, you should find editor interviews in Part II a satisfying read. These interviews are laden with quotes from real, on-the-job editors and filled with tips on how you can be more successful at freelancing.

The magazine chapters in Part II are, for the most part, self-explanatory. However, like any other business, magazines are unique. If from one chapter to another, you spot inconsistencies in the information, that's due to the magazines' different styles and preferences.

You'll note that some magazines use the term "department" while others use "column." Each editor was specific about what term he or she wanted to use, and there is no apparent global distinction between their meanings.

The payment rates for departments/columns are typically summed up in one line because the same rate applies to all of the magazine's columns/departments open to freelancers. In other instances, the rates vary greatly, so they are individually listed for each department/column. In some cases, if numerous departments/columns paid the same, a general rate that applies to those is listed and others that have different rates are so noted.

Writing for and selling your work to top magazines isn't easy. But the Part II magazine editor interview chapters that complete this book should give you the edge you need by letting the editors "speak" directly to you. If you "listen" carefully, you may soon be among the ranks of those to *Get Published.* Good luck!

Part II

Getting It in Print

Alaska Airlines Magazine

2701 First Avenue #205
Seattle, WA 98121
(206) 441-5871

Published: Monthly

Circulation: 45,000

Query: Paul Frichtl, editor

Query response time: 4 to 6 weeks

Buys: About 135 articles/stories out of approximately 450 unsolicited queries/manuscripts received annually

Guidelines: Available; send SASE

Rights purchased: First NAS

Pays: On publication

Expenses: Pays phone and approved travel

Kill fee: 33⅓ percent

Rates:

Type of Article	*Word Length*	*Payment*
Major Feature	4,500	$450 - 600
Column	1,500	250 - 350
News Brief	300 - 500	150

Alaska Airlines Magazine focuses on the people and places of the American West and the issues, trends, and events that shape this region. It spotlights the cultural and visual diversity of Alaska Airlines' markets: from Alaska, the Pacific Northwest, and Southern California, to Mexico and the Russian Far East.

As a travel, lifestyle, and business publication, *Alaska Airlines Magazine*'s audience is a mixture of business and leisure travelers. "We primarily see them as middle-aged business travelers who look to the magazine for some kind of entertainment while they are on the plane. If they can be educated too, that's great," says Editor Paul Frichtl.

Sixty-eight percent of Alaska Airlines' travelers are male and 32 percent are female. The median age is 42, and the average income is about $60,000. Almost 60 percent of the passengers stay away from home at least five nights per trip, and 22 percent travel five to 10 times in a month—for both business and leisure.

How to Slant Your Ideas to *Alaska Airlines Magazine*

"We try to be a regional publication and in doing so we work with writers and photographers who live and work in the regions we cover," says Frichtl. "They know the area best, and we want that kind of expertise. It's nice to have a well-defined region to cover because we can really concentrate on what is most attractive, fun, and entertaining. The West Coast is a phenomenal area for travel because the diversity between Baja Mexico and Alaska is immense. And some of the most innovative businesses in the country lie between the Silicon Valley and Seattle. Even when we take on national trends and issues we give them a Western focus."

Travel coverage in *Alaska Airlines Magazine* is presented in a way that allows the reader to get involved. "We don't just want a list of things to do that you could find in any book in the airport," says Frichtl. "We want the piece to be a good read so the person says, 'Yeah, I want to go to Nome, Alaska, or Cabo San Lucas—I've got to check this out.' We weave in information about where to go and what to eat in a textual way so that copy is not bogged down with lists of phone numbers. We just want the reader to get there in the first place."

Feature articles are varied and have ranged from "Getting the Picture," describing the Pacific Northwest as the location of choice for Hollywood filmmakers; to "Harbor of Hope," telling of how Vladivostok, perched on Russia's Pacific Rim, is on the edge of the change to a free-market economy.

"We started traveling to the Russian Far East in 1990, and while there is not a great volume of traffic going there, it certainly is one of the more exotic places to travel to in terms of unknown areas," says Frichtl. "Anything you get out of there is new, wild, and scenic. And business in the Russian Far East is wide open. There are a lot of similarities and differences between the cities in that region and those on America's West Coast."

In addition to its "Features" category, the magazine, which is more than 90 percent freelance-written, includes a "Destination" section and "Columns" section.

"The 'Destinations' section includes travel information, reviews, short itineraries, and great side trips for one particular destination," says Frichtl. "Every year we cover Seattle, Portland, San Francisco, Los Angeles, Palm Springs, San Diego, and Phoenix. Twice a year, in March and September, we run a special section called 'Great Escapes.' Here we group together fantastic travel articles about places that are great to visit to have a good time. They are often first-person travel essays."

The following *Alaska Airlines Magazine* columns are open to freelancers (not all columns are included in every issue):

- **Alaska Inside** is a monthly piece highlighting Alaska, ensuring that the airline sticks close to its foundation. It might cover a wonderful place to visit, a personality, or a community.

  "We ran a piece about a couple who devoted their lives to preserving the native languages in Alaska and ran one of the poems they translated from Yup'ik to English," recalls Frichtl.

  Another piece profiled Homer, Alaska, resident Tom Bodett, voice of the "We'll leave the light on for you" Motel 6 commercial, who had recently debuted on a new national radio program.

- **At Large** is a showcase of first-person essays about the West, written by top-notch writers. Though founded in travel, the column may also relate personal experiences or observations on certain areas or trends, such as one article that recapped a father and son's visit to Arizona for baseball spring training.

- **Autos** describes the experience of driving, giving background on design and function rather than straight statistical data or product reviews. One column looked at the evolution of automobile wheels; another discussed the resurgence of interest in American cars.

- **Being There** is a compilation of brief stories on culture and the arts, detailing museums, exhibits, and events specific to the West Coast. The column has covered such varied subjects as The Barbie Hall of Fame; the Vintage Fashion Expo; scuba diving in Alaska in February; and the work of space photographer Roger Ressmeyer.

- **The Business Enthusiast** is an upfront section of short business-oriented features including profiles of innovative West Coast executives and companies. Close-ups have shed light on such businesses as a new company that is streamlining the laborious translation of Japanese documents; and an outfit that is the only commercial banana grower in the 48 contiguous states.

- **Sports** deals with the world of professional, recreational, and spectator sports. Topics have ranged from golf and youth soccer to baseball and Olympic previews.

- **Tools of the Trade** is a business column that presents leading-edge technology and trends. One article, "Facsimile Technology Sends Communications to New Heights," described the business dealings now possible with the use of FAXes and detailed the features available on the latest equipment.

- **Travel** focuses on areas within the Alaska Airlines route system. Some destinations presented have included Mazatlan, Phoenix, and Barrow, Alaska. The pieces are generally first-person and offer an individual's perspective of an area.

How to Query *Alaska Airlines Magazine*

One page preferred; include good leads for photography if you have them.

In Frichtl's mind, an enticing query is one that includes a very brief introduction, a sample lead that indicates style, tone, and direction, and brief supporting facts.

"A tight, solid query should indicate some level of initial research," he says. "It tells me the writer knows there is a story to be had and that he or she has thought enough about it to get a focus on it and present it clearly. We get too many queries that say, 'How would you like a story on Cabo?' Writers need to differentiate their idea by telling me exactly what they want to say about Cabo, because I get at least 20 queries on a place like that each month."

It is also essential to include a few sample clips with your proposal. "We pass queries among several editors, so we give them the best shot," says Frichtl. "It may be that one editor sees something in a story that another does not."

Frichtl encourages beginning writers to query the columns because that's where the volume of purchases lies. Some of the features, he says, are assigned a year in advance.

"Prove yourself in the columns and work at developing long-term relationships with the editors," he says. "We like to be able to call a writer and assign an article idea we come up with in house, but getting to that point takes time."

If the staff wants to pursue your idea, you'll receive a phone call from an editor who will discuss the story with you and may offer suggestions for refocusing, if necessary. The editor will follow up with a contract confirming the assignment and terms.

How to Write for *Alaska Airlines Magazine*

"A lot of people view us as a travel magazine, and in most respects we are," says Frichtl. "But we do not present the kind of travel writing you see in newspapers. Our articles are not lists of things to do and see; they include discussions about what the writer is seeing and experiencing. Contributors need to talk to local people, make sophisticated observations, and then weave all that into an interesting piece of narrative. Our writing style is thoughtful and crafted."

Frichtl uses an example to make his point. "A writer doing a story about a charter fishing boat experience should talk to the skipper on the boat as well as to groups of people to find out what is interesting. First person is fine, but still there shouldn't be too much of the writer in the story; it needs real-world personality to come alive."

When it comes to travel experience, Frichtl says he wants someone who has been around enough to be awed but not overwhelmed. "The writer needs to be able to add a literary touch to what he sees and experiences and to do so with a degree of brevity and conciseness."

Business writers must be equally experienced. "It requires a certain amount of understanding to shape the personalities and issues of a business story into a literary piece," says Frichtl. "We don't like to rely too heavily on quotes and tired descriptions."

The writer's contract for *Alaska Airlines Magazine* stipulates that a list of sources and phone numbers must be submitted with the manuscript assignments for fact-checking purposes. "We call each source to verify quotes and information, so we demand accuracy," says Frichtl.

The magazine gives writers who don't hit the mark with the first manuscript a chance to rewrite. "But we still assume the right to rewrite, edit, and pare down the article for space considerations," the editor notes. "If we make major cuts, we sometimes send out an edited version to the writer to ensure that we retained elements essential to the story. And in any case, we'll send galleys to a writer who wants to see them."

Americana

29 West 38th Street
New York, NY 10018
(212) 398-1550

Published: Bimonthly

Circulation: 100,000

Query: John D. Sicher, editor-in-chief

Query response time: About one week

Buys: About 30 articles/stories out of approximately 2,500 unsolicited queries/manuscripts received annually

Guidelines: None available

Rights purchased: First NAS

Pays: On publication

Expenses: Pays phone and pre-approved travel

Kill fee: No standard practice

Rates:

Type of Article	*Word Length*	*Payment*
Major Feature	1,800	$500 - 700*
Short Feature	100 - 200	50
Department	750	350

**negotiable*

Americana is a treasure trove for those who enjoy American collectibles. In addition to enjoying profiles of collectors, readers get to explore trends in collecting, decorating with American collectibles, and collecting while traveling. It's a history and travel text, as well as a decorator's dreambook.

Americana's audience is split almost evenly between males and females. Nearly 70 percent of its mature readers have attended college and are married. They have an average net worth of $344,500.

How to Slant Your Ideas to *Americana*

The predominant focus of *Americana* is on American collectibles and decorative arts. Articles include information on how and where to buy and sell certain pieces and how to assess their value. The history of items profiled is an added point of interest for readers.

Travel is an important component in *Americana* and much of the editorial in any given issue is devoted to that. "We profile interesting places with some historic significance," says Editor-in-Chief John Sicher. "A travel piece can also give tips to collectors on how to pursue a particular interest."

Such pieces include a comprehensive history of an area and its early founders. For instance, an article on Aspen, Colorado, described Aspen's origin in 1879 as a tent city of 35 silver miners and how it grew and developed into a modern-day metropolis. Travel articles include sidebars on what to do, where to stay, and where to buy antiques and collectibles.

Sicher suggests that freelancers with a love of American collectibles study the magazine and come up with ideas on topics with which they are particularly intrigued. "Whether a writer profiles an interesting collector, a collectible item, or a landmark, it helps if he or she is interested in the topic," says Sicher.

An accepted article on vintage pens (written by a freelancer who was previously unknown to the magazine) included information about collectors, resources such as periodicals and clubs, and discussed the invention and history of the fountain pen. The article even included the names of several companies that repair antique fountain pens.

Another freelanced story was on collecting and renovating old American-made electric fans. Details about where to find these fans and how to renovate them were crucial to the piece. "Many of the vintage fans have beautiful Art Deco and post-Deco design," says Sicher. "Writers should include information that the avid collector will need to get started and outline the full range of costs a reader can expect."

According to Sicher, all of the magazine's features and departments are open to writers. "We believe in very extensive use of freelancers," he says. "It is a great way to build a diverse and eclectic magazine."

Departments open to freelancers include:

- **Collecting** profiles collectibles from Depression glass to Barbie dolls to Windsor chairs.
- **In Jest** features tongue-in-cheek essays on what it would have been like if a modern broadcast news team had covered certain specific historic events. For example, what if CBS News had covered the Boston Tea Party?
- **Passages** gives a then-and-now perspective, such as a recent feature on Litchfield County, Connecticut, which depicted the area's transformation from an industrial community to a chic venue for entertainment and political luminaries.

- **Preservation** includes essays about preserving America's heritage. A recent article in this department chronicled the plight of America's decaying landmarks.
- **Revising the Record** is an opinion column that sets the facts straight about historical events. An example includes a feature on why a U.S. battalion of Irish immigrants changed sides during the war between Mexico and the U.S. in the 1840s.
- **Travel** looks at places with historical interest such as the previously mentioned story on the development of Aspen.

How to Query *Americana*

One-page query letters preferred; send photo/art information to increase the chance of earning an assignment.

Sicher judges a writer's work by the query letter. "Submitting a well-written proposal is very important," he says. "It should have lots of detail and show that the writer has already done the research necessary to do the article."

Query letters that interest Sicher also include anecdotes and quotes. "I keep all good query letters," he says. "Often I will assign a topic to someone whose query letter attracted my attention because it was close in subject matter to an article idea generated in house."

Sicher suggests that freelancers read the magazine and submit ideas that are consistent with what has run in recent issues. He also advises writers to include clips with their proposals.

The editor assigns articles by phone, unless the writer lives in the Northeast. "If they live close enough, I try to get them to come to New York to discuss the assignment," he says.

How to Write for *Americana*

Sicher wants concise prose in an easy, open writing style. "My biggest objection is when a writer submits overblown, overwritten, 'Hollywood' writing," he says. "I prefer a minimalist style."

American Health

28 West 23rd Street
New York, NY 10010
(212) 366-8900

Published: Monthly, except February and August

Circulation: 850,000

Query: Call the magazine's receptionist to ask which editor handles the column or feature section you want to query

Query response time: 4 weeks

Buys: Less than 5 percent of its material from approximately 1,500 unsolicited queries/manuscripts received annually

Guidelines: Available; send SASE

Rights purchased: First NAS

Pays: On acceptance

Expenses: Pays items if reasonable, and as approved in advance

Kill fee: 25 percent

Rates:

Type of Article	*Word Length*	*Payment*
Major Feature	2,500	$2,000 - 2,500
Short Feature	1,500	1,000 - 1,500
Column	1,500 - 2,500	1,750 - 2,000
"Personal Trainer"	750	750
News Brief	200 - 400	250

American Health, with its subhead "Fitness of Body and Mind," covers health in the broadest sense of the word. It's written for upscale baby boomers who have embraced health as a core value. The underlying editorial thesis is that good health generates the energy and vitality essential to achieving success, pleasure, and satisfaction in every facet of life.

The median age of the *American Health* reader is 43, and 71 percent of the readers are female. Research shows that 51 percent have attended college; 29 percent are professional/managerial; and one-third of the readers have household incomes in excess of $60,000.

How to Slant Your Ideas to *American Health*

The editors give little encouragement for freelance writers trying to sell to the magazine. Only five percent of articles are written by freelancers previously unpublished in *American Health.* Ten percent are written in house, and the vast majority (85 percent) come from a well-entrenched freelance pool.

American Health reports the latest developments in medicine, psychology, dental care, fitness, food and nutrition, personal and family relationships, stress, and the environment. Beyond that, the editorial looks at all aspects of health and quality of life that lead to integration and balance.

Another facet of the magazine is its coverage of offbeat health-related pieces, such as what it takes to be a fighter pilot; teenage suicides; the biology of homosexuality; and how to avoid having an automobile accident.

What *American Health* wants most from writers is health news. The magazine receives timely news releases and abstracts of the latest medical studies from medical institutions and universities across the country, so editors look to writers to find information they won't necessarily know about from those sources.

"A good way to find ideas is by reading scientific journals and noticing something that a consumer magazine hasn't covered yet," suggests Cynthia Moekle, assistant managing editor. "While those journals can be difficult to read, they usually have a synopsis of the study at the beginning that is relatively easy to understand. Attending scientific conferences and listening to researchers deliver papers on a finding not yet published is also a way writers sell ideas to us."

One of the best ways to break in is through news brief pieces of about 200 to 400 words. The following paragraphs contain basic information on the magazine's many sections of short news items that flank the feature well:

- **Dental** reports the latest information on teeth and gums. One study found that most people who wore braces had a recurrence of crowded teeth, and that long-term retainers were necessary to keep straight teeth in line.

- **Family** looks at issues such as single mothering; sibling rivalry; working out with baby; childcare; and teen health.

- **Fitness** reports fitness news as well as the latest trends, such as the treadwall, an exercise machine that simulates mountain climbing. Other topics have included body image disorders; how to maintain fluids while working out; and new ways to stay fit during pregnancy.

- **Looking Good** covers skin and hair and includes topics such as cosmetic surgery, skin cancer, liposuction, and the health risks of certain beauty products.
- **Medicine** offers late-breaking medical news. Because the magazine receives reports from the top medical universities and major medical journals, writers need to uncover ideas before public relations practitioners and trade journal editors release the news. Sample topics are deadly food allergies, and a new drug that minimizes nausea and vomiting caused by chemotherapy.
- **The Mind** covers any psychology-related health topic. New research on subjects such as bulimia, migraines, stress, PMS, and male and female differences are a sampling of what editors are after. One issue included women in politics; the passive-aggressive man; and the health consequences that crime victims suffer.
- **Nutrition** presents all sides of food and nutrition. Examples are calcium and kids, and the relation of zinc-deficient diets to would-be fathers.

The following is a list of columns open to freelancers:

- **Healthy Cook** features a particular cuisine, cooking style, or ingredient, accompanied by healthy recipes.
- **First Person** is a personal narrative often written by a person undergoing a particular medical ordeal. While many of the articles in this section fall into the disease category, writers should try to think in new directions. One editor wrote a humorous column on buying cosmetics. A freelancer wrote about listening to his inner voice warning him to postpone hip surgery, only to discover that he had a mitral valve infection that could have taken his life if he had gone ahead with the original plan. The word length of this column is 1,500 words.
- **Personal Trainer** focuses on one body part each month. Pieces include an anatomical drawing and brief explanation of how the part works, as well as exercises recommended to strengthen it. A past issue featured the calf muscle.
- **Profiles** takes a close-up look at one person doing something unusual in a health-related field. In addition to performing innovative work, the individual featured must also have an intriguing personal life. "We don't air every single aspect of someone's private life, but we make sure our profiles are interesting all-around," says Moekle.

For example, the magazine ran a profile of Byllye Avery, Ph.D., founding president of the National Black Women's Health Association. "This story worked because Black women's health has been neglected, and Avery's personal story of how she became devoted to the cause was moving as well," explains Moekle. "Activists often make very good profiles. We often run profiles of laypeople who are leading crusades for neglected areas in health. Since our readers are mostly laypeople, it's often easier for them to relate to a person who is not a medical expert."

Dr. Spock made a good profile not only because of his legacy in child health, but because of his political ideology as an anti-Vietnam activist. The magazine also ran a vignette on Rae Grad, head of the National Commission to Prevent Infant Mortality, who is working to reduce the appallingly high infant mortality rate in the United States.

"We get a lot of queries about profiles of people who have overcome horrendous, personal health problems, such as a physically challenged rock climber," says Moekle. "Those individuals are wonderful, but to fit our 'Profile' column, they have to have done something more, like start a national organization to help others in a similar situation. In other words, the person's efforts have to have national consequences."

- **Second Opinion** is a well-reported essay about 1,500 words in length in which the writer takes an opinion on a health issue. Past columns have featured topics such as doctors with AIDS; pesticides and produce; and the need for warning labels on psychoactive drugs such as Prozac and Halcion. "The column can take on all sorts of forms, but typically they read much like a newspaper op/ed piece," says Associate Editor Rebecca Norris. "Opinions are backed up by expert quotes and specific examples."

Columns closed to freelancers include: "Ask American Health," "Checkups," "Close Encounters," "Editor's Rx," "Klass Act," "Medicine Chest," "Moments," and "Weight and See."

How to Query *American Health*

One page or less preferred.

"When reading queries, we often get the feeling that the writer plans to send the idea to a wide range of magazines," says Moekle.

"He or she doesn't seem to be putting a lot of effort into tailoring it specifically for *American Health.*"

Moekle says that the best queries for this magazine are short and straightforward. "We get a lot of queries that have two or three paragraphs of the proposed article's lead, as a way for the writer to show his or her writing style," says the editor. "That doesn't do much for us. A much better way to show writing style is to send a few appropriate clips. In a query, we want to read the raw idea, without a lot of padding."

While the needs of the magazine depend on the individual column or news section you are querying, Moekle says most stories tend to be service-oriented. "We have a few columns that are 'good reads' without a practical application, but most of what we run is designed for our readers to learn something they can use in their daily lives," she says. "For that reason, queries have a better chance if they have something to do with common diseases that affect a lot of people, such as heart disease, cancer, and women's health. In addition, the idea must unveil an unusual study or something else that hasn't been covered everywhere else. We don't want queries on rare diseases that don't affect a large percent of our readers."

How to Write for *American Health*

American Health is known for reporting the latest health and medical information, quoting top experts in the field, while maintaining the highest level of medical integrity and thoroughness. Yet it maintains a style that is deliberately geared to the average person. The magazine directs the reader where to go next for information.

"We like the writing to be tight and fairly simple, without a lot of clichés and extra words," says Moekle. "We don't want writing that is too bouncy or cutesy. We run a few columns in which stylish writing is the key. But for the majority of stories, the most important thing is to convey information as succinctly as possible."

Moekle says that because *American Health* likes personal stories, the editors look for anecdotes about people who have had the disease that the feature highlights. "That's one way to avoid a dry, scientific story and liven up the writing," she says.

The magazine's fact-checking process is rigorous, so be prepared to have your work triple checked.

The American Legion Magazine

P.O. Box 1055
Indianapolis, IN 46206-1055
(317) 635-8411

Published: Monthly

Circulation: 2,900,000

Query: John Greenwald, editor

Query response time: 2 to 3 weeks

Buys: 50 to 75 percent of its material from approximately 3,000 to 4,000 unsolicited queries/manuscripts received annually

Guidelines: Available; send $2 for sample copy of magazine

Rights purchased: First NAS

Pays: On acceptance

Expenses: Pays items agreed upon in advance

Kill fee: 25 to 100 percent (depends on reason)

Rates:

Type of Article	*Word Length*	*Payment*
Major Feature	1,000 - 2,200	$750 - 2,000
Short Feature	600 - 750	300 - 700
"Legion News"	500	250

The American Legion Magazine is an issue-oriented, general interest publication. It is published by the American Legion for its three million members—military wartime veterans who belong to 16,000 community-level posts.

"Our readers are interested in the same subjects every American cares about, such as national security, foreign affairs, education, social issues, family, and the community," says Editor John Greenwald. "And since they are service veterans, they also care deeply about the welfare of veterans, their spouses, and their children. We are not a military magazine, though we write on military subjects as part of our interest in national defense issues. We devote 20 to 30 percent of the magazine to issues of concern to veterans. Half of the readers are World War II vets; one-quarter are Korean War vets; and one-quarter are Vietnam vets (a prime growth audience for the magazine)."

The magazine focuses on current trends affecting the United States, the free world, and the way we live. It also reports on topics such as business, hobbies, health, ethics, and the arts. The average *The American Legion Magazine* reader is male, about 60 years old, who is married, devoted to his family (which probably includes two or three children), and earns about $30,000 a year in a white- or blue-collar job. At least 75 percent of the readers graduated from high school and 33 percent attended college or earned one or more college degrees. About 70 percent are employed; 30 percent are retired. They are community-oriented, perhaps even more than their neighbors. About 90 percent of *The American Legion Magazine*'s readers vote.

Four words—"For God and Country"—tucked below the magazine's title, sum up the aims of this monthly publication and the organization that produces it. Greenwald adds, "Our audience spans the socioeconomic and educational spectrum, but every reader has these commitments in common: a strong national defense, proper veteran care, morality, community service, and concern for the nation's youth. The magazine reflects those interests while it strives to maintain a varied editorial mix. We consider ourselves 'The Magazine for a Strong America.'"

How to Slant Your Ideas to *The American Legion Magazine*

The American Legion Magazine publishes commentaries, opinion pieces, analytical articles, and reportage. Ground rules include no exposés, no partisan politics, and no articles that ridicule the opinions, appearance, or activities of any person or group. The publication addresses only the issues, not the partisans involved.

Greenwald says he looks for trends that get his readers ahead of the news. "We've done pieces that focused on Europe, the new nanotechnology (tiny computers and machines), and the resurgence of single sex schools," he says. "We don't just cover a topic that's interesting—we look at what is happening next, what impact it will have down the road, and how we can prepare."

A writer who knows his subject is one who will break into *The American Legion Magazine.* In addition, he or she must be willing to work with Greenwald to focus the story. "The best ideas happen when a few people can talk and bounce ideas off of one another," he says.

The American Legion Magazine will also consider purchasing interviews conducted with prominent national and world figures who address topics of current concern to its readership. Remember, the magazine has at least a three-month lead time.

Each month the publication contains at least eight features. One is staff-written on a subject of special interest to veterans. Three of the remaining seven are from ideas generated by the editors; the others evolve from writers. Topics have included aid to Russia; food irradiation; prison boot camps; collecting memorabilia; commentary and debate on popular culture; over-prescribed surgeries; and the best WWII movies.

"Big Issues," "Parting Shots," "Veteran's Update," "Washington Watch," and "Your American Legion" are all written in house or by regular contributors. "Legion News," short items about The American Legion, may occasionally be written by an outside source. "If you have an exceptional, offbeat piece of local Legion activity, send it in," says Greenwald.

How to Query *The American Legion Magazine*

One and one-half pages at most; don't send photo/art suggestions; query six months in advance for seasonal material. The magazine buys very few unsolicited manuscripts.

A query that captures Greenwald's attention is one that makes him want to read the article now. "I want to immediately know what your article is about," he says. "Set up the reader's needs in the first paragraph and then tell how you're going to satisfy those needs in the next. If I'm not hooked by the first two paragraphs, there is no way to interest me. A third or fourth paragraph of background is fine to help cinch the sale, but limit the query length to one and one-half pages. Suggesting a headline for the story is a good way to quickly communicate your angle."

What doesn't work for Greenwald is an all-purpose query that could have been sent to any magazine. "Those writers make it clear that they haven't read our magazine. They have an interesting subject in mind, but really haven't thought about how it pertains to *The American Legion Magazine* reader."

If the subject you propose is highly specialized, Greenwald expects you to be knowledgeable about it. "An article about the nation's press should be written by an authority on the subject," he says.

Competent writers with no particular expertise in a topic area will receive an assignment if they prove they can research well and interview the right people. Credentials are important to include in your query, whether they are clips of published work, or a résumé detailing a career in the subject about which you want to write.

If the editorial staff warms to your idea as a major piece, expect a call from an editor to talk the article through ahead of time. "We want ideas that are fully formed in the query stage, but we want to discuss if there's a better way to treat it than the way you've suggested," explains Greenwald.

Before being assigned an article, writers may be required to submit an outline showing the general thrust of the proposed article. The outline does not need to be long, but it must be thorough and demonstrate a writer's firm understanding of the proposed topic and the particular slant being recommended. If the editors agree, they will send an assignment letter, confirming the details of the story and giving contract information, such as fee, deadline, length, and rights purchased.

The magazine occasionally takes a chance on unpublished writers, but on speculation only.

How to Write for *The American Legion Magazine*

The American Legion Magazine places a premium on good taste, objectivity, and accuracy. Articles should be written to a sophisticated reader with strong knowledge of national issues. "Don't make assertions if you aren't an expert in the field," says Greenwald. "If the Secretary of Defense says something, that's one thing. But if you think something else, back up your statements with Pentagon sources, reports, or other experts."

Read the magazine to see how articles are organized. "Note how we write our lead paragraphs, transitions, and quotations from sources," he suggests. "Analyze how sharply the stories are angled and the depth of detail they cover."

Articles generally adhere to a three-part editorial format: the problem; how it will affect readers; and what solutions are potentially feasible. The editors like to see these points summarized early in the article, then expanded as needed to include vivid examples, facts, and expert opinions to report the story in a dynamic, interesting manner.

"Make sure your article has a point of view," urges Greenwald. "It should be easy for the reader to see why the subject is important enough to invest time reading about it. Show that you're excited about the idea."

The editor says that among the things writers do wrong is write sentences and paragraphs that are too long, include too much passive voice, and get caught up in the jargon of the industry. *The American Legion Magazine* looks for solid reporting and a lively writing style.

If during the writing process, you have a question for Greenwald, call him. The editor doesn't like surprises, so it's important to make sure you are on target before you send in your article.

Greenwald says he seldom requests full rewrites, but 25 percent of the pieces he buys require some "touching up."

"We want writers to master our style so we don't have to edit much," says Greenwald. "Know how to make the lead compelling and how to get the nut graph up really high. Understand what we want, but also realize that we want you to stretch our thinking a little bit, too. And delivering stories on time is a must."

Writers are required to include documentation of pertinent facts and citations verifying the accuracy of quotes in the article. This is especially important when quoting people whose professional reputations could be damaged if misquoted or quoted out of context. Before an article is purchased, a writer may have to submit additional documentation and clearances as required by either the editor or the Legion's legal counsel.

American Visions

2101 S Street, N.W.
Washington, DC 20008-4011
(202)462-1779

Published: Bimonthly, plus supplements

Circulation: 125,000

Query: Joanne Harris, editor

Query response time: 2 to 3 months

Buys: 20 to 30 articles out of hundreds of unsolicited queries/manuscripts received annually

Guidelines: Available; send SASE

Rights purchased: Varies

Pays: Within 30 days of publication

Expenses: Pays phone and travel, when discussed in advance

Kill fee: 25 percent

Rates:

Type of Article	*Word Length*	*Payment*
Major Feature	2,000 - 2,500	$400 - 600
Short Feature	1,250 - 1,750	200 - 400
News Brief	under 500	100
	under 250	50
Department	1,250 - 1,750	100 - 400
"Arts Scene"	100 - 200	50 - 100
unsolicited manuscripts	any length	100 - 200

American Visions is an African American cultural magazine. Its editorial is upscale with a focus on the arts (broadly defined), history, literature, travel, lifestyle, and cuisine—all filtered through the prism of the African American experience.

Readers of *American Visions* are between the ages of 25 and 54. Readership is almost evenly divided between men and women. Nearly 90 percent of the audience attended college, and household incomes range upward from $60,000.

How to Slant Your Ideas to *American Visions*

Editor Joanne Harris says that when you think of ideas for *American Visions,* understand that you are writing for readers whom she describes as "culture vultures."

According to Harris, the *American Visions* audience is proud of its culture and find that this magazine promotes aspects of it that have been and continue to be neglected. It provides a refreshing change of pace and perspective to many loyal readers.

"They are people who are starved for more African American culture," she says. "They want to know more about themselves and what we're doing in the world culturally. Our readers are people who frequent art galleries, museums, and the theater. They want to be on top of who is out there and who is hot. When it comes to travel, people read *American Visions* to learn the specific African American history of a site, which is generally not well known. If you're talking about a trip to Mexico, give readers an understanding of how African Americans from the Diaspora have influenced that region."

In each issue, *American Visions* includes three to five features, each freelance-written. One is always a major art piece, usually on an artist or sometimes on a style of art, like West African adobe architecture. "Soulscapes by Gorden Parks," looked at the recent photographs of the 80-year-old photographer, writer and composer, and film director.

There is also always a history piece, such as the history of Blacks in baseball or the impact that first ladies have had on African Americans through the years. In "Standing Up in the Heart of America," political scientist Ronald Walters shared his accounts of the "first" sit-in, in Wichita, Kansas.

Of the remaining articles, there is typically one on the performing arts, and the other topics vary. One article, for example, featured eleven noted painters who used their talents to challenge traditional perceptions of Christian themes. Another profiled Bryant Gumbel, anchor of NBC's "Today" show. Yet a third discussed how renewed interest in Black history is changing the perception of a cemetery as a place to avoid.

The following *American Visions* departments are open to freelancers:

- **Arts Scene** is a potpourri of articles on current events in theater, film, television, dance, music, visual arts, and more.
- **Cuisine** approaches African American cuisine as an art form, discussing specific foods and offering profiles of Black chefs and restaurants. Although the column is not a how-to section, recipes are often included. One article on Afro-Brazilian cuisine looked at Africans in Brazil and the foods they brought with them, how they made do with indigenous foods, and what emerged when the two cultures mixed. This department occasionally features extended

restaurant reviews that not only critique the food, but also give a behind-the-scenes look at the owners and chefs.

- **Film** covers both television and screen films and filmmakers. The column includes profiles of actors, producers, directors, and technicians as well as reviews of theatrical releases. It may also discuss issues in the film industry, such as Black exploitation in films during the '70s.
- **Profile** typically looks at a person in the arts, but may occasionally profile someone who makes a difference in African American society on a larger scale. A recent article told of a professional at Xerox Corporation who gives grants to people in the community.
- **Spotlight** focuses on organizations or institutions that are making a difference in the lives of Blacks. A recent article examined the categorization of African American music and the fact that not all such music can be pigeonholed into soul, funk, or rhythm-and-blues.
- **Travel** gives an historical and pleasure guide to areas of interest to African Americans. The magazine is looking to branch out into sights that don't have a specific African American history, but which are destinations of cultural interest.

"Books/Recent and Relevant" and "Music Notes/Earworthy" are closed to freelancers.

How to Query *American Visions*

One-page queries preferred, with clips. Send SASE for correspondence if more information is needed. First-time writers send résumé and three writing samples that most closely reflect the type of writing found in *American Visions.*

Before you send an idea to *American Visions,* take time to familiarize yourself with the magazine's editorial content and writing style. "So many people who query us obviously have not picked up one issue of the magazine," says Harris. "The best writers for us are those who tackle subjects with enthusiasm."

You do not need a background in the arts to write for *American Visions,* nor do you need to be African American. You must, however, demonstrate in-depth knowledge of the subject matter or show that you are capable of doing the research and making contact with the people who will give you the story.

Harris says she is not as picky about query style as she is about the idea. "As long as the writer gets the specifics of the idea across and how he or she expects to present it, we don't really have any query letter rules," she says. "A lead paragraph that serves as an introduction to the piece often works well because it gives us a sense of style as well as information about the idea. If the writer has no writing samples to send, we prefer a completed manuscript to a query letter."

Though she doesn't shy away from a query or manuscript that is a simultaneous submission, Harris wants to know up front if that's the case and which other magazines are considering the piece. "If you're selling a story to another magazine but you're varying the theme or giving it to a regional publication, that's fine," she says. "But if the idea will be appearing in a national magazine with a wider circulation than ours, we will shy away from it—unless you've made the idea very different for us."

Harris encourages writers to be pleasantly persistent. "Ours is a small staff with a colossal mission. We get a lot of ideas and are more likely to rely on people we know and not branch out, unless you remind us you're there," she says. That means sending a résumé and clippings, queries, and following up with a phone call when the timing is appropriate.

How to Write for *American Visions*

An assignment for *American Visions* always begins with a phone conversation, which allows Harris to get an idea of how articulate and spontaneous you are, as well as of your enthusiasm for and commitment to the subject. The conversation will be followed with an assignment and contract.

Harris is looking for upscale, straightforward, direct writing that is at the same time chatty. Though the magazine frequently includes an historical perspective on a topic, it is not a scholarly publication. Writing is reportorial, current, and objective, rather than academic or polemical.

"Give our readers a view of the subject they may not see normally," she says. "If you are an expert in the field, let it show. Share with readers specific knowledge that's not readily available. If you are not the expert, get quotes from people who are."

Harris wants writers who are attentive to detail, verify facts, and really get into the story. "One writer pitched a story about amateur night at the Apollo Theater in Harlem," she recounts. "She did a great job interviewing—from the people who conceived the idea, to the actors and right down to the ushers. She made the article personal and fun."

American Way

P.O. Box 619640
Dallas–Ft. Worth International Airport
Dallas, TX 75261-9640
(817) 967-1804

Published: Bimonthly

Circulation: 300,000 printed; 1.6 million readers per issue

Query: Doug Crichton, editor

Query response time: 2 to 3 weeks

Buys: About 200 articles out of approximately 100,000 unsolicited and assigned queries/manuscripts received annually

Guidelines: Available; send SASE

Rights purchased: First World

Pays: On acceptance

Expenses: Pays all, up to a contracted-for ceiling

Kill fee: Approximately 25 percent of contract fee

Rates:

Type of Article	*Word Length*	*Payment*
Major Feature	2,500 - 3,500	$1,500 - 2,000
Short Feature	1,000 - 1,500	750 - 1,000
Department	1,200	1,000
News Brief	300 - 400	200
"Sojourns"	300 - 400	200

American Way prides itself on being a "real" magazine, not just a marketing arm of American Airlines. "We could easily be sold on the newsstand, and, as such, we use only top-echelon writers," says Editor Doug Crichton. "We are predominantly freelance-driven, but we look for those who are very writerly, such as Carlos Fuentes, Calvin Trillin, Wallace Stegner, and James A. Michener. Our tone is more literary, but for those writers who have that style, we are open to new talent."

With an average household income of $107,000 plus and a median age of 42, this in-flight magazine's demographics exceed both *Fortune* or *Forbes.* The readership is divided evenly among men and women. More than half are college graduates or beyond and in top or middle management. The average reader, who is a business or affluent traveler, makes about 15 airline trips per year.

How to Slant Your Ideas to *American Way*

American Way's editorial content is 55 percent travel. Business-oriented material accounts for 15 percent, and the remaining 30 percent covers personalities, sports, culture, entertainment, and general interest.

"I get so many queries that have no theme or focus but simply say, 'I'm going on vacation to outer Mongolia. I thought you might like a piece,'" says Crichton. "We're not a travel agent or vacation facilitator. We look for writing credits. Approach us as you would any other major magazine."

The following departments are open to freelancers:

- **Culture** explores cultures by finding an intriguing news peg and developing it in a new way.
- **Environment** tackles issue-oriented articles. An example is a feature that the magazine ran on the Nevada desert, boasting the last clean air in America.
- **Food** includes full-length features that look at food as a way to explore a culture. An example is an article on pulque, an almost extinct liquor made in Mexico, and its heritage and meaning to the people.
- **Journeys** are travel pieces of 1,000 to 1,500 words. As with all *American Way* travel articles, these must have a novelistic hold, be cohesive, and have direction. They are written in a narrative voice, not a destination-oriented style.
- **Sojourns,** a front-of-the-book section subtitled "A Traveler's Companion," provides writers with the path of least resistance into *American Way.* The 300- to 400-word shorts have covered topics such as The Dog Museum in St. Louis; the myth and history behind the strong-smelling Camembert, one of France's soft cheeses; and Manhattan's exceptional quality bookstores.

"Books," "Celebrated Places," and "Story Corner" are closed to freelancers.

How to Query *American Way*

One page; do not send photo/art information.

As a high-profile in-flight magazine, *American Way* receives hundreds and hundreds of queries a week, of which it accepts less than .05 percent. Most of the writers come to the magazine by referral. Many are part of a stable core of contributing editors who receive assignments.

Crichton says that what catches his eye are straightforward queries and strong clips from magazines like *Vanity Fair, Esquire, Time,* and *The New Yorker.* "If you have a style compatible with one of these magazines, then you are set apart from the rest of the writers and you have a good shot at publishing in *American Way.*"

How to Write for *American Way*

A writer accepted into the inner circle of *American Way* is one who can transport a reader outside the airline cabin with his or her prose. Most stories are almost novelistic in tone, with emphasis on building the story to a climax, classic dénouement, and a strong narrative style.

"We want simple writing with intelligence and a point of view," says Crichton. A former Associated Press editor, Crichton expects writers to be accurate and to provide a list of sources for fact checking. "If we have significant fact-checking problems, we don't reuse that writer," he says. "You've got to be as good a reporter as you are a writer."

America West

7500 North Dreamy Draw Drive, Suite 240
Phoenix, AZ 85020
(602) 997-7200

Published: Monthly

Circulation: 110,000

Query: Michael Derr, editor

Query response time: 3 to 6 weeks

Buys: About 120 articles out of approximately 2,500 unsolicited queries/manuscripts received annually

Guidelines: Available; send SASE. Sample magazines are $3 and require a 9"x12" SASE

Rights purchased: First NAS

Pays: Within 30 days of acceptance

Expenses: Pays phone, mileage, and all else if approved in advance

Kill fee: 15 to 25 percent

Rates:

Type of Article	*Word Length*	*Payment*
Major Feature	1,800 - 2,200	$900 - 1,200
Department	1,000 - 1,800	600
"Close-up"	500	75 - 250
"Inside Business"	500 - 1,000	200 - 600
"Quick Fixes"	300 - 500	150

America West is a general-interest magazine designed to capture the character of the regions served by the airline that shares its name. America West Airlines operates hubs from Phoenix, Las Vegas, and Columbus, Ohio, and flies to 50 American cities. In addition to its hub locations, other top destinations include San Francisco, San Diego, Chicago, New York/Newark, and Los Angeles.

Business travelers constitute 75% of passengers; 24 percent travel for leisure. The average reader makes 15 trips per year. Nearly 70 percent are executives, managers, and professionals. The average age is 45 and 61 percent of the audience is male. Just over 50 percent have college degrees or beyond, and their median household income is $67,090.

How to Slant Your Ideas to *America West*

Since most *America West* readers are executives and professionals, the magazine concentrates heavily on business issues. It targets well-educated, sophisticated readers, by covering topics such as the arts, education, the environment, lifestyles, travel, and issues of the future.

The magazine wants tightly focused subjects that educate and entertain. Articles should have a newsworthy theme, involve trends, innovation, or offbeat content, or encompass creative people or fresh ideas. Highly controversial subjects (politics, religion, and downbeat themes, for example) are not appropriate. It does not want derisive commentary or preaching. Issue-oriented articles are welcome if they're balanced, thought-provoking, and offer constructive discussion of an issue.

The magazine runs two to three features and six departments per issue. Subjects are geographically and thematically balanced.

Because the magazine is four-color, editorial ideas are judged with regard to their graphic possibilities. Color slides are preferred and graphs, charts, and illustrations are welcomed.

The magazine's guidelines, most of which are excerpted here, are friendly and encouraging. The editors uncharacteristically encourage writers to keep the ideas coming and say they are eager to work with you!

America West includes a number of regularly published categories that can work either as a feature (1,800-2,200 words) or as a department (1,000-1,800 words). The sections, all of which are open to freelancers, include:

- **The Arts** focuses on the visual or performing arts, architecture, and other art forms and entities. Not strictly the fine arts, its emphasis is more on "everyman's culture." Past articles include a piece on the Houston Grand Opera's image as a popular, unpredictable theatrical company; and a story on how San Francisco turned a former military site into a wide-ranging and financially self-supporting cultural organization.

- **City Life** is a stylish profile on an America West destination. It's a close examination of a narrowly focused and symbolic aspect of life in a city—not an all-you-ever-wanted-to-know article or travelogue. Past articles have featured Los Angeles cafes that make for hip breakfast hangouts; and San Francisco's North Beach as a tale of two cultures—Italian and Chinese. People, places, attitudes, neighborhoods, lifestyles, trends, and experiences are all good fodder. The articles can be humorous or serious; they should be thoughtful, descriptive, insightful and spicy, but not cynical, negative, or sarcastic. They should evoke a true sense of place and a strong, positive feeling about life in that city.

- **Close-Up** is a photo essay, sometimes with text of up to 500 words. Content consists mostly of close-in shots offering details of life in an urban environment, those things that make the target city distinctive, special, and unusual. The photos should be artsy, stylish, and evocative.
- **Education** looks at creative trends, programs, individuals, and concepts that revolve around learning. One article was on professionals who've found rewarding second careers as high school teachers, thanks to innovative certification programs. Another looked at a program that brought seniors to the classroom in a special format structured just for them; while another featured an audio-tape series designed by two teachers to help undergraduates master tough courses like calculus, accounting, and economics.
- **Food** gives information on trends or distinctive concepts in the food industry. Articles have focused on a Chicago college for chefs; revitalizing one of Kansas City's grand restaurants; and a Napa, California, winery that grows organic foods to improve the marriage of cuisine and wine at its restaurant.
- **Inside Business** comprises as much as 75 percent of the magazine. It typically features a profile, trend piece, or article exploring a topical issue. There are also numerous shorter articles covering entrepreneurs (typically a little-known inventor); high technology; management; sales; books and authors; advice; trends; essays; and comeback stories.
- **Nature** looks at newsworthy natural resources indigenous to regions within the America West area. Examples include the decline of America's wetlands; efforts to save the endangered sea turtle of Florida; Iowa's roadside nesting box program for the kestrel, North America's smallest falcon; and Omaha Zoo's new rain-forest exhibit.
- **Quick Fixes** features refreshing escapes that last a weekend, an afternoon, or an hour. Each piece is up to 300 words, so it must be focused, concise, and cleverly written. Topics have included Midwest farm vacations; a Colorado climbing school; and island-hopping in Puget Sound.
- **Science** covers new concepts, trends, or topics of current interest written in plain language. The department has

featured efforts to revive the electric car; an archaeological search for the first flower; and progress in predicting earthquakes.

- **Sport** tackles a particular sport, trend, or issue, often with regional significance. Examples are the college football alliance between conferences and the bowls; and Major League Baseball's rising injury trend.

How to Query *America West*

One page preferred. Submit ideas at least five months in advance to a proposed publication date. Assignments are made three to five months prior to publication and articles are generally due a month after being assigned. Send photo/art information.

First-time writers for *America West* should submit at least three clips. Inexperienced writers will generally be asked to write their first piece on speculation. Once an idea has been accepted, writers will receive a letter confirming the assignment, pay, deadline, length, and other details. Send a large 9"x12" envelope if you want a manuscript submitted on speculation returned.

How to Write for *America West*

The magazine's goal each month is two-fold: to offer diverse, upbeat content that identifies closely with the regions the magazine serves, and to engage readers in subject matter that is innovative, newsworthy, or distinctive. Fresh reporting that stimulates fresh thinking is the key.

America West has detailed fact-checking guidelines. Put a check mark over names, titles, firms, numbers, foreign and technical terms, dates, and other vital information so the editors know you've double-checked them for accuracy. Writers need to provide a list of sources and phone numbers for the staff to further fact check.

American Woman

1700 Broadway
New York, NY 10019
(212) 541-7100

Published: Bimonthly

Circulation: 180,000

Query: Lynn Varacalli, editor

Query response time: 5 to 6 weeks

Buys: 10 to 15 articles/stories out of 3,000 to 4,000 unsolicited queries/manuscripts received annually

Guidelines: Available; send SASE

Rights purchased: One-time NAS

Pays: Upon publication, but pays sooner for writers who work on a semi-regular basis

Expenses: Pays phone, FAX, overnight mail, and meal expenses within reason

Kill fee: 20 percent, but rarely used

Rates:

Type of Article	*Word Length*	*Payment*
Major Feature	1,600 - 2,400	$350 - 900
Short Feature	800 - 1,200	200 - 500
Department	500 - 900	150 - 400

American Woman began in spring 1991 and is establishing itself as a national lifestyle magazine that speaks directly to today's evolving woman. As a newer woman's magazine on the scene, the publication is targeted to women who want to reach their potential on both a personal and professional level.

The reader of this how-to publication is typically 31 years old. Although 70 percent of the readership attended college and 75 percent work full time, many scan the magazine to learn how to get a better job or start a new career. The majority of women readers are the head-of-household and either single, divorced, or separated (60 percent); the remainder want to know how to improve their marriage or relationship. Just over half have children older than five. The median household income is $30,000.

Editor Lynn Varacalli describes the readers of this publication as women ready for change in their lives. "These women are looking for answers," says Varacalli. "They may have just gotten out of a relationship or quit a job, and they're looking for someone or something new."

How to Slant Your Ideas to *American Woman*

To meet the diverse needs of today's American women, the magazine's diverse editorial content covers relationships of all sorts, self-esteem and self-improvement, careers, starting a business, finances, health and beauty, fashion, and leisure and private time. Nearly half of *American Woman* readers are on a diet of some sort.

Because readers of the magazine tend to juggle a relationship, job, friends, and family, they want a magazine they can browse through when they have a free moment. For this reason, articles are quick and to the point.

"Our niche is advice," says Varacalli. "It's informational and intimate, without being preachy." She continues, "We're a very supportive, solution-oriented magazine. We like to describe a situation that many women can relate to—whether it has happened to them, could happen to them, or has happened to someone they know—and give practical answers."

The editor's idea of a dream writer is someone who knows the subject matter well enough to accurately cover it. "I'm not interested in a writer who knows something about everything. I want someone who has a specialty and can put heart into the topic," says Varacalli.

Sample cover lines have included: "When He's Wrong for You But You Just Can't Say No"; "The No-Hassle Holiday Shopping Guide"; "Seven Subtle Signs That Say He's Cheating on You"; "Why Am I Such a Bitch?"; and "The One-Hour Orgasm."

The majority of the articles in *American Woman* (85 percent) are generated from ideas developed in house. All of the following departments are open to freelance writers:

- **Careers & Money** offers quick-tip pieces on how readers can improve their work life, live better on a budget, save money, and still indulge themselves. For instance, "The Best Businesses You Can Start—For Under $500" shared five success stories of women who started their own businesses with $500 or less, and now have potential earnings in the five digits. "We need more entrepreneurial articles," says Varacalli, "like stories about a woman who lost her job and used her savings to start a business in her garage . . . but an *interesting* business, not selling computer supplies. And we use career strategy articles like how to deal with a horrible boss and how to get a raise."

- **Diet & Health** covers how-to tips to lose weight and stay in shape; ways to deal with or prevent PMS; and information on sexually transmitted diseases, among other topics.

  One piece, "The Fast-Food Diet," listed seven ways to go from fat to fit on fast food and gave recommendations for breakfast, lunch, and dinner—a diet that averaged 1,500 calories a day with 50 grams of total fat. "Get off Your Butts," a personal fitness article, offered quitting strategies and programs for smokers. The piece also gave advice on how to cope with a cigarette craving.

- **Fashion & Beauty** is a potpourri of tips and pointers on designer cosmetics, clothing, hygiene, and grooming. Past titles have included, "Be Beautiful for Less," a guide to buying top-brand make-up at discounted prices; "Vested Interest," a look at different styles of vests for spring; and "Frosty Beauty," a piece on cleansing and moisturizing routines to help skin survive a long winter.

- **Lifestyle** covers miscellaneous topics that affect women's everyday lives or pique their curiosity. "A Sneak Peek Inside Men's Topless Bars" explored the question "Do topless bars make men cheat?" and included a sidebar titled "Mommy by Day, Stripper by Night."

- **Men & Relationships** fills the majority of *American Woman*'s editorial pages. Articles are written to the single, married, and divorced woman. "We're always looking for unique angles," says Varacalli. "How I Got My Husband Back from the Other Woman" was a first-person account of one woman's strategy to win her husband back from his young receptionist—and it worked! "Caught in a Love Triangle: You, Him . . . and His Mother" explained that whether a man chooses you because you're just like his mom or because you're her complete opposite, be sure of one thing—her influence is always there. "Don't Talk to Me Like That" gave pointers on how to speak up when your man puts you down, and included a quick test to help determine if you're experiencing verbal abuse in your relationship.

- **Self** discusses ways in which women can build self-esteem or become better in-tune with themselves and those they care about. One piece, "Mad About Everything" used anecdotes to describe the best ways to release anger—whether it's toward siblings, friends, parents, co-workers, or men. "When Your Kids

Are Buzzing About the Birds & the Bees" gave 10 tips on talking to children about sex.

How to Query *American Woman*

One page maximum; do not send photo/art information.

The elements a query must have for *American Woman* are: short in length, to-the-point, and a grabbing lead. "Tease us in your query, and if we're interested, we'll call you to get more information," says the editor. "One writer's proposal started with, 'What would you do if your husband walked out on you after 20 years of marriage?' That grabbed our attention."

Ideas for this market need to be well-thought-out and conveyed in as few words as possible. "Don't just say, 'I want to write an article on how to have a long-lasting marriage,'" the editor warns. "We do not do pieces that have been done a million times and can be found in just any magazine." Before querying *American Woman*, you should have a general familiarity of the magazine. "Pick up a copy and browse through it," says Varacalli. "That way, you can get a feel for what we're looking for and a general sense of our readership."

A bad tendency of writers querying this magazine is to state a topic or problem, but not explain what they want to do about it, or what direction their article will take. "If you envision the piece having a quiz format, say so. If you plan to interview sources, tell us that," advises Varacalli. "And you should know that we give suggestions through anecdotes and experts."

Published samples should accompany queries from writers trying to break into this market. "They should somewhat relate to our subject matter," says the editor. "If you're going to send me a clip of an article you wrote on your trip down the Amazon, you might as well save the extra postage."

Varacalli makes assignments via phone call.

How to Write for *American Woman*

Writers should note that the tone of the articles in this publication is always positive, even if the topic is a difficult one, like divorce or losing a job.

"We get a lot of unsolicited manuscripts," Varacalli notes, "and some really stand out above the rest." One writer who the editor had not worked with or heard of previously, submitted a short query on a fresh topic. "The woman had never met her father and was aggressively trying to track him down. They were reunited after being apart for 27 years," recounts Varacalli. "The true-life idea was very dramatic and had a lot of potential, so we took a chance with the writer and ultimately it worked."

When it came to the writing process, Varacalli recalls that the first draft didn't have a lot of emotion. "But the writer understood what she needed to add and took direction well. The rewrite was perfect."

American Woman's fact-checking procedures require writers to provide a list of individuals who contributed to the article, with their titles and phone numbers. If statistics were included in the piece, the source must be cited as well as a phone number to verify the information.

The Atlantic

745 Boylston Street
Boston, MA 02116
(617) 536-9500

Published: Monthly

Circulation: 500,000

Query: Articles and "Reports and Comment": Jack Beatty, senior editor or C. Michael Curtis, senior editor
Poetry: Peter Davison, associate editor, poetry

Query response time: 1 to 5 weeks

Buys: About 200 articles out of approximately 5,200 non-fiction unsolicited queries/manuscripts received annually; buys very few poems a year from the 10,000 to 12,000 poetry submissions received; purchases 12 to 14 fiction pieces a year from about 12,000 fiction submissions

Guidelines: Not available

Rights purchased: First NAS

Pays: On acceptance

Expenses: Pays if reasonable, when discussed in advance

Kill fee: Approximately 25 percent

Rates:

Type of Article	*Word Length*	*Payment*
Major Feature	3,000 - 6,000	$3,000 - 6,000+
Short Feature	1,000 - 3,000	1,000 - 3,000

The Atlantic, founded in 1857, is a general interest magazine covering a broad range of topics. The magazine positions itself, in part, as a national reality check. It questions what we believe about America's economic role in the world, what constitutes our national interest, our military commitment and obligations, the relationship of government to business, what normal family life should be, and what is important for our children to learn.

The magazine also functions as a forum where scientists, politicians, businessmen, academics, writers, and members of the clergy, military, and other institutions can gather and listen to each other. It sees its role as a barometer, alerting readers (and other media) to new developments on the horizon.

The Atlantic attracts readers who live an educated lifestyle, actively pursuing a wide range of interests. And so, the magazine speaks to those interests with features on all types of music and literature, short fiction, and articles on travel and design. Research shows that 57 percent of *The Atlantic*'s readers are male. The median age is 41, 64 percent are married, and 37 percent have children. Eighty-four percent have attended college, and 70 percent have attended graduate school. The median household income is approximately $58,500.

"We tax readers of *The Atlantic* with sometimes dense or technical material, and they seldom complain about it," says Senior Editor C. Michael Curtis. "Because they enjoy such a variety of articles on many subjects, we conclude that our readers are not predictable ideologically. We work very hard to avoid an ideological cast in the magazine, so we often get letters from people who don't agree with one thing or another."

How to Slant Your Ideas to *The Atlantic*

"We are primarily a magazine interested in information, rather than opinion," says Curtis. "People proposing pieces to us should bear in mind that we don't have an editorial stance to speak of. While we gladly consider and publish works from writers who have very distinct points of view, we like our articles to make their case through a judicious presentation of evidence. In other words, through the facts rather than by way of strongly held opinion. We publish writers who are often identified with the far right or far left and others who identify with neither. It's in the editing where we work toward producing articles and other pieces of writing that are, generally speaking, free of ideology."

Curtis says that one of the most frequent mistakes writers make in pitching ideas to *The Atlantic* is failing to understand that because the magazine is monthly, it can't keep abreast of breaking news. "We turn away quite a few manuscripts and proposals pegged to topical events," he says.

The Atlantic aims its editorial at readers who are willing to read and are interested in reading poetry, fiction, criticism and views of culture as well as careful, thorough reporting on politics and many areas of public interest.

"Our readers tend to be active politically, in the sense that they vote, run for office, or participate in political campaigns," Curtis says. "They are interested in public policy-oriented material that points toward a solution, assigns responsibility, or suggests new thinking. They seem a bit less interested in scandal and sensation, and that suits us, because on the whole, we aren't either."

Except for "Other Departments," the entire magazine is open to freelance writers. "We get people all the time who want to do puzzles or word pieces, but we turn away even good ideas because we don't want them to conflict with our departments," says Curtis.

Here are the five sections of the magazine to which freelance writers may contribute:

- **Arts and Leisure** is not conventional coverage of film, television or other art forms. Instead, it provides a retrospective of someone's work as a whole, triggered by an event such as the reissue of an old book or perhaps publication of a new biography. "We don't publish the conventional review because that would seem peculiar in a magazine that doesn't cover the arts on a regular basis," says the editor.
- **Books** reviews two or three books a month. *The Atlantic,* however, is not a great market for freelancers, because the magazine is very careful about whom it assigns to write review essays. "Our reviews are more ambitious than most; they don't just assess the achievement of the book, but go on to make larger points about its subject matter. We are reluctant to assign these pieces to writers whose work we don't know. Most reviews are written by an established authority on the subject, a reviewer with a reputation for wisdom in the area. That may mean an academic, or someone who has written a great deal about the topic," Curtis says.
- **Humor and Poetry** features some of the finest writers in the nation and abroad. "Since making a judgment about poetry is, for the most part, subjective, I can't easily explain how we make our selection," says Curtis. "We look for clear writing and interesting characters. We don't like stories that are open-ended and don't move toward a resolution."

  The only restriction put on poetry is a preferred length of no more than a column, and since the magazine receives such a high volume of poetry, the editors are able to be very selective. Humor, Curtis says, must be work that the editors find sophisticated, amusing, and clever. That's a tough order to fill, since many say good humor is the most difficult style of writing there is.
- **Main Text** comprises more lengthy articles that make up the center of *The Atlantic.* Here, Curtis says, writers should bear in mind the difference between information and opinion. "We want specific, factual detail, new ways of looking at familiar subjects," he says. "We frequently publish articles on political, economic, and social issues."

Topics have ranged from a look at the politics of overpopulation, to an argument that the feminist campaign to outlaw pornography is based on faulty and potentially dangerous assumptions, to a report on the tough decision wildlife managers increasingly have to make: whether to slaughter one species to save another.

- **Reports & Comment** assesses the condition of an area, city, town, or country, or discusses progress in a certain field, such as agriculture. The articles, often written in essay form, argue, reflect upon, or simply present a variety of issues, from international policy and medicine to social questions and moral issues. One issue included topics ranging from sentencing guidelines in the courts now and in the past; the strange romance of idiosyncratic dictionaries; and a journey with historian Suzanne Massie through the streets of St. Petersburg.

  "The important thing is that the author's treatment of the topic should be persuasive, thoughtful, and useful," Curtis says. "This section of the magazine can and will accommodate the expression of opinion, provided it's well supported."

How to Query *The Atlantic*

Two pages or less preferred; do not send any photo/art information; query six months in advance for seasonal material.

The best approach to use in presenting ideas to *The Atlantic* is a proposal that is understated, deliberate, reflective, coherent, and focused. "We don't like ideas that jump off the page," says Curtis. "We want calm writing. We worry if a writer is too energetic, wild-eyed, or trying too hard to press a case. In those instances, we believe the writer's shrillness will be reflected in the final piece, and we tend to be wary."

Curtis says that many proposals tell the editors more than they need to know about the subject, without telling how the subject will be approached.

"Write a few paragraphs to get to the core of the idea—setting up the premise and the circumstances," says Curtis. "Then let us know the proposed angle of vision—exactly what you intend to examine. We want to know what can be said about your topic that has not been said elsewhere. Give names or sources, if that is what's involved. And tell us a bit about your credentials. Why should I be respectful and trustful of you on this particular subject?"

Though Curtis likes to receive completed manuscripts, he knows writers prefer to send queries first. "We don't encourage pieces that we don't feel confident will work out, and we discourage many more ideas than we encourage," he says. "The majority of our responses say, 'Sorry, we're not the right place for your idea,' or 'We'd be glad to consider a manuscript, but can't offer an assignment.' Very few of the queries we review result in an outright assignment."

How to Write for *The Atlantic*

"I think this magazine is much easier to write for than a lot of writers do," Curtis comments. "But an awful lot of able writers don't click with us because they don't understand that we are more concerned with information and coherence than with splash and dash. If you're writing for magazines that consciously attempt to shock or startle, you're not likely to make a connection here; we simply don't respond to that.

"On the other hand, we will spend a great deal of time with a writer who has useful information on a public issue of some kind or simply has expertise in an area, provided the information or expertise suggests new developments or new insights," he says.

According to Curtis, the editors care a great deal about original reporting, as distinct from a piece that essentially takes facts from other newspaper or magazine articles and pulls it together in summary fashion. When preparing a piece for *The Atlantic*, go to the source of the original information or research, if you are not that person.

"A smart writer will give us a sense of what the person featured in the article looks like or what his office, farm, or factory is like," says Curtis. "We want our reader to visualize the source of the facts and see what's happening there."

Audubon

700 Broadway, Fourth Floor
New York, NY 10003
(212) 979-3000

Published: Bimonthly

Circulation: 500,000

Query: Michael W. Robbins, editor

Query response time: About 3 months

Buys: 10 to 20 articles/short pieces out of approximately 1,000 unsolicited queries received annually

Guidelines: Available; send SASE

Rights purchased: First NAS

Pays: On acceptance

Expenses: Pays reasonable and pre-authorized items

Kill fee: 30 percent

Rates:

Type of Article	*Word Length*	*Payment*
Major Feature	2,000 - 4,000	$1,500 - 3,000
Short Feature	800 - 1,500	750 - 1,200
Book Review	500 - 800	300 - 500
"About Audubon"	500 - 1,800	250 - 900
"Essay"	1,500 - 2,000	800 - 1,000
"P.S."	600 - 700	800
"A Sense of Place"	1,200 - 1,400	1,200
"Reports"	300 - 750	200 - 500

Celebration of the beauty and mysteries of nature with a balanced view of the issues presented by humanity are the mainstay of this magazine for members of the National Audubon Society and, increasingly, newsstand readers.

"We used to be more focused on nature," says Mary-Powel Thomas, managing editor. "But we've undergone major editorial and design changes in the last couple of years. Our content has changed a lot to reflect the expanding concerns of our readers."

Audubon has an upscale, educated audience with a good income, college education, and a home. The readership is split nearly evenly between males and females. The average *Audubon* reader is married and about 40 years old. More than half are birders and photographers, which reflects the original heritage of the Audubon Society. They are active people who read for education and action as well as pleasure.

How to Slant Your Ideas to *Audubon*

In addition to being a magazine of nature, Thomas notes that it is increasingly environment-oriented, without being radical. An editorial profile written for the advertising sales staff describes the magazine as exploring "the linkages among environmental issues and politics, commerce, cultural traditions, national aspirations, ideals—and nature itself."

A recent article, "Keepers of the Past," reported on a mother and daughter of the Palouse Indians in the Pacific Northwest, who were fighting to retrieve ancestors' remains that had been taken from the Indians' burial area and placed in a university anthropology department.

Another article, "A Town Called Morrisonville," concerned a city-turned-ghost town in Louisiana commonly called "Cancer Alley" because of the high number of cancer diagnoses in that town that may be related to industry. Dow Chemical has a plant in Morrisonville, and its owners decided that the best way to avoid medical problems in the surrounding community would be to buy out the town. The company was almost completely successful in decimating the town: there are fewer than a dozen homes still occupied there, and only one of the churches still has a congregation.

When considering ideas for *Audubon*, remember that it covers items of interest from around the world, not just the nation.

If you're approaching *Audubon* for the first time, Thomas suggests you develop angles for a brief piece in "Reports." "Our longer pieces go to writers with whom we have a relationship or whose work we know from elsewhere. An writer unknown to us is highly unlikely to receive a major assignment from us on the first try."

The following columns are open to freelancers:

- **About Audubon** reports on Audubon Society activities from around the nation. You may be able to break into this competitive market by following a local issue that the magazine hasn't yet discovered. It should have an Audubon Society angle to it—something that the local chapter has done to bring the issue to light, for instance. One article, "Listen to the Sound," was about the pollution of the Long Island Sound. The regional office of the Society managed to join hands with local union officials and presented legislation to Congress that would help preserve the environment *and* create new jobs.

- **Essay** is an introspective column in which nearly any appropriate topic can land. Thomas remembers a particularly nice one on building the first road into wilderness, and how that road inevitably spawns more roads. Another favorite was about canaries on the prairie.
- **P.S.** is a column that editors call "one person's informed ranting." It must be something about which the author knows a great deal and feels strongly. "If it is controversial, that's fine," says Thomas. Recent pieces addressed sky pollution—when there are so many lights from the city that the natural lights from the sky are obscured—and one author's outrage that power companies have the right to cut down trees on a property owner's lot in order to clear a path for power lines.
- **Reports** is the magazine's news brief section. Pieces may be about something that is of interest to readers but not so compelling that it merits feature length; or about a quirky piece of legislation about which readers are likely to want to know.
- **A Sense of Place** can be about a swamp, a backyard, a national park—anywhere there is an interesting natural history angle and where the author has a personal connection. The article relies heavily on description to take the reader to the spot and feel its uniqueness.

"Incite," "True Nature," and most book reviews are written by regular contributors.

How to Query *Audubon*

One page preferred for one-idea queries, or send two or three ideas at one time. Always send two or three clips.

"It sounds obvious, but a well-written query is a big plus," Thomas says. "Tell the story in a paragraph or two in the same style you would use in the article.

"Know the people you'll contact, what direction you would take, and what the article would accomplish," says Thomas. "If you have personal involvement or knowledge of the subject, let us know."

The magazine has a query tracking system in which every query received is logged in a book and, if all goes right, followed through the consideration process. If you know which editor handles the type of article you're proposing, use his or her name. But otherwise, all queries addressed to Editor Michael Robbins will be opened by editorial assistants and routed to the appropriate editors. If you haven't heard anything in three months, Thomas suggests you call or write to inquire about your query.

How to Write for *Audubon*

"We want writers who will ask tough questions of all sides of an issue," says Thomas. "A lot of people don't question their own side or point out that the other side has good arguments, too. Our sympathies are clearly on the environmental side, but we don't want to lose credibility by ignoring other viewpoints."

Senior editors recruit quality writers when they see a good article in another publication. "We want good writing—neither fluff nor newspaper reporting—but the best words to make the point. Actually, a reporting background is helpful. But we don't want newspaper-style writing," says Thomas.

Because the magazine is bimonthly, it must avoid overdone topics, Thomas says. "We have to take a longer view," she notes. "We can't report on breaking environmental or conservation issues the way a weekly or monthly could. But the beauty of a bimonthly magazine is that we have time to hone an article before publication."

Audubon tries to vary its mix of articles with some short pieces and others that can range to 4,000 words. Serious and simple, introspective and controversial, even first-person articles work here, provided the topic is right and the writing is excellent.

Better Homes and Gardens

1716 Locust Street
Des Moines, IA 50336
(515) 284-3000

Published: Monthly

Circulation: 7.6 million

Query: Features: Margaret Daly
"Building and Remodeling": Joan McCloskey
"Decorating and Crafts": Denise Caringer
"Food and Nutrition": Nancy Byal
"Garden": Douglas Jimerson
"Health and Education": Paul Krantz
"Automotive, Home Electronics, Money Management": Margaret Daly

Query response time: 1 to 3 weeks

Buys: 100 articles out of several thousand unsolicited queries/manuscripts received annually

Guidelines: Available; send SASE

Rights purchased: All, with few exceptions

Pays: On acceptance

Expenses: Pays items as discussed in advance

Kill fee: $100 to $200

Rates:

Type of Article	*Word Length*	*Payment*
Major Feature	1,500 - 2,500	$1,125 - 2,500
Short Feature	500	375 - 500
Department	2,000 - 2,500	1,500 - 2,500

Home service is the theme of *Better Homes and Gardens.* Its readers are people whose home and family represent their greatest investments in emotion, time, and money; its charge is to help the readers make the most of them.

"Our direction is very straightforward," says Managing Editor Lamont Olson. "We are a home service- and family-oriented publication. We publish articles about decorating, gardening, building, food, and crafts. Our feature area includes pieces on travel, money management, education, cars, health, pets, and parenting children today."

Today, after some 70 years of publication, *Better Homes and Gardens* still sticks to the words of its founding father: "No fiction, no fashion, no piffle, no passion." It carries no romances, no fashion stories, and no hair or cosmetic roundups.

The audience of *Better Homes and Gardens* is married men and women who are homeowners and parents. The group has a median income of $37,400 and an average age of 42.

The editors get to know the readers well by the hundreds of letters they receive every day. "It's a very loyal and close relationship," says Olson. "When they write to us, it's often on a first name basis, and the tone is like that from a good friend. And, that's the way we try to edit the magazine. We try to sound like a letter from a good friend."

How to Slant Your Ideas to *Better Homes and Gardens*

Better Homes and Gardens has a real-life focus. Every article has a call to action, inviting readers to do something—try a new recipe, start a new project, take a vacation, send for information.

"We are often compared with the 'Seven Sisters' (the seven major women's magazines), but the main difference is that they are women's service magazines and we are a home and family service magazine. We try to edit our book so that men will feel comfortable reading it. We're very strong in some of the traditionally male-interest areas, like cars, building, and finance. But today, men are interested in much more than that, and women are interested in more than food and decorating."

Only about 10 percent of *Better Homes and Gardens'* editorial material comes from freelance writers, artists, and photographers; the rest is staff-written. The best chances for freelancers are cars, money management, and health.

The following departments are open to freelancers:

- **Cars** concentrates on easy-care topics, such as protecting your car's finish with the proper products. Pieces on buying and selling cars and what to look for in a new car are common staples, such as best family sedans in the $10,000 to $15,000 price range. Automotive tips, such as improving your mileage; how to drive safely in certain conditions; and how to avoid a carjacking, are also regularly included.
- **Health** uses approximately 30 freelance stories per year from experienced health writers. The department likes to use

family-oriented topics. As the baby boom generation ages, more and more readers are interested in topics related to their advancing age.

"For freelancers, that's a good area to mine," says Olson. "We'll often look at a story that has had a lot of controversy or conflicting opinions in the past, and try to take a new, but even-handed, look to find the medical consensus that our readers can rely on."

The column focuses on topics such as fitness and nutrition, though major technological breakthroughs and serious illnesses are periodically featured. "We like to cover ways in which a person can be involved in his or her own care," says Olson. "Our readers want to be able to go to a doctor and know the right questions to ask. Topics should relate to both men and women."

- **Money** offers the reader financial-planning and money-management articles, such as "The Top 10 Mutual Funds for Small Investors."
- **Pets** is a service-oriented section for pet owners. Care of the pet, choosing the right pet, and topics such as grooming and training are standard fare.

Building, crafts, design, education, environment, food, gardening, home decorating, parenting, and travel articles are almost exclusively staff-produced or written by regular contributors.

How to Query *Better Homes and Gardens*

One page or less preferred; do not send photo/art information; query one year in advance for seasonal material.

"A sample lead is an effective way to sell your story idea to an editor," says Olson. "It gives the writer a chance to sell his or her writing ability, and the editor a chance to see if the writer understands our market."

Olson suggests making the sample lead part of a one-page summary that describes your article and tells what problems it solves or ideas it offers. Tell what has happened in the area to make it necessary for readers to have fresh information about the topic. Also give the editor the names of a few people you plan to interview for the article.

Better Homes and Gardens prefers to work with writers who specialize in certain areas—someone with strong interests and contacts in a particular field.

Most pieces from new writers will probably be requested on speculation. But the editors only ask writers to do work on spec if they have serious intentions about it. "If the manuscript comes in and isn't on target but has merit and potential, the editor involved will critique it and give the writer explicit instructions on how to approach a rewrite," explains Olson. "If the rewrite comes in and is good, we buy it. If not, sorry; we send it back."

How to Write for *Better Homes and Gardens*

To write for *Better Homes and Gardens,* it's imperative to offer a national perspective. Talk to people all over the country, and get different reactions from different areas.

The *Better Homes and Gardens* writing style is warm and conversational. "I don't mind an occasional sentence ending with a preposition, yet we don't want our style to be too folksy or too colloquial."

Writing must also be tight. "We can't have articles that go on and on," says Olson. "You must still get all the information in, but in far fewer words than one would be allowed in some other publications. The ability to maintain an authoritative voice and write in a compressed style, yet still sound like a good friend, is a must in all areas."

Thorough research is also a must, but Olson says that unfortunately, some writers' research is too shallow. "We have 7.6 million subscribers and a total readership of 30 million a month," he says. "If a writer makes a mistake, no matter how obscure, someone will notice in an audience that size."

For that reason, Olson wants every fact double-checked before it is submitted. Then the editors will check it again. A source list with names and addresses for that purpose must be submitted.

Olson says that although most of the magazine is written in house, the editors still look for freelancers who are willing to do the kind of hard work the magazine requests. "We don't like to send back for revisions; we'd rather have it right the first time. That's why we develop writers and hold on to them by giving them a lot of work."

Black Elegance

475 Park Avenue South
New York, NY 10016
(212) 689-2830

Published: 9 times a year

Circulation: 275,000

Query: Depends on geographical location—

Eastern Writers: Sharyn Skeeter, editor-in-chief
(send correspondence to address above)

Western Writers: Sharon Blount, managing editor
12024 Kling Street, #202
North Hollywood, CA 91607
(818) 508-4366

Query response time: 4 to 12 weeks

Buys: About 45 articles out of approximately 300 to 400 unsolicited queries/manuscripts received annually

Guidelines: Available; send SASE

Rights purchased: First/Second Serial

Pays: On publication

Expenses: Negotiates items, if the article is assigned

Kill fee: 25 percent

Rates:

Type of Article	*Word Length*	*Payment*
Major Feature	1,500 - 2,000	$175 - 250
Short Feature	500 - 1,000	50 - 175
News Brief	250 - 500	25 - 50
"Arts and Entertainment"	500 - 600	75
"Man Talk"	1,200 - 1,500	175

Black Elegance is a lifestyle magazine for contemporary Black women between the ages of 25 and 45. Its articles cover topics of interest to career women, mothers, wives, and singles.

The magazine, which began in 1986, highlights the dignity and self-esteem of Black women. Most of the readers (68 percent) work outside the home and 75 percent have had two years or more of college. The median household income is $27,200.

How to Slant Your Ideas to *Black Elegance*

"Our reader strives for achievement and quality in her career and lifestyle," says Editor Sharyn Skeeter. "She is interested in relationships but also in arts, entertainment, education, parenting, personal finance, career paths, health, cooking, beauty, and fashion. She wants to know as much as possible about the world."

Skeeter says her ideal writer is someone who understands how to write to the woman she has described. "You need to be able to connect to our reader, but you don't necessarily have to have the same background," she says.

Although the magazine has a small staff, much of the material is written in house or by a cadre of permanent freelancers. The staff generates 80 percent of the ideas for the magazine and assigns them to known writers. Still, the magazine is eager to work with new talent.

"We often read other publications and find writers who can handle certain subject areas well," says Skeeter. "Other times, writers send us ideas or manuscripts and we pick which ones will work for us. One Irish writer sent us a number of career ideas; we liked a few and gave her the go-ahead."

The best way to break into *Black Elegance* is to propose a relationship article. One article took an intricate look at a young couple in Los Angeles who were having a Yoruba wedding, a traditional African celebration. This piece was especially appealing because it also dealt with a current aspect of Black history. Another relationship article offered tips for how to keep it together after the honeymoon; while a third talked about "married valentines"—giving tips to keep romance alive through the years. The article "Can a Man Be A Sex Object?" discussed how more men are going through what women always have—pressure (often media-induced) to have the perfect face and body in order to get a second glance from women.

Other sought-after freelanced feature topics include careers, parenting and family.

Most departments in the magazine are staff-written, but two areas open to freelancers are:

- **Arts and Entertainment** focuses on African American arts of national appeal which will still be timely at least three months from the time of submission. The department includes short reviews of music and theater from around the country, as well as features on celebrities and artists. Since the magazine has offices on the East and West Coasts, it is particularly interested in arts and entertainment originating in other areas of the country which will be touring major cities throughout the country.

- **Man Talk** is a prime forum for Black male writers (or interviews with Black males) who have a strong opinion about Black men today. For instance, one writer lamented the fact that men always get stuck with the barbecuing; another described his plight to win visitation rights with his children; yet another talked about how he felt taken advantage of by his girlfriend.

  The column is also a place for Black men to share their perspectives in areas beyond relationships. Musician Bobby Short talked about his life and feelings about Black music; Paul Stewart described how he developed the idea of starting the Black American West Museum in Denver. "Man Talk" queries should be sent to Sharon Blount at the West Coast office.

"Beauty," "Fashion," "Health Beat," and "Your Money's Worth" are closed to freelancers.

How to Query *Black Elegance*

No more than two pages; photos/artwork appreciated, but not necessary.

Before you query, study six back issues of *Black Elegance*, suggests Skeeter. "Develop a sensitivity to the magazine," she says. "It's annoying when writers suggest ideas we've just done."

A business-like approach will work best when writing to *Black Elegance*. Quickly define your subject, then tell how you intend to approach it. Tell why you are the person to write the piece, why the readers need this information, and what contacts you have. "I like to be sold," Skeeter says.

If your writing has been published, send clips with your query. If you are new to writing, Skeeter prefers to see a completed manuscript.

How to Write for *Black Elegance*

Talk directly to the reader without talking down. "The *Black Elegance* reader has a full life with a job, child, and maybe a man," says Skeeter. "Articles should be relatively short so she can get as much information as possible in as little space as possible. Yet you have to do this without sounding like an encyclopedia; the prose must be lively."

You don't need to be African American to write for *Black Elegance,* but must know the readers' points of reference. "You must understand who our readers are so the writing sounds natural. We want as much ethnic reference as possible, and we have a lot of writers with varied backgrounds who are able to do that."

Skeeter asks writers to turn in a source list that includes names of those interviewed and their phone numbers. She wants you to fact check your articles before submitting them, with the knowledge that the staff is small and will spot check only when necessary.

Black Enterprise

130 Fifth Avenue
New York, NY 10011
(212) 242-8000

Published: Monthly

Circulation: 256,000

Query: Alfred Edmond, Jr., managing editor

Query response time: 4 to 8 weeks

Buys: 35 to 50 articles out of approximately 300 unsolicited queries/manuscripts received annually

Guidelines: Available; send 9"x11" SASE

Rights purchased: "Work made-for-hire," as defined by U.S. Copyright Act

Pays: On acceptance

Expenses: Varies

Kill fee: 25 to 35 percent

Rates:

Type of Article	*Word Length*	*Payment*
Major Feature	5,000 - 6,000	$1,000 - 5,000
Short Feature	3,200 - 3,500	600 - 1,000
News Brief	600	175 - 225
Departments	500 - 600	125 - 600

Black Enterprise is a business-service magazine for African American professionals, corporate executives, middle managers, entrepreneurs, and policymakers in both the public and private sectors. Since its inaugural issue in 1970, the magazine considers itself the "Black American's Guidebook for Success." Its mission is to provide readers with information on how to improve their success potential in all aspects of their lives.

"We provide economic, entrepreneurial, and money management news and advice to help African Americans prosper in whatever they do. That may be boosting their household income, advancing their careers, or building a business," says Alfred Edmond, Jr., managing editor. "We cover economic, political, and public policy, such as minority business development, bank discrimination, and issues like the Supreme Court decision that restricted minority set-aside programs."

The average subscriber to *Black Enterprise* is approximately 39 years old with an average household income of $54,000; 56 percent of subscribers are men, 44 percent women. Of its readers, 58 percent are professionals or managers of their companies and 17 percent are partners or owners of their businesses; 66 percent are college graduates, and 70 percent own their own homes.

How to Slant Your Ideas to *Black Enterprise*

Before you attempt to write for *Black Enterprise,* send for its "Free-lance Writers Orientation Manual," which is undoubtedly the most comprehensive set of writer's guidelines ever created by an editorial staff. This 12-page compendium details the 10 major subject categories covered by the magazine, the three special annual issues, the special reports, and the special sections. It also gives specific elements for writing a *Black Enterprise* feature, as well as tips on how to organize the article. Details for writing service pieces, profiles, and news analysis/trend features are also included.

It's also important to know that Edmond is looking for solid business writers who have expertise in the basics of finance, money management, and career development. "Writers must understand that this is a business publication," he says. "We get a lot of people suggesting human interest stories about successful Black persons who have served as role models. We almost never run individual profiles. Instead, we write about trends in which individuals serve as examples. In a story on executives leaving corporate America to start their own businesses, we might point to one executive as an example. While many of the people who appear in our pages are role models, our magazine does not just celebrate their successes. It offers real strategies for readers to duplicate those types of successes in their own lives."

One article that profiled a Miami entrepreneur did so because he was the only African American business owner in the coffee industry. The article focused on what it meant to take on a trail-blazing challenge during a time when the coffee industry was flat, thus tackling the larger issue of building a business during an economic decline.

Edmond divides *Black Enterprise*'s business editorial into two types of coverage. One is for the largest 100 Black-owned businesses that have grown beyond $10 million a year. The other is for the mid-size emerging business. "Black ownership no longer implies a small business," says Edmond. "In the last five years, we have made a real effort to address not only the executives at a

$30-million publishing house, but also the owner of a $3-million office supply company.

"Before you send us an idea, ask yourself why it would be useful to our readers," Edmond suggests. "It's not enough to be inspired. Our readers want to know, 'How do I get enough money together for my kids' college education?' 'What should I do now that I've lost my job?' 'What can I do to improve cash flow in my business?', and 'What do I need to do to write a business plan?' In fact, when we did an article on business plans, we illustrated it with anecdotes about companies that had written business plans and how they used them to avoid problems and see solutions."

Past articles have also included "Hot Industries for Small Businesses," which forecasted consumer and business needs over the next decade; "Putting People First," in which 16 African American leaders explored how the Clinton economic agenda would impact jobs, finances, and business; and "It Is the Shoes . . .," which asked why there are so few Black executives in the $30-billion sporting goods industry.

In addition to the major features section, the following *Black Enterprise* departments are open to freelancers:

- **Book Review** covers primarily nonfiction books of particular interest to African Americans. Subjects include business, politics, civil rights, biographies, essays, history, commentary, and current affairs. Each review offers a basic summary of the book and an evaluation of the writing, reporting, and research. A review also discusses the relevance of the book in today's society and interesting information about the author. Although this column is typically written by regular writers, send a query if you have a good idea.

- **In the News** covers fast-breaking news material, trends, cutting-edge stories, and news analysis. Stories must be written specifically for *Black Enterprise* and may not have appeared in other publications. National and international news, politics, and policy are common fare.

  "This column is the easiest place for freelancers to test their reporting skills," says Edmond. "If we feel comfortable with what a writer is doing for us in this column, we may ask that person to write other freelance stories."

- **Making It** profiles at least two small Black-owned enterprises each issue. The companies must have been in business between two to six years, employ a minimum staff of three people in addition to the founder, and boast gross sales of $350,000 to $10 million a year.

"Even in these profiles of companies, the goal is to talk about the issues they had to deal with, such as getting financing and setting goals," says Edmond. "It is not just a pat on the back. We give readers who want to start a small business a glance at what the guy next door is doing."

- **Travel** covers topics that are determined by July 31 of the year prior to publication. They are assigned monthly to a variety of freelance writers. Travel articles cover a wide range of subjects and approaches, from destination travel pieces, such as Florida or Bermuda, to theme stories, such as "Family Ski Vacations" or "Cruise Incentive Travel Programs." Articles include travel logistics and recommendations for lodging, dining, and entertainment.

  Two travel guides, "The *Black Enterprise* Executive Travel Guide" and "The *Black Enterprise* Guide to Caribbean Travel" are published annually in March and May, respectively. Sample topics from an "Executive Travel Guide" include "Is It Worth It to Fly Business Class?"; "Courting the Executive Traveler" (hotels that try to lure business clientele); and "Presentation Equipment" (the latest in show-and-tell apparatus).

- **Verve** is an array of lively, timely feature articles on lifestyle trends and leisure activities. "Here, readers find things they need to know between 5 p.m. and 9 a.m. that will enhance what they do from 9 a.m. to 5 p.m.," says Edmond.

  Executive lifestyle articles in "Verve" focus on health and fitness, sports, collecting, fund-raising events, convention and meeting planning, and business entertainment. Your piece should contain anecdotes and advice from real people as well as from experts in the field, along with concrete examples, instruction, or how-to information.

"Economic Perspectives" is closed to freelancers. A computer guru or electronics wizard might consider sending in ideas for "Tech Watch," or an accountant or financial planner might submit queries for "Personal Finance."

How to Query *Black Enterprise*

One page preferred; do not send photo/art suggestions.

About 65 percent of the major features in *Black Enterprise* are written in house. "We've recently expanded our staff to bring in greater quality control," says Edmond.

Most stories assigned to freelancers are from ideas developed on the inside. If you have an idea to submit, Edmond wants straightforward query letters. He says some anecdotal information is helpful, but that sample quotes are not needed.

"The first thing I look for in a query is whether the writer has a sense of the level of sophistication and instruction our audience expects," says Edmond. "We get a lot of queries that could have also been sent to *Essence, Ebony,* and *Emerge*—as if all books for African Americans have the same mission. That isn't true for *Forbes* and *People,* and it's not true for us."

Edmond encourages writers to read *Black Enterprise* carefully. "The most succinct pitches we get are from writers who have read recent issues and are familiar with what we have covered," says Edmond. "We got a letter from one writer suggesting that since we already did an investment club story, perhaps we would like to run an article on how to *start* an investment club. This person took the next logical step in giving readers investment options.

"When *Black Enterprise* decides to work with a writer who has sent in a good idea, the editor sends an assignment letter that explains the package he wants. If the writer is interested, we formally assign the piece," says Edmond. "Since we are the only publication that focuses consistently on Black business issues, we have many contacts and we pass along to the freelancer the names of expert sources to contact for interviews. We give the writer six to eight weeks to complete the first draft. When it comes in, we review it, and send it back for necessary modifications. The writer then prepares what is the second, and hopefully final, draft."

How to Write for *Black Enterprise*

"We look for writers who can pull together a lot of information from a wide variety of sources and create lively, concise articles," says Edmond. "We demand quality and depth of reporting. We don't just gloss over topics; we focus on what our audience needs to know. When readers put down an issue of the magazine, they should be able to decide what specific action they can take to make an immediate difference in their business."

As with most other magazines, Edmond cautions writers, show it, don't tell it. "Our goal is to put the reader into the story," he says. "We want them to feel as though they are in the other person's shoes and are able to identify with the problems and recommended solutions. In other words, our writers should empathize with our readers."

Edmond does not insist on just one style for his magazine, but the magazine's writer's guidelines suggest the following organization for a *Black Enterprise* feature:

- An exciting and provocative lead paragraph that isn't too long.
- A billboard paragraph that tells the reader what he'll get out of the story and motivates him to read it.
- Any history and background that is relevant to the topic today.
- The pros and cons of the issue at hand, or the how-to steps (whichever is applicable).
- The impact of the subject on future events.
- A summary of what it all means and final conclusion.
- A kicker or end. "Please make it good," the guidelines stress. "Our readers dislike wimpy."

Edmond warns, "Don't make the reader waste time wondering why he is reading your article. Focus on what you want to deliver to the reader, and if you are fulfilling that promise, the writing of the story almost takes care of itself."

Edmond says he is flexible about the types of leads, imagery, and gimmicks used to tell the story, but he doesn't like inside jokes. "Sometimes, writers get so cute they forget that they have something to tell the reader. I'd rather have simple writing that we spruce up in house than writing that sacrifices facts and advice in exchange for style."

When preparing your article, think about material that could be set aside for a sidebar. "We use a lot of charts, statistics and at-a-glance elements," says Edmond. "Breaking large features into manageable chunks by using sidebars is less demanding on our readers' time and attention."

Sidebars to complement how-to stories may include a listing of resources—names of individuals, organizations, agencies or companies, addresses, phone numbers, and a brief description of the resources available.

Boys' Life

1325 West Walnut Hill Lane
P.O. Box 152079
Irving, TX 75015-2079
(214) 580-2000

Published: Monthly

Circulation: 1.4 million

Query: Major Features: Scott Stuckey, executive editor
Columns and Back-of-the-Book Feature: Douglass Daniel, articles editor

Query response time: 4 to 6 weeks

Buys: About 100 articles out of approximately 2,000 unsolicited queries/manuscripts received annually

Guidelines: Available; send SASE. Send $2.50 and 9"x12" envelope for sample magazine or check the children's section of the library

Rights purchased: First NAS

Pays: On acceptance

Expenses: Pays items if reasonable, and as discussed in advance

Kill fee: Rare

Rates:

Type of Article	*Word Length*	*Payment*
Major Feature	750 - 1,500	$500 - 1,500
How-to Feature	up to 500	200
Department	300 - 750	150 - 300
Comic Page	one-page script	150

Boys' Life is published by the Boy Scouts of America to make available to all boys the highest caliber of fiction and nonfiction; to stimulate an interest in good reading; and to promote the principles of Scouting. Most readers are boys between the ages of eight to 18. While readers are predominantly male, girls read the magazine too, and are quite vocal in their letters telling this publication what they like and don't like.

How to Slant Your Ideas to *Boys' Life*

The subject matter covered in *Boys' Life* is as broad as the program of the Boy Scouts of America. A look at the Boy Scouts' over 100 merit badge pamphlets gives an idea of the wide range of subjects possible. "The establishment of values and education are our number one priorities," says Executive Editor Scott Stuckey. "But keep in mind, we are a positive, happy group, and that's reflected in the subjects we choose."

The magazine covers practically every interest of boys—aircraft, archaeology, books, camping, collecting, dinosaurs, entertainment, exploring, history, monsters, music, sports, weight training, and more. A sampling of recent articles includes a close-up of the Kansas City Chiefs' speedy linebacker Derrick Thomas; a feature on old movie monsters; an article on cave exploring; and a story about a rock climber who, though he lost both lower legs to frostbite, continues to climb using artificial limbs.

According to Stuckey, the magazine takes the pulse of what its young readers want through their reactions in the letters they write to Pedro, the *Boys' Life* mailburro in the column "Hitchin' Rack." Writers might take the hint and glance at letters to Pedro to get to know what's on the minds of the magazine's loyal following.

Except for the magazine's letters section, all other departments are fair game for freelancers. The best chance of breaking into this magazine for kids is through the dozens of short articles and back-of-the-book how-tos it buys each year. Hobby how-tos, such as wood carving, model building, painting, and crafts, include step-by-step photos or sketches.

Just like earning merit badges, you've got to earn your way up in this organization; most of the 50 or so major pieces purchased annually are assigned to regular contributors. Each issue contains at least one full-length piece about Scout activity—mountain climbing, canoeing, hiking, bike touring, or camping, for instance. Depending on the season, the magazine also uses athletic profiles of both adults and kids; how-tos on fishing, camping, money-making, and game playing; as well as history, humor, and hobbies.

The front-of-the-book columns are also good venues for new *Boys' Life* writers. On average, each issue uses seven columns. Column headings and examples of past article titles include:

- **Bicycling**—"Know Your Tires" discussed the different types of tires available for bicycles.
- **Cars**—"Monster Makers" described a monster truck team.
- **Computers**—"Creating Illusions with Supercomputers" appeared in a past issue.
- **Earth**—"Keeping Watch for Polluters" was about a group that monitors rivers and bays.

- **Electronics**—"Compass of the Future" spotlighted a high-tech satellite tracker.
- **Entertainment**—"Toon Talk" featured people who provide voices for cartoon characters.
- **Health**—"Get a Grip on Motion Sickness" gave tips on staying well while traveling.
- **History**—"The Buffalo Soldiers" examined the Black troops that guarded the West.
- **Nature**—"Trouble for the Monk Seal" focused on a species faced with the threat of extinction.
- **Pets**—"You Can Train Your Cat" shared tricks you can teach your kitty.
- **Science**—"Phony Fido" was a brief (150 to 200 words) on an artificial dog used to breed fleas. (*Boys' Life* buys a collection of four to five briefs from the same writer, runs them together, and treats them as a column.)
- **Space & Aviation**—"Return to Mars" offered experiments in planning new probes to the red planet.
- **Sports**—"Spotlight on Sumo" highlighted Japan's favorite sport.

Writers may also submit one-page scripts for the comic pages. Large format comic strips (not newspaper style) are requested. The script must describe the page layout, action, characters, and dialogue. Three types of comics include:

- Monthly: "Pee Wee Harris," about Boy Scouts; "The Tracy Twins," about Cub Scouts.
- Nonfiction features: Half- or full-page cartoon. Titles include, but are not limited to, "Dinosaur Hall of Fame," "Space Adventures," and "Sea Creatures."
- Serial: Usually science fiction with a boy protagonist. Runs consecutively for 12 to 15 months.

How to Query *Boys' Life*

One page preferred; send step-by-step photos or sketches with how-to craft pieces.

Even *Boys' Life* writer's guidelines remind readers that no written explanation about the magazine can substitute for careful reading of as many back issues of the magazine as possible. In addition to children's sections of libraries, the magazine is also obtainable at some Waldenbooks stores and at Boy Scouts of America council offices.

Query rather than submit a manuscript, which might duplicate a topic already in the works or one the editors simply do not want. "Writing an article without an assignment wastes a writer's time and energy," says Douglass Daniel, articles editor. We rarely, if ever, buy manuscripts that haven't been assigned." He continues, "A straightforward query that quickly gets to the point and samples of previous work, if available, allow us to see your writing style and get an idea of how you would treat the material. Whether you're a novice or a veteran, sell your idea—and yourself—in a query letter."

Boys' Life truly is interested in fresh talent. "There are new writers debuting in almost every issue," says Daniel. "Read the magazine and the writer's guidelines, and pitch an idea via a query letter."

If your idea piques the editors' interest, you will receive an assignment letter explaining what they are looking for in your article, along with an agreement for you to sign. The magazine even goes so far as to send a blank invoice for you to fill in, if you don't have your own billing system established.

How to Write for *Boys' Life*

Put simply, write for a boy you know who is about 12 years old. *Boys' Life* readers want crisp, punchy writing in relatively short, straightforward sentences. The editors demand well-reported articles that demonstrate high journalistic standards and follow *The New York Times Manual of Style and Usage.*

"The writing in *Boys' Life* is upbeat," says Daniel. "Articles should inform and entertain our readers."

A common pitfall of inexperienced *Boys' Life* writers is wordiness. "We know a good writer when we see one because that person knows how to express himself or herself clearly and briefly in a way a young person can relate to," says Daniel. "The writing has to be crisp and accurate. Kids will spot an error quickly—and boy do they have fun telling you.

"Writers who are used to working with us know what we want and need, and they get the facts across in an interesting way," the editor continues. "They don't write down to our audience. Most of our readers are in the 11-to-14 age category, though there are lots of younger and older readers too. If we get a piece that needs too much work, we will refuse it. This is not amateur hour—not with our circulation and a readership of 6.5 million."

Bridal Guide

441 Lexington Avenue
New York, NY 10017
(212) 949-4040

Published: Bimonthly

Circulation: 375,000

Query: Features and "Planning Your Wedding":
Erica Buchsbaum Goldberg, managing editor
"Home & Design": Cathy Cook,
"Travel": Lisa Gabor

Query response time: 4 weeks

Buys: About 60 to 80 articles out of approximately 500 unsolicited queries/manuscripts received annually

Guidelines: None available

Rights purchased: First NAS

Pays: On acceptance

Expenses: Pays phone and mail

Kill fee: 20 percent

Rates:

Type of Article	*Word Length*	*Payment*
Major Feature	1,200 - 1,500	$900 - 1,200
Short Feature	750 - 1,000	525 - 750
News Brief	300 - 500	375 - 500
"Groom With a View"	750 - 1,000	350
"Love & Money"	1,000	750

Bridal Guide devotes its pages to women engaged to be married. It is a compendium of how-to advice to help brides plan a wedding with the individual look, style, and personality they desire. Its goal is to make that one day so many women have dreamed about for years turn out to be perfect in every way. It's one of the biggest days of a woman's life, and the magazine wants to ensure it comes off as she always imagined.

Most readers comb through at least three issues of *Bridal Guide* in their first six months of wedding planning. The median ages of the bride and groom who read the magazine are 24 and 26. The majority (94 percent) are engaged. Nearly 70 percent of readers attended college, and 86 percent are employed. Their average projected household income is $44,850.

How to Slant Your Ideas to *Bridal Guide*

"When a bride picks up a copy of our magazine, she should be able to completely plan her wedding," says Managing Editor Erica Buchsbaum Goldberg. "Each issue is geared toward a new reader—telling her how to plan her budget, giving advice on how and where to register for gifts, and updating her on the latest in wedding etiquette."

Just a few of the planning topics freelancers have covered for this magazine include how to choose a photographer, flowers, invitations, and children attendants.

The magazine carries relationship articles with a marriage twist. For instance, one might address how a bride can work with her future mother-in-law who may want wedding details handled differently than she does. Others may answer questions about bedroom politics and other couple relationship issues, such as when marriage means moving, or mastering the fine art of apologizing. It also addresses personal topics for the bride, such as how to beat post-wedding blues, and what to consider before taking his name.

In its "Home & Design" section, *Bridal Guide* offers decorating advice for the new home a woman will share with her mate. How-to home decorating articles, some of which are written by freelance writers, include how to buy a mattress or tabletop; what to look for in a vacuum cleaner; and big ideas for small spaces.

"We give tips on how to get along when sharing home and hearth with the one you love," says Goldberg.

The travel section is all freelance-written. "We are locked into a schedule that is prepared a year in advance each January," says Goldberg. "While destination pieces are typically written by a stable of writers, the magazine is looking for informative pieces, such as how to pack, the best luggage to buy, or what to look for when purchasing a camera."

The following departments are open to freelance writers:

- **Groom with a View** is a personal account of a man telling how he felt about his engagement and getting married. "It's an eye-opener," says Goldberg. "Nearly everything in the wedding planning is geared around the bride. Well, how does the groom feel about it all? This column is always written by an engaged or married man and gives his understanding of and perspective on the wedding."
- **Love & Money** discusses practical money-management ideas for couples. The column has looked at how to merge money styles; all you need to know about checking accounts; and reception budgets ranging from $3,000 to $10,000.

Beauty and fashion articles are written in house as well as "Bridal Style," "Etiquette," "Just Married," and "Sex and Your Health."

How to Query *Bridal Guide*

Send several ideas at once, summarizing each in a few sentences. Do not send photo/art suggestions. Include clips and background information.

Half of the stories in *Bridal Guide* are generated by freelancers. If you're bubbling over with ideas for brides-to-be, *Bridal Guide* is the place to send them. Goldberg's favorite queries are little capsules of ideas that are two to three sentences long. She likes to see several ideas at once as well as clippings of past work.

If the editors are interested, they will contact you about the idea to make sure you are both thinking along the same lines.

The magazine's contract stipulates that once you have written an article for *Bridal Guide*, you may not write on the same subject for another magazine for at least six months.

How to Write for *Bridal Guide*

Bridal Guide's writing style is upbeat, yet realistic. "It's not all fairy tale," says Goldberg. "Practicality is the key. A reader should be able to go through an issue and learn a million things on how to plan a wedding. Virtually all of the women who turn to the magazine are looking for a dress. Once they're hooked by that, they look for all the other information they need to plan their wedding."

Goldberg wants writers to quote experts and weave in one or two anecdotes of engaged couples to make a point. "But don't go overboard," she says. "A few examples are fine, but the bulk of the article should be straightforward information."

The type of writer Goldberg searches for is one who, once he or she has been given an assignment, can complete the article without much supervision.

"One of my pet peeves is missing a deadline," says Goldberg. "If a story takes a different direction once the research is done, call and say that the original idea is not appropriate. It's important to stay in touch with the editor rather than not deliver on time or turn in something that's off the mark. Sticking to the word count is also imperative. If I assign a 1,200-word article that comes it at 3,000 words, it's almost automatically a kill."

"We depend on freelance writers," says Goldberg. "We have 130 pages of editorial and an incredibly small staff. We value writers and I think we're good to them."

Bride's & Your New Home

350 Madison Avenue
New York, NY 10017-3799
(212) 880-8532

Published: Bimonthly

Circulation: 400,000

Query: Features and News Briefs: Andrea Feld, managing editor
"Travel": Sally Kilbridge, editor

Query response time: 6 to 8 weeks

Buys: About 160 articles out of approximately 2,600 unsolicited queries/manuscripts received annually

Guidelines: Available; send SASE

Rights purchased: All for features; First or Second Serial rights for book excerpts, fiction, and poetry

Pays: On acceptance

Expenses: Pays phone calls up to $50; mailing expenses (Federal Express and Express Mail); and photocopying

Kill fee: 20 percent; first-time writers for the magazine write on speculation

Rates:

Type of Article	*Word Length*	*Payment*
Major Feature	1,500 - 3,000	$800 - 2,500
Short Feature	1,000	500 - 1,000
News Brief, "Etiquette," and "Home Tips"	300 - 800	100 - 300
"His View" and "Insight"	700 - 800	500
"Reader Weddings" and "Wedding Diary"	100	100
Poetry and wedding ideas	varies	25

Bride's & Your New Home is a magazine written for both first- and other-than-first time brides and grooms, and their families and friends. Its goal is to help the couple plan their wedding and adjust to married life.

The magazine covers the three areas involved in planning a marriage: the wedding, honeymoon, and home.

"Our readers love the idea that a bridal magazine also allows them to focus on decorating and combining households," says Managing Editor Andrea Feld.

Research has shown that many brides take over a year to plan their wedding, while others spend only three months. That means some brides-to-be purchase six to seven issues of the magazine, while others buy only one.

"Each issue is a complete encyclopedia on weddings, but that ensures that each edition is different," says Feld. "It's our job to make sure that those who consistently buy the magazine are not reading the same articles over and over again."

The average *Bride's & Your New Home* reader is a 24-year-old woman who will be married within the next year. Typically, she is living at home with her family (58 percent) and is attending college or has already graduated. According to a reader survey, two-thirds of the weddings that took place in 1991 consisted of first-marriage brides and grooms.

The average wedding costs ring in at $15,811, and traditional weddings continue to be the trend. Florida and Hawaii are the hot honeymoon travel destinations, with newlyweds spending an average of $3,004 on a nine-day vacation.

"*Bride's & Your New Home* blends fantasy and reality," says Feld. "Somewhere in its pages, we want to offer the fantasy a woman has always had—the dream of how she'll look on her wedding day. At the same time, most of our readers will invest a substantial amount of money in the first year of marriage. They and their families and friends will spend an average of $20,000—buying everything from appliances and furniture to crystal, silver, and electronic equipment. So, although we want to help our reader fulfill her fantasy, *Bride's & Your New Home* also helps her become a wise consumer."

How to Slant Your Ideas to *Bride's & Your New Home*

Almost any topic, when slanted to the engaged or newly married couple, can work for *Bride's & Your New Home.* Subject areas include wedding planning, travel, home, relationships, and romance.

The Wedding Planning Section covers the how-tos of preparing for a wedding, from writing wedding vows and selecting silver, to choosing music and sending thank-you notes. It also covers etiquette and customs.

The magazine devotes a lot of space to the Honeymoon Section. "The four editors in our travel department visit each destination every time the magazine reports on it," says Feld. "But if there is a destination they want to cover but can't get to, they assign freelancers to go. While the editors have their own list of assignments, they are also open to unique ideas."

One marital and sex therapist proposed a roundup of the most appealing and sensual honeymoon suites at major destination sights. She won the assignment and wrote "Hot Beds for Newlyweds," a piece that proved extremely popular in reader surveys.

Another travel article, "True Tales of First Night Fumbles," gave real-life accounts of honeymoon nightmares, from brides and grooms who got locked out of their rooms in their underwear, to celebrating guests who wouldn't leave the honeymoon suite.

Other popular travel articles have covered honeymoon cost-cutters and barrier-free honeymoon destinations for the disabled.

The pages reserved for the Home Section of the magazine are very visual, giving brides and grooms specific ideas for selecting items for their homes and combining households and styles. "Through art and editorial we show various ways to decorate a room or set a table, plus service spreads on bedding, furniture, curtains, paint, glassware, china, or a silver trousseau," says Feld.

One whimsical article gave insights on how a spouse's lovemaking style is revealed by his or her preference in sheet patterns—bold stripes, leopard spots, delicate flowers. Another article, "Living Naturally," offered tips for creating an environmentally safe home. Past articles have also given suggestions for breakfast in bed, catalog shopping, and weekend meals served when lounging around together.

Relationship and marriage articles fall under the Home category and cover a broad range of subjects: finances, careers, housing, health, fitness, nutrition, sex, pregnancy, entertaining, and lifestyle. Topics may include blending religions; coping with holiday stress; or handling step-relationships. Tips on confronting jealousy, infidelity, or fear of commitment, as well as how to improve communication, are also appropriate here.

Romance, of course, is a mainstay. Article topics have covered creative ways to propose marriage; tips for keeping intimacy alive during the wedding planning months; and 100 ways to say "I love you."

The magazine does not shy away from provocative, realistic subjects. Past issues have addressed AIDS; breast cancer and marriage; the warning signs of partner abuse; as well as what an abortion in a bride's past may mean for her future. And while these couples are just starting their lives together, *Bride's & Your New Home* does cover pregnancy and infertility. "We were extremely pleased with one article entitled, 'Surviving Infertility: How to Keep Your Love Alive,'" says Feld. "While many articles on the subject examine the medical realm of infertility, this one addressed the blaming and dissatisfaction that can occur between a man and woman in this stressful situation."

When it comes to word count, the general rule is that ideas focusing on a specialized subject that may not affect every reader—such as age difference in marriage—run about 1,000 words. Broader topics incorporating issues most brides and grooms face when planning their lives together—dealing with in-laws or setting marriage goals—run about 1,500 to 3,000 words. Psychological and problematic pieces are approximately 3,000 words.

The magazine welcomes any qualified writer to query for feature articles. Newly marrieds are especially encouraged to contribute ideas to the following sections (all other columns are written in house):

- **His View** and **Insight** are essay pages where women and men relate their wedding or marriage insights—on topics like remarriage, pregnancy, or gaining a daughter-in-law.
- **Love**, a poetry column, includes topics such as the day the bride and groom met, the wedding proposal, the honeymoon, their careers, or their feelings toward their parents.
- **Reader Weddings** looks at various wedding sites—a boat, hotel, country inn, ranch, or mansion—and wedding styles, from Renaissance weddings to Texas barbecues. The editors depend on readers to submit their wedding stories. Brides should send their photos and may also send a query letter. The staff may call for interviews or ask for a 100-word account of the wedding.
- **Wedding Diary** is a place where couples can recount a memorable moment (getting married on rollerskates); a "wedding nightmare" (a blizzard or damaged wedding dress); or give a roundup of wedding ideas (wreaths, pumpkins, backyard torches, proposals, invitations, shower themes). In addition, it covers news notes, such as a touring exhibit of Chinese wedding gowns from the Ching Dynasty.

How to Query *Bride's & Your New Home*

One paragraph to one page preferred; photo/art information is optional; query six months in advance for seasonal topics.

Send a detailed outline or query describing how you will go about researching and writing the idea you've proposed. Feld looks for queries that have very specific slants. "We get so many general queries," she says. "Tell me what your unique angle will be and whether you've experienced what you want to write about."

You don't have to be a seasoned writer to write for *Bride's & Your New Home.* In fact, the magazine uses many unpublished individuals who, through their experience in planning or taking part in a wedding, have become somewhat expert in the field.

"Weddings bring out a lot of emotion in people—whether they are brides, grooms, fathers, mothers, siblings, or friends," says Feld. "We had one Midwest writer who, after attending his old girlfriend's wedding, got very sentimental and realized he was ready for a long-term relationship of his own."

The magazine is also open to articles written by cutting-edge wedding professionals—photographers, florists, caterers, and the like—who can offer 10 hot tips, or how-tos for doing something spectacular for a wedding.

Professional writers and beginners should send several clips of past work so that style can be evaluated. "Even if that sample writing piece is a community handout or college newspaper, it helps us see the way you use verbs and adjectives," Feld says. "Your style might be absolutely right for a research piece, but not for a first-person essay."

Be patient if the magazine doesn't respond to your query right away. "We put good ideas in folders for seasonal issues or for the yearly 'Groom's Issue' (April/May), in which we may need a piece on your topic," says Feld. "So if you don't immediately hear back from us, it could be that we liked your idea, but we're caught up in deadlines and haven't been able to get back to you. If you haven't heard from us in two months, call the office."

How to Write for *Bride's & Your New Home*

Along with reading the magazine to get a sense of its writing style, Feld suggests you understand the magazine's view of marriage. "It's not 'Donna Reed' or 'Leave It to Beaver,'" she says. "In today's economy, most wives and mothers work. The worst thing a writer can do is not be aware of our contemporary slant. If you are writing 'How to Have a Good Sex Life,' make sure your advice is relevant and current."

Bride's & Your New Home

When writing for *Bride's & Your New Home,* don't quote secondary sources in your articles. Use magazines and books as background reading only, to educate yourself on a specific topic. Feld says the magazine likes to use couple anecdotes and "slice of life" vignettes.

"Give us lots of dialogue," she encourages. "We love quotes from newlyweds and engaged people. Let the couple discuss the issue, rather than tell the reader what the couple says. We also like first-person accounts. As a bride planning a wedding, you may actually become an expert on selecting a site or planning an interfaith wedding—even if just for this year."

When writing bride-and-groom anecdotes, use first names only and include occupations, ages, city, state, and wedding date.

Issue-oriented and relationship articles should include quotes from marriage counselors, doctors, or financial counselors commenting on the problem. Introduce expert sources with their complete name, degree, affiliations, city and state, and any book titles with publisher and year of publication. Include a source list with names and phone numbers for fact checking.

Organize your material into related subheads. An article on planning a reception might be broken into these subtopics: food, decor, music, and flowers. Or, an article on buying a first home might include: budgeting, searching for the house, moving, and making mortgage payments. Include a sidebar or box, dos and don'ts, or 10 tips.

When writing third-person narratives, think of intriguing ways to present your material. For example, consider a diary-style article with his-and-her viewpoints. Or, create a quiz for couples to take together on topics such as parenting, lifestyles, or eating habits. Articles always have a positive resolution or a discussion of how a couple can compromise to deal with a conflict. "Think about your topic in a very different, creative way before you propose to us," adds Feld.

Brides Today

3400 Dundee Road, #230
Northbrook, IL 60062
(708) 498-0618

Published: Bimonthly

Circulation: 150,000

Query: Debi Lewis-Kearns, managing editor

Query response time: 4 weeks

Buys: About 40 articles/stories out of approximately 300 unsolicited queries/manuscripts received annually

Guidelines: Available; send SASE

Rights purchased: First NAS

Pays: On publication

Expenses: Pays photography when requested, fee negotiated

Kill fee: 10 percent

Rates:

Type of Article	***Word Length***	***Payment***
Major Feature	2,000	$ 500
Short Feature	500	100
Department	250 - 750	200 - 400
News Brief	50 - 150	50

Brides Today began publishing in 1992 to offer Black women a look at the wedding scene through their eyes. With the subtitle "For Brides of Color," the magazine is targeted to the growing population of influential African American women between the ages of 24 and 35. The reader has a median family income of $27,000, is well educated, and professionally employed. More than 70 percent of the readers are single and have never been married.

"Our demographics are wide-reaching," says Managing Editor Debi Lewis-Kearns. "The audience is women of all ages who are getting married, contemplating marriage, have been married, or think they will marry in the near future. It is also a resource for people interested in the historical aspects of marriage as they relate to the African American community. We go further than any other publication to provide that kind of information."

Published in the United States, *Brides Today*'s distribution has expanded to England, the Caribbean, South America, and elsewhere.

How to Slant Your Ideas to *Brides Today*

Brides Today features how-to and planning articles covering the engagement, wedding, and honeymoon. It focuses the concerns of today's bride on one of the most important times of her life—her wedding. Readers will find informative articles on wedding planning, honeymoon travel, marriage, family issues, sex, health, and finance.

"We might do an article on getting married with a young child; how to buy a car; or on blending two families in marriage, which is very much a part of the African American tradition," says Lewis-Kearns. "We also look for pieces on how brides are weaving African rituals and heritage into their African American weddings."

The team at *Brides Today* develops the magazine's editorial calendar a year in advance, but remains flexible to new issues that arise and to ideas submitted by hopeful contributors. The magazine does not have staff writers, but it does have a stable of proven writers to which it assigns 60 percent of the editorial content. The remaining 40 percent goes to freelancers who earn assignments by proving they are dependable, flexible about rewrites, and can deliver a good product.

Lewis-Kearns says she looks for freelancers to write not only on bridal topics, but to write articles aimed at improving the rate and success of marriages in the African American community. "We work to do whatever we can to provide positive images and information not available elsewhere," she says. "We want our readers to think and plan as much as possible before they marry and, therefore, have happier, more successful marriages."

Travel writers as well as writers interested in African American history are also good candidates to sell to this magazine. In addition, Lewis-Kearns looks for poetry and wedding vows to help couples write affirmations and meditations on marriage.

Almost all sections of the magazine are open to freelance writers, such as the following:

- **Celebrations & Happenings** spotlights celebrity weddings that feature African American couples. The magazine pays for writing and photography but does not pay the celebrity. Well-known weddings covered have included those of actress Debbie Allen and Los Angeles Laker Norm Nixon; famed hair designer Zainab Abdul-Hafiz and budding stylist Thomas E. "Troy" Moore II; and the renewal wedding celebration of Bishop Jessie Delano Ellis II and his wife Sabrina Joyce Ellis.

- **Decorating & Giftware** is usually staff-written. But, if you are a decorator who loves to write about decorating issues as they relate to new couples, send your story and photograph ideas for this section.
- **Fashion & Beauty** features bridal beauty articles related to the African American woman. While a lot of this section is done in house, freelancers are welcome to submit ideas. One writer wrote a published story about beauty regimens for mothers-of-the-bride.
- **Food & Entertaining** welcomes well-written food articles for the wedding and for new lives as a couple. Menu planning and entertainment tips are provided.
- **Grooms** is open to men who want to write about situations of interest to grooms. It may cover how they feel about getting married, improving communication skills, or understanding the history behind African dress.
- **Honeymoon & Travel** gives options for honeymoon destinations. "We are particularly interested in getaways close to urban centers that readers could get to within two hours," says Lewis-Kearns. "We've covered spots like Aspen, Quebec City, Disney World, and Caesars Pocano Resorts. Find places that are romantic and scenic and where couples can have a wonderful time, meet new and interesting people, and create terrific memories, but aren't thousands of miles from home."
- **Lifestyle Planning** is one area where expert interviews are key. Topics include psychological, medical, family, legal, and financial issues.
- **Wedding Planning** is handled primarily by Lewis-Kearns, the magazine's resident bridal consultant, who worked in that field for 20 years before assuming her editorial role. "I'm looking for any unique ideas for wedding planning, and I love submissions on ways to customize weddings," says the editor. Past articles have covered designing your own wedding gown, African drums to "A(fro)ccent Your Wedding," and marrying in a Baptist church.

The column "Miscellaneous" is staff-written, but "Tips and Tidbits" is a forum where brides and grooms warn other couples of how to avoid the wedding mistakes or mishaps that happened to them during their wedding.

How to Query *Brides Today*

One page preferred; send photo/art information; do not send actual photos. Query six months to a year ahead of time for seasonal material.

The simpler the query the better. "I am not attracted to nor do I have the time to review long proposals," says Lewis-Kearns. "Be concise and to the point and present your idea in a way that is easy to read and gives me confidence in you as a writer. I'm still amazed at the horrendous errors that occur. People are so anxious to get the idea out the door that they don't take time to proof their own work."

If you can include short sample anecdotes and still write in an abbreviated form, all the better. "The key to good writing is to attract someone's attention and to keep it by making your point quickly," says Lewis-Kearns. "Your query letter is an indicator to an editor that you can put out good work."

If your idea merits an assignment, you'll receive a contract from the magazine and an assignment letter that stipulates the details.

How to Write for *Brides Today*

"When you write for *Brides Today*, you are writing to a neglected market about issues that have rarely been written about before," says Lewis-Kearns. "You're talking to people who have never been asked how they feel about the topic of marriage and relationships. In that vein, our readers want both serious and upbeat writing; hilarious and somber prose. We are all these things; there is so much to be done in this market. We're playing catch-up."

Because there is so much to be said, the editor says that the biggest mistake writers make is trying to put every thought into one article. "Don't give too much information," she cautions writers. "Most of these topics deserve a book."

While Lewis-Kearns says it's nice to have experts quoted in articles, she is just as impressed with a writer who gathers knowledge through research. "If you painstakingly come up with information, it is not necessary to have it verified by an expert," she says. "There has been so little done on these topics that the writers become the experts. Don't write just off the top of your head, however. We need substance, not just rhetoric or pontification."

One perfect example of the writer becoming the expert is a man who was lounging by the pool at a resort and began talking with another man who had honeymooned at the same spot 40 years earlier. "That sparked his curiosity, and he proposed an article looking at where Black people went on honeymoons in this country before the civil rights movement," says the editor. "Where were African Americans comfortable going? What did they encounter when they got there? Was it difficult for them? His article, 'Chicken Bone Beach and Other Honeymoon Adventures,' took readers from the early 1900s through post World War II. It was an article we cherished. And the writer traced our American history primarily through university libraries."

Once you've turned in a completed piece to the magazine, the editors take two weeks to review the article. If you don't hear from the magazine within that time frame, you can assume your article was acceptable and will be published in the future.

"We are really open to new writers, no matter what your experience," says Lewis-Kearns.

child

110 Fifth Avenue
New York, NY 10011
(212) 463-1000

Published: 10 times a year

Circulation: 575,000

Query: Child behavior and development, "Child's Play": Miriam Arond, senior editor
Education, health: Yanick Rice Lamb, senior editor
Lifestyle, trends, children's media: Mary Beth Jordan, deputy editor

Query response time: 8 weeks

Buys: About 50 articles out of approximately 500 unsolicited queries/manuscripts received annually

Guidelines: None available

Rights purchased: First-time only

Pays: On acceptance

Expenses: Pays phone

Kill fee: 25 percent

Rates:

Type of Article	*Word Length*	*Payment*
Major feature	2,500	$ 1,500
Short feature	1,500	800 - 1,000
"Child of Mine"	1,000	800 - 1,000
"Child's Play"	800 - 2,000	1,500
"Health"	800 - 2,000	1,500
"Love, Dad"	1,000	800 - 1,000

"We are distinctively different from other parenting books," says Stephanie Wood, executive editor of *child.* "Many of our readers are working; those at home were professionals before they started their family. In any case, they are very career-oriented. Essentially, they are a better educated and more aware audience than the reader of other magazines in this category."

child readers are college-educated, married mothers of a child or children under 6. More than 60 percent work in a professional capacity. They are about 32 years old, with a median household income of $55,000.

"Our readers are very serious about the kind of information they want," Wood continues. "As a result, we rely heavily on recent research, rather than on the formula child-rearing articles that appear so often. While other magazines may feature a cut-and-dried approach to issues like potty training and temper tantrums, we try not to over-simplify advice; there is no single right way to do any of those things. Parents need to adopt their own approaches to their children's personalities and individual comfort level."

How to Slant Your Ideas to *child*

A minimum of four or five feature-length articles appear in every issue of *child*, according to Wood. Two revolve around child behavior and development; one is on parenting; and another is a trend piece about something happening in the world that affects a parent and her children. Learning disabilities, education, finances, health, playtimes, developmental stages and skills, and other topics are featured.

The following departments are open to freelancers:

- **Child of Mine** alternates the back page slot with "Love, Dad." It is a personal essay about some aspect of mothering. It may at times be funny, introspective, or simply be a portrait of the poignancy of parenthood. Past essays have included one on feeling torn between providing activities for kids but knowing that unstructured playtime can be the most fun; thoughts on living with infertility; and a reminiscence of the moment a mother realized she had bonded to her child.

- **Child's Play** is a short feature about playtimes. The articles take a theme and offer tips or instructions on playing. One piece featured 40 group games every kid should know, and included tips on parents' involvement in organizing and participating in the games. For this column, keep in mind that the reader may have children ranging from newborn to 12. The editors frequently want articles to be broken into developmental stages or age ranges. For instance, in the games article, a handful of games was offered for each of four age ranges.

- **Health** columns discuss the range of childhood difficulties, from disease to injury to preventive measures regarding both. Articles have covered immunization and vision, for instance, and often feature a chart or sidebar listing the various options or symptoms of the topic.

- **Love, Dad** gives fathers a chance to sound off on their parenting experiences. Like "Child of Mine," this is a back-page essay told in the first person. It can be funny, touching, or even strident, as long as it's a man talking about young children. One memorable essay discussed the terror of every parent—traveling by airplane with your toddler.

"Discoveries," "The First Year," "Learning," "MediaKids," "Mom & Pop Quiz," "Parent-Child Connection," "Pediatric News," "Stages," "Time for Yourself," and "Travel Notes" are written in house or by regular contributors, as are the food and fashion pages.

How to Query *child*

In addition to a one-page query, the editors require a résumé or background information about your experience, and published clips to demonstrate your skill.

Unfortunately, Wood says that her personal experience with over-the-transom queries is poor. "I could count on one hand the times I have assigned an article on the basis of a query in the last four years," she says.

"We've thought of most ideas by the time a query arrives proposing something," the editor continues. "There are millions of things we could write about, so I'd rather know about what the writer brings to the topic personally. I like to talk to people and find out things that I don't always see in a résumé and clips. Then the other editors and I can keep the person in mind for topics that fit the writer's experience."

How to Write for *child*

About 80 percent of the article ideas in *child* are generated in house and assigned to known writers. But that leaves an additional 20 percent for those who haven't yet written for the magazine.

When you receive an assignment, your editor will send an assignment letter and contract. "We try to be as specific as possible," Wood says. "We have, at times, given the writer the theme paragraph, subsections, and suggestions for sidebars. Since a lot of ideas are large in scope, we help the writer understand what we want to focus on. We offer sources, copies of articles, plus background information to get the person started."

You can expect to revise your manuscript at least once, and this magazine's lead time is short. "Most of the articles we assign are slotted for a specific issue already," Wood explains. "So we're specific about allowing four to six weeks to write the piece and a week or two for revisions, at most. We try to send the writer the edited manuscript as time allows."

Christianity Today

465 Gundersen Drive
Carol Stream, IL 60188
(708) 260-6200

Published: 15 times a year

Circulation: 193,000

Query: Features: Carol Thiessen, administrative editor
"Books": Michael G. Maudlin, associate editor
"Church in Action": Timothy Jones, associate editor
"News": Tim Morgan, associate editor

Query response time: 2 to 3 weeks

Buys: 40-plus articles out of approximately 600 unsolicited queries/manuscripts received annually

Guidelines: Available

Rights purchased: First NAS

Pays: Prior to publication but not on acceptance

Expenses: Pays any that are arranged and approved in advance

Kill fee: Varies

Rates:

Type of Article	*Word Length*	*Payment*
Major Feature	3,000	$300 - 500
Short Feature	1,500	150 - 250
"Books"	varies	50 - 150
"Church In Action"	1,200 - 1,500	varies
"News"	1,000	40 - 200
"Speaking Out"	600	75

Christianity Today provides editorial coverage of religious doctrine, issues, trends, current events, and news from a Christian perspective. The magazine is a forum for the expression of evangelical conviction in theology, evangelism, church life, cultural life, and society.

"We follow a news magazine model to a certain extent," says Managing Editor David Neff. "We run essays, reportage, and news. But no matter what the format, the question we always ask is, 'What is new or different about what you are saying?' We don't want to recycle old material. A lot of denominational publications include devotional material that has the tendency to sound the same as what was printed 10 or 20 years ago."

"In essay or devotional content, we want to know the news hook or social trend, or we want to see that you have an absolutely fresh way of looking at the topic," Neff says. "And since *Christianity Today* is of evangelical conviction, we are going to look at social trends, public policy, and every other topic from the standpoint of what the evangelical church brings to bear on those items."

The *Christianity Today* reader is reasonably well educated and trained to think critically about issues. "This is what distinguishes us from other religious magazines," says Neff. "Our readers are not specialists in theology or Biblical studies, but laypeople who think critically about current issues. Of the readership, 88 percent are church leaders (past or present clergy); members of governing boards; teachers of adult Sunday school classes; or opinion shapers or direction setters for the church. People come to us to determine how to think about specific issues."

The median age of *Christianity Today* subscribers is 46; 65 percent are male; 69 percent are college graduates; and 48 percent have a graduate degree. The median household income is $37,101.

How to Slant Your Ideas to *Christianity Today*

Christianity Today focuses a fair amount of its editorial on news. "We are looking for writers experienced in news reporting who can give us balanced, even-handed reporting," says Neff. "We are not looking for news that has too much of a viewpoint; we want a sense of objectivity. Writers must be able to let the sources and interviewees create the flavor and balance, rather than injecting too much of themselves."

Neff is also seeking major reportorial articles in the feature section of the magazine. He wants trends from the Christian viewpoint. "That takes a lot of skill, a lot of information gathering, and an eye for the kind of revelatory detail that can make the reader feel as if he or she is present," he says.

A recent piece on crisis pregnancy centers, though staff-written, is an article Neff points to that did not have a wide variety of viewpoints, but had a lot of detail that came through good reporting. "The writer found a caring network of women working for women," says Neff. "Because general reporting on this topic has been one-sided, we tried to present an alternative viewpoint without being strident in tone. We presented the story from the other vantage point—something you wouldn't hear from listening to Diane Sawyer on the CBS News."

In an article entitled, "Washington's Pro-Family Activists," it would have been easy for *Christianity Today* to take potshots at the three major organizations profiled—Concerned Women for

America, Family Research Council, and Christian Coalition. "Instead, we got an even-handed profile of the three groups' work," says Neff. "The author told us how these groups were into family values before family values were cool. He raised questions about the groups without being hard-hitting, yet it wasn't a puff piece either. It was the model of balanced reporting. Questions emerged from the piece, but readers didn't feel as if they were reading an exposé."

Neff is also interested in personal-experience stories when they speak to a larger social trend. One article, "Why Sex Education Is Failing Our Kids," was written by a public health educator. She wrote what she encountered trying to work with public schools on sex education. "It was not major reportage; it was her personal experience," says Neff. "But it touched a chord with every family in America."

Another broader, personal-experience article, "Casualties of the Abortion Wars," written by a pastor, described how he found himself put off by the manipulative techniques used by Operation Rescue during its visit to Buffalo, New York. "It did not include a lot of research, but it discussed a topic of concern to many," says Neff.

In each issue, two to three of the half-dozen feature articles in *Christianity Today* are freelance-written. The articles tend to be three to four pages, although the editors occasionally run a longer piece.

The following are descriptions of a number of other opportunities for freelancers in this magazine:

- **Books** looks at religious books or books about social trends, but the work needs an evangelical Christian angle for the magazine to be concerned about it. The book must also cover new research, a new angle, or the new formulation of an idea.

  The lead book review is 800 words; the second is 600 words; and the third is 300 words. The space devoted to a book depends on how important the editors feel the work is to their readers and whether they want to critique it or just call their readers' attention to it. "That's why it's important to query first and let us help you shape the book review," explains Neff.

- **Church in Action** features descriptive pieces about a person or ministry that is low profile but is accomplishing something of interest.

  "If we get something that has a strong crusading feeling, chances are we will reject it because it doesn't fit our tone or purpose," says Neff. "The real question is 'Who is the reader of the magazine?' In our case, we write for people who take the Christian faith seriously, who think critically but are not specialists in the field."

- **News** is a large back-of-the-book section of about 15 pages. Because of its timely nature, you may query "News" by phone or FAX. (Call the magazine for the appropriate FAX number to query this department.) "News writing is a skill, so don't try it unless you have had a news editing course in high school or college. If you've never done it you might be at a loss," says Neff. "We want observant writers who can capture something that has just happened or is a part of a broader trend. All of our news must have a religious overtone."
- **Speaking Out** is the best place for new writers to break into this Christian market. "It's very similar to *Newsweek*'s 'My Turn,'" says Neff. "We want 600 tightly written words that make a strong statement of opinion. There needs to be a religious element to it, but a wide variety of topics fit here. The key is to argue your position in a very short space—the kind of thing syndicated columnists do every day of the week." One column entitled, "Why Pick on Hillary?," said that evangelical Christian women were uncomfortable with the first lady. The author wrote that it was not because of her religion, résumé, or marital situation, but the fact that she defines herself as a professional while they see themselves as homemakers first, even if they work outside the home.

Editorials are staff-written.

How to Query *Christianity Today*

One page preferred; do not send photo/art information.

The most important thing you can do in a query letter directed to *Christianity Today* is to let the editor see at a glance what you want to write about. Don't pitch a broad topic—suggest a narrow slice. It is also essential to say briefly why you are qualified to write the piece. Tell what contribution you can make that others haven't.

Neff suggests sending a list of previously published work and several clips that show you've published in the right magazines. "But if your letter is extremely well written, it alone will convince us," says Neff. "What I want to see is that we are on the same wavelength and that you can communicate religious beliefs. Your query should give me a feel for your case and the way you will frame the topic."

You must be brief, however. Neff rarely reads into the third paragraph. "Give me all I need to know up front," he says. "The old inverted pyramid news style works well for queries."

Anecdotal material helps to make your case, and citing authorities tells the editor whether you are familiar enough with the territory to know the authorities. "That helps to build my confidence in the idea and in you as a writer," says Neff. "If you tell me whom you plan to call for comments, it shows me you will rely on authorities, studies, and statistics—the kind of writing we run."

If you are a new writer to *Christianity Today*, you will be asked to create your article on speculation. Agreements are verbal, not written.

How to Write for *Christianity Today*

Christianity Today seeks writers who have high regard for language and style, words, punctuation, and grammar. The editors work to make sure the writing is colorful, vivid, and moving as well as simple, clear, and readable. No technical jargon or academic language is allowed.

Articles should relate to real-world problems and needs, yet apply to Christian values and principles. Build your case point by point, with strong transitions, show the reader where you are going and why, and make clear what you are trying to prove.

Neff says if there is one major thing writers do wrong when writing for this magazine, it is stating their own opinions over and over again, without getting credible sources to give the hard facts. The ability to use experts skillfully to buttress a point is very important. "That's what makes *Christianity Today* a journalistic magazine," he says.

Academic authors—and *Christianity Today* deals with a large number of them—often have difficulty keeping the layperson's knowledge base in mind.

If you are reading back issues of the magazine to mirror its style, Neff suggests you first note the degree to which there seems to be a uniform versus an individual voice. Secondly, ask yourself the purpose of the magazine—is it to inform with a viewpoint, stimulate thought, address a particular issue, or entertain?

Condé Nast Traveler

360 Madison Avenue
New York, NY 10017
(212) 880-8800

Published: Monthly

Circulation: 1 million

Query: Features: Alison Humes, features editor
"Getaways": Irene Schneider, senior editor
"Stop Press": Cliff Hopkinson, executive/news editor
"Word of Mouth": Catherine Kelley,
"Word of Mouth" and beauty editor

Query response time: 6 to 8 weeks

Buys: About 10 department articles out of 1,500 to 2,000 unsolicited queries/manuscripts received annually

Guidelines: None available

Rights purchased: First World for major features;
All for other material

Pays: On acceptance

Expenses: Pays as necessary, when discussed in advance

Kill fee: 25 percent

Rates:

Type of Article	*Word Length*	*Payment*
Major Feature	5,000	$ 5,000
"Getaways"	300 - 500	300 - 500
"Stop Press"	1,000	1,000
"Word of Mouth"	50 - 150	50 - 150

Launched in 1987, *Condé Nast Traveler* set out to distinguish itself from others in the travel field with the credo, "Truth in Travel."

"Our aim is to tell the truth and to be utterly independent from the influences of the travel business," says Cliff Hopkinson, executive/news editor. "To that end, we accept no discounts or free trips. Writers pay their own way and travel incognito, going to great pains to produce objective reporting."

A review in *AdWeek* sums up the magazine this way: "A winning combination of eye-candy photography, consumer guides and entertaining features, *Condé Nast Traveler* has triumphed for yet another year as the most in-depth book an airport magazine browser could hope to find. For those who aren't going anywhere, but like to look, *Condé Nast Traveler* has steadily entrenched itself as an elegant and well-written addition to the coffee table. Investigative stories that rival those in the news magazines and a well-done news section make *Condé Nast Traveler* more than just fluffy copy and gorgeous shots of exotic locales."

This destination-oriented magazine is targeted to sophisticated, intelligent, upscale readers who are financially able to enjoy travel. The audience is almost evenly split between men and women, with a few more male readers (53 percent). Approximately 58 percent of the readers are married and the average age is 41. The median household income is $55,300.

How to Slant Your Ideas to *Condé Nast Traveler*

"*Condé Nast Traveler* is a hard magazine for anyone to break into," says Hopkinson. "We cover very specialized subject matter and have a large number of experts in the field who contribute on an exclusive basis. We are not reluctant to try experienced freelancers on rare occasions, but this is a difficult field for a beginning freelancer."

Venture inside this compendium of travel insight and you'll become intrigued by such reads as "Secrets of Sintra," describing a sensuous decadence lurking in the mist-shrouded hills above Lisbon; "An Island of My Own," a sail into a Greek sanctuary of privacy and luxury; and "Impromptu Provence," in which a traveler's whim allows him to discover France's walled city of Avignon.

All *Condé Nast Traveler* departments are open to freelancers. They include:

- **Getaways** features domestic or overseas destinations appropriate for three to four days. "We have a fairly large net, but in general we deal with the venue, the attractions, and what the area itself has to offer," says Hopkinson. "We cover several venues in every issue, each running between 300 and 500 words."
- **Stop Press** is reports, news, and developments that affect travel. A sampling of snippets here include a 10-city test of how taxi scams work; a look at provincial new rulings that could let pilots take controlled naps—one at a time!; and an update on how to treat snakebites (sucking out the venom by mouth or with suction gadgets is definitely out).

- **Word of Mouth** is a potpourri of 50- to 150-word briefs that give a sophisticated view of travel. It covers cultural events, restaurants, new destinations, and quirky revelations about destinations for the well-heeled. The TaxiBike that slips through London's jammed traffic, herb and vegetable seeds from foreign countries, and the return of the aviator jacket as a hot fashion ticket are a few of the updates that have been included.

How to Query *Condé Nast Traveler*

"Unsolicited manuscripts and queries come in and go out," says Hopkinson. "They are reviewed but almost none can compete with the material we already have in our large inventory and the ideas presented by contributing editors. Occasionally, in the case of a writer with status who has an interesting idea, a successful approach is made through an agent. For a writer unknown to us, the idea would have to be uniquely interesting and the material presented in an authoritative, intriguing, and clear manner. The odds against success are very high."

New writers are advised to introduce themselves with clips, a résumé, and letter of expertise.

How to Write for *Condé Nast Traveler*

"Read the magazine thoroughly and understand its level of intelligence and discrimination ," Hopkinson suggests. "We aren't doing the same things as other travel magazines, and we find it's difficult to inculcate the right attitude in a writer from a distance."

In a fifth anniversary editorial note, Publisher Thomas A. Florio wrote, "With truth and independence as our principal values, *Condé Nast Traveler* has transcended the travel category in many respects to become a magazine of the world. Our readers enjoy an insider's perspective on travel and are also challenged with political, social, cultural and environmental perspectives on global issues that affect worldly Americans."

Cooking Light

Box 1748
Birmingham, AL 35201
(205) 877-6000

Published: Bimonthly

Circulation: 1 million

Query: Katherine Eakin, editor

Query response time: 3 to 4 months

Buys: About 140 articles out of approximately 480 unsolicited queries/manuscripts received annually

Guidelines: Available; need to be specific as to area

Rights purchased: All

Pays: On acceptance

Expenses: Pays none

Kill fee: 25 percent

Rates:

Type of Article	*Word Length*	*Payment*
Major Feature	1,400 - 2,000	$1,600 - 2,000
Short Feature	900 - 1,000	650 - 900
Food Feature 8-10 recipes	350 - 400	750 - 1,000
News Brief	150 - 250	200
"Books, Etc."	200 - 300	100
"Downfall"	800	300 - 500
"Fast Food" 6-8 recipes	200 lead	650 - 800
"For Two" 6-8 recipes	275 lead	650 - 800
"Heartbeat"	150 - 200	50 - 200
"Kids' Fitness"	1,200	600 - 700
"Profile in Fitness"	1,500 - 1,800	1,500 - 1,800
"Taking Aim"	1,800	700 - 900
"Technique" 6-8 recipes	200 lead	700

The subtitle, "The Magazine of Food and Fitness," sums up the editorial slant of this magazine. *Cooking Light* presents a mainstream approach to better living through a balance of exercise and proper nutrition.

"We look at all elements of a person's life, from regular exercise and recreation, to mental health and body care," says Editor Katherine Eakin. "Our objective is to present nutrition, health, and fitness information in a very positive voice to help our readers make wise choices about the way they are living their lives."

The *Cooking Light* staff includes the editor, who is a professional home economist with a background in food science and nutrition, three registered dietitians, a fitness editor with a background in psychology, and five test kitchen home economists.

This astute staff directs the magazine content to a well-educated woman (80 percent of the magazine's readers are female), approximately 45 years of age. She is probably married and works in a professional or managerial position. She is very interested in balancing her work, home, and family, and in feeling good about her choices. Time is a major concern to her.

How to Slant Your Ideas to *Cooking Light*

Cooking Light is divided into two general areas: food, which includes recipes and nutrition; and fitness, which covers health, recreation, and exercise.

For technical articles, the editors look for writers who have expertise in the area, be it nutrition, behavior modification, psychology, exercise physiology, or other specialty.

If you're a recipe developer or dietitian, *Cooking Light* has very specific guidelines to follow when creating recipes. The magazine follows the general guidelines of the American Heart and American Diabetic Associations in terms of what "healthy" means from a diet perspective. The magazine strives to keep the percentage of fat in its recipes to no more than 30 percent. All recipes also list types of fat, number of calories, percentage of calories from fat, carbohydrates, protein, calcium, and other basic nutrients.

"Our main recipe criteria are that the recipes be tasty, nutritious, and heart-healthy," says Eakin.

All recipes are tested by the staff. If they don't pass, the staff goes back to the recipe developer for additional recipes. "We pay for the initial testing, but do require a color photograph of the product so we have something to aim for in the test kitchen," says Eakin.

Columns open to freelancers are many, as follows:

- **Books, Etc.** reviews and rates books and videos on a five-point star system within the magazine's editorial purview. The magazine receives many books and typically assigns reviews to writers.
- **Downfall** is a back-page humorous essay, recognizing occasional setbacks of plans to live a healthy lifestyle. One

woman wrote of a theory that if her intentions are good, the extra calories she consumes don't count.

- **Fast Food** includes quick and easy recipes. The recipes use ingredients likely to be on hand.
- **For Two** includes 6 to 8 recipes that yield 2 servings; it may be a romantic menu or brown bag lunches for a duo.
- **Heartbeat** includes short articles on health and fitness news. Most articles are generated by the University of Alabama at Birmingham staff members at the medical center, but the magazine is contracting more and more with freelance contributors.
- **Kids' Fitness** is written to parents and has covered subjects such as weight training for kids, exercising as a family, and the use of steroids in team sports.
- **Profile in Fitness** is specific to individuals or families. One article dealt with a family that went to work at a ranch as part of a vacation; another interviewed experts about why diets don't work; a third profiled Nolan Ryan and how his lifestyle impacts his longevity on the baseball field.
- **Taking Aim** is an individual's story of a goal he or she is trying to reach or an obstacle to overcome. One article chronicled a woman's crusade to take morning walks, which turned from drudgery to delight.
- **Technique** is a step-by-step article that gives directions for variations on proven recipes. It has covered new ways to make scones, bagels, popovers, and angel food cake.

"Make It Light," "Menu Planner," "Recipe Exchange," "Recipe Index," and "What's Cooking?" are closed to freelancers.

How to Query *Cooking Light*

Any length is acceptable; photo/art suggestions are optional. Query six to 12 months in advance for seasonal material.

"First and foremost, your query must be personalized. It's obvious if someone is blanketing a query to all similar publications," says Eakin. "Second, be specific about the area in the magazine you want to write for."

Eakin has no preference for query style, but reminds writers to sell themselves. "Send a résumé and samples of published material," she says. "If you're interested in developing recipes for us, send examples of some you have created and your specific areas of interest and expertise."

The *Cooking Light* editorial staff typically comes up with ideas in house and then looks through their files of freelancers to pair up a story idea with a writer. In fact, 75 percent of the assignments occur that way.

The other 25 percent of assigned articles come from writer-generated ideas. "When people query us, we put the ideas into a notebook," explains Eakin. "Then as we are planning, we go back to that person who sent the query."

When a *Cooking Light* editor calls about an idea, she will be working from a focus sheet that spells out the concept. If you agree to accept the assignment, that sheet is mailed to you along with a contract. If recipes are involved in food stories, you will be asked to send recipe proposals before you pursue final development. For fitness articles, you will be required to submit an outline of your research before you start to write.

How to Write for *Cooking Light*

"Our articles must have application to daily life," says Eakin. "No matter how long or short the piece, we want readers to find some action they can take in their own life or the life of a family member."

When writing for *Cooking Light*, be certain to go to primary sources for information. Do not depend on news releases, articles, or books. In articles with quotes from health professionals, be sure to include the quote first and the attribution last. Sending research information to the editors for fact checking is a must.

"The bottom line is we are looking for the type of research that will substantiate whatever statement is made in the magazine," says Eakin. "But, try to avoid a preachy or instructional tone." She adds, "Our mission is to ensure that we can provide very credible and accurate information to defuse the wide variety of misinformation in the media. We go back to the original source to make certain we are not repeating someone else's misinterpretation."

Cosmopolitan

224 West 57th Street
New York, NY 10010
(212) 649-3570

Published: Monthly

Circulation: 2.7 million

Query: Features: Guy Flatley, managing editor and Roberta Ashley, executive editor
"His Point of View": Irene Copeland, senior articles editor
"On My Mind": Myra Appleton, senior articles editor

Query response time: 2 weeks

Buys: Several articles/stories out of 2,000 to 3,000 unsolicited queries/manuscripts received annually

Guidelines: Available; send SASE

Rights purchased: All

Pays: On acceptance

Expenses: Pays items if reasonable

Kill fee: 15 percent

Rates:

Type of Article	*Word Length*	*Payment*
Major Feature	2,500 - 3,500	$ 1,500+
Short Feature	1,000 - 2,000	500+
"His Point of View"	1,000 - 1,100	750 - 1,000
"On My Mind"	650 - 1,300	500+

"The format for *Cosmopolitan* has not changed appreciably since my husband and I created it in 1964," says Editor Helen Gurley Brown. "The *Cosmo* woman is traditional in many ways: she loves men and she loves children, but she doesn't want to live *through* them. She wants to be known for what she does in life; she wants to achieve."

Readers are between the ages of 18 and 34. Nearly half are married and 47 percent have a college education.

"Our reader is sophisticated, intelligent, and interested in having a career if she doesn't already have one," adds Managing Editor Guy Flatley. "She seeks as healthy a personal and professional life as possible."

"The single *Cosmo* girl wants to have a relationship, to be married eventually," Flatley continues. "Right now she may have one or more men in her life, and she wants information on how to deal with them."

"We talk a great deal about love relationships in *Cosmo,*" Brown notes. "We do that consciously because we don't feel that life is wonderful unless you have somebody to love. And we all know there are not enough men to go around."

How to Slant Your Ideas to *Cosmopolitan*

"*Cosmo* is a service magazine," Flatley says. "We give the *Cosmo* girl suggestions on how to cope with the psychological crises in her life, like how not to feel frustrated in a deadend job, how to get out of that job and into another more suitable one, and how to make her way through a variety of emotional situations.

"We publish eight categories of major articles in every issue," he continues. "The well of the book always leads off with a major celebrity profile. Then there's a major article on sex, followed by two articles on emotional topics, one concerning the nonsexual aspects of male-female relationships and the other focusing more on the woman herself. Past articles have included what to do when the man in your life is jealous of your job, and learning how to handle rejection."

In addition to those four full-length articles, *Cosmo* includes a major feature on health, beauty, or exercise; one on careers; a piece dealing with colorful trends or glamorous personalities; and a factual, informational article that doesn't fit into the other categories, such as a look at how sperm banks operate or the world of the psychic. Medical pieces cover subjects such as new cures for depression, food fads and phobias, and an update on hypnosis.

"I once heard Frank Sinatra say that he's in favor of anything that helps you get through the night," says Brown. "And that's us—we help the *Cosmo* girl get through the night."

The following columns are open to freelance contributors:

- **His Point of View** is a man's-eye-view column. These personal, 1,000-word pieces let *Cosmopolitan*'s female readers in on what men are thinking, so they can better understand and get along with them. "His POV" essays convey the writer's own experiences, feelings, and opinions, and can also incorporate the experiences of men he knows. The tone may be humorous or serious; in either case, the writing must be succinct.

- **On My Mind** is *Cosmo*'s opinion essay page. Like most other articles in *Cosmo,* ideas for this column usually originate in house, although queries are accepted and read by the senior editor who edits the column. By *Cosmo* standards, the article is short— usually 650 words. Past columns have included "Is It Sexual Harassment or Flirting?" and "Should Good Girls Finish Last?"

"Beauty Bar," "Books," "Dieter's Notebook," "Health Memo," "Horoscope," "Irma Kurtz's Agony Column," "Money Talk," "Movies," "Travel Update," "What's New in Beauty," and "Your Body" are written by regular contributors or the staff.

How to Query *Cosmopolitan*

One page preferred; do not send photo/art information; query six months in advance for seasonal material.

Cosmopolitan is open to a very select group of writers, most of whom are hand-picked by the magazine's editors. Although the staff reads every query that is submitted, very few items sent in over the transom are purchased.

When Brown and her husband launched *Cosmopolitan* 30 years ago, the idea was so innovative and controversial that not even the editors on staff were able to grasp its slant consistently. So Brown started "idea notebooks," into which she put ideas she thought would work well in the newly organized magazine. Editors then followed up on those ideas and assigned them to writers. Soon, the editors began submitting their own ideas and today, every editor is expected to contribute to the notebooks. Now, there are several notebooks divided into categories such as general, emotional, major features, and minor features.

When an editor at *Cosmo* notices a writer's work in another publication and thinks the person has potential as a *Cosmo* contributor, the editor invites the writer to leaf through the idea notebooks. The writer selects about six ideas and, with the editor, narrows the field to the one the writer is best suited to do.

"Almost every idea we use comes from the staff," Flatley says. "We don't say that we won't consider ideas from writers—we occasionally buy them—but we don't really solicit queries, either.

"The best way to bring yourself to our attention," Flatley suggests, "is to send us no more than five tear sheets of articles you've had published, with a cover letter introducing yourself. You should be aware of the *Cosmo* style first, however, and you must have clips that relate to the kinds of articles we publish."

How to Write for *Cosmopolitan*

"There are a lot of people who don't want to write about a renaissance in their sexual life, about sexual boredom, or about why women love bad men," Brown says. "The best writers for us are the ones who respect what we need to do and are able to write on those subjects. *Cosmo* writers differ from other magazine writers because they are willing or able to write about emotional subjects as if they understand and have experienced them themselves."

"Our text editors are superb," Flatley says, "and most writers are grateful for the editing they do. We don't edit for the sake of changing something, however. We work over the articles to shape them into suitable form.

"We prefer and urge writers to rewrite their material, rather than having us do the first revision," he continues. "But ours is a difficult style; the writer has to be very skilled. And since we are on a schedule, we can't always promise the writer a second chance to rewrite. If the piece has a good chance to get into print, we offer the writer lots of advice. Often it's just a matter of the writer having gone off on the wrong tangent. If we can point out the problem, we do so."

Nearly half of the articles assigned by the editors are killed, and the writer receives fifteen percent of the original fee. "We hope that every idea we assign will be successful," Brown says. "But if it isn't, we give a kill fee and start over again.

"Our editors are very good at assigning the right people to do the right articles," Brown says. "And after those good writers finish their work, we put every one of our articles through intense editing. We work hard to give the *Cosmo* girl a whole lot for her money."

The Costco Connection

10809 120th Avenue NE
Kirkland, WA 98033-9777
(206) 828-8100

Published: Monthly

Circulation: 1.6 million in the U.S.; 250,000 in Canada

Query: David Fuller, editor

Query response time: 1 to 4 weeks

Buys: About 40 articles out of approximately 500 unsolicited queries/manuscripts received annually

Guidelines: None available

Rights purchased: First NAS

Pays: On acceptance

Expenses: Pays reasonable phone and overnight mail or express mail; some travel when discussed in advance

Kill fee: Not applicable

Rates:

Type of Article	*Word Length*	*Payment*
Major Feature	1,000 - 1,200	$ 500
Short Feature	800	300
Department	400 - 800	150 - 300
News Brief	350	150

The Costco Connection is a monthly tabloid-style magazine for members of Costco, a wholesale warehouse, who are owners or operators of small businesses. It is sent to members who live in 16 states, primarily on the West and East coasts, and four Canadian provinces where Costco warehouses are located. The edition for Canada is printed in both English and French.

The readership is slightly weighted to the male side; the average age is 48.

"Our broad underlying purpose is to enhance members' affiliation with Costco," says Editor David Fuller. "This is our sole means of communicating with them on a regular basis. It is truly a value-added benefit of membership."

How to Slant Your Ideas to *The Costco Connection*

The primary editorial slant of *The Costco Connection* is useful articles that help small business owners run their companies more successfully. Secondarily, it is designed to provide articles that will relate to their personal lives.

"Our small business owners run the gamut from doctors, dentists, accountants, and marketing consultants to owners of small publishing companies, beauty salons, construction companies, and gas stations," says Fuller.

Fuller prefers writers with a business-writing background. "Experience with regional markets is acceptable, but a background writing for national business publications is even better," he says. "Occasionally we work with new writers, if the idea is outstanding."

The majority of ideas you see in *The Costco Connection* (80 percent) are developed in house and assigned to writers. Subjects have included how to talk to the media; how to market your product through schools; and how to set up a 401K retirement fund.

The easiest way to break in is to suggest a profile of a Costco member. "If you can find an interesting member from an area other than the Northwest, you have a fairly good chance of publishing here," he says. Two examples include a feature on the author of a new book, *What Do They Say When You Leave the Room,* and another on a man who created an innovative service that gives small businesses quick access to government files.

Most cover stories feature a nationally known person who has achieved success in some walk of life, such as one that featured Annette Funicello's fight against multiple sclerosis and another that profiled Speaker of the House Tom Foley.

Departments open to freelancers are:

- **Arts & Entertainment** runs profiles of entertainers or issue-related stories on subjects such as freedom of speech and adult literacy. Book reviews are also included.
- **Food** addresses issues of food, nutrition, and health in a balanced manner. "Recently we did an article called, 'The Milky Fray,' discussing the positive and negative health aspects of this popular drink since experts see it both ways," says Fuller. "It's surprising and unique to see a commercial wholesale retail company talk about the pros and cons of an issue. But we know our readers are smart, sophisticated people who can make their own judgments."

Each issue also contains a special section, the topic of which rotates throughout the year. "Automotive," "Health & Nutrition," and "Home and Garden" are each featured twice a year. "Debate," "Dialogue," "Product Profile," "Special Events," and "What's New" are staff-written.

How to Query *The Costco Connection*

One page preferred. Do not send photo/art suggestions, unless extremely striking or unusual.

"A dream writer is one who can send me a fabulous one-page query, adjust it according to my whim, and accomplish the adjusted assignment with a minimum of fuss and bother on my part," says Fuller.

Fuller wants queries that are to the point. "Tell me who the story will appeal to and demonstrate that you have read my publication and understand my reader," the editor requests. "I don't need a sample lead, but anecdotes have some appeal, as long as they aren't gimmicky. And sending clips is important for me to judge your writing style."

Fuller wryly says that a query that lands on his desk goes through a patented aging process. "It is slotted and reslotted, according to seasons, categories, and subjects," he says. "We may get an idea that is right for us and call the writer right away to start working on it, or it may take a while to find the right issue for a good idea."

How to Write for *The Costco Connection*

When preparing to write for this magazine, Fuller suggests that one of the keys in reading back issues is to look at more than just the writing. "Examine the subheads, captions, pull-quotes, display elements, and editor's notes," says Fuller. "All those elements give you clues about the editorial staff's personality. They are really one of the key ways an editor has to shine through in his publication, and they say a lot about what an editor may want from writers."

When it comes to style, Fuller wants journalistic writing. "We typically run third-person narrative, how-to articles with catchy grabber leads," he says. "But we also like humor and the occasional first-person piece."

Because *The Costco Connection*'s headquarters is in the Northwest, Fuller says the magazine fights a regional perception. "Since we are distributed throughout the United States and Canada, we really want a North American perspective," he says.

"Scatter your experts; you don't have to find them just in the perceived 'Costcoland'—you can draw from across the United States and Canada."

It's also ideal, according to Fuller, to find anecdotes from Costco members. "We will search our membership files by company to give freelancers a starter set of people to interview, and then they can build from that," he says. "In most of our stories there are direct Costco ties, be it quoting business experts who are members, profiling a celebrity who is a member, or getting quotes from nonprofit organizations that are members."

Although for the most part, Fuller prefers to receive articles that are ready to publish with some light editing, he says he stands ready to help a writer work through a problem in the direction of a story or in making contacts with sources.

Country Victorian Decorating & Lifestyle

1700 Broadway, 34th Floor
New York, NY 10019
(212) 541-7100

Published: Bimonthly

Circulation: 225,000

Query: Florine McCain, editor

Query response time: 1 to 8 weeks

Buys: About 10 to 20 articles/stories out of approximately 100 unsolicited queries/manuscripts received annually

Guidelines: Available; send SASE

Rights purchased: First NAS

Pays: On acceptance

Expenses: Varies

Kill fee: 25 percent

Rates:

Type of Article	*Word Length*	*Payment*
Major Feature	1,200	$300

Country Victorian Decorating & Lifestyle provides a plethora of ideas and information for those who want to recapture the ambiance of the Victorian age.

This magazine's editorial mix includes articles on Victorian home design and restoration, decorating, home furnishings, remodeling, crafts, needlework, woodworking, antiques and collectibles, food and wine, fairs and festivals, travel, gardening, and fashion.

Country Victorian Decorating & Lifestyle magazine is designed and edited especially for those who want to emulate, or simply read about, the romance, graciousness, and traditional values of that bygone time.

Virtually all (98 percent) of the subscribers are female; however, 32 percent of the overall readers are males. The median age is 39. The majority of readers (71 percent) are married and the median household income is $37,600.

How to Slant Your Ideas to *Country Victorian Decorating & Lifestyle*

Country Victorian Decorating & Lifestyle is reflective of the way ordinary people lived 100 to 150 years ago. Decor then, as now, was a mixture of many periods. "The average family home in the Victorian era was decorated with a blend of new items and family heirlooms," says Florine McCain, editor. "The magazine shows readers how people lived and decorated at that time."

Country Victorian Decorating & Lifestyle readers are romantics and, therefore have a romanticized view of what that time was like. "Our readers don't want to read about the negatives, like slavery and child labor," says McCain. "They like to be reminded that people wrote letters and had tea, instead of watching TV." Past ideas that have sold to *Country Victorian Decorating & Lifestyle* are a mixed bag, from Victorian decorating to customs to personality profiles. A few specific topics submitted by freelancers have been Victorian women's skin care and how the rise of the bicycle led to the decline of the corset.

"The words 'affordable' and 'budget' are words that appeal to our readers," says McCain. "Although we occasionally cover an influential or historically important style, such as high-end antiques, we are more interested in low-cost decorating tips and collectibles."

The magazine's two main feature sections, "Decorating" and "Victorian World," are both open to freelancers. Each section contains several articles. *Country Victorian Decorating & Lifestyle* also accepts features on antiques and collectibles.

The following subject areas are open to freelancers:

- **Antiques** and **Collectibles** includes details about when and how an item became popular, how it was used, and where you can find it today. Stories have included Victorian napkin rings; valentines of the past; discovering Victorian board games; and crochet instructions for a Victorian tablecloth.

  "A piece on 19th-century flatware, for example, should emphasize its availability and low price, include historical background, names of major manufacturers, plus information about dealers, care and preservation, and reference materials," says McCain.

- **Decorating** looks for pieces that give an historical overview and fully explain how things were done in the past and how they can be re-created today. Stories for this section should include specific how-tos and plenty of resources for reference.

"A story for the decorating section could be on how a particular room, such as a nursery or a dining room, would have been decorated," says McCain. "We want a lot of detail. Writers need to know things like what kind of flooring and window treatments were typical and where you can find a company that makes copies of Victorian rug patterns today."

Other story examples for this section include "Windows and Walls," a feature on historic patterns; and "Family Values," the story of how the restoration of an 1888 Missouri house became a family project.

This section also regularly features a story and photos about a home, inn, or bed & breakfast, either historic or authentically decorated. According to McCain, many of the homes featured are found and submitted by freelancers. "We pay a finder's fee when we use a home submitted from a freelancer," she says. "And, we frequently ask that person to do the story if the query letter is well-written. Those stories are usually very decorating-oriented."

- **Victorian World** features topics about Victorian fashion, customs, lifestyle, sports, activities, and personalities. A piece on calling cards included details on the elaborate etiquette and rules of "paying calls," a daily ritual for middle-class Victorian ladies.

  The editor is very interested in brief biographies or portraits of glamorous, scandalous, or infamous notable Victorian women. "We are not interested in doing stories on 'worthy' women in this section," says McCain. "We don't want a story on the first woman architect. We want to know about the love affairs of Lily Langtry. We want a great deal of drama and soap opera."

  Other stories in this section have included a piece on the 1893 World's Fair; true stories of White House pets; a history of the invention of photography; and 19th-century mourning customs and costumes.

How to Query *Country Victorian Decorating & Lifestyle*

One-page queries preferred; photos should be sent for historic home submissions; photos and/or illustrations should be sent for antique or collectible submissions, and with other queries that require visuals.

Freelance writers are encouraged to send one or two paragraphs on a number of story ideas if they have them. "I love it when people send me more than one idea," says McCain. "We are extremely pleased when we find competent writers. Once we find writers we like, we start assigning articles to them."

Always send clips when introducing yourself to McCain.

How to Write for *Country Victorian Decorating & Lifestyle*

The writing style in *Country Victorian Decorating & Lifestyle* is conversational and personal. McCain wants writers who can give detailed information in a chatty tone, without writing in a history-book style. The writer may add a touch of humor, but it should be affectionate.

"There were things about that period that were silly," says McCain. "Writers can be gently humorous, but we want to avoid being negative."

According to McCain, writers need to have a genuine affection for, interest in, and extensive knowledge of the period. "My dream writer is someone who is romantic enough to empathize with our reader," she says. "Our readers, like many of our writers, have the feeling that they were born 100 years too late."

When McCain receives a query that makes the grade, she will call and assign the article over the phone. She doesn't follow up in writing unless what she wants is extremely detailed. Normally, she has very little contact with writers during the writing process, unless there is some problem. When a piece needs editing, she will do it herself, although she may call and ask the writer for more information.

Since *Country Victorian Decorating & Lifestyle* does not work with a contract, the writer should send one of his/her own. It can be a simple confirmation letter detailing the assignment, including length, due date, rights sold, expenses paid, and fee.

D&B Reports

299 Park Avenue
New York, NY 10171
(212) 593-7011

Published: Bimonthly

Circulation: 75,000

Query: Patricia Hamilton, editor and associate publisher

Query response time: 1 to 2 weeks

Buys: About 10 articles out of hundreds of unsolicited queries/manuscripts received annually

Guidelines: Available; send SASE

Rights purchased: All

Pays: On acceptance

Expenses: Pays none

Kill fee: None

Rates:

Type of Article	*Word Length*	*Payment*
Main Feature	1,800	$650 - 800
Regular Feature	850 - 1,600	500+
Special Feature	900	500

D&B Reports offers concrete advice and practical how-tos to owners and managers of small companies. "The Small Business Administration defines small businesses as companies that employ 500 people or fewer," says Editor and Associate Publisher Patricia Hamilton. "From subscriber surveys, we've found that our readers have annual sales of $12 million or less. They are not mom-and-pop companies but sophisticated owners and managers. At the same time, they are quite different from the top positions at Fortune 500 companies. Our readers wear many different hats, from human resources and purchasing, to finance and marketing. They don't have an army of specialists to help them. They work long hours, and find it difficult to keep up on the kind of information they need."

According to Hamilton, most readers are customers of the Dun & Bradstreet Corporation, the world's leading supplier of business information. But a fair number find out about the magazine from business contacts and become subscribers. A limited number of magazines are sold on the newsstand.

The majority of *D&B Reports* subscribers are men (69.7 percent); the median age is 42. More than 90 percent have attended college and more than two-thirds have earned a four-year degree.

Just over half of the subscribers are in top management and 42.7 percent are in middle management. They have a median annual household income of $73,400—well above the national average.

How to Slant Your Ideas to *D&B Reports*

To help readers run their businesses better, *D&B Reports* offers management information that can be applied to everyday business. Practicality is paramount.

"We've carved a special niche in the marketplace by offering more of the type of information small businesses need than any other magazine," says Hamilton. "When we run a profile, we don't just say how a business developed out of the garage and three years later earned a zillion dollars. Those types of articles are fun to read, but we always try to include something the reader can take away and apply to his or her business. We want to report on strategies the company used to succeed or, conversely, any mistakes the reader doesn't want to duplicate."

The magazine's tag line on the table of contents page reads, "Keeps small businesses from making big mistakes."

D&B Reports breaks its editorial into three sections: "Main Feature," "Special Feature," and "Regular Feature," the latter of which is more column-oriented material. Each issue is based on a theme, such as training, innovation, or cost control.

For instance, an issue on innovation included main features on a nonprofit group making capitalists of Amazon farmers; three start-up airlines carving out niches in a tough business; and an amateur designer taking on toy-market experts. The "Special Feature" looked at portable technology and how the car has become an office for many managers.

"Writers sometimes have the best chance with the 'Special Feature' section because we often don't have time to write that in house," says Hamilton. For a *D&B Reports* that focused on training, the editors needed a "Special Feature" on language training for international business. If you were a writer who had a background in that area and had called ahead for an editorial calendar, you might have won an assignment.

While the major stories in *D&B Reports* are open to freelancers, the columns are semi-closed. In other words, the magazine doesn't want to discourage great suggestions from writers who have expertise in the topic categories. But it doesn't want to unduly encourage submissions either, since it primarily depends on staff writers and regular contributors to fill those pages.

"If you are someone who can report on up-to-date trends, policies, laws, or on new strategies in insurance, taxes, or marketing, send us your ideas," says Hamilton. "We also have a short 900-word column on good management ideas."

The four center pages of the magazine contain information solely provided by the Dun & Bradstreet Corporation and its economic analysis department.

How to Query *D&B Reports*

One-page queries preferred. Do not send photo/art suggestions. Query five to six months in advance, remembering that *D&B Reports* is a bimonthly publication.

Hamilton encourages writers to call for an editorial calendar and writer's guidelines. "But don't query over the phone, we don't pay attention to ideas presented that way; we must see them in written form," she cautions.

Queries for *D&B Reports* shouldn't be too detailed. "What really interests us more are clips and a résumé sent with a concise proposal," says Hamilton.

The editor wants to groom a few good new freelancers for the magazine, but she says often it is a matter of timing. Serendipity may cause a sale if you come to her at exactly the right time with a story proposal that fits into a forthcoming issue. You must also present your ideas with impressive clips from established publications whose editorial judgment she trusts. Those magazines don't have to be business or consumer publications; they can be a women's magazine or trade journal that has pages devoted to management or careers.

"A writer we just commissioned to write 'Legal Briefs' sent a résumé and clips just at the right moment," says Hamilton. "She had the expertise we were looking for. It never hurts to send your background information to us. On a separate occasion, we wanted to start a column on partnerships. We looked through the story proposals and clips we had on file and selected one capable writer. When his query first arrived, we had nothing for him, but it turned out we started using him regularly."

How to Write for *D&B Reports*

"*D&B Reports* seeks normal, straightforward English, not 'corporate-speak-type language,'" says Hamilton. "I'm sick of terms like 'right sizing,'" says Hamilton. "I have no patience for buzz words in a business magazine."

The editor also encourages writers to get right to the point. "A lot of people beat around the bush. They write long leads to get into the stories," she says. "Get on with it; tell us what you are writing about."

D&B Reports does not overuse anecdotes, but if you have a short case history that proves a point, include it. "If your article is discussing a marketing strategy, it works well to include a brief description of how a small business owner implemented that strategy," says Hamilton. "In addition, we want a number of expert sources in each piece." Send a list of sources and phone numbers for fact-checking purposes.

Eating Well

Ferry Road
Charlotte, VT 05445
(802) 425-3961

Published: Bimonthly

Circulation: 525,000

Query: Scott Mowbray, editor

Query response time: 1 to 8 weeks, depending on urgency and timing; most within 3 weeks

Buys: 55 to 60 features/shorter stories out of thousands of unsolicited queries/manuscripts received annually

Guidelines: Available; send SASE

Rights purchased: First NAS, plus rights to use stories or recipes on TV and in other promotions

Pays: On acceptance

Expenses: Pays items as discussed in advance

Kill fee: 25 percent

Rates:

Type of Article	*Word Length*	*Payment*
Major Feature	2,500 - 4,000	$1,800 - 3,750
Department	250 - 350	200 - 300
News Brief	300	200 - 400

Plus special assignments paid by the word or by the hour

Described as a new-generation epicurean magazine, *Eating Well* is edited for members of the baby boom generation who are entering their middle years. "We are a food magazine, not a 'health-food' magazine," says Editor Scott Mowbray. "We cover the pleasures of cooking and eating with the added benefit that the food we feature is healthy. We are about taste and health and preserving both."

Mowbray describes his readers as sophisticated cooks. "About 80 percent of our readers also use the recipe editorial of this book," he says. "They spend a lot of time in the kitchen and in the armchair with our magazine. They read not only about food and nutrition, but about issues related to the two. And, they don't let us get away with anything. They are careful readers, and occasionally take us to task to argue or discuss a point in one of our features."

Eating Well's readers live active, health-conscious lifestyles. They are interested in indoor and outdoor activities, home remodeling, sports, travel, and more. The majority of readers are female (82 percent) with a median household income of $61,000. Most are over the age of 35 and are married; 75 percent have attended or graduated from college; and four out of five own their own home.

How to Slant Your Ideas to *Eating Well*

Each issue of *Eating Well* contains a mix of journalistic profiles, nutrition, health, and science reports, investigative articles, and travel pieces, as well as cooking/recipe-oriented service features.

Mowbray says he is hungry to find more good writers who understand food and the food/health connection. "We get a lot of people who write in and say, 'I never eat sugar or flour and I want to write for your magazine'," says Mowbray. "What we need are writers who can understand sophisticated scientific issues, have aesthetic interests, and are technical experts. And, we also need them to have the ability to spin a good tale."

The editor encourages writers to pay attention to the types of articles in the magazine. "Telling writers to 'read the magazine' sounds trite," he says. "But I have freelanced, and I remember times when I got lazy and didn't pay attention to the fact that the story I was suggesting just ran two issues ago."

One out of 10 articles you'll read in *Eating Well* are from ideas generated by freelancers; the other nine are developed in house. Mowbray assigns articles to writers he has worked with in the past, but he also looks through clips and résumés sent in with queries to find new writers. "In the last 10 months, six out of 10 feature stories have been written for us by writers who had never sold to *Eating Well* before," he says.

All features in *Eating Well* are ripe for freelance picking. A survey of past issues turns up articles on why the nation's school lunch program is failing our children; a reporter's visit to a radical health-food convention; a journey to find the "healthy English chef"; a tour of New York City with a food inspector; a profile of Alice Waters; and a look at hospital food.

Recipes are a standard ingredient in many *Eating Well* articles. "If you are assigned a piece with recipes, you will be working with our food editor," says Mowbray. "We expect writers to test the recipes and make sure they are written as much as possible to meet our nutritional and aesthetic standards. We don't expect nonnutritionists to do detailed analyses, but we expect them to be reasonable. If the recipes don't work when they come in, you will never work for us again."

Examples of recipes include light versions of classic chocolate cakes; low-fat pizzas; new approaches to classic sauces; an updated treasury of fruit desserts; a Korean menu; rich-tasting soufflés; and a collection of Mediterranean dishes.

Eating Well departments open to freelancers are:

- **Nutrition Letter**, subtitled "The Science of Eating," contains short nutrition updates with emphasis on exciting new research. It's a great place for new *Eating Well* writers to break into the market. A sampling of topics covered includes eating and aging; the USDA food pyramid; a study linking childhood breakfast habits and adult heart disease risk; and possible neurological explanations for fat cravings.
- **Observer** focuses on other news from the world of food and health—new product reviews, market trends, book reviews, and labeling laws—and is also a perfect venue for untried writers. Examples of reports include how advertising food icons like the Campbell's Soup Kids and Tony the Tiger have slimmed down and shaped up over the years; a study of attitudes toward food among health gurus; a survey of healthy airline food; and a look at the risks and marketing of megavitamins to body builders.

"Healthy Skeptic," "Nutrition Sense," "Rush Hour," "Rx for Recipes," and "Q&A" are closed to freelancers.

How to Query *Eating Well*

Submit two or three ideas at once, writing a few paragraphs (or longer) on each.

Queries that sell to *Eating Well* must tell what the story will be about, not merely give a topic. "We often get queries proposing to do something on cholesterol testing or cancer," says Mowbray. "My answer is that those story ideas are a dime a dozen. What do you want to *say* about the topic? Who will appear in the story? What is the special angle? We are a bimonthly and print far in advance of distribution. We have to make stories our own and make them *Eating Well* specific, or they won't seem timely."

While Mowbray prefers that writers send several ideas at once, he wants each idea to be thoughtfully presented. "Talk to several people who are experts on the subject or who will be players in the story," Mowbray says. "Instead of saying you know an interesting heart researcher at Harvard with a new theory about iron, tell us specifically what Dr. So-and-So has been doing. Give us details."

If doing that kind of research means your query has to extend to two pages, that's fine with the editor, as long as the topic is fascinating. "You don't have to mimic the style of your proposed article," he says. If your query is well-written, it suggests that you are an able writer.

Mowbray encourages writers to send clips, "even if you are world famous." Explains the editor, "We may know you, but refresh our memories about your writing style by sending a recent article on a related topic that appeared in another magazine. We prefer magazine experience over a newspaper background. But, you can make the transition from newspaper to magazine feature if you are the right kind of writer."

If Mowbray likes your idea, he will most likely ask you to send an outline that more clearly develops the theme. Then, if you're still on track, he will write you an assignment letter that outlines his expectations of the final piece in great detail. When you turn in your manuscript, Mowbray will critique it and most likely send it back for a rewrite.

"Except in the case of superb writers, rewrites happen at least once and maybe twice," the editor says. "I call the writer and send a written detailed analysis—sometimes as long as four to five pages—that includes a page-by-page critique with tedious amounts of direction.

"Writers are typically appreciative of that kind of detailed input," he says. "And if ultimately we have to kill the piece, we feel we have done everything we could to save the patient."

How to Write for *Eating Well*

When it comes to writing style, this magazine wants a strong journalistic voice that brings authoritative, timely coverage of nutrition issues. *Eating Well* avoids the "for women only" tone in many food magazines, and its healthy recipes emphasize good ingredients, simplicity of preparation, and full flavor.

At the same time, *Eating Well* prefers its articles to be stories. "We need to involve the reader with real situations, real people, and not simply to offer topics," says Mowbray. "And, we need the story told in a balanced way. That's a lot to demand, especially since food writing has not always incorporated science and health. We are finding a new type of writer for a new category of articles."

Incorporating scientific data to back up information in your article is also essential when writing for *Eating Well.* "Make sure you use appropriate attributions," says Mowbray. "This is especially important when it comes to controversial issues. Beyond that, give it style and tone. Make sure your prose is clear and concise, not over-embellished. We are not a health-food magazine and are not given to the type of exaggeration seen in that type of publication. We use butter, sugar, meat, and alcohol in our recipes; we are not radical vegetarians, although we are interested in those readers."

Mowbray expects writers to turn in a detailed source list with the completed manuscript. He wants names, titles, and phone numbers of experts, as well as photocopies of original materials used in research. "We don't pay until you turn in your source material," he says. "That's fulfilling your obligation." Mowbray doesn't need your notes, but suggests you keep them in your files for at least two years.

Emerge

1700 North Moore Street, Suite 2200
Arlington, VA 22209
(703) 875-0430

Published: 10 times a year; January/February and July/August are combined issues

Circulation: 150,000

Query: George Curry, editor-in-chief
Florestine Purnell, managing editor
Alvin A. Reid, senior editor

Query response time: 6 weeks

Buys: 80 articles out of approximately 300 to 400 unsolicited queries/manuscripts received annually

Guidelines: Available; send SASE

Rights purchased: First NAS

Pays: On publication

Expenses: Pays phone, FAX, and meals when they're in conjunction with interviewing subjects and discussed in advance

Kill fee: 25 percent

Rates:

Type of Article	*Word Length*	*Payment*
Major Feature	2,000 - 2,200	$1,000+
Department	650 - 700	325+

Since the magazine's première in October 1989, readers look to *Emerge* for fresh insights into the issues and events affecting African Americans. The magazine sees itself as a primary source of thoughtful, sophisticated commentary and in-depth reporting about African American life in the '90s.

Emerge readers are Blacks (56 percent male) between the ages of 25 and 40. The majority (86 percent) have attended or graduated from college, and 63 percent work in a professional or managerial position. Their annual household income is $60,500, and 76 percent own their home.

How to Slant Your Ideas to *Emerge*

"Our major topics are politics, environment, economics, and religion," says Alvin A. Reid, senior editor. "Very rarely does a Black magazine offer critical analysis of Black issues and what Black people do. We are serious in our coverage. No matter what we discuss—books, records or movies—we are probing and analytical."

Since it has been 30 years since the civil rights era, *Emerge* can draw upon a plethora of writers who understand the issues Blacks face. The professionals from whom the magazine buys articles have either worked at other news magazines, are graduates of the best schools, or are good writers and competent thinkers.

"We wouldn't have been able to publish this magazine 25 years ago, because our ideal writer is someone who is a product of what we are writing about," says Reid.

Feature articles for this magazine focus on current issues, ideas, or news personalities that are of interest to the successful, well-informed African Americans who make up the target audience.

The magazine also runs feature-length interviews with notable individuals—entertainers, businesspeople, and scholars, among others. These interviews appear in editorial and Q&A format. A 500-word introduction must present the essence of the individual's work and ideas and their distinctive impact on or contribution to the African American community and/or world in general. Occasionally *Emerge* assigns shorter-format interviews to run in one of the publication's departments.

A rundown of *Emerge*'s departments, most of which are open to freelancer's ideas, includes:

- **Capital Scene** is written by Ken Cooper of the *Washington Post*, but *Emerge* does accept queries for the department and can run additional stories in it. Recent topics include the ramifications of free trade on the Caribbean Islands; Black politicians' new power base in Washington; and the current Black Caucus' pressure on presidential budget plans.
- **Cinema** covers what's new and interesting to African American movie-goers and in home videos. In addition to criticism, the column offers behind-the-scenes-reporting on the film industry.
- **Cover to Cover** reviews and provides news on new books or magazines.
- **Destinations** is a travel section showcasing experiences and adventures in far-off places or unique approaches to familiar destinations.

- **Dialogue** is a short Q&A with African American newsmakers or scholars. It usually runs two pages in the magazine and can be up to 1,000 words with a 200-word introduction. Past departments have featured Kgosie Matthews, Alcee Hastings, and John Lewis.
- **Diaspora Watch** runs along the department "International," and usually centers on stories from Africa of interest to *Emerge* readers. Two examples of topics included here are the Barundi elections, and Cuba and its efforts to keep African culture.
- **Education** contains news and trends in teaching and academics and how they pertain to the African American community. Black colleges and desegregation, and African American administrators at predominantly white private schools are examples of topics covered here.
- **Etcetera** are stories or insights that are often humorous and which do not fit into an existing category. Past "Etcetera" pieces have included a feature on how Blacks act at national conventions, and the story of the man next to Martin Luther King, Jr. during the "I Have a Dream" speech.
- **Friendly Fire** offers humorous or satirical commentary on newsmakers and current events, written in a personal editorial tone. While this section is produced by a contributing editor, $50 is offered for ideas used within the department.
- **International** covers all corners of the globe, from an Afrocentric perspective, taking a special interest in Third World and African Diaspora. It runs 650 to 1,200 words, although it is occasionally longer. Sample fare includes Haiti and its deposed president, Black soldiers in Somalia, and racism in Japan.
- **Media** features television and radio shows, their stars, and creators. Sample topics are how the media networks portray African Americans, the new shows for the season that star Blacks, and Hate Radio in St. Louis.
- **Minding Our Business** highlights stories on African American enterprises and entrepreneurs; unique start-up businesses or established businesses that have broken new ground. The department also contains a column by Leon Wynter of *The Wall Street Journal.* One example out of this department includes a story about a New York African cloth company.

- **Perspective** offers writers a chance to include personal thought and experience. Articles may examine a current news topic or center on a topic of the author's choosing. Why African Americans join cults and President Clinton's abandoning civil rights after the election were two contributions.
- **Portfolio** provides critical perspective and news about visual arts and artists. One department covered Jamaican artists, for example.
- **Religion** examines the church and the role it plays in the African American community. One recent issue took a look at Afrocentric stained glass windows in a Dallas church; another featured Black nuns in America.
- **Speaking Volumes** is an interview with the author or publisher of a new book.
- **Sports** highlights newsworthy and current sporting events and people who stage and star in them. One story tallied graduation rates; another put together a Bottom 25 of Division I football teams; and another focused on the retirement of Clarence "Big House" Gaines.
- **Stage Presence** spotlights the world of theater and dance.
- **Take Note** looks at artists, new releases, and trends in the music industry. Features on Ice T and James Brown are just a sampling of what's included here.
- **The Last Word** is a full-page opinion piece that can be on any topic the author chooses. Recent topics have included why gay people should not be in the military, and parents fighting racism.

How to Query *Emerge*

One page or less preferred. Send photo/art ideas.

Although the editors will consider completed manuscripts, they prefer query letters detailing your ideas for a story, accompanied by samples of your published work. When submitting story ideas, keep in mind that a three-month lead time is necessary for meeting a monthly magazine deadline.

"We have several regular freelance contributors, but we are always interested in new writing talent," says Reid.

How to Write for *Emerge*

All articles are judged on newsworthiness, although a number of departments accommodate a writer's opinion and personal observation. Articles that include charts and graphs are well received.

The hallmark of an *Emerge* story is a sophisticated journalistic approach. That means well-written, detailed features that are tightly written and lend themselves to the use of photos, charts, and/or graphics.

"Our readers expect fresh and detailed information from our magazine that only original, diligent reporting can provide," says Reid. "While point of view need not be absent, we feel pure polemics are a poor substitute for real information."

Endless Vacation

3502 Woodview Trace
Indianapolis, IN 46268-3131
(317) 876-1692

Published: Bimonthly

Circulation: 861,000

Query: (Mr.) B. Ancil Davis, associate editor

Query response time: 6 weeks

Buys: About 60 articles out of approximately 2,500 unsolicited queries/manuscripts received annually

Guidelines: Available; send $5 and a 9"x12" SASE for sample

Rights purchased: First NAS

Pays: On acceptance

Expenses: Negotiates items on a case-by-case basis

Kill fee: 25 percent

Rates:

Type of Article	*Word Length*	*Payment*
Feature	1,500 - 2,000	$ 1,000+
Department	800 - 1,200	600+
"Compleat Traveler"	500 - 700	400
"Facts, Fads & Fun Stuff"	200	100 - 300

Endless Vacation is a magazine for vacation travelers who own timeshare resort condominiums. It is published by Resort Condominiums International, Inc., which banks timeshares of more than 2,000 resorts worldwide. Published six times a year, the publication's editorial is focused on travel, recreation, and leisure lifestyle.

The magazine's readership is split evenly between men and women who travel an average of 40 days a year. They own at least one week of timeshare property and are global travelers. The median age is 45; 85 percent are married with an average household income of $57,000. Half have attended college and/or graduate school. Most readers are active in sports, especially fishing, golf, and tennis; enjoy cultural activities; and like to shop while on vacation.

"The people who read our magazine have the means to spend money on recreation and entertainment," says Associate Editor B. Ancil Davis. "Whatever inspires our readers to seek value in vacation ownership also makes them look for value in other areas of their lives. They enjoy a pleasant lifestyle inside and outside the home. They invest in stereo systems, cameras, video recorders, and computers."

How to Slant Your Ideas to *Endless Vacation*

Endless Vacation helps readers find new resort destinations and activities they can participate in while on vacation. Every issue devotes one feature of its editorial to timeshare vacationing, as well as to other vacation ideas.

"We don't focus as much on destinations as we do on vacation ideas surrounding destinations," says Davis. "In other words, the articles are not geared for the armchair business traveler. Our readers are doers, not dreamers. We provide ideas people can definitely do while on vacation, whether it is cultural, sports-related, or dining. The ideas writers send must generally be accessible to most travelers."

The magazine recommends vacation areas to which others have given the thumbs-up. "Our readers don't want to be the first ones on the beach, but to come in just behind the explorers," says Davis. "They want someone else to have ventured there and to have said it's okay."

The magazine offers a mix of mostly North American (70 percent) and some foreign (30 percent) vacation activities. Because in the '90s, people don't seem to be traveling as much internationally, Davis is primarily looking for new stories on destinations in the United States, Canada, and Mexico. "How much people travel tends to be in direct correlation to how strong money is at the time," he says. "We help readers rediscover a place that is not terribly expensive, but still exciting."

One example of a new twist on travel to familiar destinations is a recent feature article that highlighted the African American heritage of four cities—Philadelphia, Washington, D.C., New York City's Harlem, and Atlanta. "The presentation of African American culture had not before been highlighted in *Endless Vacation* as a tourism option," Davis says.

Other slants on tried-and-true vacation spots included a look at Tucson, Arizona as a golfer's escape from the board room atmosphere of Phoenix's courses; and at Fiji's evolution over the last few years as a South Seas paradise. The magazine has also covered the attraction of Colonial Mexico's rich historical and cultural sites, as opposed to the traditional Mexican beach vacation; and a look at Las Vegas as a fun and inexpensive place for families to vacation, highlighting its water park, circus entertainment, and chocolate factory.

"Since the mission of our magazine is to enhance timeshare exchanges for our readers, each issue includes at least one timeshare story," says Davis. "For example, we covered the best beaches in the Canary Islands and the timeshare resorts there."

Departments open to writers include:

- **Compleat Traveler** includes unique travel experiences and gives tips about how to avoid travel hassles and obstacles. It has covered how to put a pet aboard an airplane; how to avoid the pitfalls involved in losing your credit cards during international travel; and an inside look at flashy race car driving schools and jet training schools.

- **Facts, Fads & Fun Stuff** is a compendium of cutting edge tips and trends and is a terrific place to break into this market. News briefs have covered the new space center in Houston; the Cleveland Metro Park Zoo; the Aztec exhibit at the Denver Museum of Natural History; a day trip to Belize, a tiny Central American democracy off the Caribbean Sea; and a look at the new luxury cruise ship, the SSC Radisson Diamond. These are short, newsy items of 200 words.

- **Family Vacationing** is a service-oriented column that looks at ideas for the whole family, such as things to do in cities around the country when you have a four-hour layover in the airport; YMCAs that are open to family vacationers; the best discounts on family airfares; and how to traipse through Egypt with an eight-year-old. Pieces run between 800 to 1,200 words.

- **Healthy Traveler** is open to ideas from freelancers ranging from the best health care on cruise ships to how to avoid ski injuries on the slopes. Length is approximately 800 words.

- **Weekender** is a regional column focusing on either the Northeast, South, Midwest, or West, depending on where its readership is geographically located. Each of the four editions offers short getaways during the timeframe of a weekend, and provides an insider's view of the sports activities, culture, restaurants, and hotel accommodations. This column's information is for the reader who isn't planning to stay in a timeshare, but in a hotel. Column length is 1,200 words.

"American Icons," "Exchanges," and "Traveler's Journal" are closed to freelancers.

How to Query *Endless Vacation*

One page preferred. Most photographs are assigned to independent photographers or bought from a network of stock houses. Only send photo/art ideas to photo editor Connie Boehm if they are terrific. Send seasonal ideas one year in advance.

Queries for this market should include three to four concise paragraphs, indicating the approach, focus, and tone of the proposed article. While Davis doesn't mind writers pitching ideas to him on the phone, he does not want you to call to say you are going to Sweden and wonder if he needs anything. Nor does he want your itinerary; he can't assign a story based on that.

"It's really difficult to tell me what you will write about before you go on a trip because you'll probably have no idea what you will experience," says Davis. "I need you to have a carefully planned vacation idea. But even if we talk about it first, I'll need you to send me at least one written paragraph of how you will approach it. Tell me what your story will contain and, if I haven't worked with you before, I usually like a sample lead and clips."

The majority of articles in *Endless Vacation* are based on topics suggested by freelance writers. When an idea seems right to Davis or another editor, it is brought to an editorial meeting where the potential of the story is discussed.

"We talk about how it might work for us, which issue it would fit into, and if the writer has what it takes to do the piece," says Davis. "If so, we call the writer and go over the story on the phone. We discuss what we like and determine if we are on the same wavelength. A follow-up letter detailing the assignment and a contract is then sent."

How to Write for *Endless Vacation*

"The lead is crucial," says Davis. "If the first sentence doesn't grab our attention, we may never get to the second."

Davis says *Endless Vacation* is looking for a specialized type of writing, primarily from seasoned travel writers. "A lot of people think they can write travel, but there is a vast gap between someone who is a good writer and someone who can write interesting, compelling prose that will make others want to go to that place."

Davis says that a good writer has an awareness of everything around him. "I'm not interested in being shown what I want, but being shown something I don't know I want," he says. "You've got to be able to turn a cliché inside out and make the reader see something in a new, provocative way that compels people to travel."

Upbeat personal experience is key to this magazine. "It brings humanity to the story," says Davis. "It doesn't necessarily have to be your own experience; it can be that of someone you met along the way."

Submit all source material for fact-checking purposes.

Entrepreneur

2392 Morse Avenue
Irvine, CA 92714
(714) 261-2325

Published: Monthly

Circulation: 360,000

Query: Rieva Lesonsky, editor-in-chief

Query response time: 6 to 8 weeks

Buys: About 75 articles/short pieces out of more than 1,000 unsolicited queries received annually

Guidelines: Available; send SASE, and mark the envelope "Attention: Writer's Guidelines"

Rights purchased: First World

Pays: On acceptance

Expenses: Pays phone

Kill fee: 20 percent

Rates:

Type of Article	*Word Length*	*Payment*
Major Feature	2,000	$500
"Business Beat" profile	450	200

Entrepreneur is targeted to small business owners and those who want to begin businesses. It is idea- and action-oriented, offering advice from experts and analysis of new opportunities. Topics cover a broad range, and include office technology, finance, management techniques, business financing, and others.

Nearly 70 percent of the magazine's readers own a business; three-quarters of them intend to start a new or additional business. The median age of readers is 39, with a household income of $62,500.

How to Slant Your Ideas to *Entrepreneur*

Entrepreneur publishes 11 or 12 articles, minimum, per month, and has run more than 20 in one issue at times. In addition, it publishes about 37 columns.

"Because we run so many articles and columns, over half the queries we receive get rejected since we've already done the topic," says Maria Anton, senior managing editor. "You really have to keep up with the magazine and know what we've covered if you're serious about breaking in.

"The magazine's readers are looking for new ideas or strategies to incorporate into their businesses," Anton says. "They want to know about trends, what's hot, advertising, any changes in the business world that affect their industry, and more."

Unlike most magazines, columns and shorter articles are not the break-in point at *Entrepreneur*. Instead, columns are written by regular contributors, and features are purchased from freelancers or are written by one of five staff writers.

The following are some areas open to freelancers:

- **Birth to Billions** profiles highly successful entrepreneurs in a feature of about 2,000 words. Business moguls recently covered include Nike footware founder Phil Knight and the makers of Ben & Jerry ice cream. Although the bulk of this article is the story of the person's road to success, it must be educational as well as informative.
- **Business Beat** is one of the best break-in points in this publication. The lead story to this section at the front of the magazine is a short (about 450 words) profile on a business owner with a unique product or service. One column featured a man who recycles light bulbs into miniature replicas of hot air balloons.

The magazine's remaining 35 to 40 departments are written by regular contributors.

How to Query *Entrepreneur*

One page only; do not send photo/art information.

"We'll take a chance if you have a good idea and your query looks like you can write. But if your query is badly composed, we'll reject it," Anton says. "We have so many good writers who satisfy our needs that we can be picky about new writers."

If your query arrives and it is immediately considered inappropriate, you may have an answer in a week or so. If not, the query may have gone into what Anton refers to as "the query basket." Promising queries collect in the basket for about six weeks until the four top editors hold a "query meeting," where they toss around the ideas and see how the suggested ideas might fit into future issues of the magazine.

Even then, most queries are sent a polite "no." Those writers who earn assignments receive a phone call followed by an assignment letter reiterating the details.

How to Write for *Entrepreneur*

"We need writers who can look beyond the obvious angle and find a new story," Anton says. "We'd reject a query on how to negotiate with your vendor—that's too simple and overdone. But we jumped at a piece that had a news peg—new legislation—and asked, 'Are you suddenly breaking laws by doing the same thing you always have?' That was a fresh angle."

Anton subscribes to most major city magazines and business journals. "I've basically seen it all," she says, warning, that you'll need a unique business angle that hasn't been covered yet.

"Write for a person who owns a small business," Anton urges. "The needs and interests are very different if you are the one responsible for the success or failure of a business."

The feature well is where you'll find psychological articles, general business how-tos and other topics that warrant more length or won't land in a column. For instance, the magazine has published articles on how to keep your staff's spirits up when business is down; how to achieve "flow" (a psychological term for an adrenalin rush); and dealing with the bank when shopping for expansion capital.

Entrepreneur has a stable of writers who specialize in tax, law, and other technical topics, so you're better advised to propose articles in other areas.

"Everyone is entitled to a first time and we're willing to try new writers who have promise," says Anton. "But we probably choose not to work a second time with 80 percent of the writers we try out. We give everyone one chance to rewrite an article, however, and kill only one or two articles per year.

"Because we are a national magazine, writers must be certain to cite experts and others from around the nation, not just near their home," Anton says.

"Many people mistakenly think we are a franchise magazine," Anton says. "But we cover all phases of small business." The magazine publishes a special franchising issue in January, and a business opportunities issue in July. The rest of the year is devoted to general small business topics.

Essence

1500 Broadway
New York, NY 10036
(212) 642-0600

Published: Monthly

Circulation: 950,000

Query: "Back Talk": Gordon Chambers, assistant editor
"Brothers": Audrey Edwards, editor-at-large
"Health": Linda Villarosa, senior editor, health
"Interiors": Valerie Wilson Wesley, executive editor
"Windows": Stephanie Stokes Oliver, editor
(All other queries should be directed to the editor of the appropriate section)

Query response time: 4 to 6 weeks

Buys: About 400 articles/short pieces out of more than 10,000 unsolicited queries received annually

Guidelines: Available; send SASE

Rights purchased: First NAS or One-time

Pays: On acceptance

Expenses: Pays, with prior approval

Kill fee: 25 percent

Rates:

Type of Article	*Word Length*	*Payment*
Major Feature	1,500 - 2,500	$1,500 - 2,000
Parenting Feature	1,000	1,000
Short Feature	750 - 1,000	750 - 1,000
News Brief	250	250
"Back Talk"	800 - 1,000	800 - 1,000
"Brothers"	800	800
"Essentials"	250	250
"Health"	1,000	1,000
"Interiors"	750	750
"Parenting: Gazette"	250	250
"People"	250	250
"Windows"	800	800

The *Essence* reader is a Black woman, 18 to 49 years old, with a median age of 33. More than half of all Black women earning $50,000 or more read the magazine. These readers are well-educated, most of them having attended college. More than a third are married; half have children in the home.

"She is a striver," says Editor Stephanie Stokes Oliver. "She looks to *Essence* to help her move her life forward."

Most of the major features in the well of the magazine begin as ideas from the staff. "The big pieces are usually assigned to writers who have worked with *Essence* before, at least on smaller pieces," Oliver says. "We need to know that someone can bring an additional element to the table once we've presented the idea."

That doesn't mean the magazine is closed to new writers. In fact, the editors are happy to discover new talent. New writers simply start out with a column piece or brief article. About 90 percent of the book is freelanced, and Oliver says the magazine offers a good chance for unpublished writers.

"For example, if you write a short piece for "Parenting: Gazette" and we decide to publish it, you stand a good chance of writing for us again," the editor says.

How to Slant Your Ideas to *Essence*

"The most important thing a prospective writer must know about *Essence* is that it is specialized in a way similar to *Working Woman* or *Esquire*," Oliver says. "For instance, in the health area, the top 10 killer diseases are different for Black women than they are for White women. Our magazine speaks especially to the Black woman in ways a writer should understand."

That isn't to say that the color of a writer's skin determines assignment, Oliver notes. "Any writer who can bring to us solid information about and for Black women can get published in this magazine," she says. "Expertise is important."

Essence publishes a one-year editorial calendar revealing the 12 issue themes for the upcoming year; it is available from the advertising department, not the editorial staff.

The following columns and sections are open to freelancers:

- **Back Talk** is an opinion page for anyone with a strong point of view. Oliver says she likes the column to be controversial and provocative as well as artfully written. The most successful essay she recalls from this column was one by a Black writer, a Harvard-educated attorney, who felt that, in response to the racism he experienced, he overtipped and was oversolicitous with Whites. The column attracted so much mail the magazine ran another reader's response to the first "Back Talk."

- **Brothers** opens a page to African American men. The editors look for essays of about 800 words in which the author shares his feelings about an issue. For instance, one essay was by a man who had agreed at marriage not to have children; now his wife was pregnant and he was angry. Another man wrote about the men whose friendships he had shared since childhood. Because this is an essay, a writer should submit a full manuscript. The editors note that they need more of these essays.
- **Essentials** is often written in house. When the three or four briefs are written by a contributor, they are about 250 words long and can cover everything from using the appropriate bug repellent, to a quiz testing the reader's knowledge of hip-hop words and their definitions.
- **Health** topics, as mentioned earlier, are similar to those covered by other women's magazines. But these articles, about 1,000 words long, should have an awareness that the reader is a young Black woman concerned with health issues that are relevant to her.
- **Interiors** explores a woman's interior world. The articles should be intimate, about subjects close to the heart. Past topics have included the ambivalent feelings of an expatriate about moving back to the United States from Italy; and the outrage of a prominent poet and writer on being denied entry to vacation in a Caribbean country because she wore dreadlocks. The essays should be 750 words long, and the editors ask you to submit a complete manuscript.
- **Parenting: Gazette** features 250-word items of service to new mothers, in particular.
- **People** items, about 250 words long, cover people of note in the arts, as well as entertainers, community activists and book authors.
- **Windows** is a forum for women of diverse cultures who share their ethnic experiences with *Essence* readers. For instance, a Jewish woman wrote about her bat mitzvah; while a Chinese-American woman wrote about feeling "outside" this country's discourse on race because she was not Black or White.

Beauty and fashion pieces are produced in house. "Essentials," "Graffiti," "Health" questions and answers, and "Horoscope" are written by staff members or regular contributors.

How to Query *Essence*

One page preferred, with one idea only; do not send photo or art information; query at least six months ahead for seasonal or theme material; include SASE and daytime phone number.

Oliver asks that prospective *Essence* contributors review several issues of the magazine and request writer's guidelines before attempting to query the magazine. She wants a concise, one-page query that answers the questions, "what, how, who?"

"First, the writer has to sell us," the editor says. "The first paragraph should cover the 'what' of the query—what the story is about. The second paragraph should tell us why *Essence* should cover it, and how it should be done. Finally, we need to know who the writer is, and what credentials he or she has that qualify him or her to write the article."

Most writers submit what Oliver calls a chronology, beginning with an anecdotal lead and continuing through the query as though it were a miniature article. "We just don't have the time to read long queries here," she says. "We want writers to get to the point immediately."

How to Write for *Essence*

Oliver says that her magazine does not have trouble getting the articles it needs. "The editors each have a section for which they are responsible and for which they have to generate ideas," she explains. "So we can assign to known writers and don't have to rely on just queries."

There are some areas, however, for which Oliver is always interested in seeing more. Those include humorous articles that are both entertaining and informative; articles on financial topics, such as how to stay out of debt; and business pieces.

"Since we are a women's service magazine, we will always be interested in how-to, self-help, bulleted articles, and any of those '10 ways to do something' pieces," she adds. "We want to know what women are doing around the country and how African American women are making a difference."

First-time contributors to *Essence* will be asked to write on speculation. After that, regular contractual arrangements are made. Certain articles, such as special sections and food pieces, are assigned on a work-for-hire basis.

Exploring

P.O. Box 152079
Irving, TX 75015-2079
(214) 580-2000

Published: 4 times a year (January, March, May, and September)
Circulation: 350,000
Query: Scott Daniels, executive editor
Query response time: 2 weeks
Buys: About 12 articles out of approximately 200 unsolicited queries/manuscripts received annually
Guidelines: Available; send SASE
Rights purchased: First NAS
Pays: On acceptance
Expenses: Pays all reasonable
Kill fee: None
Rates:

Type of Article	*Word Length*	*Payment*
Major Feature	1,250	$350 - 600
Short Feature	800	250 - 300
"Career File"	750	350
"Dateline: Exploring U.S.A."	250	75 - 100
"It's Easier Than You Think"	750	250 - 350

Exploring is published for registered members of the Exploring program, the young-adult division of the Boy Scouts of America. The purpose of Exploring is to provide community organizations with an effective young-adult program designed to improve character, citizenship, and fitness.

The magazine is written for teenage boys and girls between the ages of 14 and 21 who join Explorer posts. The posts are organized by businesses, industries, religious groups, government agencies, professional societies, civic clubs, labor unions, and other community organizations.

The Explorer post programs match the interests of the youth with the adult expertise and program resources of the organization. For example, a computer center could design a program in data processing and invite young adults interested in this field to join. Or a church might have a number of adults interested in outdoor activities who could provide leadership and program help in an outdoor Explorer post.

How to Slant Your Ideas to *Exploring*

This 12-page magazine, devoid of advertising, strives to display articles of interest to teenagers. It deals with subjects such as careers, entertainment, recreation, and items of particular interest to the Explorer post program.

"These young people are grouped into posts by career interest (medicine, law, nursing, law enforcement, science); or by avocation (photography, art, baseball, surfing, scuba diving, skiing, backpacking, hiking, rafting, canoeing). That is how we look at our editorial as well," says Executive Editor Scott Daniels.

Explorer post event-related stories are easiest to sell to this magazine. Daniels says writers should have no qualms calling up local Explorer executives to learn what kinds of exciting activities are going on in the posts. "In such cases, never say that you are writing for *Exploring* magazine, but that you are trying to sell an idea to *Exploring* and wonder if they have anything going on," says Daniels.

He gives a hypothetical example. "A writer in Seattle might have learned that a group of Sea Explorers is planning to take a spring break cruise on a small-masted sailing ship through the San Juan Islands," says Daniels. "He would contact the local Boy Scout Council (listed in the white pages under Boy Scouts of America) to learn about the trip. If the writer were to contact me five or six months ahead of time, I might be interested. I would check out the story and the writer's clips to see if he could handle the assignment. If I felt he could, I might negotiate a fee for him to cover the adventure. I'd pay for rental car, lodging, and food for as long we decide the person should be on the assignment."

Exploring activities covered include a mock disaster played out by dozens of Explorers and the Columbia, South Carolina, fire department; drills and tests included in the National Law Enforcement Explorer Conference; and the serious side of cold-weather camping as taught at a Scout ranch in New Mexico.

While part of the magazine is Explorer-related—whether covering an activity or giving details for how to do things in Explorer post programs—the rest of the editorial is of interest to all teens. "We like good pieces on relationships with peers and parents, how to handle money, or how to get into the college of your choice," says Daniels.

Exploring is also intrigued by personality profiles of young Explorers. "Look for dynamic individuals who have been recognized by the Exploring program for doing the unusual," says Daniels. "One writer queried us on a member of a police Explorer post who was recognized by the Governor of Illinois for outstanding service." It was ideal. It included comments from friends and described the kinds of activities in which that police Explorer post became involved.

Another way to give your article a fighting chance with this magazine is to make sure it has strong visuals that can be photographed or illustrated. "To be honest, teens are attracted by art. It pulls them in. The article has to be visually stimulating as well as have interesting editorial," says Daniels.

As a rule, the magazine runs one or two one-page features, two two-page features, and one three-page feature. Daniels determines the length of articles based on the topic proposed and the availability of quality photography or illustrations.

Following are the regular sections open to freelancers:

- **Career File** reviews up-and-coming careers. "We utilize the *U.S. Department of Labor Occupational Handbook* to see what career job titles currently offer faster-than-average growth opportunities," says Daniels. "We don't want to be in the business of promoting careers that are outdated."

  A sampling of career fields the magazine has covered includes child care, correction officers, financial planning, flight attendants, hotel management, nursing, physical therapy, and speech pathology.

- **Dateline: Exploring U.S.A.** is the inside cover news brief section. It includes one to five items relevant to Explorers, be they interesting occurrences, activities, or upcoming conferences. Daniels says it is rare that he gets submissions for this column, but he is open to writers who have short, relevant items.

- **It's Easier Than You Think** discusses typical business, protocol, and organizational topics that come up at Explorer meetings, such as how to introduce a guest speaker, brainstorm a super activity, or raise money for a trip.

How to Query *Exploring*

One-page queries preferred; describe ideas for photo/art; pitch ideas three months in advance of an event and six months in advance for seasonal stories.

"Your query letter should get right to the point," says Daniels. "We don't need sample leads or quotes, but it must be evident that you know the market. And don't send manuscripts. It's ridiculous to think that you would pound out a lot of effort before you knew if I was interested in the topic."

Most of the pieces in *Exploring* are assigned to a dependable stable of freelance writers. "We reject 99 percent of the queries and manuscripts we receive over the transom," says Daniels. "Mainly it's because the writers have not seen the magazine and are unfamiliar with the Explorer program."

Each year, however, Daniels says the magazine picks up one or two new writers. "They send solid queries that are on target as far as word length, tone, and style, and they send clips that let me see where they've been published in the past," says Daniels.

How to Write for *Exploring*

When writing for *Exploring,* remember that you are writing for teens. The tone should be upbeat and bright and the action should move along rapidly, but don't write down or simplify your language. Be succinct.

Less is usually more in most cases. "When you only have 1,200 words to work with, you need a fast start, lively writing, and bright quotes from youths, typically 16- to 17-year-olds," says the editor. "Teens prefer to read what other teens have to say. If an adult has expertise on the subject, fine. But when possible, bring out quotes from the Explorer post member in charge of the activity. *Exploring* prides itself in being a youth-operated program."

Family Circle

110 Fifth Avenue
New York, NY 10011
(212) 463-1000

Published: 17 times a year

Circulation: 26 million

Query: Susan Kelliher Ungaro, deputy editor

Query response time: 1 to 2 months

Buys: More than 200 articles/short pieces out of more than 10,000 unsolicited queries received annually

Guidelines: Available; send SASE

Rights purchased: All

Pays: On acceptance

Expenses: Pays usual items with prior approval

Rates:

Type of Article	*Word Length*	*Payment*
Major Feature	1,000 - 2,500	$1,000 - 2,500
Special Reports	2,000 - 5,000	2,000 - 5,000
"Women Who Make a Difference"	1,500	1,500 - 2,000
Essay	750 - 1,500	750 - 1,500

"Our readers are active, involved women in their communities," says Susan Kelliher Ungaro, deputy editor. The majority of the magazine's 27 million readers fall between the ages of 18 and 49, with the median age hovering around 43. Nearly three quarters own their home and have a median household income of $36,000. The majority of readers are employed; nearly 25 percent are working mothers.

Family Circle offers readers advice and practical information to assist them in managing the many relationships they juggle with their husbands, children, parents, friends, and community.

With this kind of mission to guide its editorial mix, you'll find *Family Circle* covers a variety of topics, including parenting, health, diet and fitness, money and jobs, education, the environment and community issues, family vacations, the home —including decorating, gardening, arts and crafts, and cooking— as well as beauty and fashion.

How to Slant Your Ideas to *Family Circle*

"We don't underestimate our reader's intelligence," says Ungaro. "We believe that our readers are well informed. They watch the news or read a newspaper, so they know what's going on in their community and beyond."

As part of its editorial mix, *Family Circle* publishes a journalistic "Special Reports" in every issue. Contemporary social issues are most often the subjects of "Special Reports." Articles falling under this category include teen sexuality, migrant workers, domestic violence, right-to-die issues, and adoption scams. "This is the place where we report on problems that people and society are facing, plus offer insight into what you need to know to protect yourself and your family, or to take action," Ungaro explains.

Special sections on subjects such as health care, child care, and education are also scheduled six to 10 times a year. They are usually comprised of several articles on one general topic. The pieces, published together in the magazine, range from lengthy research updates to collections of brief sidebars, often written by more than one person. The sections generally run about 3,000 words, including sidebars.

"Special sections are almost always assigned to freelancers," notes Ungaro. Examples of special sections on health that have appeared include "Your Breasts: A Good Health Guide," "Body Image Obsession," and "What Scares Men Most: The Truth About Prostate Cancer."

The magazine also is well-known for its dramatic narratives of ordinary people overcoming difficult challenges. These articles have ranged from a woman who rescued an elderly neighbor from a terrifying fire; women who brought hope and help to a devastated poor community in the days after Hurricane Andrew; and one woman's narrative of how she turned her life around after marrying "Mr. Wrong."

Writers who can capture what's going on in the world outside of the Big Apple and in small-town America hold a special appeal to editors like Ungaro. "We crave writers who are living in places outside of New York, Los Angeles, and Chicago, who can tell us what people are concerned about. The best reporters help our editors—who aren't getting out of our offices as much as they'd like to—tap into trends and social issues concerning middle America."

The following types of articles are sought by the editors of *Family Circle*:

- **Child care and teen years** features help readers cope with the anxieties and frustrations of raising children and teenagers.
- **Diet and body-shaping** reports share new fitness tips with readers. With expert sources who will grant you an interview your copy could find a fit here.
- **Elder care** articles address the challenges faced by the "sandwich generation," who must care simultaneously for their own young children and their aging parents.
- **First person or as-told-to** articles chronicle the personal battles waged and won by courageous women. These stories, many told in first person, explore problems experienced by many women—problems that can seem hopeless and insoluble. Articles in this column have covered diet struggles, loss of a job, and poor self image.
- **Health** articles are a good spot for freelancers to target. These pieces cover a range of health news topics that are pertinent to every age group. Past features have included new ways to put an end to chronic pain, and how to cure mystery rashes. To succeed in getting an assignment in this section, you'll need qualified medical sources, proven ability to research a topic, and good case studies to tell the story.
- **Humorous essays** are always in demand. The essays *Family Circle* seeks target readers' funny bones, chuckling at some of life's lighter moments. While Andy Rooney and other well-known humorists are sometimes featured, essays by freelancers who are not household names have also been published.
- **Money and personal finance** articles offer readers tips on ways to get more for their money. Articles have reported on how to save money with credit cards and updates on financial planning. Contributors must have access to financial experts to get an assignment.
- **Psychology** reporting gives readers a helping hand with problems that everyone is likely to face at one time or another. For example, one column offered advice on how to get along with people who bug you.
- **Special Reports** provide in-depth, investigative coverage on topics that are of vital importance to readers' health and well-being. A diversity of subjects—from toxic schools to migrant worker exposés—have been featured here.

The following regular columns are open to freelancers:

- **Pets** is a periodic column that updates animal lovers on how to take good care of a pet.
- **Pharmacy Facts** is designed to safeguard readers' health with practical information concerning prescriptions and over-the-counter drugs. "Dangerous Medication Mistakes Parents Make," written by a freelancer, shared useful advice on safely administering medicine to children.
- **Women Who Make a Difference** appears in every issue and captures what *Family Circle* is all about. The successful women profiled here are role models who *volunteer* their time for a special cause or service. Their contributions to education, ecology, disaster relief, and the poor make the world a better place to live. The magazine editors are eager to profile women from across the country. If you know of a hometown hero, you've got the makings of a good query for this section. Send along local newspaper clips about your subject, if available. This is one of the best places to break in at *Family Circle.*

"Circle This," "The Early Years," "Full Circle," "Medical News," "Priorities," "Shop Smart," "Your Money," and beauty, fashion, craft, garden, and home decorating features are written by regular contributors or staff writers.

How to Query *Family Circle*

One- to two-page queries preferred. Do not send photo/art information. Query up to one year in advance for seasonal material.

"Generally, a good proposal starts out with a dramatic statement, a shocking statistic, or something that's going to make me, an editor who reads so many proposals and articles and other publications, take notice," says Ungaro. "You need to sell your ideas in the initial letter."

Yet it's surprising how many people don't take this advice to heart, as she says. "Many writers think that they don't have to do very much research to propose a story. That shows in the query," comments Ungaro.

"If you really want to sell a story, I don't think it's unreasonable for a person to make a few phone calls to verify their information. Listing whom you will interview isn't enough," says Ungaro. "To be able to write an intelligent proposal, you should be interviewing and quoting an expert or two. These interviews will help you formulate a good proposal. The expert may even give you the name of a patient or client, or someone in the community whose story will grab the editor's attention."

Ungaro passes along another useful tip for beginning freelancers: "It's very smart to send your query to somebody low on the masthead. Try sending it to an editorial assistant or associate editor. They're trying to move up, and they're looking for good story ideas. These staff members receive less mail than senior editors who are swamped with material," adds Ungaro.

When a good query reaches the desk of a senior editor, the idea is passed along to Ungaro. If the proposal meets Ungaro's requirements, it's routed to Jackie Leo, editor-in-chief. "If Jackie thinks it's a good idea then the senior editor will be given a go-ahead to assign the story," says Ungaro. This process can take up to two months before a writer hears a response.

How to Write for *Family Circle*

"The key thing for any writer to understand is who the editor believes is reading her magazine," says Ungaro. "Our reader cares about the world around her, but also wants to know about solutions.

"Writers for *Family Circle* have to approach any story with a fresh angle," Ungaro continues. "For it to be of interest to us and to our reader, it must have a news hook, new research or findings, or identify a new trend. Our stories look for the positive.

"Ultimately, people want to be well informed. But reporting on devastating hunger and sicknesses in society exclusively gets us nowhere. We report on the serious issues of the day. But there must be a takeaway point so the reader and her family will be more aware, better prepared, or more compassionate about each problem," the editor says.

Family Circle encourages writers and editors to stay in touch once an assignment has been made. "I think it's a mistake for a writer not to call an editor if she has a question when working on a piece," Ungaro says. For example, if you're considering three different leads to a story and can't decide which is best, call the editor for some guidance. "I think that's smart," the editor concludes. "As long as your call doesn't take an hour, it's a good idea to keep the relationship going. You have to have respect for the editor's time, but editors are going to respect writers who want to get the story right."

Family Fun

P.O. Box 929
Northhampton, MA 01060-0920
(413) 585-0444

Published: Bimonthly with an additional four special issues per year

Circulation: 400,000

Query: Alexandra Kennedy, executive editor

Query response time: 4 to 8 weeks

Buys: About 60 articles/stories out of approximately 2,500 unsolicited queries/manuscripts received annually

Guidelines: Available; send SASE

Rights purchased: First NAS

Pays: On acceptance

Expenses: Pays items if reasonable; as determined at time of assignment

Kill fee: 25 percent

Rates:

Type of Article	*Word Length*	*Payment*
Major Feature	3,000	$1,500
Short Feature	1,500	750
News Brief	300	100
"Family Almanac"	300	150
"Family Traveler"	100 - 200	75
"Mom, Dad & the Kids"	1,500	1,000+
"My Great Idea"	1,200 - 1,500	1,000

Family Fun targets active parents with children between the ages of three and 12. The editorial surrounds all the great things that families can do together—travel, sports, cooking, parties, celebrations, learning projects, home computing, and arts and crafts.

The magazine aims to be a resource for parents who are dedicated to the idea of having a good time with their children. Almost 90 percent of readers are married; 86 percent have attended college; and the median household income is $47,150. The average number of children per reader household is two; and 89 percent of these children are between the ages of three and 12.

How to Slant Your Ideas to *Family Fun*

The magazine's readers are parents who are looking for ideas and information on how to spend quality time with their kids. "Our readers want step-by-step how-tos for the activities that we feature," says Alexandra Kennedy, executive editor. "They also want suggested books to read and phone numbers to call for more information."

This magazine does *not* offer advice for child-rearing. "The biggest mistake a writer can make is to send us a query on sibling rivalry or how to discipline a three-year-old," says Kennedy. "There are plenty of good magazines that offer tips on raising children. We want *Family Fun* to be a resource for parents on everything from fun craft projects to great places to go camping."

Family Fun readers are budget-conscious and smart about how they shop. "We avoid ideas that require parents to go out and spend $100 on supplies before they can start a project," says Kennedy. "Writers should submit ideas for projects that can be easily managed by a family on a Saturday afternoon or a weekday night."

One freelanced piece, "A Child's Magic Garden," told how to give kids a garden space of their own. It suggested creative ideas for a child-friendly garden, including a bean teepee and pumpkin tattooing. Another article idea that hit the mark was a family crafts piece on how to make a "Little House on the Prairie" homestead with sticks, stones, and acorns. It was simple, but clever. "We want straightforward, classic ideas with great twists as opposed to wild, obscure ideas," says Kennedy. "We are more likely to do a story on a national park adventure than a trip to Bali."

The editors turn to an established stable of freelance writers for most feature stories. Although Kennedy says *Family Fun* would rarely assign a feature to a new writer, there are several smaller columns at the front of the magazine that freelancers can use to prove themselves. An established book author, who has written on a specific topic, however, can land a major feature without having written for the magazine before.

The following departments are open to freelancers:

- **Family Almanac** is a great section for new writers to make an entry into the magazine. This section is a hodgepodge of 300-word blurbs on short projects and creative learning activities, from how to build a cardboard-box playhouse, to simple experiments to do in rainy-day puddles.

  Sometimes, when a writer has submitted successfully several times to "Family Almanac," he or she will get an assignment to pursue a feature article. Occasionally, according to Kennedy, a query to this section warrants a longer article and a writer earns a feature assignment.

- **Family Traveler** is full of brief newsy blurbs on fun family trips. The subhead to the section, "What's new, what's great and what's a deal" sums up the kind of contributions the editor seeks. Past contributions have included everything from guided walks to see elephant seals off the California coast, to visiting a working farm in North Carolina, to a winter getaway at a Minnesota lodge.
- **Mom, Dad & the Kids** looks for essays about the things that make families special, such as traditions, trips, and nature experiences. Humorous essays about family life also can find a home here. One writer/parent sent confessions of his life as an elementary school carpool driver; another sold a tongue-in-cheek piece on how his children grew up and developed talents that he and his wife never expected them to have.

  A third winning submission was an essay on a family's white water rafting trip in which the writer described what he learned about his children by going on such a family adventure. Another writer wrote about his family's tradition of attending minor league baseball games as a way to instill his love of baseball in his own children.
- **My Great Idea** shares the innovative and creative ideas families have devised. "Oliver's Trail" told of a family that cultivated a tiny nature preserve right in their own backyard. They let a small corner of the yard overgrow and made signs describing plants and maps to guide the way. "This idea is so original and fresh, yet very simple," says Kennedy.

  Another idea for this section included a story about a family writing, photographing, and producing a creative picture book called *My Tyro.* The article explained how a man and his two sons wrote a poem about having a tyrannosaurus for a pet and included snapshots to illustrate it. Working together, they created a wonderful family book.

"Family Computing," "Good Sports," "Home Cooking," "Learning Together," and "Reviews" are written by regular columnists.

How to Query *Family Fun*

Any length queries can be sent; do not send photos/art.

Query letters should clearly explain what makes the idea special or particularly satisfying for the writer's own family. Kennedy likes a query letter to reveal that the writer has spent time reading the magazine. "I love it when a writer studies the magazine carefully and has a good sense of how and where the article would fit in," Kennedy notes.

By reading the magazine, prospective writers will learn that quoting experts will not win points with Kennedy. "I don't want opinions from psychologists," she says. "This magazine is about parents talking to parents. We avoid child-rearing jargon."

Appropriate clips of previously published work should accompany your query letter.

How to Write for *Family Fun*

Family Fun's writing style is upbeat and straightforward. Kennedy wants writers who are good reporters and who have tested out their ideas. "Our writers have to have a sense of what parents want and what is going to attract them," says Kennedy. "The ideal writer is a parent who has already tried what he or she is suggesting with his or her own family. We have one writer who picks an educational topic, does ten projects on that subject with her kids, and picks the family's top three favorites to write about."

Assignments are given over the phone with a written follow-up letter and contract. Whether or not Kennedy has contact with a writer during the writing process is relative to the deadline. "If the deadline is tight, I normally want to communicate with the writer during the process to make sure that we are going to get what we need," the editor explains.

Field & Stream

2 Park Avenue
New York, NY 10016
(212) 779-5285

Published: Monthly

Circulation: 2 million

Query: Articles: Duncan Barnes, editor
Regional edition articles: Cathy Meyers, associate editor

Query response time: 4 to 6 weeks

Buys: About 250 articles out of approximately 3,500 unsolicited queries/manuscripts received annually

Guidelines: Available; send SASE

Rights purchased: First NAS

Pays: On acceptance

Expenses: Pays only with written consent of editors; regional editions pay the portion of phone and postal research expenses exceeding $25

Kill fee: Only on assignment; most work done on speculation

Rates:

Type of Article	*Word Length*	*Payment*
Feature and photo package	1,500 - 2,100	$ 800+
Back-of-the-book	900 - 1,200	500
Regional edition	300 - 750	250 - 600
"By the Way"	50 - 600	75 - 450+
"Field & Stream Junior"	25 - 600	50 - 500+
"Finally"	500 - 750	750+
"Food"	750 - 1,200	800 - 1,000
"Guest Shot"	1,000 - 1,500	800+
"How It's Done" filler	500 - 900	250
"Humor"	1,000 - 1,200	800+
Cartoon		100

Field & Stream is an outdoor service magazine. "The big difference between our publication and others in this field is that we stress the magazine's literary tradition and emphasize the *whole* hunting and fishing *experience*," says Editor Duncan Barnes. "We have been a leader in conservation and sporting ethics for 100 years and that will continue."

Field & Stream readers are active outdoorsmen. Nearly half of the magazine's readers are college-educated and work at the professional manager level. The average age is 38.

"The magazine is read and passed along to friends," says Barnes. "We have two million paid subscribers, but our readership is 14.5 million."

How to Slant Your Ideas to *Field & Stream*

How-to articles for *Field & Stream* must be national in scope plus offer some special insights or a new slant or idea on fishing and hunting. "This is an excellent market for both men and women writers, but you have to know something about fishing, hunting, and the outdoors," says Barnes. Pieces range from 1,200 to 2,000 words.

The magazine also publishes nostalgia and descriptive writing or ("mood pieces") on hunting and fishing. "Yesterday's Bass" was one writer's look at the changing world of bass fishing, suggesting that readers tired of fishing in the fast lane should step back and slow down.

Profiles are also common fare. A recent piece described the late Jim Corbett, who hunted India's man-eating tigers, and as a pioneer conservationist, helped save those animals from extinction. Profiles on interesting living people with direct ties to hunting and fishing are also in demand.

Recently, *Field & Stream* changed the graphic design of the magazine, which significantly impacted the editorial as well. "We are always looking for new ways to present the material," says Barnes. "Study the magazine. Look for how we're integrating art and photos into the text and how we are making more use of sidebars. Note that the sidebars now lean to new and unusual ideas. Instead of a deer-hunting sidebar discussing the kind of rifle used or clothing worn, you're more likely to find addenda on how a deer hunter can study cloud formations to predict the weather."

The editors place heavy emphasis on the quality of the writing. The following departments are open to freelancers:

- **By the Way** is a national column that uses short articles about natural history as it relates to hunting or fishing, as well as how-to shorts and offbeat outdoor material.
- **Field & Stream Junior** is published every other month for young sportsmen ages nine to 12. One issue covered fishhook facts; why geese fly in a V-formation; and collecting tracks to keep a record of wildlife in the area. This section also uses short real-life adventure pieces and profiles on

wildlife experts. "Be careful," says Barnes, "younger readers are less experienced, but don't underwrite as if you are talking to a six-year-old."

- **Finally** is published six times a year. It is a short, self-contained essay of 500 to 750 words. Pieces are highly opinionated or evocative.
- **Food** looks at the way interesting outdoors people use cooking techniques or recipes that relate directly to hunting and fishing. The "chefs" must be knowledgeable outdoors people or else cook for them—and they must have something interesting to say.
- **Guest Shot** is a mood piece or philosophical essay that appears on a fairly regular basis. "We want these pieces to be personal," says Barnes. "There is no absolute formula, but the articles we publish convey a wide range of hunting and fishing experiences. How-to does not belong in this department. For this section, we prefer finished manuscripts over queries."
- **How It's Done** are fillers of fishing and hunting tips and news items. They tell how an outdoor technique is accomplished or a device is made.
- **Humor** must revolve around some aspect of a hunting or fishing experience. The piece should be short and touch on some foible or situation that most readers could relate to. This is the hardest category to pull off and the editors prefer the full manuscript over a query letter.
- **Regional Edition** articles are designed to provide specific where-to-go regional hunting and fishing information, plus small doses of relevant how-to.

  "We are looking for specifics in regional stories to help readers plan their trips," says Barnes. "We want the names and addresses of places, guides, bait shops, shooting supply stores, campgrounds, and Chambers of Commerce. Writers must submit all reference material and a list of contacts so the facts can be updated if necessary."

How to Query *Field & Stream*

One page preferred, double-spaced; send photos with query whenever possible; 35 mm color transparencies preferred.

"Most queries are turned down because they are not focused," says Barnes. "Make sure the point of your story comes across clearly. The editors need to be able to grasp your point."

Barnes says that slant, organization, and good writing are essential in a query, as is brevity. "We want a short, compact query lead that explains what you are going to write about," the editor continues. "Clearly state your angle. Brief sketches of some of the anecdotes you might use in the completed article can help an editor judge your material and your writing ability. Three to five short paragraphs should really do it."

Barnes is less interested in clips than in a well-written query. "The quality of the query sells the idea," he says. Acceptance of a query at *Field & Stream* is almost always on speculation. A go-ahead letter will be sent that contains suggestions on ways the editor would like the article developed or elements that should be included, but writers should be warned that this in no way guarantees that the final article will be purchased. Articles are occasionally returned with suggested revisions. If the article is subsequently purchased, the writer will receive a contract. At the discretion of the editors, unacceptable pieces may be returned with a kill fee.

How to Write for *Field & Stream*

Barnes says *Field & Stream* publishes the best writers in the business. "These writers have great command of the English language, a tremendous amount of practical experience as hardcore hunters and fishermen, and an ability to combine how-to tips with power writing."

Most manuscripts rejected are because of poor grammar, spelling, and punctuation, lack of originality, and unsuitable subject matter.

Writing styles vary in the magazine. Filler stories are written in a how-to tone; feature articles give in-depth information on hunting or fishing, or on issues such as game and resource management. Mood pieces, reporting, and profiles require different styles.

"Study the style of writing the magazine typically uses for the type of article you plan to write," says Barnes.

First for Women

270 Sylvan Avenue
Englewood Cliffs, NJ 07632
(201) 569-9094

Published: 17 times a year

Circulation: 1.5 million

Query: Jane Traulsen, editor-in-chief
Teresa Hagan, managing editor

Query response time: 4 weeks

Buys: About 150 articles out of approximately 5,000 unsolicited queries/manuscripts received annually

Guidelines: Available; send SASE

Rights: First NAS, but buys All when appropriate

Pays: On acceptance

Expenses: Pays mileage, phone, and other items when approved in advance

Kill fee: 20 percent

Rates:

Type of Article	*Word Length*	*Payment*
Major Feature	2,500 - 3,500	$2,500 - 3,500*
Short Feature	750 - 1,200	750 - 1,200
"Nutrition"	300	300
"Profiles"	300	300

**Longer, more difficult stories pay more*

"*First for Women* broadens the definition of the service magazine by folding human interest stories and entertainment into traditional service topics," says Jane Traulsen, editor-in-chief. Three-fourths of the women who read *First* work outside the home. The median age is about 33, and the median household income is about $35,000. More than 40 percent have attended college, and 53 percent have children living at home.

How to Slant Your Ideas to *First for Women*

"Out of the 124 pages we run each issue, 80 are editorial, which means we offer a larger editorial well than most service magazines—and the magazine is published every three weeks," says Traulsen. "If you know of a good story that illustrates a compelling problem and an interesting resolution, send it to us. Or, if you just have a good story about the way people cope today, I'd be interested in seeing it."

While the staff writes a lot of the magazine in house, Traulsen says virtually all of the magazine is open to freelancers. "We are looking for entertaining stories that women will find interesting and amusing," she says. "For example, we run a number of shorter articles on love, sex, and marriage in which we try to have fun with the latest behavioral research. If you learn of a new study, don't just report it; try to apply it to our magazine and develop a compelling second-day angle for it. Discover a new twist that readers will find interesting even after they've read headlines on the subject in their daily newspaper or in a news magazine," the editor-in-chief adds.

Other article categories include health, behavioral topics, parent/child relationships, love relationships, consumer tips, and travel. In addition to advice from experts, *First* likes to offer insights and solutions from real people. An article on infertility gave couples' experiences with various forms of treatment and reported the costs they incurred.

"We also like to use celebrities as an element in service packages," says Traulsen. "In an article on coping with stress, we interviewed Deborah Norville and included the coping mechanisms used by Reba McIntyre, Delta Burke, Michael Jackson, and Shannen Doherty of 'Beverly Hills 90210.'"

The front of the book includes shorter, newsier items about health, nutrition, beauty, and entertainment.

The following columns are written by regular contributors: "Crossword," "Doctor on Call," "Horoscope," "Numerology," and "Talking About Sex."

How to Query *First for Women*

One page or shorter preferred; send photo/art suggestions if they are unique to the idea; send seasonal material five to six months in advance.

Traulsen says she has no preconceived notion of how a query should be structured. What's most important is that it captures an editor's attention.

How to Write for *First for Women*

"It's very important for writers to develop their own voice, unless they are experts reporting on a topic in their field," says Traulsen. "We don't like to have one style overtake the magazine. Some articles are newsy, others are emotional, still others are straightforward. Some move along at a quick pace; others work with a more leisurely tone. It all depends on the writer and the subject matter."

Fitness

110 Fifth Avenue
New York, NY 10011
(212) 463-1903

Published: Bimonthly

Circulation: 400,000

Query: Rona Cherry, editor-in-chief

Query response time: 3 to 4 weeks

Buys: About 15 to 20 articles/stories out of approximately 800 unsolicited queries/manuscripts received annually

Guidelines: Available; send SASE

Rights purchased: All

Pays: On acceptance

Expenses: Pays phone and travel

Kill fee: 20 percent

Rates:

Type of Article	*Word Length*	*Payment*
Major Feature	1,500 - 2,000	$1,500 - 2,000
Short Feature	1,000	1,000
Department	650 - 1,200	650 - 1,200
News Brief	150	150

You don't have to look further than the title on the cover of this magazine to get a glimpse of its editorial stand. Tucked inside the letter "F" in "Fitness" are the words "Mind, Body, Spirit." A publication of *New York Times* Women's Magazine Group, this relatively new book grew out of a *Family Circle Great Ideas* annual supplement. It went quarterly in 1992 and bimonthly in 1993, under the editorial direction of Editor-in-Chief Rona Cherry.

"This magazine contains news and articles that feed a reader's mind as well as her body," says Cherry. "It's important for us to reflect the realities of the nineties and to help keep readers thinking actively, in the same way they are exercising their bodies actively. We have a much more holistic sense of fitness. When we say 'mind, body, and spirit,' we really touch all of those areas. Editorial integrity and good journalism are paramount."

The woman who turns to this magazine is not an exercise fanatic. Rather, she is a mainstream woman who shoulders many demands. She's not obsessed with a hard body, but taking care of herself is an important part of her life.

"Some readers are very active and committed to fitness," says Cherry. "Others know what they should be doing to stay in shape, but with all the demands on them, they find it tough to do."

Demographics show that 90 percent of *Fitness* readers are women; the median age is 30. Readers are almost evenly split between marrieds and singles, and 30 percent have children. Most are employed outside the home, with a median household income of $42,300.

How to Slant Your Ideas to *Fitness*

Before approaching this magazine, Cherry suggests reading several back issues to get a clear sense of the tone.

Then, step into the mind of a 28- to 32-year-old woman and try to determine whether your angle seems fresh enough and strong enough to interest her.

"Unlike the baby boom generation, which grew up debating such controversial concepts as the link between diet and cancer and the mind/body connection, these are just a part of life for today's 20- and 30-year-olds," says Cherry. "Health-food stores used to be for health fanatics, now there is one in every shopping mall. Today, there's a different attitude about fitness, but there's still a lot of confusion. That is where the magazine steps in to help. With solid reporting, we answer questions like, 'Should you get beta-carotene from pills or food?' or 'Do fat-burning drugs really work?'"

Each issue of *Fitness* includes full workout regimens like "Streamlined by Summer," an eight-week workout to sculpt hips, thighs, and buttocks. "Just Add Water," offered the latest information on water workouts, including equipment, exercise swim tapes, and fashion—from suits that cover every move you make, to high-style suits that show off workout payoffs.

The magazine also includes a 16- to 24-page workbook printed on a different weight and color of paper to distinguish it from the rest of the book. It covers specific fitness topics in depth. For example, one issue included the workbook, "Dropping 10 Pounds Now!" The piece started by warning readers that they might not even need to lose 10 pounds in the first place. It offered a quiz to help readers find out if they'd really be happy 10 pounds leaner or if they have an obsession with a too-thin physique. The remainder of the pages offered progressive steps for gaining muscle and speeding the fat-burning process. Finally, it ended with new look-thinner clothes to wear while losing weight—or until starting to loose it.

In addition to workouts, Cherry is looking for well-reported, health-oriented features that are provocative and solidly researched. The article, "The Pill and Breast Cancer," examined the renewed debate over the possible connection between the rise in breast cancer incidence and the increase in the number of women who rely on contraceptive pills as their primary method of birth control. Another piece, "The Tobacco Industry's Last Frontier—Us!" told how selling cigarettes as a diet aid, funding female fitness, and supporting female candidates have all paid off for tobacco companies. In "Covering Your A__," the writer looked at the juxtaposition between excessive clothing of yesteryear that hampered women's workouts to today's bare-backed thong leotards.

The magazine's table of contents is divided into categories with these six labels: "Exercise & Sport," "Fashion & Beauty," "Food & Nutrition," "Health & Medicine," "Love & Sex," and "Mind & Body." Within those categories, you'll find a mix of features and columns. Columns are not identified on the contents page, but are called out inside the book by slugs at the top of the pages.

"I like to keep the departments fluid," says Cherry. "I can run a column one month and not the next, and if something comes along that I think would make a new department, I create one. Most of the time, I prefer to respond to an idea and figure out where to put it, rather than having the writer try to determine just where a piece fits."

The following is a sampling of *Fitness* departments open to freelancers:

- **Behind Closed Doors** covers sexual topics as they relate to fitness, but the emphasis is on relationships. One article talked about how exercise has a tremendous impact on losing sexual hang-ups. Another told how men and women can enhance sexual pleasure if they both learn to do Kegel exercises.

- **Bouncing Back** provides inspiration for anyone who has felt let down, such as a story about Olympic gymnast Kim Zmeskal, who slipped from the balance beam at the 1992 Games in Barcelona and shattered her dream of becoming an Olympic gold medal winner.

- **Breaking Away** is a travel department with a fitness angle. "My First Time" was a first-person story about a novice bike tourer's inn-to-inn experience. The department has included service sidebars on buying a bike, tour packages, and exercises to get in gear.

- **Eating Right and Light** offers information and recipes about different types of food. "Entertaining Mediterranean Style" combined the knowledge of a scientist and nutritionist to discuss the merits of this kind of food. The piece then talked about why Mediterranean food is so appealing and gave directions for easy-to-prepare-ahead meals. In another article, "Spa Salads To Go," four spa chefs gave tips on how to make nutritious salads. It was accompanied by the sidebar, "Cool Carriers," showing how to tote salads to work in style.
- **Living Naturally** includes topics such as "Nutritional Bodyguards," a report on the importance of beta-carotene's anti-oxidant effects in preventing cancer, heart disease, and cataracts.
- **Look Good, Feel Good** pieces have covered topics like "Over-Exercised Hair," which gave pointers on keeping sweat, salt, and the sun from turning hair into straw; and "Post-Workout Fragrances," which offered advice on new, invigorating scents that can extend your after-gym "up."
- **Mind Fitness** delves into the psychological realm of fitness like how early sports experiences can haunt a woman later in life, and three ways to boost exercise determination.
- **Standouts** salutes endeavors to promote fitness. One piece gave kudos to businesses that take workers' health to heart by profiling the wellness programs at 10 large companies.
- **Thrills** covers fitness adventures. One writer wrote about her experience during a three-day sea-kayak and camping trip.
- **Vital Questions** is an interview with a leading expert who provides answers to questions like, "Are you protein deficient?" and "Do healthy women jiggle?" The first article delved into how women who eat lots of fruits and vegetables and exercise may actually not be consuming enough protein. The latter offered views on how fatness and fitness are connected and how women can develop a more healthful approach to weight loss.

"Testing," a column that rates consumer fitness products, is written by a regular contributor. "Fitbuzz," the upfront news section, and "Fitpoll" are also generally written in house.

*H*ow to Query *Fitness*

One-page queries preferred; do not send any photo/art information. Query six months or more in advance for seasonal material.

"It's important to me that writers present clean, well-written queries," says Cherry. "I want to learn the idea for the piece, the experts to be interviewed, a sense of how the story will be organized, and what the person has written in the past. A query is like a résumé. It's got to be strong because that's all I have to get a clear sense of the writer."

If the editors of *Fitness* want you to pursue a piece for them, you'll get a phone call to discuss the parameters, followed by a written contract.

*H*ow to Write for *Fitness*

"Our writing style is direct, authoritative, friendly, lively, and upbeat. And, it's chatty—like standing by the backyard fence to talk with a neighbor," says Cherry.

Articles must also be well-reported and balanced. "We want solid, current information—not studies from 20 years ago."

Cherry wants writers to turn in a hard copy of their manuscript, along with a disk formatted for the Mac computer. A list of sources and an annotated manuscript for fact checking is also required.

Friendly Exchange

1912 Grand Avenue
Des Moines, IA 50309-3379
(702) 786-7419

Published: 4 times a year

Circulation: 5.9 million

Query: Adele Malott, editor

Query response time: 4 to 6 weeks

Buys: About 32 articles out of approximately 1,200 unsolicited queries/manuscripts received annually

Guidelines: Available; send five first-class stamps and a 9"x12" envelope to request a sample copy

Rights purchased: All

Pays: On acceptance

Expenses: Depends on assignment

Kill fee: 25 percent

Rates:

Type of Article	*Word Length*	*Payment*
Major Feature	1,200 - 1,800	$700 - 800
Short Feature	400 - 800	400 - 500
"Health and Safety"	600	500
"Trends of the Times"	750	500
"Weekends on the Road"	400 - 800	400 - 550

Friendly Exchange is a magazine designed to open communication between the Farmers Insurance Group of Companies and its customers. It is distributed to policyholders who live in the 28 states that stretch from Tennessee, Alabama, Virginia, and Ohio to California. It explores travel and leisure topics of interest to active families.

The magazine's readership is 52 percent women and 48 percent men. The average reader is 35 to 45 years of age; 65 percent are college-educated; and the median household income is $37,900. Seventy-five percent of the readers are homeowners; 67 percent are married; and 45 percent have children. Youngsters are more likely to be in junior high or high school.

How to Slant Your Ideas to *Friendly Exchange*

Friendly Exchange provides readers with helpful facts and information they need to live well, receive full value for their dollar, and get up and go. While mainly filled with domestic travel articles, it also includes reports about home, automobile, food, health and safety, consumerism, heritage, and education.

"Our articles give the reader the feeling that he can do whatever the article proposes, so we don't want anything that is too odd or dangerous," says Malott. "The information we share serves as a catalyst to action—be it taking a trip, improving home safety, or trying a new recipe."

Each issue of *Friendly Exchange* contains seven to eight freelance-written pieces; two usually center around family getaways. The first provides a tight focus on a single activity, interest, or locale.

"We typically focus on something universal that can be done in most parts of the country, yet is based on an individual experience. A past article on a sand castle competition was told through the example of a Southern California competition, yet included a sidebar of other competitions across the country," Malott says.

If the magazine were to feature Harry Truman's home in Independence, Missouri, it would include a sidebar listing homes and libraries of other presidents open to visitors. If a feature described cross-country skiing in Colorado, the magazine would run a sidebar of additional cross-country skiing locations. "The stories are highly graphic, which gives us an opportunity to use strong photography," says Malott.

The second family getaway piece is a smaller version of the first or may include a geography quiz or a consumer subject, such as how to shop for a family ski package.

When it comes to travel, *Friendly Exchange* is not looking for a description of a single property, such as a review of a bed and breakfast, nor is it looking for a big sweep of a region. "If we were to feature San Diego, California, we wouldn't look at the whole city but we might describe a trip to the Point Loma Lighthouse and all that it has to offer. We need a fine focus; we don't have a lot of words to spend."

The following magazine sections are open to freelance writers:

- **Health and Safety** features articles about health or safety topics affecting a family's leisure hours. Past issues have included pieces on how to protect yourself from the sun; preventing bee stings; RV safety techniques; and how to pack a traveler's medical kit. To write for this section, include your credentials or expertise in the health arena.

- **Trends of the Times** is a section devoted to nuts-and-bolts communications with Farmers' policyholders. Most issues include four guest experts authoring articles on planned insurance topics. But Malott says she can use freelancers to help write for this section, which might include topics such as no-fault auto insurance, teenage drinking and driving, and cleaning up crime areas.
- **Weekends on the Road** is a regular section that includes short, regionally based pieces. The geographic divisions include California, other western states, central U.S., and south central U.S. The magazine does not have circulation in the Northeast or Southeast. These 400- to 800-word articles describe something a family can do within the region over a weekend. *Friendly Exchange* seeks a balance of subjects, locations, and activities in every issue. In other words, it would not run four weekend topics all on restored mining towns, even if they were in different states or regions.

  "A few California stories have included a trip to the Pinnacles National Monument; an inside out volcano north of Santa Barbara; and a story about people helping to build the Tahoe Rim Trail," says Malott. "We might also cover unique festivals, cooking competitions, or nature walks that can be a weekend trip on the road."

"Ideas to Go On" and "What's Cooking?" are both closed to professional writers. They are designed to be a forum where readers can exchange information with other readers, the editors, the sponsoring company, and the advertisers.

How to Query *Friendly Exchange*

Three paragraphs to three pages, depending on the depth of the topic.

According to Malott, your query should describe the subject matter, the geographical region to be covered, and tell why you should be the person to write on the topic you propose.

Query length doesn't matter as much to Malott as to other editors. "I don't mind a long query because it gives me a sense of the writer's ability to handle the language," says Malott. "The key element in a query is a strong hook. Tell me what your focus is and what direction you see the story taking. I don't want a piece on Chicago or even Chicago's Gold Coast, but I did buy a story about a walking tour of Chicago that focused on outdoor sculpture. It was something anyone could do that didn't cost money."

When it comes to errors writers make in queries, Malott says it's either not giving enough information or suggesting topics outside the regions the magazine covers. "One writer queried me on a dollmaker," says Malott. "That's all the information the letter had. It didn't tell me where the dollmaker lived, what made her special, or why readers would be interested."

The editor doesn't mind taking a chance on beginners if they prove they know the magazine. "One new writer queried me about a Santa Claus truck driver," shares Malott. "This man spends lots of time on the road, and every Christmas he dresses up and helps fellow drivers in distress. The piece tied into travel and safety, yet still had a strong human element."

Nearly 75 percent of the articles in the magazine are from ideas generated by freelance writers. "Send me a query the first time, and if you execute the assignment, I will probably call on you if I have a niche to fill in your neighborhood," says Malott.

When you work with Malott you can expect an assignment letter detailing the specific approach and deadline. "Call if you have any questions or concerns," she says. "I want to know about a change in direction ahead of time, and once I assign a piece, I assume it will come in on schedule."

How to Write for *Friendly Exchange*

To provide the action-oriented information *Friendly Exchange* demands, your writing must be factually accurate and based on current data. Writing for *Friendly Exchange* should be reportorial but also colorful and warm.

In the magazine's writer's guidelines, Malott describes what she is looking for from freelancers. "We want our writers to strive for a people orientation in every story," writes Malott. "When you can, use people to tell the story. And use emotion. We want to make our readers laugh or cry—as long as we don't make fun of a group or individual. Use applicable anecdotes and pointed quotes as primary ingredients in your story. Use action-oriented words and avoid the passive voice. The third-person approach is almost always preferred. First-person treatment is accepted only if agreed upon in advance. Destination approaches should be avoided in travel articles."

To learn how to write for *Friendly Exchange*, analyze how it talks travel. "Be a critical reader," says Malott. "Learn the areas we cover and how we approach our topics. Try to understand our attitude."

Malott pays writers when she is satisfied they have done what she has asked—usually no longer than one month after she receives the manuscript.

Glamour

350 Madison Avenue
New York, NY 10017
(212) 880-8800

Published: Monthly

Circulation: 2 million plus

Query: Pamela Erens, articles editor

Query response time: 6 to 8 weeks

Buys: Approximately 50 articles out of 3,000 unsolicited queries/manuscripts received annually

Guidelines: Available; send SASE

Rights purchased: Exclusive First NAS and exclusive right to distribute the issue throughout the world

Pays: On acceptance

Expenses: Pays phone, photocopying, and travel

Kill Fee: 20 percent

Rates:

Type of Article	*Word Length*	*Payment*
Major Feature	2,500+	$ 2,500+
Short Feature	900	750+
News Brief	250	150+
"His/Hers"	1,000	750 - 1,000
"Medical Report"	1,000	varies
"Viewpoint"	800	500
"Women Right Now"	300 - 500	250 - 500

Glamour is aimed at women in their twenties and thirties who are interested in fashion, beauty, and the latest trends and issues that affect them, their families, friends, careers, and lifestyles.

More than half of the magazine's readers have some college education; about 55 percent work at jobs outside the home. Approximately 50 percent of *Glamour* readers are married; 25 percent have children. The average family income exceeds $39,000 a year.

Glamour is a thick magazine of women's service issues which, according to Articles Editor Pamela Erens, "eats up ideas." Most of its features and columns are written by a cadre of contributing editors or freelance writers with whom the editorial staff has developed good working relationships. "But we are always open to new ideas and newcomers," reassures Erens.

The magazine's healthy appetite is both good and bad for freelance writers. While *Glamour* uses more articles than many other magazines, the probability is high that before you submit your idea, the editors will have a similar piece in inventory or will have just assigned a comparable idea to another writer.

How to Slant Your Ideas to *Glamour*

Since one million *Glamour* magazines are sold on the newsstand each month, Erens says that stories with fresh, timely angles that can be turned into cover lines are most heavily considered. "We distinguish ourselves from the competition by tackling tough women's issues," says Erens. "We publish pieces on abortion, rape, contraception, and sexual harassment. At the same time, we do a fair number of relationship and service pieces in almost every issue. For example, most of the feature well in one issue focused on how to take control of your life. We included pieces on sex, health, and keeping a clear perspective on your career. We are devoted to keeping the reader informed with accurate and timely articles on all subjects that are of immediate concern to them."

The best way to determine if your idea might be appropriate for *Glamour* is to use the magazine as your guide. "See if we publish articles of the same style, format, length, and approach as the idea you have in mind," says Erens. "If we do, your chances of selling to us are better."

Major subject categories open to freelancers include health, relationships, women's issues, consumer topics, women in the workplace, childbirth, and early parenthood. *Glamour* also occasionally runs a first-person narrative, such as "Should Rapists Ever Be Set Free?" a story by a young woman who lived with the memory and fear of her rapist who was about to go on parole.

Although *Glamour* wants its articles to be timely, the magazine has a four-month lead time. "We are looking for material that is fresh, but we have to cover topics in such a way that they will engage readers when the banner headlines are no longer running in their local or national newspapers," the editor says.

Fashion and beauty pieces are usually staff written, so articles in these two areas would have to be extraordinary to be assigned to a freelancer. The magazine does not buy travel articles, celebrity profiles, fiction, or poetry.

The following *Glamour* columns are open to freelance contributors:

- **His/Hers** offers a man's or woman's opinion on a pertinent topic of the day, or on a very personal subject. "This column is literary and highly anecdotal," says Erens. "It's a tough spot for new writers because style is so important." In the column "Separate Journeys," a writer chronicled his emotional state while his girlfriend was with a film crew in Africa for two months.

- **Medical Report** devotes 1,000 words each month to a single health topic. While this column is often written by regular contributors, the editors do look through unsolicited queries and discuss ideas with freelancers. The subject must relate directly to women. For example, a story on cholesterol would have to provide information about cholesterol and women. Chronic fatigue syndrome would be fair game because women suffer from this illness far more than men do.

  "The real criterion is that you have a health-reporting background that is demonstrable through clips," says Erens. "Or, you have to turn in a well-written query that marshals enough evidence that you can report on health subjects."

- **Viewpoint** presents the widest opportunities for new writers. This opinion page works best when the writer presents a strong argument to support her stand on a timely yet controversial issue. Articles should be well thought out and of interest to a broad range of readers. In one column, "Let's Put an End to 'Public Stripping' of the Disabled," a woman with cerebral palsy decried the practice of submitting disabled patients to public medical exams. Another, "Should I Donate My Eggs to Michael and Linda?" explained why one woman refused to become part of her married friends' fight against infertility. Mark the outside of the envelope "Viewpoint Editor."

- **Women Right Now** is usually staff written, but the editors will consider freelance ideas. These pieces surround offbeat, often controversial, topics that you would *not* find in the *Los Angeles Times* or *Washington Post.* One column, "AIDS: Its Menace Is Growing for Women," included a profile of a woman who contracted AIDS through date rape; information on a newsletter for women with AIDS; and a close-up on a teenager whose best friend died of AIDS and who has since became an advocate of condom availability and AIDS education in public high schools.

All other columns under the table of contents category "In Every Issue," as well as all health and fitness columns, are written in house or by regular contributors.

How to Query *Glamour*

Double-spaced queries preferred, no length limit; do not send photo/art information; query six months in advance for seasonal material.

"I prefer a detailed proposal that mirrors the type of article you want to write, which means I like to see a sample lead, lively anecdotes, good quotes, and a sketch of how the article would be structured," says Erens. "Write your proposal as long as is needed to explain your idea adequately. Include the names of experts you'll interview, and relevant facts and figures about the subject and their sources. Make sure that you've clearly communicated your idea."

Erens says poor writing, inadequate research, and insufficient familiarity with the types of articles *Glamour* publishes are immediate signs of inexperience. Let the editor know why your article will interest her readers and convince her that she should assign it.

Before assigning an article, Erens says she and other editors must be sure the idea meets certain criteria. She suggests that writers ask themselves the following questions before submitting a query:

- Is the idea timely?
- Is your approach to the topic fresh? Does it have a news angle?
- Does the story need research? If you're suggesting a reported story, be sure to include enough information to persuade the editors of the merit of the piece.
- Is the idea presented in the best form—narrative, interview, first person?
- Are you qualified to write the piece?

How to Write for *Glamour*

"We buy only first-rate, quality writing," says Erens. "We look for incisive reporting and the latest information on a subject. We want it fleshed out with anecdotes about women who have experienced a certain situation and quotes from experts in the field."

Other words Erens uses to describe the *Glamour* writing style include: straightforward, well argued, persuasively written, and logically organized.

"We also want the piece to be entertaining in the sense that the writer has a good ear and can appreciate a colorful quotation," the editor explains. "In addition, it is essential that a writer have solid factual information as a frame for the story, and the talent to shape a piece to emphasize what is new."

Most articles for *Glamour* are written more than once. "We almost always request a rewrite after an editor reads the piece for the first time," says Editor-in-Chief Ruth Whitney.

"We're looking for writers who are meticulous researchers and strong reporters, who can write with great style and warmth," she concludes.

Good Housekeeping

959 Eighth Avenue
New York, NY 10019
(212) 649-2265

Published: Monthly

Circulation: 5 million

Query: Articles and Features: Carolyn Kitch, senior editor
"The Better Way": Erika Reider Mark, "The Better Way" editor
"My Problem": address to "My Problem"

Query response time: 4 to 6 weeks

Buys: About 100 articles out of approximately 10,000 unsolicited queries/manuscripts received annually

Guidelines: Available; send SASE

Rights purchased: Varies, but generally All

Pays: On acceptance

Expenses: Pays reasonable phone, travel, and lodging

Kill fee: 25 percent

Rates: The general rule is $1 a word. This varies, depending on the length and difficulty of the assignment and on the writer's relationship with *Good Housekeeping*. Individuals who have been writing for the magazine for a long time receive higher pay than first-timers.

Good Housekeeping is written for the new traditionalist—a contemporary woman with traditional values. The magazine characterizes its reader as thoughtful, responsible, and a doer—active in her neighborhood or community. She feels deeply about issues and reacts to them personally. She enjoys improving and decorating her home, but doesn't want to be a slave to it. She's concerned about her family's health, and keeping fit is a part of her lifestyle. She shops conscientiously, takes environmental concerns seriously, and is involved in her children's schools.

"The *Good Housekeeping* reader mirrors the female American population," says Carolyn Kitch, senior editor. "The average age of our reader is about 41, and she has a combined household income in the high $30,000s. She is more likely than not to be working outside the home full time, though we do have a significant number of readers who work part time. Most of the women who read *Good Housekeeping* are mothers, but their children may be grown.

"Our reader is an activist in a local sense," continues Kitch. "She wants to improve her community and life for her family. She reads *Good Housekeeping* as an information source, so we emphasize service, not just advice. Every time we cover a topic, we want to educate her by giving hard-core data and resources. It's a constant challenge to give her the best information and current developments, whether it's about breast cancer or environmental concerns."

How to Slant Your Ideas to *Good Housekeeping*

Good Housekeeping relies on freelancers for issue-oriented discussions of a political or social issue of the day. "We typically explain the issue through one woman who faced the problem, in a personal, narrative format," says Kitch. "The strength of the story lies in the woman featured. We need freelancers to bring us women's stories from throughout the country."

The dramatic narrative is the number-one category of writing *Good Housekeeping* buys from writers. "In this kind of story, a woman faces and overcomes a problem that is common to many women or families," says Kitch. "The way she handles the problem has to offer something that educates others, whether it is information, a new point of view, or an inspiration."

Kitch describes a story the magazine ran on homelessness. "We wanted to do something on this topic, and we received a query from a Washington, D.C. writer who found an atypical woman whose family had become homeless," the editor explains. "Her husband, a cameraman, had been laid off from a local television affiliate. They lost their home, had to sell many personal belongings, and lived in a public campground for six months. This made a good story for two reasons. First, the writer found a woman who shattered the myth about the homeless by showing how easily it could happen to anyone. And second, because the woman used her experience to organize a group that successfully lobbied to get unused Pentagon land as a place to build homes for the homeless."

Medical and health problems are also covered regularly by *Good Housekeeping*. "We rarely buy health-issue overviews from freelancers who are new to us; instead, we'd turn to one of our regular writers or top science and medical experts," notes Kitch. "But if a new writer comes to us with a powerful one-woman's experience that has some unusual angle to it, we might be interested. We need the story to have an extra dimension of inspiration, surprise, or outrage to make a common subject come alive. In general, the story must illustrate or illuminate a national issue, as seen through the eyes of one person who overcame it."

Kitch recalls one story about a nurse and her husband and two children who appeared to live a typical American life. But in reality, they were incredible drug addicts. One of their children was born addicted, and finally, the couple hit bottom and went for help.

While *Good Housekeeping* runs essays—the biggest category of unsolicited ideas sent to the magazine—Kitch says the odds run against you if you want to sell an essay. "When faced with a choice of what to put in the magazine, we'll opt for more timely pieces than the subjects covered in most essays," she says. "However, if you have a seasonal essay, say pegged to a holiday, and send it far enough in advance, you have a chance."

Good Housekeeping also buys short human interest features that are "so inspiring, funny, or interesting, you can't help but read them." An example of this was an article by a woman in Georgia who worked part time as a night court judge. "She got all the crazies in her courtroom and wrote an interesting, funny piece detailing the cases," says Kitch. Another piece was about a woman who, because she did scientific research on pig farming, began a correspondence with a pig rancher in Montana and fell in love. "Their mutual love of pigs brought them together," says Kitch. "We know these stories when we see them. They make us laugh or gasp or feel inspired.

"One feature we ran in this category for Father's Day was about a man who took advantage of family leave benefits offered by his employer. Though he had always worked very long hours, he decided to save enough money to take six months of unpaid leave to stay home and get to know his children. The story described how that decision changed his life. He supplied many photos, and it resulted in a positive, fun piece that was almost like a photo feature," Kitch says.

"All major women's magazines use the expert voice and service journalism," says she. "But I think we tend to call on the expert voice more than the other six sisters. [The "seven sisters," of the women's magazine world are: *Better Homes and Gardens, Family Circle, Good Housekeeping, Ladies' Home Journal, McCall's, Redbook,* and *Woman's Day.*]

"For service material we cover on a regular basis—food, fashion, beauty, nutrition—we have a full-time staff of experts who work specifically on those subjects. We also have regular columnists, such as Dr. Joyce Brothers on psychology and Heloise on household hints. So, writers might sell more service pieces to other women's magazines than to us," the editor explains.

Kitch recommends studying the magazine's masthead to find a list of its experts by category. Look over that list, and see if the subject area you have in mind is covered by one of the experts.

"If you want to sell a home-care topic, we wouldn't be interested because we have an expert in that area. On the other hand, we do not have an education editor," Kitch explains. "So, if you've written a book on how to pick a top college for the best education dollar, we might take an article on this subject from you."

Except for the "Articles and Features" category, almost all of the other material in *Good Housekeeping* is written in house or by regular contributors.

The following are two sections open to freelancers' queries:

- **The Better Way** covers consumer news with a strong service angle, in a reportage style. Health topics, for instance, emphasize understanding newly available medical advances and tell readers where to find them. The section is big on giving resources and offering the latest information from top experts. A story on teenage drug abuse would give readers an understanding of the problem, offer advice from experts, list warning signs, and give resources of where to go for more information.

  Writers for "The Better Way" must have strong credentials in consumer reporting, whether in health, financial advice, education, careers, or travel. Pieces run between 500 and 1,000 words.

- **My Problem** features real problems and how they are solved, in about 1,500 words. This is a very good venue for freelancers. "Whether it is your problem or someone else's, there are no bylines," says Kitch. "The subject of the story remains anonymous."

Kitch says the problems the magazine runs range from very serious to lighthearted. It has covered childhood sexual abuse, drug abuse, alcoholism, battered spouses, and relationship issues with spouses, children, parents, and other relatives. Most problems have something to do with the family, although occasionally the column features a workplace issue or a personal problem, such as an addictive behavior or fear.

"The best way to figure out how to write for this column is to read a whole year's worth of back issues and get to know the writing style," says Kitch. "Think of your job as a writer as that of a storyteller. Use dialogue, set scenes, and give details. It's essential to make sure your problem has a solution or resolution—something that happened that allowed the person to recover, change, or move on to the next step. If we cover a marital problem, the couple doesn't always work it out and get back together, but a resolution occurs in the woman's mind. Some stories call for seeking counseling, but it's boring if everything ends in therapy. The article needs to show that the woman's thinking changed, not that someone else modified his or her behavior or that the problem just went away."

How to Query *Good Housekeeping*

Two pages or less preferred; do not send photo/art information; send seasonal material four to six months in advance.

As with most magazines, make sure your queries are in writing. Kitch says she has a pet peeve with writers who call out of the blue and say, "Do you have a minute?"

"If you are pitching me a story when a final page proof is on my desk, my mind will not be on your idea," she says. "And only FAX your idea if it is extremely urgent."

When putting your thoughts on paper, Kitch encourages writers to remember that a query letter is, in fact, a writing sample. For *Good Housekeeping*, it should mirror the style of the magazine and the piece you want to sell.

"If you say your article will be amusing and your query isn't, we have a hard time believing you," says Kitch. "Likewise, if you're trying to sell a powerful, suspenseful rescue piece and your query is dull and hard to understand, we know you will have trouble writing in a dramatic narrative format that is chronological and fast-paced."

Kitch encourages writers to take the query stage seriously. "Do some research ahead of time," she says. "Don't just say you will find out how many women at the college in your community have experienced date rape; deliver the goods in the query letter. We are toughest on writers at this stage because we don't want to kill stories later if the writer doesn't deliver."

If your query captures the editors' interest, you will receive a phone call indicating that the magazine wants to assign the article to you. "The slant of the piece and financial arrangements will be discussed at that time," says Kitch. "Then we'll send an assignment letter that serves as a contract. It details the deadline, financial agreement, kill fee, and rights. We'll also explain how the article should be written, giving very specific directions to prevent misunderstandings."

How to Write for *Good Housekeeping*

For the three categories of writing *Good Housekeeping* most often purchases from freelancers—personal narratives, essays, and short human-interest features—the tone of the writing is always very personal.

Kitch says that some of the magazine's best nonfiction writers employ the fiction techniques of plot, dialogue, and scene-setting to advance the narrative. She advises that personal narratives be told in chronological fashion.

"Write the article as if you were explaining the story to a respected friend," Kitch directs. "Many women have been loyally reading *Good Housekeeping* for years and have an emotional investment in the magazine. When they call us, they expect to find an ally on the other end of the phone. So, the relationship between the magazine and reader needs to come through in our articles. This doesn't mean we don't cover serious subjects and that the articles aren't carefully done. A piece on breast cancer will, of course, be more deeply researched and include more factual information than a human interest pet story. Yet both will communicate in a conversational, straightforward manner and be very accessible. It's important to note that *Good Housekeeping* readers are well informed and expect sophisticated information. A freelancer who writes too plainly is missing the mark."

Guideposts

16 East 34th Street
New York, NY 10016
(212) 251-8100

Published: Monthly

Circulation: 4 million

Query: Articles: James McDermott, senior staff editor
Shorts: Colleen Hughes, features editor

Query response time: 1 to 4 weeks

Buys: About 125 articles/stories out of approximately 60,000 unsolicited queries/manuscripts received annually

Guidelines: Available; send SASE

Rights purchased: All

Pays: On acceptance

Expenses: Pays everything for writers with a track record with *Guideposts*

Kill fee: Minimum $25/maximum $250; varies with writer and effort expended

Rates:

Type of Article	*Word Length*	*Payment*
Major Feature	1,500	$300 - 1,500
Short Feature	100 - 900	100 - 900

Guideposts is the only exclusively personal-story format magazine that illustrates how people can make their lives better through faith in God. This nondenominational publication was founded by Norman Vincent Peale.

"Of all religious magazines, we have a more general readership," says Senior Staff Editor James McDermott. "I believe our stories appeal to a broad spectrum of people because they have no particular axe to grind, and we try to make them as engaging as possible."

To keep in touch with what is on people's minds, *Guideposts* runs an outreach prayer fellowship. "Anyone can write to us and express any sort of dissatisfaction, disappointment, or tragedy in his or her life, and can expect to get a letter back addressing the problem," says McDermott. "In fact, we respond to an average of 6,000 prayer requests per year. But they fluctuate wildly depending on the circumstances. For example, during Desert Storm, we received 1,000 in one week."

The nonprofit magazine carries no advertising. It is supported through subscriptions, sales of books, and a small number of contributions, which are typically used to help fund outreach projects.

"While most of our subscribers are women, surveys have indicated that 50 percent of our readers are men who read the magazines their wives buy," says McDermott.

The average *Guideposts* reader is 49. About two-thirds of them have at least some college education. "They are much savvier than what is typically expected of a reader of an inspirational magazine," the editor notes.

How to Slant Your Ideas to *Guideposts*

Guideposts addresses problems readers face in their lives by showing how others have overcome a similar situation—whether it is an unruly child, drug addiction, having a child out of wedlock, or a marital problem.

"For every piece considered for the magazine, we ask, 'What is in it for the reader?'" explains McDermott. "We want to know what little nugget of practical/spiritual advice a story can prove to our audience.

"We get a lot of queries about people doing worthwhile things, such as starting a soup kitchen for the homeless," the editor continues. "While we greatly admire people like that, what good will their stories do for our readers, other than make them feel guilty? People are amazed when we turn down such stories, but unless a person has gone through something where he has gained an insight, it's not a *Guideposts* story. Each article has to have what we call a 'takeaway' message."

A great example of that was the lesson imparted in "To Finish First," a story about a TV anchorwoman's drive to succeed. It wasn't until after she lost her marriage and her job that she realized that God's idea of being first was very different than hers. After volunteering for a year at a service agency for the homeless, she got back into television. She doesn't have the glamour or the salary of earlier jobs, but she has found something better—love, happiness, and peace-of-mind in being the parent of a five-year-old girl, whom she adopted from a Honduras orphanage.

"We bill our magazine as a practical guide for successful living," says McDermott. "I feel that much of what is in the Bible is not always easy to do, but it's always practical. It's tough to turn the other cheek, but it's in the Bible because it works."

McDermott illustrates his point through a *Guideposts* story written by a Black woman in upstate New York who bought a home in a lovely community. Four days after the family moved in, they woke up to these words spray-painted on their house: "Die Nigger, Die. KKK." The message was devastating to the woman, but she refused to let it defeat her. Instead of lashing back, she expressed her sorrow and disappointment to reporters. By the end of the day, her neighbors responded with flowers and food, and she got a chance to meet every one of them. Even the kids who committed the hurtful deed came over, and one in particular was really impressed by the way the family reacted.

"She didn't feel like 'loving her enemy,' yet she knew it was the right thing to do," says McDermott. "By rigorously adhering to a Biblical truth, she created a beautiful happy ending to the incident."

In addition to longer features, *Guideposts* runs a number of regular shorter pieces including "His Mysterious Ways," "The Quiet People," "This Thing Called Prayer," "Why Don't We," and "Words to Grow On." While the magazine's writer's guidelines briefly describe each section, McDermott says that Rick Hamlin, the senior editor who developed many of these short features, prefers that writers not worry about how to categorize their work.

"Rick thinks it's a mistake to try to pigeonhole a featurette into one of these categories; it's like putting the cart before the horse," says McDermott. "Instead of trying to slant something to one of the titles, just tell your story and make your point. Let us worry about putting the label on it."

How to Query *Guideposts*

One-page queries preferred. Send queries for longer features; send completed manuscripts for shorter stories. Do not send photo/art information. Query six to eight months in advance for seasonal material.

It may surprise you to learn that this magazine, for all its emphasis on telling true stories, prefers query letters that don't use any storytelling devices. Simply spell out the idea and get to the point. "We are interested in a business-like letter that says, 'Here is my idea,' telling us as much about the narrator and the story as you can in one typewritten page," says McDermott.

"I think the query technique that uses anecdotes and quotes as would be used in an article is dated, overdone, and should be given a decent burial," the editor says. "But I wouldn't hold that against someone who writes that type of proposal."

McDermott also does not care about seeing clips. "It's good to list your best credits in a cover letter, but samples don't mean that much to us. We're more interested in what you can do for us, and dull clips can work against you," he explains.

All new writers whose ideas intrigue the editors will be asked to write on speculation the first two times they work with *Guideposts*. "The good news is it's fairly easy to get an assignment from us if you've got a good situation. The bad news is we are a different enough magazine that writing for us takes some getting used to, so we can't pay advances and expenses."

What surprises McDermott is that of every 50 on-spec invitations he gives out, only 20 percent of the freelancers ever deliver. He assures writers they shouldn't be scared off by an on-spec request or by the fact that it may take several rewrites to hit the mark. "One frustrated writer asked me if any freelancer *ever* places in *Guideposts*," McDermott says. "Of course, many do. We have a large network of writers who place material with us regularly, some as often as three to four times a year."

According to McDermott, after a writer publishes several pieces in *Guideposts*, the magazine starts to give assignments, which means paying for expenses and offering a kill fee.

In even-numbered years, *Guideposts* announces in its April issue a writer's contest with a June 1 deadline. The following September, 15 winners are treated to an all-expenses paid, week-long writer's workshop that serves as a training ground for *Guideposts* writers.

"Over the years, we've trained some 200 writers, 50 of whom are active, 25 of whom are very active," says McDermott. "The pay scale for stories evolves with their success. The first piece after our workshop pays $600. Every time a writer publishes twice in a category, the fee is increased by $100. We have one woman who is paid $1,500 per story placed. If someone is placing six stories a year, we'll generally have him or her sign a formal contract with a fixed rate."

McDermott says that even writers who have not attended any workshop, but who sell regularly to the magazine, are offered the same pay increase.

When you are asked to pursue a story for *Guideposts*, don't expect a lot of initial editorial direction. "We depend on the writer to bring a story to life," says McDermott. "We like to give writers a chance, but we're not into bottle-feeding. The onus is on contributors to prove themselves to us."

How to Write for *Guideposts*

Guideposts stories make for simple reading, but don't be fooled; they require a great amount of effort to write. As McDermott would contend, sometimes it's more challenging to be simple than complicated.

The magazine's writer's guidelines warn freelancers not to try to tell an entire life story in a few pages. The key is to focus on one specific event in a person's life. Always written in the first-person—whether it's your story or someone else's—stories emphasize one individual. In a disaster piece, stick to the viewpoint of one rescuer or the rescued individual. If the piece is about an organization, tell it through the eyes of one worker or one person who has been helped.

Classic story ingredients are implemented, including narration, description, characterization, dialogue, suspense, conflict, climax, and conclusion. At the beginning of the article, the character and the problem are presented. By the end, the character is changed and the solution revealed—one the reader might adapt to his or her own life. The message must be presented subtly and naturally, without pontification.

"Our stories are told in straightforward narration, but every story has a double layer," says McDermott. "If it is a dramatic story of how someone survived being lost in a cave, we would expect the writer to convey the despair and suspense. We would also require that the freelancer be able to get inside the person's head and experience the growth and development that takes place because of the stressful incident."

McDermott's ideal *Guideposts* writer has a good head for detail, the ability to play a minor psychologist, and a fairly good knowledge of Biblical scripture. "It is essential," the editor notes, "that all of our stories prove the value of the tenets of the Bible, but to do it in such a way that they present a practical side to the Bible's messages."

McDermott says the magazine also likes to surprise the reader whenever it can. "We covet the element of surprise as much as fiction editors do," he says. "And, though it's cliché, true events are often more surprising than fiction."

McDermott offers two more essential attributes for success at this magazine: patience and good humor. "It's not unusual for a piece to have to go through three revisions—even *Guideposts* writers with a vast amount of experience will occasionally deliver a story that requires a lot of work," says McDermott. "We do not delight in torturing people, but it often takes this kind of work to discover the meaning of a person's experience. Sometimes it takes a little sorting out. Every manuscript is a learning process for me, as an editor, and for our contributors. We spend a lot of time worrying out the meaning of a story; it's often like putting together a puzzle. And if a writer has patience and good humor, it makes the process enjoyable for both of us."

McDermott wants to bring writers on board because *Guideposts* wants new voices. "We need people who can tell the same old scenario of someone getting up from the bottom of a cave or down from a failing airplane in fresh ways," he says. "We really only have five or six basic story lines, so we have to make sure our approach is unique, and new voices help us do that.

"I doubt there's another magazine in America that reads 60,000 manuscripts a year. We do it out of a sense of enlightened self-interest. We love it when someone with a fresh slant comes to us totally out of left field."

McDermott recounts a story of a woman who sent in an idea about being in a bad relationship with a man and taking a trip to the Gulf of St. Lawrence in Canada. "She looked in the dark, trusting eyes of a white seal and determined that if God could make something that clean and pure, she couldn't continue to go against God's law," he explains. "It was a magical moment for her and we were delighted with the story."

Similarly, a rancher submitted a story about releasing a trapped coyote, and told how that experience helped free him from the bitter feelings he was having because he had been forced to sell his ranch.

"Those are two examples of why we read so many submissions," says McDermott. "We lust for these kinds of stories, with strong individual voices."

Guideposts does its own fact checking, but writers are on the honor system here. "We are different from most publications in that we show every finished story to its narrator for approval," the editor says. "So, in that regard, our fact checking is self-accomplished. We take pride in representing subjects' experiences accurately. Very often, someone gives *Guideposts* a story because he wants to help others, so we make every effort to cast the story just the way its narrator experienced it. Sometimes we have to jump through hoops—especially in the case of celebrities—but in the end, we always have a meeting of the minds."

Harper's

666 Broadway
New York, NY 10012
(212) 614-6500

Published: Monthly

Circulation: 203,000

Query: Lewis Lapham, editor

Query response time: 4 weeks

Buys: About 60 articles out of approximately 2,000 unsolicited queries/manuscripts received annually

Guidelines: None available

Rights purchased: First NAS

Pays: On acceptance

Expenses: Pays if reasonable and discussed in advance

Kill fee: 33⅓ percent

Rates:

Type of Article	***Word Length***	***Payment***
Major Feature	5,000	$3,000 - 5,000
Short Feature	3,000	1,500

"Our readers enjoy *Harper's* because they find in it things they don't find in other publications," says Lewis Lapham, editor. This magazine, founded in 1850, is still ahead of its crowd in reporting the events of the day in a unique manner which other publications often try to copy.

"We assume an intelligent and well-informed reader," the editor adds. *Harper's* readers are well-educated; more than half have attended graduate school and nearly all have attended college, and all are serious about reading. Lapham says that an average reader is likely to read a major daily metropolitan newspaper as well as a news magazine, *The Economist, New Republic,* and various trade journals during a month. The reader also buys an average of 23 books a year.

About two-thirds of the readers are male, and their median age is about 45; median household income is nearly $80,000.

How to Slant Your Ideas to *Harper's*

"We're trying to make a magazine that will add to the reader's store of knowledge," Lapham says. "We won't repeat something he or she has seen elsewhere in the media.

"Our readers like to think for themselves," he continues. "There is no point in trying to astonish them with one-day sensations or the wonders of celebrity."

The magazine is divided into short pieces at the front of the book, called "Readings," and lengthier features in the center well. The back of the book might offer a short story one month, and then, in another month, a memoir or an essay. "Readings" is the best spot for a new contributor with a sharp eye who can find something published elsewhere that would be of value to *Harper's*.

The following *Harper's* sections are open to freelancers:

- **Essay** is a form that the magazine particularly likes, Lapham says. "The use of the first person singular allows the writer to follow his thought in many directions," he says. "We have published essays that also could be described as sermons, progress notes and field guides."
- **Readings** is a mosaic made of "found" texts, Lapham says. Items may come from meetings, internal corporate memos, poems, speeches—any number of places where words of some interest appear. "Today, people express themselves more naturally in memos and speeches. You don't have to seek out literary forms to learn about society."

  One "Readings" section included, among other items: congressional testimony, a questionnaire distributed by an Arkansas welfare office, and an internal memo from a furniture manufacturer.
- **Reports** are lengthy, researched articles on urgent topics of the day. *Harper's* is known for examining trends and issues in this section, only to be followed months or even years later by other publications that notice the trend.

How to Query *Harper's*

Up to three pages for queries; full manuscripts accepted. Do not submit photo/art information.

"I read all letters addressed to me in the hope of finding interesting reading for my readers," Lapham says. "I can tell within the first page or so whether that writer is appropriate to *Harper's*."

Likewise, manuscripts are read at this magazine. "Any well-turned manuscript that arrives in this office will be received with gratitude," he says. "I can tell within three pages whether the manuscript is of the kind I want to publish in *Harper's* magazine."

How to Write for *Harper's*

"We commission and buy a great many manuscripts," Lapham says. "This magazine is created *ex nihilo* [Latin for 'from nothing']. The system is by no means closed. Certainly, we publish some of the best writers and those on the leading edge of thought and opinion. But we often find ourselves scrambling to put a magazine together."

Regarding the editorial mix of the magazine, Lapham smiles and says, "We buy any good manuscript that comes along. We look at what we have on hand and see if there is a place for it in the next issue. If a long, serious essay comes in on a matter of public policy, we also may publish a humorous short story, or use an annotation from the entertainment or cultural world in the same issue. We try to address different aspects of the culture every month."

Lapham says the magazine is neither conservative nor liberal in its leanings. "If we show a bias it is in our suspicion of the conventional wisdom in whatever form," he says. "We address our remarks to the citizen, who is free to take or leave the information. We are deeply suspicious of the proscriptive conditional tense—you should, or shouldn't, must or must not."

Harrowsmith Country Life

Ferry Road
Charlotte, VT 05445
(802) 425-3961

Published: 6 times a year

Circulation: 200,000

Query: John Barstow, editor
Gardening: Karan Cutler, senior editor

Query response time: 6 weeks

Buys: About 50 articles out of approximately 400 unsolicited queries/manuscripts received annually

Guidelines: Available, with sample copy; send SASE

Rights purchased: First NAS

Pays: Within 45 days of acceptance

Expenses: Pays reasonable expenses when approved in advance

Kill fee: 25 percent

Rates:

Type of Article	*Word Length*	*Payment*
Major Feature	4,000	$ 2,000
Short Feature	1,500	600
"Country Careers"	1,200	600
"Gazette"	300 - 500	100 - 150
"Screed"	1,200	600
"Sourcebank"	300 - 500	100 - 150
"Wild Lives"	1,500	600 - 800

Harrowsmith Country Life celebrates country and rural living in a literate, thoughtful voice. Not to be mistaken for one of the many country-style shelter magazines, this publication focuses on life in the country—indoor and outdoor living, gardening, the environment, and the sense of community a small town can offer.

The readership is split evenly between men and women, most of whom are in their mid-40s and married. The vast majority attended or graduated from college, and have incomes of about $40,000. They live in the northern tier, north of the Mason-Dixon Line. (There is a sister magazine also named *Harrowsmith* in Canada, and the publications share a limited amount of editorial.)

The readers look to the magazine for articles relevant to their climate, lifestyle, and home. Nearly all of the readers garden. In fact, the average size of their home property is more than three acres, and half of the readers devote up to one-quarter of an acre to a garden area.

"We like to think that our readers are the same people who tune in to public radio and television stations," says John Barstow, editor. "They are less concerned with the status quo and more interested in choosing a different approach to living than city or suburban life. Some people who move to the country do so because they value a slower pace, a smaller-scale community where they can get on the school board if they want to, and actually make a difference. Our readers are involved."

How to Slant Your Ideas to *Harrowsmith Country Life*

The bulk of the pieces published in the magazine fall into six categories: gardening, shelter, natural history and wildlife, community-based topics, food, and the environment. Fully a third of the articles in each issue are devoted to gardening topics, although only a portion of those are actual how-tos. Gardening pieces appear as examinations of a particular family of plant, profiles of plant breeders, and even an occasional essay about gardening.

Cover stories tend to be about an unusual aspect of country life. For instance, the magazine has published articles on the role of small hospitals in remote rural areas, food-buying co-ops, and the dilemmas facing small-town schools.

Shelter articles feature a house that is remarkable in some special way, frequently incorporating an energy-saving or environmentally responsible angle. This is an area of the magazine where the subject is sometimes out of the readership's general geographical area; if a house is special enough, Barstow says the magazine will go further south or west for the piece.

Natural history and wildlife topics are covered in "Wild Lives," written most often by a group of regular contributors. Lengthier features that warrant more coverage also appear in the well. Environmental issues are such a part of country living that the topic is woven through many of the articles.

The following columns and features are open to freelance contributors:

- **Country Careers** is a regular feature whose title makes the topic rather self-evident. These profiles are not just of people who have a job in the country, but a chronicle of those who worked elsewhere and were able to move—along with their profession—to a country lifestyle. It is a detailed article on what they do, how it translated to country living, and, if possible, how much they earn.

Again, the celebration of life in the country is present—an essay-style piece about a trout-farming family in south-central Missouri described the couple's 42-year vision and the troubles they weathered before eventually succeeding.

- **Gazette** copy is *Harrowsmith*'s magazine-within-a-magazine, according to Barstow. "These news briefs are so topical or rapidly changing that we can't do a feature on them for a while, but need to report on them," he says. "The best way to get in the door of this magazine is to find an issue, researcher, or country resident who is doing something of note and get a 'Gazette' assignment."

  Topics for "Gazette" range widely. They have included research showing that honeybees that walk through beneficial bacteria-laced pollen may be useful in inoculating fruit trees from certain diseases; a report dispelling the myth that potato peels carry the most nutrients in the vegetable and showing that toxins in the peel actually make removing it the healthier approach; and an article about the 10 remaining grizzlies in Montana's Mission Mountains.

- **Screed** is the place for strong opinions. Barstow describes the column as, "letting loose a little more, giving an impassioned opinion without being balanced or trying to report in such a way that takes the passion away." Topics have included property rights; military flyovers near national park land; and gun control.

- **Sourcebank** bills itself as "A compendium of useful tools and ideas." Many of the brief reports in this section are written in house, where access to information about the latest in hoes, renovation lighting, or organic seed distributors is likely to be broader than your own. However, Barstow is open to suggestions and contributions.

- **Wild Lives**, though technically an open column for freelancers, is a tough area to crack. Barstow says he tends to rely on a small group of regular writers whom he already knows and trusts. However, if you can write about an animal or a plant in the essay/first person/ informational style of the column, Barstow says he wants to see your ideas. Subjects covered during one four-issue period have included lichen, ospreys, centipedes, and roadrunners—all written by regular contributors to the magazine.

"Home Ground," "Kitchen Garden," "Pantry," "Queries & Quandaries," "Stock Answers," and most "Sourcebank" and food pieces are written by contributing writers or the staff.

How to Query *Harrowsmith Country Life*

One to two pages preferred; send information on photo/art availability; query six months in advance for seasonal material.

"An idea is fine, but we look for what distinguishes this article from every other article about the same subject," Barstow says. "For instance, for a piece on solar hot water, we didn't rehash everything that had been written before. We felt there had been progress in the systems and that there was good reason to reconsider solar hot water as an option in our homes."

Barstow looks, foremost, for queries from people who clearly understand his magazine and its readers. The first step he appreciates from a prospective contributor is a written request for writer's guidelines and a few sample copies. After you've studied the style, topics, and personality of the magazine, Barstow asks for a well-written letter and clips.

"I like to see some evidence that you have a handle on the story," he says. "Don't just have an idea, but show me that you've gone to some trouble to get some hard facts about the piece. At times, a good lead can help draw me in, but it is the preparation of the writer that sells a piece to me."

Barstow doesn't mind receiving letters suggesting three or four topics and offering a lengthier proposal if he is interested. "It can be a good way to start a dialogue about an article," he says. "But don't send me a shotgun-approach list of 25 ideas that have nothing to do with the magazine and have been sent to a dozen other places."

How to Write for *Harrowsmith Country Life*

"We try to let freelance writers have their own voice, in order to let the magazine be a journal of different voices," Barstow says. The editor tries to describe the personality of the magazine with a string of words—thoughtful, careful, sensible, thorough—then laughs and says, "That doesn't make us sound very interesting, does it?"

Along with those very careful-sounding words, Barstow tells writers, "We put a very high premium on having interesting facts and lots of information. But just as important as those factors is high-quality expository writing. I still require a beginning, middle, and end to each article, whether it is an essay or an article about tent camping."

First-time writers without clips sometimes are invited to submit a manuscript on speculation. If the piece interests the editors, an assignment will be made when the article is sent back for revisions.

Health

301 Howard Street, Suite 1800
San Francisco, CA 94105
(415) 512-9100

Published: Bimonthly, plus a special issue in October

Circulation: 900,000

Query: Articles: Cassandra Wrightson, editorial assistant
Family: James Scott, senior editor
Fitness: Bruce Kelley, senior editor
Food: Sheridan Warrick, managing editor
Mind: Lisa Davis, senior editor
Vanities: Barbara Paulsen, senior editor

Query response time: 2 months

Buys: About 12 articles/short pieces out of more than 600 unsolicited queries received annually

Guidelines: Available; send SASE

Rights purchased: First NAS, plus stipulation that splits sales on foreign, reprint, dramatic and commercial rights

Pays: On acceptance

Expenses: Pays as agreed upon; always phone and photocopying

Kill fee: 25 percent

Rates:

Type of Article	*Word Length*	*Payment*
Major Feature	N/A	
Department	1,200	$1,800

"The magazine has two missions: to help readers take control of their health with practical information and to wake them up to important issues with powerful storytelling," says Sheridan Warrick, managing editor. "We try to be mainstream, yet cover health in as wide a way as possible."

The magazine is the newest incarnation of a magazine that began in 1987 as *Hippocrates.* It was then called *In Health* until it bought the title and circulation list to the *Health* magazine which had been published for a number of years. It has been called *Health* since the February/March, 1992 issue.

Health readers are fit and active professionals with college experience or degrees and incomes in the $40,000 range. More than 80 percent of the readers are women, and their median age is 43. Most have pre-teen or teenaged children and are concerned about the health problems of their kids, their aging parents, and themselves.

When Warrick thinks of his reader, he says he imagines Washington Senator Patty Murray, who has described herself as "just a mom in tennis shoes," and as "caring for my own children and my parents at the same time."

How to Slant Your Ideas to *Health*

"Until recently, our trademark had always been the offbeat or different approach to health topics," Warrick says. "That won't go away entirely, but we are becoming more mainstream. And we will always offer service pieces and articles on basic issues relevant to our readers' lives.

"We publish the fewest articles on birth and childhood issues because our readers are past that point," the editor continues. "We want to talk about things that really cater to their interests so we leave most articles on younger kids to the parenting magazines."

The following departments are open to freelancers:

- **Family** covers the gamut of family issues facing readers. The pieces can examine an issue like raising an only child or confronting teenage addiction. But it has also featured an introspective essay by a writer who accompanied his mother to the doctor the day she learned of a terminal illness.
- **Fitness** reports on exercises, avoiding injury, and equipment shopping. But true to *Health*'s determination to stretch its boundaries, it publishes other articles relevant to fitness, such as a piece discussing a program to help athletes apply their training to academics.
- **Food** is a nutrition column, devoted to dispelling myths about certain foods and dispensing information about others. In one long column by a contributing editor, the topic was beer and other liquor. It probed whether or not there is a scientific basis to the beer belly, which led to a discussion about how alcohol is metabolized. The column has recently covered yogurt, sugar, Chinese food, Kosher food, and sulfites in wine.
- **Mind** is unlike the typical psychology or self-help column. Instead, it looks at how the mind works and how the reader might benefit from the increased understanding. Warrick notes that, of the departments open to freelancers, this is the one he has the most trouble filling, making it a good mark for someone with an idea that suits his need.

A "Mind" piece that Warrick recalls as particularly appropriate was about lie detectors. "That hit the nail," Warrick says. "It was topical at the time because of the Clarence Thomas/Anita Hill hearings." Another, on procrastination, was good because it looked at a habit nearly anyone would like to eliminate.

- **Vanities** is all about beauty and looking better, again covered with the breadth and creativity that gives *Health* its mark. It has covered the history and improvement of the bra; the possible hazards of hair dyes; breast implant risks; manicures; and skin cream myths.

"Healthy Cooking," "Rounds," "Stitches," "Vital Signs," and "Vital Statistics" are written by regular contributors.

How to Query *Health*

One or two pages; do not send photo/art information.

"I always tell freelancers who haven't worked with us before to query on departments, not major features," Warrick says.

Your query to *Health* should get specific about the structure of the article and your sources for it. The editors want the query to reflect the eventual tone and style of the article you suggest. "A query that works proposes a story with a narrow focus with broad appeal," Warrick says simply. "Take a topic or event from your own backyard and connect it to bigger issues."

The query-reading process begins with an editorial assistant, who sorts queries and rejects those that are clearly inappropriate for the magazine. Those queries receive a "thanks, but no" form letter. The vast majority of queries stop here, Warrick warns. "There just aren't a lot of queries from new writers that make it," Warrick says.

The remaining queries are routed to various editors according to their specialties. Many of those queries are also rejected. "If a person has a good idea but we've just done it, or the topic won't work for some reason, we may send them a note encouraging them to try again," Warrick says. "But the truth is that letters from someone we don't know or who doesn't have a track record at other major magazines hardly ever work out."

How to Write for *Health*

"The important thing for people to know about *Health* is that we treasure good writing and a likeable voice," Warrick says. "We also value good research and a writer who puts a lot of time into accuracy.

"We don't expect objectivity from our writers. We look for a point of view. But along with that we require the writer to justify his or her view," he adds.

If you receive an assignment from *Health*, an editor is likely to call you to discuss details and approach. An assignment letter and contract will follow.

In addition, you'll receive a four-page "Guidelines for Writers on Assignment." It discusses keeping in contact with your editor, the manuscript review process, rewriting expectations, and shows how stringent the fact checking will be. Finally, it offers the writer some suggestions on annotating his or her completed manuscript to key quotes and facts to their sources. (See Chapter 5, Writing Articles That Command Attention, in Part I for more about annotating a manuscript.)

Much is expected of writers at *Health*, but the talent and work invested is not taken lightly. "I have a hell of a lot of admiration for freelance writers," Warrick says. "It's a tough row to hoe. Despite all my stern words about people who don't take the query system seriously, I know it's a difficult business."

Hemispheres

1301 Carolina Street
Greensboro, NC 27401
(919) 378-6065

Published: Monthly

Circulation: 500,000

Query: Kate Greer, editor-in-chief

Query response time: 6 to 12 weeks

Buys: About 250 articles/stories out of approximately 2,000 unsolicited queries/manuscripts received annually

Guidelines: Available; send SASE and $5 for a sample copy

Rights purchased: First World

Pays: On acceptance

Expenses: Pays reasonable documented incidental expenses agreed upon in advance

Kill fee: 20 percent

Rates:

Type of Article	*Word Length*	*Payment*
Major Feature	2,000	*(individually*
Short Feature	700 - 1,000	*negotiated)*
Department	900 - 1,200	

This magazine, published under the auspices of United Airlines, identifies itself as presenting a global perspective, practical information, and editorial with an attitude. It directs its contents to its primary reader—the frequent flyer—a business professional and decision-maker.

Hemispheres' audience is 60 percent male, more than 70 percent of whom are business travelers. The median age is 48. Almost 60 percent are college graduates, and the median household income is $111,500.

To Editor-in-Chief Kate Greer, in-flight is a mode of delivery, not a genre of editorial, so she cautions writers against thinking that all in-flight magazines are alike in their editorial focus.

"When people travel a lot, their lives are different," says Greer. "It changes the way they do business and handle their personal lives. So, we've tailored *Hemispheres* to serve their specific needs. We offer a sophisticated level of editorial without being intimidating or stuffy. While we cover business, we don't do it with a news focus as *The Wall Street Journal* does, but with a more reflective state of mind and a service orientation."

How to Slant Your Ideas to *Hemispheres*

Hemispheres' editorial mix features travel, business, family, and leisure. To learn how the magazine slants its ideas, Greer suggests studying several back issues. But, the editor requests that you don't call and ask the staff to send copies to you. If you don't fly United or know someone who does, you can send $5 to Pace Communications at the address listed at the beginning of this *Hemispheres* listing and request a sample issue.

The magazine avoids press junket journalism. "We have an international network of writers who give us insider information," says Greer. "Don't call and say you are going to Paris in a week and want to know if you can do something for us. When we want something on Paris, we are likely to call a person who lives there to do it, versus a writer who is going into town for a week."

The key to a good idea for *Hemispheres* is that the reader benefits from reading the article. "Though we favor service, we want a slightly off-the-wall approach," says Greer. "We look for a unique slant on things—a twist.

"A piece we did on post-modern marketing looked at the trend to 'buy a hat and save the planet,'" Greer continues. "The story took the tack that most of the green movement these days is highly dubious. The only benefit may be keeping the environment on people's minds. When readers finished the story, they had read quotes from several experts who've been observing the trend and could then devise opinions for themselves."

Hemispheres boasts a jam-packed table of contents with more than two dozen article categories. Virtually the entire magazine is open to freelance contributions.

The following is an editorial breakdown:

- **Aviation** covers anything that has to do with planes, aviators, airports, and other aviation-related subjects. "It could be future-oriented, nostalgic, or up-to-date," says Greer. "For example, we did a piece on airport designators, trying to discern how airports arrive at their three-letter identification codes. Another article looked at the new technology used to design the Boeing 777 on a computer, without making a prototype."

- **Case Study** covers a group of companies or an institution that has pulled off something rather remarkable. "It might be a profile of a company that was going bankrupt and after making numerous changes, its stock doubled," says Greer. But it doesn't necessarily have to be a turn-around story. One issue featured Hewlett Packard's climb to the top.

- **Executive Secrets** may be an interview with various people or just one person's viewpoint. It attempts to step inside an executive's mind. One article described the kinds of questions top executives ask when doing interviews. Another looked at what two executives involved in a personal relationship do when one gets transferred.
- **Eye on Sports** offers a worldwide view of sporting, including polo, hockey, cricket, football, soccer, and others.
- **Making a Difference** is a direct interview with a world-class leader. Figures featured in past issues are Carlos Salinas, president of Mexico; Boutros Boutros-Ghali, secretary general of the United Nations; and John Sawhill, president of The Nature Conservancy.
- **Of Grape and Grain** provides information on wine, distilled liquor and beer. "We approach the topic in a sophisticated way without being stuffy—which is definitely passé," says Greer. Topics have included art labels, Beaujolais Nouveau, cognac, and the trend to micro-breweries.
- **Savvy Shopper** is a location-based shopping guide. "We try to use people from the locations we cover because they know the ins and outs of the stores," says Greer. A few shopping meccas covered are Florence, Mexico City, and Santa Fe.
- **Science, Technology**, and **Computers** alternate each month to offer gee-whiz, leading-edge technology that has an application to people. It covers the wonders of discoveries and how they improve our lives, including new computer products, and subjects such as virtual reality, ergonomics, and medical breakthroughs.
- **Three Perfect Days,** the magazine's signature feature, gives readers a structured itinerary for how to spend three great days in a particular city. "Business people always say they're going to spend a few extra days at their destination before or after their business trip to get in a little leisure, but they never know what to do," explains Greer. "We tell them exactly where to stay, where to go, and what to do, hour by hour, day by day. We give them the best there is so they will tear out the article and file it. One feature that covered Hong Kong made me wish I had had the information when I was there; instead, I did all the usual things in the guidebook. The

writer gave the city such verve and sophisticated energy. It was naughty in places and had character and personality."

- **Vintage Traveler** aims to reach the more mature, experienced traveler, providing information about journeys that offer more luxury, more service, and more intellectual stimulation. The Andalusian Express, a luxurious train that travels through Spain; elder hostels; and the Thai floating market have all made the grade.
- **Weekend Breakaway** offers action weekends just an hour or two outside major cities to allow business people to make the most of travel layovers. "These people are sitting around air-conditioned offices all week, and when the weekend comes, they're ready to move," says Greer. "This column offers athletic adventures without having to travel too far. We've covered sea kayaking outside of Miami; attending a polo school 20 minutes from Heathrow; and participating in a wealth of outdoor activities at Ashinoko, a lake in the wooded foothills of Mt. Fuji."

"Artist Profile," "Artist's Showcase," "Children's Story," "Collecting," "Cultural Icons," "Family Counselor," "Fairways and Greens," "Personal Growth," "Point/Counterpoint," "Roving Gourmet," and "Travel News" are written by regular contributors or staff writers.

How to Query *Hemispheres*

One-page queries preferred. Do not send any photo/art information.

Greer likes well-thought-out queries that describe the story angle, why the magazine should want the idea, and what it will do for the reader in a way that reflects the writer's knowledge of the magazine. "Write about places where you have connections, and you'll come up with a framework that is far more interesting than a tourist would."

Since United flies all over the globe, the magazine is not tied only to destinations on its routes. "We fly globally and have connections to very obscure places," Greer says.

Remember that the magazine's desire is to be service-oriented and speak with a worldly voice and an international perspective.

How to Write for *Hemispheres*

"We like writers who have a strong personal style, and we do our best to let it shine through," says Greer. "We are not looking for uniformity in tone but rather in intellect, always keeping in mind our high-end, well-educated reader. We have writers who have various styles—humorous, literary, and poetic. Our success lies in finding a balance."

Greer prefers writers who don't have to be heavily edited. "We expect light editing on occasion, but if we have to do a lot, the writer rarely gets a second chance," the editor says.

Highlights for Children

803 Church Street
Honesdale, PA 18431
(717) 253-1080

Published: 11 times a year (July/August are combined)

Circulation: 3 million

Query: Beth Troop, manuscript coordinator

Query Response Time: 2 to 4 weeks

Buys: About 200 articles/stories out of approximately 10,000 unsolicited queries/manuscripts received annually

Guidelines: Available; send SASE

Rights purchased: All

Pays: On acceptance

Expenses: Pays

Kill fee: Pays only occasionally

Rates:

Type of Article	*Word Length*	*Payment*
Major Feature	800	$150+
Short Feature	400	125+
Activities	varies	15+
Poetry	varies	25+

"Fun With a Purpose" is the cover slogan for this children's magazine, founded in 1946. Geared to kids from ages two to 12 years, *Highlights for Children* is sent by mail to the homes of children whose parents subscribe, as well as to virtually every school and library. It also is seen in most doctors' and dentists' offices throughout the U.S.

One reason for the magazine's popularity, says Coordinating Editor Rich Wallace, is its stability. Packed with science, sports, arts, activities, puzzles, crafts, and fiction, it's substantive entertainment. "People who subscribed as kids are now buying it for their children and grandchildren," he says. "The magazine has high name recognition."

Highlights for Children includes no advertising because the publishers do not believe in it for this age group. Its editorial is based on the belief that learning and reading shouldn't be drudgery, but lifetime habits of pleasure. Instead of teaching isolated reading skills, it takes the view that kids will read stories that are enjoyable. For children too young to read, picture items are available. All of the content is created to be both fun to listen to or to be read alone.

How to Slant Your Ideas to *Highlights for Children*

The magazine seeks all types of fiction that will appeal to kids, including simple picture stories for younger children and advanced literary fiction for older kids. "An ideal story is one that an older child might enjoy reading while a younger one enjoys having it read to him," says Wallace.

Nonfiction stories go beyond what you'd find in a textbook or encyclopedia. "We want the personality, event, or process to really come to life," the editor notes. "The nonfiction stories can't be dry; they must be as accessible to the readers as the fiction."

Good past examples include articles on chimpanzee expert Jane Goodall; a novelist's efforts to save wild mustangs; an alternative feed for cows; and the art of voice acting as told by one actor who creates voices for cartoon series.

"These stories were by people involved in the areas they were writing about; they did not include second- or third-generation information," says Wallace. "We need writers to get as close to the subject as they can and bring the reader there as well. Don't use the encyclopedia or another magazine article to get your information—you'll be removed from the subject. If you want to profile Jesse Jackson, interview him and follow him around for a few days. Don't rely on someone else's research."

Wallace cautions that most articles do not focus just on a personality. The goal is for children to learn about the process in which the figure is involved—whether be it art, science, or sports.

The magazine's editorial includes the following feature categories, which are all open to freelance writers:

- **Art** or **Music** often focus on one artist, whether a painter, sculptor, or musician. "It doesn't have to follow a format," says Wallace. "Rather than writing a biography on the famous French artist Henri Matisse, one writer took a close-up look at one aspect of his work."
- **Biography** tends to be pieces about historical figures, so that the article teaches both history and a lesson about a great person. A biography of a Japanese woman named Michiko

Ishimure described her nine-year fight in the 1950s against a chemical company that refused to accept responsibility for making people sick.

- **Crafts, Parties, Plays**, and **Quizzes** are all part of the magazine's "Fun with a Purpose" philosophy. The magazine wants simple craft projects children can do with items found in any home. The parties provide activities for a wide range of ages. Finger plays or action verse should be easily understood and able to be illustrated in the magazine. *Highlights for Children* publishes only one or two party plans a year, though crafts and finger plays appear more regularly. One craft gave instructions on how to create a Christmas stocking out of a grocery bag.

  There is a great need for quizzes, but they have to be something other than topics you would find in the back of a textbook. Both the questions and the answers should be fun and informative.
- **Science** and **Nature** articles are frequently written by a scientist. A piece in each issue often focuses on a particular animal, such as one Wallace wrote about the white-tailed deer. The article gave a detailed description of the graceful, gentle, yet strong deer who live in the woods near his home.
- **Sports** includes nonfiction articles about sports, as well as fictional sports stories in which the child is the central character. The sports *Highlights for Children* covers must be accessible to children. They accept articles on how to play soccer, tips on shooting a basketball, and the invention of baseball. Sports profiles look at famous athletes who are good role models. Writers must have inroads to interview the sports figures.
- **World Cultures** is included in almost every issue. If you write about a culture, bring a slice of life from the area, whether it is the Sahara Desert, Brazil, or Tahiti. "Focus on something a kid would be interested in and weave in details about the culture though the narrative," says Wallace.

"Hidden Pictures" and "Things to Make" are open to freelancers interested in arts and crafts. "Our Own Pages," "Jokes," and "Riddles" are submitted by children. All other columns are written in house or by regular contributors.

How to Query *Highlights for Children*

Any length query accepted; send photo information with query; seasonal material is purchased throughout the year.

All *Highlights for Children* material is written on speculation, so the editors say they prefer to receive completed manuscripts rather than queries. "If you want to know if we have a piece in inventory on Ray Charles, then it's worth a query to save yourself the work," says Wallace. "However, most of the time when we get a proposal on a subject not already in inventory, we say we are happy to look at it on speculation. In most cases, it's almost not worth the time to query first."

If you choose to submit a query, include the information you will cover, the sources of the information, and the way you will approach the topic. The magazine is not current-events driven, nor is it particularly time-sensitive. However, if you are proposing a timely idea, make sure to send it well ahead of time.

How to Write for *Highlights for Children*

Wallace says that *Highlights for Children* is looking for a distinctive voice in every piece it publishes. "We want to get the feeling that the writer is passionate about the subject, but in a natural way," the editor explains. "We don't want writers to invent a voice, but to develop it through experience and then not be afraid to let it shine through."

Wallace believes that some writers hold back when writing for children. "We look for good journalists who can write for kids," explains Wallace. "People make a mistake when they measure every word they use and write down to youngsters. Our approach is to lift kids to another level. If the subject is intriguing, kids will extend themselves to the next reading level. If an article in the magazine doesn't appeal to a certain kid today, he or she may go back to that piece in a year or two."

When writing nonfiction for *Highlights for Children,* Wallace says most writers go wrong by submitting what classically reads like a term paper. "We do not want a dry collection of facts that covers too much ground," he cautions. "We are interested in anecdotal nonfiction; we like kids to learn by reading about an experience that shaped a person's life. Rather than saying that Mary Jones learned to work hard to become a champion figure skater, show that she competed in her first figure skating event at age seven and, even though she fell down 16 times, she decided to go on skating and eventually won the Olympic Gold Medal."

In fiction writing, Wallace faults writers for explaining too much. Too many story writers rely on over-used plots, or invent dialogue that doesn't sound natural, or preach at readers.

Because *Highlights for Children* is often the first place freelancers who want to write for children send queries and speculative manuscripts, the editors get to pick and choose from among the very best.

"We reject a lot of good material," says Wallace.That doesn't mean that the magazine isn't open to new writers. "We continually publish writers' first articles," the editor says. "We want to take a chance on new writers and to reach out to a broader writers' community."

If *Highlights for Children* is interested in your manuscript, you will receive a letter or phone call to discuss any necessary revisions. A contract is sent once the revised piece is accepted, and pay is on acceptance of the manuscript.

Home

1633 Broadway
New York, NY 10019
(212) 767-6000

Published: 10 times a year

Circulation: 1 million

Query: Linda Lentz, articles editor

Query response time: 1 week to 1 year

Buys: About 20 articles/short pieces out of 500 to 1,000 unsolicited queries received annually

Guidelines: Available; send SASE

Rights purchased: All

Pays: Within 2 months of acceptance

Expenses: Pays phone, research, and other items with prior approval

Kill fee: 20 percent

Rates:

Type of Article	*Word Length*	*Payment*
Major Feature	1,500 - 2,000	$1,000 - 1,200
Short Feature	750 - 1,000	500 - 750
Column	1,500 - 2,000	1,000
"Building Blocks"	1,000	750

Home is for middle-class homeowners, ranging in age from their thirties through retirement. Although some of the magazine's photography could certainly set a reader to dreaming, it is not intended as a dream book or pretty picture book.

"It is more of a resource book for practical matters," says Mary Kelly Selover, senior editor. "We try to take the reader beyond the brochure level, so we offer up-to-the-minute information and resources."

The identifying trait of the audience is its use of the magazine as a guide. The reader either is aspiring to buy a home, planning changes to the home, or actually spending money on anything from minor decorating to building a dream house. In any case, the reader is actively collecting information—a key to understanding *Home*'s articles.

How to Slant Your Ideas to *Home*

"Part of our editor-in-chief's precept is that *Home* should not be a coffee table book," says Timothy Drew, managing editor. "This magazine should be ripped apart and used. We inform the reader about what he or she should know without going as far as telling them how to do the project."

Linda Lentz, articles editor, adds, "We try to make our book readable, yet entertaining, informative, and good looking."

Virtually all well articles are assigned to known writers or written in house. The well of the book includes an architecture article, one on decorating, a kitchen feature, and a bath story, and one piece on a design detail such as comfortable chairs.

The following columns are open to freelancers:

- **Building Blocks** is a one-page report on one product. Past items have included wool, concrete, outdoor wood, and glass tile products.
- **Home Ecology** reports on a home-related issue and advises what to do. It states the issue and gives information, then offers resources that will help the homeowner. Topics have included radon, lead, and a solar update.
- **Home Economics** presents practical financial issues that affect homeowners. That might include an article about refinancing, hiring an inspector before purchasing a house, or starting your own bed and breakfast.
- **Home Office** addresses both product and trend in this increasingly important area of the home. The writer must be able to convey often confusing and complex information in an easily understood, readable (but not simplistic) manner with well-sourced national information. Topics have included: setting up a home office; computer-aided-design; home facsimiles; cellular telephones and beepers; portable computing; and computer programs that organize your money and taxes.
- **Homeowner's Diary** is your best shot at breaking into *Home*. It is a first- or third-person piece on an experience from which readers can learn. An article about surviving the aftermath of a home fire—with information about clean-up, insurance issues, and who to contact—fits here.
- **Home Report** deals with more general trends in home, housing, and design in addition to building and consumer products. These in-depth reports must be well researched and include a wide geographical range of sources for a

national audience. Roofing, pools, sun rooms, universal design, minivans, and mattresses have been addressed here.

"Home Almanac," "Home Front," "Home Library," "Homenclature," "Home Report," "Home Stretch," "Home Tech," and "Shop Talk" are written in house or by regular contributors.

How to Query *Home*

One or two pages; submitting several ideas at once is acceptable; do not send photo/art information.

Lentz knows what will get her attention in a query letter. "A concise, well-written, relaxed, conversational tone, solid information about what you want to do, and maybe a touch of humor," she says.

The editors agree that they don't mind seeing three or four ideas in one query. "The writer may get pigeonholed if I only see one idea," says Drew.

Selover adds, "I may get interested in the writer, even if the query isn't right on target. If it has a range of topics and shows that the writer understands the magazine and what he or she is writing about, that's important."

The worst queries are those that demonstrate ignorance of the magazine by mailing to the Los Angeles address (the offices moved in 1991), or suggesting something completely off base from *Home*'s needs.

An editorial assistant helps with the queries, but the editors share proposal review duties. Each editor confesses to being slow to respond to queries. "I really try," Drew says. "But in addition to putting out a magazine, we respond personally to every reader letter, so our time is short."

How to Write for *Home*

Drew advises writers to study the magazine in preparation for proposing an article. "Look at the tone," he says. "The closer you can write to the tone, the more the article will work for us."

That isn't to say that you must adhere to a rigid style, however. "There are a lot of voices in the choir," Selover says. "As long as each is on key, it's okay. If someone has a good voice on their own, we won't change it."

But Lentz adds that editing style into a piece isn't unusual. "If the article doesn't have great style and is flat but otherwise well-organized, we may have to put a little vitamin B-12 into it," she says.

Home

Resource information is important to the articles *Home* publishes. Since the reader may tear out an article and take it with him or her when shopping, a sidebar listing company names or brands has to be accurate. You may be asked to write a sidebar that includes books, organizations, and helpful phone numbers. You'll be required to submit your sources when you complete the article.

"Writers don't often realize that we're sticking our necks out when we assign to someone we don't know," Lentz points out. "If we have expertise in the topic, we might catch an error. But we really have to rely on our writers at times. We have to know we can trust them, so we tend to assign to people we know can deliver."

Breaking in is hard here, but *Home* isn't closed to new writers. "I use people I can rely on for most articles," says Lentz. "But I usually have one or two queries I'm considering."

International Wildlife/ National Wildlife

National Wildlife Federation
8925 Leesburg Pike
Vienna, VA 22184
(703) 790-4524

Published: Both magazines are published 6 times a year

Circulation: 700,000 for *National Wildlife*
375,000 for *International Wildlife*

Query: *National Wildlife:* Mark Wexler, editor
International Wildlife: Jonathan Fisher, editor

Query response time: 3 weeks

Buys: About 25 articles/stories out of approximately 750 unsolicited queries received annually

Guidelines: Available; send 9"x12" SASE for sample copies

Rights purchased: All

Pays: On acceptance

Expenses: Pays per individual arrangement

Kill fee: 33 percent

Rates:

Type of Article	*Word Length*	*Payment*
Major Feature	1,500 - 2,500	$1,000 - 3,000
Mini-feature	700 - 1,000	500 - 1,200

> "To create and encourage an awareness among the people of the world of the need for wide use and proper management of those resources of the Earth upon which our lives and welfare depend: the soil, the air, the water, the forests, the minerals, the plant life and the wildlife."
>
> —Jay D. Hair, Chairman
> Editorial Board,
> *International Wildlife/National Wildlife*

That is the editorial creed of *National Wildlife* and *International Wildlife,* magazines published by the National Wildlife Federation, the largest conservation organization in the nation. The nonprofit, nongovernment organization has a network of state affiliates and has long been a leader in educating the public about environmental issues.

Individuals who receive the magazines are members of the National Wildlife Federation. All memberships include subscriptions to *National Wildlife,* and 375,000 of the 700,000 memberships include subscriptions to both publications. The magazines are similar in the way they look and read, but their subject matter is different. As the name implies, *National Wildlife* covers wildlife and a wide range of related subjects inside the United States. Its sister publication, *International Wildlife,* covers the same subject matter worldwide, though it saves coverage of the United States for *National Wildlife.*

The magazines are aimed at people who are interested in nature. While readers include conservationists, biologists, and wildlife managers, the majority are not wildlife professionals. Demographic information is not available.

"Imagine middle-class adults who live in urban or suburban areas and are interested in nature," says Bob Strohm, editor-in-chief. "They appreciate the drama and beauty of all wildlife. Some are environmental activists, some are hunters and fishermen, and some are armchair travelers who enjoy reading about fascinating places and wildlife."

How to Slant Your Ideas to *National Wildlife* and *International Wildlife*

"We try to show people wildlife in a way they haven't thought of before," says Strohm. "We take a wise-use-of-nature approach, not a preservationist approach. The three areas we cover primarily are nature, science, and environment. Nature stories concern both animals and plants, as well as marine biology, but it's best if there is a scientific or environmental thrust. Science stories focus on the work of a scientist or group of scientists. The crux of an environmental article, whether it concerns animals, plants, water, air, or toxins, is the threat to a healthful environment and what people are doing about it. We want to cover environmental/political issues.

"The kinds of stories we carry don't always have news angles, but if you have one or one can be created, use it to give the article a patina of timeliness," says Strohm. For example, *National Wildlife* used one such article titled "Is There a Killer in Your House?"—a piece based on the age-old idea that cats kill a lot of birds. The writer made the story current by reporting new research figures from a four-year study on the impact of cats killing wildlife.

"We like seasonal pieces, and are, in fact, always in need of them, but think about an angle before sending an idea. For example, we ran one piece about the winter keeper of Yellowstone National Park, whose family lives with him isolated in a house 18 feet under snow for four to five months each winter. Another article we asked a newspaper writer to do for us covered the how-to basics of having a living holiday tree. Keep visuals in mind—they are a good way to get into our pages."

Strohm says the easiest way to find ideas for the two magazines is to identify a scientist who has done research on animals, birds, fish, flowers, or some other form of nature. "We will always do stories on the white-tail deer, but what sells easiest is new research," he says. "In fact, we spot a lot of topics in newspapers and other science magazines that we eventually cover in our own way."

While both *National Wildlife* and *International Wildlife* are connected to the National Wildlife Federation, Strohm emphasizes that neither publication is a mouthpiece of the organization. "We don't just parrot the party line, but we do report on environmental issues the Federation is working on," he says.

Neither magazine runs accounts of rescuing injured or orphaned wildlife. They aren't looking for reports about the saving of one or two animals; their interest runs broader, to habitat preservation and enhancement that saves an entire species.

One-third of the publications' editorial content is based on ideas generated by writers; another third of the ideas come from editors; and the final third are ideas that are developed to accompany visuals that photographers submit. "If a photographer writes to say he has the best pictures of the ruby-throated hummingbird, we will want to see them. If they are great, we will come up with a text assignment," the editor explains.

Although both rely heavily on freelancers, *International Wildlife*, because of its broad scope, has many more scientists and photographers authoring articles. "If a couple spent seven years in Africa researching the brown hyena, it's best for them to write the article," says Strohm.

Each issue of the two magazines includes approximately eight to 10 feature articles of 1,500 to 2,500 words and a one-page mini-feature of about 700 words. There are no regular columns.

National Wildlife breaks down its editorial into the following:

- **People and the Outdoors** describes people who have been involved in environmental concerns or conservation in interesting ways. Examples include the last of the old decoy makers and a day in the life of an Oregon forester.
- **People Who Make a Difference** profiles private citizens who have gone beyond the call of duty to protect wildlife and habitats or to prevent environmental contamination.

- **What You Can Do** offers articles that show readers how to get things done. Examples include how a city was cleaned up, a park area that was saved, and a legislature that was educated in the need for sound environmental laws.

Many articles look at a single species, like whether or not the grizzly can survive the 20th century; the battle between diminishing habitats and human encroachment; and adventure narratives involving wildlife. (The latter can include hunting, but it should not be the main focus of the narrative.)

International Wildlife does not adhere to such a breakdown of editorial, but a few examples of articles include: "The Sheer Wonder of Penguins," tales and tidbits about the world's coolest birds; "Dr. Ant," a study of the work of Harvard's E.O. Wilson; "How We Invented the Lion," showing how art through the ages attached nobility and bravery to lions; and "Running for Their Lives," a look at whether the worldwide ivory ban will save Africa's elephant population.

How to Query *National Wildlife* and *International Wildlife*

One page preferred; photos are important—send information on photos you have available or tell if you know who can supply the art.

Good ideas are what sell to *National Wildlife* and *International Wildlife.* The best queries, Strohm says, are one page long, describe the scope of the story, and have a very specific peg on which the story will be hung.

When it comes to writing queries for these publications, the writer's guidelines for *International Wildlife* put it best: "Too much environmental writing is self-serving and dull. Yet even the dullest subject can be made interesting. The challenge is to come up with new approaches, new slants, new angles. We appreciate creative thinking and novel ways of covering conventional subjects. Even more, we appreciate proposals on unconventional or unusual subjects."

"Most writers fail by proposing broad topics, such as 'I am going to Montana this winter and thought I'd do a story,'" says Strohm. He wants writers to tell him in their queries whom they plan to quote in their articles. He prefers to see sample anecdotes, especially from new writers, and notes that a sample lead is a great indicator of how good the story and the writer can be. "Generally if the lead is terrific, the writer has a great story," he says. "Sample quotes are not necessary, because I assume writers can get them during the interviews."

Both magazines are visual, so it's essential to send photos or have photos available. "If you are proposing a story on box turtles or endangered plants in the Marshall Islands, it's easier for us to think about assigning the piece if you have photos or know who has photographed them," says Strohm. "Our standards for photography are as high as other top magazines."

While both magazines like writers to send samples of past work, Strohm says that clips reflect a person's best writing and often substantial editing. "We wonder if this is a great writer or editor at work," he muses. "Our premium is good writing, and one or two clips are fine to show us that."

How to Write for *National Wildlife* and *International Wildlife*

The best prototype to follow when writing for these two magazines is the front page, center column article of *The Wall Street Journal.* "It is superb writing with a great lead, good kicker, terrific quotes, and the right kind of examples," says Strohm. "Another way to think of it is to adopt news magazine style. We are after vital, active reporting that holds the reader once the dramatic photography and art work have attracted initial interest in the story. We want writers who can do a comprehensive job of covering the five Ws and have a heavy anecdotal style. Some of our very best writers are from *People* or *TV Guide.* They are solid reporters and good writers."

The magazines' writer's guidelines encourage contributors to use the phone to get information from primary sources. "Don't be satisfied with general quotes; get colorful comments that say something," the editors tell freelancers. "Get the latest statistics and numbers. Cover all sides, but don't get so close to the story that you can no longer distinguish what is important. And, avoid the lingo of biologists or wildlife managers. Remember, our readers, no matter how well educated are 'just folks.'"

Says Strohm, "One editor at our publications has a saying—'Never underestimate a reader's intelligence, but never overestimate a reader's comprehension.'"

One area where most writers go wrong, according to Strohm, is not reading the assignment letter carefully. "We are fussy," he admits. "We often send a two- to four-page letter that suggests the kind of lead, the authorities to talk to if it is a reporting piece, and the content we want and don't want. We put a lot of effort into those letters; they are not loaded with a boiler plate."

Strohm says the magazines normally condense pieces 20 to 30 percent. "We find that we produce the best text if we ask the writer for 2,500 words and then cut in house to 2,000," he says. "About one out of three stories is rewritten at least once by the writer before we begin editing. When that is needed, we send very specific instructions of what we want the writer to do."

Both magazines expect writers to rigorously check facts. After the text is edited by the staff, it is sent to three to six outside experts, the names of whom the writer must supply. "These people could be sources used to write the piece or other experts," he says. "If they require money for their trouble, we will pay them. That, however, only happens a few times a year."

Once the story has been final-edited, the editors send it back to the writer. "We think it is important for writers to see how their work will appear," says Strohm. "Sometimes editing creates errors and misimpressions, so passing it by the writer one last time produces a better final product."

Islands

3886 State Street
Santa Barbara, CA 93105
(805) 682-7177

Published: Bimonthly

Circulation: 170,000

Query: Joan Tapper, editor-in-chief/associate publisher

Query response time: 4 to 6 weeks

Buys: About 30 articles/short pieces out of more than 1,500 unsolicited queries received annually

Guidelines: Available; send SASE

Rights purchased: All; open to splitting reprint rights after one year

Pays: On acceptance

Expenses: Pays for features, not for departments or "Logbook"

Kill fee: 25 percent

Rates:

Type of Article	*Word Length*	*Payment*
Major Feature	2,000 - 4,000	$1,000 - 2,000
Department/Column	1,200 - 2,000	600 - 1,000
"Encounters"	925	462
"Escape Artist"	150 with photo	150
"Logbook"	500	250

This magazine's mission statement says that it aims to be the best publication for island travelers and dreamers. Joan Tapper, editor-in-chief and associate publisher, adds, "Our readers are those who are interested in islands, those who travel to islands, and those who dream about islands. Most of our readers actually travel quite a bit. But they also like to fantasize about places they may never get to or haven't visited yet."

The magazine's readership is 61 percent male and 39 percent female, with a median age of 47 years. The reader has the money to travel—the median household income is $74,700, and the average net worth nearly $900,000. A little more than 20 percent of the readers own property on an island. Most hold a valid passport and nearly all have traveled beyond the 48 U.S. continental states in the last three years.

How to Slant Your Ideas to *Islands*

Once they've arrived at their destination, these readers are active, enjoying sailing, snorkeling, golf, and exploring. Tapper emphasizes that, although *Islands* is a destination magazine, it does not cover resorts or publish the typical travelogue.

"We don't cover every detail about an island. We expect to meet characters and see places—not fictional ones, of course—but those that illustrate the author's point of view about what's really characteristic about a place," the editor says.

Tapper discourages writers who haven't worked with *Islands* from querying for features. There are numerous columns and departments in which a newcomer stands a better chance. Not all columns appear in every issue.

The following columns and departments are open to freelancers:

- **Arts** tends to be about an indigenous art form, not an artist. Past topics have included seagrass baskets from South Carolina, textiles in Indonesia, and tapa cloth in Samoa. Tapper asks that the article tell about how the art is made, include a bit of history or information about its uses, and possibly identify some characteristics of a high-quality piece.
- **Culture Shock** highlights unusual cultural juxtapositions on various islands. Tapper offers as examples an article about country/western bars in Japan and a look at how urban Manila differs from what you'd traditionally find in the Philippines.
- **Encounters** offers a personal anecdote that gives the reader a sense of the character of an island. This is not a travel memories column, but rather a place to examine such topics as the aesthetics of unusual Japanese food. Other pieces have discussed growing up on a Long Island beach, and coming across an idiosyncratic church in Iceland.
- **Escape Artist** is a long caption that accompanies a photo. The subject of the photo is an island dweller with an interesting story. One was about a retired business owner and diver who discovered 138 sunken ships and now lives on a volcanic knob in the Virgin Islands.
- **Food** features a local cook—not a restaurant owner or famous chef—who is known for his or her expertise in the local cuisine. Pieces have covered the experience of a typical Bahamian breakfast, and the story of an Irish woman who is rewriting old cookbooks found in the basement of her family's castle.

- **Island Hopping** is a featurette about a destination too far off the beaten path to warrant a full article. Often, the places are interesting but lack the potential for widespread interest. This is the only department that is destination-oriented. Past examples include an article about little-known City Island in the Bronx, which has an interesting sailing history; and a piece on Anticosti Island at the mouth of Quebec's St. Lawrence River.
- **Life-Style** is an eclectic department covering interesting aspects of island life that don't fit easily into other categories. An article on the rebuilding of Kauai, Hawaii, after Hurricane Iniki is a good example of a relevant, timely article.
- **Logbook** is the magazine's front-of-the-book briefs department. "It is the only section that approaches a journalistic tone," Tapper says. The short pieces cover all manner of topics about islands—new museums, festivals, environmental issues, scientific discoveries, architecture, and more. "These tend to be topical or somewhat offbeat," Tapper adds.
- **Nature** looks at unusual natural history aspects of an island or islands. A recent piece explained how an island is born, featuring Surtsey, off the coast of Iceland, which surfaced suddenly in 1965.
- **Islanders** are profiles about notable people with an island connection. Past columns have featured a *New York Times* outdoors columnist who lives on Martha's Vineyard; and a musician who travels the world recording island music.
- **Sports** covers unusual and frequently amusing sports and contests native to an island. For instance, how about going mud-walking on Frisian Island near the Netherlands? Or attending dragon races in Hong Kong? Get the idea?
- **Trails** offers the reader somewhere to walk for the day. This column isn't the place for backpacking articles, but for day hikes. The walk can be around a city, exploring its culture or history, or into wilderness areas to appreciate a particular type of wildlife or natural phenomenon.

"High Seas Letter" and "Readings" are written by regular contributors.

How to Query *Islands*

One or two pages with several feature-oriented clips, rather than travel pieces, to show writing style. Although no photo/art information is necessary, editors appreciate hearing about local sources.

"We will look at a query for a feature," Tapper allows. "But if you don't have great clips or some way to demonstrate your experience and talent, chances are very small we'd assign a feature to an unknown writer."

The good news is that Tapper is open to less-experienced writers for the departments and columns. "The smaller the piece, the better the chances of breaking in," she says. "'Logbook' is a good place to start.

"I like to see the idea, your focus, why you should be the one to write this article, and some good clips to back you up," Tapper states.

"Most islands have been around for a long time," she adds with a laugh. "So chances are we've covered them. You need to tell me why we need another article on this place now."

There's an element of luck and timing in selling an article, the editor says. "For instance, as Eastern Europe began to open, I received a query for a piece on an island off the Estonia coast," she recalls. "It was accompanied by good clips, so I assigned it. Two weeks later, I received another query with equally good clips for the next island over. Obviously, I couldn't use both articles, so the second one lost out purely by chance."

Queries to *Islands* go to either Tapper or a senior editor. If an editor thinks it has merit, the query and clips will be passed to another editor or two. "We have a small staff but we have a wide array of interests and expertise," Tapper says. "So I'd go to the editor most likely to be familiar with the place or topic suggested."

Tapper warns that several things will turn her away immediately: a laundry list of 20 ideas that have no relevance to *Islands*; articles proposing resort stories; and queries riddled with travel clichés.

"Give me proof that you can write an interesting story," Tapper says. "If I can't understand the query or the clips you send are dull, I'll assume your article would reflect that and reject the query."

How to Write for *Islands*

"I happen to believe in using the finest writers possible," Tapper says. "They aren't always the ones you would think of for a travel magazine. I like essayists, novelists, science and nature writers, as well as those who specialize in travel."

Some of those writers Tapper has published include Paul Theroux, Jan Morris, and numerous writers based in other countries and, coincidentally, on many islands.

"It's not easy to write an article for us," Tapper admits. "We look for an individual voice that will help the reader distinguish one place from another. So one piece might be very lyrical, another straightforward, and another exuberant.

"A good author gets to the heart of a place, the thing that is crucial about it, that makes it memorable," says Tapper. "Our best pieces share a sense of place and the author's personality. An article should take you there—reveal some detail of the background and beauty of the place. However, the writer must describe his or her experience in a very subjective way. Good articles are memorable because the writer chooses to focus on a detail—a rare flower, what's in the shop windows, or a special person who embodies the culture," Tapper says.

Once an article is assigned, an editor will talk with the writer to flesh out the approach to the piece. If the writer is new to the magazine, a letter will follow recapping the approach of his article.

Occasionally, Tapper will ask a new writer to do an article on speculation, particularly if it is a good idea for a short piece, but the writer has no clips. "If someone has done the legwork already for an article that is only going to be 500 words or so, he or she may think the work is worth the chance to break in," she says.

Articles that need work are nearly always returned to the writer with extensive instructions. But, Tapper assures prospective writers, she almost never kills a piece. "I hate that," she says. "Sometimes we have to polish it, but if we get to the point of an assignment, it nearly always works out."

Ladies' Home Journal

100 Park Avenue
New York, NY 10017
(212) 351-3500

Published: Monthly

Circulation: 5 million

Query: Pam O'Brien, features editor, or appropriate department editor

Query response time: 2 to 10 weeks

Buys: About 135 articles/stories out of approximately 17,000 unsolicited queries/manuscripts received annually

Guidelines: Available; send SASE

Rights purchased: All

Pays: On acceptance

Expenses: Pays if reasonable

Kill fee: 25 percent

Rates:

Type of Article	*Word Length*	*Payment*
Major Feature	2,000	varies widely
Short Feature	300 - 500	varies widely
"Kidspeak"	100 - 200	$ 50
"A Woman Today"	1,500	750
"Woman to Woman"	1,000	750

Ladies' Home Journal is targeted to the intelligent woman who wants to be up-to-the-minute on issues she cares about most—family, relationships, education, health, the environment. She also enjoys thought-provoking coverage of the people she wants to know more about. The magazine supports a woman's determination to be the best she can be.

The median age of readers is 43, with 73 percent having attended college. More than 60 percent of the *Journal*'s audience is employed outside the home. The median household income is $38,213.

How to Slant Your Ideas to *Ladies' Home Journal*

"The most important thing a writer can do is to get to know the magazine and target the correct section and editor," says one editor. "Look at recent issues to familiarize yourself with our content and style. Our human-interest columns are usually a good place for new or first-time freelancers to start," the editor adds.

The following columns are open to freelancers:

- **Kidspeak** includes short, true anecdotes relating funny things children say.
- **A Woman Today** is a first-person column detailing a significant crisis or life-altering event in the writer's recent past. One article profiled a busy businesswoman, mother, and grandmother who invested in the stock market, turning $300 into $100,000 and boosting her self-confidence as well. Another writer told of the miracle that saved the life of her Siamese twins. A third woman, whose house was damaged by Hurricane Andrew, wrote about the ordeal and how her family rebuilt their lives.

  Contributors should address submissions to Box WT at the New York address listed at the beginning of this *Ladies' Home Journal* entry. Include your name, address, and daytime phone number on the manuscript, with an SASE.
- **Woman to Woman** is a column of true first-person stories about intimate events that occur in a woman's life. The topic should be one about which a woman would confide only in a close female friend. Identities are kept anonymous, and pseudonyms should be used for persons included in the story. A couple of examples include "My Husband Left Me for the Town Tramp" and "The Strangest Obsession of All" (about a young woman's battle against the compulsion to pull out her hair).

  Address submissions to Box WW at the New York address listed previously. Include your name, address, and daytime phone number on the manuscript, with an SASE.

Beauty, fashion, food, and lifestyle articles are written by regular contributors.

How to Query *Ladies' Home Journal*

One to two pages preferred. Do not send any photos/art suggestions. Query seasonal stories five to six months in advance.

Queries to *Ladies' Home Journal* should be brief and specific. After writing an enticing lead, describe how you will research and develop your story. If you've been published previously, include samples of your writing, a list of credits, and a résumé.

Editors will not respond to a submission unless it is accompanied by an SASE with proper postage. They ask that writers do not call to follow up on a submission, and reassure them that every query is read carefully.

How to Write for *Ladies' Home Journal*

Due to the volume of submissions received, *Ladies' Home Journal* was unable to offer information for this section.

Lear's

655 Madison Avenue
New York, NY 10021
(212) 888-0007

Published: Monthly

Circulation: 500,000

Query: Nelson Aldrich, Jr., articles editor

Query response time: 4 weeks

Buys: Less than a dozen articles out of many unsolicited queries received annually

Guidelines: None available

Rights purchased: First NAS

Pays: Within 30 days of acceptance

Expenses: Negotiates items on a case-by-case basis

Kill fee: 25 percent

Rates:

Type of Article	*Word Length*	*Payment*
Major Feature	4,000-5,000	$4,000 - 5,000+
Other Feature	1,200-2,500	1,200 - 2,500+

"I can't emphasize enough that this is one of the last general interest magazines in America," says Nelson Aldrich, Jr., articles editor. "We are, in theory and in practice, open to anything."

That kind of open-minded attitude to new ideas is what also characterizes *Lear's* readers. "We like to think of the *Lear's* woman as a woman of any age who is engaged in politics, her work, and in the life of her local and global society," Aldrich says.

Lear's primarily targets female readers 35 years old and older with a mix of celebrity profiles, personal stories, money management tips, reports on contemporary social issues, the arts, health, and stories about women who are making a difference in the world. Fashion and beauty coverage takes a back seat to features that stimulate readers to think about their role in the world around them.

Frances Lear founded the magazine in 1987 to fill a void of publications devoted to women over 35. Although she's not active in the daily workings of the magazine, her imprint is still visible in the topics and people covered.

How to Slant Your Ideas to *Lear's*

Each month Frances Lear takes her readers and a stimulating guest to lunch. Her candid, thought-provoking conversations with Pulitzer Prize-winning journalists, directors, physicians, and authors is summarized in "Lunch," a column that captures the essence of what this sophisticated magazine is all about.

Freelancers interested in writing for *Lear's* will get a good sense of the flavor of this magazine by reading "Lunch." Her guests tackle everything from the growing influence of women, to the future of television, and combining demanding careers with motherhood.

The rest of the editorial mix in *Lear's* is no less thought provoking. "We look for an emotional and intellectual engagement and commitment to the subject by a writer," says Aldrich. "If you're really, really hot to write about something the chances are good that it's going to show.

"We look for some connection between the would-be contributor and the subject they want to write about," he explains. "If you say you want to do a profile of Jay Leno, tell me why you want to write about the entertainer. I know people are interested in Jay Leno, but why are *you* interested?"

This kind of emotional attachment between the author and the subject matter of a story shows up frequently in *Lear's*. In one issue, a writer shared her story of traveling to Bulgaria to adopt a baby girl. "That was an interesting story because the narrative threw such a surprising light on adoption," Aldrich recalls. "This was also a story about what it means to adopt and some of the not very pleasant things you may learn about yourself in the process."

On another journey closer to home, a New York writer and her ten-year-old daughter traveled south of the Mason-Dixon line to meet their southern kinfolk. The trip forged a bond between mother and daughter as they discovered a new culture within their own country.

In addition to personal sojourns, *Lear's* looks for informative articles that update readers on important issues or provide them with news that makes life easier. These articles run the gamut — from how to pick a good running shoe, to how our medical records aren't as confidential as we once believed, and to the trials of reentering the dating scene at 40.

While most features are written by established writers known to *Lear's* editorial staff, new freelancers are accepted if they are excellent reporters and strong stylists, and can offer compelling ideas.

The following columns are open to freelancers:

- **A Woman for *Lear's*** is one of the magazine's most interesting columns, and a feature that distinguishes this publication in the women's market. Readers have met political activists, photographers, bankers, TV producers, novelists, military officers, and even a dog sled driver from Alaska in this section. These empathic and intimate pieces explore the work and personal lives of inspirational women who, though they have not yet achieved widespread fame, have stories that will capture the imaginations and admiration of their peers. The stories highlight strategies these women used to overcome obstacles in their lives.
- **Fitness/Sport** offers readers news of the latest trends in exercise to feel good and stay in shape. Topics have included everything from yoga to ballet to in-line skating. If you know your topic and have sources who are fitness experts, you'll have a shot at this one.
- **Money & Worth** is written by financial experts who offer investment tips and guidance to achieve financial security. Freelancers must be knowledgeable and write engagingly about money.
- **Shopping** pokes fun at America's passion to "shop until we drop." The column features humorous personal accounts of "shopaholism," disastrous purchases, shared dressing rooms, and other perils of the eternal search for that perfect item.

"Economies," "Health" and "Places" are written by regular contributors or staff writers.

How to Query *Lear's*

One or two pages preferred; no photo/art information needed.

"Access to our printed page is very difficult," admits Aldrich. "We generally rely on a stable of favorite writers." He notes that at least 25 percent of each issue comes from regular contributors.

If you're an unknown to *Lear's*, your best bet is to use the query process, says Aldrich. "Our associates read through the submissions, and if we get something that sounds good, we commission it."

Aldrich passes on a piece of advice that may sound unusual to many freelancers. "Stop sending queries that you think the magazine's editors and readers will be interested in. It's a disaster.

The ideas look dead on the page. Instead, writers need to dig deeper," he says. "There must be an emotional, intellectual connection, some reason a writer wants to write a story."

How to Write for *Lear's*

"The watch words at *Lear's* are high spirited, aggressive, confident, and humorous," says Aldrich.

In other words, you've got to write with passion. And have the persistence to rewrite when necessary. "Typically, there are three rewrites," notes Aldrich. "And that's with the good writers."

To get writers started on the right track, *Lear's* editors spend time talking to them about the story. "We try to talk it through so they know what we want and we know what they want," Aldrich says. I'm a writer myself, so I tend to be sympathetic to freelancers. I can help turn a story into English, but I can't do a writer's reporting."

Longevity

1965 Broadway
New York, NY 10023-5965
(212) 496-6100

Published: Monthly

Circulation: 350,000, with 64 million readership

Query: Features and all other areas: Susan Millar Perry, editor
"Anti-aging News," "Childwise," "Longevity Advisor": Marie Hodge, senior editor

Query response time: 2 to 3 weeks

Buys: About 2 articles out of approximately 1,000 unsolicited queries/manuscripts received annually

Guidelines: Available; send SASE

Rights purchased: Exclusive First NAS in English, nonexclusive worldwide periodical rights to publish work in all languages; other nonexclusive rights; all rights retained for short pieces

Pays: On acceptance

Expenses: Pays reasonable expenses approved at time of assignment

Kill fee: 25 percent

Rates:

Type of Article	*Word Length*	*Payment*
Major Feature	1,500 - 2,500	$1,500 - 2,500
Column	650	650

Longevity readers are baby boomers who have noticed that they aren't 20 years old anymore. Three-quarters of the readers are female, and the median age is 39. Their household income is about $43,000, and 67.5 percent work. They are an educated audience; more than half attended or graduated from college.

Marie Hodge, senior editor, comments, "Our readers are people who want to live long, productive lives. They don't see aging as necessary, and what they look to us for is the latest research findings in life extension; it is our job to translate that data to their everyday lives—from what they eat to how they exercise."

Patricia Lynden, executive articles editor, says, "We deal with both the quantity and quality of our years. For instance, we publish articles on facelifts, with the belief that if you feel better about yourself, you'll live better, and your chances of living longer are better. We also do it to report the latest techniques, and offer good consumer knowledge in this new way to spend the medical dollar."

The magazine is published in Europe, Australia, and South Africa in addition to the United States.

How to Slant Your Ideas to *Longevity*

Few writers grasp the unique slant of the magazine which is news/trend-oriented.

All articles and shorts must be pegged to cutting-edge research, nutritional or scientific findings, or a trend that affects one's health and longevity. Most of the article ideas are created in house and assigned to a number of contributing editors and other regular contributors. Many of the remaining articles come from those regular contributors who have taken the time to learn the magazine's style.

Medicine, science, food, nutrition, fitness, beauty, and lifestyle pieces make up the four or five well articles each month. In addition to news briefs at the front of the book, the magazine has a changing roster of about a dozen columns, most about 650 words long.

The following columns, while often produced by frequent contributors, are open to queries:

- **Air, Earth, Water** is an environmental column of 650 words. Topics may address what the reader can do to improve her responsible lifestyle or about a danger to the reader, but must have a newsy, cutting edge slant. Articles have covered subjects such as the danger of batteries, the military's contribution to pollution, and cleaning up your car's act.
- **Anti-aging News** is the news brief section at the front of the magazine. Although most pieces are written in house or by regular contributors, writers with anti-aging information and current research briefs may query.
- **Childwise** covers parenting of kids from birth to adolescence. Topics range widely, but have included cosmetic dentistry for children, pediatric PMS, and kids and cholesterol. Again, *Longevity* looks for a newsy slant for this column.
- **Last Word** is a backpage personal essay. It may be about coming to terms with childlessness as one approaches menopause, how much it costs to maintain one's

beauty-product collection, or becoming too old to play in major league baseball—but young enough to run for president. The idea is to offer a final 650 to 750 words—happy, sad, or funny—but always eloquent, about your state of life, and always with an age angle.

- **Marketing Youth** explores beauty products and their value to the consumer. Many of these columns are written by a beauty editor or a regular contributor. Past topics have included the pros and cons of dermatologists selling their own products, a piece on facials, and an article on the value of firming creams.
- **Medicine** reports on new medical advances and trends. One piece looked at computer-generated drugs; another examined the medical breakthroughs that have come out of the space program.
- **Travel/R & R** falls under the *Longevity* category of "destressing." The articles usually have a spiritual or physical renewal angle. There are no "Seeing Europe in Seven Days" articles that are exhausting to read, let alone attempt. The focus is on finding a calming, restful place, or a spot to do the physical or adventurous things you've been putting off.

"Beauty News," "Health Style Setters," "In Shape," "Longevity File," "Long-life Ideas," "Love and Longevity," and "Mind, Body, Spirit" are written by regular contributors. Celebrity profiles are written by *Longevity*'s West Coast editors.

How to Query *Longevity*

One or two pages preferred; no photo/art information needed.

Like most editors, the editors speaking for this magazine agree that a writer's first obligation is to read the magazine. Lynden says, "I want to see that you've taken the trouble to look through it and figure it out. A lot of people just read the masthead and query someone.

"What many people fail to understand is that, although we are a health and fitness magazine, there always must be a longevity spin to every article. A general piece on herbs won't work for us, but an article on new research findings proving the medicinal benefits of an herbal remedy might," the editor explains.

Therefore, your query should focus on the life-extension aspect of your topic. The editors want to know who you plan to interview, and what direction your proposed article would take. They also want to see any evidence you have that you understand or have written about living a long, healthy life, and always expect to see your clips that reflect that.

How to Write for *Longevity*

"A lot of people read this magazine and think it is easy to write for," says Lynden. "It's actually hard. The articles have to be easy to read, but must be packed with information. This is not a place for beginners. Even the beauty pieces are full of information, not just fluff."

Managing Editor Penelope Weiss notes, "*Longevity* doesn't neglect the negative things we all must face. But our articles always offer a positive self-help angle with a lot of underlying science and solid research to back it up."

Two full-time researchers will follow up on the information you include in your article, so sources and facts must be squeaky clean. Once your article is accepted, you'll be asked to submit transcripts of interviews, source names and phone numbers, and book citations where they've been quoted or used as background.

McCall's

110 Fifth Avenue
New York, NY 10011
(212) 463-1000

Published: Monthly

Circulation: 4.6 million

Query: "Health Report," "Staying Fit," "Vital Signs": Ann Ranard, health editor

Other features: Lynne Cusack, executive editor

Query response time: 4 weeks

Buys: About 100 articles out of approximately 3,100 unsolicited queries/manuscripts received annually

Guidelines: None available

Rights purchased: First NAS

Pays: On acceptance

Expenses: Pays if reasonable

Kill fee: 20 percent

Rates:

Type of Article	*Word Length*	*Payment*
Major Feature	2,500 - 5,000	$2,500 - 5,000
"Health Report"	2,500	2,500
"Inside Story"	2,500 - 5,000	2,500 - 5,000
"Personal Journey"	2,500 - 5,000	
Total Health section		
"Special Report"	2,500	2,500
"Staying Fit"	750	750
"Vital Signs"	750	750

All ages of women read *McCall's*, according to Lee Lusardi Connor, special features editor. "We think of her as in her early 40s, married and working, with a couple of kids," she says. "She feels good about herself, so we don't publish 'thigh anxiety' stories that make her feel vulnerable about some alleged difficult part of her body.

"We try to take a positive point of view for our readers," Lusardi continues. "We want to give her a sense that there is pleasure out there and she can find it."

How to Slant Your Ideas to *McCall's*

"We're a strategies-oriented magazine," Lusardi says. "Articles that offer 34 ways to do something better or faster are popular with our readers. Even in an investigative piece or a dramatic human-interest story, we like to offer the reader something she can learn from, often in the form of an accompanying sidebar."

About 70 percent of the magazine's story ideas are created in house; the remainder come from freelancers. The editorial mix includes relationships, sex, health, personality profiles, and fashion, beauty, home, food, and decorating.

The following columns and sections are open to freelancers:

- **Inside Story** offers sensational, dramatic, or investigative stories with a larger meaning to them. One article dealt with a female oncologist who was instrumental in identifying some of the early cases of AIDS in New York City. While it told her professional story, it wove in her personal story of polio at age five and her lifelong fight to live as normally as possible.
- **Personal Journey** is a first-person account of an extraordinary experience that proved to be a turning point for the person involved. A past article asked the question, "When a Woman is Attacked, Why Does *She* Get Blamed?" Another dealt with a mother surviving her daughter's murder. Betty Ford wrote about staying recovered from alcoholism.
- **Total Health** includes "Staying Fit," "Special Report," and "Vital Signs." In one issue, the "Vital Signs" piece looked at home testing kits and other self-monitoring techniques in less than 1,000 words. "Staying Fit" was about "low-cal" foods that really aren't; the piece was about 500 words long. And "Special Report" covered cosmetic surgery in about 1,500 words, plus a brief sidebar and a chart listing the costs and risks of various procedures.

"Betsy McCall," "Between Friends," "The Confident Parent," "Personal Style," "Pet Life," "Secrets of a Marriage Counselor," "True Colors," "Your Healthy Child," and "Your Home," as well as celebrity profiles, fashion and beauty, food and entertaining, and home decorating articles are written by regular contributors or the editorial staff.

How to Query *McCall's*

One or two pages preferred; do not submit photo/art information. Submit seasonal material any time during the year.

Lusardi recommends that writers study the magazine carefully before querying. Being able to suggest which section of the magazine your piece might fill, along with a catchy proposed headline, will demonstrate your familiarity with the masthead, and win points with the busy editors.

The editor is equally clear about things that don't work in queries: letters that begin with "Dear Editor" and demonstrate that the writer hasn't taken the time to look at the publication; queries that suggest a topic that is too broad to cover in one article; proposals noting that the writer read about this issue in another magazine and thinks *McCall's* should now cover it; and writers who cannot offer credentials or published articles to back up their proposal.

Lusardi explains that the key to breaking in to the magazine may be at your back door. "Spouse abuse is an important issue, for example, that we have covered over the years," she says. "In your query, we would want to know what you could offer that was new—little-known research, or examples on a particularly good or enlightening story that you found in your area. Combining that with a working title, compelling writing in the query, and the correct editor's name will catch our eyes."

How to Write for *McCall's*

"We know good celebrity profile writers and good reporters who can write about the latest research," Lusardi says. "But we can't know everything that is happening across the country. So the best way to break in at *McCall's* is to find a personal story—yours or another woman's—and link it to an issue."

Lusardi cites prenatal testing and childhood sexual abuse as examples of issues that are of national concern and which *McCall's* effectively told from a personal point of view. Another example, she adds, is a piece about a woman who lost a custody battle for her son because she was a working mother. At *McCall's,* this story was treated with a personal touch that expanded into the greater issue and offered a sidebar on the impact of such custody decisions on the courts and society.

"Start by earning some clips at smaller publications," she suggests. "Then do some small pieces for us—in '*McCall's* Tells All' or 'Total Health.' In time, you'll prove your merit and the editors will consider you for larger articles."

Once you've earned an assignment, an editor will follow up with a very specific letter that carefully outlines what the magazine is expecting. Deadlines are usually six to eight weeks away. "A good editor talks to a writer two to four times during the writing and editing of an article," Lusardi comments. "And writers are obligated to call us if the idea isn't working out. We don't want surprises when the piece is turned in!"

When your piece is completed, you'll be asked to submit a contact list with names, titles, telephone numbers, and copies of research, and even tapes or transcripts for fact checking.

Men's Health

33 East Minor Street
Emmaus, PA 18098
(215) 967-5171

Published: 9 times per year

Circulation: 650,000

Query: Steven Slon, managing editor

Query response time: 2 to 4 weeks

Buys: About 100 articles/stories out of approximately 1,500 unsolicited queries/manuscripts received annually

Guidelines: Available; send SASE

Rights purchased: First NAS

Pays: On acceptance

Expenses: Pays reasonable phone

Kill fee: Usually pays 25 percent

Rates:

Type of Article	*Word Length*	*Payment*
Major Feature	2,500	$750 - 2,000
Short Feature	1,200	200 - 1,000
Department	500 - 1,500	250 - 1,000
"Back Talk"	600 - 800	750
"Malegrams"	100 - 200	50

In the last few decades, men have experienced dramatic lifestyle changes—the fitness boom, two-career households, getting married at an older age, involved fatherhood, and a change in traditional male/female roles. Many men are juggling competing roles as husband, father, and worker. They are increasingly self-reliant and more health- and fitness-conscious than the men of yesterday. Thus, they turn to *Men's Health*, a magazine designed to give the male gender answers about coping and evolving in today's world. Through *Men's Health*, men seek information and insights into improving the quality of their lives.

In 1988, *Men's Health* began as a quarterly magazine. Today, it's a fast-growing publication published nine times a year and reaching 2.3 million readers (when pass-along rate is factored in). The typical subscriber is a 35- to 49-year-old college-educated urban or suburban male professional. He is as likely to be single as he is to be married, and is actively involved in all sorts of sports and a variety of other activities.

How to Slant Your Ideas to *Men's Health*

The magazine positions itself as the first men's publication to talk to the reader in a credible and informative way about his physical, mental, and emotional self. It serves as an authoritative voice on all aspects of men's health, and assists men in the management of their health and the quality of their lives.

Its editorial covers the health perspective on a variety of lifestyle areas: careers, family relationships, time and stress management, leisure activities, travel, sexuality, fitness, nutrition, and contemporary medical practices.

The editors are not eager to promote the magazine as a good market for untried freelancers. They encourage writers to study back issues and to earn credits at other publications before attempting to sell to this magazine.

If you are a seasoned writer with health credits and a bent toward this market, you may want to consider developing ideas for its columns, all of which are open to freelancers:

- **The Active Traveler** is offbeat, real advice with a health/fitness slant.
- **Back Talk** is a back-of-the-book humor piece that will provoke readers to laughter. "Clothes Make the Mess" was a tongue-in-cheek piece handing out fashion rules for the taste-impaired. "The Enemy Within" looked at cholesterol, free radicals, plaque, and floaters—all substances that wreak havoc on our bodies.
- **The Cook** instructs readers on how to prepare healthy dishes and enjoy them.
- **Couples** provides new takes on major relationship issues.
- **Eating Well** provides information on the healthful aspects of food, which as the magazine states, should be "the kind of food men already eat."
- **Fathers** is about being one or having one.
- **Looks** gives practical and health-related tips on grooming and dressing.
- **Malegrams** are short takes relevant to men. They cover nutrition, exercise, work and relationship issues, and clinical and research advances in health, medicine, psychology, and sports performance. Topics from one issue included insomnia; switching to one-percent milk; tooth whiteners;

and insights on the human growth hormone. "Malegrams" offers the best chance for freelancers tackling this hard-to-crack market.

- **Man-to-Man** is a simple, first-person story about manhood, manliness, machismo, and momentary lapses. In other words, the wiser you are, the more of a wiseguy you can be. One example, "Deere Hunting," described how traditional masculine skills, like working with and discussing heavy equipment and hardware, become instruments of extreme sensitivity among males. Another, "The Rites and Wrongs of Dating," discussed the do's and don'ts involved in having a successful first date.
- **Q&A** is an interview with a man who is changing men's lives, or with a celebrity or athlete whose lifestyle is exemplary. One "Q&A" dealt with the topic of whining, and included responses from famed TV/radio psychiatrist David Viscott.
- **Remedies** explains and clarifies health and medical problems, as well as how to prevent, treat, and cure them.
- **Self-Care** tells a man what to do so he doesn't have to call on a doctor.
- **Sports** offers lessons for men's lives from all areas of professional athletic performance.
- **Time Off** offers tips to readers about learning to unwind and regain control of their lives. One example, "Choose to Snooze," talked about naps being one of life's small pleasures.
- **Working** tells how to succeed, how to fail, and how to know the difference. An example of a past article is "10 Things Bosses Want and How to Give It to Them." Another piece offered readers suggestions for how to avoid getting pigeonholed in their job.

"Life's Lessons" is written by a regular columnist.

How to Query *Men's Health*

The editors are clear that it is not easy to break into *Men's Health.* Most unsolicited queries fail because they don't address the specific *Men's Health* reader.

Follow this three-point outline to structure your article proposal:

1. Start with the lead you expect to put in the piece.
2. Write a summary of where the article will go from there.
3. Give specifics on whom you plan to interview; what types of real-life anecdotes you'll include; what research sources you plan to use; and the conclusion the story might reach.

Assignments are made only if the idea is on target and you have sent one or two of your best published clips for the editors' review. Writing samples don't have to be health or medical articles. The editors' goal is to see how well you report, write, and interpret stories.

How to Write for *Men's Health*

Men's Health relies on writers who seek out the right experts and can get good anecdotes. Articles are written in the third person as well as from the first-person vantage point. The tone is that of a peer who has spoken to a few authorities on the subject at hand. "Imagine you're relating that information to the reader, one on one, over a beer or at dinner," the editors recommend.

Make sure you have solid research to back up your statements. All quotes and health information are carefully fact checked by the editorial staff.

Military Lifestyle

4800 Montgomery Lane, Suite 710
Bethesda, MD 20814-534
(301) 718-7600

Published: 10 times a year; combined July/August and December/January issues

Circulation: 530,000

Query: Hope Daniels, editor

Query response time: 6 to 8 weeks

Buys: About 80 articles out of approximately 1,500 unsolicited queries/manuscripts received annually

Guidelines: Available; send SASE

Rights purchased: First NAS

Pays: On acceptance for regular contributors; on publication for first-time writers for the magazine

Expenses: Pays portion when agreed upon in advance and the writer is on assignment; does not pay expenses for articles written on speculation

Kill fee: 25 percent

Rates:

Type of Article	*Word Length*	*Payment*
Major Feature	1,500 - 2,000	$500 - 800
Short Feature	800 - 1,000	300 - 600
Department	1,000 - 1,200	400 - 600

Military Lifestyle is the quintessential niche market magazine, according to Editor Hope Daniels. It is directed to a military spouse between the ages of 18 and 34, who has a part-time or full-time job, young children to raise, and is dealing with the vagaries of the career his or her partner has chosen. About 60 percent of the readers are men, and the median household income is $44,500. More than half of the readers have attended or graduated from college.

"Our readers move frequently and often don't get to choose their next location," says Daniels. "When their spouses are on maneuvers, they are left alone to handle the household chores, the children, and a job. They usually don't have time to plan for things and lead a semi-chaotic life."

Military Lifestyle has one worldwide edition.

How to Slant Your Ideas to *Military Lifestyle*

As the title implies, *Military Lifestyle* focuses on articles that have a military families slant. While many contributors are military spouses or service members, the magazine works regularly with a number of freelancers who are not. These writers go the extra mile to tailor material to this special audience.

"Having a military background gives writers an inside track, but we've had a lot of success with freelancers who are interested enough in our magazine to put themselves in the position of a military spouse, and make the material work," says Daniels. "If you are a good writer and reporter, that shouldn't be a problem."

Since *Military Lifestyle* is a lot like other women's service publications, it covers the full gamut of food, fashion, travel, marriage, self-help, and lifestyle stories. "Just be aware that readers are in the military, and include pertinent details or references specific to that population," says Daniels.

Daniels says she looks for writers who are willing to go the distance to find a distinctive idea that makes the readers say, "Wow, this is great information. I'm going to file this article away."

A sampling of article topics in just one issue of the magazine included adoption expenses the military will reimburse; what "Mommy, I don't feel good" can mean on school mornings; a special program that smooths the jump from military to civilian life; and how to buy automobile tires.

The following departments in *Military Lifestyle* are open to freelancers:

- **Food** is usually freelance written. It covers a wide range of topics, but steers away from anything too gourmet or expensive to prepare. "Family meals are the focus," says Daniels. "We cover nutritional topics, preparing well-balanced meals, and feeding a crowd. In the summer and during the holidays, we outline party packages. We've run articles on sending invitations, planning a menu, hosting an open house, and preparing for a backyard barbecue. Ethnic dishes go over well with our readers, too."

  Food stories usually include 600 to 800 words of copy and 10 recipes. Daniels, who used to be a food editor, prefers that you test the recipes or tell where you found them. Often, the magazine staff tests the recipes as well.

- **Your Child** appears in every other issue and focuses on a topic of interest to parents. It is typically geared to mothers and fathers with children ranging in age from infancy through early grade school. Topics covered include lying; peer pressure; and toys that can help babies learn by playing.

- **Your Money** deals with everyday financial concerns. The column has covered how to balance a checkbook; income tax filing tips; and how to deal with poor credit.
- **Your Pet** covers health, grooming and training issues, as well as the logistics and problems involved with moving a pet to a new home—sometimes across the country or across continents. One article, "Is There a Cat in Your Future?" told how to be sure if a pet of the feline persuasion is right for your family.
- **Your View** is a first-person article focused on a particular issue, similar to a newspaper op/ed piece. One woman addressed the issue of how she dealt with family members who think the military lifestyle is crazy when she, in fact, enjoys it. "Let your personality come through," says Daniels. "This column covers issues of interest to women everywhere."

"Now Hear This" and "Take 5" are written in house.

How to Query *Military Lifestyle*

One-page queries preferred. Do not send photo/art information. Query six months in advance for seasonal stories.

To capture Daniels' attention in a query, your idea has to have spark. It's got to be intriguing enough to make her stop and think about what she's reading.

"The ideal query starts with one or two paragraphs of summary copy that makes me understand what the proposed article is about," says Daniels. "Then it states why the writer sending it is the perfect person to be writing the piece. Next, it should include one or two paragraphs of substantiation, quoting the sources the writer tends to interview for the article. The style of writing should be conversational."

If your idea has merit, Daniels will call you to go over the piece and then send you a form follow-up letter detailing the assignment, publication date, terms, deadline, and additional instructions.

First-time writers for *Military Lifestyle* typically write on speculation. "Once an individual has successfully written an article for our magazine, I frequently go back to that writer and ask for more. The savvy writer also contacts me soon after his article is published to say, 'You have just published my article on such and such and I have another idea for you.' I'm much more open to working with writers I've already worked with in the past. It pays off for them to do these kinds of things to keep my attention."

How to Write for *Military Lifestyle*

"Our readers are busy people; they have more than enough to do," says Daniels. "That means articles have to be clearly written, relatively short, and enjoyable. They must offer ideas and information to enhance their lives that they can't get anyplace else."

Conversational writing that brings out the writer's personality is what Daniels seeks. "We want our writing to be lively, not boring. But steer clear of clichés," she warns.

When Daniels assigns a piece to a writer, she typically asks for an outline first. "I want the writer to tell me the hook, where the article is going, and how it will work chronologically," the editor explains. "If I receive that before the writer starts writing, I can tell if he or she is on the mark or where things may possibly go off track. The outline often alleviates the necessity for rewrites later."

In the search for experts to interview for *Military Lifestyle*, Daniels suggests that you first attempt to find someone with a military background or connection. It is essential to maintain a geographical balance with sources and, if at all possible, to make sure that quoted sources are distributed evenly through the four branches of the service—Army, Navy, Air Force, and Marines. Military experts must be correctly identified by rank, duty title, and military installation. All other experts must be fully identified by first and last names, professional titles (if applicable) and city and state where they reside.

Daniels likes writers to use anecdotes if they are relevant and enhance a point.

The magazine's writer's guidelines explain how and when to work with military public affairs offices. They also explain what to do if quotes obtained in interviews must be reviewed by military personnel.

Before you turn in a manuscript, double-check the spelling of proper names, geographical names, and military acronyms. Also send a one- to two-sentence writer autobiography, which will appear beside the article to identify you to readers. Any connections you have with the military or with the article's subject matter should be included. Example: "Air Force wife Sherry Watson is a financial counselor. She lives in San Antonio, Texas."

"I prefer to work with writers who have 'bendable egos,'" says Daniels. "I want to be able to work together with them to produce the best story possible," she says. "If a writer is concerned about every 'a' or 'the,' he's probably not the kind of person we're going to want to deal with on a long-term basis."

When a rewrite is needed, the editorial staff works closely with the writer. "It may be that we have to go through two or three rewrites," says Daniels. "We don't like wholesale rearrangements of copy. However, if a piece needs work but has potential, we'll send it back for a rewrite with detailed annotated notes. We call to make sure the writer understands how to beef up the piece and make it work. When the idea is good enough for this extra effort and the writer is willing to do the extra work, everyone benefits."

Mirabella

200 Madison Avenue
New York, NY 10016
(212) 447-4600

Published: Monthly

Circulation: 622,000

Query: The magazine's policy is to read unsolicited queries only if extensive writing samples are included

Query response time: Generally no more than 6 weeks

Buys: About 10 articles out of approximately 1,500 unsolicited queries/manuscripts received annually

Guidelines: None available

Rights purchased: First NAS

Pays: On acceptance

Expenses: Pays some; varies with article

Kill fee: 25 percent

Rates:

Type of Article	*Word Length*	*Payment*
Major Feature	1,500 - 2,500	$1,500 - 2,500
Short Feature	300 - 1,000	300 - 1,000

"We try to avoid categorizing our reader," says Stacy Morrison, associate features editor. "There is a perception that she is an older woman, because people align sophistication with age, but that's not the case. We don't speak down to our audience; we assume sophistication and keep the reading level elevated.

"The writing in *Mirabella* is as important as the subject being written about," Morrison adds.

The magazine is the brainchild of Grace Mirabella, who created the magazine after 17 years as editor-in-chief of *Vogue.* She, too, has resisted attempts to describe her reader in demographic terms. She prefers, instead, to say that women are changing, and fashion magazines must change with them.

Ah, but despite a founder's or editorial staff's determination to allow the reader to be who she will be, there are demographic surveys that give specifics about the *Mirabella* reader: she is about 33, college-educated, very fashion-conscious, and affluent. (Her median household income is more than $50,000, but about a third of the readers have household incomes of more than $75,000.)

She's only slightly more likely to be married than not, but not likely to have children. About a third of the readers work in professional or managerial positions.

She buys clothing, cosmetics, and other luxury items at a much greater pace than the average American woman. She also reads quite a bit and has interests that reach beyond fashion. That's where *Mirabella* comes in—with a mix of fashion and politics; beauty and issues; luxury travel and arts news.

How to Slant Your Ideas to *Mirabella*

This is not a magazine for beginners. Morrison says that most of the writers who receive assignments from *Mirabella* are known to the editors or have had some contact with them. All feature ideas are developed in house and assigned to a stable of writers. Morrison adds that, of 100 ideas, 60 are generated in house, and nearly all of the remaining 40 come from that reliable stable.

"Our political writers also write for publications like *The Wall Street Journal*, *Time*, or *Newsweek*," she explains. "Other writers come to us from *Vanity Fair*, *Esquire*, and other major publications. Agents are also a source of some of our writers. Writers are, almost without exception, very well-established."

Arts and entertainment, books, fashion, food, "Q&A," travel, and all medical and health articles are assigned to selected writers. Only the occasional feature or essay is purchased from a writer without prior contact with the magazine.

How to Query *Mirabella*

Editors prefer an introductory letter and clips demonstrating proficiency in an area.

How to Write for *Mirabella*

"Thinking is what makes the *Mirabella* writer," Morrison says. "We get our writers through word-of-mouth—meet with them if possible—and see how well-seasoned and thoughtful they are."

Morrison adds that what sets her type of writer apart is the ability to take an assignment a step further than someone else might have, into another realm, whether that means creating an essay from what could be simply a reportage piece or finding a new way to approach a topic that has been written about dozens of times before.

"Despite the fact that we don't use most unsolicited ideas, we will always be interested in hearing from established writers who have something unique to bring to the magazine," says Morrison.

Modern Bride

249 West 17th Street
New York, NY 10011
(212) 337-7000

Published: Bimonthly

Circulation: 351,556

Query: Mary Ann Cavlin, managing editor

Query response time: 4 to 6 weeks

Buys: About 25 articles out of approximately 500 unsolicited queries/manuscripts received annually

Guidelines: Available; send SASE

Rights purchased: First NAS

Pays: On acceptance

Expenses: Pays reasonable phone

Kill fee: 25 percent

Rates:

Type of Article	*Word Length*	*Payment*
Major Feature	1,500 - 2,000	$650 - 1,500
Short Feature	700 - 1,000	300 - 500

Modern Bride is a service magazine designed to help engaged couples plan their weddings. "We give brides and grooms lots of ideas to accomplish what they want for that special day—within their budgets," says Managing Editor Mary Ann Cavlin.

The bride-to-be who subscribes to or purchases *Modern Bride* is approximately 25 years old, college educated (90 percent), and employed (94 percent). The average household income that she and her soon-to-be husband will share is $50,500.

Today's emphasis in weddings among first-time brides is on tradition. A whopping 98 percent of *Modern Bride* readers have formal weddings, and 86 percent are married in a church or synagogue. Virtually all have receptions, hosting an average of 186 guests. The total cost of a formal wedding approaches $17,000.

Because *Modern Bride* is a planning guidebook for weddings, honeymoons, and a new lifestyle as husband and wife, readers spend a lot of time with the publication. Women traditionally buy the magazine to study current wedding fashions—especially wedding dresses. Nearly 70 percent look through an issue four times or more, with more than one and one-half hours spent reading the magazine. Most women buy the magazine for six months to a year before their marriages to help them make decisions and purchases related to their weddings.

How to Slant Your Ideas to *Modern Bride*

"Couples today want their wedding to be incredibly special, and they want to celebrate in a way they will always remember," says Cavlin. "They are willing to make compromises to have the wedding and reception of their dreams. Because of that, we want ideas, tips, and trends that are up-to-date and affordable."

There are certain basic wedding-planning topics *Modern Bride* addresses in each issue: buying the wedding dress; choosing a florist, caterer, and photographer; and planning the reception.

Consumer education is an integral part of the information newlyweds need to start a home and life together. "We give our readers guidance on using the bridal registries in department and specialty stores, and offer advice on buying flatware, crystal, dinnerware, housewares, linens, and furniture—everything to set up your new home," says Cele Goldsmith Lalli, the magazine's editor-in-chief. A special section titled "Your First Home Together" is published in every issue, and the magazine also provides thorough resources on honeymoon travel.

Modern Bride also runs relationship articles about what to expect after the wedding. "The majority of the articles I assign to freelancers deal with relationships—from living together to dealing with in-laws," says Cavlin. "They are either psychological or how-to pieces that include interviews with experts and anecdotes from engaged or newly married couples across the country.

"Our readers are savvy, but they know that sharing their life with someone means entering uncharted territory," says Cavlin. "They want to know how to do it right. One piece covered how to avoid financial mistakes during the first year of marriage. Another told how marriage changes family ties."

The magazine also devotes space to remarriage. An example in that category is "Remarriage With Children: Healthy Ways to Deal With the Challenge."

Cavlin also likes personal experiences. "A father of a bride wrote about watching his daughter plan her wedding, and what went through his mind on the wedding day," she recalls. "We also like to have men write articles from the groom's point of view. But, first-person experiences could be from anyone involved in the wedding—the mother, maid of honor, best man, bridesmaids, groomsmen, sister, or the bride herself."

All *Modern Bride* columns are written by staff or regular contributors.

How to Query *Modern Bride*

One page preferred. Send photo/art information.

Before you query *Modern Bride,* Cavlin suggests you get a feel for the mindset of engaged and newly married couples today. Then, search for a slant that will immediately catch their interest.

"I like brief queries that outline in bulleted form what the writer wants to achieve and express why the article is good for our readers," says Cavlin. "A sample lead and anecdotes help us to evaluate the writing style, as do copies of previous work. Clips do not have to be from other bridal magazines. Most writers who have sold to us repeatedly offer several ideas at once."

Modern Bride asks most freelancers new to the magazine to write on speculation. "At least 80 percent of the query letters I receive are from writers trying to break in," says Cavlin, "and they offer to work on spec."

How to Write for *Modern Bride*

Though brides' heads may be in the clouds when they dream about their wedding day, *Modern Bride* wants writers to keep their feet on the ground. The tone should be practical and purposeful. Keep a balance between the reality of marriage and the excitement and fantasy that surrounds a wedding celebration.

"Know what points you want to get across and write as succinctly as possible," says Cavlin. "Get to the core of the theme quickly."

Cavlin looks for writers who will deliver an article that follows what the query outlined. "Some writers submit a proposal that is direct and to the point, but their manuscripts go off on tangents," the editor says. "They ramble and lose their focus. That, along with misspellings are my pet peeves."

Modern Bride likes the editorial to be upbeat but doesn't mind a writer presenting the pros and cons of an issue. "We know nothing is ever one-sided," says Cavlin.

Anecdotes about brides and grooms give zest to a piece. Confirm that the couples you include are relatively new at the marriage game. "One writer pitched a great idea, but when the article arrived, the anecdotes featured people who had been married for a very long period of time. It was more like an article for *Modern Maturity* than *Modern Bride.*"

When finding experts, strive for a balanced geographical mix.

Modern Maturity

3200 East Carson Street
Lakewood, CA 90712
(310) 496-2277

Published: Bimonthly

Circulation: 22.5 million

Query: General editorial: Tom Dworetzky, executive editor
Regional issues: Leslie Yap, regional editor

Query response time: 4 to 8 weeks

Buys: About 100 articles/stories out of approximately 20,000 unsolicited queries/manuscripts received annually

Guidelines: None available

Rights purchased: One-time NAS

Pays: On acceptance

Expenses: Pays phone up to a preset limit; and travel for longer pieces

Kill fee: 25 percent

Rates:

Type of Article	*Word Length*	*Payment*
Major Feature	2,000 - 3,000	$2,000 - 3,000
Short Feature	1,000 - 1,500	1,000 - 1,500
Department	150 - 500	150 - 500
News Brief	150 - 300	150 - 300

If you are over age 50 and a member of the American Association of Retired Persons (AARP), you receive a monthly subscription to *Modern Maturity*. Because a lot of married members share a joint membership, the readership of this magazine climbs to approximately 30 million.

The median age of the magazine's readership is 64. Just over 56 percent are women. About 40 percent have a college education, and more than 60 percent are married. Although this association may be geared for senior adults in retirement, one-third of its readers are employed. The median household income is $31,700.

How to Slant Your Ideas to *Modern Maturity*

"Our pieces appeal to anyone who is mature in the psychographic sense," says Executive Editor Tom Dworetzky. "The age issue has become muddied over the years. One of our recent issues featured an extensive report on seeking work after the age of 50. This magazine is not exclusively dedicated to retired adults. Many 65-year-olds can't afford to retire, and even people with pensions are still working."

In other words, make sure you study this market before approaching the editor with ideas. Don't underestimate the quality and scope of the editorial content or the caliber of its writing. "Freelancers are in competition with the best writers in the business," says Dworetzky. "We use only established magazine writers for features or columns, and there is really not much of a chance to sell a short front-of-the-book piece here unless you are a polished professional."

A few article examples paint a picture of the type of journalism the magazine seeks. Just prior to the 1992 elections, *Modern Maturity* ran a piece in which a liberal economist from Harvard and the editor of *The Wall Street Journal* took opposing viewpoints on the economy. Concurrent with Los Angeles riots that same year, the magazine came out with the piece, "America: The Fabric of a Nation," speaking about cultural diversity.

"Those stories could have appeared in any quality magazine," notes Dworetzky. "We make certain that every cover story reports on a hard-hitting issue that is of some importance to our readers. We also include a Q & A in each issue. One issue included an interview with Studs Terkel, Chicago's acclaimed interviewer and author; and another featured a chat with Nobel Prize winning economist Gary Becker."

One mainstay of the magazine has always been practical information on finance and health. A piece on viruses, for example, discussed how viruses spread, especially as people travel great distances, and gave an overview of the virology war. The magazine has also run an article on the oriental art of Tai Chi. Moneywise, you'll find pieces on mutual funds and various housing options available to people as they age.

Travel is another regular topic, but the magazine is leaning toward running more essays and travel reportage and fewer destination pieces. "Occasionally, we will include a shorter service piece on an important topic such as what to do if you get into trouble while traveling abroad," explains Dworetzky.

The best spots for established freelancers who are new to this market are the 12 regional editions of the magazine, which span the entire country—from New England to Hawaii. "We want experienced writers who can write short features or bits about travel, events, or issues that are of interest to people in various geographical areas," says Dworetzky.

A few *Modern Maturity* departments open to freelancers include:

- **Health** columns tend to be reader-service pieces. "If there is a new treatment out on something, writers must make sure it is geared to some extent to middle-aged or older people," says Dworetzky. Past issues have featured health information on the symptoms and side effects of lupus and the fact that W.C. Fields' red nose was not necessarily a sign of heavy drinking.
- **Highlights** are bits and pieces of information included in the front-of-the-book matter. "They can really be about anything of interest to our audience," the editor notes. Examples include "Bebop on the Bayou," a summary of New Orleans' finer points; "Down By the Old Mill," a look at how a part of America's history has become a travel destination; and the story "A Little Guy Wins," is an explanation of how the intermittent-windshield-wiper came to be.
- **You Asked** is a freelance-written column in which a writer responds to a question posed by a reader. Questions are assigned to writers chosen by the magazine. One column looked at the topic of dating services for seniors; another gave tips on traveling with pets.

"Voices" is a column of reprints of previously published articles relevant to *Modern Maturity* readers.

How to Query *Modern Maturity*

One page preferred; do not send photo/art information. Query ideas a year in advance.

"The typical mistake most writers make in a query is to give the editor a general topic rather than a specific spin on a topic," says Dworetzky. "Really think about the story and tell me what is new about it."

To help your angle grab the editor's attention, Dworetzky suggests pitching a sample head and deck to the story—just as you would see on the first page of a major magazine feature. "That helps focus the editor," says Dworetzky. "It immediately tells me the point of the story. If the head and deck don't get me, there's no chance of convincing me with a lot of writing."

Thinking far ahead is another key to success at this magazine. "Because we are a bimonthly, we're planning issues at least six months ahead of time," says Dworetzky. "We need writers to think about what is going to happen next year. It is not as hard as it sounds, but it's essential to this market."

How to Write for *Modern Maturity*

When it comes to telling freelancers how to write for his market, Dworetzky is brief and to the point. "I like good writing, as we all do," he says. "I want lively, clear, accurate prose. Tell me an intriguing story and avoid the passive construction."

Mother Jones

1663 Mission Street, Second Floor
San Francisco, CA 94103
(415) 558-8881

Published: 6 times a year

Circulation: 110,000

Query: Feature articles: Jeffrey Klein, editor-in-chief
Investigative articles: David Weir, investigative editor
"Outfront": Katharine Fong, managing editor

Query response time: 3 to 4 weeks

Buys: About 60 articles a year, most assigned by the editors; does not accept unsolicited manuscripts, but encourages queries

Guidelines: Available; send SASE

Rights purchased: Varies with article and author

Pays: On acceptance

Expenses: Pays when authorized in advance

Kill fee: 33 1/3 percent

Rates:

Type of Article	*Word Length*	*Payment*
Major Feature	3,000 - 4,000	$2,400 - 3,200
Short Feature	1,500 - 3,000	1,200 - 2,400
"Outfront"	200 - 450	160 - 360

Mother Jones digs into the worlds of corporate and government policy and glad-handing to report stories not found in traditional publications. With a feel to it like an alternative newspaper that grew up and became a magazine, *Mother Jones* publishes quality investigative reporting, national news, and profiles of people in the center of those storms.

The magazine's readers are active, not armchair intellects. The median reader age is 39, and the readership is split almost evenly at 55 percent male, 45 percent female. Most attended college; and the average income is $34,700. Ninety percent make financial contributions to various causes and 95 percent participate in community activities.

How to Slant Your Ideas to *Mother Jones*

The magazine's politics and articles are decidedly left-leaning, so you are not likely to find an audience for causes or articles that land on the more conservative side of things. However, the magazine is open to intelligent critiques of progressive sacred cows.

The writers who contribute to *Mother Jones* are on top of what's going on. They have contacts within government agencies, think tanks, foundations, and the countless cause-related organizations that dot our national map.

Evidence of the finger-on-the-pulse investigative work that is essential for writers interested in *Mother Jones* is an article called, "Unhappy Meals," which concerned contaminated meat at fast food restaurants. Several months after it was published, a number of people in Washington state became ill and two died when contaminated meat made its way into fast food restaurants there.

In addition to politics, government, and investigative reporting, other areas of interest the editors mention include: culture, current controversies, family, environment, individual liberties, and personal choices.

The best place to break into *Mother Jones*—and virtually the only place—is "Outfront." (All other columns are closed to freelancers.) "Outfront" is a front-of-the-book briefs section that features quirky pieces that illustrate the same issues covered in larger articles, but don't merit more than a few hundred words. Some past examples include a piece on workplace sabotage; one on a Department of Energy project to mark nuclear waste sites for future generations; and a pointed question-and-answer phone call between a reporter and a clinic doctor who claims to help gays go straight.

How to Query *Mother Jones*

One or more pages preferred; no phone or FAX queries accepted; no unsolicited manuscripts; query at least four months in advance for timely material.

The editors look for a national or international interest in all stories. However, they are open to articles about a specific city's experience that is of national relevance, such as the 1992 Los Angeles riots.

If you are querying for a certain section, make sure you mention the section and indicate, by your angle and approach to the story, that you know how that column usually appears. If the topic has been covered in this or other magazines in the last few years, state why it needs more attention now.

The magazine's "Guidelines for Writers" is very clear about the type of queries the editors want, so your first step should be sending for the guidelines. In sum, the editors say they are looking for answers to the following:

- How do you plan to cover the topic?
- What is your style and approach to this piece? (Your query should echo that.)
- Why are you qualified to write the article? What contacts or experience do you have?
- Why does the *Mother Jones* reader need to know this information?
- Can you prove and provide documentation that supports your reporting?

How to Write for *Mother Jones*

The magazine publishes five to eight features six times a year—roughly 35 or 40 total. Unless you have journalistic experience that qualifies you to write in-depth or investigative pieces, it's best to target areas you know. Some excellent journalists from around the world contribute to this magazine, and competition is stiff.

There are issues in your own city or neighborhood that could be the first step toward an article of national interest. For instance, the magazine published an article about the nursing profession in the United States. The author was a well-published writer already well-versed in her subject. But the main topic of the article is well known to many aware Americans: nurses do far more than they are credited for, and are capable of even more.

Ms.

230 Park Avenue
New York, NY 10169
(212) 551-9595

Published: Bimonthly
Circulation: 211,000
Query: Manuscripts editor
Query response time: 2 to 3 months
Buys: 25 to 30 articles out of 5,000 unsolicited queries/manuscripts received annually
Guidelines: Available; send SASE
Rights purchased: World rights
Pays: On acceptance
Expenses: Pays reasonable expenses when approved in advance
Kill fee: 20 percent
Rates:

Type of Article	*Word Length*	*Payment*
Major Feature	1,500 - 3,000	$1,000 - 3,000
Departments	400 - 2,000	300 - 1,500

"*Ms.* has changed over the years," declares Barbara Findlen, managing editor of the publication that broke ground in 1971 as the nation's first feminist magazine. "We're breaking ground again." While many mainstream publications now cover feminist issues regularly, *Ms.* is still leading the pack with a new style of feminist journalism.

"The *Ms.* reader obviously is someone who is interested in feminism; we believe this encompasses a whole range of issues and concerns," says Findlen. "We look at a feminist angle in all kinds of stories, not just what are commonly thought of as 'women's issues.' One of our objectives is to be thought-provoking in a way that moves people forward."

Being a leader in the feminist movement hasn't been easy. The magazine has encountered plenty of bumps along the way, with a flurry of ownership changes, suspension of the publication for seven months in 1990, and finally a decision to publish six issues a year without advertising beginning in July, 1990.

Now supported entirely by reader subscriptions (circulation dropped to half of its half-million high in the 1980s), the new *Ms.*

has lost some of its glitz and glamour. The publication uses less costly uncoated paper, and less color inside, with full color only on the covers. But less is more in this case. The substance remains. The new *Ms.* has an attractive, scholarly look that communicates a serious magazine with a purpose.

"We offer a hundred pages of pure editorial, and it's a great product," Findlen says proudly. "One of the exciting things about not having advertising is that we are accountable only to our readers, not to advertisers or anybody else. We conduct reader surveys and pay very close attention to the letters we get. We take into account our readers' ideas for what they want to see in the magazine. I think we have a more direct relationship with our readers than magazines supported by advertising."

How to Slant Your Ideas to *Ms.*

Not surprisingly, *Ms.* readers—at least 95 percent are women—are involved and active in causes close to their feminist hearts.

The majority of *Ms.* readers are well acquainted with feminist issues. They look to the magazine to update them on a wide range of new national and international developments from a feminist perspective as well as profiles and essays that celebrate women and share their experiences and achievments.

Today's *Ms.* covers thought-provoking news about the arts, feminist writers, sexual harassment, women in the military, the law and women's rights, apartheid, and more. "Our reader is someone who wants to be challenged," notes Findlen.

What you won't find are stories about women who are succeeding in stereotypical male careers. "A lot of the ideas that are rejected seem to be based on the idea that if a woman is doing something, that's news. That's not true for us," Findlen says. Fashion and beauty tips won't find a place on the pages of *Ms.*, either.

Ms. isn't afraid to tackle the personal problems today's women face. "We did a major package on the politics of breast cancer, for instance," the editor says. "Another article, written by a writer who works at home, shared the author's sense of violation by friends who interrupt her and don't take her work seriously because she's at home. We published a report about feminist activism on campus. And a recent cover story explored the experiences of feminist mothers raising sons."

One of the best ways to break in at *Ms.* is to target a particular department. Department articles vary in length between 400 and 2,000 words.

The following departments and columns are open to freelancers:

- **Ecofeminism** covers environmental issues from a feminist viewpoint. One contributor outlined the connections between feminism and the animal rights movement.
- **Feminist Theory** expresses opinions on feminist ideas and the state of feminism in today's society. A recent column discussed why young women are afraid to be labeled feminist due to the lack of education about women in history.
- **Guest Room** features short essays that describe personal experiences that give some insight on feminism. This is a good column for freelancers.
- **Inner Space** explores women's spiritual and emotional lives from a first-person perspective.

The global and national news sections are a little more difficult for freelancers to target. With only six issues a year, much of the news section content is pre-planned so that articles remain timely. Freelancers have a better chance of succeeding with national rather than international news. Overseas news is usually written by writers from their respective countries.

How to Query *Ms.*

One- to two-page queries preferred. Clips and a résumé are requested.

Findlen notes that there are several faux pas that are likely to land a hopeful query in the reject pile at *Ms.* "The most common problem is that the piece isn't angled to *Ms.*," she says. "Many of the queries we get are clearly simultaneous submissions, with no particular target at all. Frequently, freelancers fail to understand that *Ms.* is not just a women's magazine, but a feminist magazine."

The more detail writers can offer in their query, the better, says Findlen. "Angling the query to a particular department is very helpful." Providing as much background about the research as possible, listing who you will interview, and giving other pertinent details will increase your chances of assignment.

Ms. takes the query process seriously. That's probably because most of the queries tend to come from regular *Ms.* readers. "Queries are divided among two assistant editors who work with a team of interns, and everything is read," Findlen promises. Queries that make the first cut get passed along to editors. Responses can take from two to three months. Fiction and poetry are not accepted.

How to Write for *Ms.*

"Our guiding principle is to empower and celebrate women, and to work to eliminate women's second-class status," Findlen states. With a mission of that magnitude, it wouldn't be surprising if all *Ms.* articles took a serious, no-nonsense tone. Fortunately, that's not the case.

"There's a vast world of feminist writing and commentary out there, and we're always looking for something a little different, maybe even funny, or an unusual way to tell a story," says Findlen. "Readers unfamiliar with *Ms.* might expect us to be heavy-handed. But we like a humorous approach and enjoy being a little wry sometimes. We try to vary our tone a lot. We can be serious when it's warranted because part of our mandate is to bring news that a lot of other media ignore about women, and a lot of it is bad news. But we also want to be enlightening, entertaining, and energizing."

Ms. editors work closely with their writers to ensure a quality finished product. "Typically, before we make an assignment, we discuss the piece extensively to make sure that we have a mutual understanding about what it's going to be and to outline it," Findlen says. There are a lot of questions to ask and answers to get before the work begins, she adds. After that initial conversation, the editor writes an assignment letter that summarizes the discussion. Depending on the complexity of the article, a *Ms.* editor may have a number of follow-up conversations with the writer. If substantial revisions are needed, the writer is responsible for rewrites.

Ms. very thoroughly fact checks all freelance submissions. "It is vitally important to our fact checkers that writers provide documentation of all factual information, including photocopies and printed back-up materials as well as interviews, tapes, or transcripts and telephone numbers of sources used in writing the piece," she says. As a rule, even with transcripts or tapes, sources will be contacted by a *Ms.* fact checker.

Findlen says *Ms.* isn't afraid to expose differing feminist opinions about controversial issues such as contraception, abortion, pornography, and health care. "We are becoming more of a forum for controversy," she claims. But the magazine remains true to its feminist principles. "We won't publish something that is anti-woman or hurts women, just as we won't publish racist or homophobic articles."

National Geographic

17th and M streets, NW
Washington, D.C. 20036
(202) 857-7000

Published: Monthly

Circulation: 9.7 million

Query: Robert M. Poole, associate editor
"Expeditions": Peter Million, senior editorial staff

Query response time: 6 weeks

Buys: 30 to 35 articles out of 7,000 to 8,000 unsolicited queries/manuscripts received annually

Guidelines: None available

Rights purchased: Exclusive First World

Pays: Half on initial submission of article; the remainder on final acceptance

Expenses: Pays all reasonable

Kill fee: Negotiable

Rates:

Type of Article	*Word Length*	*Payment*
Major Feature	8,000 maximum	$12,000+
Short Feature	2,000	2,000+

"The National Geographic Society founded its magazine in 1888 for the increase and diffusion of geographic knowledge," says William Graves, editor. "Gilbert Grosvenor, the man who did more than anyone to develop *National Geographic,* said that geography means the whole world and everything that's in it. Today, that concept encompasses the entire universe."

National Geographic's readership is as broad as its editorial content. "Our readers are fairly well educated, and most of them are members of the National Geographic Society," explains Graves. "They are family people (more than 90 percent are married), and each copy of the magazine is probably read by three or four family members. We have an estimated readership of 30 to 40 million people in 100 countries. Our pass-along rate is relatively low because readers tend to collect the magazines so that they may refer back to them later."

The readership is almost evenly divided between males and females. The median age is 45, and the median household income is $87,000.

How to Slant Your Ideas to *National Geographic*

National Geographic promotes education through a mix of articles on science, archaeology, geography, adventure, and natural history. It covers the people and places of as many geographical locations as possible.

"We are doing what we have always done, but we constantly try to do it better," says Graves. "We want to give readers something of value and relevance, so we try to focus on timely but vital subjects."

Each issue of the magazine features a modern geography story which focuses on a place or person in the news. The goal of the publication is to delve beneath the daily headlines. "The idea is to get to the heart of a trend or change and to help people understand something big going on," says Graves. "For the article 'The Broken Empire,' a staff writer spent several months traveling around Russia, Kazakhstan, and the Ukraine talking to ordinary people about how their lives were changing as a result of the collapse of the Soviet Union. This was not something you would find in a weekly news magazine, but a long-range view to help readers understand what they were seeing in the daily newspapers and evening news."

In another modern geography story, a writer went to Easter Island to cover the area, its culture, and new thoughts on archaeology. Two other examples in this category include a report on how nations in the Middle East are competing for a shrinking water supply and how the end of the Cold War has changed immigration in Europe.

National Geographic also runs general-interest stories about specific locations. Although the articles are used as background by people who travel, it is not specifically aimed at travel. In a piece on Wyoming, the magazine looked at what sort of people live in America's least populated state. Another travel-related piece, "Earth's Deepest Canyon," featured an inventor who took kayaks and rafts through Colca Canyon in Peru.

Other articles have covered topics such as nomads in Mongolia, beekeepers in the United States, wildlife research taking place in a remote region of Tibet, and the latest scientific thinking on dinosaurs. One issue featured a close-up look at money—how it works, what it means, and how that varies throughout the world. In the article, "The Ogallala: Wellspring of the High Plains," the magazine gave readers an update on the aquifer, a huge underground water resource under the high plains of the United States that is being slowly depleted and, in some spots, polluted by ground water contamination.

Writers considered for assignment by *National Geographic* must have an understanding of and background in the subject area. Most natural history pieces are written by people who specialize in the study of a particular animal. The majority of science articles are written by scientific experts.

"We are looking for people with imagination, sufficient knowledge on a subject, and familiarity with the magazine's editorial content," says Graves. "Most of all, they must have ideas that will work."

How to Query *National Geographic*

One and one-half to two pages preferred; include photo/art information; query one year in advance for seasonal material.

"Because photographs are a prerequisite for any *National Geographic* feature, the ideal proposal should describe how the subject can be covered both editorially and photographically," Graves says. "Tell us what the story is about, why *National Geographic* should be interested, why it would make a great story, and why you are just the writer to do it for us. If you come through with a successful story suggestion, we will try to help photograph it.

"Look at the magazine and get to know what we do," the editor advises. "If you're serious about wanting to write for us, get the magazine's index, which is available through our office and is carried by some libraries. That way, you can see what we've covered, and you won't send proposals on topics we've already published."

Although your proposal should indicate which magazines you've written for, don't send clips. "We have an editorial review group that meets once every month or so to review story suggestions," Graves tells contributors. "We consider forty to fifty proposals at once, and don't want to be inundated with paper. First, we like to see the query. If the idea is well presented, we might ask to see articles you've sold to other publications."

According to Graves, editors at *National Geographic* normally assign work, rather than asking for it on speculation. Half of the fee is paid when the manuscript is delivered. The balance is paid after revisions suggested by the editor are completed.

How to Write for *National Geographic*

Writing for *National Geographic* should be straightforward and concise. Avoid long sentences and paragraphs and take an informal, nonacademic approach. Be willing to condense, fact check, and rewrite.

"The real test of a story is whether or not it engages you as a reader," says Graves. "We don't apply any formula; individual style is important. We don't want to be stereotyped as only buying a certain style of writing. If you want to write for *National Geographic*, read and write for *The New York Times Sunday Magazine, The Atlantic*, or a first-class newspaper. That's probably the best training and background you can have.

"The editors want a sense that you've been to the place about which you're writing. Your participation and involvement are important," says Graves. "It's always better to do something yourself than to interview others about what it's like. We like a sense of adventure and humor. Use dialogue to reveal more about the place and its people."

National Geographic supports its writers' efforts by providing both staff and freelancers with background research material. "The best writers know as much as possible about their subject before they go into the field," says Graves. "That way they make the most of their time. Anyone who lives near a good library can do book and periodical research on a subject."

One special characteristic of *National Geographic* stories is that the magazine allows its writers and researchers to stay with a story long enough to get a true sense of what is really happening. They may spend three weeks to three months in the field, depending on the length and scope of the story.

"We can afford to do that because we are not racing to meet a weekly deadline," says Graves. "A longer lead time allows us to go deeper and get to the fundamentals which will hold up years from now. And we hope that is why people keep the magazine around for the long term."

Nation's Business

1615 H Street, NW
Washington, D.C. 20062-2000
(202) 463-5650

Published: Monthly
Circulation: 850,000
Query: Roger Thompson, assistant managing editor
Query response time: 4 to 6 weeks
Buys: About 50 articles/stories out of approximately 700 unsolicited queries/manuscripts received annually
Guidelines: Available; send SASE
Rights purchased: All
Pays: On acceptance
Expenses: Pays all authorized expenses for assigned articles
Kill fee: Varies
Rates:

Type of Article	*Word Length*	*Payment*
Typical Feature	1,800	$ 1,400+
Short Feature	800	550+
Department	800	600 - 800

Founded in 1912 and published by the U.S. Chamber of Commerce, *Nation's Business* is the country's oldest business magazine and boasts the largest circulation. It bills itself as "The Small Business Advisor," and covers three principal areas: managing people; managing money; and managing logistics. The average reader spends more than one and one-half hours reading each issue.

"*Nation's Business* is designed to provide hands-on management information to small businesses," says Assistant Managing Editor Roger Thompson. "We are different from our competitors because our emphasis is on practical advice."

With that agenda, the magazine gears its editorial to the owners and managers of small- and medium-size firms in all types of business. Most of the readers are in charge of established, growing companies, rather than start-ups. More than 60 percent own a business or a franchise. Most readers are men (82 percent), with a median age of 46. The median income is $75,700 with a median net worth of $371,700.

Median gross sales for the companies reflected by the readership are $2.5 million. Almost three-quarters have fewer than 100 employees.

How to Slant Your Ideas to *Nation's Business*

The magazine's four editorial goals are to: 1) provide direct guidance on day-to-day business operations; 2) report on strategies and techniques used by successful business people; 3) impart personal advice in areas such as finance, taxes, and health; and 4) alert readers to legislative or regulatory changes that will impact their business.

Nation's Business rarely accepts outside manuscripts that cover Washington issues. It is not interested in academic or legalistic reports, speeches, annual reports, or biographies of company presidents or CEOs.

"The best writers for us are ones who have a feel for writing small business management stories, not consultants who happen to know a topic," says Thompson. "Typically, the latter person does not give the piece the kind of anecdotal flavor we need. We want stories brought to life through the words and examples of small business owners and managers. Just offering advice isn't good enough."

Most of the articles are staff written. Each issue includes three to four freelance-written articles.

The magazine's table of contents page is packed with articles. In addition to the cover story, there are articles under various business headings: "Benefits," "Business," "Insurance," "Management," "Politics," "Regulation," "Retailing," "Small Business Computing," "Special Report," and "Women in Business." It also includes a monthly survey and its results.

"The key is not to think in terms of category or department, but to come up with a good idea that would help a small business run better, and let us decide where it should go," says Thompson.

In addition to feature articles, the following departments are open to freelance ideas:

- **Making It** profiles two to three growing businesses that share their experiences in short articles about creating and marketing new products and services.
- **To Your Health** provides advice on how to manage your own health. One article looked at the signs and symptoms of diabetes and discussed major treatments for the disease.

"Entrepreneur's Notebook" and all other departments are written in house or by regular columnists or contributors.

How to Query *Nation's Business*

One-page queries preferred. Do not send any photo/art information. Do not FAX queries. Staff members produce time-sensitive material.

To win an assignment through a query letter, Thompson says writers must be very familiar with the magazine. "It's clear through the proposals we receive that most people who submit ideas don't have a clue about what kind of magazine we are and the kinds of stories we run," he says. "They simply get our name and address from someplace, and send in material that is totally out of bounds. It's a waste of my time and their own to put postage on the rejection letter if they can't take the time to become acquainted with our editorial focus."

Once you are sure your idea is a fit, outline in your query how you plan to approach the topic. State the basic theme, your specific angle, and the article's usefulness to readers. Tell who you plan to interview for the article. At this point, it is not necessary to include sample quotes from sources or anecdotes about companies. But it is essential to let Thompson know who you are.

"Assuming I'm intrigued by the topic, I am more inclined to respond favorably if the writer describes his or her experience in the subject area," the editor says. "I am most interested in people who have a background writing about business for newspapers or magazines."

Thompson cites an example of a California newspaper writer who proposed a story on alternative dispute resolution (ADR), a low-cost alternative to taking business disputes to court. "This was very useful to our readers," he says. "In addition to describing what ADR is and how it works as a quick, less expensive alternative, the writer included a box of information on where to write or call for more details."

On the opposite coast, a former newspaper business writer from Florida suggested a story on employee leasing. Thompson saw this as a hot topic for small companies because it allows them to turn over paperwork, regulatory problems, and benefit and worker's compensation issues to a leasing organization. It ran as the cover story.

How to Write for *Nation's Business*

"Every publication has a unique style, and so do we," says Thompson. "You may be a successful business writer somewhere else, but to be one here, you must read the magazine."

Nation's Business readership is well educated but nontechnical. They don't have time to read long, complex articles. Hence, the key is tight writing.

The mistake consultants and professors make, Thompson says, is approaching business management in an academic manner. It's essential to find business owners who can give you anecdotes about their experience that will help tell the story.

The hands-on management advice *Nation's Business* tries to cultivate means including explanatory sidebars, boxes of names and addresses for more information, and chart/graph material. "It lets the reader take the next logical step to find the help he needs," says Thompson. "This takes an extra bit of work but it is the way we approach business writing."

At the end of your manuscript, include a brief autobiography, citing the basis of your expertise for writing on the particular subject covered.

Thompson wants each article to be accompanied by a source list for fact checking. He asks writers to send a hard copy of the article, as well as the disk in ASCII format.

New Body

1700 Broadway
New York, NY 10019
(212) 541-7100

Published: 7 times a year

Circulation: 120,000

Query: Nicole Dorsey, editor-in-chief

Query response time: Rejections—2 weeks, with SASE; queries with potential may be kept up to 6 months.

Buys: About 40 articles out of 500 to 600 unsolicited queries/manuscripts received annually

Guidelines: Available, with editorial calendar; send SASE

Rights purchased: First NAS or All

Pays: On publication, which is usually within 8 to 12 months

Expenses: Pays if reasonable

Kill fee: 20 percent

Rates:

Type of Article	*Word Length*	*Payment*
Major Feature	1,000 - 2,000	$200 - 500

"Health, fitness lifestyles for women on the go!" is the tagline on every *New Body* cover, and the editors aren't kidding. Readers of this magazine receive information on working out, sports, health and nutrition, dieting, and a host of other fitness-related topics. More than 90 percent of the magazine's 120,000 copies are sold on the newsstand, so good query titles that can become cover lines will catch the editor's eye.

The average reader is 24 to 30 years old, and fully half of them own gym memberships. Many use exercise videos and nearly 80 percent incorporate walking into their regimen. They are low-fat, low-calorie, vitamin-taking eaters, the vast majority of whom want to lose another 10 to 20 pounds.

The audience is fairly evenly split between single and married women. More than a third of the readers juggle job, children, home and still have to find time to work out. The majority attended or are presently attending college.

You won't find any couch potatoes on this editorial staff. Nicole Dorsey, editor-in-chief, is proud that every member of the staff is dedicated to fitness. Staffers work out regularly, train with weights, walk—even take gymnastics. Dorsey, a certified aerobics instructor and personal trainer, teaches aerobics three nights a week, and is completing a Master's degree in exercise physiology and research.

How to Slant Your Ideas to *New Body*

Think fitness, not fads; lifestyle changes, not just dieting. This is a magazine edited by and for women with realistic attitudes about maintaining their health. Dorsey says that there is an assumption throughout the magazine that the reader is trying to better herself. But that assumption is tempered by the understanding that almost no one makes it to *every* workout, or *always* eats what is best for her.

The editorial mix in each issue of *New Body* is fairly consistent: a major diet article; a question and answer celebrity profile; two or three health-oriented pieces; a food and recipe article; and three articles on exercise, health, or sports medicine. There are also three four-page exercise sections.

The exercise sections are always written by Dorsey; most of the other articles are open to freelancers:

- **Diet** articles are always concerned with losing weight in some way. Some past articles have covered beating the gain-back odds; overcoming the afternoon energy slump; and 25 ways to stop midnight munchies.
- **Exercise** articles often accompany the photographic exercise sections Dorsey authors. Typical pieces might be about overtraining; spring sports; preventing injury to a particular part of the body; or an article on a specific sport, like in-line skating or scuba-diving.
- **Food** columns will always cover low-fat, low-calorie foods. Dorsey doesn't believe in encouraging the occasional chocolate pigout. So even a piece on desserts should concentrate on packing the most enjoyment into the healthiest desserts.
- **Health** articles cover a broad spectrum of topics, including new contraceptives, skin care, dental care, and AIDS.
- **Profile** takes a question-and-answer format and features a celebrity who is committed to a healthy lifestyle. Dorsey warns that writers must have access to the subject before querying. Past articles have profiled Cher, Winona Ryder, and Andie MacDowell.

The following columns are written by regular contributors: "Dieter's Workshop," "Fit Beat," "Health Scene," "Personal Trainer," "Stargaze," and "Vid Biz."

How to Query *New Body*

Accepts completed manuscripts as well as queries; will consider simultaneous submissions that are so noted; send photo/art information; send for editorial calendar to know about upcoming topics.

Dorsey breaks just about every query rule a freelancer comes to expect from an editor. Her favorite query of all time was one on dehydration, which the writer sent to her in a water bottle—and he won the assignment! Different colored paper or envelopes also catch her eye.

"Maybe it's because I really like my job and even opening the mail can be fun, especially if there's a query on purple parchment!" Dorsey laughs.

Dorsey also likes to receive completed manuscripts—though she cautions that she throws away any that are not accompanied by an SASE.

Dorsey warns writers not to call her with story ideas. "I hate to talk on the phone about a story idea. The interruption irritates me," she says. Her staff teases her because she answers the phone with an edge in her voice and says, "This is Nicole. *How* can I help you?" she admits.

Queries that reflect the look and beginning of the proposed article cause Dorsey to pay more attention. "I like to see a headline, the deck, and a lead," she says. For instance, one article was headed, 'Overweight versus Overfat,' with a deck that read, 'why some overweight people aren't fat at all!' If a writer can do that, he or she probably knows the magazine and our readers."

Dorsey wants to see two or three clips with queries, preferably those that show that you are knowledgeable about fitness.

How to Write for *New Body*

Dorsey says she appreciates a writer who is a little bit funny, well-informed about his or her subject, and writes just enough over the assigned amount that she can edit superfluous material.

"I like to see sources, with phone numbers or documentation that shows me that you've done your research," she says. "Because of the size of our staff, we have to rely on competent writers who deliver accurate information," she adds.

Once you've received an assignment, you'll get a letter detailing the desired article. At that point, Dorsey likes to stay in contact to prevent problems later.

"I always end my letters to new writers with, 'Any questions, call me pronto!'" she says. "Then, I don't mind the phone call."

New Woman

215 Lexington Avenue
New York, NY 10016
(212) 251-1500

Published: Monthly

Circulation: 1.3 million

Query: Check the current masthead for appropriate department editor

Query response time: 6 to 8 weeks

Buys: About 120 articles out of approximately 6,300 unsolicited manuscripts/queries received annually

Guidelines: Available; send SASE

Rights purchased: Exclusive first NAS, plus certain periodical rights in the United Kingdom and Australia, and worldwide print syndication rights for six months following the off-sale date of the issue in which the article appears; publisher pays the author half of all net proceeds received by publisher

Pays: On acceptance

Expenses: Pays reasonable minor expenses; any large expense must be negotiated

Kill fee: 20 percent

Rates:

Type of Article	***Word Length***	***Payment***
Major Feature	2,000 - 2,500	$2,000 - 2,500
Short Feature	800 - 1,500	800 - 1,500
Health, Money and Relationship	1,000 - 4,000	1,000 - 5,000
"Viewpoint"	800 - 1,500	800 - 1,500

"I regard our reader as a thinking person," says Kathy Green, managing editor of *New Woman.* "Our research shows that relationships, including her relationship with herself, are very important to her. She's introspective, and wants to grow and change. She's not the *Self* fitness-oriented woman or the *Glamour* fashion and news reader.

"She is trying to do her best at her career and has or may want a relationship with a man, but also wants to feel good about herself," Green continues. "She isn't interested in a lot of frivolous things; she wants to read about psychology, relationships, and self-discovery."

New Woman readers range in age from 25 to 49 years; the median age is 36 years old. The readership is evenly split between unmarried and married women. About three-quarters of the readers are employed; they have a median household income of $36,445.

How to Slant Your Ideas to *New Woman*

Because the magazine is so relationship and self-oriented, there has to be a very human element in every piece, Green explains. "A piece on going on a safari wouldn't work for us—but an article about what one woman discovered while on safari might," she says. "We published an article about a father and daughter who went on a cross-country bike trip, telling how they reconnected after years of being distant. The angle was the relationship, not the biking."

New Woman has many features and columns each month, and the majority of them (except for the fashion and beauty layouts) are written by freelancers. The sections include: "Careers and Money," "Food," "Health & Diet," "Love & Sex," "Relationships," and "Self-Discovery." The items listed in the table of contents under "Regular Features," are closed.

"Love & Sex" articles are all about relationships between men and women—anything from how to meet men to how to put life back into your sex life.

"The *New Woman* attitude toward sex and relationships is unique in that we always put the woman's needs and desires first," Green says. "We do not tell women to do whatever is necessary to get and keep a man. Her self-esteem is always our first concern. However, our readers are interested particularly in how to maintain good relationships with men.

"'Self' articles are our forté," the editor continues. "We cover all aspects of self-esteem, personal growth, and self-discovery. The articles are written in a positive and supportive, but not preachy, tone. Our readers turn to us for advice and insight into how to make their lives better."

The following areas are open to freelancers:

- **Health** articles cover the latest news and research about the full range of health and medical topics. Basic ailments are discussed here, like headaches, and treating the common cold. But other pieces can be hotter, like an article that discussed RU-486, the abortion pill.

- **Money** is, clearly, about finances, but even this area sometimes takes a relationship angle to money issues, rather than simply explaining how to invest for the highest yield. An article should offer concrete steps to take in overcoming a problem.
- **Relationships** articles concern those with anyone—siblings, parents, co-workers, neighbors, or others—except romantic liaisons between men and women. The latter relationships are covered more thoroughly in the well of the book. In one article, a man wrote about feeling left out of part of his wife's life that she reserved for her best friend.
- **Viewpoint** is *New Woman*'s opinion and thought-piece column. Past topics have included "Making Sense of Censorship," "Suing Over an S.T.D.—Will You Win?," and a piece on being a confident mother.

"Beauty Marks," "Bookshelf," "Careerwise," "Celebrate With Food," "Celestial View," "Eating Right," "Getting Physical," "Good Advice," "In Brief," "In Style," "Mind & Body," "Money Matters," "Not for Men Only," "Previews," and "Profile" are written by regular contributors or the staff.

How to Query *New Woman*

One to two pages preferred; do not send any photo/art information.

"We prefer a rather detailed proposal, not just five quick ideas on a piece of paper," Green says. "Instead, we like to see one idea that has been well developed. Is it going to offer case histories? Interviews with experts? A first-person slant to a topic our readers want to know about? Be able to cite the experts you're thinking of interviewing, and tell us what the article will accomplish."

Although the beginning of this chapter states that *New Woman* buys 120 articles a year from freelancers, Green warns that only about six are from writers completely unknown to the magazine who simply query over the transom. The vast majority go to writers sought out by the magazine.

Why? Because the vast majority of queries simply don't fit the magazine's needs. "Most often, the angle is wrong," Green says. "The query is written for someone too young or too old to be our reader, or something about the idea makes it clear that the writer doesn't understand our magazine well enough to write for it."

Green says that using an anecdote in the query helps to illustrate how you'll handle the human interest part that is integral to every *New Woman* article. "But we don't want all our stories to have anecdotes," she adds. "We're also interested in looking at shorter advice pieces, like a quick, fun piece on 100 ways to be more romantic."

If you haven't been published before, Green recommends that you aim your query at one of the editors lower on the masthead. "Stephanie (von Hirschberg, senior editor) and Donna (Jackson, editor-at-large) have their own lists of writers they use," she explains. "But the features associate and assistant editors are more open to receiving material."

How to Write for *New Woman*

"The *New Woman* voice is always friendly, helpful and warm," the managing editor says. "A lot of readers have referred to this magazine as their best friend. Our articles are usually very informative, yet still emotional and personal."

The editors note that they are sticklers about fact checking. "We're royal pains, actually!" Green warns with a laugh. "There are usually one or two revisions, then we need a list of contacts and research sources for fact checking.

"It's hard to get your foot in the door," Green admits. "But once you do, we treat our writers well. Everybody here is nice, and we all really like to work with writers."

Off Duty

3303 Harbor Boulevard #C2
Costa Mesa, CA 92626
(714) 549-7172

Published: 31 times among 4 editions (Europe, Pacific, United States, and National Guard Reserves)

Circulation: 662,000

Query: Gary Burch, managing editor

Query response time: 8 weeks

Buys: About 10 to 15 articles/stories out of approximately 250 unsolicited queries/manuscripts received annually

Guidelines: Available with SASE; send $1.75 for sample magazine

Rights purchased: One-time Worldwide

Pays: 30 days after acceptance

Expenses: Pays phone, if approved in advance

Kill fee: Assignments are never killed but may be postponed

Rates:

Type of Article	*Word Length*	*Payment*
Major Feature	1,800 - 2,100	$360 - 420
Short Feature	700 - 900	140 - 180

Off Duty is distributed door-to-door to military personnel and families who live on base in the United States or overseas. As the title states, the magazine's editorial focuses on the off-duty lifestyle of those in the military.

"Our readers aren't as different as everyone thinks," says Gary Burch, managing editor, who's invested a dozen years at the publication. "They have careers that take them around the world, so they are more mobile and transitory. Their job also demands tremendous personal sacrifice. But their concerns and interests are just about the same as the average person's. They want to nurture their families, protect their health, save money, make wise purchases and investments, travel, and have fun."

In terms of the magazine's readership, about 88 percent of active-duty personnel are male, 60 percent of whom are married. "We have a high percentage of female readers as well," notes Burch.

How to Slant Your Ideas to *Off Duty*

Look for lifestyle issues that affect military personnel but aren't too controversial. The magazine has covered adopting children while in the military, making transition plans for civilian careers, preparing military spouses to return to college, and giving your new automobile some "TLC."

"You don't have to have been in the military to write for *Off Duty*, but you must learn about our audience," says Burch. "Take time to know the subject areas we cover, and do some research to get to know your topic."

An article on New Year's tax resolutions included strong military points; another on stretching a pay check included taking advantage of ways to lower food bills by shopping at the commissary and using base beauty salons and auto repair centers.

Burch says he welcomes ideas concerning consumer electronics. These include cameras, stereos, TVs, videocameras, and computers—any products sold in military exchanges. One piece, for example, covered the new trend to simplify VCR programming.

"These pieces have most often been staff written, but we are considering using more freelancers," he says. "Writers must talk to personnel at the exchanges to get the information."

Historical articles are another avenue the magazine pursues when space allows. "We've done pieces on Desert Storm two years after the war ended; Pearl Harbor 50 years later; and the retirement of the Jeep from the military."

When it comes to sports, *Off Duty* runs previews of the major sports seasons, such as basketball and football, as well as articles slanted to recreational sports. One piece talked about avoiding workout injuries, while another reviewed sports shoes and how they've changed over the years.

Health topics are also worth considering. The magazine has covered surviving a cold; dental care; cardiovascular fitness; and stress reduction. No military angle is needed here.

In addition to lifestyle topics, *Off Duty* is interested in travel articles that fit its particular needs. "We get more queries about travel than anything else, and they usually fall short because writers don't know our approach to travel," says Burch. "When covering domestic travel, don't zero in on one destination; use a theme to tie together three to four destinations. For example, cover a number of ski resorts or write a piece on fun side trips while on the road, such as visiting military museums."

Overseas articles can have a more limited scope. "The attraction that being stationed overseas has for military personnel is the chance to see as much as they can during the two or three years they live somewhere," the editor explains. "So we cover one area in depth. For instance, we ran a piece on northern Sweden and another on Vladivostok, Russia."

All *Off Duty* departments are closed to freelancers. The bulletin board page is filled with news that is typically sent by public relations professionals.

How to Query *Off Duty*

One page preferred; send photo/art information, but do not send actual photos or negatives.

Burch favors a query that outlines the idea. Tell him the military angle and why you can write the article better than anyone else. The magazine works from an editorial calendar, but Burch prefers not to share it with writers. "We would rather get a query on a topic and say, 'Perfect, we have that idea planned,'" he says. "We normally make purchases from freelancers when they send something in that fits an upcoming need rather than buy a new idea that doesn't fit our editorial plan."

Off Duty depends on a regular cadre of freelancers the editors know they can count on and trust. "It's tough to break in. You've got to hit on one of the topics we are planning and for which we don't have another writer in mind," says Burch. "But once you get an assignment and do a good job, we will consider you for another idea we have in store."

The editor recalls one new freelancer who sent in an idea for a multigenerational military family piece which was very similar to a topic the staff had planned to do. "We assigned her the piece and she did a terrific job. Then we asked her to cover the topic of military marriages when both spouses are on active duty. She included interesting anecdotes and good quotes," he relates.

How to Write for *Off Duty*

A conversational tone is the key to writing articles for this market. "Tell me a story," says Burch. "Don't give me a speech."

Burch is impressed by writers who can do enough research to come up with really good quotes from experts, versus those who use whatever quotes they get from the first few sources they contact. If the article is based on basic advice, there is no need to find experts with a military background. However, if the topic has to do with the military (such as child-rearing problems that arise from frequent moves), it would be best to talk to a specialist, such as a military psychologist.

When applicable, offer how-to tips. Always include names, addresses, and phone numbers to contact for more information.

"As a writer, you alone are responsible for fact checking, so don't wait for someone to follow up behind you," says Burch. "Get things straight the first time."

Omni

324 West Wendover Avenue
Greensboro, NC 27408
(919) 275-9809

Published: Monthly

Circulation: 700,000

Query: Keith Ferrell, editor

Query response time: 4 to 6 weeks

Buys: About 800 articles/stories out of approximately 5,000 unsolicited queries/manuscripts received annually

Guidelines: Available; send SASE

Rights purchased: First NAS and overseas *Omni* edition rights; all rights for "Continuum" and certain electronic rights; pays re-usage fees if material used in a book or a syndicate

Pays: On acceptance

Expenses: Pays all reasonable, when discussed in advance

Kill fee: Negotiable

Rates:

Type of Article	*Word Length*	*Payment*
Major Feature	3,000	$3,000
Column	750	750
"Continuum"	200	100

"*Omni* is a science magazine that takes in all of the universe and all aspects of human nature as its stomping ground," says Editor Keith Ferrell. "We also publish fiction, which sets us apart from any other science magazine.

"We are determinedly futurists," the editor continues. "We seek pieces that speculate about the consequences of technology, new discoveries, and theories. In addition to our wonderment about astrophysics, genetics, and biochemistry, we consider the human side of the equation. For example, we've looked at how technology affects the world economy, how new telecommunications are reshaping the structure of the corporation, and how various approaches will work to solve the health care crisis in the United States."

Ferrell describes *Omni* readers as inquisitive people who want to know about a subject early on—before anyone else. Some work in science, many are professionals of one sort or another, and all are interested laymen fascinated with scientific discoveries.

"The real world is drawn to *Omni* because our speculation is always grounded in research and because we are interested in more than one field. We are generalists versus specialists," says Ferrell. "If you were a biologist, you might also love articles about astrophysics, yet you may not be able to follow all the technical literature in the science magazines. That is where our ecumenical approach helps; we embrace all of the sciences."

Omni's total adult readership is 3,763,000, two-thirds of whom are male. The median age is 34. Nearly 67 percent of the readers attended college, and 25 percent hold a professional or managerial job. The median household income is $41,247.

How to Slant Your Ideas to *Omni*

"What we add to the scientific equation is a willingness to speculate and to cover topics that are frowned upon by other science magazines," says Ferrell. "We are solidly-grounded, but we are aware of the public's fascination with unexplained phenomenon. We are a poetic magazine—not in language but in imagination. We look for writers who can persuade scientists to speculate on the consequences of scientific discoveries. That is the center of our magazine and it is what brings about new thought."

Ferrell recalls one freelancer who approached the magazine with the topic "Techno Wizards and Couch Potatoes," a piece which posed a question about the potential for abuse with new digital video technology. "He wondered how special effects, the magnitude of those used in 'Terminator II,' might be used to control and manipulate the public and was especially curious about political abuse," the editor explains. "The piece was solidly based yet it had a level of speculation."

Another article, "How to Build an Alien," written by Ferrell himself, brought the reader to a conference where many anthropologists, scientists, and science fiction writers were designing a serious planetary environment and deciding what creatures and cultures might evolve there.

To make the grade as an *Omni* feature, a story must have a dramatic subject strong enough to be flagged on the cover. It needs broad appeal and a variety of expert sources quoted. Of course, the material must carry the weight of a 3,000-word piece.

A few *Omni* cover lines have included "Hot Science: Touring the Volcano," "Killer Comets: Was Chicken Little Right?," and "Brain Gain: Pills That Boost Intelligence."

Topics of narrower focus are directed into one of the many 750-word *Omni* columns. Not every column appears in every issue. These are the ones open to freelancers:

- **AI (Artificial Intelligence)** is a computer column that explores the far end of science. "We are not interested in next year's chip but next century's chip," says Ferrell.
- **Antimatter** tackles unexplained phenomena on the fringe of science and reality. "This is where we cover UFOs," the editor notes.
- **Continuum** is a collection of short pieces varying in subject matter. Past issues have discussed the difference in taste between microwaved food and food cooked in conventional ovens; a preventive medicine to cure cataracts; and why we may want to avoid sleeping with electric blankets or in waterbeds that have an electrical component. This is a good venue for those who are new to this market.
- **Digs** taps into the fields of archaeology, anthropology, and field science.
- **Earth** is an environmental column. One piece, "Talk is Chief," told how the words attributed to Chief Seattle, Earth Day's patron saint, have been as distorted as they would be if kids were playing a game of "telephone."
- **Funds** covers how science and technology are exerting enormous pressure on the world economy in terms of how money is managed and how stocks are sold. It is also a science fiction investment column where writers speculate about how to invest in a private enterprise in outer space or what challenges lie ahead for biotech companies.
- **Mind** delves into what's new in psychology, such as computer psychoanalysts and technology neurosis.
- **Space** covers space technology—not tomorrow, but a decade from now. It has looked at the best material from which to build a space craft of the future, such as a ship of ice.
- **Stars** offers innovation and speculation about astronomy and astrophysics.
- **Style** looks at how science and technology are changing fashion. One article focused on breeding cotton for color to avoid using toxic dyes. Another looked at computerized tennis shoes that monitor such things as heart rate and distance traveled.

- **Transportation** explores future evolution of all forms of transportation other than automobiles. One column speculated about the return of the blimp as a cargo vehicle; another wondered about the possibility of transcontinental subways.
- **Wheels** is devoted to how cars are changing in response to technology. "We've reached a point where many cars have more computing power than many companies did a decade ago," says Ferrell. That's evidenced in one column that debuted a new Volkswagen prototype claiming to be the first self-parking car.

"Electronic Universe," "Forum," "Games," and "Political Science" are closed to freelancers.

How to Query *Omni*

One-page queries preferred; send photo/art information if possible, but 95 percent of the art is generated by the staff.

"First and foremost, make sure your query can pass the test of basic literacy," says Ferrell. "We receive a number of queries in which our names are misspelled. I spent eight years as a freelancer and that is basic. An editor once told me that magazine editors look for any reason to get a query off their desk, and I can verify that that's true."

Ferrell prefers proposals that let him see immediately that you know *Omni* and are excited about the story you're suggesting. "Don't say you're enthusiastic; show in every sentence why our reader will benefit from reading your article," he says. "It's also helpful for us to know that you have a strong sense of who your interview sources will be. And we need to be convinced that you understand the science you are dealing with."

A straightforward business letter is fine to sell to this market, as long as you give a sense of how the article will be organized. If you're an untried writer, it would be wise to let the editor see a few takes on how you'd approach the topic through a sample lead or two. Also send a résumé or good clips.

If your idea strikes a chord at *Omni,* an editor will call you to discuss the approach, deadline, length, and any travel, which the magazine will book for you. "Then, go out and buy a nice dinner and celebrate," says Ferrell.

How to Write for *Omni*

"One of the things we try to do is make *Omni* a real writers' magazine," says Ferrell. "If we feature 10 different writers, we don't mind an equal number of writing styles. A good magazine should be a little like going to a good party, where you can circulate and hear different voices. We have copyediting rules, but we like a writer's personality to shine through."

Ferrell says it is fine for writers to transport themselves into their stories, but they must remember that they are not the expert but a conduit for information. "Don't let yourself get in the way of the story," he says.

Additionally, a solid *Omni* writer communicates excitement without seeming excitable. "Because we so often deal with the ultimate—the beginning and end of the universe—we want a rational, understated, calm voice. The magazine has a fluidity and grace to its prose that I'd stack against any other publication," says Ferrell. "But use the active voice; we are not flowery."

Scientific terms must be explained, which means the magazine wants writers who can popularize science without pandering or talking down to readers. "We look for writers who have a gift for using the simile and metaphor that relates to something in the reader's life," says Ferrell. "One great example is a writer who compared the firing rates of neurons to the up-and-down sequence of a wave at a baseball stadium. That sort of gift is rare, and we treasure it."

Omni fact checks as hard as any other magazine. "Writers must provide a source list and documentation, meaning transcripts, tapes, correspondence, and other research material all keyed to the manuscript," he says. "We expect writers to fact check, and then the piece is verified through two more fact-checking processes at the magazine."

Ferrell believes freelancers will find the editorial process at *Omni* very exacting and intense, but respectful. "We really enjoy working with writers to make sure the very best of their prose and the very best aspects of the story blossom."

Outside

1165 North Clark Street
Chicago, IL 60610
(312) 951-0990

Published: Monthly

Circulation: 400,000

Query: Features: Laura Hohnhold, articles editor
"Bodywork": Andrew Tilin, associate editor
"Destinations": Kathy Martin, assistant editor
"Dispatches": Alex Heard, senior editor

Query response time: 4 to 6 weeks

Buys: About 200 to 300 articles/stories out of approximately 3,000 to 4,000 unsolicited queries/manuscripts received annually

Guidelines: Available; send SASE

Rights purchased: First NAS

Pays: On acceptance

Expenses: Pays travel, phone, and research

Kill fee: 25 percent

Rates:

Type of Article	*Word Length*	*Payment*
Major Feature	4,000 - 5,000	$2,500 - 7,000
Short Feature	2,000 - 3,500	1,500 - 3,500
News Brief	200 - 1,000	100 - 1,000
"Bodywork"	1,500	1,000 - 1,500
"Destinations"	300 - 1,200	250 - 1,000
"Dispatches"	300 - 1,200	200 - 1,000
"The Outside Review"	300 - 1,200	250 - 1,000

"There is no other magazine like *Outside*," says Articles Editor Laura Hohnhold. "In a time of specialty magazines, we devote ourselves to the world. We are unique in that we consider everything from travel to environment to camping to adventure."

Outside is written for active, educated adults who are curious about the world and concerned about its preservation. It's dedicated to inspiring people to enjoy fuller, more rewarding lives through year-round editorial coverage of sports, travel, events, people, politics, art, and literature of the world outside. The magazine provokes readers to develop an appreciation and sense of responsibility for the natural environment.

"Our readers love engaging in all sorts of sports, whether they play themselves or are armchair participants," says Hohnhold. "They can pick up the magazine and dream about sailing to Tahiti, even though they know they may never do it themselves. We attract individuals who have hungry imaginations and a healthy interest in life."

Readers are predominantly male (73 percent), with a median age of 35. More than 80 percent are college-educated; nearly 60 percent are in professional/managerial/sales positions. More than half of the readers are married, and the median household income is $56,000.

How to Slant Your Ideas to *Outside*

Of the articles in *Outside*, 60 percent are developed by the staff and assigned to experienced writers. However, the editors are always interested in new writers and their ideas.

The magazine publishes articles on all aspects of the outdoors. In particular, the staff looks for solid seasonal service pieces. Articles may be on outdoor personalities, regions, lifestyles and activities, or in-depth investigative stories on environmental issues.

"We want writers who go out and actually do the things they write about," says Hohnhold. "They must have a wonderful sense of the absurd and a healthy curiosity about the world and all the diverse people in it."

Hohnhold says she likes to break new writers in through the departments. "We get people started on something short—for their sake and ours," she says.

One feature, "Eddy Matzger's Ten-Wheel Drive," profiled the world's best in-line skater who, at age 25, is making a comfortable living competing in races, ranging from five kilometers to 95 miles. Another article offered tips on the 15 best places to pitch a tent, how to read a map, and what to do when you reach your destination.

"Chase of the Tornadoheads" examined the tornado, the most powerful and destructive weather phenomenon in our atmosphere and one that occurs over every land mass on earth. This piece included the schedule for a tornado chaser—one who spends thousands of dollars on video equipment and fearlessly drives through lightning, rain, and hail for a chance to get as close as possible to the source of such amazement.

In addition to five to seven full-length features in each issue, the magazine also carries the following freelance-written departments:

- **Bodywork** focuses on health and fitness with a sports bent. One issue included a guide on when to work hard and when to rest easy, with a sidebar on how to gauge one's level of effort and establish a target heart rate.
- **Destinations** is a travel column, typically covering domestic locales. It offers places, news, and advice for the adventurous traveler. The pieces are short and usually cover what can be done once an individual arrives at the given location. Each month the column also describes a select inn or lodge.
- **Dispatches** includes news, event coverage, and short, timely profiles relevant to the outdoors. It's the magazine in microcosm, with coverage of sports, adventure, and the environment. Samplings from one issue include: "Neither Crevasse, nor Terrorist, nor Typhoon Marge . . . Could Wreck a Good Adventure"; "The Age of Greenpeace"; "What's Left Out There: The Last Great Unknowns"; and "Amazing Disgrace: Natural Disasters of the Human Kind."
- **The Outside Review** examines outdoor equipment and includes field evaluations of specific products. The writers describe the equipment after trying it themselves; they don't just write from press releases.

"Field Notes," "Natural Acts," and "Out There" are written in house or by regular contributors.

How to Query *Outside*

One page preferred. Separate guidelines are available for prospective photo and illustration contributors. Request them directly from the photo or art department.

To get noticed at this magazine, make your query straight to the point and present a clear idea. "Make sure you have a piece of reporting; don't just tell us about your trip or experience," Hohnhold states.

"Sample leads do nothing for us," says Hohnhold. "How can we judge anything from a paragraph? Your query doesn't have to show a lot of style; that can be reflected in your clips. But the proposal must be well thought out and presented. Sample quotes aren't important; we assume you'll do all the necessary reporting."

Hohnhold says that most queries the magazine receives are of too-general interest. "We believe our readers have a certain knowledge about the outdoors and the environment," she says. "We like to have the writer teach them something they don't already know."

If you get the go-ahead from *Outside*, you will most likely have several conversations with the editor prior to starting your reporting. Typically, you will also be sent an assignment letter.

How to Write for *Outside*

"We take a different tack, always trying to find a weird angle on things," she notes. "We like our stories to have several layers. For example, a profile shouldn't just bring the person to life but should also have a really strong point of view. A piece by Jon Krakauer called 'A Cure for Baldness,' told of his climbing a mountain in South America at age 40. It was as much an adventure story as it was a personal essay. Another article, 'No Cannibal Jokes, Please,' was an author's tale of visiting a Stone Age tribe. It was classic armchair adventure, but it also described the landscape and the people in a provocative way."

Send a list of sources with your piece so the editors can fact check the article.

Parade

750 Third Avenue
New York, NY 10017
(212) 573-7000

Published: Weekly

Circulation: 37 million

Query: Fran Carpentier, senior editor

Query response time: 4 weeks

Buys: About 150 articles/stories out of approximately 12,000 unsolicited queries/manuscripts received annually

Guidelines: Available; send SASE

Rights purchased: First NAS

Pays: On acceptance

Expenses: Pays

Kill fee: Seldom needed

Rates:

Type of Article	*Word Length*	*Payment*
Major Feature	1,800	$3,000 - 5,000
Short Feature	1,500	3,000

Every Sunday, nearly 75 million Americans reach for their newspapers and pull out *Parade,* a magazine supplement filled with news, reportage, and personality profiles.

"We are a full-scope magazine that boils down a universal concern so that it's accessible—and meaningful—to the individual," says Senior Editor Fran Carpentier.

She continues "*Parade* has the largest circulation of any magazine in the country, and it's frustrating when people think of us as a photo contest magazine. In reality, we carry important, thoughtful pieces. We don't steer clear of controversy, and you can't accuse us of fitting into a do-gooder formula.

"We cover serious subjects such as a national survey we conducted asking the question, 'Will the Supreme Court Make Abortion Legal?' and a piece by Nobel Peace Prize Winner Elie Wiesel in which he pleaded against bigotry and racism. That's what *Parade* is at its best," the editor says.

How to Slant Your Ideas to *Parade*

"The world is our oyster. We can cover anything—and therein lies the challenge," says Carpentier. "When you pick up *Parade,* it's rare that you don't find a good read. We give people hope. If there is a wrong, we provide a means of redress. If there's a problem, we give them resources to help solve it."

Even celebrity profiles, a genre reserved for tried and true *Parade* writers, give the reader something to which they can relate. It's not enough that a person is a celebrity; there's got to be a story behind the story. For example, a feature on actor Joe Pesci, of *Home Alone* and *Lethal Weapon* fame, talked about the very human message of striving to please Mom and Dad.

In every issue, *Parade* runs three or four features that are possible venues for freelance writers. Yet most writers are turned down by the magazine because, as Carpentier puts it, "Writers propose subjects; we want clearly focused ideas."

The editor challenges freelancers to do a bit of homework before proposing a specific area to explore. Whether it is a social issue, a profile, or a medical breakthrough, turn the idea upside-down and inside-out. Just taking one idea—gangs—Carpentier quickly thought of several different takes on the subject.

"It might be the story of one teacher who helped put an end to gang problems in a community; a round-up of five to 10 cities throughout the country who have stopped gang violence; or a story we ran by a gang member who did time in prison and then turned his life around," she rattled off in less than a minute.

Carpentier tells a story about turning down a proposal by a regular contributor on gun control. "I told her we couldn't possibly rectify that controversy in 1,500 words," remembers Carpentier. "Then the writer went on to tell me that, as a single mother of an 11-year-old son, she had become frightened and went out and bought a gun. Now *that* intrigued me. Instead of running a story on 'Should Americans Bear Arms?' we ran the cover article, 'Why I Own a Gun.' To give the story balance, we ran a sidebar on where gun control legislation was at that point, with quotes from the National Rifle Association and FBI statistics on gun-related accidents and homicides. You couldn't turn away from this story, whether or not you cared about gun ownership."

Examples of other *Parade* articles are: "When Drugs Hit Home," a story about a narcotics detective who found that his 16-year-old daughter was using drugs; "She Turns Kids' Lives Around," a piece about a woman who started the Skating

Association for the Blind and Handicapped; and "We've Got These Kids All Fired Up," about an impoverished urban school in El Paso, Texas, where, in 1992, five students were accepted by MIT and all received substantial financial aid.

"A piece we did called 'Men Who Love Babies' was a narrative by a single man who, with 10 other guys, volunteers at a local hospital to help with the babies born to drug-addicted mothers," says Carpentier. "It was a lovely idea that came over the transom and turned out to be a fabulous piece."

How to Query *Parade*

One page preferred. Send photo/art information.

"Many writers have a story to tell, but they don't pitch it the right way," says Carpentier. "They don't think of all the possible ways to tell the story that will make it marketable to our publication. You've got to decide how to focus your idea so that the story is worth telling to 75 million readers. What is it that makes your idea matter to everyone? What difference will it make in people's lives? What can readers do with the information? On the one hand, focusing your idea is the most difficult to do, yet in another way, it is so simple. It's a skill writers have to develop."

Query letters need to reflect the same sense and tempo as the magazine's articles. "It's great if you can spark controversy and pique my interest," Carpentier says. "Don't be cutesy. Tell me how you will approach the topic. For example, if you are pitching a medical topic, tell me if you will interview the sufferers and survivors, and let me know what medical experts you will talk to. We also like sidebars, so it's a good idea to pitch those in your article proposal."

Carpentier wants to see clips, but she doesn't rely on them to foretell a writer's ability. "I'm aware of how much work I have to do when editing articles," she says. "I look at a writer's credits and the quality of the idea. There is no substitute for talent and real professionalism; it just shines off the page."

How to Write for *Parade*

"The key to good writing is to take the incidental and make it universal," says Carpentier. "There is so much wisdom in that approach."

Parade seeks to develop a dialogue between writer and editor. "We have to communicate with one another so that the writer learns exactly what the publication needs. In fact, some of our best writers turn in an outline first, so we know exactly where they are taking the piece."

Regarding its style, *Parade* presents stories "straight on." "We tell things just the way they are with clean, concise, lively prose," says the senior editor. "We are lean and mean, never running features that are more than 2,000 words. Almost every piece pulls at heart strings, but we do not run what I call, 'Lassie-Come-Home' journalism. We also don't do 'gripes.' If we try to right a wrong, we provide the reader with the information he needs to take action. At the same time, we don't proselytize. We never present something as 'the only' answer."

Because *Parade* generally likes to tell its stories through the individuals involved, Carpentier encourages writers to learn to be good interviewers. "Get your subjects to open up a bit to tell you the *real* story," she encourages.

Parade prides itself on integrity and accuracy. "Everything is fact checked by the staff, but writers still should strive for accuracy, or they may not get another assignment," says Carpentier. "We request a source list with every manuscript."

Asking a writer to fine-tune an article after the editors have read it is par for the course at *Parade.* "If I buy a fabulous dress or suit, chances are I'm going to take it to a tailor for a couple of nips and tucks to get it to really fit," says Carpentier. "The same could be said of an article—so, don't take rewrites personally."

Parenting

301 Howard Street, 17th Floor
San Francisco, CA 94105
(415) 546-7575

Published: 10 issues per year, plus one annual special issue, *Parenting's Summer Fun*

Circulation: 875,000

Query: Articles editor

Query response time: 4 to 6 weeks

Buys: About 100 articles/stories out of approximately 4,000 unsolicited queries/manuscripts received annually

Guidelines: Available; send SASE

Rights purchased: First NAS

Pays: On acceptance

Expenses: Pays all reasonable items

Kill fee: 25 percent

Rates:

Type of Article	***Word Length***	***Payment***
Major Feature	2,000+	$800+
Short Feature	800 - 1,500	500+
Department/Column	75 - 1,200	50+
"News"	75 - 500	50+

"As a parenting publication, we try to present smart, in-depth service," says *Parenting*'s Managing Editor Bruce Raskin. "Readers come to us for the breadth and depth of our reporting. But what differentiates us from others is that we also run articles on social and political issues that appeal to mothers and fathers as members of the larger parenting community."

Such articles have included the devastating effects of Hurricane Andrew on families; reactions to the 1992 Los Angeles riots; and an article on "bright flight," the trend in which white and minority middle class families are fleeing public schools.

"We don't preach," says Raskin. "We provide intelligent information and give a point of view, but we let parents make up their own minds."

Three-quarters of *Parenting*'s readers are women; the median age is 31. The median household income is $37,634.

The majority have children from age newborn to six, but the magazine also publishes articles that appeal to parents of kids older than six.

How to Slant Your Ideas to *Parenting*

Parenting editors build the magazine's backbone from this list of core topics:

Activities
Behavior
Child Development
Current Affairs
Day Care
Discipline
Education
Entertainment
Environment
Food/Nutrition
Health/Medicine
Mother Care
Pregnancy

"The key is to develop a unique slant within these areas," says Raskin. "It's easy to come up with a basic article on picky eaters, but we've already done that subject from several angles. The trick is to find something unusual about finicky kids that will also reach a broad range of parents."

One article Raskin points to as an example of a tight angle is "When Kids Talk Back," a round up of smart aleck tactics kids use and advice on when they happen, why they occur, and how to deal with them.

A few other examples of articles that made the grade are "Chill the Whine," about dealing with whining in ways that respect kids' needs and parents' nerves; "Pippi Power," a look at what makes Pippi Longstocking such a plucky kids' heroine through a profile of her Scandinavian creator; and "Kids and AIDS," which included suggestions for how to teach young children about AIDS in words they can understand.

The jam-packed table of contents reveals at least 10 features, including a major cover story, and 25 departments and columns. Most departments are open to freelancers, such as the following:

- **Ages and Stages** gives age-specific advice on the entire gamut of *Parenting* topics. The sections are divided from birth to six months, six months to age one, one to two, three to five, six to eight, and nine and up. A quick sampling of topics reveals: home-made birth announcements; breaking the bottle habit; the truth about fibbing to kids; healthy responses to "playing doctor"; and the contact-lens decision.

- **Discovery** is an activity department that is often written by a regular group of freelancers, but open to writers who come to the magazine with a good idea and healthy clips. One piece on handpuppets told how to turn stray socks, wooden spoons, spare gloves, and even pinecones and sea shells into characters that bring oodles of storytelling entertainment to young kids.
- **Learning Curve** leaves no aspect of education neglected, from preschool through the elementary school years. Sample coverage includes the latest word on whole language learning and parents bringing art programs back to life.
- **Money's Worth** offers consumer and financial tips. The key here is to find a family/parenting hook and not to be generic. Two examples are using allowances to teach kids about money; and a report on a day-care-provider tax break.
- **Mother Care** devotes its pages to women's health and beauty. Stories have included how adoptive mothers can use breast pumps to stimulate breast milk production; how to face the harsh winds of autumn without chapped lips and flyaway hair; and how monthly reading groups can make indulging in novels part of mom's daily routine.
- **News** takes a brief news perspective on any one of the magazine's core topics. It presents new occurrences, studies, and trends, such as current thinking on Sudden Infant Death Syndrome; kids' magazines; the increase of single moms; and the bashing of the bashfulness theory.
- **One Family** profiles an individual family that has an interesting story to tell. The magazine has run features on disabled parents; Arab American parents; and parents who home school. One article told how a family's open contact with their adopted children's birth parents gave new meaning to "extended family." Another focused on the challenges a young mom and older dad—sprouting a second family tree—faced as they parented their children.

  "There needs to be some sort of tension in the story, meaning a problem has to be addressed, then partially or fully resolved," says Raskin. "We once tried a story on two parents who were psychologists, but there was no real drama to the story—no real hook—so it wasn't interesting enough."

- **On the Job** is a column for working parents, giving advice ranging from how to negotiate a part-time deal with your boss, to how to move up on the mommy track, and what a job interviewer is allowed to ask about your home-life circumstances.
- **Passages** presents a brief description of a major turning point in a parent's life. One mother shared her thoughts as she and her husband scrambled to pack memories and necessities while a fire raged toward their Oakland, California, home.
- **Single Parents** and **Step Parents** are reserved for parents without partners and for stepparents. Topics have included what you must know to collect child support, and how to introduce a stepchild to a new sibling.
- **Tactics** is a catch-all service column that includes everything from how to prepare a home for a new baby, to how to tell if your kids are conning you.
- **Up in Arms** is a reader speak-out column, giving parents a chance to air their feelings on topics ranging from the Clintons sending Chelsea to a private school, to mothers who were incensed by public places that cater to families but don't include changing tables in rest rooms. In "Stars and Bribes Forever," a reader presented the case that once parents start doling out rewards, kids only reach as far as the next prize.
- **What's Cooking** presents recipes, nutrition guidelines, and tips for choosing healthy food. Ingenious bean dishes, weaning kids from caffeine, and sizing up the options in breakfast cereals were on the menu in one issue.
- **Whole Nine Months** gives advice on preparing for and living through pregnancy. Topics have included the safety of drinking caffeine, what to do about stretch marks, managing morning sickness, and quizzing your obstetrician.

"Medical Mysteries" and "Q & A" are written by regular contributors.

How to Query *Parenting*

One-page queries preferred; do not send any photo/art information; query five months to a year or more in advance for seasonal material.

Short, organized, well-thought-out proposals catch the eye of this editor. Raskin pays close attention to how a writer proposes to package the story. He doesn't just want 3,000 words of gray text, but a story that has been made more intriguing to the eye with sidebars, graphs, and charts.

Doing a little background research prior to writing a query is a necessity according to Raskin. But he warns writers not to mention the name of the magazine to potential sources until they've earned an assignment. Instead, present yourself as a writer approaching a national magazine directed at parents. Then, when you are assigned the piece, you can feel free to tell sources that you are writing for *Parenting*.

Raskin says the magazine is cautious about assigning reportorial pieces. "We need the writer to prove to us that he or she has a track record in this kind of writing before we'll send him or her to cover a political, social, or environmental issue," the editor explains.

Once you've won the editors' confidence to cover any type of feature story for *Parenting*, you'll be sent a contract and an assignment letter. Expect a call from an editor to talk the piece through with you as well. And, if you're a new writer, you may be asked to submit a letter further outlining the topic and the approach. Smaller assignments for departments and columns do not include as much instruction.

How to Write for *Parenting*

The perfect *Parenting* writer is someone who has paid attention to the magazine, figured out how its various sections work, and understands its voice.

"Ideally, the writer has kids or has spent time with children, and likes to do service writing," says Raskin. "Writers sometimes do a lazy job in terms of organization, reporting, and phrasing. Many freelancers prefer to write personal essays and profiles rather than service pieces. But there's no good reason why they can't write creative service pieces, making them exciting, readable, and interesting. We want anecdotes, good quotes, and intriguing language to carry the reader from start to finish."

For service pieces, Raskin suggests writers use subheads when appropriate, to ease the transition from section to section.

"I'm disappointed when freelancers turn in manuscripts that are underwritten, underreported, and dull," says Raskin. "It takes time for the writer to put that extra polish on a piece, but it's worth it—it's what makes the writing professional."

Raskin suggests that if an unexpected turn in the road appears during the writing process, the freelancer call the assigning editor with an update. All writers are asked to turn in a list of sources, copies of notes, and an annotated copy of their manuscript keyed to the notes. Don't worry; a letter from the magazine spells out the how-tos of this process. (See Chapter 5 in Part I, Writing Articles That Command Attention, for more about annotating a manuscript.)

"We cross-check every fact with the writer's sources as well as with experts we find," says Raskin.

Parents

685 Third Avenue
New York, NY 10164-1027
(212) 878-8700

Published: Monthly

Circulation: 1.75 million

Query: Editorial department

Query response time: 6 to 8 weeks

Buys: 12 to 20 articles out of approximately 2,500 unsolicited queries/manuscripts received annually

Guidelines: Available; send SASE

Rights purchased: First NAS with an option for worldwide syndication for an additional fee

Pays: On acceptance

Expenses: Pays reasonable phone and mail when approved in advance

Kill fee: 25 percent

Rates:

Type of Article	*Word Length*	*Payment*
Major Feature	2,000	$1,500 - 3,000
Short Feature	1,000	750 - 1,500
First-person Article	700 - 1,800	750 - 2,000

"Our reader is a first-time mom, and sometimes dad, with a median age of 31; she has attended some college before starting her family," says Pamela Abrams, executive editor. "Although the magazine runs pieces about divorce or stepparenthood, 90 percent of the magazine's readers are married; two thirds of them are working mothers.

"*Parents*' editorial is aimed at informing and educating readers: not telling them what to do, but showing them the pluses and minuses of various child-raising issues," the editor adds. The magazine addresses all steps of parenthood, from pre-birth to 18 years, with an emphasis on the younger years.

How to Slant Your Ideas to *Parents*

Imagine a young woman who has just learned she's pregnant: what does she want to know? The articles in *Parents* break down very roughly into four categories: how experts advise you to do something ("As They Grow" articles); how another mother or father experienced something (first-person pieces); health and safety pieces; and general articles on family life.

"We look for creative ideas about what parents do with their kids," says Abrams. "Among other topics, we're interested in strong opinion pieces, creative activities for cold indoor winter days, and new slants on old classics like child development, choosing a preschool, and starting kindergarten."

Parents' table of contents is a good guide for the freelancer looking for a home in its pages. Although about 75 percent of its article ideas are generated in house, the editors are eager to read well-thought-out, targeted proposals that indicate a familiarity with the magazine.

The following sections or columns are open to freelancers:

- **About Fathers** is a first-person account of a story that sheds light on a man's experience as a father. Past topics have included one dad's experience as the family chauffeur and a piece on how dads act differently from moms on the playground.

- **First-Person Parent** is a touching, wry, or humorous look at being a parent. "You Know You're a Mother When..." was one piece; another followed a family's trip to South Korea to help their adopted son seek out his past.

- **My Story** is one parent's experience, frequently a crisis or hardship, and how they have grown from the experience. Past stories have included raising a child with spina bifida, and a piece on delivering a breech baby.

- **Special Report** is the magazine's investigative and journalistic section. Topics covered in the past include how secondhand smoke affects kids, what kids learn in sex education, the latest about AIDS, and whether hospitals are equipped to deal with children in a medical crisis.

- **Work** offers suggestions to working parents, advice to moms who stayed at home but are considering working again, and ideas for moms who want to have it all—staying at home and working. One article asked whether today's workplace was really "family-friendly" while another offered ideas on working for a temporary agency.

"Your Family" is a non-age-specific section that addresses family finances, education, and other issues that deal with family life. The section includes "First-Person Parent," "My Story," and "Work," among other features. "Family Pet," "News," "Our Problem," and all beauty, home decorating, and food features are written by the staff or regular contributors. "Read-Aloud Book" is purchased through literary agents or known writers.

How to Query *Parents*

One- to two-page queries preferred. Submit a full manuscript for first-person or humor articles. Include relevant photos, but no original art or negatives. Query at least seven months in advance on seasonal material.

"Give me a sample lead, the names of the experts you'll interview, and cite new research if your topic is on a familiar theme," Abrams says. "Tell me why *Parents* should do this article now, and why you should be the writer."

Abrams says the most important thing a writer can do before querying is to read the magazine. "Understand which columns are open to freelancers, and be able to suggest the space your written piece would take in the magazine," she says.

Queries are assigned alphabetically to various staff members. Assistant editors read many, and associate editors get their share. Queries with promise eventually are passed up the editorial chain of command. The editor-in-chief signs off on all new assignments.

Queries that don't work are those whose topics have been covered recently or are too similar to another article in the hopper.

Inevitably, topics are repeated, but editors try not to repeat too many of the same approaches to a topic within a three-year period. So, for instance, coverage on kids and sleep might concentrate on a narrow problem area one time, offer straight how-to information another time, such as getting a child to sleep through the night, or appear as a round-up of several short articles on various related topics in a later issue.

Abrams notes that the summer months are a bad time to query, since the editors are busy with back-to-school and holiday issues. Instead, follow the school calendar roughly: query between Labor Day and Memorial Day.

How to Write for *Parents*

"We don't want one homogenous voice at *Parents.* The voice of the magazine changes depending on the topic and author, and we strive for a balance of warmth and authority throughout the magazine," Abrams says. "The 'As They Grow' section tends to be more authoritative, since that is where experts are often our authors or are cited in articles. Freelanced pieces tend to be more conversational and warm; of course, the first-person pieces, by definition, are personal.

"We prefer to work with writers who come to us with good and relevant clips about kids," says Abrams. "But we are open to new voices. The best opportunity to break in is to have a unique idea and to be the only person who can possibly write this piece. That usually means a first-person experience article.

"We are very open to working closely with a writer during the writing stage of an article," Abrams adds. "Often, if the writer has a good, solid query, she can go with little additional advice from us at the magazine."

Occasionally, an editor will call someone to assign an article, then ask the freelancer to write his understanding of the conversation and submit it to the editor. Most often, the assigning editor follows an assignment with a detailed letter to give the writer a general blueprint to follow. Although the typical article is assigned outright, Abrams says that first-time contributors, especially beginners, are occasionally asked to write on speculation.

"If we're on the fence about something but the writer looks good, we may ask for an article on spec," the editor says. It is standard procedure at *Parents* to have one rewrite, whether it's a fine-tuning or an all-out reworking of your article.

"We follow a 50 percent rule," Abrams says. "If the article is 50 percent there, we'll go for a rewrite—sometimes two if the writer is really trying and we want the piece. But if the article isn't 50 percent there, we kill it without rewrites. It seems less painful for everyone that way."

Popular Mechanics

224 West 57th Street
New York, NY 10019
(212) 649-3121

Published: Monthly
Circulation: 1.6 million
Query: Deborah Frank, managing editor
Query response time: 2 months
Buys: About 60 articles out of 1,000 queries/manuscripts received annually
Guidelines: Available; send SASE
Rights purchased: All, including copyright, on a work-for-hire basis
Pays: On acceptance
Expenses: Negotiable; depends on the article
Kill fee: 25 percent
Rates:

Type of Article	*Word Length*	*Payment*
Major Feature	1,000 - 2,000	$750 - 1,500
Short Feature	800 - 1,000	500 - 600
News Brief	300 - 500	300
"Tech Update"	100 - 400	300
Finder's Fee		200

Dubbed "the original men's service magazine," *Popular Mechanics* satisfies its readers' (mostly men) appetites for information on cars, boats, planes, tools, home improvement, science, electronics, and technology. Even after celebrating its 90th anniversary in 1992, the magazine shows no signs of slowing down, says Deborah Frank, managing editor.

"Our editors do a lot of hands-on testing," she says. "Our automotive and boating editors conduct firsthand drive reports of new vehicles." But these are no ordinary test drives. Readers have chugged down the Mississippi River in a bass fishing boat and four-wheeled through the Yukon in a souped-up off-road vehicle.

While the majority of readers are male, a growing segment of the magazine's readership are women, who are primarily interested in automotive and science news. Readers, on average, are between 35 and 55 years old, with a median income of $38,000. Increasingly, the magazine is targeting a younger audience.

Though in recent years the magazine has focused greater attention on high-tech military developments and laboratory discoveries, some things never change. "A lot of our readers are into do-it-yourself projects at home," Frank says. "Our 'Home Improvement' department is one of our most popular sections." *Popular Mechanics* readers are just as likely to tackle projects like building a bookcase or restoring an old car for the personal satisfaction they gain as they are for the money they save.

Frank adds that the magazine will publish more about the telecommunications industry, expanding its electronics department from six to twelve pages to accommodate the change. Car care and home improvement will decrease by two or three pages to make room for the new coverage.

How to Slant Your Ideas to *Popular Mechanics*

"A freelancer looking to break into our magazine would have to come up with a topic our editors haven't gotten around to yet," notes Frank. "We run a lot of stories that could have been freelance stories, but unfortunately, somebody on staff thought of doing it first."

That's no surprise considering *Popular Mechanics'* staff. The editorial staff has expertise in all areas of technology, regularly attends industry conventions and has numerous contacts at universities, research labs, industrial manufacturers, and within the military. The magazine's low turnover rate makes it less dependent on outside talent than some other publications.

That's not to say that the editors aren't interested in fresh ideas. "Our magazine tries to focus on subjects that are very technically advanced. We're not interested in the ordinary, simple things that a hobbyist would tinker with," Frank reports. "Articles are written in layman's terms, but because our readers are technically knowledgeable, the subject matter has become much more advanced."

Readers are hungry for details on what makes the technology work, adds Frank. She cites just one example from a story the magazine ran on wind turbine technology. "I got letters from as far away as Ireland and Saudia Arabia wanting more information on how aerodynamic the devices were, the angle of the blades, and suggestions on how to increase energy output. That's the sophistication of thinking among our readership. Our editors have to concentrate on that level of expertise and publish articles that our readers can relate to."

Unlike most departments at *Popular Mechanics*, there is one area that encourages freelance submissions. "Tech Update" is a seven-page section that consists of an eclectic grab bag of military, science, and aerospace news that hasn't yet been reported by the mass media. Many are the direct result of technical breakthroughs in military or industrial research.

Each month "Tech Update" features more than a dozen news briefs ranging from 100 to 400 words. The section has updated readers on flight simulators that train pilots to navigate Air Force fighter jets; futuristic personal rapid transit systems; a device able to export water from Alaska to California; and a technique that helps police prove that a suspect fired a gun.

Frank passes along a valuable tip to freelancers looking to get published in "Tech Update." "Get to know a professor at a university or develop a contact with someone at a research lab," she suggests. "These are really good contacts to have. Find out what's going on before the public relations department distributes a news release. Send us a query on the topic or send in a brief write-up. The copy for 'Tech Update' does not have to be something that's very polished. It can be rough, because our science writer will rewrite it to fit our style. Contributors will get credit for the submission."

All other sections of the magazine are written by staff editors or regular contributors.

How to Query *Popular Mechanics*

One or two pages preferred. Diagrams can be helpful to illustrate complex subject matter.

"We do have room for freelancers. We just don't have enough people querying us on the topics we're looking for," notes Frank. "The majority of queries I get seem like the writer hasn't looked at the magazine in about ten years." They still think we're the *Popular Mechanics* that their grandfathers read.

"A query letter has to show that the writer knows what he's talking about," adds Frank. "You've got to have expertise in the area you want to write about."

During the Persian Gulf War, a writer queried the magazine on a new high-tech device that tracked troop movement. The editorial was devoted to the Gulf War. "The writer wrote the story overnight, followed by a flurry of FAXes and overnight mail to ready the story for publication," recalls Frank. "This story was one of the rare electronic features we purchased. Most freelance material goes into the 'Tech Update' section."

While it definitely helps to have an inside track on your subject matter, the magazine shies away from inventions created by hobbyists in a home basement lab. "People will send in their inventions, and even if it's patented we won't pick it up because of the possibility of lawsuits," Frank notes. "We're typically more interested in technical developments that big industries are doing or that are coming from universities."

A Princeton University graduate student recently tipped off *Popular Mechanics* editors to a new compound that can store solar energy. She received a $200 finder's fee for the information that was later used in an article written by the science editor.

How to Write for *Popular Mechanics*

Writers who can skillfully write about what they know in layman's terms, and who can put a technical spin on their subject and still make the information understandable and intriguing have the best shot at getting published in *Popular Mechanics.* Frank is the first to admit that's no easy order to fill.

Meeting those kinds of requirements comes easiest to writers who have specialized expertise in their fields, she says. Take the freelancer who wrote a story about his personal ice climbing adventure, with an in-depth look at the clothing and gear needed to master this daring adventure sport. The first-time *Popular Mechanics* writer was manager of a chain of mountain climbing and sporting goods stores. "Most of the feature stories we accept from freelance writers are from people who specialize in the field they want to write about," notes Frank.

It helps to be able to stretch the imagination when searching for topics suitable for *Popular Mechanics.* It is much more than a magazine targeted to car tinkerers and weekend hobbyists.

Fact checking at *Popular Mechanics* is done by the editors, who are considered experts in their fields. That means you have no room for mistakes or fudging a little bit to get through a particularly technical paragraph.

Frank notes that *Popular Mechanics* periodically includes articles with an historical twist. One issue took readers back to the age of Columbus, exploring how the Niña, the Pinta and the Santa Maria were built. Another issue appealed to car buffs with a look at the autos used by former U.S. Presidents. An aviation feature took readers back to the most famous half-minute in history, when a squadron of B-25 bombers took the first offensive crack at the Japanese in World War II. The story helped readers relive the daring attack, and explained the many engineering modifications that made the plane suitable for its mission.

"Readers enjoy reminiscing about the past as well as what's in store for the future," says Frank. "Our 'Time Machine' section is our most popular page."

Frank and the rest of the *Popular Mechanics* editorial staff seem to have no trouble dreaming up new topics to keep this veteran publication lively reading. On a trip to Hoover Dam, Frank and Editor-in-chief Joe Oldham noticed a sign stating that the American Society of Civil Engineers claimed the dam as one of the seven engineering wonders in the United States. "He said to me, 'What are the other six?' I didn't know, but we're looking into it now as a possible story," Frank says.

Popular Science

2 Park Avenue
New York, NY 10016
(212) 779-5000

Published: Monthly

Circulation: 1.8 million

Query: Richard Stepler, executive editor

Query response time: 4 to 6 weeks

Buys: About 40 to 50 features and 300 news briefs out of approximately 5,000 unsolicited queries/manuscripts received annually

Guidelines: Available; send SASE

Rights purchased: First NAS

Pays: On acceptance

Expenses: Pays, up to a preset limit

Kill fee: Varies

Rates:

Type of Article	*Word Length*	*Payment*
Major Feature	1,500 - 4,000	varies; competitive
Short Feature	500 - 1,000	
News Brief	150 - 300	
Department	100 - 800	
"What's New"	50 - 100	

Founded in 1872, *Popular Science* reports on cutting-edge technology in a number of fields to an audience of nonspecialist readers. "The magazine provides detailed coverage of a wide range of areas that competing magazines do not cover," says Richard Stepler, executive editor.

The *Popular Science* readership is overwhelmingly male (83 percent), with a median age of 40. One-third have graduated from college, and 24 percent hold professional/managerial positions. The median household income is $43,460, and 73 percent are homeowners.

How to Slant Your Ideas to *Popular Science*

About three-quarters of the ideas that lead to *Popular Science* stories are generated in house. Freelance writers are assigned about 40 percent; the rest are staff written.

Stepler describes his readers as people who want the inside track on what led to the development of various products, ranging from computers to automobiles. They also like learning about basic advances in science and technology.

The article, "Superconductivity Goes to Sea," described the Yamatoo 1, a new class of oceangoing ships and submarines characterized by high speed (115 mph) and stealth (its superconducting thrusters are silent).

Another feature, "High-tech Harvest," brought readers up to date on scientists' work to genetically engineer vegetables, fruits, and grains. A special section on "Tech TV" told how TV has been virtually reinvented. It covered engineering that eliminates ghosts, digital technology that makes home-viewing more like the movies, and how interactive technologies will affect TV's future.

Almost all sections of the magazine are open to freelance contributors, except "Looking Back." The following departments are open to freelancers:

- **Automotive Newsfront** looks at basic research into how automobiles can be redesigned to meet various new requirements, including environmental and economic needs. It also looks at features, power, and performance.
- **Computer Newsfront** leaves no computer technology uninvestigated. "In the 120th anniversary issue, we published a 1967 *Popular Science* article entitled, 'I Used a Real Computer at Home,'" says Stepler. "Back then that was a radical idea, but within 15 years our cover photo featured the first computer under $100."
- **Electronic Newsfront** devotes its editorial to home entertainment hardware, including TV, VCR, and CD-ROM drive, among others.
- **Home Newsfront** examines the role technology plays in improving the comforts at home while reducing expenses in maintenance, heating, and cooling. The department reports new advances in appliances, furnaces, windows, and building materials.
- **Science Newsfront** covers developments in a wide range of areas, from aviation and space to government research at national labs. "Our coverage is worldwide and looks at basic science, biotechnology, genetic engineering, aviation, space, environment, and geology," says Stepler.
- **What's New** offers short captions about a wide variety of products—from a recycling system for high-rise buildings, to

a CD storage rack for cars, to a circular chess game. Though the column is typically written in house, freelance ideas are considered.

How to Query *Popular Science*

One page preferred. Send photo/art information.

Stepler says the best query letters are those that tell what the article is about, why the freelancer is exactly the person to write the piece, and why the topic should be covered at this particular time. Let the editors know what has happened recently that should make them care about your subject.

"It's hard for a writer to tell us something we don't already know," says Stepler. "But if you can get the inside track on something and offer us unique access to someone who has valuable insight, you'll have an advantage. In fact, we'll even overlook shortcomings in writing ability to work with a freelancer who offers a new take on an idea."

Stepler says your proposal should read as if it is a condensed version of the article, complete with an attention-grabbing lead. Include facts, figures, and sample quotes from sources.

Equally important, make sure that you demonstrate through your query a familiarity with the kinds of articles the magazine publishes. "It's discouraging to get a query on a topic we just ran," the editor says. "The most successful writers know what we have covered recently."

If your idea captures the editors' interest, you will be sent a contract and a detailed assignment letter.

How to Write for *Popular Science*

Stepler's dream writer is someone who has superior story-telling skills as well as a curiosity about the way things work. "We look for writers who are not intimidated by high technology, and who also have a gift for language."

When it comes to writing style, Stepler says *Popular Science* offers a "real voice." "We want the writer's personality to shine through," he explains.

Turn in your story on disk or via computer bulletin board. "Our editorial assistants get upset if they have to rekey a piece," says Stepler. "Don't worry about the format; we've never run across a disk we couldn't translate."

Also submit a list of contacts for fact checking. "We want recent research based on fact, not on the writer's inference," says Stepler. "It's frustrating to check facts and find out that the writer hasn't spoken to the source in years."

Profiles

376 Boylston Street
Boston, MA 02116-3812
(617) 424-7700

Published: Monthly

Circulation: 400,000

Query: Anne W. Studabaker, editor

Query response time: 4 weeks

Buys: About 100 articles/stories out of approximately 1,300 unsolicited queries/manuscripts received annually

Guidelines: Available; send SASE

Rights purchased: First International Magazine

Pays: On acceptance

Expenses: Pays phone, transportation, lodging, and meals on assignment only

Rates:

Type of Article	***Word Length***	***Payment***
Major Feature	750 - 2,000	$750 - 2,000
Department	400	300 - 400
News Brief	150 - 250	150 - 250

Profiles, the in-flight magazine for Continental Airlines, has a subtitle that reads, "The best in global business travel and entertainment."

"As the name implies, we use a lot of faces in *Profiles,*" says Robert S. Benchley, editorial director. "We are not a personality magazine, but the human element is a strong component. All of our articles profile a person, place, or thing, which also can be a product or company. We tell our stories through people, whether the person lives at a particular destination, runs the company, or invented the product."

From a statistical standpoint, the publication sees its reader very narrowly: a 40-year-old male traveling on business. "We also have Great Aunt Tessie, families going on vacation to Disneyworld, and women on business flying Continental, but by sheer number of bookings, our readers are good corporate male soldiers flying the airplane three to five times a week," says Benchley. "Fair or not, our research tells us our primary audience is the businessman, but naturally we include articles of interest to everyone."

The reader is college educated (81 percent), is more likely to be in a professional or managerial position, and has a median household income of $57,500.

How to Slant Your Ideas to *Profiles*

"It's hard to know how people feel when they get on an airplane," says Benchley. "When you step on board, you lose a certain amount of control—whether you're a frequent flyer or not. The plane crew tells you when to sit down, stand up, eat, and go to the bathroom. It's like being a small child in school again. On top of that, you may be concerned about being late, apprehensive about facing bad weather, wondering how the food will taste, or worried about an upcoming appointment.

"We feel that when the normal patterns of life are interrupted, people are vulnerable to new experiences. When they are strapped into that seat heading across the country or the ocean and the office can't reach them, business travelers might read something they wouldn't normally," says the director.

He adds, "We run articles on business, people, sports, and entertainment. The most response comes from our 'Global Frontrunners' section, which includes short items on people, trends, ideas, and innovations. It's hard to say whether reading our cover feature on Gregory Hines actually makes anyone go to his show. But when we run a news brief on an entrepreneur who invented a better mousetrap, we invariably hear that the company was deluged with phone calls and letters. We think that because readers are stuck in their seats, they are receptive to new ideas. If they find a product or service that excites them, they want to take advantage of it."

Benchley recalls that when the magazine ran an article on a man who started a government access information network, a woman flying coast-to-coast who read about the company actually *deplaned* on what was only to be a brief stop, rented a car, and drove to his office. The two are now working together on an international venture.

"That one article brought us more response than anything else we've published," says the editorial director. "We feel heartened as a magazine when we can put people together like that. Another man we featured, a high-tech sleuth who investigates white collar crime, says people come up to talk to him in airports because they recognize his face from the magazine."

Profiles

Because Continental is a global airline, Benchley says the magazine is interested in stories that are not confined to the place where the subject of the story is located. "If the entire impact of a particular business is in a 10-block radius of its location, it is not a candidate for *Profiles,*" he says. "The kind of business story we want was exemplified in an article we did on L.L. Bean, a clothing catalog company based in New England, which moved into Japan and is going gangbusters."

Each issue of the magazine includes one to three profiles of people doing significant things. If the person is an entertainer, chances are good that he is known throughout the world. If it is a business person, then his company's products have international appeal.

Just a few of the magazine's profiles have included those of American producer Marla Ginsburg, who runs a French television company; Celestial Seasonings' guru Mo Siegel; and actor Michael Palin who has journeyed from the North Pole to the South.

"It's easy to find someone to do a hack job on a celebrity profile, but those are yawners," says Benchley. "We need a competent journalist who can pull something out of the person to create a piece that you wouldn't find elsewhere. For example, an interview with Sting was very introspective. He talked about how his new album revealed a lot about himself, including his creative songwriting process and how middle age got him thinking."

Another regular feature is "Great Escapes," a get-away piece to somewhere wonderful. "Here, we generally talk about the place, not about business," says Benchley. "We bring in the nature of the city and the feel of the culture. Some are first-person accounts, some are more standard destination features. We ran a feature on hiking in New Zealand, another that encompassed the entire state of Alaska, and a city piece on Munich."

"Trends," another major article category, is a big business story that analyzes a trend. One writer examined cars which are built with recyclable auto parts—with the intention that when they've outstayed their welcome, their parts will be ground up and turned into something else.

"An international business flavor is fun when possible," says Benchley. "It's easy for us to make this a very United States-oriented magazine, yet we fly to Europe, Asia, and Central America, so we need to keep our global focus."

Another feature category that appears somewhat regularly is "Voices," a book excerpt. *True Confessions,* in which celebrities reveal all, was one such excerpt.

All *Profiles* departments and features are open to freelancers. They include:

- **Business Report** focuses on business topics in three different cities on Continental's route. "The idea is not to write about Cleveland as a business city, but about some business issue going on in Cleveland," says Benchley. "It's got to be something very focused."

  For example, the magazine looked at how hospitals in Cleveland were competing against one another in their marketing to attract patients. Another report told how San Diego was building business from the ashes of the defense cutbacks. A third illustrated how companies are copying Rochester-based Xerox's total quality management program.
- **Family Fun** reviews different cities on the Continental route where fliers may invariably end up with their kids and want to do something fun. Article topics have ranged from snorkeling in the South Pacific to history and environment on the shores of the Timucuan Ecological and Historic Preserve in Jacksonville, Florida.
- **Global Frontrunners** are fun, interesting tidbits about people, ideas, and innovations. Coverage has included glass artist Dale Chihuly and his largest exhibit of glass in the history of Taiwan; edible roses made from cookies; and St. Moritz, the Swiss resort that protected overuse of its exclusivity by becoming the first city to register its name.

How to Query *Profiles*

One-page queries preferred. Send photo/art information if it is truly spectacular.

"The style of the query doesn't matter to us; it can be straightforward or anecdotal. And we don't mind getting one to five ideas at a time—as long as they are polished," says Benchley. "What *does* matter is that the freelancer has looked at the magazine and thought the idea through, and is presenting something useful.

"We get many more good suggestions than we have room to publish," he says. "Therefore, we reject many ideas based on what we know we'll be doing in the next three to four issues. If we just completed a piece on Cincinnati, we know it will be a while before we cover it again, so we return the idea to let the writer sell it elsewhere. We are a tough magazine to break into because of the comparatively small number of articles we buy. We use about 12 freelance-written pieces a month, but that includes all the news briefs we buy. There is a lot of competition out there and the cream rises to the top fairly quickly."

Half of the article ideas in *Profiles* are staff generated and the other half are freelance driven. "We often seek out a writer in a certain geographic area to cover that place," says Benchley. "We either look for someone we have worked with successfully in the past or for someone who has a particular area of expertise."

Benchley says the magazine likes to know that photos are available if they're truly great. "Most writers are not photographers, but if you just got back from the jungles and you think you took wonderful photos, mention it in your query."

If the editors take a liking to your idea, you'll get a confirmation phone call, followed by an assignment letter. And before the article appears in the magazine, you'll receive a courtesy copy of the final draft for fact-checking purposes.

How to Write for *Profiles*

"Even though our readers appear to be a captive audience, they are easily distracted by flight attendants throwing peanuts and the captain making announcements," says Benchley. "The writing has to be lively and, ideally, entertaining and informative so the flier will turn the page and read it. Our style is not literary or 'businessy.'

"My belief is that all in-flight magazines are, for better or worse, versions of each other. All carry the same mix of business and leisure articles. So, it is essential for us to clearly differentiate ourselves from the competition, and we've done that with our profile focus. Since most of our articles look at the people behind the story, it's essential for the writer to breathe life into them," Benchley says.

Psychology Today

24 East 23rd Street, 5th Floor
New York, NY 10010
(212) 260-7210

Published: Bimonthly

Circulation: 225,000

Query: Articles and Features: James C. Mauro, senior editor or Hara Estroff Marano, executive editor

Query response time: 4 to 6 weeks

Buys: About 12 articles/stories out of approximately 250 unsolicited queries/manuscripts received annually

Guidelines: Available; send SASE

Rights purchased: Prefers World; will negotiate First NAS

Pays: On publication

Expenses: Pays reasonable phone and FAX

Kill fee: 20 to 25 percent

Rates:

Type of Article	*Word Length*	*Payment*
Major Feature	2,500 - 4,000	$2,000 maximum
"Body," "Mind," "Spirit"	1,500	1,000

In January 1992, Sussex Publishers re-introduced *Psychology Today* after a two-year hiatus. The magazine, which had a 25-year track record, set out once again to be the authoritative magazine on human behavior.

"We are very conscious of the fact that we have a tremendous legacy," says James C. Mauro, senior editor. "A wealth of information and talent has been contributed to this magazine for all these years.

"*Psychology Today* has had four reincarnations," the editor continues. "At one point, it became so serious that today we say the magazine lost its ability to smile. The rebirth has let the air in a little. We try not to get tangled up in research but to balance the presentation of new evidence with an explanation of what it means to the reader. We have conducted numerous reader surveys to make us mindful of what our readers want."

According to Mauro, *Psychology Today* sees its editorial mission in the following light: "To provide readers with the latest insights and information on why people act the way they do, and show them how to transform these insights into powerful personal strategies for more successful living."

The editors describe their readers as people who energetically seek ways to realize their potential by reading, listening, and participating. They are active consumers who are especially receptive to ideas and products that involve learning and self-improvement—both physical and intellectual. Nutrition, exercise, and every form of mind exploration are integral to their lifestyle.

"We target our editorial to the person who is not only interested but curious about new topics that tell us how to improve ourselves and our relationships," Mauro sums up.

Statistically, demographics identify a reader whose median age is 37 and who has a median household income of about $37,200. The audience is almost evenly split between single and married people, and more than 40 percent are college graduates.

How to Slant Your Ideas to *Psychology Today*

Many of the story ideas you'll see in *Psychology Today* are generated in house. "We attend conferences and read tons of newspapers about what is going on in the field," says Mauro. "But we are building up a base of freelance writers. A background in psychology is helpful but not necessary.

"In fact, a good journalist might have an advantage," he continues. "When we work with professionals in psychology, usually Ph.D.s, we have to translate an awful lot of information into readable, presentable material that allows our readers to learn. The experts who write for us are typically one-time writers whom we contact because they are doing a unique study. For example, we may ask a dream researcher to write about something new and tremendous about sleep and dreams. We may never use that individual again, or we may get back in touch in another five years when something new about dreaming is revealed."

If you are a new writer, Mauro says the best way to tap this market is through its columns ("Body," "Mind," and "Spirit"). "Find someone who is doing interesting work on a particular topic and send your idea," he explains.

For more experienced writers eager to secure a feature assignment, the editor encourages you to do a fair amount of legwork ahead of time. "Pick a subject you are passionate about and do some research," says Mauro. "Interest us in your topic and sell it through your presentation. You can't do that through cold reportage; it will show."

Being timely is also critical. "We cut deadlines to the bone. We typically only have four to six weeks between the time a story is assigned and goes to press," Mauro says. "We want to be the first one to report new findings. For example, one editor working on a story about how the brain dictates the food we eat had just one month to research and write the story before we sent it to press. On another occasion, I had three days to write an article on the psychological effects of Hurricane Andrew. Being timely paid off, but I respect the fact that some writers can't work at that pace."

A few sample titles from the publication include "The Lowdown on Handwriting Analysis," which allowed a graphologist to peer into the lives of several *Psychology Today* editors and flaunt her stuff; "The Decline and Fall of Personality," which described how the FAX, phone, and VCR are taking us beyond ourselves; and "Ambition," which reported on how to manage success and failure throughout our lives.

There is definitely a trend toward New Age and spirituality in the magazine's pages. "Our editor is interested in New Age topics because a good population of our readers want to learn about that," says Mauro. "Psychology is so different today than what it was. The big stars are gone and new figures are coming forward. To us, New Age is anything that deals with the spirit and the soul, including traditionalism."

The following columns, any two of which generally run in each issue, are open to freelancers:

- **Body** takes into account the body/mind connection. Sample topics have included acupuncture and massage.
- **Mind** is very open. "We cover any subject that relates to psychology, which is basically any subject," says Mauro. Past articles have covered child abuse and an interview with Salvador Minuchin, a family therapist.
- **Spirit** deals with spirituality—anything that puts readers in touch with their spiritual side. The focus has been on New Age topics and religion.

"News & Trends" is written in house.

How to Query *Psychology Today*

One page or less preferred. Do not send any photo/art information.

Writing queries for this magazine is an exercise in brevity. Mauro wants three paragraphs, max. In business letter style, tell him who you are, what you have done or the work about which you will write, whom you will talk to, and the timeliness of the piece. The editors aren't interested in discerning your writing style from a query letter.

"That's the purpose of sending clips," says Mauro. "Anyone who tries to be overly stylized in a query bothers me. We don't have time for that here. On the other hand, writers shouldn't be too vague. Don't send queries that say, 'I want to write an article on depression.' And worse yet, avoid writing, 'My brother is manic-depressive, and I'd like to write about my personal experiences with him.' That could be wonderful, but chances are it won't be."

If your article proposal passes the litmus test, the editors will follow up with a phone call. "We almost always send the writer additional materials and ask him or her to expand on the original idea," says Mauro. "There are interesting topics we want to report on, but we need to make sure they are covered well. If the writer comes through with additional information, we take the proposal to an editorial meeting for review. If it passes that step, we assign the piece."

How to Write for *Psychology Today*

If you have a good journalistic background and are able to deal effectively with science topics, you may be a contender for *Psychology Today*. "Our writers synthesize information and research and present it clearly and concisely," says Mauro.

Mauro says *Psychology Today*'s goal is to present information in a readable, accessible style. "There is a certain element of good writing involved, but here writing is almost mathematical," he says.

Freelancers who make it through the assignment process find their pieces rarely get killed. Pieces that do are usually authored by writers who know so much about the subject that they can't step back from it and present it in a readable fashion.

"Like getting caught in quicksand, they get mired down in the information," he says. "You've got to be able to look at a subject like a journalist and not get too involved in what you are writing about.

"Turning in a source list is necessary," the editor adds. "We rely heavily on freelancers to get the facts right, but there are certain circumstances that raise questions, and we call to verify facts. Since we have a very small staff, we see thoroughness as the writer's responsibility."

Reader's Digest

Pleasantville, NY 10570
(914) 238-1000

Published: Monthly

Circulation: 16.25 million in the United States; combined worldwide readership is about 100 million

Query: Features: Select a senior editor or senior staff editor from the masthead of a current issue. "All in a Day's Work," "Campus Comedy," "Humor in Uniform," "Life in These United States," "Toward More Picturesque Speech": Send to editor of that department. Anecdotes, brief excerpts, quips and quotations: Excerpt Editor

Query response time: 3 to 6 weeks

Buys: 180 original articles and 180 pickups out of thousands of unsolicited queries/copies of published stories received annually. *Unsolicited manuscripts not welcomed, acknowledged, or returned*

Guidelines: Available; send SASE

Rights purchased: All World for all forms of print and electronic publishing media

Pays: On acceptance for originals; on publication for pickups from other published sources

Expenses: Pays reasonable items when approved in advance; some advances given when needed for research or travel

Kill fee: $500

Rates:

Type of Article	*Word Length*	*Payment*
Original Feature	4,000 - 5,000	$3,000+
"Drama in Real Life"	4,000 - 5,000	3,500
"It Changed My Life"	1,000 - 2,000	3,000
"Unforgettable Character"	4,000 - 5,000	3,500
Feature-length Reprint	varies	600*
		*per full *Digest* page
Short department item:	up to 300	400
"All in a Day's Work"		
"Campus Comedy"		
"Humor in Uniform"		
"Life in These United States"		

"Toward More Picturesque Speech"

Original	word length varies	$ 50
Reprint	word length varies	10*

**per one-column Digest line, minimum $50*

Payment for "It's Human Nature," "Laughter, the Best Medicine," "Notes From All Over," "Personal Glimpses," "Points to Ponder," "Quotable Quotes," and fillers is $35 to the first contributor of an item from a published source or from TV or radio. Payment for original material is $30 per *Reader's Digest* two-column line, with a minimum payment of $50.

The offices of *Reader's Digest* are nestled among rolling hills of green grass and mature trees three-and-a-half miles north of a village named Pleasantville, New York, about an hour north of busy Manhattan. The long driveway leads you to a brick building with white wood trim reminiscent of an exclusive school. And in a way, that's what *Reader's Digest* is: a place where the basics get a lot of attention, and where it takes persistence, great story ideas, dramatic writing, and some salesmanship to gain admission.

It's difficult to pin down the demographics of a magazine that reaches one out of every four American households and attracts 100 million people worldwide. The editors report their readers have a median age of 46.2, the readership is fairly evenly split between males and females, and in many ways mirrors the United States population. To reach such an audience, the editors look for stories that have universal appeal and cut across all age groups and occupations. Topics range from dieting and health to financial management, politics, religion, marriage and parenting, success on the job, and many others.

How to Slant Your Ideas to *Reader's Digest*

Co-founders DeWitt Wallace and Lila Acheson Wallace wanted their *Digest* to provide "an article a day of enduring interest." Since 1922, the staff of the magazine has aimed toward that goal. Of its roughly 30 articles published in each issue, only about half are original; the rest are book excerpts and reprints from other publications.

Regular contributors and roving editors write some of the 15 original articles a month. But the *Digest,* as it is often called, has traditionally made room for new voices whose talents call out loudly enough to gain the attention of an editor.

"We don't like the word 'formula,'" says Clell Bryant, senior editor. "Rather than follow the tired approach of beginning with two anecdotes, introducing the theme, following that with a paragraph of explanation and so on, we prefer to follow a story line. The best articles tell the experience of one individual who exemplifies the situation, and with whom the reader can become emotionally involved."

The editor warns writers not to rely on years-old *Digest* copies for studying the magazine. Although the core of the magazine retains the same values, Bryant says there have been subtle but important shifts in the emphasis and style of the stories.

"We look for key turning points in our articles," Bryant explains. "Create a scene and tell the reader what it feels like for the person whose story is being told. That also gives a story the peaks and valleys that keep it from being flat."

Bryant likes to say that the *Digest* carries on the ancient storyteller tradition. "Storytelling usually begins at the beginning," he says. "However, sometimes a story will start at the most dramatic moment and then step back to the beginning and build to the suspenseful end.

"At the beginning, the protagonist is introduced, and the plot begins to develop, gradually unfolding through scenes, building up detail and dialogue as it moves chronologically through the events," the editor continues. "It finally leads up to the dramatic moment or the meaningful message. The best devices of theater—suspense, foreshadowing, dialogue—combine to tell a great story."

Bryant adds that all stories aim to offer a "*Digest* point," an inspiring message, moral, or insight that readers can use to improve their own lives or careers.

The "Drama in Real Life" is a *Reader's Digest* staple. Bryant descibes it as a story of the triumph of the human spirit, a dramatic narrative of ordinary people thrust into extraordinary situations, from which they extricate themselves by courage and character.

"It Changed My Life" is a shorter feature that runs occasionally. The story tells of one incident—a moment in time, or perhaps a summer—that drastically changed the author's life. The topic should be one to which readers can relate. The lesson the author learned should be applicable in anyone's life.

"Unforgettable Character" often, but not always, features a celebrity-bylined story about someone—famous or obscure—who deeply affected the author and whose colorful life celebrates a principle that readers can admire and emulate in their own lives. These pieces are often ghostwritten. If you have access to such a story, a call to an editor or a query is appropriate.

The following short departments are open to freelancers. Submit the full manuscript for these departments:

- **All in a Day's Work** covers humor on the job.
- **Campus Comedy** looks at life at college.
- **Excerpts** are taken from magazines, newspapers, and newsletters, and may fall into any of these categories.
- **Humor in Uniform** is a salute to life in the armed services now and then.
- **Life in These United States** needs true, unpublished stories from your own experience that are relative to adult human nature.
- **Toward More Picturesque Speech** is for the reader who wants to increase his vocabulary and his understanding of the language.

How to Query *Reader's Digest*

One page preferred; if the editors are interested in your idea, you then will be asked to submit a six- to eight-page outline. Do not submit photo/art information; query on seasonal items at any time in the year.

"You'll get a careful reader, no matter to whom you write," Bryant says. "Whomever takes your first story idea and sponsors it through the process becomes your sponsoring editor. Each of us works with a group of writers and wants his or her writers who succeed."

If the editor to whom you query believes that your story has merit, he will contact you for an expanded proposal, usually offering detailed suggestions. Your proposal may be returned to you several times until your editor believes it is acceptable.

You're not in the game yet, but your position on the bench gets closer to the coach when your sponsoring editor submits your proposal to the editor-in-chief. Your editor will, in effect, act as your agent, explaining the value and "takeaway" of the story.

Even after your proposal has reached the editor-in-chief, fewer than half of the proposals move on to assignment. If you're among the fortunate who receive an assignment, you'll usually receive a call first, followed by a contract and the editor's very detailed instructions on how to pursue your story.

"The secret is to listen carefully to what the editor says," Bryant notes.

How to Write for *Reader's Digest*

Assistant Managing Editor Philip B. Osborne likes to tell about a conversation he had when he was first hired at the *Digest.* He was given a manuscript to edit and realized that it was going to need substantial revision. The piece was written by a woman who had contributed many pieces to the *Digest* through the years, so Osborne dreaded calling her with his rewrite requests.

More than a little apologetic, Osborne called the woman and explained that he had to ask her to do some additional work on the manuscript. The woman paused, then asked Osborne if he was new on the block. When he said yes, she laughed and said, "Honey, I learned a long time ago that you don't write for the *Digest,* you *rewrite* for the *Digest*!"

When you write a story for the *Digest,* expect to submit 4,000 - 5,000 words of copy for a piece that will eventually be 2,000 to 2,500 words long. The *Digest* doesn't just edit: the editors examine every word to make sure that each one carries weight.

The work is done with care and respect for the writer's words and individual voice. A saying is heard in the halls of the editorial department at least weekly, Bryant says. Coined by a *Digest* editor named Ken Payne many years ago, it has become a theme for the editors: "If it is not necessary to change it, it is necessary not to change it."

Bryant balances that philosophy with the tongue-in-cheek sign he once spotted hanging over the desk of an editor in the *Reader's Digest* Paris bureau: "The strongest drive is neither love nor hate; it is one person's need to change another's copy."

Bryant explains, "That quote is by John Dyson, one of our roving editors. I keep it near my desk to remind me of what it was like when I was a writer. When I'm editing someone else's copy I invoke that quote along with Ken Payne's quote and try to strike a balance between the two.

"All writers, everywhere, use extra words to tell a story," Bryant says. "Some writers digress; others just take a long time to tell the story. We take the writer's best effort and condense it to pack more information, drama, and anecdotes into a smaller space. It gives the reader more value for his money. In the process of making the piece more dense, we are careful to be true to the original intent of the writer and to retain his authentic voice."

Don't worry, you'll see the edited and condensed version of your story before it goes to press. Once your piece is edited, *Reader's Digest* takes fact checking to new heights. In an average issue, the editors estimate that the staff of more than 60 researchers checks 3,500 facts with 1,500 sources. There is no room for error or fabricated information; if such offenses are found, they are corrected. If they are too numerous, the article will be killed.

How Reprints Are Selected at *Reader's Digest*

If your article appeared in a major American newspaper or magazine, it has probably been considered for reprinting in *Reader's Digest.* Since half of the articles in any issue are reprints, the magazine's reading staff scours hundreds of publications each month, including most national and many regional magazines, major metropolitan newspapers, and 2,000 books a year.

Nonetheless, if you think your article is a good candidate for reprinting, submit a tear sheet to an editor whose name you select from the masthead. Enclose an SASE.

Redbook

224 West 57th Street
New York, NY 10019
(212) 649-3449

Published: Monthly

Circulation: 3.2 million

Query: Features: Diane Salvatore or Sally Lee, senior editors
"Happy Endings": Ellen Seidman, associate editor
"A Mother's Story": Christina Ferrari, features editor
"You and Your Child": Toni Gerber Hope, articles editor

Query response time: 4 to 6 weeks

Buys: About 50 articles/stories out of approximately 5,000 unsolicited queries/manuscripts received annually

Guidelines: Available; send SASE

Rights purchased: Generally First NAS; sometimes All

Pays: On acceptance

Expenses: Pays if reasonable

Kill fee: 25 percent

Rates:

Type of Article	*Word Length*	*Payment*
Major Feature	2,500	$2,000 - 2,500
Short Feature	1,000	750 - 1,000
"Happy Endings"	600	600
"A Mother's Story"	750	750
"You & Your Child" opener	200	150 - 200

With the youngest audience of all the "seven sisters," *Redbook*'s median reader age is 37. "She's bright, hip, and puts her family first in her emotional hierarchy, without being a slave to it," says Diane Salvatore, senior editor.

This reader is happily married with a young child or two, but is still interested in sex—having it and reading about it. She wonders if other men are attracted to her. More than 42 percent of the magazine's readers attended college. You can assume that two-thirds of the readers work, even if they don't need the money. The median household income is $34,915.

How to Slant Your Ideas to *Redbook*

This 90-year-old service publication for women has changed over the years. It has been an all-fiction magazine; one for young married couples, and today is a guide for women juggling career and family duties.

Redbook unveiled a new look in the fall of 1991, with the arrival of Editor-in-Chief Ellen Levine. "The words I use to describe the redesign are energetic, compelling, and provocative," says Levine. "It's more sexy than service-y."

The tone and voice of the magazine have become more intimate. "Writers need to pay attention to these characteristics to see how our presentation of articles differs from other magazines," says Salvatore. "We're talking to the woman who spends time reading the magazine to pamper herself, as a way of putting herself first. In everyday life, she probably comes last—after her job and family."

The senior editor explains that the editorial staff only wants to do a story if it's a *Redbook* story. "We don't want to see any more 'one size fits all' queries or stories that could be sent to *any* women's magazine," says Salvatore. "We're doing edgier pieces that were previously considered taboo." "Why I Date Your Husband," "The Sex Urge Married Men Satisfy . . . Alone" (about male masturbation); and "Your $2,000 Egg: How Fertile Women Profit" are just a few cover lines that have titillated readers since the makeover.

Salvatore recommends that writers read at least six back issues of the publication to capture the savoir faire for which it strives. "We're looking for excellent, thorough, critical reporters who are also very stylish writers," she says. "These people bounce ideas off me that can work for the magazine, without waiting for me to call them."

If you're not sure your idea is strong enough, you might consider doing what the editor-in-chief does when determining whether or not a query is suitable for the magazine. She calls it the 10 p.m. test. Levine tries to read manuscripts and queries at 10 at night because that's when the majority of *Redbook* readers finally get time to themselves and crawl into bed with the magazine in hand. If the idea or manuscript holds her interest at that time, then the writing has gone the distance.

"We're always interested in reporting on news events and interpreting them in a way that brings them home to our readers," says Salvatore. "And timing is also key. Don't tell me you want to do a piece on the World Trade Center bombing after every newspaper across the country has reported on it, unless you can bring something fresh to it."

Editors are making an effort to use writers new to the magazine for nonfiction features.

Mary Bounds, for example, an Atlanta newspaper reporter who was not previously known to Salvatore, was recommended to her by another writer for a story on Atlanta child protection activist Faye Yager. In a feature titled "Driven by Guilt," Bounds proved she could make the transition from daily news reporting to magazine writing. A thorough and exhaustive piece, Bounds unfolded Yager's crusade—how she was arrested for her aggressive methods of rescuing sexually abused kids, and how her trial revealed the insensitivity and ineffectiveness of the criminal justice system in this case. "The writing had a baroque style appropriate for the material and typical of Southern novelists," says Salvatore.

Departments open to freelancers include:

- **Happy Endings** is reserved for the last page, as a way of ending each issue on a high note. Ellen Seidman, associate editor, is intrigued by human interest stories that have an unfavorable beginning and evolve into an uplifting outcome. "We don't want ideas too rooted in sadness or melodrama," says Seidman. "And they should have a quirky or dramatic twist; there's not one formula." The timeliness of your ideas is an important criterion. If a story happened two years ago, it needs an updated angle to be considered for this column. One "Happy Ending" described a couple who met through a computer. The Colorado woman had just been jilted by her husband, and the man was going through a divorce. They shared their stories via a computer network, and met when he passed through Denver on a business trip. The article was published just after they'd married.

  Make sure you explain what makes your "Happy Ending" angle unique. For example, one unusual story told of a young woman who was in desperate need of a kidney transplant. Her father wanted to give her one of his kidneys until doctors discovered he had a serious heart condition and needed to be operated on immediately. In the end, the girl saved her father's life—and then her brother saved hers by donating his kidney.

  "A Second Chance" uncovered the secret of James Sanders, a family man who was wanted by the FBI. His wife,

Randy, had no idea of her husband's past life until he called her at work to tell her he'd been arrested. Randy, their daughter, and the community rallied to James' side, and a parole board decided unanimously to set him free.

Queries for this section should be written in the third person and should include demographics of the individual(s) involved—for example their ages, where they live, and if they have children.

- **A Mother's Story** is a strong human interest narrative focusing on a mother, usually involving some aspect of parenting. The story must have resonance beyond one woman's life. Writers can find a mother's case and be assigned to write it "as told to."

  One piece, "Always Something There to Remind Me," was the bittersweet story of actress Carol Potter. The widowed mother of a one-year-old son, Potter found the strength to love again, four years after her husband's death. "Eyewitness to Murder" recounted one mother's tale of observing a drug dealer kill a man in cold blood, and her inner turmoil about going to the police.

- **You & Your Child** is closed to freelancers, except for the introductory page that opens the section. There are generally three to four short items that offer useful parenting advice or product information from reliable sources—other moms. Openers have included translating teen slang, ending supermarket showdowns, and new shows kids are sure to love (which parents will also approve of).

Columns that appear under the headings "Beauty & Fashion," "Food & Nutrition," "Health & Healing," "Love & Sex," "News & Views," and "Stars & Entertainment" are closed to freelancers.

How to Query *Redbook*

One- to three-page queries acceptable; always enclose clips.

When submitting a proposal to *Redbook*, you need to show you've done the leg work by shaping a subject into an article idea. "I want writers to come to me with part of the answer already—not just a question," says Salvatore. She advises writers to include examples in their queries. "What gets my attention are riveting anecdotes that make me laugh or help to illuminate an issue in a personal way."

About 90 percent of *Redbook* ideas are generated in house. But, if Salvatore is interested in using a writer whose own queries haven't yet hit the mark, she may call on her to flesh out an idea born in house. But even in cases like that, a proposal is required before an article is assigned.

Contributors to this market need to prove they have experience and tenure—clips from national consumer magazines are the best evidence of that. "If you're making the leap from news reporting to magazine writing, your query has to be even stronger," says Salvatore.

Two or three editors review all items being considered for assignment before the editor-in-chief sees them. In some cases, an editor will go back to a writer and ask for more information, such as "What's your connection to the topic? Has it happened to you or someone you know? How far does the trend extend?"

As you wait with anticipation to hear from the magazine, your time will be better spent sitting by the telephone than standing by the mailbox. Salvatore's initial contact with writers is made via phone. She then follows up with a letter detailing the story-line.

How to Write for *Redbook*

What warms Salvatore's heart are writers who employ fresh language. "We appreciate humor and wit when appropriate. We live in dread of clichés."

One distinctive characteristic that sets *Redbook* apart from other magazines in this genre is its avoidance of pseudonyms. Salvatore forbids composites—merging anecdotes into a fictional person. Authors must use their own name and are highly encouraged to include subjects' real names, both first and last, as a way of giving every article credibility and authority.

The senior editor doesn't mind periodic updates once a piece has been assigned, if that's what it takes to avoid numerous rewrites. She generally expects one revision will be necessary, as part of the give-and-take between editor and writer. However, a second rewrite usually means there's been some kind of breakdown. "I don't want to lose critical lead time, and I especially don't want to feel like I'm teaching someone how to write," she concludes.

Redbook considers itself to use a scrupulous fact-checking process. Writers are required to submit all phone numbers of sources, and transcripts or tapes of interviews. Books or articles that assisted the writer in producing the piece must be made available as well.

Robb Report

One Acton Place
Acton, MA 01720
(800) 229-7622

Published: Monthly

Circulation: 45,000

Query: Robert Feeman, editor

Query response time: 4 to 8 weeks

Buys: About 55 articles/stories out of approximately 350 unsolicited queries/manuscripts received annually

Guidelines: Available with SASE; send $6 for sample magazine

Rights purchased: Standard contract buys All

Pays: On publication, which is usually within 90 days

Expenses: Standard contract pays $50 in expenses; other expenses negotiated with writer

Kill fee: 50 percent

Rates:

Type of Article	*Word Length*	*Payment*
Major Feature	2,500	$700 - 850
Short Feature	1,500	500
Department	500 - 1,500	75 - 250
News Brief	500 - 1,000	100 - 250

Knowing that *Robb Report* grew out of a newsletter for Rolls Royce owners gives you a headstart in understanding the discriminating tastes and interests of those who turn to this magazine.

"We reach a broad spectrum of upscale readers whose rallying point is the exotic automobile, the likes of Ferrari, Lamborghini, Mercedes, BMW, and Lotus," says Robert Feeman, editor. "We are the magazine they reach for when they're done with their business reading and want to have fun. They pick up *Robb Report* to learn about the best hotel in Europe; the latest trend in art investments; or the fastest boat in the world. Every issue presents our readers with a variety of facts and information about how to enhance their leisure lifestyle."

More than 90 percent of the magazine's readers are male; the average age is 41. About three-quarters are entrepreneurs or presidents or CEOs of companies, and the remaining quarter are doctors, lawyers, or other professionals. Their average annual income is $422,000, and their average net worth tops $2.6 million.

"Essentially, our readers are the nouveau riche; they're not old money," says Feeman. "They network a lot, and they love to talk about the latest car or the newest gadget. They're very bright, fairly aggressive and, in a sense, risk takers. Our typical reader is like the executive we heard about who lives in New Hampshire. He owns a computer company and works 60 hours a week. Instead of slowing down on weekends, he pushes just as hard, going parachuting, hiking, speedboating, flying, and sport fishing."

How to Slant Your Ideas to *Robb Report*

While automobile coverage abounds and is territory covered by four or five regular writers, Feeman says he is open to a unique perspective or angle that a freelancer might develop. Speed and style are most important to this audience. "We sell more newsstand copies when we have an exotic car on the cover than when we show a luxury auto," says Feeman. "Our readers like to make a bit of a statement with something that is unique, different, or discriminating. We look for all those things when writers send us their ideas."

Robb Report also covers luxury boats and yachts, private aircraft, the arts, and profiles of movers and shakers. "Whether they are successful entrepreneurs, celebrities, CEOs, or chairmen of the board, we want to know how they got where they are and information about their lifestyle away from the office," says Feeman.

Unfortunately, only a small percentage of freelancers who approach the magazine are able to grasp its angle. "They haven't taken the time to see what we are after," the editor notes. "For example, we get a lot of travel proposals similar to, 'I'd like to write about our tour up the coast of France.' That's nice, but there needs to be a *Robb Report* spin that has a pro-active lifestyle slant. Our stable of freelancers is just the opposite. The writers can suggest a dozen story ideas for us and at least half are on target."

Along with becoming familiar with the magazine's style, Feeman gives writers another exercise that could either be extremely fun or terribly depressing. "The best thing you can do if you want to write for us is to pretend you have a million dollars and the accompanying discriminating taste," he suggests. "And forget about taking care of the kids or picking up the groceries. Imagine where you could spend the best weekend in the world, visit the fanciest spa, or eat food prepared by the world's best chef."

Feeman admits he doesn't pay his writers well enough for them to afford that lifestyle, but nevertheless hopes that they can understand and envision it. In other words, a *Robb Report* writer will know how to live vicariously through the eyes of the reader. If you are interested in that quest, you may want to contact the magazine for its editorial calendar, which maps out the themes for the year.

A few examples of *Robb Report* features include "A Toast to Champagne," in which the writer consulted the vintners of the world's finest champagnes on their own chalky turf in Reims, France. In "Style Counsel," three Chicago professionals allowed the magazine to assess their wardrobes and create whole new looks based on their individual personalities. "Caribbean Golf" undertook a discriminating investigation of the most beautiful and challenging golf courses in the world.

While the majority of the magazine's regular departments are written in house or assigned to regular contributors, Feeman is open to anything, if you have the right idea. Here are the departments in which a freelancer has the best chances:

- **Great Escapes** contains more destination-oriented pieces than the experiential travel features in the well of the book. The column covers a wide range of travel subjects, including hotels and restaurants, spas, cruises, general travel information, and travel books. "Our reader is not the kind of person who goes to a resort to spend the weekend on the beach," says Feeman. "He travels with a purpose and wants to get involved and experience something."
- **Investibles** targets a variety of collecting hobbies, not just antiques but the entire realm of investments. For example, one article looked at the unveiling of one of the world's largest emeralds, newly sculpted by gemstone carver Thomas R. McPhee. Another issue gave pointers on collecting old stock certificates.
- **Lifestyles** features anything from real estate and home furnishings to fashion and personal grooming. It has devoted its pages to male manicures, a $60,000 pool cue, a London jeweler who turns everyday items into miniature conversation pieces, and curious condiment sets of sterling silver and 18-karat gold.
- **Recreation** includes sports-related essays written in the third-person. Topics deal with outdoor activities like cycling, fishing, hiking, hunting, and kayaking.

> Sports is an area that Feeman wants to expand. He is open to a variety of angles. Past issues have covered the best seats at various stadiums, a profile of Michael Jordan's off-court life, investing in the best sports teams, and the prime places to stay for baseball spring training. "We're also looking for more profiles of successful people," the editor adds.

"Autos," "Boating," "The Cutting Edge," and "The Robb Reports" are typically assigned to a contributing editor.

How to Query *Robb Report*

One-page queries preferred; do not send any photo/art information.

"Don't worry about impressing me with skill; tell me your idea," says Feeman. "Every editor judges a writer by the query, so there should be some sort of style or format. And, though it sounds rudimentary, it's remarkable how frequently writers spell the editor's name wrong and how much that means to an editor. When I was a freelancer, I heard editors harp that if writers can't spell their names right, how could they expect writers to have what it takes to put a story together? And now I ask myself the same question," says Feeman (who notes that his name is often misspelled.)

Feeman says that if he reads a query that offers a great idea and is well thought through but blandly written, he will buy it over a proposal that is organized and has great stylized writing but a lackluster angle. He also requires an SASE, and he will not return a query without one. When Feeman spots a good freelance idea, he calls the writer to discuss the story and then sends a written contract. "We try to give writers two to three months to complete an assignment," says Feeman.

How to Write for *Robb Report*

"When a reader picks up a magazine, he wants to read the articles, but he's fighting the distractions of life," says Feeman. "My goal as an editor is to keep the reader involved from the beginning to the end of the story. If I do that, I've succeeded.

"The biggest weakness I see in writing is the lead—it's got to grab the reader," Feeman continues. "I often ask writers to pump up the lead. Another major problem is a lack of organization in articles and the segue from one idea to another."

Feeman likes to involve his readers, to give them a "you are there" sense. "We constantly tell writers who test-drive cars to let the reader feel, hear, smell, and see the car as much as possible. And I think that can be said of all pieces. The reader needs the experience to come to life."

Lively, upbeat, and a little off-the-wall are all characteristics of *Robb Report* pieces. "We are tongue-in-cheek sometimes and readers love that kind of stuff," says Feeman. "We are a leisure publication, so we don't take ourselves too seriously. We like to enjoy life and have fun, and writers can build on that."

And just because the editorial is geared to men doesn't mean women writers can't break in. "Our senior editor is a woman," says Feeman, "and she is responsible for writing a monthly arts column. However, if a woman is knowledgeable on one of our other subjects, we'd welcome queries. We don't have any female auto writers and encourage women to query."

Scouting

1325 West Walnut Hill Lane
P.O. Box 152079
Irving, TX 75015-2079
(214) 580-2000

Published: 6 times a year

Circulation: 1 million

Query: Ernest Doclar, editor

Query response time: 1 to 2 weeks

Buys: About 60 to 80 articles/stories out of approximately 150 unsolicited queries/manuscripts received annually

Guidelines: Available; send SASE and $1 for a sample copy

Rights purchased: First NAS

Pays: On acceptance

Expenses: Pays for previously approved travel, meals, mileage, and lodging

Kill fee: Never applies

Rates:

Type of Article	*Word Length*	*Payment*
Major Feature	1,200 - 1,800	$500 - 1,000*
"Family Quiz"	varies	125+
"Front Line Stuff"	varies	60
"The Way It Was"	1,500	200 - 250
"Worth Retelling"	varies	10

**depends on author's experience, complexity of the assignment, and length of travel time required to complete the research*

The Boy Scouts of America publishes *Scouting* to help adult volunteers do the best job possible as Scout leaders. This magazine is delivered to the homes of one million Scout leaders as a membership benefit.

Two-thirds of the readers are male, one-third female, with a median age of 39.6 years. Total readership is up to 2.4 million. Almost 90 percent of the readers are married with two children, and the average household income is $53,500.

How to Slant Your Ideas to *Scouting*

If you know the Scouting program, have been a parent or a long-term Scout leader, and can write magazine-quality material, you're the perfect candidate to write for this magazine.

"One of our writers is a 70-year-old Scoutmaster who's a bachelor, but he knows what kids and parents are interested in reading," says Editor Ernest Doclar. "Another writer is a child psychologist and former newspaperman who writes on counseling children and on how to deal with a death in the family. He exhibits expertise that would serve families well."

Scouting carries news, program ideas, Boy Scout policy interpretations, and Scouting leadership hints. In addition, it features articles on outdoor programs, American heritage, health, safety, and Scouting's educational role in building the character and citizenship of boys.

A sampling of the general interest topics includes home schooling, the timber wolf, and low-pressure baseball programs for kids.

"The magazine also likes stories with an Americana theme," the editor says. "One writer proposed a story about Scout troops visiting presidential libraries. That information could be put to use by both Scout leaders and families, but also would be of interest to any reader. Another all-American story covered the history of the 'Star-Spangled Banner.'"

A major focus of the magazine is providing coverage of Scouting topics and events. "We report on what has worked successfully in Scouting programs across the nation and interpret parts of the Scouting program to help parents lead troops more effectively," Doclar says.

A few of these headlines include: "Canoeing the Mighty Chattooga," about a North Carolina troop that took on the "Deliverance" river; "The Beat Goes On," describing how musical groups from posts and troops continue a long Scouting tradition; and "Here's to the Have Knots," showing how to add fun and excitement to teaching the practical skill of tying a knot.

According to Doclar, the most common mistake people make in approaching his magazine is assuming it's written for kids. "The Boy Scouts of America publishes *Boys' Life* for children," he says. Although 90 percent of the ideas in *Scouting* are developed by the magazine staff, Doclar says he gets great ideas from volunteers working in the Scouting program. That doesn't mean there aren't openings for writers not associated with the Boy Scouts who take the time and initiative to get to know the market.

"Develop a rapport with us," says Doclar. "Understand the Scouting program and present your work professionally. We have three regular contributing editors who started with us 20 years ago as freelance writers."

The following columns are open to freelance writers:

- **Family Quiz** offers a variety of topics in a question/multiple-choice format, including sports, entertainment, television commercials, ships, airplanes, and Scouting trivia.
- **Front Line Stuff** is a Scouting problem/response column that runs a question one issue and follows up with readers' responses in a later issue.
- **The Way It Was** recounts Scouting history. You have to know or be able to find and develop historical instances about Scouting. This is a perfect area for retired Scout leaders to contribute to.
- **Worth Retelling** is a combination of humorous and serious things that have happened to Scouts and Scout leaders. One example told how a Cub Scout leader, dressed in uniform, was mistaken for a park ranger. Another described a troop's venture to Beverly Hills to conduct the opening flag ceremony at a major council event.

"News Briefs," a recap of general Scouting news, is written in house.

How to Query *Scouting*

One page preferred. Send photo/art information.

Query letters for this market should be terse and show evidence that the reader has examined the magazine.

"I'd be impressed with a sample lead, but what intrigues me most is a provocative topic that I think will make a good article for our readers," says Doclar.

In most cases, Doclar will ask a new freelancer for *Scouting* to write a piece on speculation. "The only time I wouldn't is when the writer has submitted quality samples and has impressed me with his or her ability by having a professional approach," the editor says.

When you are asked to write a piece for this magazine, you'll get a personal letter that spells out the terms, deadline, length, and payment. You will also receive several sample copies of the magazine.

How to Write for *Scouting*

"We want professional-caliber writing," says Doclar. "We like manuscripts that require very little work and can almost be put right into the magazine. In addition, a writer needs to speak the Scouting language. We have a jargon of our own. For example, a freelancer might call a kid a Scouter, but when we say Scouter, we mean adult leader, either a professional or volunteer. We are more likely to use a piece if the writer uses the correct terminology. But if the piece is well done in other ways, we can doctor-up terminology."

Doclar prefers a relaxed writing style. "We tend to think of our readers as good-natured people because they deal with kids," the editor explains. "They have to have a lot of patience to do their jobs well, and be fairly easy-going. So, our style ought to match that way of life. It's not too formal; for example, we vary the term 'boys' with 'kids.'"

Scouting keeps its articles short and sweet. "Our readers automatically get this magazine; they don't subscribe to it. So we have to pull them in with attractive titles and get to the point with valuable information. You'll seldom find an article longer than 1,500 words," the editor says.

Fact checking is paramount. Doclar requires writers to turn in a source list.

"We must be sensitive to the concerns of the 330 local Scouting offices, which are autonomous but a part of the Boy Scouts of America," says Doclar. "Because of that, we send articles to Scouting professional associates in the field to make sure that we don't offend them or their supporters."

Sesame Street Parents' Guide

One Lincoln Plaza
New York, NY 10023
(212) 595-3456

Published: 10 times a year

Circulation: 1.1 million

Query: Development/Psychological pieces: Susan Schneider, senior editor
Essays: Nadia Zonis, associate editor
Medical pieces: Douglas S. Barasch, senior editor

Query response time: 8 weeks

Buys: About 50 to 100 articles/stories out of approximately 750 unsolicited queries/manuscripts received annually

Guidelines: Available; send SASE

Rights purchased: Depends; from work-for-hire to First NAS

Pays: On acceptance

Expenses: Pays items if reasonable

Kill fee: 33 percent

Rates:

Type of Article	*Word Length*	*Payment*
Major Feature	1,200 - 2,400	$1,000 - 2,500
Short Feature	500 - 750	300 - 750
"Body Basics"	700 - 1,200	500 - 1,200
"Brothers and Sisters"	700 - 1,200	500 - 1,200
"A Conversation With"	1,500	1,000 - 1,500
"The Elementary Years"	700 - 1,200	500 - 1,200
"Family Portrait"	750 - 1,200	500

If you think kids learn a lot from the loveable television characters Big Bird, Cookie Monster, and Bert and Ernie, then you won't be surprised by the wealth of insight parents discover in *Sesame Street Parents' Guide.*

This magazine is available only to subscribers of *Sesame Street Magazine*, a monthly publication of games, activities, and stories for two- to six-year olds. As a companion publication, the *Sesame*

Street Parents' Guide (SSPG) is narrowly focused to parents of children who are within that same age range.

"One of our great strengths is that we do *not* offer information on caring for babies or tips for parenting teenagers," says Ira Wolfman, editor-in-chief. "We concentrate on the preschool to early elementary years."

And it's all kid stuff. The entire magazine focuses on parent/child relations. "We are 100 percent parenting," says Wolfman. "We don't include fashion or beauty or cover other topics traditionally found in women's and parenting magazines."

Most *SSPG* readers are married middle-class parents who are 25 to 34 years old and who have one or two young children between the ages of two and six. The average reader has attended college, is employed, and has a median household income of $42,800.

"Our research shows that we have a large pass-along rate to fathers," says Wolfman. "Because of this, we make a definite point of talking to both parents, more so than other parenting magazines."

How to Slant Your Ideas to *Sesame Street Parents' Guide*

"Following the Sesame Street tradition, *SSPG* mixes education and entertainment," says Wolfman. "We help parents relate to both the *Sesame Street* magazine and TV show. For example, the column, 'Variations on a Theme,' deepens a parent's understanding of the theme presented in the most recent children's magazine. Each issue also offers information on the wide range of things done on the television show to educate kids."

In addition, the magazine helps parents understand their child's development. "As a parent, you are the expert on your kid," says Wolfman. "We digest a lot of information and then present it in a way that gives moms and dads insights about their child's needs, concerns, and worries at a particular age. Most articles have developmental material built into them; the ages of the kids are bolded for a parent's easy reference."

Along with child development, the magazine offers practical advice and ideas on discipline, education, nutrition, health, and curriculum areas, such as reading and writing.

Writers who are parents have an advantage when querying *SSPG*. "Living with children is different from intellectualizing about them," says Wolfman. In other words, if you're writing on the subject of toilet training, you'll understand it better and be more compelling if you have a track record of getting a child through that momentous experience.

"Our focus is what to do with this little child in front of you," says Wolfman. "We are very much a service magazine, offering parents tips for how to live with, encourage, and develop their children. Obviously, however, we want our own unique slant on ideas. It needs to be exciting—different."

Wolfman cites a topic all parents' magazines cover every fall—back to school. "We looked at the things parents worry about and explained why they didn't have to worry, in a light and fun way. We also brought together five eight-year-olds to talk about their feelings about starting school. In another vein, when covering the topic of lead poisoning, we said, okay, you know lead in paint is a problem, now here are concrete steps you can take. We outlined whom to call if you have a problem and what to expect. We took the parent moment-by-moment through the process—including what to do if no one answers the phone when you call your local Health Department. Parents today are incredibly busy. They don't want to know simply what is going on, but their options for taking action as well," he says.

The clearer and sharper the focus of the idea you want to propose, the better. "Take one aspect of a popular and interesting topic and apply it to our slice of the population," Wolfman advises. "For example, when author Deborah Tannen wrote 'You Just Don't Understand,' a book about miscommunication between men and women, we looked at how that might be true in preschoolers. On another subject, how schools shortchange girls, we asked, 'Hey, how does this affect the youngest children?'"

These *SSPG* departments are open to freelancers, although not every department appears in each issue:

- **Body Basics** seeks journalistic writing on medical issues. Writers should be experienced in translating medical information into layman's language. Subjects have included easing the discomforts of the common cold and what to do when your child runs a temperature.

- **Brothers and Sisters** looks at any issue affecting siblings. It ranges from first-person essays to journalistic reports. In one column, a mother looked back at the dollhouses, tea sets, and other gender-appropriate toys she had bought her daughter in the '60s, only to wonder how the young woman turned out to be so good at math and science—and was unwilling to cater to her brother.

- **A Conversation With** is a bimonthly department presented in a Q&A format. It presents the views of prominent educators, psychologists, authors, performers, and others who affect the lives of children.

The following departments appear in every issue and are open to freelancers:

- **The Elementary Years** tackles issues that school-age kids face, such as making the most of the parent/teacher conference, home schooling, and the move toward year-round schooling.
- **Family Portrait** is a first-person column written by readers and is an excellent break-in spot for writers new to this market. It offers true accounts of how a parent coped with a particular situation. For example, one father shared the queasy feelings dads get when their children get sick. Topics can range from everyday situations such as teaching siblings to share, to larger concerns, such as coping with a disabled child. For this column, the magazine prefers a completed manuscript over a query letter.

Columns not open to freelancers include "Newsbriefs" and "What's Cooking." "Practical Parenting" is a reader-contributor column; "Your Child's Health" is written by doctors at a number of children's hospitals.

How to Query *Sesame Street Parents' Guide*

One to one and one-half page queries acceptable. Do not send photo/art information. Query six months in advance.

Rule number one when querying SSPG: Realize that all ideas must be targeted to kids ages two to six. Including anecdotes or quotes about infants or 10-year-olds is a sure sign that you haven't studied the market.

Rule number two: Send general-interest clips if you have them to show you are a well-established writer. They should be at least 1,200 words in length, except for first-person essays.

Rule number three: Tell why your idea is relevant to the magazine's audience and how you plan to write the final piece. It's important for proposals to include a parent's voice.

Rule number four: Plan to interview nationally recognized experts. "*Sesame Street*'s name opens doors—we have access to leading experts," says Wolfman. "For that reason, writers need to quote the best in the field. If you're writing about kids' fear of the dark, rather than looking for a psychologist who works with children, find someone who has written a book on the topic or is known for his expertise in that field."

If your query leads to an assignment, you will receive a contract and an assignment letter.

How to Write for *Sesame Street Parents' Guide*

"One way we save our readers is by trying to get into the child's head and present the world looking out from his point of view," says Wolfman. "That means writers have to talk to child developmental specialists to find out how to see the world from a kid's vantage point."

SSPG articles range from about 800 to 1,500 words; the longest is 2,400. "We're not interested in being encyclopedic," says Wolfman. "We focus our pieces to be specific and service-oriented. For example, we did a five-part series on play that both helped parents understand children's needs, then offered specific tips for better communication between parent and child," the editor says.

When it comes to writing style, *SSPG* prefers to provide parents with options, rather than a rigid approach. Avoid using terms like "must" or "should." Be supportive, not critical. The magazine steers away from the "he/she" problem by using the words "children" and "they" as often as appropriate.

If you've received an assignment from *SSPG* and wonder where you're going to find three mothers of three-year-olds, the magazine's Parents' Network can supplement your search. It includes some 2,000 parents who have agreed to be interviewed for articles and serve as resources for the magazine.

When it comes to attributing quotes, give the expert's full name and title, organization or affiliation, and any book authorship. For books, cite the title, author, and publisher. When referring to research done on a particular subject, the study must be cited. If you are referring to a body of research, be as specific as possible. All phone numbers of sources must be included with your finished piece.

Once an article is turned in to the staff, it undergoes a careful review. "Members of our Advisory Board—all experts in early childhood—review every article that goes into the magazine," says Wolfman. "Including staff review, every piece is circulated to about 25 people." That means the magazine is thorough and any writer for this market would be wise to follow suit.

"We can't tell you what changes must be made to your manuscript for about three to four weeks, so please be patient," says Wolfman. "If an assignment is deemed unacceptable, we give writers a chance to rewrite.

"We think our magazine is a terrific place to showcase your writing. Our readers care deeply about the material. We try to develop our writers with tender loving care, too."

Seventeen

850 Third Avenue
New York, NY 10022
(212) 407-9700

Published: Monthly

Circulation: 1.75 million

Query: Catherine Cavender, executive editor

Query response time: 6 to 8 weeks

Buys: About 80 articles out of approximately 3,500 unsolicited queries and manuscripts received annually

Guidelines: Available; send SASE

Rights purchased: One-time

Expenses: Pays items agreed upon in advance

Kill fee: 25 percent

Rates:

Type of Article	*Word Length*	*Payment*
Major Feature	2,000	$1,500 - 2,500
Short Feature	1,200	1,000 - 1,200
News Brief	150 - 500	75 - 800

"Our job is to inform teenagers, but not in a heavy-handed way," says Catherine Cavender, executive editor. "We don't want to sound like their teachers."

Seventeen's editors attract readers by entertaining them with informative articles and appealing graphics. With plenty of fashion and beauty news pages, the publication looks a lot like MTV in print.

The nation's third leading fashion and beauty magazine reaches 6.6 million teens each month—nearly half of the country's females between the ages of 12 and 19 years.

Seventeen's editorial content is targeted to teens between 13 and 19 years old, although a large percentage of readers are actually in the 15 to 16 age group, says Cavender.

How to Slant Your Ideas to *Seventeen*

"If there's a voice that we claim as our own, it is probably that of an older sister rather than parents or teachers," says Cavender.

That voice needs to be entertaining as well as informative and readable, no matter the subject.

Target your articles to more sophisticated teen readers, Cavender advises. "Our readers are thinkers; they are interested in issues and open to finding out what's going on in the world." *Seventeen* publishes one or two major articles a month, and those usually are by freelancers. The magazine always tries to include one article on a major social issue each month, usually written by a freelancer. These articles cover such topics as alcoholism, incest, dropouts, and runaways.

Relationships is another hot category with editors, says Cavender. "We can never get enough stories about relationships with friends, siblings, parents, boyfriends, teachers, and school. For example, an article about what to do when your teacher hates you is a good one."

The following columns are open to freelancers:

- **Entertainment** is tough for a freelancer to crack unless you have connections with celebrities. The key here is to focus on entertainment figures who are popular with young female audiences.
- **Guys** is also open to freelancers. Of particular interest are short, funny articles highlighting the differences between the sexes.
- **The Spin** features briefs on "news that makes your world go 'round." This section incudes a potpourri of current events that are of interest to young adults. "The Daily Planet" is a regular section that covers environmental news. Other topics that have been addressed here include "Pot: illegal and unhealthy, but popular again"; gays in the military; endangered species; and rape verdicts that were based on the use of condoms. There is a lot of interesting reading here, and good opportunity for freelancers.

"Relating" and "Sex & Body" are written by regular columnists. Beauty and fashion layouts are handled by the staff.

How to Query *Seventeen*

One- to two-page queries preferred; do not send art/photo information. Query at least six months in advance on seasonal material.

Cavender reports that, while only a few queries from unknown writers are accepted at *Seventeen,* it does happen. "If someone writes in with a good idea and has quality clips from other assignments, we'll consider the query," she says.

Cavender's assistant passes along all ideas that show potential. At that point, Cavender even rejects another 95 percent of these queries.

Writers who sound old won't survive *Seventeen*'s rigorous screening process, says Cavender. "If a writer talks about teens as a 'them,' or is removed from the audience, we won't be interested."

How to Write for *Seventeen*

"Writing for *Seventeen* is about entertaining. People forget that," says Cavender. The editor notes that freelancers can significantly improve their chances of getting published if they pay better attention to *Seventeen*'s style. "Our writers must read our magazine, become familiar with it, and show a sensitivity for the reader," the editor says.

If an idea from a freelancer is accepted, the writer will receive a call from one of *Seventeen*'s editors. The editor will want to learn how you plan to approach a story. She may suggest slanting the story in a different direction.

A letter will follow the phone conversation to confirm the assignment, with further details on what the editor is looking for in your story.

"When a piece comes in, three or four editors read and comment on the story," Cavender notes. "A revision letter usually will be sent to the writer asking for changes. Editors then review the second draft. Occasionally we'll decide to kill a piece when it becomes clear the writer can't handle the assignment. But only about five percent of articles are killed." *Seventeen*'s editors do their best to steer a writer in the right direction. "We always try to make a piece work once we're committed to publishing it," says Cavender.

Shape

21100 Erwin Street
Woodland Hills, CA 91367
(818) 884-6800

Published: Monthly, plus special pregnancy edition in Spring

Circulation: 800,000

Query: Peg Moline, editorial director

Query response time: 4 weeks

Buys: About 60 articles/stories out of approximately 1,000 unsolicited queries/manuscripts received annually

Guidelines: Available; send SASE

Rights purchased: All

Pays: On publication

Expenses: Pays phone and additional approved expenses

Kill fee: 30 percent

Rates:

Type of Article	*Word Length*	*Payment*
Major Feature	2,500 - 3,000	$ 1,200
Short Feature	1,500	1,000 - 1,200
Department	1,000 - 3,000	varies
News Brief	100 - 300	75 - 100

Women's health and fitness are the focus of *Shape.* Readers committed to an active lifestyle can find everything from sports and fitness activities to the latest information on health, psychology, and nutrition. Other issues that *Shape* explores with a health and fitness slant are travel, family, leisure, career, and the environment.

The readership of *Shape* is 90 percent female; readers are between the ages of 18 and 49, with a median age of 32. More than 50 percent are married and 44 percent have children. Over 50 percent of *Shape* readers have attended or graduated from college and 78 percent are employed.

How to Slant Your Ideas to *Shape*

Shape's mission is to help its readers develop a healthy and fulfilling lifestyle through care of the body and mind. The heart of the publication is explaining and demonstrating exercise routines and workouts. According to Peg Moline, editorial director, *Shape* talks to people in a personal way.

"We give a lot of information on the best way to do specific exercises and what those exercises will do for readers, both physically and mentally," she says. "What makes us unique is that we explore the mental side of fitness—how exercise affects mood and personality."

Shape readers expect information they can immediately use and apply to their lives. "I advise writers to look at past issues for ideas that have worked, and then give me a new angle," says Moline. "I like surprises." She is also looking for cutting-edge issues. Features on the latest in techniques, equipment, food, travel, and leisure will get her attention.

Although most departments are open to freelancers, the majority of workout stories are done in house. "Because the exercise stories require close collaboration with the art department, they are hard to assign to freelancers," says Moline. Beauty and fashion stories are also primarily done in house.

All departments are open to freelancers. They include:

- **Diet & Nutrition** features four articles each month that help readers eat for optimal health benefits. "Recipe Makeover" is a regular feature that takes traditional high-fat temptations, such as quiche and asparagus soup, and gives an alternative recipe with reduced fat, salt, and sugar content.

  "Shopping Smart," another regular feature, helps readers sort through the health-food hype. Examples include an article comparing health-food store products to their grocery store counterparts; and another comparing nutritional contents of breakfast cereals.

  Other titles that have run in this section include "The Non-Diet Diet," a feature on a realistic approach to eating right; "Mealtime Tactics," a story giving 10 tips for eating on the go; and "Chez Lean," an article on celebrated chefs who are slimming down their menus.

- **Mind/Body Health** includes several articles each month that focus on the psychological side of fitness. "Mind/Body Health" also features a news briefs section, "In Shape," which is a compilation of several short columns on a variety of topics including health, nutrition, sports medicine, fitness trends, and psychology. "In Shape" material can consist of blurbs on items such as new products, books and videos, survey and research findings, and quick tips.

Past articles in this section have included a story about the facts of childhood obesity, learning how to get a good night's sleep, and the results of a woman's search for an alternative to having a hysterectomy.

- **Sports & Adventure** includes a monthly fitness-related travel piece. Stories for this section should highlight stimulating destinations with an emphasis on action. "When our readers go on vacation, they want to know what activities are available," says Moline. "Frequently, their vacations are specifically planned around an activity such as white-water rafting."

  Examples of articles that have run in this section include "Happy Trails," a feature on how a city slicker found her cowgirl soul on a cattle drive; and "The Ultimate Glide," a guide to cross-country skiing.

How to Query *Shape*

One-page queries preferred; send photo/art suggestions when appropriate.

Knowledge of *Shape* and insights into where an idea will fit in the magazine are part of what makes a query letter sell to Moline. "I require that new writers send clips, but I generally don't trust clips because of the editing filter," she says. "A query shows me how well a person can write and how they would handle the proposed story."

Moline appreciates anecdotes and quotes from experts when they are right for the story. "I'm always looking for good writers with lots of ideas," she says. "If a good writer who knows the magazine and its tone sends me an idea I don't use, I may still assign the writer another story if his idea was right on the mark."

How to Write for *Shape*

Moline's dream writer has an instinctive and educated knowledge of fitness and health. She wants organized writers who can write in a creative, personal way, but not necessarily in the first person.

Writers who want to impress Moline should employ a conversational tone with crisp journalistic style, and avoid the jargon. "Writers should be comfortable with technical and medical terms, but must not write too technically," she says. "They need to be able to write medical information in an understandable way for the reader."

Shape

The editor looks for freelancers who have magazine experience and an understanding of how to write, while keeping the magazine's graphics in mind. "I need people who are very visual and know how to include sidebars, subheads, and pull-quotes," she says.

Moline assigns articles over the phone initially, followed by a letter of agreement.

Sierra

730 Polk Street
San Francisco, CA 94109
(415) 776-2211

Published: 6 times a year

Circulation: 500,000

Query: Marc LeCard, managing editor

Query response time: 4 weeks

Buys: About 50 articles out of approximately 1,500 unsolicited queries/manuscripts received annually

Guidelines: Available; send SASE

Rights purchased: First NAS

Pays: On acceptance

Expenses: Pays up to $1,000 for feature articles only

Kill fee: 20 percent for first draft; 25 percent for rewrite

Rates:

Type of Article	*Word Length*	*Payment*
Major Feature	3,000 - 4,000	$1,500 - 2,500
Short Feature	1,000 - 2,000	800 - 1,000
Column/Department	800 - 1,000	400

"We reflect the totality of environmentalism," says Annie Stine, deputy editor of *Sierra.* "That is, we cover conservation, politics, and outdoor adventure on a global basis. And we do so through standard journal contemplative writing, essays, and personal reflections.

"*Sierra* reinterprets the classic definition of the environmental movement. We joke that the typical article in this genre is, 'There is a blank in my blank, so we'd better blank before we all die.' We try to get away from the stereotype of what environmentalists do and who they are," Stine says.

The magazine's connection to its publisher, the Sierra Club, is to draw strength from the organization's activities. While it celebrates the work of the Club, it is not a house organ or mouthpiece. Sierra Club membership includes a subscription to the magazine; a magazine subscription alone is $15 per year.

"In terms of political coverage, the Sierra Club has bi-annual conservation priorities," the editor explains. "We see it as our job to make those issues come alive for our readers. If one of the

Club's goals is wilderness preservation, we might do an adventure story on a wilderness area that the Club is trying to save. We would delve into the politics of that region and send nature writers out there to observe and ruminate."

Most readers are Sierra Club members, although the magazine's per-issue newsstand sales reach 30,000 copies. "The people who read *Sierra* are just about as diverse as a cross-section of the country," says Stine. "They have in common a love of the land. Yet, they include Republicans and Democrats and hold pro-nuclear and anti-nuclear energy sentiments. Our readers are independent individuals who don't like to be told how to think or what to think. Much more, they like to be informed, so we stay away from being preachy. They are demanding in terms of truth and accuracy, insofar as these can be revealed. For any one article we run, we will have 10 letters saying it's ridiculous and just as many saying it's the best story we've ever done."

By pure demographics, the readership is almost evenly divided between men and women. The median age is 45. Almost 80 percent have graduated from college, half are married, and the median household income is $53,900.

How to Slant Your Ideas to *Sierra*

"It's becoming harder to sell to us because as many as 80 percent of our ideas are ones we come up with internally and assign to writers we know," says Stine. "However, each bimonthly issue probably has one or two writers who are new to the magazine."

Stine says the magazine gets barraged with very parochial ideas. "We can't talk about everybody's backyard or polluted creek, or the recycling efforts at a local elementary school," she says. "We understand the importance of small-scale, local changes, but it isn't the kind of story that will make it into the magazine."

All the slots in the feature well are open to writers. These articles lend themselves to greater length, photography, and a more extended narrative. A few examples of some features from past issues are: "Gambling with Tomorrow," a piece about the federal government's plans to bury high-level nuclear waste in a remote western desert; "A Grizzly's Place," an article about the bear's dwindling habitat; "In Name Only," an insider's view of what's wrong with the EPA; and "A Return to the Peaks," an essay by a stalwart octogenarian who encourages today's activists to take greater risks and reap more rewards.

"Afield" is Sierra's front-of-the-book department that consists of six regular columns; those written by the staff or regular contributors include "Body Politics," "Hand & Eye," and "Ways & Means." Freelance contributions are considered for the three other "Afield" columns:

- **Good Going** is a destination/travel column that takes on more of a personal essay style than a Sunday newspaper journalistic approach. It offers reflective travel writing that looks at what it means to be in a different culture or a different place.

  "Writers should ask themselves what can be learned from the experience and what remains hidden," explains Stine, "rather than focusing on chronological-type prose that consists of 'the first day we did this and the second day we did that.' It's got to be creative."
- **Hearth & Home** is light and lively coverage of how to be an environmentalist at home without being smug about recycling. It ranges from worm composting to safe paint strippers to what to do with old oil when changing the oil in the car.
- **Whereabouts** is a first-person meditation on one's home ground. Writers share images of where they live and reasons why they live there. In "One Hour," the author offers his perspective on life in New Hampshire.

Other departments open to freelancers are:

- **Outdoors** provides insights on equipment and techniques in the area of outdoor recreation. No equipment reviews are included. "If we did a story on tents, we might talk about various materials and different weights and their applications," says Stine. "In the piece we did on water filters for camping and backpacking, we looked at how they work and what they do."
- **Priorities** is open to established political writers who can deal with a regional issue that has national significance. Most often it is written in house.

"Clubways" is closed to freelancers.

How to Query *Sierra*

One to one and one-half pages preferred. Send photo/art information, but no photos or slides.

"It's really heartening to get queries from writers who read the magazine and know us," says Stine. "They have a sense of our departments and don't send us a proposal for a story we just did. Writers must convey their familiarity with the magazine, as much as that's possible from the outside.

"Be careful with your query," Stine encourages writers. "That goes all the way from spelling our names correctly to writing to an editor who still actually works here. The query itself should be a piece of writing of which you are proud—that means intriguing and thought-provoking.

"It depends on the topic, obviously, but if you want to write about a recent adventure, the query must illustrate your tone, attitude and humor. We wouldn't want you to state, 'I just got back from going to Antarctica by kayak. Do you want the story?' We need to see the drama. There is a danger of overwriting, sure, but the query is an introduction to us. It lets us know who you are on paper," she continues. (Make sure you send quality clips along with your proposal.)

If your query piques an editor's interest, it will be circulated among five editors. "We operate collegially here," says Stine. "We have a query meeting each week, during which we talk about maybe four of the 30 or so queries we received the previous week. If we decide to proceed with an idea, an assigning editor will call the writer to see if he or she is still up to it and to offer our terms. If the writer agrees to those terms, we send an assignment letter that serves as a contract."

How to Write for *Sierra*

"You can't pigeonhole our readers, so we use a lot of different voices in the magazine," says Stine. "We try to speak to the hard-core activist as well as to the more spiritual wanderer, and to everyone in between."

Stine has trouble with writers who think the magazine is more one dimensional than it is, or not as much fun as it strives to be. "We get many manuscripts in which the first draft is dry. We go back and ask the writer to add color and humor and he or she responds, 'Oh, I didn't know you wanted that.' That's like saying, 'Oh, I didn't know you wanted it to be good and interesting.' It's such a blessing to run into a good writer, and when we do, we are encouraging and open," she says.

Stine says that personal writing can be the most difficult. "It takes a more experienced writer for that genre because language plays such a crucial role," she notes. "There is a very thin line between putting poetry into the expression of feelings and getting too misty. It's a risky venture. Sometimes it works and sometimes it doesn't."

Stine tells writers the phone line is always open once you've received an assignment. "We'd much rather hear about problems early," she says.

When you send your completed manuscript to *Sierra,* it circulates among the five editors. "Usually the assigning editor is much less subjective and can be blind to the manuscript's faults," Stine explains. "So we work together to reach a consensus about whether the manuscript should be accepted. Afterward, the assigning editor gets down to the business of editing. It is then sent out for expert review and fact checking. Discussions go back and forth between the editor and the writer until all questions are answered and problems solved.

"We are very hands-on, and some writers are appalled at what a group grope it is here, but it serves us well," Stine says.

Ski

Two Park Avenue
New York, NY 10016
(212) 779-5000

Published: 8 times a year (Monthly Sept.-Feb., combined Mar./Apr. and May/June. The latter covers activities at mountain resorts during summer months.)

Circulation: 444,000

Query: Steve Cohen, editor

Query response time: 2 weeks to 6 months

Buys: Dozens of articles/stories out of approximately 200 unsolicited queries/manuscripts received annually

Guidelines: None available

Rights purchased: First NAS

Pays: On acceptance

Expenses: Pays all negotiated in advance for assigned articles only

Kill fee: 30 percent

Rates:

Type of Article	*Word Length*	*Payment*
Major Feature	3,000	$1,500 - 2,000
Short Feature	1,000 - 1,500	500 - 1,000
Department	25 - 400	25 - 300
"Going Places"	100 - 350	75 - 250
"Last Run"	800	800
"My Turn"	750	225 - 375

If you ask readers of this magazine what they do in their leisure time, they'll tell you they ski—even if they only hit the slopes one day out of 50. They've been captivated by this exciting sport, and they turn to *Ski* as their cold weather lifeline to tell them how to get the most out of the adventure.

Ski is a lifestyle-oriented magazine aimed at the ski enthusiast who doesn't live in or near a ski resort, but who participates in the sport an average of 10 to 20 days a year.

Because snow skiing demands special abilities, *Ski* readers are physically active and often younger than other major sports participants. The median age is approximately 34. The sport is almost evenly divided between men (54 percent) and women (46 percent). The majority have attended college, and 68 percent report annual household incomes of more than $40,000.

How to Slant Your Ideas to *Ski*

"Skiing is a difficult sport to participate in because it's not something you can do in your own backyard, like tennis, golf, or jogging," says Steve Cohen, editor. "In most areas outside of Colorado or Utah, there is not a lot of information on the sport. A small number of newspapers have a ski column a few times a week, but for the most part, readers turn to ski magazines for information."

Ski is a combination travel/sports magazine for skiers. It tells its adventuresome readers where to find the best skiing or ambiance. The magazine gives secrets to better skiing, offers commentary on certain aspects of the sport such as ski racing, gives money-saving ideas, takes a look at personalities in the game, covers the unique skiing adventures of experienced skiers, and evaluates ski equipment.

"Our instruction pieces are primarily written by certified instructors, so a freelancer needs a novel approach and a lot of expertise," says Cohen. "When we cover ski equipment, we tend to highlight the people who test the equipment. We talk about Jim or Mary testing the equipment. Our sister publication, *Skiing* (also a Times Mirror publication), talks about the 162-pound tester. We are left of center compared to them."

Cohen says he assigns most features to writers with whom the magazine has worked in the past. But occasionally a query with a unique angle from a freelancer unknown to the staff will shine bright. "One writer had a special Christmas angle on Banff Springs Hotel in Alberta," the editor recalls. "She'd been there, had good clips, sold it hard, and we assigned it to her."

Under the table of contents heading "Where to Ski," you'll find articles such as: "Skiing in the Cradle of Civilization," a piece on skiing in Israel, Greece, and Rome; "Rooms at the Top," a peek at the finest rooms at great hotels in ski country; "Missing Link," a look at the addition of high and steep Parseen Bowl at Winter Park, Colorado; and "Bon Appetit!" a review of France's Haute Savoie, where planning a ski day means checking the menus as well as the trail maps.

The October issue is *Ski*'s "Vacation Planner," and includes a compilation of short articles touting new ski programs, activities at ski resorts, and travel tips. "The articles here are almost 100 percent travel-oriented," according to Cohen. "The majority of the editorial is about the skiing available at various destinations, and most features concentrate on the totality of the resort, including the restaurants, accommodations, and ski diversions."

One "Vacation Planner" gave a photographic record of the animals in Yellowstone National Park. Other articles have included "One-Stop Shopping," a list of ski resort hotlines for hassle-free vacation reservations; and "Packing It In," a review of new cargo bags and a dozen no-sweat packing tips to make one-duffle ski vacation travel a snap.

Occasionally, *Ski* features a "Special Feature" section, the ideas for which are usually generated in house. "Wild Women," was a "Special Feature" that profiled the lives of four fast, fearless females who made it to the top by living on the edge. Other articles in this category have included "The 100 Greatest Things That Ever Happened to Skiing," a look back at the innovations, personalities, equipment and good times that have shaped American skiing; and "Manhattan Transfer," a story about New Yorkers who left the fast lane and took sanctuary in Colorado's Summit County.

The magazine also includes "In Your Region," which gives readers a look at skiing in their part of the country. "We are looking for good eastern writers," says Cohen. "We need to cover New England, yet most ski writers cover the Rockies, where the skiing is the best."

Under the "Department" category, the following are open to freelancers:

- **Cool Stuff** critiques new ski accessory items. It is typically staff written; however, if you discover new items and can write several great paragraphs about it, you might try your hand here.
- **Going Places** offers unique vacation experiences. Past issues have included heli-skiing in the former Russian Republic; midnight skiing in a Scandinavian country; and discoveries of exotic places to lodge. This column runs about three times a year and is written by freelancers and *Ski* staff.
- **Hotline** is a breaking news page of 75- to 100-word items covering travel, airline changes, or new developments at ski resorts. If you have something hot, phone queries are accepted between the tenth and fifteenth of the month.
- **Last Run** presents humorous essays on a variety of topics. One writer gave a fitness plan only a couch potato could love. Another pointed tongue-in-cheek at Vail's tug-o-war over the decision to put in a stoplight. (It remains one of the last civilized places on earth that gets by with no form of electronic traffic control.)

- **My Turn** is an opinion column for any writer who has 750 great words in mind. "This is your opportunity to editorialize about something that has to do with skiing," says Cohen. "It could be a piece about the propensity of people to litigate, the fact that you don't like snow boarders, or some grievance you have with an airline. We need more people to submit to this column. It's a great opportunity to make your name known with us."
- **Ski Life** features short, humorous news ranging from 25 to 500 words. Pieces include news reports on problems facing ski resorts, such as getting water withdrawal rights for streams, as well as a quick look at new products, such as a virtual-reality skiing helmet. One fun piece told how a cable TV installer, who bought a house on two acres in Sturbridge, MA, spent eight months building his own ski slope and lift.

"A Skier's Journal" is closed to freelancers.

How to Query *Ski*

One page preferred. Do not send photo/art information.

"Don't send me queries about the first time you went skiing but hated it, or how you've been away from the sport for 20 years and you've made a comeback. I get 10 of those a week," Cohen yawns.

Instead, send a proposal that shows your knowledge of the sport as well as your ability to dream up a different angle. "I want ideas I can't think of on my own," Cohen encourages. "Give me something that is outside the realm of what we do. A lot of writers send queries that say, 'I just skied Steamboat Springs and I'd love to do a feature on it.' Well, so would 15 other writers who have worked for us for 15 years."

To break into this market, writers need to have a unique approach backed by solid research. "Tickle me with a terrific lead," says Cohen, "and you're halfway there."

According to the executive editor, most writers don't have a strong enough angle; they dash off queries without taking the time to make the writing titillating. They also have to be willing to break into the news section to earn the right to a feature.

"Like anything else, you've got to show you have novel concepts, know the subject matter, and can work hard," he says. "Our departments are the proving ground."

Out of the dozen years Cohen has been at this magazine, he says there have been a few feature articles bought from over-the-transom submissions. And he has discovered some new writers.

The bulk of the editorial, however, is generated in house based on a major editorial planning conference held well in advance of ski season each year. Afterward, the staff sends a general letter to regular and casual contributors, outlining key areas the magazine plans to cover. "This eight-page outline is designed to stimulate thought," says Cohen. "A good 60 percent of what we do is accounted for before the season even begins."

If you earn an assignment from *Ski*, you will receive a letter up to three pages long, reviewing the salient points you should cover and suggesting sources for you to talk to for research.

How to Write for *Ski*

"Writers for *Ski* have to be avid skiers, more or less, so they can speak the language," says Cohen. "They've got to be able to know what would interest the skier and present what we call 'bar facts.' That means that if a guy in an Oklahoma bar says, 'Hey, did you know they put a bunch of T-bars in the back bowls of Vail?' the writer knows what he's talking about."

Ski captures readers with a snappy, somewhat sophisticated, in-the-know writing style. "We tend toward the wry and witty," Cohen says.

If you are on assignment for the magazine, Cohen encourages you to call when you have questions or face a stumbling block. "It's not a bad idea to send in the first few pages to see if you are on the right track," says the editor. "That shows me you are trying hard and want to make sure you give me what I really want."

Sky

600 Corporate Drive
Ft. Lauderdale, FL 33334
(305) 776-0066

Published: Monthly

Circulation: 500,000

Query: Lidia de Leon, editor

Query response time: 1 to 4 weeks

Buys: About 300 articles/stories out of approximately 3,000 unsolicited queries/manuscripts received annually

Guidelines: Available; send SASE

Rights purchased: One-time

Pays: On acceptance

Expenses: Pays phone and other miscellaneous expenses

Kill fee: 100 percent when cancellation is through no fault of writer

Rates:

Type of Article	*Word Length*	*Payment*
Major Feature	1,800 - 2,000	$500 - 700
Short Feature	1,500 - 1,700	400 - 500
News Brief	200 - 300	75 - 100
"Communique"	225	50 - 100

Sky, the in-flight magazine for Delta Air Lines, reflects the global perspective of its carrier routes. The preponderance of readers are business oriented. The majority are males between the ages of 25 and 54 who hold managerial positions. They have household incomes of approximately $75,000.

How to Slant Your Ideas to *Sky*

Editor Lidia de Leon estimates that 80 to 90 percent of the ideas in *Sky* are generated by freelancers. She has broken in many good writers and is extremely open to new talent.

"Sometimes we work on spec with new writers; other times on assignment," says de Leon. "Most of the time, our own experience with freelancers has been good. And if my experience with a writer is good, I will definitely be open to using him or her again."

One writer new to the magazine sent de Leon a query on the 100th anniversary of the Ferris wheel. "It was very charming and he did a wonderful job on the final piece," she notes.

According to de Leon, one reason the Ferris wheel story worked is that it lent itself to great art. "A combination of a wonderful story and beautiful art is unbeatable," she says.

The more international flavor your idea has, the greater its chances. A sampling of the topics *Sky* has covered include creative use of architectural glass, the debate over whether chimps can use language, the 50th anniversary of the movie "Casablanca," and an update on Europe's Formula One Grand Prix.

Each issue also looks at various destinations in such articles as: "Tokyo: In the Spirit of Edo," which covered a very charming side of the metropolis; "Taking in Tel Aviv," which explored the wide mix of diversions in Israel's cultural enclave; and "Detroit: Renewal of Renaissance," a look at how the city is reclaiming its heritage.

Here's a brief overview of the columns and departments open to freelancers:

- **Communique** presents timely news and information on the arts, consumer news, books, and destinations. "Often, they are pieces that are too limited for a feature," says de Leon. "It's the perfect place for new writers to break in."

  The department has covered Cook, Nebraska, deemed "The Best Small Town in America," the Owls Head Transportation Museum near Rockland, Maine, and an L.A. artist who infused his bank account by painting portraits of pets.

- **Finance** focuses primarily on personal finance. It covers everything from mutual funds to annuities to buying a second home. Two past columns looked at why it pays to shop around for a good insurance policy and why variable annuities may be a way of saving for the long haul.

  "We bring the topic down to a personal level," says de Leon. "However, we also run broader pieces, such as how the stock markets are developing in Eastern Europe."

- **Living** is an all-encompassing column that makes room for articles whose graphic possibilities are too limited for the feature well. Fare has included how the United States is moving toward metric standards, Russian hoteliers coming to America to learn the business, commuter marriages, and nanotechnology.

- **Managing** includes anything relevant to a manager. "Because our passengers read other business magazines, we have to

> come up with fresh angles to spark their interest," says de Leon. "We cover theoretical and practical concepts. We've done stories on networking to build long-term business relationships, the fear of not repeating or maintaining achievement, and the ISO9000 international quality standards that will be asked of companies wanting to compete with European businesses."

Sky doesn't accept travel queries, but interested freelancers are encouraged to submit for consideration a list of destinations they're equipped to handle.

How to Query *Sky*

One-page queries preferred. Send photo/art information. Submit ideas six to nine months in advance.

"Queries that strike my fancy are to the point. They grab my attention right away by presenting a fresh idea," says de Leon. "Since I've been with the magazine for a decade, you can imagine that it's a challenge to present something new to me. It's also difficult to find writers who can meet our lead time of six to nine months."

In terms of style, de Leon prefers straightforward summations of ideas. Tell her what will be in the story, whom you will use as sources, and why the angle is appropriate for *Sky*. If you can cite a few sources, all the better.

What bothers de Leon most are writers who send in queries but have not bothered to look at the magazine or its editorial guidelines. "Come to us with knowledge about this market," she says. "Tailor your query to *Sky* specifically; don't send the same proposal to 52 markets. And let me know if you are aiming your idea to one specific column. If you say it is for 'Finance' or 'Managing,' then I know you've done your homework."

If de Leon likes your proposal, she will notify you that it's under consideration and channel it to an idea file, which is divided into categories—lifestyle, sports, arts, etc. "Once a quarter, I go to these files and plan for three upcoming issues," she explains. "For each issue, I develop a mix of topics. Two to three months prior to the publication date, I assign the story. I phone first and then send a formal assignment memo that recaps the basics—deadline, word length, and slant. I also send guidelines and several issues of the magazine so the writer is well apprised of what I want."

How to Write for *Sky*

"Our dream writer," says de Leon, "is someone who gives us the perfect story at the perfect time. Good writers have a knack for coming up with great ideas and working from beginning to end in an enjoyable, seamless way. They deliver what they promise."

De Leon doesn't pigeonhole the tone of her magazine. Generally, it has a narrative, straightforward style. "There is not a lot of latitude for individuality when a writer is taking the third-person approach, so good organization is the key," she says. "We like a broad use of sources, solid research, and to have the material presented in an exhaustive way within the designated word count."

Prior to publication, the magazine provides writers an opportunity to review their story in galley form.

Smithsonian

900 Jefferson Drive
Washington, DC 20560
(202) 786-2900

Published: Monthly

Circulation: 2.4 million

Query: Marlane A. Liddell, articles editor

Query response time: 6 to 8 weeks

Buys: About 110 to 120 articles and 12 backpage humor columns out of 12,000 unsolicited queries/manuscripts received annually

Guidelines: Available; send SASE

Rights purchased: One-time NAS

Pays: On acceptance

Expenses: Pays all expenses agreed upon with story editor in advance

Kill fee: 33-1/3 percent

Rates:

Type of Article	*Word Length*	*Payment*
Major Feature	4,000 - 5,000	$2,500+
Short Feature	1,500	1,500, no kill fee
Profile	2,500	2,500

"Curiosity is the one word that can describe what all of our readers have in common," says Articles Editor Marlane Liddell. "They want to know about a variety of subjects, so they read *Smithsonian* where they can sample some aspect of the arts, history, science, and culture in virtually every issue."

Smithsonian readers are well educated and the readership percentages are equally split between men and women. The average reader is about 40 years old and falls into the upper-middle class income category. In addition to *Smithsonian,* they may subscribe to the news weeklies or a specialized magazine such as *Scientific American.*

"We seek offbeat, entertaining articles on a wide range of subjects that would interest a national audience," the editor notes. "Our readers seem to enjoy our unpredictability; they never know what to expect when they open the magazine. It is our hope that at least one or two articles in each issue will attract them to topics they haven't considered before."

How to Slant Your Ideas to *Smithsonian*

Though the subject range of the magazine reaches beyond the walls of the museums of the Smithsonian Institution, the scope of the exhibitions provides a glimpse of the variety available to visitors. The Smithsonian Institution is sometimes called the nation's "attic," and is responsible for collecting, preserving, and chronicling American history. The museum complex presents exhibits that cover everything from airplanes to political campaign buttons. A few of the more intriguing items on view include Fonzi's leather jacket, Dorothy's red shoes from *The Wizard of Oz*, a moon rock, and the inaugural gowns of the First Ladies.

"We cover any subject the Smithsonian Institution is, or should be, interested in," Liddell states. "That includes fine arts, cultural history, archaeology, physical sciences, the environment, wildlife, and international topics that fit our range of interest. However, we do represent the Institution, so we stay away from politics and current events; material that is covered by the daily press. We also cover controversial subjects that fall within our purview, particularly as they relate to the environment."

According to Liddell, the best way to get published in *Smithsonian* is to suggest a subject that doesn't seem obvious for the magazine. "The editors are well informed about upcoming art exhibitions, scientific research, and major environmental issues, so we are looking for something that surprises us, that offbeat idea that entertains us," she says. "For example, we've done a piece on a surfing museum and another on the history of mannequins."

A typical issue of *Smithsonian* carries eight to 10 features. One or two of those usually covers history; two or three science, ecology, wildlife, etc.; and the others art, generally to coincide with art exhibitions at the Smithsonian, or other major museums and galleries.

A sampling of articles from one issue includes "Taking the Wal-Mart Cure in Viroquo, Wisconsin," a description of the strong medicine it took to make this town's economy healthier; "The Time is Right to See Matisse," a preview of a showing at New York's Museum of Modern Art; "Croquet: A Civilized Way to Whack Your Pals," a discussion of why this venerable game is more than child's play; and "A Good Frog Is Hard to Find," a discussion of the mysterious disappearance of amphibians in many areas.

Smithsonian readers enjoy profiles, so most issues offer one or two. "We look for someone whose contribution has made a difference in our lives," Liddell remarks, "but they don't have to be well known or elderly. We've featured a guitar maker, a fossil-tracks paleontologist, and a primatologist who has rehabilitated lab chimps to the wild."

One profile looked at a New York couple (he was a postal worker, she a librarian) who mined New York's lofts and small galleries for 30 years collecting 2,000 art works mostly by minimalists and conceptual artists. Now they've pledged their collection to the National Gallery of Art.

The back page of the magazine is devoted to a short humorous essay. "It is difficult to tell from a query whether or not the subject will work, so we need the full 750- to 800-word piece," says Liddell. "It should be amusing and genial; a mini-essay rather than a one-joke list of anecdotes. The best ones concern subjects that deal with an aspect of society that strikes the author as odd, funny, or worth musing about."

Another section open to freelancers is book reviews. "Send in samples of book reviews you've written so the book review editor can evaluate your interests and capabilities," explains Liddell.

None of the magazine's monthly columns are open to freelance writers.

How to Query *Smithsonian*

One- to two-page queries preferred; if available, include photo/illustration possibilities; query six months in advance for seasonal material.

"Your proposal should sell me on your idea and provide compelling reasons why *Smithsonian* should cover the subject," Liddell advises. "It's also important to convince me that you should be the person to write the article. I need to be able to evaluate how you will treat the subject and whether you can write a 4,000- to 5,000-word narrative in a stylish manner. It is always helpful to send writing samples and/or clips.

"All freelance writers send written proposals whether or not they have written for us before," continues Liddell. "The only exceptions are writers commissioned by an editor on a subject the editor has come up with."

Liddell emphasizes that it is essential to study the magazine carefully before you query. "Look at the type of pieces we run and tailor your query to us," she says. "It takes time, but it could prove worth the effort. We may take an obvious subject and put our own angle on it. For example, when we ran an article on St. John the Divine, it wasn't about the architecture of the building. We covered a 'year in the life' of the community within the walls of the cathedral and the neighborhood that surrounds it."

All unsolicited queries are evaluated; even a writer turned down receives a rejection letter. "If we like what a writer sends us but we can't use it for some reason, we tell them specifically why," says Liddell. "If you get that kind of response, consider it as encouragement."

Half of the magazine is devoted to photography and illustrations, so it is helpful to mention the visual possibilities in your query.

"If we decide to commission the writer for an article, we have what I call a 'writer-friendly' contract that spells out the details of what an editor wants in an article," according to Liddell.

Scheduling an article can be unpredictable. There is always a balance of subjects in each issue, so depending on the backlog, or timeliness of a topic, scheduling can vary from a few months up to a year.

How to Write for *Smithsonian*

"Writers frequently make the mistake of thinking that writing for a magazine called *Smithsonian* means they must be formal or academic in their writing style," says Liddell. "They are wrong. All of our articles are anecdotal, narrative in style, and tell a story in an entertaining way."

There is not just one *Smithsonian* voice. "We like to run a variety of writing styles to give pace to each issue," says Liddell. "Even if I have to rewrite or heavily edit a piece, I try to preserve as much of the writer's original wording as possible."

Liddell says if an article misses the point, the writer is always given the first chance to rewrite it.

The final draft of a manuscript turned into this magazine must be accompanied by an annotated copy that clearly explains the writer's sources. (See Chapter 6 in Part I, Using the Library to Your Advantage, for more information on annotation.)

"Each article goes through an elaborate research process," says Liddell. "Every word is checked and every fact verified before the piece ever goes to press. We have to be ready to stand behind everything we publish. And, since we represent the Institution we feel a strong responsibility to be correct."

Snow Country

5520 Park Avenue
Trumbull, CT 06611
(203) 373-7253

Published: 8 times a year; January to August, bimonthly; September to December, monthly

Circulation: 460,000

Query: Ron Rudolph, senior editor

Query response time: 4 weeks

Buys: About 25 to 50 articles out of hundreds of unsolicited queries/manuscripts received annually

Guidelines: Available; send SASE

Rights purchased: First NAS

Pays: On acceptance

Expenses: Pays items if reasonable and approved in advance

Kill fee: 10 to 25 percent

Rates:

Type of Article	*Word Length*	*Payment*
Major Feature	1,200	$600 - 1,200
Department Feature	800	400 - 600
"Mountain Ear"	150 - 250	25 - 75
"Snow Country Store"	200	75 - 150

Snow Country skiers have been at their sport for an average of 16 years and are interested in year-round mountain living as well as snow sports. Nearly three-quarters rank themselves as advanced skiers or better and they take day- and week-long ski trips totalling as much as a month of skiing in the winter.

The subscribers (of whom 70 percent are male and 30 percent are female) are well educated, the majority holding at least one degree, and are financially capable of maintaining their sports activities. Their median household income is $62,000, with an average net worth of $228,000. They are slightly older than the readers of *Ski* and *Skiing*, the magazine's closest competitors. *Snow Country* readers are nearly 40 years old.

How to Slant Your Ideas to *Snow Country*

"*Snow Country* is a year-round publication," says Robert J. LaMarche, managing editor. "Since we have two summer issues, we can cover mountain biking, climbing, and offer a scenic-drive issue."

Ron Rudolph, senior editor, adds, "We're broader than *Ski* and *Skiing* which are more concerned with turning left and right on the mountain. Our readers already understand that basic technique. *Snow Country* is a more overall mountain sports and lifestyle magazine.

"Mountain living is quite important in the magazine," Rudolph continues. "We publish articles on what kind of house to build in snow country, how to take your business to snow country, and what items craftspeople are making in the mountains."

The following columns and topical areas are open to freelance contributors:

- **Back page** items require a good photograph, usually supplied by a professional. The short pieces offer a snippet of mountain or skiing life like the article on snow-grooming devices that, instead of being used to compress snow, are now being employed to build moguls, children's areas, and intermediate-level rolls.

- **Environmental/political** pieces concerning mountain living are welcome at *Snow Country*. The editors aren't afraid of a little controversy here and there. For example, a feature on wood stoves made the point that although most mountain homeowners are attracted to quaintness of the stoves, smoke can pollute mountain valleys when air inversions occur. By weaving in personalities and plenty of quotes, the article noted that various mountain towns had to regulate their stove usage in order to maintain local air quality. Another environmental piece told of the possible noise pollution caused by heli-skiing—a daring sport in which skiers are dropped from a helicopter in the hope of finding untouched snow.

- **Mountain Ear** is a section of short, quirky pieces—one or two paragraphs—that relate obscure and often humorous mountain-related items. Many of the pieces are gleaned from resort papers and written in house. But the editors are happy to see your contributions. (Submit the entire manuscript.) One piece, for instance, told about an executive who sued a resort hotel for removing carpeting without warning, causing him to trip and hurt his ankle. He claimed the injury prevented him from entertaining skiing clients.

- **Profiles** are of people who have made the move to the mountains and continue their profession from there. One piece was about a man who publishes a travel newsletter from Sun Valley; another featured a man who decided he could conduct his business involving 28 companies in the former Soviet Union just as well from Vail as from New York City. LaMarche notes that the magazine is always looking for people to profile. "They don't have to be millionaires," he says. "We're interested in the fascinating people who decide to work by FAX, modem, and mail from mountain dream homes rather than staying in the city."
- **Snow Country Store** publishes two or three featurettes per issue about artisans who work in the mountains by creating handmade goods. The distinction, according to Rudolph, is the craft they sell, whether it is sculpture, art, stained glass, or leather goods.

"Datebook" and "Travel Watch" are primarily written in house. "Follow Me" is written by ski instructors and other accomplished athletes and is often ghost-written by freelance writers. Many, though not all, of the equipment, automotive, real estate, and resort articles are written by contributing editors.

How to Query *Snow Country*

Will accept full manuscripts, although one-page queries are preferred. Do not send photos or art, but mention their availability. Submit seasonal material 6 to 12 months in advance.

"There's no reason why the lead of your query should be different from the lead of your eventual story," says Rudolph. "I like to see the lead and a sample paragraph in the query—get to the point quickly."

LaMarche adds, "Since we feature people in nearly everything we publish, it helps if the writer weaves in something about who is involved in the story and whether it is a technique piece or a profile."

How to Write for *Snow Country*

Many of the lengthy articles in this magazine are written by people associated professionally with skiing or mountain living. There are several contributing editors, as well as a host of ski instructors, Olympians, and others to whom the magazine looks for technical articles.

Your best chances of selling to *Snow Country* are with the shorter pieces and the more unusual articles the editors may not have concocted. For instance, one writer won an assignment for a piece on where to soak in snow country—reviewing the hot springs and spas in cold places.

"Most writers are from mountain areas and are familiar with the type of recreation they write about," LaMarche says. "Whether it is skiing, mountain biking, or something else, the writer needs to know the mountains."

If you receive an assignment, an editor will call you, then follow up with a letter that serves as a contract. The editor may give directions about the angle or people to interview if the magazine has sources in a particular mountain area. Articles nearly always go back for one rewrite and, occasionally, for a second. Pieces are killed only when they have been worked on so much or for so long that they have lost their punch or timeliness.

Spirit

P.O. Box 619640
DFW Airport
Dallas, TX 75261-9640
(817) 967-1804

Published: Monthly

Circulation: 200,000

Query: John Clark, editor

Query response time: 1 to 2 weeks

Buys: About 5 articles/stories out of approximately 3,600 unsolicited queries/manuscripts received annually

Guidelines: Available; send SASE

Rights purchased: First NAS

Pays: On acceptance

Expenses: Pays 15 percent of story fee

Kill fee: 15 percent of story fee

Rates:

Type of Article	*Word Length*	*Payment*
Major Feature	3,000	$1,800 - 2,000
Department	1,700	800 - 1,000
"Omnibus"	300 - 400	200

"To tap the vitality of life with stories that capture the unconventional spirit of Southwest Airlines."

This is the mission of *Spirit,* the magazine of Southwest Airlines. It is published by AA Magazine Publications, which also publishes *American Way*, the magazine of American Airlines.

"We are a general interest magazine that features contemporary subject matter," says Editor John Clark. "We don't publish fiction, poetry, or history."

The Southwest Airlines passengers who turn the pages of this magazine are between the ages of 35 and 55. The majority are male (54 percent), with a median household income of $103,800.

"Our readers work hard and play hard," Clark says. "In some ways, they have distinctively different tastes from *American Way* readers. They're a little looser—for example, they're more likely to own a pick-up truck than a Lincoln Town Car.

How to Slant Your Ideas to *Spirit*

As a general interest magazine, *Spirit* seeks ideas in a wealth of areas—adventure travel, arts, business, culture, fitness, health, lifestyle, and technology.

"Our basic job is to be entertaining enough to draw people into the story, and informative enough to give them something they can take away," says Clark. "The information we provide can't be too obvious or simplistic. And there's got to be a solid hook—a reason for them to care about the subject right now. In addition, we want to make sure that our articles are as far out in front of a trend as possible."

No matter what the topic, your article has to include people if you want to add this market to your list of credits. "People are interested in other people," says Clark.

"I like first-person narrative, but it has to make sense in the overall context of the piece," says Clark. "It must fit the concept of the story." Sample first-person essays include "River of Rainbows," a reminiscence about a father-son fishing trip in the lush hills of the Arkansas Ozarks and "The Aha! Moment," which described a visit to a celebrated Arizona health spa where movie stars, business wizards, and everyday "sluggards" try to regain control of their bodies and guide them to physical perfection. Other features were "Want Ads," a piece that took an offbeat look at some of the things people might have envisioned as they examined the classifieds; "Home Away from Home," which looked at the socially significant work of homeless shelters; and "Head 'Em Up," a realistic piece that gave readers a glimpse of a week on a working cattle ranch—*City Slickers* it was not!

Celebrity profiles contribute to cover-story fodder. "The Thing" profiled stand-up comic and TV star Jerry Seinfeld and his passion to make people laugh. "Talked Out" looked at the reasons why comedian Dennis Miller's late night talk show didn't make it. Other cover stories have featured country music star Clint Black, Cuban-born movie star Andy Garcia, and mega-restauranteur Norman Brinker.

Spirit's travel pieces are not destination-oriented or travel guide stories. Rather, they transport the reader into another world through quality storytelling techniques. "One article we did was about a man going to the woods outside Chicago where there were supposed to have been werewolf sightings," says Clark. "He talked about what it was like being there and interviewed people who had supposedly seen the werewolves, to bring a sense of adventure as well as entertainment to the piece."

The magazine's departments cover the same broad spectrum of general interest topics as the feature well, but in a shorter format. The column topics rotate each issue, and the following are open to freelancers:

- **Business** tackles different business and personal finance topics. One column discussed how a fast-growing sector of the economy succeeds in business without ever leaving home. Another took readers inside a tiny San Francisco shop called The Universe of You, which sells machines that mechanically induce meditation.
- **Eats** has featured articles such as "Haute Tamales," a look at the Chicago trend toward menus based on dishes from the interior of Mexico, and "Cactus Confidential," a close-up on how cactus-fruit margaritas have made the prickly pear a new cash crop. "Don't Talk, Just Chew" described how Southwestern-cuisine chefs are exploring new territory by borrowing recipes from Italian, French, Russian, and even Oriental cooking.
- **Health** brings readers up-to-date on topics such as how botanical adventurers bio-prosect for plants that may help conquer major diseases, and how new research hints at a possible method for preventing noncontact knee injuries to high-risk athletes.
- **Music** has brought readers profiles of both itinerant singer-songwriter James McMurtry and up-and-coming Austin musician Chris Wall.
- **Omnibus** covers leisure information for the business traveler. It has reviewed the National Bowling Hall of Fame and Museum in St. Louis and the Liberace Museum in Las Vegas. In addition, the column has given an update on where to hear accordion and fiddle music and where to learn Cajun dancing in New Orleans. Other articles have presented suggestions for how to stay fit on the road and how to infuse personal style into your wardrobe.
- **Sports** topics range from Phil Mickelson, the hottest young pro on the PGA tour, to an intimate interview with Dave Wannstedt, the coach of the Chicago Bears.
- **Technology** has looked at NASA's use of microelectronics to tune into the microwave region of the electromagnetic spectrum and the new generation of digital audio recording formats.

- **TV** profiled tele-therapist David Viscott, whose television "group therapy" has gained a cult following in Los Angeles. It also took readers behind the scenes of HBO's hit comedy series "Dream On."
- **Wheels** has taken readers to the Jim Hall Kart Racing School, where more than 13,000 students have earned their Go-Kart racing stripes, and given passengers a look into the world of concept cars built to demonstrate design and engineering ideas.

All other departments are closed to freelancers.

How to Query *Spirit*

One page preferred. Do not send photo/art information.

Clark cautions writers that the outlook at *Spirit* may not be as good as at other magazines. Most stories are assigned to writers who are regular contributors.

If you do send a query, you'll pique this editor's attention if the idea has a news hook and matches the focus of the publication. Your work samples must be comparable to what the magazine publishes, and your résumé should show an impressive track record. If your idea doesn't fit but your experience and writing style do, the editor may call you to pursue an idea the staff has developed.

Clark describes how one new writer caught his eye with a great idea for the "Wheels" column. The query suggested a piece about a Santa Fe man who had invented a suspension system for a motorcycle that was eventually purchased by Yamaha. "There are a few things that made that story work for me," the editor recalls. "First, the writer sent clips I liked. Second, he gave me plenty of lead time so that I could publish the story right when the motorcycle was released to the market. Finally, I appreciated the underlying theme of a modern-day lone inventor who was succeeding in a world that has moved away from such a philosophy."

That brings us to an important point. All queries for this market should clearly spell out the theme of the story and how the writer intends to approach it. Don't just give the subject.

The go-ahead writers receive from Clark is typically a telephone call, followed up by a short note outlining the assignment, and a contract.

How to Write for *Spirit*

"We look for writers with a strong sense of narrative flow," says Clark. "They can inject fiction style into a nonfiction piece. They're good storytellers as well as good reporters."

Anecdotal leads that put the reader in the middle of the scene or in the midst of the action are preferable over a fact-based newspaper-style start. The first paragraph or two should unfold the theme in an intriguing way that will continue throughout the piece.

Clark is not crazy about a story heavy in quotes. He looks for a reader to interpret the information using good observation and descriptive skills of the people and the surroundings. Facts should be interspersed in the action, which is used to move the story along.

"If any problem at all arises when you are writing the piece—the theme changes or your direction is different—call," Clark encourages writers. "Don't just write the story."

When you turn in your final draft, send along a source list that includes names and phone numbers for fact-checking purposes.

Sport

8490 Sunset Boulevard
Los Angeles, CA 90069
(310) 854-2265

Published: Monthly

Circulation: 800,000

Query: Cameron Benty, editor

Query response time: 6 weeks

Buys: About 75 articles/stories out of approximately 500 unsolicited queries/manuscripts received annually

Guidelines: None available

Rights purchased: First NAS

Pays: On acceptance

Expenses: Pays some travel

Kill fee: 25 percent

Rates:

Type of Article	*Word Length*	*Payment*
Major Feature	1,500 - 2,500	$750 - 1,250
Short Feature	700 - 2,000	350 - 1,500
News Brief	100 - 500	50 - 250
"One on One"	1,200 - 1,300	600 - 650
"Sport Talk"	100 - 700	100 - 350

Sport is a monthly sports magazine for professional and amateur athletes. Rather than giving recaps of what happened in the world of sports last week, this magazine gives previews and predictions of what will happen this month, next month, and next year. It offers the ultimate sports aficionado in-depth profiles, solid investigative reporting, and lively features about action on and off the field. All that is tempered with humor, gossip, trivia, and dramatic sports photography.

Who are the people making sports such a major part of their lives? It's no surprise that more than 87 percent are men; the median age is 33. A little more than half are married, 44 percent have attended or graduated from college, and the average household income is $38,700.

"We are not a sports fan magazine," says Editor Cameron Benty. "We are geared toward the fan who has an interest in a particular sport. Generally, our readers are in their 30s, although our demographics reach widely into the 60s and the teens. Our photography shows players in interesting active situations."

How to Slant Your Ideas to *Sport*

"We attempt to be as high-impact as possible," says Benty. "Nothing about sporting events these days is subtle in any way, and we try to emulate that in the magazine, both editorially and visually," he says. "Our pages are action-packed."

Benty encourages writers to stick to topics surrounding baseball, football, and basketball. Hockey, motorsports, golf, tennis, and boxing are typically covered by staff writers or regular contributors.

The magazine uses a blend of interviews, season previews, player and team evaluations, and behind-the-scene reports on both professional and collegiate sports. Freelancers have the best chance of selling sports profiles, but it takes more than gaining access to a well-known sports figure to land a story here.

"The key question a writer has to ask is, 'Will this person make interesting reading?'" advises Benty. "Most of the people we cover are interesting because they have something controversial to say. Hank Aaron, all-time home run record holder, for example, is not newsworthy for his baseball efforts but for his outspoken criticism of baseball's hiring practices. We asked him why he only hired white managers even when he had a chance to do otherwise. Those kind of interviews make for interesting reading."

The magazine often does comparison question/answer articles. In separate interviews, it asks two people who are having problems with each other questions about their difficulties. "In interviews with basketball players Patrick Ewing and Michael Jordan, it was not so much what they said about each other but what people were saying about them," explains Benty. "The coach for the Chicago Bulls was saying Ewing, who plays for the New York Knicks, was a loser—not a nice thing to say. In this case, Jordan didn't agree with his coach, so we gave him a chance to respond. We also asked Ewing to tell us how being called a failure affected his game."

Just after four-time Super Bowl champion and future Hall of Fame quarterback Joe Montana was traded to the Kansas City Chiefs, *Sport* did simultaneous interviews about the controversy between Montana and San Francisco 49ers quarterback Steve Young. Young took over for Montana while he was injured and was named Super Bowl Most Valuable Player.

What Benty wants most from freelancers is the ability to tackle ideas from a regional perspective. "If you live in Chicago, give me news from your backyard," he says. "We pretty much have L.A. and

New York covered, but we don't have stringers in other areas of the country. Help us get stories from other areas."

Three times a year, *Sport* adds an extra 60 pages of "Bonus Section," which opens up more room for stories. Benty groups stories together by topic—baseball, basketball, or football—and directs freelance ideas into the "Bonus Section" if they warrant coverage.

"We bought one great over-the-transom piece from a writer who took a trip on a decrepit bus with the minor league ball club, The Salt Lake City Trappers," Benty said. "He chronicled what he called the 'road trip from hell,' as the team traveled from Salt Lake City to Alberta and back again. It fit perfectly into our '1993 Baseball Preview Bonus Section.'"

The following departments are open to freelancers:

- **One on One** is a profile that draws the reader as close to the personality as possible. The column used to be called "Beer's With . . ." because the whole point is to write the story so the reader feels like he's taken the person out for a pizza and a few beers. Today, the name is different but the mentality is the same.

  A feature on the Bulls' power forward Horace Grant showed how this basketball player doesn't sugarcoat his words when he speaks his mind about being kept out of the offensive flow.

  "We assign most of these features to writers we know, but we are willing to listen to freelancers who have great sports profiles to offer," says Benty.

- **Sport Talk** is a catch-all for sports news, thoughts, and a touch of humor. "Give us a line on photography if you have it,"says Benty. Topics covered have been a short Q&A with Michael Jordan on what it meant to turn 30; an update on Chicago Cubs center fielder Willie Wilson's successful baseball career, after coming back from a stint in jail for cocaine abuse; and a "turn-about is fair play" story, after Deion Sanders dowsed CBS TV's Tim McCarver with ice water three times during the World Series, describing all of the practical jokes McCarver played during his days with the St. Louis Cardinals.

"Motor Sport," "Sport Beat," and "Sportscope" are written in house or by regular contributors.

How to Query *Sport*

One-page query with multiple ideas preferred. Send photo/ art information.

A bulleted list of various one-paragraph descriptions of story ideas is the type of query Benty prefers. The editor places all of the ideas that pique his interest onto a computer bulletin board for the rest of the staff to review. Decisions on which queries to pursue are made at regular staff meetings.

When *Sport* decides to give a writer a chance, an editor will call to discuss the story and ask for a longer description of the direction it will take. Upon receipt of the fleshed-out idea, the editor will write a letter listing the elements that should be covered and will send it along with a formal contract.

How to Write for *Sport*

Entertaining and informative are the two main descriptors of *Sport* journalism. Since most stories center on sports celebrities, writers must be sure to secure details about the athlete's career as well as to discover key things in the individual's personal life that can paint an intriguing picture.

"It's truly entertainment that we go after," says Benty. "We are fairly loose and conversational. Statistics are woven into the copy; we are not looking for a sports biography. For example, a piece we did on Dallas Cowboys head coach Jimmy Johnson talked a little about his role in the Super Bowl and the mentality of how he picks players. But it primarily focused on his relationship with his sons and his collection of tropical fish. We wanted insights into the man."

Benty asks writers to turn in a source list that includes names and phone numbers of persons interviewed. "Our fact checkers check quotes when they can, especially if they have the potential for being scandalous or libelous," the editor explains.

Sports Afield

250 West 55th Street
New York, NY 10019
(212) 649-4000

Published: Monthly

Circulation: 530,000

Query: Tom Paugh, editor-in-chief
"Almanac": Frank Golad, associate editor

Query response time: 4 to 8 weeks

Buys: About 60 articles out of approximately 2,500 unsolicited queries/manuscripts received annually

Guidelines: Available; send SASE

Rights purchased: First NAS

Pays: On acceptance; "The Almanac" and fillers pay on publication

Expenses: Negotiable; generally pays some travel

Kill fee: Negotiable

Rates:

Type of Article	*Word Length*	*Payment*
Major Feature	1,500 - 2,000	$800 - 1,500
True Adventures	1,500 - 2,500	800+
Short Feature	500 - 1,000	500 - 1,000
News Brief	200 - 300	200
"The Almanac"		200
One-page Fillers		500

The majority (about 88 percent) of *Sports Afield* readers are male and about 40 years old. Nearly 72 percent are married, and 45 percent have children. Almost three-quarters of the readers are employed and homeowners; they make about $35,000 a year.

Tom Paugh, editor-in-chief, believes that *Sports Afield* has two kinds of readers—the fall reader, who is interested in deer hunting, and the spring reader who is fascinated by fishing, particularly bass and trout fishing. "We prefer to think that both the spring and fall readers are well-rounded sportsmen, interested in all aspects of the outdoors," he says. Eighty percent of *Sports Afield*'s half a million circulation is from subscriptions, so many hunters are interested in fishing, and vice versa.

How to Slant Your Ideas to *Sports Afield*

"To get our attention, be familiar with the magazine," Paugh says. Serious freelancers may request the magazine's editorial calendar from the advertising department. Contributors can expect most issues to feature a special section—deer hunting in August, game hunting in the fall, waterfowl hunting in November, and fishing and wild turkey hunting in the spring.

"We've also changed *Sports Afield* so that it is a read-through magazine, with almost no stories that 'jump' to elsewhere in the book," says Paugh.

A good way to break into this market is with survival and nature pieces. "We're very interested in back-to-nature stories, like, 'What would you do if you were lost in the woods?'" the editor says.

In addition, Paugh is looking for sustained true-life adventures that preferably take place in the United States. Though the stories vary greatly, they should be suspenseful, contain noteworthy information, and run approximately 2,500 words.

The magazine also runs features on wildlife artistry. "Creating Knives From Stones," offered information on the materials and techniques used to shape decorative and useful tools.

Back-of-the-book items are referred to as "flexible pages." These fillers supplement the advertisements that appear on those pages. "It's a way for us to get fishing pieces into our hunting issues," says Paugh. "The Barbless Hook Ethic" was a venue for readers to tell how barb bending makes catch and release easier. "Improve Your Wingshooting" showed how practicing your eye motion and follow-through helps increase your hits.

The following areas are open to freelancers:

- **The Almanac** features 60 short features each month, so this is a good place to break in. A past "Almanac" included tips on how to see game before it sees you. "When you contribute to "The Almanac" you create a connection to the magazine," says Paugh. "If you have an idea later for another section, you can ask the editor of 'The Almanac' to whom he thinks it should be pitched."
- **Backcountry** is a back-of-the-book essay written primarily by freelancers. According to Paugh, it has evolved into a reservoir of nostalgia—for instance, a father might share his memories and feelings about things he and his son did on their first hunting or fishing trip. "The Fish Hunters" told of one man's determination to catch a fish and his encounter with two young brothers. "The Rack" was a father's recollection of his six-year-old son's initiation to hunting.

- **Reports Afield** carries the subhead "Conservation and Outdoor News" and occasionally contains freelance items. One piece discussed the hardships that Pacific coast sea mammals face as a result of the shifting currents that affect weather worldwide.

"A Hunter's View," "Ecowatch," "Gundogs," and other front-of-the-book columns are written by regular columnists or the in-house staff.

How to Query *Sports Afield*

One-to two-page queries preferred. Send any photo/art information when relevant; query a year in advance for seasonal material.

"When you query, be clear about where you think your idea might fit. Do you imagine it as a feature, action adventure, or memoir?" Paugh asks. "We have freelancers who work with us on a fairly regular basis because they send their seasonal ideas far enough in advance, and they know where their ideas belong. Don't worry about querying too far ahead; if we're interested in your proposal, but don't have room for it in the next issue, we'll assign it and tell you when we want to see it," the editor says. If you're unknown to this market your query needs to separate you from the pack. Its presentation and the inclusion of clips give the editorial staff a feel for your talent.

The magazine has a couple of readers on staff to do a first review of all queries. They are responsible for distributing queries to the various editors, but it will help if you address your letter to an appropriate editor when possible.

How to Write for *Sports Afield*

"It's typical for new contributors to do at least one revision, if not a second one for fine tuning," says Paugh. An editor will explain to the writer exactly what needs to be done to make the piece work. It's not uncommon for new writers to be asked to work on spec, but kills are rare after an article has been assigned. If an editor holds on to a submission for any length of time, he'll generally go back to the author to see if the idea is still newsworthy. "Very often, we ask a writer to do additional work, or to add a sidebar to the material already proposed in the query," Paugh says.

Tennis

5520 Park Avenue
Trumbull, CT 06611
(203) 373-7242

Published: Monthly

Circulation: 800,000

Query: Donna Doherty, editor

Query response time: 6 to 8 weeks

Buys: About 10 articles out of approximately 100+ unsolicited queries/manuscripts received annually

Guidelines: None available

Rights purchased: All

Pays: On publication

Expenses: None paid for unsolicited material; expenses for assigned articles are negotiated

Kill fee: 33-1/3 to 50 percent

Rates:

Type of Article	*Word Length*	*Payment*
Major Feature	1,000	$800 - 2,000
Short Feature	850	400 - 850
"My Point"	700	500 - 800
"Passing Shots"	100 - 300	25 - 125
"Tennis Tips"	200	75
"Winners"	700	400 - 800

Tennis is an all-around service magazine for the hard core recreational tennis player and tennis fan. The readership is just slightly more weighted toward men, with a split between the sexes of 53 to 47 percent. The average age is 36. *Tennis* readers are upscale, with a median household income of $49,273.

"Our readers are avid tennis players who are on the courts three times a week," says Editor Donna Doherty. "They are people who can afford to go to pro tournaments and take tennis vacations."

How to Slant Your Ideas to *Tennis*

The only tennis magazine on the newsstand (at time of publication), this book offers a rich mix of instruction, fitness, travel, and profiles. It shows readers how to improve their game with tips from the pros, and gives the latest insight into the lives of professional tennis players.

"The problem with freelance contributions is that people take an incident that happened to them and don't realize we just got 10 similar submissions," says Doherty. "If you suggest the idea, 'I got to hit with Bjorn Borg,' you've got to make it read like no other article about an amateur having a chance to hit with a pro. And that's tough to do unless you are a really fine writer."

The tennis instruction in this magazine comes from a pro who has been around the court a few times, including superstars such as Chris Evert, Billie Jean King, and Stan Smith, and coaches like Tim Gullikson and Vic Braden. Premier sports psychologist James Loehr, Ph.D., who has worked with many professional athletes, gives insight into the inner game of tennis.

"You don't usually get mental toughness training from a club lesson," says Doherty. "This is the one place tennis players can turn to for that kind of information."

Equipment coverage also scores big with readers. Just like people buy *Car and Driver* to see what's hot in automobiles, tennis players turn to *Tennis* to find exactly which racquet, strings, shoes, and clothes are right for them.

"We are considered the Bible of tennis racquets," explains the editor. "Each March, we publish a compendium of 75 racquets, and in May we cover about 100 shoes."

Though many writers propose articles featuring instruction ideas or profiles of tennis pros, Doherty doesn't encourage those kinds of stories. "Freelancers are hard-pressed to come up with an original, compelling idea that competes against the magazine's panel of experts," the editor explains. "They don't have the kind of access to the pros that the magazine does."

Doherty actually dissuades writers from approaching this magazine in general, simply because of a lack of space in the book. But if you're a writing tennis buff itching to serve up a winning piece, think grass roots tennis coverage—or, in other words, human interest.

The editor cautions that human interest doesn't mean the types of letters she receives regularly about how tennis made someone fight the battle. "Again, that's interesting but not unique," she says.

"However, one writer sold us a great story about a teaching pro who, on his way to his certification test, had a terrible car accident and lost his leg," recalls the editor. "It was a long road back, but he ultimately got that certification, playing with a prosthesis. We also ran a fun piece about Lars Ulrich, the drummer who founded the heavy metal group Metallica and is the son of Torben Ulrich, a really bizarre, well-known tennis player of the '60s."

The politics of tennis and the inside business of the game are other genres here, but Doherty says those pieces are typically more popular with the staff than they are with readers. Successful articles in these areas have included a piece on the heavy recruitment of foreign players into United States college teams, and another about the battle of tennis at a big-time football school.

Travel articles are big with this crowd but, except for regional ideas which Doherty would like to see, most travel remains the turf of two frequent contributors and staff writers. Doherty recalls when the magazine sent a writer to Wimbledon on a ridiculously low daily rate. "He related his travels and travails as he used his ingenuity to get into the matches, since you can't purchase tickets," says Doherty.

If you are a freelancer who has a compelling idea coupled with tennis expertise, you may consider submitting ideas to these four departments:

- **My Point** is an opinion column typically written by staffers, tennis beat writers from other media, and players' agents or coaches. But if you are a writer with an opinion on the game and you can articulate it and present it well, try lobbying your idea here. One column, "Award Style and Even the Score," rallied around the idea of awarding extra points in tennis for the way you win a point, such as by displaying a special aesthetic quality, uniqueness, or even some abnormal danger in your stroke.
- **Passing Shots** is the front-of-the-book news section, which covers the pro tour, grassroots tennis, and industry and amateur happenings. Readers sometimes contribute quirky stories, hometown tennis events with a bizarre bent, or fun photos. Most photos, however, are from pro tour photographers.
- **Tennis Tips** is completely freelance written, but only open to certified teaching pros. There has to be a strong visual gimmick to sell a tip—such as imagining attacking a fencer when you're at the net. These one-page instruction pieces usually contain 40 lines of text and cover a certain stroke or strategy that could fix a game.
- **Winners** focuses on people who are doing something great for the sport of tennis or using tennis as a way to share a piece of humanity. An outstanding column Doherty recalls told about a young Black women's tennis team in Chicago that fought

some tough odds to achieve a winning record. Another told about a Chinese-American boy who blew away the crowd at a junior's tournament talent show by demonstrating that he was not only a master on the court, but at the piano keyboard as well.

"Scoreboard" is closed to freelancers.

How to Query *Tennis*

One page preferred; do not send photo/art information.

"I like a query letter that shows me the writer's style," says Doherty. "I know they are hard to write—in fact, the query letter is probably the hardest letter anyone has to write to get someone's attention. You must have a clear idea of what you will do in the story and be able to express it in concise terms. You've got to sell your idea quickly. If you come across as a writer who beats around the bush, we'll consider you as someone who never gets to the point in your articles. I also must see samples of work."

What Doherty doesn't want is writers calling her to ask her for an answer. "It takes us six to eight weeks to get back to freelancers," she says. "If we really like something, we'll hop on it and you'll hear from us right away. We don't let anything good fall by the wayside. But no editor wants to be pestered. The squeaky wheel may get the grease, but it can also turn an editor against you."

How to Write for *Tennis*

First and foremost, to write for this magazine you must have a passion for tennis or an interest in the people playing the game, whether amateur or pro. With that understanding, the ability to craft a quality story comes in a close second in prerequisites.

"Fine writers have an eye for seeing life from a different slant and they bring that to their work," says Doherty. "They have a unique combination of observational and expository writing skills.

"But don't try to write the great American novel if you don't have the talent," she continues. "In such a case, it's better to be simple and plain but get your point across."

Notes and a source list must be turned in with your completed manuscript for the magazine's fact checker to refer to. "Inaccuracies in copy make me crazy," says Doherty. "If the fact checker finds lots of mistakes, we will not look forward to using that writer again. Accuracy is basic, but you'd be surprised how often it doesn't occur."

Upscale

P.O. Box 10798
Atlanta, GA 30310
(404)758-7467

Published: 9 times a year

Circulation: 235,000

Query: Sheila Bronner, editor-in-chief

Query response time: 3 months

Buys: About 600 articles/stories out of approximately 1,000 unsolicited queries/manuscripts received annually

Guidelines: Available; send SASE

Rights purchased: All for one year

Pays: On publication

Expenses: Pays depending on assignment

Kill fee: None

Rates:

Type of Article	*Word Length*	*Payment*
"Special Feature"	1,800 - 2,400	$200 - 400
"Regular Feature"	1,000 - 1,800	150 - 200
Department/News Brief	500 - 1,000	75 - 150

"The Successful Black Magazine" is the subhead for *Upscale,* a publication which defines its purpose as lifting the self-esteem of its readers. Established in 1989, the magazine provides a forum for insightful exploration of the Black experience. As a resource for empowerment of the African American community, *Upscale* is dedicated to cultural awareness, family commitment, and a can-do mental attitude.

"What makes us unique is that we are a positive publication," says Editor-in-Chief Sheila Bronner. "Yes, there are a lot of negative things going on in the world. We address those negatives and tell readers what they can do to help turn around circumstances. While other publications talk about problems in the community, we try to offer various solutions. We also like to address the positive things people are doing.

"*Upscale* is designed for two types of people—those who are successful and those who want success," continues Bronner. "In many cases, success is determined by the way one thinks. We believe being rich or poor is a state of mind. A rich state of mind will eventually yield a rich bank account. A poor state of mind will eventually exhaust the largest bank account. We try to reach the people who know they can make it. There are a lot of people who may be on the runway to success. We offer insight and inspiration to get them airborne."

Upscale's following is divided as 61 percent female and 39 percent male. Readers range from teens to individuals in their 50s, but the median age is 31. The majority, 58 percent, are married and most, 54 percent, have children. Almost 60 percent have graduated from college; the average household income is $31,500.

How to Slant Your Ideas to *Upscale*

Upscale is dedicated to generating upward mobility within the Black community. The magazine is founded on the principle that African Americans have unlimited talent, creativity, spiritual strength, and financial ability, and is committed to analyzing contemporary concerns that affect the African American lifestyle. It dispels stereotypical myths and infuses its audience with truthful and culturally relevant information.

The publication gives its readership an exclusive glimpse into the lives of celebrities, while providing the latest news in the areas of fashion, hair care, health care, home improvement, business/financial updates, and personal and professional development. Most of all, the magazine wants to present its readers with useable information.

"Our readers are curious about their surroundings and conscious about what is going on in our world," says Bronner. "They want to make today better and the future brighter for their children. They are looking for articles to read that will show them how to make a difference."

The cover feature in the magazine is always a celebrity, the likes of Eddie Murphy, Mario Van Peebles, Wesley Snipes, Tina Turner, and Janet Jackson. Freelancers must be certain to bring out the positive aspects of the personality as well as be informative and entertaining.

Freelance submissions are also welcomed for all articles included in the section called "Special Features." "Usually, the editorial staff decides what will go into the next issue, looks for freelancers who have sent in samples, and calls them to ask if they are interested in writing for us," says Bronner.

"Special Features" covers a broad range of topics. A few headlines have included, "The New Black Family: A Return to

Tradition," "Modern Day Philanthropists: Embracing the Spirit of Charity," and "NAACP Image Awards: Honoring Our Own."

The section titled "Regular Features," is divided into main categories with one or more articles included in each. Following is a sampling of the topics covered, all of which are open to freelance submissions:

- **Beauty for Her** and **Beauty for Him** are both open to writers who can give tips on hair, style, and make-up. One piece, "Mind Over Body," told men how to use visioning and imaging to keep stress under control and maintain a healthy body and mind. A piece for women called "Cosmetically Speaking: A Colorful Hue," talked about cosmetics as color compliments.
- **Bookmark** is not often done by freelancers, but if you like to write book reviews and have an intriguing book or new release in mind, send a brief query or outline summarizing what the book is about.
- **Business Profile** features a successful businessperson or company. "We try to present what the business means to an individual, the downfalls, and the secret to success despite many downfalls," says Bronner.

  One piece centered on Bradley Backus, a senior business and estate planning consultant for Metropolitan Life Insurance in New York. Another brought readers inside information on the life of Mary-Frances Winters, an entrepreneurial woman who runs a nationally recognized public relations and research firm.
- **Fine Arts** covers music, dance, and art. "Black Organized Dance in America" talked about the difference between "Black dance" and "Blacks in dance," and the roots of African American dancers in the United States. "Opera Ebony" discussed the work of Wayne Sanders, musical director of the world-renowned opera company, Opera Ebony.
- **Food** is primarily done in house, but Bronner would like to see writers present different ideas. The recipes are targeted to health-conscious people and have included soups for the fall season, spicing up meals with cheese, and vegetarian dining.
- **Health** covers the latest research and information on health topics. Articles have included "Cholesterol: What's Soul Food Got To Do With It" and "Allergies." A piece on aroma therapy talked about how different fragrances can mitigate headaches and help you sleep and relax.
- **Home** provides helpful information for beautifying the homefront. "We want readers to pick up the magazine and

be able to use the insights, whether it's for hanging wallpaper, choosing place settings, buying antique rugs, or remodeling bathrooms," says Bronner.

- **Financial Profile** gives details on financial subjects, but in simple terms. Topics covered have included buying or refinancing a home, getting a car loan, coping with credit, or understanding the dollar side of divorce. "We try to find writers in the financial field or those who have an interest in writing about the topic," says Bronner.
- **Marketing Profile** introduces readers to new products, such as Cross Colours, a new line of clothing that took the market by storm, or African Royale hair-care products. The newer the product, the better. One feature on Hanes talked about how the company has developed a new group of hosiery colors for darker skin tones to capture the Black consumer.
- **Sports Profile** focuses on one sports figure—such as David Justice of the Atlanta Braves—or a sporting event—such as baseball or a golf tournament. Updates on the world of sports are also featured, such as in the article, "The Real Deal," which discussed what was behind the NCAA'S academic mandate.

These departments and news briefs are open to freelancers:

- **Finance News** gives readers tidbits of financial information to broaden their economic knowledge base. These shorts have included searching for a financial planner, understanding interest rates, and investing for retirement.
- **Perspective** gives writers a chance to present experiences on serious subjects in as much detail as 700 words will allow. One column discussed how having a pure, focused motive can help you complete the most formidable task with relative ease. Another discussed how every effort should be made to fortify the homefront.
- **Positively You** presents one writer's positive, uplifting experience in 700 words. One man wrote, "Divorce and Me," in which he shared his feelings about divorcing his wife—and now friend—and the learning experience it has brought him. In another story, "From Visions to Victory," a woman encouraged readers to accept the possibility of a dream coming true in order to make it a reality.
- **Sports News** are briefs on the world of sports. Coverage has included Sam Lacy's induction into the writer's wing of the Major League Baseball Hall of Fame, and two Black college

quarterbacks who were rated among the top 50 quarterbacks of the college game—at numbers 12 and 17.

- **Viewpoint** voices a writer's opinion on an issue or situation. In "Rebuilding Family Leadership," a writer espoused that role models and leaders of tomorrow will develop from the leaders within our homes today. "Reflections in an Elevator" gave a writer a chance to decry the distorted perception of African Americans in society. The essay was based on an incident that occurred when he boarded the elevator occupied by only an elderly woman. The woman looked at him, her hands began to quiver, and she collapsed to the floor, saying, "Here take my purse—just don't kill me."

"Business News," "Entertainment," "Executive Suite," "Fine Dining," "Gospel," "High Notes," "Horoscope," "Marketing News," and "Upwardly Mobile" are written in house.

How to Query *Upscale*

One-page proposal and cover letter preferred. Send photo/ art information.

"We prefer a brief letter of introduction and a summary of the idea you have in mind on the second page," says Bronner. "Samples are also very important to gauge writing style."

Bronner discourages writers from sending the entire manuscript, though many do. "It takes too long to go through them," she says.

If your idea hits the mark at this magazine, expect a call from an editor, who will discuss the scope of the piece, length, price, and due date. There are no formal contracts.

How to Write for *Upscale*

"*Upscale* is leisure-time reading. We want upbeat, lively, informative, and interesting writing that is easy to read," says Bronner. "If you are doing a health piece, steer clear of technical terms and jargon. Keep the language simple so that a high school graduate and Ph.D. can both enjoy it."

Bronner also appreciates writers who turn in a source list to facilitate fact checking.

USAir Magazine

1301 Carolina Street
Greensboro, NC 27401
(919) 378-6065

Published: Monthly

Circulation: 450,000

Query: Terri Barnes, editor

Query response time: 2 to 4 weeks

Buys: About 130 articles/stories out of approximately 2,500 unsolicited queries/manuscripts received annually

Guidelines: Available; send SASE

Rights purchased: First NAS

Pays: After acceptance, before publication

Expenses: Pays per agreement, amounts vary

Kill fee: 25 percent

Rates:

Type of Article	*Word Length*	*Payment*
Major Feature	1,800 - 2,500	$600 - 1,000
Department	1,500	400 - 600
Art Feature	800 - 1,000	400 - 600

What do readers want from a magazine when they're traveling on business? "Some say business travelers are in the work mode and want to read business articles," says *USAir Magazine* Editor Terri Barnes. "Others argue that they want a brief respite and a diversion."

USAir Magazine caters to both camps, with editorial that covers travel, business, and general interest. Those who reach for the magazine from the airplane's seatbacks are typically business people between the ages of 35 and 55. About 60 percent are male, with a median household income between $60,000 and $70,000.

USAir flies to 40 states, the District of Columbia, Puerto Rico, Bermuda, Bahamas, Canada, France, Great Britain, and Germany. Most of the magazine's copy relates to those areas.

How to Slant Your Ideas to *USAir Magazine*

The most distinguishing feature of *USAir Magazine* articles is that even the nontravel ones have a travel slant. "When we did an article on salsa, we ran a sidebar of hot food stores where readers could pick up unusual fiery tastes while traveling."

To pique the interest of this editor, make sure your idea is molded specifically for her magazine. "Show me that you know the magazine by detailing in your query why the idea fits *USAir Magazine* and, even more specifically, tell me what section of the publication you see it in," says Barnes. "I always choose a writer who streamlines an article over someone of equal ability who doesn't make the effort."

Barnes recommends that writers not categorize in-flight or travel magazines as one amorphous group. "Writers often send the same idea to 20 markets without discerning the differences between the magazines," she says. "If they would spend more time on fewer magazines, they'd probably be more effective."

To familiarize yourself with this market, take a look at the feature well. Its first story surrounds the arts, with a topic that is slightly off the beaten path and is located within the airline's flying territory. One piece, "Art Imitates Light," focused on artist Tom Christopher's New York City scenes.

"We make arts pieces into travel articles by listing exhibitions where travelers can go to see the artist's work," says Barnes.

The next feature is a profile of someone of merit. Coverage of this person should not have been overdone by the media, and the story could be about something of lesser note regarding a popular personality. Past issues have featured jockey Julie Krone, author P.D. James, and artist William Wegman. When the magazine featured actor Tony Randall, it profiled him in respect to his perhaps lesser-known work with the National Actor's Theater, not his well-known work as a celebrity.

How did the magazine go about the business of turning those profiles into travel pieces? For the jockey story, it included a sidebar on the Triple Crown as the hook. The P.D. James profile turned travel by noting that the author was coming to the United States from London for a book signing tour, and listed where readers could see her.

Among the features each month are two travel articles. One is a business traveler's guide to a particular city, written by someone intimately familiar with the area. "This piece begins with 200 to 300 words about the city, then tells where to stay, eat lunch, work out, and what to do with free time after a business meeting," Barnes says.

The other travel feature takes a narrower focus on a particular region, area, or city. Coverage has included the 200th anniversary of Paris' Louvre, Napa Valley's wine train, and how to learn your way around Bermuda.

The final well feature is open for discussion. Topics have included job performance reviews, an update on the car industry, and a guide to the spa experience.

Not all departments in *USAir Magazine* run every month. The following are open to freelance writers:

- **Destination** pieces are narrow travel articles covering specific sites in USAir routes, such as Hershey Park, Pennsylvania; Solvang, California bakeries; and Ponce, Puerto Rico.
- **Food** offers sharp, fun pieces with recipes to draw in the hungry reader. Tempting culinary delights have included wild foods (mushrooms, dandelions) and comfort foods (hot chocolate and grandma's meatloaf).
- **Health** covers how-to topics, with quoted experts if the piece is of a serious nature. Past issues have addressed biofeedback and yoga.
- **Leisure** describes ways to spend leisure time, whether it be visiting a museum or collecting souvenirs on vacation. Past issues have covered Universal Studios, Hollywood, and the opening of the Freer Gallery in Washington, D.C.
- **Sports** has ventured into rock climbing, falconry, and billiards.
- **Strategies** is a business column that offers pointers such as brushing up on office etiquette, nurturing talent in your organization, and quitting your job.

"Psychology" is written regularly by a psychologist.

How to Query *USAir Magazine*

One page or so preferred. Do not send photo/art information unless it's for the art feature.

"I prefer one-page queries, but I don't want one paragraph or 10 ideas in one letter," says Barnes. "Sending me one query a day is better than a number of ideas in one letter because I will skim the latter."

A sample lead will always catch Barnes' eye, as will a description of whom you plan to quote in your piece. "Get to the point immediately and tell me why your idea is a good fit for *USAir Magazine*," says Barnes.

If your query is a winner in Barnes' eyes, she'll send you a form letter indicating that your idea is under consideration and a time frame for when it might appear. "If I can't run the piece for a while, I'll call the writer and tell him that, but reassure him that I will assign it when the timing is right," the editor explains. "When

I do assign the piece, I call the writer, review what I want, get ideas from him, and discuss price, length, and due date. I follow up with an assignment letter that serves as the contract, and sample copies of the magazine."

How to Write for *USAir Magazine*

Making your piece informative and enjoyable are the keys to writing for *USAir Magazine.* There is no pat writing style, but Barnes looks for a sharp tone, and anecdotes and examples that lure the reader into the piece.

"When the writing doesn't hit the mark, the freelancer has usually waited too long and has rushed the assignment," says Barnes. "He hasn't taken the time to polish it."

Barnes says she has been fortunate to work with a lot of good writers. "One essential element for success is to call me immediately if, while writing the piece, you discover you may not be headed in the right direction," she says. "You'll save us both a lot of time if you do."

Submit your article with a source list and phone numbers of anyone and anything mentioned in the article. "Send brochures, books, or relevant research to make our fact-checking job easier," says Barnes. "We double-check everything."

USA Weekend

1000 Wilson Boulevard
Arlington, VA 22229-0012
(703) 276-3400

Published: Weekly

Circulation: 16 million homes

Query: Amy Eisman, deputy editor, or a specialist listed in the masthead

Query response time: 6 weeks

Buys: About 100 articles/stories out of approximately 3,500 unsolicited queries/manuscripts received annually

Guidelines: Available; send SASE

Rights purchased: First World

Pays: On acceptance

Expenses: Pays travel and phone if agreed upon in advance; *USA Weekend* books the travel

Kill fee: 25 percent

Rates:

Type of Article	*Word Length*	*Payment*
Major Feature	2,500	$1,250 - 2,500
Short Feature	800	400 - 800
"What's Next"	250	25 - 100

USA Weekend is a fresh, timely, newsy magazine that appears as a weekend supplement in 381 American newspapers, reaching 33.5 million readers. "Our audience is pretty much the Baby Boom generation. They are people concerned about issues of the day, such as family, workplace, politics, religion, and health," says Amy Eisman, deputy editor.

How to Slant Your Ideas to *USA Weekend*

"Our articles cover important subjects, have a sharp, unique angle, and are pegged to a news event," says Eisman. "We present high-profile pieces on topics or persons of note. In addition, we look at timely issues of the day—from how to pay for college, to living with HIV, to lighter fare, such as an interview with home decorating and entertaining expert Martha Stewart.

One article, "Gathered from the Wall, Tokens of Heartbreak—and Healing" talked about a Smithsonian exhibit that showcased 600 of the thousands of treasures that visitors have left behind as the Vietnam Memorial approached its tenth anniversary.

Cover features have ranged from the debate over gays in the military, to a candid conversation with Denzel Washington, star of the movie *Malcolm X*, to an excerpt of former major league pitcher Dave Dravecky's book about his struggle to keep up his spirit after losing his arm to cancer.

Eisman seeks freelancers who can write on universal themes, looking at current thinking on an issue as well as speculating about future thought on the topic. "We need stories to have an edge and a time value," the deputy editor explains. "A successful article is one that people will talk about because it has significance to their lives and the times. Sometimes subjects are so topical that we ask for reader response. When we requested opinions to the question of whether Hollywood has lost its values, we heard from 440,000 people. When we sought opinions about the ban on gays in the military, 280,000 readers responded."

Occasionally, the magazine runs a first-person topic. In "Close Call in Yellow Springs," a writer shared her fear about her daughter's brush with death as street kids from neighboring towns threatened the local teens who hang out at the market. "The Destiny of Diego" looked at one husband and wife's experience playing the name game. On a quest to find the perfect Spanish name for their son-to-be, the dad-to-be described his answer to the question "What's in a name."

Freelancers for this market must realize that they are competing with many prominent writers. Eisman says the magazine is not looking for freelance articles on fitness; Arnold Schwarzenegger handles that beat. Food falls to columnist Lee Bailey; and environment belongs to Denis Hayes, one of the founders of Earth Day.

The best subject categories for freelancers to pursue are health trends, popular psychology, sports—including profiles of pro athletes and trends in recreational sports, entertainment profiles—typically written in a question/answer format, and destination travel pieces that cover domestic locations.

Examples in these categories have included an article in which the top-ranked female skeet shooter shared tips on feeling at home on the gun range, a getaway piece featuring Oregon's Cannon Beach, and a look at "brief therapy" to patch up marital difficulties, as opposed to "insight-oriented" therapy which can last for years.

All of the magazine's regular columns are written by staff or regular contributors, except one:

- **What's Next** offers short items about newsworthy trends that haven't been published elsewhere. The magazine has run a list of cars most likely to be carjacked in different cities, toolmakers' current effort to create tools aimed at women, and a look at new electronic toys that speak to the needs of Hispanic tots.

  This page also covers trends in books, giving an overview of several books that tackle a similar topic. For example, one issue examined about three new books that focused on child abduction by parents or other family members.

How to Query *USA Weekend*

One page preferred. Do not send photo/art information.

"I like proposals that get to the point immediately, just the way our articles do," says Eisman. "I am frustrated by writers who make me read four to 10 paragraphs before I can see the angle and news hook."

Along with sending a query letter, Eisman suggests writers new to this market include a résumé and a few clips that represent their best work and demonstrate their ability to write for *USA Weekend.* "We are looking for ideas from established writers," Eisman states.

As soon as *USA Weekend* agrees to your idea, you'll receive a letter outlining the expectations, payment, due date, and other pertinent parameters. Turn in a hard copy as well as a disk in ASCII format.

How to Write for *USA Weekend*

USA Weekend wants writers to get into their stories quickly and present material in a clear, tightly written fashion.

However, the magazine gives writers latitude. "We don't want every word in the magazine to sound the same," says Eisman. "We encourage writers to have an attitude and display personality in their writing, as long as it keeps with our general theme. Humor is difficult, but it works on occasion."

Writers go wrong when they underreport and overwrite. "We don't want extraneous information or stories that wander," Eisman notes. "Because we have a magazine style, we don't need to attribute every piece of information, but the author must write with confidence. Pieces must be supported by facts; they can't be too lightweight.

"We have had many successes when writers turn in timely, well-researched, well-packaged stories that match our unique style," says Eisman. "Part of the packaging is accompanying the article with a sidebar, headline, and pull-out quotes."

The staff reads manuscripts as soon as they come in and responds to the writer immediately. "The assigning editor will call the writer to request necessary revisions," says Eisman. "We believe writers to be responsible for accuracy, though we sometimes like a source list to be turned in as background information. When the final draft arrives, the editors edit it to length and show the writer the revised version before it is published."

Weight Watchers Magazine

360 Lexington Avenue
New York, NY 10017
(212) 370-0644

Published: Monthly

Circulation: 1 million

Query: Susan Rees, senior editor, Health & Nutrition

Query response time: 2 to 4 weeks

Buys: About 50 articles/stories out of approximately 500 unsolicited queries/manuscripts received annually

Guidelines: Available; send SASE

Rights purchased: First NAS

Pays: On acceptance

Expenses: Pays reasonable research, phone, and photocopying

Kill fee: 25 percent

Rates:

Type of Article	***Word Length***	***Payment***
Major Feature	1,000 - 5,000	$500
Short Feature	750 - 800	250 - 300
"Health & Nutrition"	1,100 - 1,300	500
"Success"	750 - 800	250 - 350

"Smart Choices for Living" is the subhead for *Weight Watchers Magazine.* This special-interest publication is devoted to self-improvement and is geared to women making healthy changes in their lives—through weight loss, weight maintenance, exercise, and proper nutrition.

"What's unique about our readers is that they pore over every page of the magazine and really act upon what they read," says Susan Rees, senior editor, Health & Nutrition. "So, we feel a special responsibility toward them."

Less than five percent of the magazine's readers are members of Weight Watchers; 95 percent of them are women. The average age is 42, and 59 percent of the readers are married. Just less than half have children under the age of 18. Two-thirds are employed and own their home, and the average household income is $39,616.

How to Slant Your Ideas to *Weight Watchers Magazine*

The magazine looks to freelancers for articles on timely health, medical, wellness, nutrition, and psychology topics based on documented research results. "We're inundated with queries on broad health issues that you could read about in *any* women's magazine," Rees says. "We consider new writers who submit stories that are geared to women losing or maintaining weight or that have a self-improvement angle. And while obesity-related topics are of greatest interest, our articles are not exclusively devoted to weight loss."

Writers for this market need fresh, imaginative, focused story ideas. Rees recommends studying the magazine to understand its style, voice, and readership. "Too many stories come in sounding like journal articles, or worse yet, like high school term papers."

Weight Watchers Magazine's feature well has included titles such as "Your Worst Critic," a moving piece on the voice inside our heads that stops us from accomplishing our goals; "The Fitness Fountain of Youth," an outline of a light workout routine to tone and firm figures; "From Here to Eternity," an exploration of the very latest advances in beauty aids that can help you retain youthful-looking skin; "Great Imposters," a collection of recipes that taste rich and creamy but have less fat; and "Why I Trained for a Triathlon," a first-person account of one woman's experience preparing for the challenge of her life and tips for beginners.

The following departments are open to freelancers:

- **Health & Nutrition** offers food for thought and information on topics such as developing a healthier lifestyle and eating right. Sample article titles have included "Eating for Energy," which presented a reduced-calorie food plan that doesn't deplete the body of energy, and "The Beauty of Strength," a piece that illustrated how firm muscles resulting from exercise can make one feel more youthful.

- **Success** profiles women who've had personal triumphs with weight loss. Before and after photographs accompany these biographical pieces to further inspire readers. Success articles appear in the magazine as a result of a reader sending in an anecdote and it being assigned to a freelance writer, or a writer submitting a query about a success story involving herself or someone she knows. One cover line, "Out of the Darkness," shared the dramatic story of a woman who overcame a life-threatening condition and then took on another challenge—losing 74 pounds to *stay* healthy.

The last page in every issue of *Weight Watchers Magazine* consists of a humorous essay. Written in the first-person voice, past anecdotal pieces have dealt with giving up certain "fat" pastimes in favor of healthier habits, and the issue of fitting workouts into one's daily routine, when there never seems to be a good time or enough time to exercise.

"Beauty," "Fashion," "Fitness," and "Food" articles are written and produced in house.

How to Query *Weight Watchers Magazine*

One-page queries preferred; do not send photo suggestions.

If you feel your idea is suitable for this market, outline it in a detailed query letter. Also send a recent research study to support your proposal, the names or affiliations of interview subjects you plan to use, and your qualifications for writing the article.

"Even if a writer's idea isn't ideal, we might consider assigning him or her a story idea *we've* developed—if he or she has convincing clips," Rees says encouragingly. "Published samples should accompany all submissions." Beginners trying to break into *Weight Watchers Magazine* should note that first submissions are always on speculation.

When the magazine's editorial staff decides to use a query idea, an editor notifies the writer with a phone call. "But," warns Rees, "it could be a couple of months before we can actually assign the piece because it may not immediately fit into our editorial calendar."

How to Write for *Weight Watchers Magazine*

"Once we assign an article, we try to flesh out the idea by developing an outline of questions the freelancer can use when he or she interviews sources," says Rees. To further assist the writer, editors offer suggestions for possible subjects to interview and chart or box ideas to enhance the piece.

"While our articles are authoritative, they are still written in a reader-friendly, positive tone," says Rees. "It's a delicate balance."

A common problem the senior editor finds with new freelancers writing on health, nutrition, or psychology is that the articles are too light. "The writers don't back up what they say with research studies or quotes from experts," explains Rees. "They don't delve deeply enough and they leave too many questions unanswered." But she also admits, "Sometimes the opposite occurs—despite the fact that it has been adequately researched, the writer renders the story dull and lifeless."

To expedite the fact-checking process, the magazine requires a second copy of the manuscript, with the telephone numbers of all interview subjects annotated in the margins. "We also ask that you include copies of all written sources, with relevant passages highlighted and referenced," adds Rees. (For more information on annotating a manuscript, see Chapter 5 in Part I, "Writing Articles That Command Attention.")

Woman's Day

1633 Broadway
New York, NY 10019
(212) 767-6000

Published: 17 times a year

Circulation: 4.3 million

Query: Maureen McFadden, senior editor

Query response time: 3 to 6 weeks

Buys: About 150 to 200 articles out of approximately 12,000 unsolicited queries received annually

Guidelines: Available; send SASE

Rights purchased: First NAS; occasionally All

Pays: On acceptance

Expenses: Pays phone and travel when approved in advance

Kill fee: 25 percent

Rates:

Type of Article	*Word Length*	*Payment*
Major Feature	1,200 - 2,200	$1,000 - 2,500
"Back Talk"	850	2,000
"Quick!"	150 - 250	150 - 250
"Neighbors"	100	75

Woman's Day is a full-scale service magazine that offers articles on community issues, family relationships, education, home decorating, health and diet, beauty, fashion, and food. Because it provides women with information they can incorporate into their ever-changing lives, *Woman's Day* is a staple on millions of shopping lists.

The median age of a *Woman's Day* reader is 43. Nearly 65 percent of the readers are married and 44 percent have children. The majority have graduated from high school and are employed. Job and career-related articles cater to the busy woman who may hold another job in addition to being a mother. The median household income is $33,573 and three quarters of the readers own their home.

How to Slant Your Ideas to Woman's Day

The magazine strives to recognize trends before they appear in the newspaper and on talk shows. It typically runs one crime story per issue. Articles on carjackings and rape survivors winning damages in civil lawsuits were written for *Woman's Day* by freelancers before much of the nation heard about the issues.

"If you think you have a unique take on how to prevent a certain kind of crime and can back it with expert advice, you might consider submitting a proposal in two forms," advises Maureen McFadden, senior editor. "One form would be proposed as a "Quick!" piece, while the other proposed a feature. Although writing a feature is more attractive in terms of compensation, a shorter piece is more readily assigned."

Woman's Day takes seriously the issues women face today. The resulting freelanced articles often require a writer's expertise in health, finance, education, or any other proposed topic. "If we were to assign a piece on phobias, we'd ask that the writer have some kind of knowledge in that area," McFadden confirms.

That's not to say that *Woman's Day* articles are only serious, journalistic pieces. There's plenty of room here for introspection, straight reportage, and drama.

During the summer months, travel articles are common fare. "77 Ways to Take the Kids...and Love It" covered everything you need to know to have a great family vacation. "Taking the Teens" gave advice on keeping adolescents happy on family trips.

The following departments are open to freelancers:

- **Back Talk** is a back-page essay dealing with a controversial subject of concern to women. The thought-provoking piece should be a very personal reflection of societal trends. "We expect our readers to consider both sides of an issue, then feel moved to respond or make a decision based on the writer's opinion and the reader's thinking," McFadden says.

  "I Want to Feel Safe Again," began, "I bought a gun today." Another "Back Talk" asked the question, "Who pays the price for working mothers?" A third essay debated the issue of whether menopause ought to be considered a medical condition requiring treatment or simply a natural part of the aging process.

- **Neighbors** is written by readers for readers; as such, it isn't really the place for writers. However, it *does* offer payment for words that are published, so here's a description: "Neighbors" offers busy women today's version of a friendly chat over the back fence. (Include a related photograph.) "To Tell the Tooth" shared one child's revelation of whom the tooth fairy was, while "Cashing in on Cleaning Up" described how one mother gave her children incentives for cleaning their rooms.

- **Quick!** delivers "News You Can Use Now," according to the subhead. It includes news on late-breaking surveys, studies, plus research, and typically has a specialist quoted. One tip alerted readers to college scholarship scams; another offered advice on how groceries should be bagged to help decrease global warming, air and water pollution, and overloaded landfills.

"Mary Ellen Says...," "Money Facts," "Women at the Wheel," and "Your Health," are written by regular columnists. Other beauty, food, fashion, and home decorating and organizing articles are written in house.

How to Query *Woman's Day*

One-and-one-half to two pages preferred. Do not send any photo/art ideas unless they help illustrate a drama or are for "Neighbors." Query six months or more in advance for seasonal material. Unsolicited manuscripts are not accepted or read, except for those for "Back Talk."

"Because editorial space is precious, stories compete with one another to make it into the magazine," McFadden notes. To be deemed worthwhile, a proposal must include preliminary reporting and should convey some sense of urgency—a heartwarming piece about a grandmother who saves puppies is no longer appropriate for this market.

"We don't have the time to take phone calls, but we're pretty good about reading queries," McFadden says. *Woman's Day* editors look for queries with a professional approach. What stands out to the editorial staff is evidence of pre-query research and interviewing. When identifying a trend, you should supply credible research statistics with experts quoted. Also explain how you plan to shape the story.

"If a writer makes sweeping generalizations or appears not to have read the magazine in the last 10 years, it indicates to us that she's either not willing or not able to do the necessary research," says McFadden. "While we wish freelancers well in their careers, this is not a writing school; this is a business and we're business people."

Woman's Day is a very difficult market to crack, and it is wise to make your first few passes at the "Quick!" section. The magazine generally assigns articles to people who have worked for them in the past and who have proved that they have what it takes to write to this readership.

"Sometimes writers propose ideas that aren't right for us for one reason or another—perhaps we have recently bought an article on a similar topic. But, if the clips are strong enough, we might be willing to try them on something else," McFadden says. "Less experienced writers who have written several 'Quick!' items and are anxious to do a longer feature may be asked to do a longer feature on an on-spec basis."

When an editor assigns a story that has been generated in house, a proposal is required. "Even if the freelancer has written a good proposal, we ask her to develop it further into story form, with some direction from us," McFadden explains.

Queries should be accompanied by appropriate clips. "If you're proposing a full-length feature, don't send us a short news brief as your clip," McFadden warns.

How to Write for *Woman's Day*

Editors make themselves available to writers who want to maintain contact during the writing process. "Freelancers are encouraged to call us if the piece is moving in a different direction or they've become so close to it they no longer know what's significant about it," McFadden says.

Occasionally, writers are asked to do rewrites. Writers must submit audiotapes and a source list for fact-checking purposes. Because the amount of time devoted to fact checking is limited, annotated manuscripts are helpful. Pieces are killed when the facts aren't substantiated and important information is missing. McFadden says that if a story neglects to report a major lawsuit or misses an entire crucial issue, it will likely be killed because it lacks credibility.

Woman's World

270 Sylvan Avenue
Englewood Cliffs, NJ 07632
(201) 569-0006

Published: Weekly

Circulation: 1.5 million

Query: Articles: Johnene Granger, managing editor or Andrea Bien, senior features editor
Health: Mary Terzella, medical editor
Travel: Jeanne Muchnick, fiction editor
Service Features: Irene Daria

Query response time: 6 weeks or more

Buys: More than 700 articles/stories annually

Guidelines: Available; send SASE

Rights purchased: First NAS

Pays: 8 weeks after acceptance

Expenses: Pays if reasonable, when discussed in advance

Kill fee: 20 percent

Rates:

Type of Article	*Word Length*	*Payment*
Feature	1,000	$400 - 500

Woman's World is the only weekly women's magazine in the United States. Directed to the average American woman, this magazine prides itself on having something for everyone.

"We offer more variety than most monthly women's magazines, and we're much easier to read," says Executive Editor Stephanie Saible. "We know she's busy and that her time is valuable. And we know we're competing for her time—that's why we make the most of it with short, snappy stories that give her all the information and emotional impact she wants without the flab."

Billing itself as having a woman's service profile in a very friendly setting, *Woman's World* attracts readers who are primarily between the ages of 25 and 54. Over 60 percent of the readers work outside the home, 63 percent are married, and 40 percent are parents. The median household income is $31,500.

How to Slant Your Ideas to *Woman's World*

Woman's World publishes anything the staff believes will fascinate the reader, touch her emotionally, or simply make her life easier or more fun. "We're always hungry for fresh ideas and for talented, prolific new writers," says Saible. "The best way to break in is simply to read the magazine to get a sense of our voice and our style. Then, come up with something original that fits in comfortably with what you've read."

Saible says that the magazine always desperately needs human-interest stories that are poignant, tender, heart-tugging, or inspiring. "And we love upbeat endings that leave the reader feeling like the world isn't such a bad place after all," she says.

Most human-interest stories and feature articles in *Woman's World* are written by freelancers, according to Senior Features Editor Andrea Bien. Especially sought are stories in the following categories:

- **Cheat Fate** is a dramatic, inspiring story of people who defied the odds and returned to their loved ones from the brink of death.
- **Happy Ending** focuses on all types of joyous resolutions of heart-rending struggles.
- **Inside Story** is a third-person account of a medical mystery, real-life drama, or medical drama told from the point-of-view of the policeman, social worker, doctor, or nurse.
- **True Love/Real-Life Romance** presents a story of real, undying love. It could be the bond between a mother and child, a husband and wife, or even a pet and owner.

Freelance contributions are entertained for other categories as well, such as celebrities and travel.

How to Query *Woman's World*

Any length is acceptable. Send photo/art information. Query at least four months in advance for seasonal material.

"We prefer a detailed query," says Saible. "In your proposal, let us know how you'd angle the story, what kinds of questions you'd ask, and what the emotional thrust would be. We love leads that synopsize stories as well and as accurately as the best book jackets. If you can't make a query interesting, chances are slim that the finished story will be fascinating."

If you haven't worked with the magazine previously, send along your résumé and clips. "If we really *love* a very well-written query from a new writer who hasn't yet accumulated clips, we'll probably go ahead and invite him to submit the article on spec," says Saible.

If you are assigned a story, be prepared to turn it around fast and without a lot of hand-holding. "We're a weekly, and that means we have tight deadlines," says Saible. "We don't have much of time to spend babysitting writers. We expect *you* to be able to take the information we give you during the assigning conversation and use it to craft your piece into a polished, ready-for-publication story. If you don't quite get what we're asking for, don't be surprised if we send your story back for a super-rush rewrite. But if you can take the pace and the pressure and still turn out great stories, expect to be kept *very* busy. We'll give you as much work as you can handle!"

How to Write for *Woman's World*

"All our articles are compact, yet complete," says Saible. "That's how we manage to fit so much great stuff into such a small package. We don't waste our reader's time with unnecessary padding and information that won't interest her."

"We're looking for stories that sweep the reader along," says the editor. "We want to make her smile and cry and leave her feeling that the world is a better place than she thought, that people are braver, that love is deeper, and that fate is kinder than she ever imagined."

Women's Sports & Fitness

2024 Pearl Street
Boulder, CO 80302
(303) 440-5111

Published: 8 times a year

Circulation: 155,000

Query: Kathleen Gasperini, editor

Query response time: 6 to 8 weeks

Buys: About 130 articles/stories out of approximately 1,750 unsolicited queries/manuscripts received annually

Guidelines: Available; send SASE

Rights purchased: Exclusive First NAS for one year

Pays: 30 days after publication

Expenses: Pays phone and occasional miscellaneous expenses

Kill fee: 25 percent

Rates:

Type of Article	*Word Length*	*Payment*
Major Feature	1,000 - 3,000	$500 - 1,000
Department	1,000	250 - 350
"Bodywise"	50 - 250	50 - 100
"Essay"	750	300
"Fast Breaks"	75 - 300	35 - 150
"Prep Talk"	650 - 750	225

The editorial goal of *Women's Sports & Fitness* is to provide information and inspiration to help women improve the quality of their lives through sports and fitness. The publication positions itself as the magazine for America's most active women.

"We focus attention on women athletes the way *Sports Illustrated* does on men," says Karen Karvonen, associate editor. "Some of our readers are professional athletes; most are recreational. All are serious about sports, devoting about one and one-half hours a day to their workouts. Our readers are fairly experienced in their sports, and even when they start a new one, they come to it with other skills to draw upon."

The median age of the *Women's Sports & Fitness* reader is 35. More than 60 percent have graduated from college, and 75 percent hold professional or managerial jobs. They have a median income of $61,900. About 45 percent are married, and more than one-third have children under the age of 18.

How to Slant Your Ideas to *Women's Sports & Fitness*

Summed up neatly, the magazine offers profiles of women athletes, plus how-to articles, nutrition and health articles, travel/ adventure pieces, and discussions about issues that affect active women. The ratio of staff-generated to freelance-submitted ideas is 70/30.

"One writer queried us on athletics and antioxidants," recalls Karvonen. "It worked because it mentioned that athletes are at greater risk of free radical damage because they take in more oxygen. Another piece we bought from a freelancer talked about new research on how women who used visualization of muscles contracting actually tested stronger than those who didn't."

Each issue of the magazine contains three or four features. A sampling includes "Polar Attraction," about a woman who conquered the North Pole and was venturing to the South Pole; "The Mettle Behind the Medals," telling how three Olympic skiers earned their medals and continue to work to stay on top; and "Cover Me," a primer on health insurance for women athletes.

Features are open to freelancers as are all departments, which include:

- **Bodywise** publishes short pieces on recent trends and research that affect women athletes. Topics have included treating sports injuries and how alternative medicine relates to women in sports.
- **Eating Well** covers nutrition of concern to women athletes. For example, "Put Some Sugar Into Your Life," discussed whether or not it is healthy to eat sucrose and glucose for quick energy. Another, "Eating Well, Mood Food," discussed how diet can affect PMS and offered 15 tips for combatting the monthly syndrome.
- **Essay** gives a woman an opportunity to express her opinion on a sports issue. It could be one that personally affects her or something that more broadly affects women and about which she holds a strong viewpoint. One issue included "To Dive For," a first-person account of the agony and ecstacy one woman experienced while watching her child take risks and compete.

- **Fast Breaks** offers timely, news-related stories with a new twist on women and athletics. Topics covered have included a threat of the world's sole women-only bicycling stage race losing its sponsor; a look at whether women can go the distance as quickly as men in endurance events; and a grant that gives underprivileged and inner-city kids a chance to participate in sports.
- **Prep Talk** focuses on aerobics and weight training for women who cross-train for other sports. Generally, this is a how-to section with step-by-step instruction. Some of the topics have been crunches, squats, and bicep curls.
- **Your Health** discusses health conditions that affect athletic women and treatments available. Columns have looked at Rolfing (deep muscle massage), eye exercises, steroids, and the Feldenkrais Method (which takes the body through a series of muscle-alignment exercises to correct body problems). "When we cover a chronic disease such as multiple sclerosis, we would focus on women out there competing with MS," says Karvonen.

How to Query *Women's Sports & Fitness*

One page preferred. Send any photo/art information; do not send photos.

To get the attention of this magazine, writers should query only after they have studied back issues and have become familiar with the subject matter covered.

"Freelancers often assume that we run articles about people who are just beginning sports and fitness programs or that we focus on diet and beauty. We don't," says Karvonen.

Ideally, writers for *Women's Sports & Fitness* also have expertise in one of the top sports—running, swimming, cycling, aerobics, weight training, and fitness walking.

When it comes to the style of query, Karvonen prefers proposals that mirror the type of article you plan to write. She likes to see a lead and then a synopsis of how you will carry out the story. Send clips from other magazines.

How to Write for *Women's Sports & Fitness*

"We expect writers to be fairly creative," says Karvonen. "We want good, eye-catching hooks for leads that will draw the reader in. Our articles are very informative. Since we try to be an authority on women's sports and fitness, extensive research is necessary. For example, in the article on how health insurance affects women with sports injuries, the writer had to become very familiar with the insurance terminology."

Karvonen says that when pieces don't work, it's typically because they are too local, not specific enough in research, or not geared toward active women.

Working Mother

230 Park Avenue
New York, NY 10169
(212) 551-9399

Published: Monthly

Circulation: 925,000

Query: Linda Hamilton, articles editor

Query response time: 2 to 3 weeks

Buys: About 140 articles out of approximately 1,500 unsolicited queries/manuscripts received annually

Guidelines: Available; send SASE

Rights purchased: First NAS

Pays: On acceptance

Expenses: Pays all reasonable—primarily phone and research fees, not travel

Kill fee: 20 percent

Rates:

Type of Article	*Word Length*	*Payment*
Major Feature	1,500 - 2,500	$1,500 - 2,500
Short Feature	500 - 1,000	500 - 1,000
"Essays"	750 - 1,000	750 - 1,000
"Kids' Health"	1,000 - 1,800	1,000 - 1,800
"Money"	1,000 - 1,500	1,000 - 1,500
"Women's Health"	1,000 - 1,800	1,000 - 1,800
"Work/Career"	1,000 - 1,800	1,000 - 1,800

Working Mother is a lifestyle magazine dedicated to showing the committed career mother how to balance the joys and challenges of both a demanding job and a thriving family. According to the publication's "Editorial Profile," it's the only magazine that supports women who opt for both career and family—and who would never give up either.

"Work is a given for our readers," says Linda Hamilton, articles editor. "They are women who have a lot to juggle, and we are a support network for them. These women need help and are not afraid to ask for it. We get an incredible amount of reader mail, and we try to answer every letter."

The median age of the *Working Mother* reader is 33. Almost 82 percent of the audience is employed outside the home; 72 percent work full time. The median household income is $39,600, and 82 percent have children who are under age 12.

How to Slant Your Ideas to *Working Mother*

An important prerequisite to writing for *Working Mother* is that you be a parent, or at least very good at interviewing others who are.

"We want our readers to feel that our writers know what it's all about," says Hamilton. "If writers aren't parents, the empathy in a piece can be missing. We want writers who know how to research as well as how to weave in quotes from experts and anecdotes from mothers to help lighten a piece."

Most of ideas that eventually become the articles in *Working Mother* are generated in house. Hamilton says, "We love it when freelancers have good ideas, but it requires being plugged into the magazine and really knowing what is going on in child rearing, childcare, health, and work issues. It is hard to break in here because it is difficult to come up with ideas that we haven't done."

A few examples of feature articles that have been included in the magazine are "Shame on You," a report on the devastating damage that can result from humiliating a child; "Building Family Memories," a piece on the rich lessons children learn from stories passed from one generation to the next; and "Family Happiness," offering the latest research on ingredients for joy and harmony at home.

"A report we ran on sick child care is a perfect example of the type of feature article we seek," says Hamilton. "It offered options on the horizon for working moms when their kids wake up sick and they don't have the flexibility in their jobs to stay home."

Because at press time for this book *Working Mother* was reformatting the magazine, Hamilton couldn't give a detailed list of the magazine's departments. She did offer descriptions of the following article categories that are open to freelancers:

- **Essays** broach any topic related to working motherhood. "We've covered putting up with unwanted advice from relatives and friends, how to decipher kid talk, and 'For Goodness Sakes, What's for Dinner?'" says Hamilton.
- **Kids' Health** has full-length pieces covering topics ranging from keeping kids healthy in day care, to what to do if your child has a fever, to dealing with an overweight child, to the issue of whether or not milk is really good for kids.
- **Money** offers insights on making the most of your dollars. It could be about managing a 401K, working your way out of debt, or knowing about pregnancy disability.

- **Women's Health** includes features on subjects such as coping with varicose veins, staying well during pregnancy, eliminating stress, losing weight after the baby is born, and overcoming sinus infections. "All health pieces are filled with solid information from doctors and other experts, yet presented in a down-to-earth manner," says Hamilton. "Even though we are presenting important advice, we want articles written in a light style so the material is not boring, overwhelming, or technical sounding."
- **Work/Career** gives tips on getting ahead on the job. Articles have presented advice on becoming an indispensable employee, coping as a commuter mom, managing job evaluations, what to do if you are suddenly fired, and how to start your own business. "Always keep in mind the working mother's predicament of knowing that her work life and family life affect one another," reminds Hamilton.

How to Query *Working Mother*

A few paragraphs to one page preferred; do not send photo/art information; query six months in advance for seasonal material.

"The format of your query isn't important; what matters is that we know immediately the focus of the article you're proposing," says Hamilton. "It helps if you can tell us what experts you plan to contact and what studies you will refer to. That always grabs our attention; we love new research."

Hamilton says that sample anecdotes and quotes can help to give the editors an idea of the flavor of your piece, but if the samples are weak, they will hurt your chances of earning an assignment. "Typically, writers who have not fully developed or thought out their ideas do not sell to us," she says.

If your proposal is worthy of an assignment, you'll get a phone call followed by an assignment letter that outlines how to approach the topic, and offers the due date, rights purchased, and payment details. After you've completed the piece, you'll receive a contract to sign and return.

How to Write for *Working Mother*

"Most of our articles are factual and packed with useful advice and tips," says Hamilton. This magazine wants its writers to seek out the latest studies and to interview top experts in the field—not to just rely on information from the neighborhood pediatrician or family doctor. "Also, we prefer pieces to be written in a conversational style, devoid of technical jargon," says Hamilton. "We won't accept dry copy. Our editors look for writers who know how to weave in anecdotes and turn a phrase to pep up a piece."

Once an article assignment is made and initial research is completed, Hamilton asks for an outline—to try and nip any potential problem in the bud. "You really don't know where an article will go until you have started researching the subject," says the editor. "We'd rather spot a problem at this point, either in content or direction, than later when the manuscript is written."

Fact checking is rigorous at *Working Mother.* Writers are expected to turn in a source list and copies of studies or pages from book research. "Our fact-checking department calls every person the writer interviewed to verify all quotes and facts," says Hamilton. "Our readers depend on us to give them correct information."

YM

685 Third Avenue
New York, NY 10017
(212) 878-8700

Published: 10 times a year, plus 2 special issues

Circulation: 1.5 million

Query: Bonnie Hurowitz-Fuller, editor-in-chief

Query response time: 1 month

Buys: About 100 articles out of approximately 8,500 queries received annually

Guidelines: Available; send SASE

Rights purchased: First NAS

Pays: On acceptance

Expenses: Pays anything approved in advance; usually phone and transportation

Kill fee: 25 percent

Rates:

Type of Article	***Word Length***	***Payment***
Major Feature	2,000	$ 2,000
Short Feature	750 - 1,200	750 - 1,200
News Brief	250 - 600	250 - 600

The *YM* reader is a young woman, 12 to 20 years of age, according to Bonnie Hurowitz-Fuller, editor-in-chief. "We cast a broad net to reach all high school and college girls. But when we edit, we focus particularly on girls in the last couple of years of high school and the first couple of years in college. The reader is someone who is interested in fashion, guys, in doing well at school and in her social life, and in knowing what's happening in the world."

How to Slant Your Ideas to *YM*

"Our articles should apply to almost any young American woman," Hurowitz-Fuller says. "They are not exclusionary but inclusionary. We try to think about what would apply to the widest number of teenage girls."

The typical *YM* issue contains a 2,000-word relationship article on a guy-girl topic that will apply to many young women. One recent topic was "Is This a Real Relationship or a Real Rut?" These articles tend to be broken into readable chunks, so a wise writer would approach the topic with three subheads, four scenarios, or some other method of keeping the reader with the piece.

The editors always seek dramatic narratives, too. These 2,000-word "as told to" articles must be about a girl near the reader's age. The editor says the format is flexible, as long as the topic is a page-turning, compelling drama. One piece was about a girl who lost 70 pounds; another told of a girl whose boyfriend was killed by a gang. However, there must be some "positive" outcome—a triumph over tragedy.

The following sections are open to freelancers:

- **The Real Life Guide** is broken into three pages, each with three items. The topics are jobs, school, love, and life. One article on each page is about 500 words long; the others are about 300 words and 150 words. "It's a place for us to talk over things that just aren't big enough for a feature, and a great way to cover seasonal topics," the editor explains. She adds that most of the topics take the approach of discussing a problem and how to solve it.
- **You and Him** is a 1,200-word relationship piece on a guy-girl topic. The column frequently features a sidebar and quiz to break up copy; be ready to suggest some approaches in your query. Hurowitz-Fuller also comments, "It's a smaller relationship story, and it's nice, though not essential, if the topic deals with a sexual issue. We've done articles on body language, guys and breasts, and lies guys tell for sex."

Advice columns, beauty, and fashion, as well as "The Inner You," "Numerology," and "Star Trip" are written in house or by regular contributors.

How to Query *YM*

One or two pages preferred; do not send any photo/art information.

Hurowitz-Fuller says that the most important feature of your query should be its tone and style. Preaching and "unfun ideas" spell rejection at *YM*.

"This magazine has a very distinct style," she says. "It is funny, very direct, and very contemporary. We look at things from the reader's perspective. What does she want to know about? A query needs to demonstrate to me that the writer can handle that style of article."

A query addressed to Hurowitz-Fuller will gain her attention, but one addressed to "Editor" or *YM* will be screened by an assistant. With the volume of queries received and the unique writing tone, the odds of a first sale here are not great. "We occasionally find something in the slush pile and assign it. But I'd estimate that that happens only about 10 times a year," she says.

"Chances are good that we've already thought of just about any relationship idea a writer can suggest," Hurowitz-Fuller warns. "But a writer with a great 'as told to' story idea has a great advantage over other writers trying to break in with more typical ideas."

The editor also notes that "The Real Life Guide" section is a good place to make your first sale to *YM.*

How to Write for *YM*

"*YM* is meant to be very usable," Hurowitz-Fuller says. "There's little in here that you would just read for the enjoyment of reading it. This is a magazine with information a girl can use. Some readers would glean information from a six-page fashion portfolio, while others appreciate the little how-to tips and model or celebrity information we sprinkle throughout.

"We take a big sister/older friend tone in the articles," Hurowitz-Fuller adds. "We love 'as told to' articles, which allow the girl's voice to emerge. And the word 'should' isn't in our vocabulary."

Regarding sexual behavior in the 12-to-20 age group, Hurowitz-Fuller says the magazine is very careful to present a balance between chastity and responsibility if a girl is sexually active.

"We bend over backward to allow for the possibility that she may not be sexually active," Hurowitz-Fuller notes. "We assume that she *may* be having sex. By the time American girls reach 18, 70 to 80 percent are having sex. That means that many are *not* having sex, though many are. So we always write 'if you've made the decison to have sex,' not 'when you do.'"

Young Sisters and Brothers

1700 North Moore Street, Suite 2200
Rosslyn, VA 22209
(703) 875-0430

Published: Monthly

Circulation: 150,000

Query: Constance Green, managing editor, or editor of department for which freelancer is interested in writing

Query response time: 6 to 8 weeks

Buys: About 30 articles/stories out of approximately 300 unsolicited queries/manuscripts received annually

Guidelines: Available; send SASE

Rights purchased: First Serial

Pays: On acceptance

Expenses: Pays phone and some travel when agreed upon in advance

Kill fee: 25 percent

Rates:

Type of Article	*Word Length*	*Payment*
Major Feature	840 - 1,200	$250 - 800
Short Feature	420 - 640	100 - 300
Department	varies	varies

Young Sisters and Brothers (YSB) targets African Americans between the ages of 16 and 24. Unique in its niche, the magazine offers a forum for youth-oriented topics, ranging in scope from political and social issues to entertainment and relationships.

YSB distinguishes itself from other teen magazines not only by its Black orientation, but by its approach to tough subjects as well as lighter ones. "We have been described as 'infotainment,' meaning we deal with serious subjects in an entertaining way," says Managing Editor Constance Green. "As a youth magazine we cover fun subjects, such as sports and entertainment, but we have our share of very hard-hitting stories. Our article on rethinking the Christopher Columbus legacy gained a lot of attention, as did a feature on why traditionally Black colleges are increasing in popularity. We try to challenge young people on issues they may not get challenged on elsewhere.

"We have a strong mix of stories to attract a wide spectrum of readers, from high school to college age and in all income groups," continues Green. "We have a lot of readers older than 24 and a lot of parents who like the magazine so much that they try to get their hands on it before their kids get it. *YSB* also appeals to other minorities and Caucasian readers."

How to Slant Your Ideas to *Young Sisters and Brothers*

Articles in *YSB* have a national focus with strong local significance. The magazine's content is a mix of what young people want and need to know.

About three-quarters of the ideas in *YSB* are dreamed up in house and assigned to writers. "We want freelancers who have good ideas, especially those who live outside the Northeast area, where we are located," says Green. "We are looking for young writers in Los Angeles, Oklahoma, and in small towns where we may not know about things that are happening."

The magazine's feature well includes five or six articles in each issue covering these subject categories:

- **Arts** has focused on the young artists who began painting the hopes, fears, and dreams of youth on furniture (whose work is now featured in galleries in New York and France) as well as on fundraising efforts to revive Black theater, and the international work of the Harlem Boys Choir.
- **Education** offers encouragement and inspiration for young students. It has given tips for starting a business, profiling young people who have launched lucrative enterprises. One cover story explored how sex education is taught in schools, while another talked with students who had dropped out of school and offered tips on getting back in and taking the GED. Other features have focused on vocational schools and jobs that don't require college degrees.
- **Entertainment Profile** ranges from music personalities to television stars and movie producers. Generally, the individuals profiled are Black or entertain a Black audience. "The subject matter is more important than race," says Green. "If the person is doing something of relevance to a Black or minority community, we want to hear about it."

- **Interpersonal Story** is generally written by a teen or young adult as a first-person account of a personal issue that today's youth struggle with. Past issues have covered thoughts about a first date, when a relationship crosses the line into more than "just friends," date rape, hazards of the prom, interracial dating, what makes a good friend, and summer romance.
- **Social Issues** addresses topics such as guns in school, young fathers, afrocentricity, abortion versus pro-life, AIDS, and teens giving back to their communities.
- **Sports** brings readers both close-ups on professional athletes and general articles on various sports-related issues. People profiled have included basketball stars Charles Barkley and Michael Jordon and the late tennis pro Arthur Ashe. Major features have looked at the lack of Black faces in baseball's front offices, and have asked whether pro athletes are worth the enormous pay they command.
- **Sportsbeat** covers profiles and issues in the world of sports. These short features are light and tied to a news hook. Articles have focused on an athlete who runs a home for disabled youth, whether athletes should be role models, and the dilemma faced by high school athletes who get caught up in the money offered by recruiters.

Most departments in the magazine are open to freelancers. They include:

- **Going Places** is a travel destination column with a twist for young people. It has covered venues such as Mexico, the Caribbean, and Egypt. In addition to information for travelers on tight budgets, the pieces always highlight an educational aspect of travel, be it historical, political, cultural, or religious.
- **Groomin'** is written by the magazine's fashion department yet is open to sidebars of information provided by freelancers. It provides tips on personal hygiene and polishing a look. Titles have included "Soft Make-Up for the Sisters," "Your Breath: Nothing Personal But This Is About You," and "Hittin' Hair for the Fellas."
- **Hype** offers brief profiles and updates that pertain to music and both the big and little screens. One featurette told about the rediscovery of the harmony-rich sounds of yesteryear. Another provided a mini-profile of avant garde dancer Bill T. Jones, whose work brings to life issues like racism, politics, AIDS, and the Black family.

- **Living Large** gives tips for staying well, eating healthy, and taking care of the body. A piece called "You Can Have Your Häagen Dazs and Eat It Too" discussed the difference between anorexia and bulimia and the importance of fruits and vegetables in your diet. "Hear Ye! Hear Ye! Video Vibes" offered a few precautions for preventing hearing loss. And, "Backing Up Your Back" suggested ways to wear a backpack to prevent back injuries.
- **Mo' Money** gives financial tips on subjects such as holiday shopping, the dangers of credit card abuse, budgeting, college financial aid, students and taxes, and youth businesses.
- **What's Going On** bills itself as "straight news with a twist." It brings readers updates on colleges, culture, museums, and other events, as well as profiles of young people doing extraordinary things. Past issues have covered McDonald's scholarships, how the Supreme Court's hate crime ruling hurt Blacks, and a look at a new word game a couple invented to help students perform better on the SAT.

"Astro," "Bookin'," "In the Mix," "Listen Up," and "Work Tip" are written by regular contributors or staff. "Reflections" is written by people well known in a given field sharing experiences from which youth can learn. Past pieces have been authored by Black author Maya Angelou, Children's Defense Fund President Marian Wright Edelman, and a celebrity rap artist.

How to Query *Young Sisters and Brothers*

One page preferred. Do not send photo art/information.

"We are looking for straightforward queries that tell us how your idea fits into *YSB* and to show us why you in particular are excited about the subject you have in mind," says Green. "It's important to write in such a way that you truly make the topic come to life. Mention tidbits you'd like to include in the story to allow us to visualize it."

Green encourages writers to take their time and avoid being sloppy. "Some writers dash something off, which makes me wonder about their writing ability. Even if they have clips, I ask myself how much they've been edited. But if a proposal is well written and the writer sounds intrigued by the topic, I figure he or she will follow through on the details of the assignment."

Green is definitely interested in new writers—especially those under age 30. "We want to give young people a chance," she says.

"This magazine is their voice, and the more young people we have writing for us, the less we have to try to manufacture an interactive tone to our articles."

Green reads most queries, then passes them along to an appropriate editor. "If the editor of that section gets excited, he or she will call the writer to work out the assignment," Green says.

How to Write for *Young Sisters and Brothers*

"*YSB* has an upbeat, personable, conversational tone of young people talking to young people," says Green. "Articles come from a youth perspective, whether we are talking about violence in the community or sex education in the classroom. We use lots of quotes from young people from around the country."

No matter what your age, make sure you are concerned about youth and their ideas, hopes, and dreams if you want to write for this market. "We use standard English, but you must be able to capture the energy and language of youth—that sometimes means not being afraid to use expressions and colorful phrasing," instructs Green. "Not every older person is able to do that or wants to do that."

In all categories, *YSB* works to bring international issues home to the young reader. "A big part of our job is to open the world to our audience," Green explains. "We like to draw parallels between what is happening in other countries to events in our own. For example, when our editor did a piece on New Zealand, a mention of the music told how it related to hip-hop and jazz. Cultural connections bring relevance to the reader. If our young people don't see how the story is pertinent to their lives, they won't think it is important enough to read."

Green looks for writing that can teach without being preachy. She says that rewrites normally occur because the tone is off or the writing colorless—usually meaning it is not youth-oriented enough.

"But we have not killed many stories yet," says the managing editor of the award-winning magazine founded in 1991. "When an editor works with a writer, most things can be fixed."

Your Health & Fitness

60 Revere Drive
Northbrook, IL 60062-1563
(708) 205-3000

Published: 6 times a year

Circulation: 525,000 plus

Query: Carol Spielman Lezak, senior editor

Query response time: (see explanation in text)

Buys: About 60 freelance-written articles/stories annually; all in-house generated ideas assigned to writers; receives only about 50 unsolicited queries/manuscripts a year

Guidelines: Not available until an assignment is made. Do not send for sample copies of the magazine; find them at the library.

Rights purchased: All

Pays: Typically after publication

Expenses: Pays on an individual, negotiated basis

Kill fee: 50 percent

Rates:

Type of Article	*Word Length*	*Payment*
Major Feature	1,500	Negotiable
Short Feature/ Department	400 - 825	$100 for first-time writers

Your Health & Fitness is a 24-page health, safety, and wellness publication sold in bulk subscription to hospitals, businesses, and managed-care plans, such as health maintenance organizations (HMOs). Subscribers may supplement and customize the publication with their own material.

"Our subscribers purchase the magazine for a variety of reasons," says Senior Editor Carol Spielman Lezak. "Hospitals use it as a public relations tool to reach out to and educate the community. Although many may produce their own newsletter in house, we provide years of experience in the field, a substantial amount of health and safety information, and editorial and design services all at a decent cost.

"Businesses see the magazine as a way to communicate wellness, health and safety information to their employees and the community," Lezak explains. "If a company is buying it for safety communication purposes, it may highlight what is being done in the organization to protect employees. For example, the company may have a variety of OSHA regulations it needs to discuss or a new safety plan it wants to unveil for certain procedures in the factory or in the field.

"HMOs generally use their custom pages in the publication to highlight coverage for members, cite rules, and regulations for obtaining benefits, and do feature stories on members, physicians, and other staff," says Lezak.

Because of this tremendous mix of subscribers, the readership of this magazine varies greatly. "Our audience mirrors whatever community is being addressed by the purchaser," says Lezak. "The magazine goes to upper-middle-class neighborhoods and inner-city areas alike—it's a mix. The client pages are what vary."

How to Slant Your Ideas to *Your Health & Fitness*

Your Health & Fitness does not approach its editorial in the same manner as a traditional magazine. Rather than having a three- to four-month lead time for article ideas, this publication plans its editorial more than a year in advance. The editors make assignments between October and December for the following year.

"Because our subscribers also use their own material in the publication, we let them know the articles we have planned well in advance," says Lezak. "That way, they can plot their copy around ours. For example, if they know we have a piece on living with arthritis planned for a particular issue, they may wish to supplement that with information about their own clinic or physician who specializes in treating arthritis. Or, if they know we will be covering that topic, they might want to highlight a completely different subject."

Lezak says the editorial staff is comprised of editors but no in-house writers, so it relies on the talents of freelancers to help fill the pages. In fact, the publisher works with more than a hundred freelancers a year for this magazine and its other publications (among them, women's, seniors', and other health newsletters).

"We have a number of freelancers right now with whom we've worked for more than three years," the editor says. "They sent in queries or letters of introduction, and they did such a good job on their first assignment that we've continued to use them. We want to encourage new writers to do the same.

"Our staff is especially interested in qualified freelancers who are knowledgeable about prescription and over-the-counter drugs and various diseases," says Lezak. "These are two areas in which misinformation literally can be deadly. All articles are reviewed by our medical editor and board of consultants, but we want writers who can draw correct information in the first place from a variety of recent and reliable sources."

The cover photo of this relatively short publication ties into a two-page article that usually falls near the beginning of the publication. Cover stories included water workouts, progress made in the United States toward a smoke-free society, and family health and medical know-how.

The "Feature Story" is the magazine's only four-page article. "Feature Highlight" serves as a sidebar to that story.

For example, one "Feature Story" about how to overcome back problems was followed by a "Feature Highlight" that covered the link between emotional stress and backaches. Another combination was a feature about understanding pain, followed by a story on how to help a chronic pain sufferer.

In addition to these feature articles, there are numerous rotating departments that cover specific subject areas. Not all appear in each issue, but most are written by freelancers. They include:

- **Coping with Disease** gives updates on conditions such as Lyme disease, Alzheimer's, and anemia.
- **Drug Data** has presented information on food and drug interactions; how to avoid mixing medications; and smart ways to give children medicine.
- **Exercise & Fitness** has looked at stair-climbing as an aerobic exercise and the fitness benefits of dancing.
- **Nutrition** has covered an overview on drinking water, its safety, and an explanation of the various types of bottled water available. Another article, "You Don't Know Beans," looked at the nutritional value of legumes, how to avoid the gastronomical distress sometimes caused by them, and gave a black bean and walnut dip recipe.
- **Psychology** has broached coping with catastrophe and facing up to change.
- **Safety & First Aid** has told of the safety hazards of craft hobbies and what to look for in bicycle helmets.
- **Traffic Safety** has given tips for the physically challenged driver as well as pointers on child safety seats.
- **Your Health Care Dollar** takes a look at health care consumer topics. It has included such topics as insurance coverage through the Consolidated Omnibus Budget Reconciliation

Act (COBRA), a law that allows employees and their families to convert their health care coverage to private insurance when the employee loses his or her job, and COB (Coordination of Benefits), a way to get the most out of coverage from multiple insurance plans.

"Safety Q&A" and "Scoreboard" are closed to freelancers.

How to Query *Your Health & Fitness*

Query letters are not necessary; all topics are assigned to writers based on the magazine's needs. Send an introductory letter, résumé, and a number of clips.

"It is unusual to write a query on the exact topic we are seeking," says Lezak. "We look at queries not so much for the idea, but to evaluate writers' abilities and to see where their interests lie."

That doesn't mean that Lezak doesn't appreciate queries. To her, the writing in a query letter is a much better barometer of a writer's style and tone than clips, which every editor knows can camouflage bad writing with the heavy hand of a previous editor.

Proposals also help the editors determine which writers are not quite right for the magazine, such as when they don't take a mainstream health approach. "*Your Health & Fitness* is orthodox in its health education coverage, generally following the American Medical Association's stance," says Lezak. "We do not cover alternative medicine."

If you prefer to send Lezak a résumé and clips, back them up with a letter of introduction. Tell her what you are interested in writing about, what topics you've covered in the past, and what publications you have written for previously.

"I don't mind if your letter is less than business sounding," says Lezak. "Don't be stuffy. I will look at your qualifications and background and if I'm interested, I'll be in touch. It may not be that year if all our assignments are made, but I keep files on writers whose qualifications meet our needs."

Each year, during the two to three months when Lezak makes assignments, she first calls the writers she wants to use. She gives them the particulars of the topic and learns of their interest in the assignment. Then a staff editor sends out assignment sheets that include the length of the article, the due date, title, fee, specific notes on what she wants the writer to cover, and sample copies of the magazine. At that point, writer's guidelines are sent. These guidelines instruct the writer on the tone and stance the magazine takes and also discuss the mechanics of turning in a piece to this publication.

How to Write for *Your Health & Fitness*

"I like to see a past history of health and/or medical writing. A familiarity with the field is an important qualification for me," says Lezak.

Lezak's profile of the perfect writer is someone who has experience in middle-of-the-road health writing.

"We want writers who can talk to people, not preach," the editor explains. "They need to realize that we are not a medical journal that goes into minute detail, nor are we a news magazine that uses scary statistics to get people to take action. We encourage and empower people to take charge of their health; we don't bully them into it.

"'Health promotion' is what this magazine is about," Lezak continues. "We want readers to be able to lead a more healthful life with the information we give them. Most HMOs and businesses want health care costs to be reduced and encourage people to use medical services sensibly. Hospitals want to direct people to use their facilities when the time has come to use them."

Lezak reminds writers that the people reading this magazine are not the ones who subscribe to it. "Because of that, we need inviting, lively writing that has a conversational tone," she says. "It is really crucial for our success to be able to show our subscribers that the readership is interested in our magazine."

To break up copy, the magazine uses lots of subheads and bulleted points. Sidebars and boxed information are utilized to draw the reader's attention.

The "For More Information" sections of the articles are written by the magazine's in-house researchers. "The listing for free or low-cost information is a real selling point for our publications and well-liked by our readers," says Lezak.

When you turn in your final piece, you are required to send a source list of individuals interviewed and publications cited. "Experts quoted in the magazine need to be book authors, government sources, or individuals of national repute, such as nutrition expert Jane Brody or researchers from major research centers in the United States," Lezak says. "Because of our wide base of subscriber clients, we avoid using sources from local hospitals or institutions."

Written sources used for research may not be more than three years old. When citing a study in your article, be sure to note the institution that conducted it and in what the year the study was completed.

If you run into a snag when working on a piece for *Your Health & Fitness*, Lezak encourages you to call. "We are always available to discuss an assignment with a freelancer; I'd prefer that to being surprised by something we don't want," she says. "Writers need to follow our directions. It means a lot of extra work if a freelancer goes way over the word count, or if the manuscript is not prepared according to our specs, or if a bibliography is not included. But most importantly, if a writer has not followed our directions on the content, tone, and slant of the article, we may need to ask for a rewrite or choose to not use the article. We work on tight schedules and know what we want—so we expect the writer to adhere to directions the first time around."

Index

AA Magazine Publications, 511
Abrams, Pamela, 436–39
Abstracts, 22–23, 113, 114–15
Adventure, articles on, 298, 336, 399, 401, 424, 487, 490, 521
Advertisers, 6
African Americans, magazines directed toward, 165–68, 194–97, 198–203, 217–21, 258–62, 271–74, 527–31, 562–66
Agents, submission by, 232
Aging, articles on, 366, 387–90
Agreement, letters of, 142. *See also* Assignment letters; Contracts
Agriculture Research Council, 66
Alaska Airlines, 147
Alaska Airlines Magazine, 147–51
  querying, 150
  slanting your ideas to, 148–50
  writing for, 150–51
Aldrich, Nelson, Jr., 4–5, 361–64
All Rights, 139
Americana, 152–54
  querying, 154
  slanting your ideas to, 152–54
  writing for, 154
American Airlines, 169, 511
American Association for the Advancement of Science, 66
American Association of Retired Persons (AARP), 387
American Dairy Council, 22
American Diabetic Association, 234
American Dietetic Association, 22, 72
American Health, 155–59
  news briefs, 156–57
  querying, 158–59
  slanting your ideas to, 156–58
  writing for, 159
American Heart Association, 234
American Legion Magazine, The, 160–64
  querying, 162–63
  slanting your ideas to, 161–62
  writing for, 163–64
American Libraries, 109, 111
American Library Association, 109
American Men and Women of Science, 115
American Society of Indexers, 105–6
American Society of Journalists and Authors, Inc., 104–5, 120, 141–42
  handbook, 142
  suggested letter of agreement, 141, 142
American Statistics Index, 118
American Visions, 165–68
  querying, 45, 167–68
  slanting your ideas to, 165–67
  writing for, 168
American Way, 169–71
  querying, 170–71
  slanting your ideas to, 170
  writing for, 171
American Woman, 176–80
  querying, 179
  slanting your ideas to, 177–79
  writing for, 179–80
America West, 172–75
  querying, 175
  slanting your ideas to, 173–75
  writing for, 175
Angle of an article, 23–28, 90
  and the angle test, 25–26
  developing from ideas, 23–25, 57
  for multiple markets, 27–28
  shaping for the reader, 26–27
  three-step approach, 24–25
  titles to help shape, 31
Answering machine, 127
Anton, Maria, 268–70
Appleton, Myra, 237
Archaeology, articles on, 399, 419, 504
Arond, Miriam, 222
Article anatomy, 86–89
Article genre, 85–86
Article style, 83–85. *See also* individual magazines
Arts, articles on
  in business magazines, 242
  in general interest magazines, 183, 469, 504

Art, articles on *(cont'd)*
in hunting magazines, 521
in inflight magazines, 149, 178, 500, 533
in magazines for African Americans, 166, 195, 261, 529, 563
in magazines about islands, 354
in magazines for veterans, 161
in magazines for young people, 339, 563
Ashley, Roberta, 237
ASJA Handbook: A Writer's Guide to Ethical and Economic Issues, 142
Assignment letters, 58, 138. *See also* individual magazines
Associated Press Stylebook, The, 128
Associations as idea sources, 22, 66
Associations, magazines for specific, 160–64, 186–89, 241–44, 300–303, 387–90, 398–401, 489–93, 503–6
Astronomy, articles on, 206, 419
Atlantic, The, 59, 181–85
querying, 184–85
slanting your ideas to, 182–84
writing for, 185
Audubon, 186–89
querying, 188–89
slanting your ideas to, 187–88
writing for, 189
Authors Guild, 105
Authorship, 106
Automobiles, articles on
care and driving of, 149, 191, 243, 441, 509, 514, 546, 569
luxury cars, 469, 471
technology, 420, 440–44, 446, 514
for teens, 205
Aviation, articles on, 206, 334, 440, 469

Bacas, Harry, 35
Barasch, Douglas S., 477
Barnes, Duncan, 51, 288–91
Barnes, Terri, 34, 532–35
Barstow, John, 324–28
Bartlett's Familiar Quotations, 117, 128
Baum, Dan, 4, 30, 100, 121
on interviews, 73, 74, 77
on writing, 82–83, 96, 97
Beatty, Jack, 181
Beauty and fashion, articles on
in health magazines, 157, 298, 331, 367, 542
in magazines for African Americans, 196, 219, 528–29
in magazines for brides, 210, 219
in magazines for teens, 482–83, 560, 654
in magazines for women, 174, 196, 238–39, 273, 279, 282, 304, 312, 359, 370, 382–83, 410, 411, 466, 544, 546
in science magazines, 419
Benchley, Robert S., 448–52
Benford, Susan Victoria ("Noonie"), 94–95
Benty, Cameron, 516–19
Better Homes and Gardens, 190–93
Freelance Fact Sheet, 33
querying, 192–93
slanting your ideas to, 27, 191–92
writing for, 193
Bible, 128, 226, 319
Bicycling, articles on, 205, 470, 553
Bien, Andrea, 548, 549
Billboard paragraph, 88
Bill collecting, 124
Biographical index and dictionaries, 115
Biography Index, 111, 115
Biological Abstracts, 22–23
Black Elegance, 34, 194–97
querying, 196
slanting your ideas to, 195–96
writing for, 196–97
Black Enterprise, 198–203
"Free-lance Writers Orientation Manual," 199
querying, 201–2
slanting your ideas to, 199–201
travel guides, 201
writing for, 202–3
Boating, articles on, 440, 469, 471
Body of an article, 88
Boehm, Connie, 266
Book Catalog (Library of Congress), 112
Bookkeeping, 132–33, 134
Book of Lists, The, 116
Books and book reviews
in business magazines, 242
in food magazines, 234, 254
in general interest magazines, 183, 505, 538
in inflight magazines, 170, 500

in magazines for African Americans, 167, 200, 259, 261, 529
in magazines for women, 239, 383
in religious magazines, 227
Books in Print, 111
Bounds, Mary, 465
Boy Scouts of America, 204–7, 275–78, 473–76
Boys' Life, 204–7
comic strips, 206
querying, 206–7
slanting your ideas to, 204–6
writing for, 207
Brada, Deborah, 46–48
Bridal Guide, 208–10
querying, 46–48, 210
slanting your ideas to, 209–10
writing for, 210
Brides, magazines for, 208–10, 211–16, 217–21, 384–86
Bride's, 18
Bride's & Your New Home, 211–16
querying, 55, 215
slanting your ideas to, 212–14
writing for, 215–16
Brides Today, 99, 217–21
querying, 220
slanting your ideas to, 218–19
writing for, 96, 220–21
Bronner, Sheila, 527–31
Brothers, Dr. Joyce, 312
Brown, Helen Gurley, 99, 237–40
Bryant, Clell, 459–61
Bryant, Mark, 28
Burch, Gary, 413–16
Business, articles on, 198–203, 249–52, 268–70, 402–5, 527–31
in inflight magazines, 149, 179, 451, 500–501, 513, 534
in magazines for African Americans, 260, 527–31
in magazines for veterans, 161
Business of freelancing, 121–22
equipment, 126–28, 133
income taxes, 133–138
insurance, 105, 106, 107, 135
making a living, 120, 121, 123–25, 133
office, setting up, 125–29, 135
record keeping, 129–33
and the "writer myth," 119
writing schedule, 122–23
Business Periodicals Index, 117
Business proposal query, 34, 35–36
Byal, Nancy, 190

Cameras, 127–28
Camping, articles on, 205, 422
Caringer, Denise, 190
Carpentier, Fran, 19, 24, 31, 33, 93, 100, 426–29
Cartoons and comics, 206, 288
Cavender, Catherine, 482–84
Cavlin, Mary Ann, 384–86
Celebrity interviews and articles
articles by (ghostwritten), 459
in business magazines, 244
in general interest magazines, 427, 469, 537
in health magazines, 375, 407
in inflight magazines, 450, 512
in magazines for African Americans, 167, 195–96, 218, 528, 563
in magazines for men, 375
in magazines for teens, 483, 563
in magazines for women, 195–96, 218, 293, 370, 549
Chambers, Gordon, 271
Chambers of Commerce, 65
Checking accounts, 133
Chemical Abstracts, 22–23
Cherry, Rona, 295–97, 299
Chestnutt, Jane, 42–43
Chicago Manual of Style, The, 102, 128
child, 85, 222–24
querying, 224
slanting your ideas to, 223–24
writing for, 224
Children, articles for, 204–7, 289–90, 336, 338–42. *See also* Teens, articles for
Christianity Today, 225–29
opportunities for freelancers, 227–28
querying, 29, 228–29
slanting your ideas to, 226–28
writing for, 229
Christian Science Monitor, 113
Citation searches, 112
Clark, John, 511–12, 514–15
Clearances, legal, 164
Clearinghouses, 115
Clippings. *See also* individual magazines
accompanying query, 5, 51, 54–55

Clippings *(cont'd)*
  earning, 8–9, 371
  filing, 131
Cohen, Sherry Suib, 7, 9, 20, 70
Cohen, Steve, 494–98
Collecting, articles on, 152–53, 201, 245–48, 336, 470
College life, articles on, 457, 460
Communications Abstracts, 115
Compact disc databases, 113–14
Comprehensive Guide and Index to the Statistical Publications of the United States Government, A, 118
CompuServe® (database), 114
Computer databases, 113–14
Computers
  diskette backups, 102
  owning, 126–27
  taking notes with, 70–71, 73–74
Computers, articles on, 205, 286, 335, 403, 419, 446
Condé Nast Traveler, 230–32
  querying, 232
  slanting your ideas to, 231–32
  writing for, 232
Conferences and seminars as idea sources, 22, 65
Confirmation letter, 58
Congressional Quarterly Almanac, 116
Congressional Record, The, 116
Congressional Staff Directory, The, 116
Connor, Lee Lusardi, 369–72
Consumer topics, articles on, 293, 305, 312, 385, 500, 538. *See also* Product information and reviews
Continental Airlines, 448–51
Contracts, 58–59, 124, 138–43. *See also* individual magazines
  sample, 142–43
Cook, Cathy, 208
Cooking Light, 233–36
  querying, 235–36
  slanting your ideas to, 234–35
  writing for, 236
Cooper, Ken, 259
Copeland, Irene, 237
Coppess, Marcia, 123
  query letters, 42–43, 59, 60–61
  idea development, 18, 19, 23
  filing system, 128–29, 132–33
Copyediting, 99
Copyediting symbols, 102
Cosmopolitan, 55, 99, 237–40
  querying, 239
  slanting your ideas to, 238–39
  writing for, 240
Costco Connection, The, 241–44
  querying, 243
  slanting your ideas to, 242–43
  writing for, 243–44
Council of Writers Organizations, 105–6
Country Victorian Decorating & Lifestyle, 245–48
  querying, 247–48
  slanting your ideas to, 27, 246–47
  writing for, 248
Cover letter with query, 34
Crafts, articles on, 190–93, 285, 340
Creativity, 93–95
Crichton, Doug, 169–71
Critique groups, 103–4
Culinary Institute of America, 22
Current Biography, 115
Curry, George, 258
Curtis, C. Michael, 60, 181–85
Cusack, Lynne, 369
Cutler, Karan, 324

Daly, Margaret, 190
Dance, articles on, 166, 261
D&B Reports, 249–52
  querying, 251
  slanting your ideas to, 250–51
  writing for, 251–52
Daniel, Douglass, 204, 207
Daniels, Hope, 377–81
Daniels, Scott, 275–78
Daria, Irene, 548
Davis, B. Ancil, 263–67
Davis, Lisa, 329
Davison, Peter, 181
Deadlines, 97–98, 122, 210
Deck of an article, 86, 389, 408
de Leon, Lidia, 37, 499–502
Delta Airlines, 499
Demographics, 6, 9. *See also* individual magazines
Dentistry, articles on, 156
Derr, Michael, 177
Dialog® (database), 64, 114
Dialogue, 94, 216, 314, 319, 342
Dictionaries, 115, 128
Directories, 115–16

Directories in Print, 116
Directory of American Scholars, 115
Directory of Medical Specialists, 116
Directory of Special Libraries and Information Centers, 111
Diskette, articles submitted on, 299, 405, 447, 538
Dissertation Abstracts International, 22–23
Doclar, Ernest, 473–76
Doherty, Donna, 523–26
Dorsey, Nicole, 406–8
Drew, Timothy, 344, 345
Dreyer, Michael, 133–36
Dues, professional, 137–38
Dun & Bradstreet Corporation, 249
Dworetzky, Tom, 387–90
Dyson, John, 461

Eakin, Katherine, 233–36
Eating Well, 253–57
  querying, 255–56
  slanting your ideas to, 254–55
  writing for, 256–57
Economics, articles on, 183, 198, 201, 419
Editing. *See also* Copyediting; Rewriting; individual magazines
  by the author, 33, 95–97, 102
  by the magazine editor, 33, 54–55, 98–101
  saving edited work, 97
  and word count, 96–97
Editorial assistants, 4, 6–7, 14, 331, 345, 412
Editorial calendar, 251, 415
Editorial content, analyzing, 11
Editorials on File, 116
Editors. *See also* individual magazines
  and deadlines, 97–98, 122, 210
  expectations of, 9–10, 14
  and idea development, 3
  and job changes, 13–14
  relationships with, 5, 6–7, 9, 13–14, 15, 408
  and writer selection, 3, 4–5, 6, 20, 189, 239
Edmond, Alfred, Jr., 198–203
Education, articles on, 179, 192, 223, 260, 312, 431, 432, 480, 544, 545
Educational expenses, 134, 137
Edwards, Audrey, 271
Eisman, Amy, 536–39
Elder care, articles on, 281
Electronic and international rights, 140
Electronics, articles on, 201, 206, 414, 440, 446
Elements of Style, The (Strunk and White), 128
Emerge, 258–62
  querying, 261
  slanting your ideas to, 259–61
  writing for, 262
Employee taxes, 134–35
Encyclopedia of Associations, 65, 66, 116
Encyclopedia of Business Information, The, 116
Ending of an article, 88
Endless Vacation, 263–67
  querying, 266
  slanting your ideas to, 264–66
  writing for, 266–67
Ensign, The, 18
Entertaining, articles on, 201, 213, 219, 370
Entertainment, articles on
  in general interest magazines, 242, 537
  in inflight magazines, 170, 449
  in magazines for African Americans, 195, 260, 531, 562–3
  in magazines for young people, 206, 483, 512, 562–3
  in magazines for women, 383, 466
Entertainment expenses, 136
Entrepreneur, 268–70
  querying, 269
  slanting your ideas to, 268–69
  writing for, 270
Equipment, 126–28, 133, 137
Erens, Pamela, 304–8
Essays, personal, 32, 85–86. *See also* Human interest stories; Humorous essays and stories; Opinion essays
  in general interest magazines, 322, 459, 460, 537
  in health and fitness magazines, 157, 366–67, 375
  in hunting magazines, 290, 521
  in magazines for African Americans, 261, 273, 530
  in magazines for brides, 214, 385–86
  in magazines for men, 375

Essays, personal *(cont'd)*
in magazines for women, 273, 281, 311–13, 359, 361–62, 370, 396, 552, 556
in military lifestyle magazines, 379
in nature magazines, 188, 154, 491
in parenting magazines, 223, 437, 556
in religious magazines, 227
in travel magazines, 148, 512
Essence, 271–74
querying, 274
slanting your ideas to, 272–73
writing for, 274
Expenses. *See also* individual magazines
deductible, 135, 137–38
payment for "reasonable," 124–25
records of, 125, 130, 132–33
Expert sources, 571. *See also* Interviews
background information, 68, 70
finding, 63–65
gaining access to, 65–67
monetary compensation for, 69, 352
treating well, 71–73
verifying facts and quotes, 77–79, 352
Exploring, 275–78
querying, 277–78
slanting your ideas to, 276–77
writing for, 278

Fact checking, 77–79, 99, 103, 131. *See also* individual magazines
annotated manuscripts, 78–79, 332, 434–35, 506, 543
errors found during, 171, 193, 526
magazines and, 180, 352, 368, 397, 421, 461–62
Facts on File, 116
Fact sources, 116
Families, articles on, 190–93, 279–83, 284–87. *See also* Parenting, articles on
family profiles, 432, 480
in health magazines, 156, 330
in magazines for women, 195, 544
in military life magazines, 378
in travel magazines, 265, 451
Family Circle, 4, 19, 279–83
articles sought, 280–81
querying, 30, 282–83
slanting your ideas to, 280–82
writing for, 283
Family Fun, 284–87
querying, 287
slanting your ideas to, 285–86
writing for, 287
Famous First Facts, 116
Farmers Insurance Group of Companies. See *Friendly Exchange*
Feeman, Robert, 468–72
Feld, Andrea, 55, 211–16
Ferrari, Christina, 463
Ferrell, Keith, 98, 417–21
Fiction, 32, 181–85, 211, 338, 417
Fiction techniques in nonfiction, 171, 282, 314, 317, 319, 514
Field & Stream, 288–91
querying, 51, 290–91
slanting your ideas to, 289–90
writing for, 291
Files and filing systems, 129–33
Film and television, articles on, 167, 239, 259, 260, 514, 564
Findlen, Barbara, 394–97
First draft, writing the, 91
First for Women, 292–94
querying, 293
slanting your ideas to, 293
writing for, 294
First North American Serial Rights, 139
Fisher, Jonathan, 347
Fishing expedition query, 48–49
Fitness, 295–99
querying, 299
slanting your ideas to, 296–98
writing for, 299
Flashmarket News, 106
Flatley, Guy, 237–40
Florio, Thomas A., 232
Folio, 13–14
Fong, Katharine, 391
Food and nutrition, articles on, 233–36, 253–57
in business magazines, 242
in health magazines, 157, 298, 330, 374, 407, 486, 541, 552, 569
in hunting magazines, 290
in inflight magazines, 170, 179, 513, 534
in magazines for African Americans, 166–67, 529

in magazines about islands, 354
in magazines for men, 374
in magazines for women, 174, 192, 312, 383, 410, 466, 541, 544, 546, 552
in military life magazines, 378
in parenting magazines, 224, 433
in rural living magazines, 327
Forthcoming Books in Print, 111
Frank, Deborah, 440–44
Freelancers, opportunities for, 8–9
Freelancers Market, 106
Frichtl, Paul, 147–51
Friendly Exchange, 300–303
querying, 302–3
slanting your ideas to, 301–2
writing for, 303
Fuller, David, 241–44
Full text databases, 113–14

Gabor, Lisa, 208
Gage, Diane, 98
and creativity, 94–95
filing system, 130–31
idea development, 18, 19, 20, 23
query letters, 35–36, 43–45, 60–61
Gale Directory of Publications and Broadcast Media, 78–79
Galleys provided to writers, 151, 224, 352, 461, 502, 539
Gallup Poll, 117
Gallup Report, 117
Gardening, articles on, 190–93, 243, 245, 279, 282, 325, 327
Gasperini, Kathleen, 551
Gaughan, Tom, 109–10, 111
General interest magazines, 160–64, 181–85, 300–303, 321–23, 426–29, 468–72, 503–6, 536–39
Geography, articles on, 353–60, 398–401
Glamour, 304–8
querying, 307
slanting your ideas to, 305–6
writing for, 307–8
Golad, Frank, 520
Goldberg, Erica Buchsbaum, 208–10
Goldberg, Robert, 55
Good Housekeeping, 18, 20, 309–14
querying, 29, 30, 313–14
slanting your ideas to, 310–13
writing for, 314
Government publications, 116–17
Grammar, checking, 53–54
Granger, Johnene, 548
Graves, William, 398–401
Green, Constance, 562–63, 564–66
Green, Kathy, 409–12
Greenwald, John, 160–64
Greer, Kate, 333–37
Greer, Rebecca, 19–20, 63–64
Grosvenor, Gilbert, 398
Guidelines for writers, 33, 128–29, 199, 202–3, 206–7, 274, 303, 332, 350–51, 380, 393. *See also* individual magazines
Guideposts, 315–20
querying, 317–18
slanting your ideas to, 316–17
writing for, 319–20
Guide to Library Research Methods, A (Mann), 65, 110
Guide to Reference Books, 110
Guide to the Use of Books in Libraries, 110

Hagan, Teresa, 292
Hair, Jay D., 347
Hamilton, Linda, 555–58
Hamilton, Patricia, 249–52
Hamlin, Rick, 317
Harper's, 85, 92, 321–23
querying, 322–23
slanting your ideas to, 322
writing for, 323
Harris, Joanne, 165–68
Harris Poll, 117
Harrowsmith Country Life, 324–28
querying, 45, 327
slanting your ideas to, 325–27
writing for, 327–28
Health, 329–32
querying, 57, 331
slanting your ideas to, 330–31
writing for, 331–32
Health and fitness, articles on, 155–59, 295–99, 329–32, 365–68, 373–76, 406–8, 485–88, 540–43, 551–54, 567–72. *See also* Medicine, articles on
in business magazines, 201, 243, 403
children's health, 223, 235, 370, 431, 437, 556

Health and fitness, articles on, *(cont'd)*
in general interest magazines, 301, 537
in home magazines, 191–92
in magazines for African Americans, 196, 273, 528–29
in magazines for seniors, 388–89
in magazines for veterans, 161
in magazines for women, 174, 238–39, 273, 281, 293, 305–6, 312, 363, 370, 410, 544, 545, 557
in magazines for young people, 206, 565
in military life magazines, 414
in outdoor sports magazines, 424
in travel magazines, 265, 513, 535
Heard, Alex, 422
Heloise, 312
Hemispheres, 333–37
querying, 336
slanting your ideas to, 334–36
writing for, 337
Highlights for Children, 338–42
feature categories, 339–40
querying, 341
slanting your ideas to, 339–40
writing for, 341–42
Hippocrates. See *Health*
Historical Statistics of the United States, 118
History, articles on, 152–54, 166, 206, 217, 245–48, 339–40, 414, 443, 503–4
Hodge, Marie, 365
Hohnhold, Laura, 422–25
Home, 14, 343–46
querying, 345
slanting your ideas to, 344–45
writing for, 345–46
Home Book of Biblical Quotations, The, 117
Home Book of Proverbs, Maxims and Familiar Phrases, The, 117
Home Book of Quotations, Classical and Modern, The, 117
Home building and improvement, articles on, 190–94, 325, 343–46, 440, 446, 528, 529–30
Home decorating, articles on, 152–54, 190–93, 245–48
in other magazines, 209, 211–16, 219, 243, 282, 312, 370, 385, 544, 546
Home office, deduction for, 135–36
Hope, Toni Gerber, 463
Hopkinson, Cliff, 230–32
Horowitz, Lois, 109, 110, 113–114
Hughes, Colleen, 315
Human interest stories. *See also* Essays, personal
in general interest magazines, 457–60
in magazines for women, 292, 310–14, 370–71, 396, 465–66, 549
in religious magazines, 315–20
in sports magazines, 524–25
Humes, Alison, 230
Humorous essays and stories, 32
in business magazines, 243
in food magazines, 234–35, 253–54, 542
in general interest magazines, 183, 323, 457, 459–60, 505
in magazines for African Americans, 260, 274
in magazines about history, 153
in magazines for women, 281
in men's health magazines, 374
in rural living magazines, 518
in parenting magazines, 437
in sports and hunting magazines, 288, 290, 496–97, 508
in travel magazines, 178–79
Hunting and fishing, articles on, 288–91, 470, 520–22
Hurley, Dan, 8, 30, 54, 59, 120, 121
Hurowitz-Fuller, Bonnie, 559–61

Ideas, developing and slanting, 17–28. *See also* individual magazines, slanting your ideas to
angles from ideas, 23–28, 57
files of clippings for, 19
for multiple markets, 27–28, 57
sources of, 17–22
timeliness of ideas, 22–23
Income, 120, 123–24, 133. *See also* Payment and payment rates
Income taxes, 136, 137–38
Indemnification clauses, 140–41
Independent Writers of Southern California, 105–6

Indexes, 23, 30, 113–14, 117, 400
Index Medicus, 117
Index to International Statistics, 118
Index to Legal Periodicals, 117
Inflight magazines, 147–51, 169–71, 177–80, 333–37, 448–52, 499–502, 511–15, 532–35
Information Please Almanac, 116
InfoTrac® (database), 23, 30, 113, 115, 117
In Health. See *Health*
Insurance, articles on, 251, 300–301, 403, 569–70
Insurance for writers, 105, 106, 107, 135
Internal Revenue Service, 136–37. *See also* Income Taxes
International Association of Business Communicators, 22
International editions and articles, 241, 324, 366, 347–52, 414–15
International issues, articles on, 160, 184, 200, 260, 391–93, 395, 396, 504, 566
International Wildlife/National Wildlife, 347–52
  querying, 350–51
  slanting your ideas to, 348–50
  writing for, 351–52
Internet® System (computer network), 112
Interviews
  asking for, 67–69
  conducting, 71–76
  following up, 74, 77–79
  in-person, 69–70, 71, 94
  notes of, 73–74, 78–79, 89–91
  personalizing, 70
  preparing for, 69–73
  pre-query, 30–31
  taping, 70–71, 73
  telephone, 68, 71, 73, 94
  timing of, 71, 72–73
Interviews, magazines publishing, *See also* Celebrity profiles and articles
  with African American leaders, 260 261
  with child-development experts, 479
  with health experts, 298
  with world leaders, 161, 335
Investigative journalism, 181–82, 226–27, 321–23, 391–93, 437
Invoices, 103, 125, 132
Islands, 353–57
  querying, 356
  slanting your ideas to, 354–55
  writing for, 356–57

Jackson, Donna, 412
Jargon, 163, 251–52, 476, 487, 557–58
Jhung, Paula, 14, 27–28, 46, 70, 87, 98, 123–24, 125–26
Jimerson, Douglas, 190
Jones, Timothy, 225
Jordan, Mary Beth, 222

Karvonen, Karen, 551–54
Kelley, Bruce, 329
Kelley, Catherine, 230
Kennedy, Alexandra, 284–87
Kilbridge, Sally, 211
Kill fees, 58–59, 89, 141. *See also* individual magazines
Killing an article, reasons for, 240, 256, 315, 439, 484, 510, 547
Kitch, Carolyn, 29, 309–14
Klein, Jeffrey, 391
Knowing Where to Look: The Ultimate Guide to Research (Horowitz), 109, 110
Knox, Margaret, 4, 100
  on interviews, 73, 74, 77
  on writing, 82–83, 96, 97
Krakauer, Jon, 8, 425
  on interviewing experts, 71, 73
  on writing, 9, 82, 84, 87, 91, 92
Krantz, Paul, 190

Ladies' Home Journal, 7–8, 20, 75, 84, 358–60
  querying, 40–41, 359–60
  slanting your ideas to, 359
Lalli, Cele Goldsmith, 385
LaMarche, Robert J., 508–10
Lamb, Yanick Rice, 222
Language, articles on, 458, 460
Lapham, Lewis, 85, 92, 321–2
Law, articles on, 251, 255, 270
Leads, writing, 84–85, 87, 192, 266, 350, 471
Lear's, 4–5, 361–64

Lear's (cont'd)
querying, 363–64
slanting your ideas to, 362–63
writing for, 364
Lear, Frances, 361–62
LeCard, Marc, 489
Ledgers for expenses, 132
Lee, Sally, 463
Legal fees, 141
Leisure activities, articles on, 201, 300, 334–36, 367, 375, 468–72, 513, 534
L'Engle, Madeleine, 61
Lentz, Linda, 343–46
Leo, Jackie, 283
Lesonsky, Rieva, 268
Letterhead and stationery, 52–53
Levey, Gail A., 64–65, 65–66, 67, 72, 77, 78, 79, 92
Levine, Ellen, 464
Lewis-Kearns, Debi, 96, 99, 217–21
LEXIS® (legal database), 114
Lezak, Carol Spielman, 567–72
Libraries, special collection, 110–111
Library, personal, 127–28
Library of Congress, 65, 66, 111–12
Library of Congress Subject Headings, 112
Library research, 109–118
biographical, 111
reference guides, 110–12
reference librarians, 109–110
research tools, 114–18
subject searches, 112–14
telephone reference, 110
Liddell, Marlane A., 503–6
Lila Acheson Wallace Library, Juilliard School, 111
Littell, Mary Ann, 43
Lively Arts Information Directory, The, 116
Longevity, 365–68
querying, 367–68
slanting your ideas to, 366–67
writing for, 368
Los Angeles Times, 28
Lusardi, Lee, 369–72
Lynden, Patricia, 365–66, 367–68

McCain, Florine, 245–48
McCall's, 54, 61, 369–72
querying, 371
slanting your ideas to, 370
writing for, 371–72
McClosky, Joan, 190
McDermott, James, 315–20
McFadden, Maureen, 544–47
Magazines as idea source, 20–21
Magazines, analyzing, 9–13, 30
competing magazines, 21, 23, 30
editorial content, 9–10, 20–21
style, 83–84
target audience, 6, 9
Magazines, numbers of, 5
Magazines, selection of, xv–xvi
Magazines, small-circulation, 8, 371
Mailing lists as idea source, 22
Malott, Adele, 300–303
Mann, Thomas, 65, 66, 110–11, 112, 114
Manuscripts
annotated, 78–79, 332, 434–35, 506, 543
appearance of, 101–3
unsolicited, 4, 32–33, 175–76, 232, 261, 277, 323, 392, 408, 546
Marano, Hara Estroff, 453
Mark, Erika Reider, 309
Marketing your writing 3–15
establishing credibility, 4–5, 6–7
identifying your market, 3–4, 6
specialization and expertise, 7–8
targeting specific magazines, 5–7
Market research, by magazines, 9
Martin, Kathy, 422
Maudlin, Michael G., 225
Mauro, James C., 453–56
Medical Library Association Directory, 111
Medicine, articles on, 157, 184, 282, 306, 367, 375, 383, 479, 568–69
Men, magazines and articles for, 373–76, 468–72
by and about fathers, 223–24, 374. 437
by and about grooms, 209, 214, 215, 219, 385–86
in magazines for women, 196, 238, 273, 305–6
men's grooming, 374, 529
Men's Health, 373–76
querying, 375–76
slanting your ideas to, 374–75
writing for, 376

Meyers, Cathy, 288
Microfilm, data on, 113–14
Military life and defense, articles on, 160–64, 377–81, 413–16, 457, 460
Military Lifestyle, 377–81
  querying, 379–80
  slanting your ideas to, 378–79
  writing for, 380–81
Million, Peter, 398
Mirabella, 382–83
  querying, 383
  slanting your ideas to, 383
  writing for, 383
Mirabella, Grace, 382
Modern Bride, 384–86
  querying, 386
  slanting your ideas to, 385–86
  writing for, 386
Modern Maturity, 387–90
  querying, 389–90
  slanting your ideas to, 388–89
  writing for, 390
Moekle, Cynthia, 156, 157–59
Moline, Peg, 485–88
Money management, articles on
  in home and garden magazines, 192
  in inflight magazines, 500
  in magazines for African Americans, 196, 201, 528, 530
  in magazines for brides, 209
  in magazines for seniors, 388
  in magazines for teens, 565
  in magazines for women, 173–74, 239, 281, 312, 361, 363, 411, 545, 556
  in military life magazines, 379
  in parenting magazines, 432
Monthly Catalog of United States Government Publications, 117
Morgan, Tim, 225
Morrison, Stacy, 382–83
Mother Jones, 4, 391–93
  querying, 392–93
  slanting your ideas to, 392
  writing for, 393
Mowbray, Scott, 253–57
Ms., 394–97
  querying, 396
  slanting your ideas to, 395–96
  writing for, 397
Muchnick, Jeanne, 548
Music, articles on, 166, 167, 182, 195, 261, 339, 513, 564

National Audubon Society, 186–87
National Center for Nutrition and Dietetics, 64
National Directory of Addresses and Telephone Numbers, The, 116
National Directory of Toll-Free Phone Numbers, The, 116
National Food Processors Association, 66
National Geographic, 398–401
  index of, 400
  querying, 400
  slanting your ideas to, 399–400
  writing for, 400–401
National League of American Pen Women, 106
National Newspaper Index, 113
National Wildlife. See *International Wildlife/National Wildlife*
National Wildlife Federation, 349
National Writers Club, The, 106
National Writers Union, The, 107, 141, 143
  Standard Journalism Contract, 141, 143
National Writers Union Agents and Publishers Data Base, 140
Nation's Business, 402–5
  querying, 35–36, 404
  slanting your ideas to, 403
  writing for, 404–5
Natural history, articles on, 188, 325, 355, 399, 400
Nature and the environment, articles on, 186–89, 347–52, 422–24, 489–93
  in general interest magazines, 504
  in health magazines, 366
  in hunting magazines, 522
  in inflight magazines, 170, 179
  in magazines for women, 192, 396
  in magazines for young people, 205–6, 340, 483
  in science magazines, 419
  in sports magazines, 508
Neff, David, 29, 225–29
New Body, 26, 406–8
  columns and sections, 407
  querying, 408

New Body (cont'd)
slanting your ideas to, 407
writing for, 408
Newspaper indexes, 113
Newspaper magazine supplements, 426–29, 536–39
Newspapers as idea source, 19–20
New Woman, 70, 409–12
querying, 411–12
slanting your ideas to, 410–11
writing for, 412
New York editors, visiting, 15
New York Times, The, 8, 81, 113
Women's Magazine Group, 295
New York Times Biographical Edition, 115
New York Times Index, 117
New York Times Manual of Style and Usage, The, 207
New York Times Reference Guide, 116
NEXIS® (database), 114
Norris, Rebecca, 158
North American Film and Video Directory, 111
Notes and note taking, 73–74, 78–79, 89–91
Nutrition, articles on. *See* Food and nutrition, articles on

O'Brien, Pam, 358
OCLC® System (computer network), 112
Off Duty, 413–16
querying, 415
slanting your ideas to, 414–15
writing for, 415–16
Office, setting up, 125–29, 135–36
Office supplies, deductible, 137
Official Guide to Toll-Free Phone Numbers, The, 128
Oldham, Joe, 444
Oliver, Stephanie Stokes, 271–72, 274
Olson, Lamont, 190–93
Omni, 50, 417–21
querying, 420
slanting your ideas to, 418–20
writing for, 98, 421
One-time Rights, 139–40
Opinion essays, 32, 86. *See also* Essays, personal
on health issues, 158
on historical topics, 154
in magazines for African Americans, 261, 272, 531
in magazines for veterans, 161
in magazines for women, 306, 396, 411, 545, 552
in military life magazines, 379
on nature and the environment, 188
in parenting magazines, 433
in religions magazines, 228–29
in rural living magazines, 326
on social and political issues, 184, 228
in sports and hunting magazines 290, 497, 525, 552
Osborne, Philip B., 461
Outdoor living, magazines on, 324–28, 507–10
Outdoor Writers Association of America, 105–6
Outline query, 41–45
Outlines of articles, 90–91, 163, 429, 460, 558
Outside, 21, 28, 422–25
querying, 424–25
slanting your ideas to, 423–24
writing for, 425

Pace Communications, 334
Parade, 4, 33, 64, 92, 93, 100, 426–29
querying, 24, 428
slanting your ideas to, 27, 427–28
writing for, 428–29
Parenting, 430–35
core topics, list of, 431
querying, 433–34
slanting your ideas to, 431–33
writing for, 434–35
Parenting, articles on, 222–24, 284–87, 430–35, 436–39, 477–81, 555–58. *See also* Families, articles on
children's health, 223, 235, 366, 431, 437, 556
in magazines for African Americans, 273
in magazines for women, 192, 195, 273, 281, 293, 305, 359, 466
in military life magazines, 378–79
Parents, 8, 436–39
querying, 30, 438
slanting your ideas to, 436–38

writing for, 438–39
Paugh, Tom, 520–22
Payment and payment rates, 120, 123–25, 144. *See also* individual magazines
Payne, Ken, 461
Peale, Norman Vincent, 315
PEN American Center, 107
Penwomen, The, 106
Periodical indexes, 113–14
Perry, Susan Millar, 365
Pets, articles on, 192, 206, 282, 370, 379
PhoneDisc® (CD ROM), 65
Photographs, 102–3, 127–28. *See also* individual magazines
Photography classes, 128
Poetry, magazines publishing, 181, 211, 214
Politics, articles on, 183, 198, 200, 259, 383, 391–93, 403, 420, 491, 508
Poole, Robert M., 398
Popular Mechanics, 50, 440–44
querying, 442–43
slanting your ideas to, 441–42
writing for, 443–44
Popular Science, 64, 445–47
querying, 447
slanting your ideas to, 445–47
writing for, 447
Pregnancy, articles on, 431, 433
Printers, 52, 126
Produce Marketing Association, 66
Product information and reviews, 243, 255, 298, 326, 344, 424, 446–47, 491, 496, 509, 524, 530. *See also* Consumer topics, articles on
Professional services for writers, 104–7
Profiles, 448–52
querying, 451–52
slanting your ideas to, 449–51
writing for, 452
Profiles of companies, 200–201, 296, 334–35, 403
Profiles of families, 432, 480
Profiles of individuals. *See also* Celebrity interviews and articles
of artists, 261, 336, 339, 509
of business executives, 269, 335, 450, 469
of environmental activists, 349–50
in general interest magazines, 459
in health magazines, 157, 541
of historical figures, 247, 339–40
in inflight magazines, 179, 334–36, 448–52, 513–14, 533
of island dwellers, 355
in magazines for African Americans, 167, 273, 530
in magazines for women, 282, 541
of sports figures, 513, 518, 525–26, 530, 564
Proofreading of query letters, 53–54
Psychological Abstracts, 115
Psychology, articles on, 453–56
in general interest magazines, 537
in health magazines, 157, 298, 330–31, 486–87, 542, 569
in inflight magazines, 534
in magazines for women, 174–75, 281, 293, 312
in science magazines, 419
Psychology Today, 8, 453–56
querying, 455–56
slanting your ideas to, 454–55
writing for, 456
Public Affairs Information Service Bulletin, 117
Public opinion polls, 117
Public policy, articles on, 181–84, 198, 259, 391–92
Public Relations Society of America, 22
Publishers Weekly, 13–14
Pull-quotes, 243, 488
Punctuation in query letters, 53–54, 291
Purnell, Florestine, 258

Query letters. *See also* ; Rejection, reasons for; individual magazines, querying
appearance of, 51–54
clips accompanying, 51, 54–55
cover letter with, 34
length of, 29, 50–51
number circulating at one time, 56–57
number received by editors, 4
pre–query research, 30–31, 76, 434, 466
purpose of, 29, 50

Query letters *(cont'd)*
  response time to, 55–56, 57–58
  samples of, 34–49
  simultaneous submissions, 27, 33–34, 168
  who to query, 12, 371, 412, 283
  and working titles, 31, 50
  writing of, 29–32, 50–51, 307, 313–14
  as writing samples, 29, 192, 307, 313, 356, 471, 492, 526, 565
Quicken® (computer program), 134
Quotation sources, 117, 128
Quotes, 71, 74–76, 77–79, 94, 481, 519

Ranard, Ann, 369
Raskin, Bruce, 430–35
Readers, knowing a magazine's, 9, 26–27, 283
Reader's Digest, 457–62
  querying, 460
  slanting your ideas to, 458–60
  submitting reprints to, 462
  writing for, 461–62
Reader's Guide to Periodical Literature, 23, 30, 113, 115, 117
Record keeping, 125, 132–33
Redbook, 463–67
  querying, 57, 466–67
  slanting your ideas to, 464–66
  writing for, 467
Rees, Susan, 540–43
Regional articles
  in general interest magazines, 300–303
  in magazines for seniors, 388–89
  in rural living magazines, 324–28
  in sports and hunting magazines, 288, 290, 507, 510, 516–17, 525
  in travel magazines, 147–51, 177–80, 265, 532–34
Reid, Alvin A., 258–59, 261–62
Rejection, reasons for, 57, 58–61, 100, 290, 389
  not targeted to magazines, 158–59, 162, 167, 202, 235, 371, 396, 404, 411, 428, 501, 546
  proofreading errors, 53–54, 220, 269, 291, 345, 420, 471, 492
  timing of subject, 196, 356, 303, 350, 356, 363–64, 438, 447, 492
Relationships, articles on 174, 195, 209, 213–14, 293, 305, 374, 385, 411, 483, 559–61
Religion, articles on, 225–29, 261, 315–20, 455
Reportage (article genre), 86
Reprint Rights, 140
Reprints, magazines publishing, 322, 389, 458, 462
Research. *See also* Expert sources; Interviews; Library research
  books on conducting, 110–111
  determining sufficiency of, 76
  notes, filing, 131
  organizing and submitting, 78–79, 103
  pre–interview, 69–70
  pre–query, 30–31, 76
Research Centers Directory, The, 116
Resorts Condominiums International, Inc., 263
Response time to queries, 55–56, 57–58
Rewriting, 98–101, 429, 439, 461
  editor's instructions for, 193, 256, 351–52, 381
Rights and contracts, 138–43. *See also* individual magazines
Robb Report, 468–72
  querying, 471
  slanting your ideas to, 469–71
  writing for, 471–72
Robbins, Michael W., 186, 189
Roberts, David, 15, 60, 64, 73, 75, 82, 100
Roget's Thesaurus, 128
Rolling Stone, 55
Rudolph, Ron, 507–10
Rural living, magazines on, 324–28, 507–10

Saible, Stephanie, 548–50
Salvatore, Diane, 463–67
San Diego Union/Tribune, 20, 28
San Francisco Chronicle, 113
Schedule, writing, 122–23
Schneider, Irene, 230
Schneider, Susan, 477
Science and technology, articles on, 419–21, 440–44, 445–47
  in business magazines, 201, 268
  in general interest magazines, 399, 504

in inflight magazines, 149–50, 179–80, 335, 513
in magazines for young people, 206
Science Sources, 66, 116
Scott, James, 329
Scouting, 473–76
querying, 475
slanting your ideas to, 474–75
writing for, 476
Sears List of Subject Headings, 112
Seasonal material, querying, 220, 282, 299, 379, 483, 509, 549
Second Serial Rights, 140
Seidman, Ellen, 463, 465
Select Home, 14
Self-addressed, stamped envelopes (SASE), 53, 360, 408, 471
Selover, Mary Kelly, 343, 345
Seniors and older adults, articles for, 336, 387–90
Sesame Street Magazine, 477
Sesame Street Parents' Guide, 477–81
querying, 480
slanting your ideas to, 478–80
writing for, 481
"Seven sisters," 191, 312, 463
Seventeen, 23, 482–84
querying, 31, 483–84
slanting your ideas to, 482–83
writing for, 484
Sexual issues, articles on
in health magazines, 297, 405
in magazines for African Americans, 561, 218
in magazines for brides, 210, 213, 218
in magazines for men, 374
in magazines for teens, 483, 561
in magazines for women, 238, 293, 410, 466
Shape, 485–88
querying, 487
slanting your ideas to, 485–87
writing for, 487–88
Shopping, articles on, 282, 335, 363
Short take query, 45–48
Sicher, John D., 152–54
Sidebars, 12, 85, 89, 203, 216, 243, 346, 428, 488, 571
Sierra, 4, 103, 489–93
querying, 491–92
slanting your ideas to, 490–91
writing for, 492–93
Sierra Club, 489–90
Simultaneous submissions, 27, 33–34, 168
Skeeter, Sharyn, 34, 194–97
Ski, 494–98, 507
querying, 497–98
slanting your ideas to, 26–27, 495–97
writing for, 498
Skiing, 495, 507
Sky, 20–21, 499–502
querying, 37–38, 501
slanting your ideas to, 499–501
writing for, 502
Slon, Steven, 373
Smith, Red, 81
Smithsonian, 4, 84, 503–6
querying, 505–6
slanting your ideas to, 504–5
writing for, 506
Smithsonian Institution, 504. See also *Smithsonian*
Snow Country, 507–10
querying, 45, 509
slanting your ideas to, 26–27, 508–9
writing for, 509–10
Social issues, articles on, 183–84, 226, 322, 361, 394–94, 483, 564
Social Science Abstracts, 22–23
Society of American Travel Writers, 105–6
Sociological Abstracts, 115
Source®, The (database), 114
Source lists, 78, 103, 131
Southwest Airlines, 511
Space, articles on, 206, 419
Specialization and expertise, 7–8
Speculation, writing on, 58, 59. *See also* individual magazines
Spelling in queries, 53–54, 291
Spirit, 511–15
querying, 514
slanting your ideas to, 512–14
writing for, 514–15
Sport, 516–19
querying, 518–19
slanting your ideas to, 517–18
writing for, 519
Sports, articles on, 494–98, 507–10, 516–19, 523–26, 551–54
in business magazines, 201
in general interest magazines, 470–71, 537

Sports, articles on *(cont'd)*
in inflight magazines, 149–50, 170, 180, 335, 449, 513, 534
in magazines for African Americans, 201, 261, 530–31, 564
in magazines about islands, 355
in magazines for men, 375
in magazines for women, 487, 551–54
in magazines for young people, 206, 340, 564
in military life magazines, 414
in rural living magazines, 424
Sports Afield, 520–22
querying, 522
slanting your ideas to, 521–22
writing for, 522
Statistical Abstract of the United States, 117–18
Statistical information, 117–18
Stepler, Richard, 445–47
Stevenson, Burton, 117
Stine, Annie, 103, 489–93
Strohm, Bob, 92, 348–52
Stuckey, Scott, 204, 205
Studabaker, Anne W., 448
Style, writing, 83–85, 91–93, 154, 163, 428, 434
dramatic narrative, 171, 282, 314, 317, 319, 514
Style books, 128
Subcontractors, 134–35
Subheads, 12, 85, 86, 216, 243, 408, 488, 571
Subject Collections, 110–11
Submissions, number received, 4
Sulich, Susan, 46
Summary of an article, 88
Summary query, 34, 36–40
Sussex Publishers, 453
Sutro Library, 111
Synonym Finder, The, 128

"Take-away" ending of article, 89, 460
Tape recorders, 70–71, 73–74, 127
Tapper, Joan, 353–57
Taxes, articles on, 251, 270
Teens. *See also* Children, articles for
articles by, 564
magazines for, 204–7, 275–78, 482–84, 559–61, 562–66
Telephone directories, 113, 116, 128
Telephone expenses, 124
Telephones, 127
for interviews, 68, 71, 73, 94
for research, 66, 110
Tennis, 523–26
querying, 526
slanting your ideas to, 523–26
writing for, 526
Terzella, Mary, 548
Theater, articles on, 166, 195, 261
Thiessen, Carol, 225
Third Person (article genre), 86
Thomas, Mary-Powel, 185–89
Thompson, Roger, 402–5
Tilin, Andrew, 422
Timeliness of ideas, 22–23, 56
Time management, 122–23
Times Mirror publications, 495
Titles of articles, 31, 84, 86
Transcribing unit, 127
Traulsen, Jane, 292–94
Travel, articles on, 230–32, 263–67, 353–57. *See also* Inflight magazines
in general interest magazines, 182, 300, 302, 470, 537
in health magazines, 297–98, 367, 374, 487
to historic places, 154, 167
in home magazines, 192
in magazines for African Americans, 167, 201, 259, 564
in magazines for brides, 209, 213, 219
in magazines for men, 374
in magazines for teens, 564
in magazines for women, 192, 239, 293, 312, 383, 545, 549
in military life magazines, 378, 414–15
in outdoor/sports magazines, 424, 491, 496, 525
in parenting magazines, 224
for seniors, 336, 388
Travel expenses, 125
Troop, Beth, 338

Ubell, Earl, 92
Ungaro, Susan Kelliher, 279–83
Unipub, Inc., 118
United Airlines, 333–334

United Fresh Vegetable Association, 66
United Nations publications, 118
United States Bureau of the Census, 118
U.S. Chamber of Commerce, 402
U.S. Food and Drug Administration, 22
U.S. government, publications of, 116, 117–18
United States Government Organization Manual, 117
U.S. Government Printing Office, 116–17
Unsolicited manuscripts, 4, 32–33, 175–76, 232, 261, 277, 323, 392, 408, 546
Upscale, 527–31
querying, 531
regular features, 529–30
slanting your ideas to, 528–31
writing for, 531
USAir Magazine, 4, 94–95, 532–35
querying, 534–35
slanting your ideas to, 34, 532–34
writing for, 535
USA Weekend, 536–39
querying, 538
slanting your ideas to, 536–38
writing for, 538–39

Varacalli, Lynn, 172–76
Veterans, magazines for, 160–64
Villarosa, Linda, 271
von Hirschberg, Stephanie, 412

Walking and hiking, articles on, 355, 470
Wallace, DeWitt, 458
Wallace, Lila Acheson, 458
Wallace, Rich, 338–42
Wall Street Journal, The, 77, 113, 260, 351
Warrick, Sheridan, 329–32
Washington Independent Writers, 105–6
Washington Information Directory, 116
Webster's Collegiate Dictionary, 115, 128
Weight Watchers Magazine, 540–43
querying, 542
slanting your ideas to, 541–42
writing for, 542–43
Weir, David, 391
Weiss, Penelope, 368
Wesley, Valerie Wilson, 271
Wexler, Mark, 347
White, Kate, 54–55
Whiteley, Elaine, 7–8, 18, 20, 75–76
fact checking system, 79
sample query letters, 38–39, 40–41
on writing, 84, 89, 90, 91, 92
Whitney, Ruth, 308
Who's Who, 115
Who's Who in America, 115
Wildlife, articles on, 326–27, 340, 347–52, 504
Williams, Gurney, III, 50, 64, 99–100, 122–23
Wilsondisc® (database), 113, 117
Wine and liquor, articles on, 245, 335
Wolfman, Ira, 478–81
Woman's Day, 7, 19, 544–47
querying, 38–39, 42–43, 57, 63–64, 546–47
slanting your ideas to, 544–46
writing for, 547
Woman's World, 548–50
querying, 549–50
slanting your ideas to, 549
writing for, 550
Women, magazines for, 172–76, 194–97, 271–74, 279–83, 292–94, 304–8, 309–14, 358–60, 361–64, 369–72, 382–83, 394–97, 409–12, 463–67, 544–47, 548–50
health magazines, 295–99, 329–32, 406–8, 485–88, 540–43, 551–54
Women's Sports & Fitness, 551–54
querying, 553
slanting your ideas to, 552–53
writing for, 553–54
Wood, Stephanie, 222–24
Word association, programmed, 94–95
Word count, 96, 214, 572
WordWrap, 106
Work and careers, magazines and articles on
in magazines for African Americans, 198–203
in magazines for men, 375
in magazines for parents, 433, 437, 555–58
in magazines for teens, 277

in magazines for women, 173–74, 195, 238, 312, 544, 555–58
in rural living magazines, 325–26
Work-for-Hire, 140, 274
Working Mother, 555–58
querying, 557
slanting your ideas to, 556–57
writing for, 557–58
World Almanac and Book of Facts, The, 116
World Cultures, articles on, 165–68, 170, 273, 340, 354, 398–99, 504
Wrightson, Cassandra, 329
Wrinkle in Time, A (L'Engle), 61
Writer, The, 14
"Writer myth," the, 119
Writer's block, 81–83
Writers' contests, 318
Writers' critique groups, 103–4
Writer's Digest, 14
Writers' organizations, 103–7
Writer's Resource Guide, 110
Writing. *See also* Editing; individual magazines, writing for
and article anatomy, 86–89
and article genre, 85–86
and creativity, 94–95
and fiction techniques, 171, 282, 314, 317, 319, 514
the first draft, 91
leads, 84–85, 87, 266, 350, 471
mistakes writers make, 182, 351, 506, 538, 542
organizing your notes, 89–91
skills, improving, 91–92, 93–94
style, 83–85, 91–93, 154, 163, 428, 434
Writing courses, 9
Wynne, Ben, 37–38
Wynter, Leon, 260

Yap, Leslie, 387
YM, 559–61
querying, 560–61
slanting your ideas to, 559–60
writing for, 561
Young Sisters and Brothers (YSB), 562–66
querying, 565–66
slanting your ideas to, 564–65
subject categories, 563–64
writing for, 566
Your Health & Fitness, 567–72
querying, 570
slanting your ideas to, 568–70
writing for, 571–72

Zonis, Nadia, 477